T0215662

A Practical Introduction to Enterprise Network and Security Management

A Practical Introduction to Enterprise Network and Security Management

Second Edition

Bongsik Shin

CRC Press
Taylor & Francis Group
Boca Raton London New York

CRC Press is an imprint of the
Taylor & Francis Group, an **informa** business

AN AUERBACH BOOK

Second edition published 2022
by CRC Press
6000 Broken Sound Parkway NW, Suite 300, Boca Raton, FL 33487-2742

and by CRC Press
2 Park Square, Milton Park, Abingdon, Oxon, OX14 4RN

© 2022 Taylor & Francis Group, LLC

First edition published by CRC Press 2017

CRC Press is an imprint of Taylor & Francis Group, LLC

The right of Bongsik Shin to be identified as author of this work has been asserted by him in accordance with sections 77 and 78 of the Copyright, Designs and Patents Act 1988.

ISBN: 978-0-367-64251-8 (hbk)
ISBN: 978-1-032-04802-4 (pbk)
ISBN: 978-1-003-12369-9 (ebk)

Typeset in Times
by SPi Global, India

Access the Support Materials: https://www.routledge.com/9780367642518.

Contents

Preface

This book is written for those who study or practice information technology, management information systems (MIS), accounting information systems (AIS), or computer science (CS). It is assumed that readers are being exposed to the challenging and continuously changing computer networking and cybersecurity subjects for the first time. A special emphasis is placed on effectively integrating two subject areas as cybersecurity can no longer be afterthoughts amid rampant cyber incidents these days. As the title implies, much focus of this book is to build a practical knowledge base of fundamental concepts necessary for a successful professional career in related fields.

The book is designed to offer an impactful learning experience. First, each chapter comes with reinforcing exercise questions. If used for a course, some of the hands-on exercises are good for individual assignments. Second, cases, examples, and figures are carefully constructed to solidify concepts and enhance learning. Third, if adopted for a course, the complementary Packet Tracer–based assignments the author developed will provide students with non-trivial hands-on experience. Packet Tracer, now freely available from Cisco, is an excellent learning platform to create networks, configure network nodes, and troubleshoot problems. The book will provide an unparalleled and very practical learning experience to readers.

Much emphasis is placed on explaining cybersecurity from many different perspectives. For this, four chapters are dedicated to cybersecurity topics in the contexts of both traditional and new computing paradigms such as the software-defined network. The remaining nine chapters also have significant cybersecurity coverages while explaining networking concepts. The computer network and cybersecurity are inseparable and the Second Edition underscores their tight coupling. The most significant changes in the Second Edition are:

- Chapter 2 is a new chapter written to introduce the fundamental concepts of cybersecurity.
- Chapters 8, 9, and 10 are dedicated to cybersecurity, significantly expanding from the first edition that had only two chapters.
- Other chapters additionally reinforce cybersecurity concepts. Examples include network address translation (Chapter 4), hardening intermediary devices (Chapter 5), Wi-Fi network protection (Chapter 6), and Virtual LANs for customized network defense (Chapter 7).

If used for a course, the book of 13 chapters contains the right amount of coverage for a semester. It balances introductory and advanced concepts essential to readers. Although the writing is moderately dense, utmost efforts were made to explain sometimes challenging concepts in a manner that can be followed through careful readings. My own students told me about relative easiness in passing the CompTIA Network+ test after studying with the book and its value in building a solid knowledge base for the CompTIA Security+ and CISSP certification.

Author

Bongsik Shin is Professor of Management Information Systems at San Diego State University. He earned a PhD at the University of Arizona and was an assistant professor at the University of Nebraska at Omaha before joining San Diego State. He has taught computer network and cybersecurity management, business intelligence (data warehousing and data mining, statistics), decision support systems, electronic commerce, and IT management and strategy. He has taught computer networking and cybersecurity continuously for more than 23 years.

His current research focuses on theoretical and practical subjects related to cybersecurity and augmented reality. His research has been funded by more than 25 internal and external grants. On cybersecurity, he has conducted and is undertaking research on designing and developing (1) a cyber threat intelligence (CTI) system and (2) an anti-ransomware solution. The projects have been partly funded by the US Navy and US Air Force. As for augmented reality, his research focuses on its adaptation to real-life contexts. For example, funded by the US Navy, he is developing an application that utilizes augmented reality for the Naval Maintenance, Repair, and Overhaul (MRO) workforce. The second AR research project that has been funded by the DHS (Department of Homeland Security) is to develop an AR-powered AI system customized for DHS border security operations.

He has been frequently listed in the global research ranking (source: aisnet.org). For example, he was as high as 20th in the world based on the five-year publication records in the basket of Top 6 Information Systems journals. He has published more than 30 articles in *MIS Quarterly*, *IEEE Transactions on Engineering Management*, *IEEE Transactions on Systems, Man, and Cybernetics*, *Communications of the ACM*, *Journal of Association for Information Systems*, *European Journal of Information Systems*, *Journal of Management Information Systems*, *Information Systems Journal*, *Information and Management*, and *Decision Support Systems*. He is a 2019–2020 recipient of the Alumni Association Award for Outstanding Faculty Contribution to the University.

1 Networking

Fundamental Concepts

1.1 INTRODUCTION

By definition, the computer network represents a collection of wired and wireless communication links through which computers and other hardware devices exchange data/information/messages. A network can be as small as the one installed in a house and as big as the Internet that spans the entire planet. The size of a particular network thus reflects the size of the place (e.g., building, campus) where it is installed. The wireless and wired network has become the artery of an organization (e.g., company, university) and the society, revolutionizing every facet of our life by facilitating resource (e.g., storage) sharing and the exchange of data (e.g., texts, videos, music) in an unprecedented manner. **Throughout the book, the three terms of *data, information*, and *message* are used synonymously**, although, strictly speaking, information is a higher-level abstract derived from data by processing, enriching, and organizing them.

With the rapid advancement of information and communication technologies (or ICTs), more electronic and mobile devices are being attached to the computer network. Among them are digital smartphones, high definition IPTVs, music and video game players, tablets such as iPads, electronic appliances, and control and monitoring systems (e.g., security cameras, CCTVs, traffic signals). The rapid growth of various digital devices is transforming the network into a more dynamic, diversified, and, at the same time, more vulnerable platform.

Besides the digital computer network, there are also other traditional network platforms that were created long before the digital revolution and are still in use. They include radio/TV broadcasting networks and public switched telephone networks. The traditional networks are, however, not the focus of this book.

Although traditional networks and digital computer networks started off on separate platforms, their convergence has been taking place. For instance, more voice calls are digitized and transported over the Internet. Think of the popularity of Internet call services and voice/video conference platforms including Zoom, Google Meet, and a slew of mobile apps. The convergence has been accelerating as the computer network has reached its stability in handling real-time traffic.

1.1.1 LEARNING OBJECTIVES

This chapter covers fundamental concepts of computer networking in terms of:

- Key elements of a computer network
- Methods used by network nodes to distribute data
- Directionality in data propagation
- Network topologies focusing on physical layouts
- Classification of networks in terms of their scope
- Subnetwork vs. internetwork
- Key measures of network performance

- Binary, decimal, and hexadecimal numbering systems
- IP and MAC addresses
- Differences between data encoding/decoding and signal encoding/decoding
- Differences between digital signaling and analog signaling

1.2 NETWORK ELEMENTS

A computer network is made up of various hardware and software components including hosts, intermediary devices, network links (or communication links), applications, data, and protocols. As a demonstration, Figure 1.1 displays a simple network in which two *hosts* (i.e., a PC and a server) exchange data produced by *applications* (e.g., web browser, webserver) using a *protocol* (i.e., a set of engagement rules) over two *network links* joined by an *intermediary device*.

1.2.1 Host

The host in this book is defined as a data-producing entity attached to a network and has been primarily a client or server computer. Often times, hosts are also called *end nodes*, *end devices*, *end systems*, or *end stations*. They have the capability of accepting user inputs (e.g., keyboarding, video feeds from a camera), processing them, generating outputs in 1s and 0s, and storing them. The outputs can be digitized texts, sounds, images, videos, or any other multimedia contents that can be transported over the network.

The host is generally a source or a destination of data in transit and has been predominantly a general-purpose or high-performance computer (e.g., PC, laptop, mainframe, supercomputer). With continuous addition of non-traditional computing and communication devices to the network, host types are much more diverse these days. They include smartphones, personal digital assistants (PDAs), game consoles, home electronics and appliances, and other peripheral devices such as network-attached printers, copiers, and fax machines. When hosts exchange data over a network, their relationship is in one of two modes: client/server or peer-to-peer (P2P) (see Figure 1.2).

1.2.1.1 Client-Server Mode

In the client/server mode, the host acts as a dedicated client or server. The client host takes advantage of resources (e.g., files, storage space, databases, webpages, CPU processing) offered by servers. The server host generally has a high-performance capacity to quickly respond to resource requests

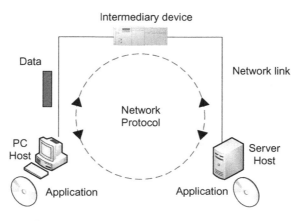

FIGURE 1.1 Key elements of a computer network

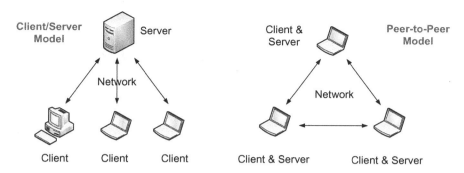

FIGURE 1.2 Client/server vs. P2P networking

from client hosts. In early days, many programs (e.g., Microsoft Outlook for email) installed in the client host were tailored to a particular server application (e.g., Microsoft Exchange).

However, the web browser (e.g., Firefox, Google Chrome) has changed it all. The browser has become an application that allows a client host to communicate with many different server applications (e.g., email, database, webservers) over the network. This *one client (web browser) to many server applications* has benefitted individuals and organizations tremendously. Above all, with the 'thin' client in which a client host needs only a web browser to take advantage of resources available from various servers, organizations can control IT spending and save efforts necessary to maintain client programs.

1.2.1.2 Peer-to-Peer (P2P) Mode

With P2P or peer-to-peer networking, each participating host behaves as both a client and server in sharing resources with other hosts. As an example, by joining P2P file sharing sites such as BitTorrent.com, anyone can download multimedia files available from other participating computers (client mode) and, at the same time, allow others to download his/her own files (server mode). As another example of the P2P technology, today's operating systems such as Windows support P2P networking among nearby computers through such standard as the Wi-Fi technology called *Wi-Fi Direct*.

1.2.1.3 Network Interface Card

To access a network, the host should be equipped with at least one network interface card (or NIC), a specialized electronic circuit board. Also called an *adaptor* or *LAN card*, the NIC is generally built into the host. Its role is to convert host-generated binary data (e.g., emails) into signals (e.g., electronic currents, lights, radio signals) and to release them to the network. The NIC also accepts signals arriving over the network, restores original data, and forwards them to the host's memory for processing.

User computers (especially laptops) come with two NICs these days: one for *Ethernet* and another for Wi-Fi to enable both wired and wireless networking. Figure 1.3 illustrates NIC cards for Ethernet and Wi-Fi. You can observe that an Ethernet NIC has one or more *ports* that allow physical connectivity of a computer to the wired network, but the wireless NIC (or WNIC) has one or more antennas for radio communications. Wireless NICs in USB are also popular. Each NIC comes with a unique address, called a physical or MAC address (to be explained).

1.2.2 Intermediary Device

Depending on the size, a network can have many different intermediary devices that conduct functions necessary to relay data between the source and destination hosts. Intermediary devices do not produce user data, but should transport them in an effective, reliable, and secure manner. Among

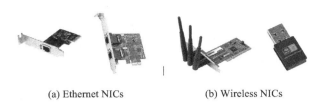

(a) Ethernet NICs　　　　　　(b) Wireless NICs

FIGURE 1.3　Wired vs. Wireless NICs (Source: Amazon.com)

the types are *modems, firewalls, multiplexers, CSU/DSU, hubs* (or *multi-port repeaters*), *switches, routers, bridges,* and *wireless access points*. Their functional details are explained in other chapters.

1.2.2.1　Intra-Networking vs. Inter-Networking Devices

The bridge, wireless access point, switch, and hub provide hosts with interconnectivity 'within' a network segment called a *subnetwork* (or subnet). Whereas, the router is used to tie different network segments (or subnetworks). The data forwarding activity taking place within a subnetwork boundary is called *intra-networking*, and that across two or more subnetworks joined by the router is called *inter-networking* (see Figure 1.4). In other words, the bridge, wireless access point, hub, and switch are intra-networking devices, and the router is an inter-networking device. More on *intra-networking* versus *inter-networking* is in Section 1.6.

1.2.2.2　Other Differences

Intermediary devices are distinct from each other in many different ways. For example, some devices (e.g., hub/repeater) transmit data in the half-duplex mode, whereas others (e.g., switches, routers) transmit in the full-duplex mode (more in Section 1.3.2). Some devices are hardware-driven in performing their primary functions, while others rely more on software capability. Software-enabled devices generally come with a higher level of intelligence to conduct networking functions than purely hardware ones. Intermediary devices are also different in their processing speeds, capacity in data filtering and security provision, and addressing mechanism used to move data.

Just as hosts, the intermediary device also has one or more internal network cards with built-in physical ports (or interfaces) to tie it to a wireless or wired network. Because of the critical importance of intermediary devices in computer networking, Chapter 5 is dedicated to cover their structural and functional features in detail. *The term, network node, is used throughout the book as an inclusive concept that refers to an intermediary device or a host.* Thus,

$$\textbf{Network nodes} = \textbf{intermediary devices} + \textbf{hosts}\,(\textbf{end nodes})$$

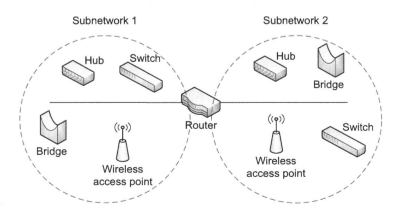

FIGURE 1.4　Intra-networking and inter-networking devices

1.2.3 NETWORK LINK

1.2.3.1 Link Types

The network link is a wired (or guided) or wireless (or unguided) connection that enables data exchange between network nodes. To form a link, various communication media have been in use. Copper wires (e.g., twisted pairs, coaxial cables) and optical fibers made of extremely pure glass or plastic are predominant wired media these days. The earth's atmosphere becomes the medium of wireless communications. Various signals are utilized to transport data through the guided and unguided media: electronic signals for copper wires and coaxial cables, light signals for optical fibers, and radio/microwave signals in the atmosphere. Details of the media are explained in Chapter 13.

1.2.3.2 Access Link vs. Trunk Link

The network link can be either an *access link* or a *trunk link*. While the access link provides direct connectivity between a host and an intermediary device, the trunk link interconnects intermediary devices (e.g., router-switch), which results in the extension of network span. The trunk link is a point-to-point connection and generally carries traffic coming from multiple access links. When two hosts exchange data through two or more intermediary devices, it takes one or more trunk links to complete the end-to-end data delivery (see Figure 1.5). Although trunk links are not necessary to create a small-scale network such as the one in Figure 1.1, most organizations rely on them to create an enterprise network.

1.2.4 APPLICATION

The application (e.g., web browser) represents a software program developed to support a specialized user task (e.g., email exchange, web surfing). Numerous applications have been introduced to support various tasks over the computer network. Many of them are designed to improve communications through email (e.g., Outlook, Thunderbird), instant messaging (e.g., Messenger), and voice and video (e.g., Zoom, Google Voice). Also, the web browser has become an extremely popular application on which countless online services (e.g., social networking, online banking, e-commerce, cloud computing) are offered over the Internet.

1.2.4.1 Application Types and Network Performance

Applications can be characterized from different angles, and their characteristics have important implications on the design of a computer network and on network performance. For instance, the majority of user applications demand one or more of the following performance requirements:

- Predictable or guaranteed network reliability (e.g., financial transactions)
- Predictable or guaranteed network capacity/speed (e.g., video conferencing)

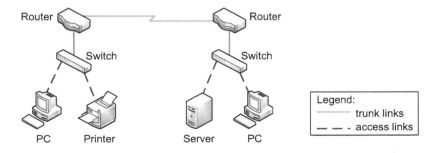

FIGURE 1.5 Access links vs. trunk links

- Little or no network delay/latency (e.g., audio conferencing, video streaming)
- Reasonable network responsiveness even though not in real-time (e.g., web browsing, instant messaging)

1.2.5 DATA/MESSAGE

Applications produce data (or messages) that need to be transported over the network. Produced data may be real-time or interactive audios/videos, or static contents such as webpages and emails. In computer networking, data are packaged in discrete message units and delivered to the destination one by one. As a simple demonstration, imagine a conversation between two persons and observe how their dialog is packaged into discrete data units and delivered over the network (see Figure 1.6).

The general name of each data unit is the *packet*. Each packet contains source data (e.g., voice message) and additional overhead information such as source and destination addresses necessary for packet deliveries. To better visualize the relationship between source data and a packet, think of a letter (as source data) contained in an envelope with mailing addresses (as a packet).

1.2.6 PROTOCOL

Host applications (e.g., web browser, email program) produce and exchange data/messages according to a *protocol* that contains a collection of detailed communication rules. For this, an application has a particular protocol built into it (e.g., HTTP embedded in the browser). The application produces outgoing data and interprets incoming data strictly based on the set of communication rules defined by the built-in protocol. There are two different types of communication rules in each protocol:

- Syntactic rules: Rules regarding the format of a message to be followed for its sharing
- Semantic rules: Rules concerned with the meaning or interpretation of the shared message

1.2.6.1 HTTP Example

For example, if a computer user enters *https://www.facebook.com* into a web browser's URL (Uniform Resource Locator), the browser produces a simple request message according to the built-in Hypertext Transfer Protocol (or HTTP). Here, the request message has syntax similar to:

GET https://www.facebook.com HTTP/1.1
Host: www.facebook.com

so that the target host (www.facebook.com server) can understand/interpret its meaning (or semantics). The semantics of the aforementioned statements is '*Please send me the main page of www.facebook.com using HTTP, version 1.1*'. The request message thus produced is then dispatched to the target server.

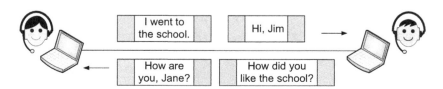

FIGURE 1.6   Delivery of discrete data units over a computer network

1.2.6.2 Standard vs. Proprietary Protocol

Certain protocols are globally *standardized* so that hardware and software vendors can incorporate them into their own products. For example, HTTP and HTTPS are standard protocols adopted by all web browsers (e.g., Firefox, Internet Explorer, Chrome) and webservers (e.g., Apache, Microsoft IIS). There are also numerous *proprietary* protocols developed by vendors exclusively for their own commercial products (e.g., the protocol embedded in Yahoo Messenger). Important standard protocols are introduced throughout the book.

1.3 MODES OF COMMUNICATION

This section explains methods network nodes utilized to distribute data/messages and the directionality of data/messages exchanges.

1.3.1 METHODS OF DATA DISTRIBUTION

The method of data distribution between network nodes is primarily *unicasting*, *broadcasting*, or *multicasting* (see Figure 1.7).

1.3.1.1 Unicasting

With unicasting, data exchange takes place between a single source and a single destination node identified by their unique addresses. The destination may be located within the same network as the source or separated from the source across multiple networks. It was explained that the co-location of the source and the destination within a subnetwork takes intra-networking for data deliveries. When the source and destination are in different subnetworks, the data exchange requires inter-networking (more in Section 1.6). The majority of messages produced by a user application are exchanged in the inter-networking mode.

1.3.1.2 Broadcasting

Broadcasting results in the flooding of data from one node to all the other nodes within a network. In fact, we have been enjoying the broadcasting service daily by tuning in to a radio or TV station. From satellites or earth stations, radio and TV companies broadcast various contents (e.g., music, drama, reality shows). Such broadcasting is also widely used by computer networks for various reasons. Prevalent examples are the Wi-Fi and cellular networks.

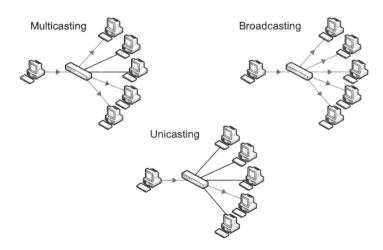

FIGURE 1.7 Unicasting, multicasting, and broadcasting

1.3.1.3 Multicasting

Multicasting from a data source results in its concurrent deliveries to a selected group of destinations. We have been using multicasting services extensively. For example, numerous online sites provide multimedia streaming for live news, music, TV programs, movies, online gaming, or SNS videos over the Internet. These services rely on a multicasting protocol so that a server can stream multimedia contents to requesting clients concurrently. With the growing popularity of such on-demand multimedia services, the usage of multicasting will only grow.

Although the demonstration in Figure 1.7 is only between hosts, intermediary nodes including switches and routers also take advantage of them to advertise supervisory information or to share information necessary to perform scheduled and unscheduled network control functions.

1.3.2 DIRECTIONALITY IN DATA EXCHANGE

Data flows between two network nodes can be one of three types in directionality: *simplex*, *half-duplex*, and *full-duplex* (see Figure 1.8).

1.3.2.1 Simplex

With simplex transmissions, data flow in one direction only. Radio and TV broadcasting services are good examples. The simplex mode of communications also exists between a computer and its input devices (e.g., keyboard, mouse). This, however, is not a prevalent mode when it comes to the computer network.

1.3.2.2 Duplex

In the duplex mode, data flow both ways between two network nodes and thus each node has the capability of sending and receiving data. Duplex transmissions are in the half-duplex or full-duplex mode.

Half-duplex: In this mode, only one party is allowed to transmit data at a time, and the other party should wait until its turn. For a good analogy, imagine the two-way traffic flow on a single lane railway. Another well-known example is the walkie-talkie, a portable radio device that communicators take turns to talk. Although used in the early generation of computer networking by the hub (or multi-port repeater), it has been largely replaced by the more effective full-duplex mode of communications these days.

Full-duplex: With full-duplex, data can flow in both directions simultaneously between two network nodes. For this, there are generally two separate channels established for a link (or circuit): one channel for each direction. It is similar to having double lanes for two-way traffic. The traditional telephone system has been using full-duplex so that two communicators on a circuit can talk and listen concurrently. Most computer networks take advantage of the full-duplex technology these days.

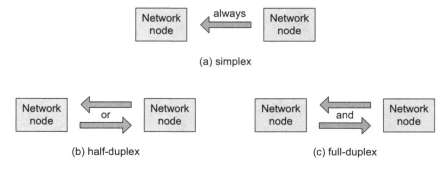

FIGURE 1.8   Simplex, half-duplex, and full-duplex transmissions

1.4 NETWORK TOPOLOGY

Network topology is defined as the physical layout of a network, a design approach utilized to interconnect network nodes (i.e., intermediary devices and hosts). The logical layout concept also exists, but we focus more on the physical arrangement of network nodes and links. The physical layout of a network can be understood in terms of the relationship between *intermediary devices* and *hosts,* between *hosts,* or between *intermediary devices.*

Many different topologies including bus, star, ring, mesh, tree (or hierarchy), and hybrid (e.g., bus-star) have been in use to arrange network nodes. Each topology has its own strengths and weaknesses, and the design process of an enterprise network should factor in various elements unique to its organizational circumstance. They include characteristics of business *locations* (e.g., number of locations, degree of their distribution), *users* (e.g., number of users), *hosts* (e.g., type and number of onsite hosts), *applications* (e.g., importance of reliability in message delivery), and *security conditions.*

1.4.1 POINT-TO-POINT TOPOLOGY

As the simplest topology, point-to-point establishes a direct connection between two nodes. There may be only two end nodes directly linked or more than two nodes between two end nodes making it an extended point-to-point connection (see Figure 1.9). A point-to-point link can be given permanent and dedicated capacity, as in the case of the phone line between a house and a telephone company. Or, it can be dynamically constructed and dismantled as needed. This dynamic formation occurs more often in the form of extended point-to-point topology. For example, a long-distance or an international call between two remote locations requires dynamic circuit formation through multiple telephone switches.

1.4.2 BUS TOPOLOGY

In a bus, end nodes are directly connected to a half-duplex common line, with a terminator device at each end of the line absorbing data remaining in the network (see Figure 1.10). Communications between any two stations, therefore, should be made via the backbone medium. Using the common

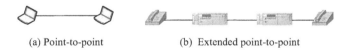

      (a) Point-to-point   (b) Extended point-to-point

FIGURE 1.9 (Extended) point-to-point topologies

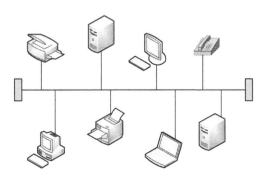

FIGURE 1.10 Bus Topology (LAN example)

line approach practically results in the *broadcasting* of data in which transmissions from a station reach all the other stations on the network, although there is only one intended receiver. This topology, therefore, allows only a single station to release data at a time to avoid transmission collisions.

With its structural simplicity, the bus topology works well for small networks. However, it is subject to traffic congestions when a network grows with more stations attached. The first generation of Ethernet LANs ran on the bus topology, but it is not used today due to inherent limitations including unnecessary data broadcasting and difficulties in cabling (e.g., installing a mainline inside the ceiling).

1.4.3 RING TOPOLOGY

With ring topology, nodes are attached to a backbone ring that may be a copper wire or optical fiber. Depending on the technology standard, a network can have a single-ring or dual-ring architecture that affords redundancy and thus higher survivability from link failures (see Figure 1.11). The ring network has technological advantages in handling high volume traffic in a reliable manner. This topology is also adequate in constructing long-haul networks.

Despite the technological advancement and availability of ring-based standards for LANs such as Token Ring, their acceptance has been dwarfed by more cost-effective Ethernet that runs on star (or extended star) topology. Ring topology, however, remains a popular choice in creating a high-speed WAN backbone with fiber optics (more in Chapter 12).

1.4.4 STAR (HUB-AND-SPOKE) TOPOLOGY

With star topology, host stations are connected to a central intermediary device (see Figure 1.12). The topology has several advantages. Above all, the topology makes it is easy to add and remove a host station from a network and also to troubleshoot network problems. It is also relatively simple to add more stations to a network. Ethernet LANs mostly run on this topology these days. With Ethernet being a dominant wired LAN standard, there are many equipment options (e.g., cabling, ports, connection speeds) with competitive pricing. As a disadvantage, the intermediary device becomes a single point of failure that can bring down a network.

An enterprise can also adopt a star to interconnect distributed LANs with WAN connections. In this case, the network node placed at the hub location (e.g., main office) mediates traffic between any other locations. Observe that the WAN topology is determined by the relationship among intermediary devices such as routers rather than that between hosts and an intermediary device.

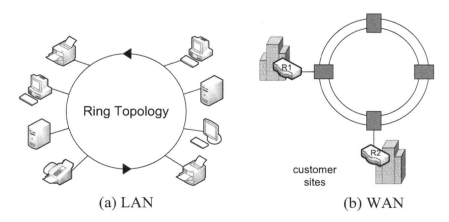

(a) LAN   (b) WAN

FIGURE 1.11   Ring topology (LAN and WAN examples)

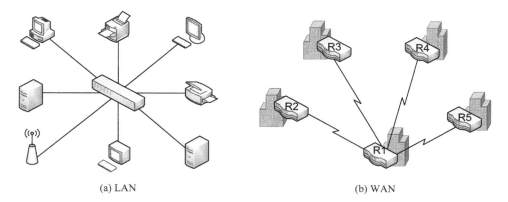

(a) LAN   (b) WAN

FIGURE 1.12   Star (hub-and-spoke) topology (LAN and WAN examples)

1.4.5   MESH TOPOLOGY

Mesh topology represents an arrangement when all possible connections between network nodes are directly linked (see Figure 1.13). This makes a mesh network very reliable through extra redundancies in which one inoperable node does not drag down the entire network. The mesh network can be a sound option when the number of nodes is relatively small. For example, with three network nodes, only three connections are required, and four nodes take six direct links.

As more devices or locations are attached to a network, the number of direct connections increases exponentially making full-mesh less practical in terms of operational costs. The partial-mesh topology uses fewer links (thus lowering the cost burden) than full-mesh but more links than the star (hub-and-spoke), making a network less vulnerable to link failures with the redundancy.

1.4.6   TREE (OR HIERARCHICAL) TOPOLOGY

With tree topology, nodes are joined in a hierarchical fashion in which the one on top becomes a root node (see Figure 1.14). There are two or more levels in the hierarchy with the number of nodes increasing at the lower level, making the overall structure like a Christmas tree. The tree structure is highly effective when many nodes (or locations) have to be interconnected using reduced direct links. This topology has been a popular choice among telephone service providers in constructing a network to cover a large geographical area of many cities and towns.

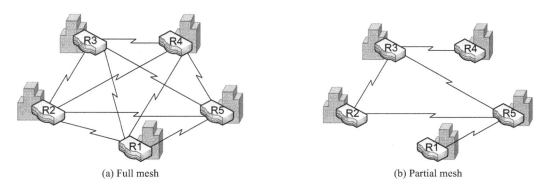

(a) Full mesh   (b) Partial mesh

FIGURE 1.13   Full mesh and partial mesh topology (WAN examples)

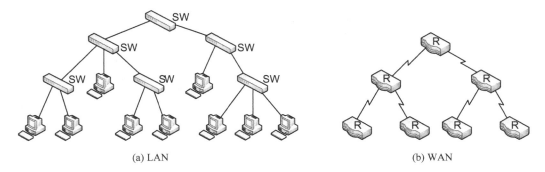

(a) LAN   (b) WAN

FIGURE 1.14   Tree/hierarchical topology (LAN and WAN examples)

1.4.7 Notes on Hybrid Network Deployment

When it comes to actual implementations, many corporate networks adopt a hybrid solution that combines more than one topology. Think of a network that covers a building of several floors. To connect a large number of end nodes to the network, star and tree topologies or star and mesh topologies can be combined. For example, the network segment of each floor can be star-based. Then, the multiple star networks from different floors can be tied to higher-speed devices in a tree or mesh structure to form a bigger LAN that covers the entire building.

In such a hybrid network architecture, intermediary devices located at a higher level generally handle more traffic and thus should be more powerful (e.g., faster forwarding rates) than those at the lower level. When the intermediary devices are interconnected in full mesh (rather than in a tree), it is called Leaf-Spine (more in Chapter 7).

1.5   CLASSIFICATION OF NETWORKS

In terms of the scope, computer networks are generally classified into four different types: Personal area networks (PANs), local area networks (LANs), metropolitan area networks (MANs), and wide area networks (WANs). Each type has widely accepted standard technologies.

1.5.1 Personal Area Network (PAN)

The PAN represents a small network whose coverage is typically a few meters or less. It has been popularized with the introduction of such wireless standards as *Bluetooth*, *Wi-Fi Direct*, *Zigbee*, and more recently *NFC* (*Near Field Communication*). For instance, NFC represents a set of short-range – generally up to 2 inches (or 4 cm) – technologies for small data sharing. NFC-enabled portable devices read tags or do credit card transactions through such tap-and-pay systems as Apple Pay and Google Wallet.

As another popular standard of the short-range PAN, Bluetooth builds a network organized around an individual and thus allows devices located in close proximity to exchange data without hard wiring. Figure 1.15 illustrates the usage of Bluetooth to interconnect computing and electronic devices in the wireless setting.

1.5.2 Local Area Network (LAN)

The LAN, in general, covers a relatively confined area to interconnect hosts located within the physical boundary of an organization or a company, making it larger than the personal area network in coverage. The size of LANs varies considerably as it is determined by the size of an organization.

FIGURE 1.15   Bluetooth-enabled personal area networks

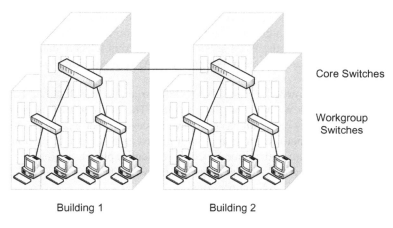

FIGURE 1.16   An illustration of a campus LAN

For example, if a company occupies only a single floor of a building, the firm's LAN is limited to the floor. If an organization uses all floors of a building, its LAN covers the entire building.

A bigger network that interconnects multiple buildings within a university or corporate campus is also a LAN. The oversized LAN is frequently termed as a campus LAN or campus area network. The campus LAN's extended scale makes its design and operations more challenging than smaller LANs. To create a campus LAN, smaller networks (e.g., one in a building) are joined by high-speed intermediary devices (e.g., core routers or switches) in a tree or mesh structure of two or three layers (see Figure 1.14).

As a simple example, imagine a relatively small-scale campus LAN of two buildings, each with a fast core switch and two workgroup switches that attach computers to the LAN (see Figure 1.16). Depending on the enterprise or university size, the actual campus LAN can be significantly more complex than the example. The dominant Ethernet and Wi-Fi LAN standards are covered in Chapters

6 and 7. As a LAN is installed within an organization's boundary, the organization fully controls any changes including its maintenance and upgrades.

1.5.3 METROPOLITAN AREA NETWORK (MAN)

The MAN is generally designed to cover a good-sized city, being considerably larger in its geographical span than the LAN. The MAN is used to interconnect LANs through land-based or wireless standards within a metropolitan area. In general, *common carriers* (or telecom carriers) such as telephone service providers (telcos) and Internet service providers (ISPs) have ownership of the MAN infrastructure. Corporate clients subscribe to the MAN service in order to access the Internet or connect to other business locations (e.g., branch offices).

Figure 1.17 demonstrates a hypothetical MAN of a common carrier in the Boston metropolitan area, which runs on high-speed links (e.g., 10 Gigabits/second) and fast intermediary devices. It shows that, through the MAN, the three client site LANs are interconnected and also can send data to the Internet and to the carrier's WAN platform.

In the past, WAN standards were technology choices for the MAN infrastructure. However, with the popularity of Ethernet as a LAN standard, the Ethernet-based technology called Metro-Ethernet has become a preferred choice for the MAN platform.

1.5.4 WIDE AREA NETWORK (WAN)

The WAN is designed to cover a state, a nation, or an international territory (see Figure 1.18). It interlinks LANs including campus networks, MANs, and even smaller WANs. In order to tie its geographically distributed LANs, a client organization (e.g., university, company) creates its own private WAN connections through the WAN service available from telecom carriers (e.g., Verizon, Vodafone). The carriers install and maintain their private WAN infrastructure to commercially offer WAN services to clients.

Separate from the carrier-owned private WAN infrastructure, the Internet has become an extremely popular platform for WAN connections as well. The Internet itself is the largest global network that no single company or nation has exclusive ownership. For example, a telecom carrier (e.g., AT&T) has its own Internet infrastructure, but it makes up just a small fraction of the global Internet backbone. With its ubiquity that literally covers the entire planet, the Internet offers significant flexibility (connect anytime and anyplace) and cost advantage (substantially cheaper than the private WAN service) in creating WAN connections.

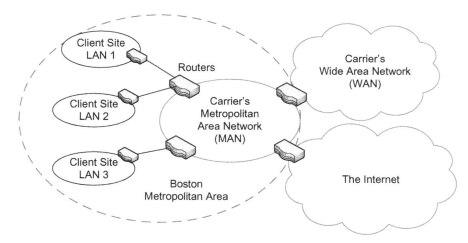

FIGURE 1.17   An illustration of MAN

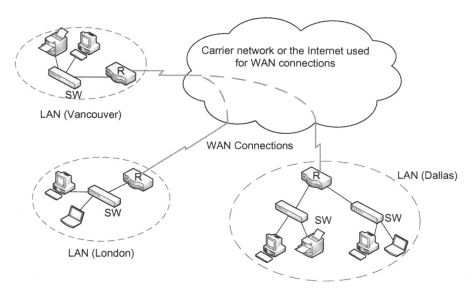

FIGURE 1.18 WAN links and an enterprise network

1.5.5 NOTE ON THE ENTERPRISE NETWORK

The *enterprise network* spans an organization to facilitate communications among employees, departments, workgroups, and other entities. An organization's units may be housed in one building or several buildings at a location, distributed in multiple locations throughout the region, or dispersed nationally or globally. Reflecting the structural diversity of organizations, an enterprise network can be any combination of one or more PANs, LANs, and MAN/WAN connections.

1.5.6 NOTE ON THE INTERNET OF THINGS (IoT)

With the prevalence of PANs, LANs, MANs, and WANs, a new paradigm called *Internet of Things* (or IoT) is rapidly rising. IoT is not a type of network/networking technology but represents a new development in which numerous devices (e.g., cars, appliances, gadgets, electronics, mobile devices, security monitoring devices, health devices, sensors) automatically detect each other and communicate seamlessly to perform a host of tasks over wired/wireless networks and the Internet. Surely, the various network types explained in Section 1.5 will bring IoT to reality, although its full swing may be years away. The emerging IoT paradigm is going to fundamentally transform the society through the transparent and automated connectivity among numerous computing and non-computing devices.

1.6 SUBNETWORK VS. INTERNETWORK

Building on the explanation of intermediary devices in Section 1.2.2, the relationship among the *network*, *subnetwork* (or *subnet*), and *internetwork* (or *internet*) is further clarified. The network is a loosely defined term whose scope covers a variety of small and large settings. Section 1.5 classified it in terms of the PAN, LAN, MAN, and WAN types. Depending on how it is designed, a network can be a single subnetwork or an internetwork with multiple subnetworks joined by one or more routers. Note that the internetwork is a generic term and thus differs from the Internet (*I* as an uppercase letter), the largest network on the planet.

1.6.1 INTERNETWORK: SCENARIO 1

Figure 1.19 is a simple demonstration in which two subnetworks are tied by a router to become an internetwork. When two computers exchange data across the two subnetworks, the data forwarding process (or activity) is called 'inter-networking'. As related, the difference between intra-networking and inter-networking was explained in Figure 1.4 in which a subnetwork contains several intermediary devices (e.g., switches, wireless access points) used for intra-networking. In summary, Figure 1.19 is a scenario in which the whole network as a LAN is an internetwork with two subnetworks.

1.6.2 INTERNETWORK: SCENARIO 2

Figure 1.20 is another scenario of a company network composed of two remotely located office LANs joined by a proprietary WAN link leased from a telco (e.g., AT&T) and thus not an Internet connection. In that setup, each LAN is a subnetwork because delivering messages within the LAN boundary does not need the router's help. This differs from Figure 1.19, in which one LAN consists of two subnetworks.

Additionally, the 'private' WAN connection is considered a subnetwork although it may be 3,000 miles long! That is, the company's enterprise network becomes an internetwork with three subnetworks. The two simple scenarios highlight the fluid relationship among the LAN/WAN, subnetwork, and internetwork boundaries.

1.7 MEASURES OF NETWORK PERFORMANCE

Network performance in effectively propagating host-produced data is a critical issue, and much consideration should be given to optimize it during the stages of network planning, design, implementation, maintenance, and upgrade. There is no shortage of stories that underscore the importance of adequate network performance, especially as the network handles more real-time (e.g., video conferencing, online gaming) and mission-critical (e.g., financial transactions, e-commerce) data these days.

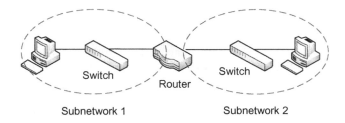

FIGURE 1.19   Scenario 1: A company's network

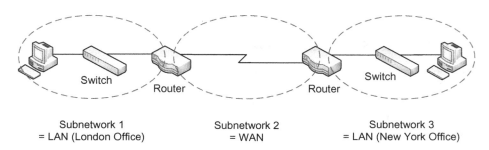

FIGURE 1.20   Scenario 2: A company's network

More applications demand a certain degree of 'guaranteed' performance regardless of the circumstance (e.g., traffic congestion). A number of measures are being used to reflect network performance from different angles, and those of *capacity* (or *speed*), *delay* (or *latency*), and *reliability* are among the most important ones.

1.7.1 Capacity

Network capacity (or speed) is gauged by the metrics of *data rate* (or data transfer rate). The data rate, shown as increasing factors of bits per second (or bps), is about how fast data can flow in one direction from point A to point B (not the combined speed of both directions). This is not to confuse between *byte* and *bit* metrics (1 byte is generally 8 bits) in which byte metrics are primarily used for data storage or memory capacity, not network speed. Table 1.1 summarizes the metrics of storage/memory capacity and network capacity.

1.7.1.1 Data Types and Data Rate

Depending on the type of data to transfer, the required network speed differs considerably in which texts take up the smallest capacity followed by audios and videos. These days, much of network traffic is in the multimedia format that combines the text, sound, graphics, image, and/or video. To put things in perspective, Table 1.2 summarizes the data rate necessary to transport audio and video data at different quality levels. MP3 and MPEC2 are popular compression standards used to encode audio and video contents.

TABLE 1.1
Metrics of storage vs. network capacity

Storage/memory capacity	Network capacity in data rate
KB (Kilobyte) = 1000 bytes	Kbps (kilobits/sec) = 1000 bits/sec
MB (Megabyte) = 1 million bytes	Mbps (Megabits/sec) = 1 million bits/sec
GB (Gigabyte) = 1 billion bytes	Gbps (Gigabits/sec) = 1 billion bits/sec
TB (Terabyte) = 1 trillion bytes	Tbps (Terabits/sec) = 1 trillion bits/sec
PB (Petabyte) = 1 quadrillion bytes	Pbps (Petabits/sec) = 1 quadrillion bits/sec

TABLE 1.2
Data rates necessary to transfer audio/video of different qualities

Type of content	Quality level	Data rate
	Telephone sound quality	8 Kbps
Audio (MP3 encoding)	AM sound quality	32 Kbps
	FM sound quality	96 Kbps
	CD sound quality	224–320 Kbps
Video (MPEC2 encoding)	DVD quality	5 Mbps
	HDTV quality	15 Mbps

1.7.1.2   Channel Capacity and Throughput

A network's transmission capacity can be measured in terms of both *channel capacity* and *throughput*.

Channel capacity: It is the maximum theoretical data rate of a link and is also called *bandwidth* or *rated speed*. Strictly speaking, channel capacity (measured in terms of data rate) is a digital concept and bandwidth is an analog concept (see Section 1.10.3). However, they are directly correlated – the bigger the bandwidth of a link, the bigger the channel capacity – and practitioners use them interchangeably.

Throughput: It refers to the actual data rate of a link. As a more realistic speed, it is lower than channel capacity due to a number of limiting circumstantial factors. Among them are the link distance, transmission interferences, and internal/external noises. For instance, Wi-Fi 6 has a theoretical bandwidth of more than 1 Gbps (see Chapter 6). However, its actual throughput is substantially lower due to various impeding factors such as the distance between two communicating nodes.

1.7.2   DELAY

Delay (or latency) represents the amount of time a network link takes to deliver data between any two nodes and is usually in milliseconds (or 1000th of a second). Delay can be measured in both a one-way trip and a round trip (e.g., a request and response cycle) between two points.

1.7.2.1   Delay Sources

When computers exchange data, there are various delay sources. Imagine the hypothetical situation in which a person downloads the landing page of *www.facebook.com*. She/he will certainly experience delays until the whole page is constructed on the browser. Among the delay sources are:

a. **Propagation delays**: It takes time for the signal carrying the webpage to travel between two remotely located hosts.
b. **Delays at hosts**: The source host should internally process the user request before releasing it to the Internet. This includes conversion of the request into a packet and then to an electronic signal for propagation (more in Chapter 3). When the request arrives at the destination host (i.e., *www.facebook.com* server), it also performs the similar internal processing to ultimately produce a response packet and convert it to a signal for delivery.
c. **Delays at intermediary devices:** Intermediary devices (e.g., router, switch) mediate data transmissions between hosts, and their message forwarding requires their own internal processing. This includes the lookup of a reference table (e.g., routing table, switch table) and subsequent forwarding path decisions. Also, when messages arrive at their port continuously, they may be temporarily placed in a queue before processing, inevitably resulting in queuing delay.

Delays are especially a sensitive issue when a network is used by time-sensitive applications. In fact, with the ever-growing popularity of real-time or near-real-time multimedia applications such as video-conferencing and online gaming, more data need to be transferred with little delay and oftentimes with guaranteed performance.

1.7.3   RELIABILITY

This performance dimension is about a network's ability to convey data in a stable manner. The reliability of data delivery is mildly or severely affected (1) when there are corrupted or lost data in the middle of transmissions and (2) when a network experiences interruptions (e.g., node failures, link failures).

1.7.3.1 Corrupted or Lost Data

Data corruption or loss takes place in different magnitudes. It can be as small as a bit change (e.g., from 0 to 1) or as big as the moderation or loss of entire bitstreams. There are a number of sources that trigger the reliability problem. Among them are the network node crash caused by certain forces, physical damage or cut of cabling, overflow of a network node's buffer space, power interruption or surge, and internal and external noise triggered by lightning, industrial noise, crosstalk, and other forces.

1.7.3.2 Network Unavailability

A network becomes unavailable when there is a node or link failure. Just as a computer crashes, an intermediary device can fail for various reasons including overload, bug(s) in the embedded software, power interruption, malicious attack (e.g., denial-of-service attack), and operational mismanagement. Also, the network link can be a source of trouble when it is accidentally damaged or when the cabling between a node and a link is unstable. When a network itself becomes unavailable either entirely or partially due to the node or link fault, this limits network accessibility.

1.7.4 QUALITY OF SERVICE (QOS)

A concept closely associated with network performance is Quality of Service (QoS). QoS represents the capability of LANs and WANs in provisioning *guaranteed performance* in terms of link capacity, latency, and reliability. It is particularly germane to the carrier's WAN (including Internet) service offered to corporate clients in transferring business data. In early days, QoS was not such a critical issue for WAN connections as network applications were not that sophisticated and mission-critical. However, as more computer programs perform business functions vital to organizations over the network, the WAN's ability to guarantee network performance has become an essential requirement.

As a simple example, Amazon.com and eBay.com rely entirely on the Internet for business transactions, and even a few minutes of Internet disruptions will directly translate into millions of dollars in lost revenue. When a carrier offers QoS to a client organization, its network should be able to provide the client with the level of 'promised' performance regardless of circumstances (e.g., traffic congestion).

The QoS-guaranteed network service is costlier than the non-QoS service to client organizations. A carrier can use such techniques as data prioritization and the dedication of link capacity to enhance service quality. Businesses, however, may not need such QoS provision if their WAN links are used mainly for general applications (e.g., emails, web surfing).

1.8 NUMBERING SYSTEMS

This section reviews three different numbering systems (i.e., binary, decimal, and hexadecimal) used to represent numeric values in networking. Although they are used altogether, there is a preference for one system over the others depending on the usage context. As we are already aware, network nodes process various data types (e.g., texts, images, videos) in binary of 0s and 1s.

Data in binary, however, are hard for humans to comprehend, and thus both decimal (with 10-base) and hexadecimal (with 16-base) numbering systems are also utilized for readability. With 16-base arithmetic, hexadecimal is more efficient than decimal in expressing binary combinations. As such, the translation between binary and decimal and that between binary and hexadecimal become fundamental in studying computer networking, especially network addressing. Table 1.3 summarizes three numbering systems and their base digits.

TABLE 1.3
Numbering systems

Numbering system	Number of digits in base	Digits
Binary	2	0 and 1
Decimal	10	0 through 9
Hexadecimal	16	0 through 9, A, B, C, D, E, and F (in which A = 10, B = 11, C = 12, D = 13, E = 14, F = 15)

Note: To differentiate decimal and hexadecimal, hexadecimal values are indicated by either *0x* prefix or *h* suffix. For example, *0x*3256 means that 3256 is hexadecimal.

1.8.1 BINARY VS. DECIMAL

The translation between binary and decimal is explained based on the unit of 8 bits as it becomes the building block of 32-bit IP addresses for the IPv4 standard. For example, an IP address of 123.45.56.89 is equivalent to 01111011.00101101.00111000.01011001. The binary-decimal conversion is demonstrated using an example of 8-bit binary (01011010) and its equivalent decimal (90) values.

1. Binary (01011010) to decimal (90) conversion

    a. First, determine the decimal position value of each binary bit using the *power-of-two* computation.
    b. Once decimal position values are in place, add up the decimal values of non-zero binary positions. In the example, the summation of 64, 16, 8, and 2 becomes 90.

Initial binary combination (8bits)	0	1	0	1	1	0	1	0
Power of two	2^7	2^6	2^5	2^4	2^3	2^2	2^1	2^0
Decimal position values	128	64	32	16	8	4	2	1
Add decimal values of non-zero binary positions		64		+16	+8		+2	= 90

2. Decimal (90) to binary (01011010) conversion

Decimal position values		128	64	32	16	8	4	2	1
a. Find the largest decimal position value that is less than or equal to 90.	128	[64]	32	16	8	4	2	1
b. Obtain the remainder value	Difference between 90 and 64 = 26							
c. Find the largest decimal position value that is less than or equal to the remainder value 26.	128	64	32	[16]	8	4	2	1
d. Obtain the remainder value	Difference between 26 and 16 = 10							
e. Find the largest decimal position value that is less than or equal to the remainder value 10.	128	64	32	16	[8]	4	2	1
f. Obtain the remainder value	Difference between 10 and 8 = 2							
g. Find the largest decimal position value that is less than or equal to the remainder value 2.	128	64	32	16	8	4	[2]	1
h. Obtain the remainder value. As the remainder becomes 0, stop here.	Difference between 2 and 2 = 0							
i. Binary numbers corresponding to the parenthesis values above are 1s and the others are 0s.	0	1	0	1	1	0	1	0

Note: 01011010 (8 bit) is identical to 1011010 (7 bit). The demonstration is based on the 8-bit combination.

1.8.2 BINARY VS. HEXADECIMAL (EXTRA)

In computer networking, hexadecimal digits are used to represent MAC addresses and IPv6 addresses. For MAC, each address is 48 bits (see Section 1.9.1), and they are converted into 12 hexadecimal digits. That is, each hex digit is equivalent to 4 bits. The following demonstrates the conversion between a hexadecimal digit and its equivalent 4 binary bits. The conversion takes nothing but the translation between a hexadecimal's decimal value and its corresponding 4 bits. For example, the hexadecimal digit 'A' is equivalent to the decimal '10', which in turn translates into 1010 in binary using the same conversion method in Section 1.8.1.

Hexadecimal		Decimal		Binary
A	=>	10	=>	1010
A	<=	10	<=	1010

To translate a binary bitstream into its corresponding hexadecimal values, the bitstream should be divided into 4-bit blocks first. Then, convert each 4-bit unit into its corresponding decimal value and subsequently find its hexadecimal equivalence. Recall that A = 10, B = 11, C = 12, D = 13, E = 14, F = 15. As an example, for the binary bitstream of 100101101000010101101:

a. Creation of 4-bit blocks: 100101101000010101101 becomes 1001.0110.1000.1010.1101.
b. Conversion of each block into a decimal value: 1001.0110.1000.1010.1101 becomes 9.6.8.10.13.
c. Conversion of each decimal value into a hexadecimal equivalence: 9.6.8.10.13 becomes 0x968AD.

1.9 NETWORK ADDRESSING

Just as postal addresses are necessary to deliver snail mails, network nodes transport data to the destination relying on its standardized address. Two different address schemes are used *concurrently* in computer networking: MAC (Media Access Control) and IP addresses.

1.9.1 MAC ADDRESS

The network interface card (NIC) of a computer has at least one MAC address assigned to it. The MAC address is also known as a physical or hardware address because it is permanently printed on a NIC and thus cannot be changed (although it can be spoofed or masked using software). The NIC for Ethernet or Wi-Fi as two most dominant LAN standards uses a MAC address of 48 bits, which is burned into the NIC's *read only memory* (ROM). When a node is started, its MAC address is copied into the NIC's *random access memory* (RAM) to enable the node's networking function.

As explained, the 48-bit MAC address is presented to people as 12 hexadecimal digits, each digit representing four binary bits. The MAC address in hex is generally written in one of three formats:

01-35-A7-BC-48-2D	(two hex digits separated by '–')
01.35.A7.BC.48.2D	(two hex digits separated by '.')
0135.A7BC.482D	(four hex digits separated by '.')

Of the 12 hexadecimal digits, the first six become an *Organizationally Unique Identifier* (or OUI). The OUI indicates a NIC's manufacturer and is assigned by the *Institute of Electrical and Electronics Engineers* (or IEEE), a leading standard-setting organization responsible for LAN standards including Ethernet and Wi-Fi. The remaining six digits represent a random combination uniquely allocated to each NIC. With this allocation scheme, no two NICs in the world should share the same MAC address.

1.9.2   IP ADDRESS

The IP address is another global standard necessary for a network node to exchange data with any other nodes. Whereas the MAC address is a physical address, the IP address is a logical address because it can be detached from a node.

Two different IP standards are used concurrently: IPv4 (version 4) and IPv6 (also known as IP next generation or IPng). While the IPv4 address consists of 32 bits, IPv6 uses a 128-bit addressing scheme. The IP address is composed of network and host identity parts. For example, in 172.232.53.8 (IPv4), 172.232 and 53.8 may represent the network and host identities respectively. Chapter 4 covers IPv4 and IPv6 addressing.

The IP address can be assigned to a node temporarily or permanently. The temporary IP address is dynamically allocated to a host station whenever it issues a request and has an expiration. Whereas, the permanent IP address allocated to a network node stays with it so that the node can perform the intended service function without interruptions.

1.9.3   PAIRING OF MAC AND IP ADDRESSES

To be able to exchange data over the network, a host or end node (e.g., PC, tablet, smartphone) needs a pair of MAC and IP addresses. Figure 1.21 illustrates their one-to-one pairing (or binding). In the case of intermediary devices, the pairing relationship is a little different and will be explained in Chapter 5.

It is natural to raise the question of why a host needs the pairing of a MAC and an IP. A rather simple answer is that MAC is for intra-networking and IP is for inter-networking. In other words, within a subnetwork, the MAC address of a destination host is all it takes in delivering a message from a source station. When a packet has to cross multiple subnetworks (for inter-networking) before reaching the ultimate destination, its IP address needs to be continuously referenced by the router(s) on the way.

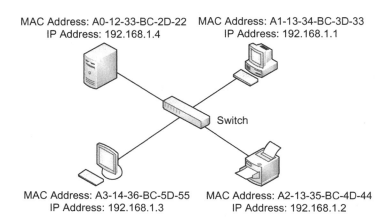

MAC Address: A0-12-33-BC-2D-22   MAC Address: A1-13-34-BC-3D-33
IP Address: 192.168.1.4   IP Address: 192.168.1.1

Switch

MAC Address: A3-14-36-BC-5D-55   MAC Address: A2-13-35-BC-4D-44
IP Address: 192.168.1.3   IP Address: 192.168.1.2

FIGURE 1.21   Pairing of MAC and IP addresses

1.10 DATA TRANSMISSION TECHNOLOGIES

Data in various formats (e.g., texts, images, audios, videos) are produced by many different sources including computers, video cameras, and smartphones. The source data are either digital or analog. As an example of the digital format, text data produced by computer keyboarding are stored as a combination of 0s and 1s. As for the analog format, such source data as the human voice, audio, and video take the wave shapes that continuously vary rising and falling in intensity with an infinite number of states in the wave.

1.10.1 DATA ENCODING/DECODING

Regardless of whether the original data are digital or analog, they are processed by computers and network nodes in 1s and 0s. This requires conversion between non-binary data contents and binary bitstreams. The term *data encoding* represents the translation process from source data (e.g., videos) to their corresponding bitstream and *data decoding* is the reverse process. The data encoding and decoding is generally the responsibility of user application programs (e.g., browser).

1.10.2 SIGNAL ENCODING/DECODING

Signal encoding represents processing necessary to transport computer-produced binary bitstreams over the wireless or wired network. The propagation of bitstreams over a network can be done in digital or analog signaling, and this requires another conversion process called *signal encoding*.

For this, signals should be patterned in a way to embed the binary source data according to the standard rules of conversion. Two different approaches are used to convey a bitstream: digital signaling and analog signaling (see Figure 1.22). Here, the signals may be electronic pulses, light pulses, or radio waves that travel over wired (e.g., optical fibers, twisted pairs) or wireless (e.g., earth's atmosphere) media. Methods of converting (or encoding) bitstreams into signals are standardized. This way, hosts and intermediary devices from different manufacturers can generate, transport, and process signals according to common encoding/decoding rules.

1.10.2.1 Digital Signal Encoding

Widely used in computer networking (especially with wired media), digital signal encoding represents binary bits in two or more discrete signaling *states*. There are two different techniques: on/off and voltage-based encoding (see Figures 1.23 and 1.24).

On/off signal encoding: On/off encoding is mainly used for bit transmissions over optical fibers. With on/off encoding, the light source (e.g., lasers) of the fiber optic system rapidly switches between on and off states to transmit bits according to exact timing. A good

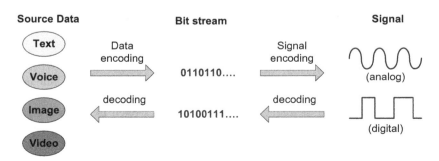

FIGURE 1.22 Data encoding/decoding vs. signal encoding/decoding

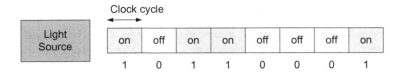

FIGURE 1.23 On/off digital signal encoding

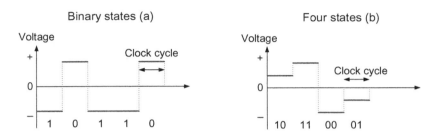

FIGURE 1.24 Voltage-based digital signal encoding

analogy of the on/off encoding is the practice of turning a flashlight on and off for communications between two sailing ships.

Voltage-based signal encoding: Voltage-based encoding is another method primarily used on traditional copper wires such as twisted pairs and coaxial cables to transport digitized source data. To represent binary bits, different voltage states that sustain the same signal strength during a timed clock cycle are used. At the end of each clock cycle, the voltage state may abruptly change to another state to reflect another bit or bit combination.

Depending on the standard, there may be two voltage states, each state indicating either 0 or 1 (see Figure 1.24a). Or, there may be more than two voltage states so that each state represents two or more data bits. For example, Figure 1.24b shows that when there are four voltage states, a state can convey (or encode) two bits of data in one clock cycle because the four states can reflect all possible combinations of two bits: 00, 01, 10, and 11. In other words, each of the four voltage states can uniquely identify a two-bit combination. Several encoding standards have been introduced to carry multiple bits in one voltage state for faster data transmissions.

1.10.2.2 Analog Signal Encoding

1.10.2.2.1 Properties of an Analog Signal

Before introducing the techniques of analog signal encoding, a basic understanding of the general properties of an analog signal is necessary. As in Figure 1.25, an electromagnetic wave has several key properties or parameters of *amplitude*, *frequency*, *phase*, and *wavelength*.

a. **Frequency** represents the number of cycles a wave has in every second. When a wave has one cycle per second, its frequency is 1 Hertz (or Hz). As an example, the human voice takes a continuous (analog) waveform and has a frequency typically ranging between 300 Hz and 3400 Hz. The magnitude of frequency decides a signal's pitch in which a high frequency results in a high pitch. As another example, a cable has a frequency range it can support. Frequency metrics are summarized in Table 1.4.

b. **Amplitude** represented by such metric as *voltage* is the indication of a signal's strength, and it is measured by the highest point of a wave.

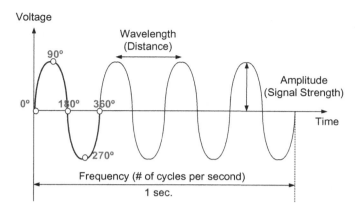

FIGURE 1.25 Analog signal and parameters

TABLE 1.4
Hierarchy of frequency metrics

Unit of frequency	No. of cycles/second
Hertz (Hz)	1 cycle
Kilohertz (kHz) = 1000 Hz	1000 cycles
Megahertz (MHz) = 1000 kHz	1 million cycles
Gigahertz (GHz) = 1000 MHz	1 billion cycles
Terahertz (THz) = 1000 GHz	1 trillion cycles

---

c. **Wavelength** is defined as the distance between two adjacent peaks of a wave. Wavelength is inversely proportional to frequency: the higher the frequency, the smaller the wavelength. Depending on the frequency of an analog signal, its wavelength varies significantly (e.g., the length of a football field or of a molecule).

d. **Phase** represents the relative position of a signal point on a waveform cycle and is measured by an angular degree within the cycle. Figure 1.25 demonstrates five different angular degrees or phases (0°, 90°, 180°, 270° and 360°) of the first cycle.

1.10.2.2.2 Modulation

For analog signal encoding (or signaling), the parameter values of *frequency*, *amplitude*, and *phase* are varied to encode digital data. The process of altering analog signal characteristics to codify source bit data is called modulation. When the frequency, amplitude, or phase attributes of an analog signal is altered to embed bitstream data, it is called *frequency modulation*, *amplitude modulation*, or *phase modulation* respectively.

Modulation techniques are also available when source data are analog (e.g., AM radio broadcasting, FM radio music), resulting in the *analog data-to-analog signal* conversion. But, our main interest is the transportation of digital bitstreams produced by computers and other digital devices, and thus the explanation focuses on the modulation of digital bitstreams to analog signals.

Figure 1.26 demonstrates amplitude modulation and frequency modulation. With amplitude modulation in Figure 1.26a, different amplitudes of an analog signal are used to differentiate source values of 0s (e.g., low amplitude) and 1s (e.g., high amplitude). You can observe that the frequency remains the same and only the amplitude changes reflecting source bits. With frequency modulation,

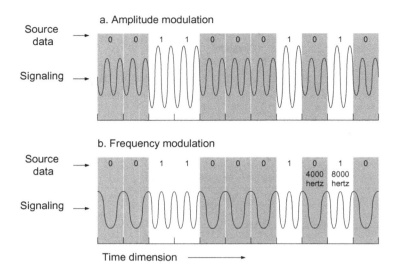

FIGURE 1.26   Amplitude (a) and frequency (b) modulation

different signal frequencies are applied to represent 0s and 1s. In Figure 1.26b, for example, 0s and 1s can be indicated by a low (e.g., 4000Hz) frequency and a high (e.g., 8000Hz) frequency respectively. Recall that each bit interval is precisely controlled by the clock cycle of a network node.

1.10.3   BANDWIDTH

In its technical definition, *bandwidth* represents the frequency range between the highest and the lowest frequencies supported by a channel or a medium. Wired (or guided) and wireless (or unguided) media including copper wires, optical fibers, and radio waves all have their frequency ranges supported. For example, if the frequency of a radio channel ranges between 30 kHz and 300 kHz, its bandwidth becomes 300 kHz − 30 kHz = 270 kHz. As another example, given that the human voice generally ranges 300 Hz through 3400 Hz, its bandwidth is 3400 Hz − 300 Hz = 3100 Hz.

Bandwidth is, therefore, an analog concept that directly relates to a channel's or medium's frequency range. It is an important concept in computer networking because the digital capacity of a medium or channel is a direct function of its bandwidth – the larger the bandwidth, the bigger the capacity in bits per second (bps). For this reason, industry practitioners have been using bandwidth and digital capacity (or speed) interchangeably. As related, there are significant differences in bandwidth among communication media (e.g., optical fiber vs. copper wire), which explains a large discrepancy in their data transmission capacity.

CHAPTER SUMMARY

* A computer network is made up of various hardware and software components including hosts, intermediary devices, network links (or communication links), applications, data/messages, and network protocols.
* Data communications between network nodes are primarily in the form of *unicasting*, *broadcasting*, and *multicasting*.
* Data flows between two network nodes can be *simplex* (i.e., one way only), *half-duplex* (i.e., two ways but one way at a time), and *full-duplex* (i.e., two ways concurrently).
* A network topology refers to the layout of network nodes and links, a design approach utilized to interconnect intermediary devices and hosts. Among different topologies are point-to-point, bus, star (or hub-and-spoke), ring, mesh, and tree (or hierarchy).

- Computer networks are generally classified into four types in terms of their scope: Personal area networks (PAN), local area networks (LANs), metropolitan area networks (MANs) and wide area networks (WANs).
- The subnetwork (or subnet) is a network segment formed when intermediary devices including bridges, wireless access points, and switches interconnect host computers. The router is used to tie different subnetworks to form an internetwork (or internet).
- The primary dimensions of network performance include capacity (or speed), delay (or latency), and reliability. As related, Quality of Service (QoS) represents a network's ability to guarantee such performance.
- Three different numbering systems (i.e., binary, decimal, and hexadecimal) are used in computer networking and a particular numbering system is preferred over the others depending on the usage context.
- Network nodes transport data relying on standardized address information, and MAC and IP addresses are used concurrently.
- *Data encoding* represents the translation process from source data (e.g., videos) to their corresponding bitstream, and *data decoding* is the reverse process.
- Signal encoding is the process necessary to transport computer-produced binary bitstreams over the wireless or wired network.
- To transmit data over the network, both digital and analog signal encoding techniques are used. The signals may be electronic pulses, light pulses, or radio waves that travel over wired (e.g., twisted pairs) or wireless (e.g., atmosphere) media.
- There are two different digital signal encoding approaches: on/off and voltage-based.
- For analog signal encoding, the properties (i.e., amplitude, frequency) of continuously varying electromagnetic waves are changed to codify bitstream data. The process is called modulation.
- Bandwidth is an analog concept and represents the frequency range between the highest and the lowest frequencies supported by a channel or a medium.

KEY TERMS

access link
amplitude
amplitude modulation
analog signal
application
bandwidth
binary
bits per second (bps)
Bluetooth
broadcasting
bus topology
campus network
capacity
channel capacity
circuit switching
client-server computing
command line interface
data rate
decimal
decoding
delay

digital signal
duplex
encoding
end device
end station
end system
enterprise network
frequency
frequency modulation
full-duplex
half-duplex
hexadecimal (hex)
hierarchical topology
host
hub-and-spoke topology
ifconfig
intermediary device
internet
Internet
Internet of Things (IoT)
Inter-networking

intra-networking
IP address
ipconfig
IPv4
IPv6
latency
local area network (LAN)
logical address
MAC address
mesh topology
message
metropolitan area network (MAN)
multicasting
Near Field Communication (NFC)
network
network interface card (NIC)
network link
network node
networking device
Organizationally Unique Identifier (OUI)
peer-to-peer computing
permanent (or static) address
personal area network (PAN)
phase
physical address

point-to-point topology
protocol
Quality of Service (QoS)
random access memory (RAM)
read only memory (ROM)
reliability
ring topology
semantic rule
simplex
star topology
subnetwork (subnet)
syntactic rule
temporary (or dynamic) address
throughput
topology
tree topology
trunk link
unicasting
wavelength
wide area network (WAN)
Wi-Fi
Wi-Fi Direct
wireless NIC (WNIC)
Zigbee

CHAPTER REVIEW QUESTIONS

1. _____ represents the layout of network nodes and links.
   A) Network node
   B) Network domain
   C) Network topology
   D) Network architecture
   E) Network blueprint
2. Choose an ACCURATE statement regarding the relationship between hosts, intermediary devices, and network nodes.
   A) Hosts are intermediary devices.
   B) Hosts are also called networking devices.
   C) Intermediary devices include network nodes and hosts.
   D) An intermediary device is either a network node or a host.
   E) Network nodes include intermediary devices and hosts.
3. Which topology is used widely when network redundancy is important to prepare for node or link failures?
   A) point-to-point
   B) partial mesh
   C) star
   D) bus
   E) hub-and-spoke
4. When the number of possible voltage states doubles in digital signal encoding,
   A) two more bits can be additionally sent per clock cycle.
   B) the effective data rate is increased by 50%.

C) the effective data rate is reduced by 50%.

D) the number of bits sent per clock cycle remains the same.

E) one more bit can be additionally sent per clock cycle.

5. Star topology is also known as:

A) ring

B) partial mesh

C) full mesh

D) bus

E) hub-and-spoke

6. Which is an access link?

A) router–router link

B) switch–switch link

C) switch–router link

D) webserver–switch link

E) wireless access point–switch link

7. The Organizationally Unique Identifier (OUI) is an element of _____.

A) MAC addresses

B) public addresses

C) IP addresses

D) global addresses

E) local addresses

8. The *throughput* of a network

A) represents the speed guaranteed by a service provider.

B) describes the strength of a signal.

C) is interchangeably used with the *rated speed*.

D) represents its maximum capacity in theory.

E) represents its actual speed.

9. In the network, data are produced and exchanged according to meticulously defined rules of communication and engagement. These rules are codified in the _____.

A) protocol

B) signal

C) network link

D) message

E) intermediary device

10. Choose an INCORRECT statement regarding the network link.

A) Copper wires and optical fibers are popular wired media these days.

B) Network links are divided into access and trunk links.

C) Creating a computer network needs to have at least one trunk link.

D) The access link provides connectivity between a host and an intermediary device.

E) The trunk link interconnects intermediary devices.

11. The campus network is a type of the _____.

A) local area network

B) metropolitan area network

C) personal area network

D) wide area network

E) wireless network

12. What is the binary combination of hexadecimal digits 'B301'?

A) 1110001100000001

B) 1011001100000001

C) 1001001100010001

D) 1011001100101001

E) 1011001100100101

13. Select an ACCURATE statement on network addressing.

A) MAC addresses of a university's PCs are the same in their first 6 hexadecimal digits.

B) The primary usage of the MAC address is for inter-networking.

C) The IPv4 address is longer in length than the MAC address.

D) An IP address should be permanently assigned to a host station.

E) A host station should have a MAC and an IP address for networking.

14. Which is TRUE regarding the MAC address?

A) It is a permanently printed address.

B) It is stored in a computer's random access memory (RAM) in 8 hexadecimal digits.

C) It is dynamically provided by a designated server to requesting stations.

D) It is determined by a computer's operating system.

E) Two computers can own the same MAC address.

15. The fiber optic cable uses _____ signal encoding.

A) multiple-level voltage

B) two-level voltage

C) on and off

D) analog

E) electronic

16. Which three terms are used interchangeably as metrics of network performance?

A) channel capacity, bandwidth, throughput

B) channel capacity, throughput, flow

C) reliability, accuracy, availability

D) channel capacity, bandwidth, rated speed

E) reliability, accuracy, latency

17. When the nearby laptop, wireless mouse and keyboard, smartphone, and digital camera exchange data, a _____ standard can be used:

A) WAN (wide area network)

B) PAN (personal area network)

C) NFC (near field communication)

D) LAN (local area network)

E) MAN (metropolitan area network)

18. Which is a legitimate MAC address?

A) ab-01-cd-ef-23-45

B) ab-01-cd-ef-23-4

C) ab-01-cd-ef-23

D) ab-01-cd-ef-2

E) ab-01-cd-ef

19. _____ represents the number of cycles a wave has in every second.

A. Amplitude

B. Phase

C. Frequency

D. Wavelength

E. Bandwidth

20. *Modulation* is used when

A) a node produces text data and the delivery channel relies on analog signal encoding.

B) a node produces sound data and the delivery channel relies on digital signal encoding.

C) a node produces digital data and the delivery channel relies on analog signal encoding.

D) a node produces analog data and the delivery channel relies on digital signal encoding.

E) a node produces digital or analog data and the delivery channel relies on digital signal encoding.

21. Which is an intermediary device designed to facilitate inter-networking?
   A) switch
   B) router
   C) wireless access point
   D) bridge
   E) network printer

22. Which is NOT NECESSARILY an accurate description of the intermediary device?
   A) It has at least one built-in network card.
   B) It also becomes a network node.
   C) It always operates in the full-duplex mode.
   D) It relies on network addressing to exchange data.
   E) It is used for either intra-networking or inter-networking.

23. Which is a right sequence of data rate metrics from the smallest to the largest?
   A) Kbps – Mbps – Pbps – Gbps – Tbps
   B) Tbps – Pbps – Kbps – Mbps – Gbps
   C) Kbps – Gbps – Mbps – Tbps – Pbps
   D) Kbps – Mbps – Gbps – Tbps – Pbps
   E) Kbps – Mbps – Gbps – Pbps – Tbps

24. There are many websites that offer audio or video streaming of TV programs and movies over the Internet. These services generally rely on the _____ technology.
   A) unicasting
   B) anycasting
   C) multicasting
   D) broadcasting
   E) dualcasting

25. Three main sources of network latency (or delay) include the:
   A) propagation delay, delay at hosts, and delay in server processing.
   B) propagation delay, delay at hosts, and delay at intermediary devices.
   C) delay at intermediary devices, delay at hosts, and delay in client processing.
   D) delay in application processing, propagation delay, and delay at hosts.
   E) delay in server processing, delay at intermediary devices, and delay at hosts.

26. The primary dimensions of network performance include _____.
   A) delay, cost, and reliability
   B) capacity, reliability, and accessibility
   C) capacity, reliability, and cost
   D) delay, capacity, and reliability
   E) reliability, delay, and accessibility

27. The following message is produced by the web browser according to the _____.
   "GET / HTTP/1.1
   Host: www.google.com"
   A) semantic rule
   B) lexicon rule
   C) syntactic rule
   D) message rule
   E) link rule

28. Which statement CORRECTLY describes network topology?
   A) Tree: All network nodes are either a hub or a spoke.
   B) Bus: All network nodes are directly interconnected.

    C) Hierarchy: Host stations are linked to a main transmission line.
    D) Star: All locations connect to a central site and thus the network is susceptible to a single
        point of failure.
    E) Full mesh: It is a cost-effective approach in creating a highly reliable network with
        redundancies.
29. Which represent key properties of the analog wave?
    A) bandwidth, amplitude, frequency
    B) frequency, wavelength, bandwidth
    C) wavelength, frequency, amplitude
    D) attenuation, amplitude, wavelength
    E) attenuation, amplitude, frequency
30. If the lowest and the highest frequencies allowed by a transmission channel are 30 Mhz and 50
    Mhz respectively, its bandwidth is:
    A) 30 Mhz
    B) 20 Mhz
    C) 50 Mhz
    D) 80 Mhz
    E) 1500 Mhz

HANDS-ON EXERCISES

EXERCISE 1.1

It is generally agreed that client/server computing has several advantages over peer-to-peer computing. Explain them in terms of the following aspects. Search the Internet if necessary.

1. Easier to protect server resources such as data
2. Better accessibility to server resources
3. Easier to back up server resources
4. More cost-effective in maintaining and upgrading server programs
5. Easier to add server resources to meet growing demands

EXERCISE 1.2

The hypothetical enterprise network in Figure 1.22 covers one main office and two remotely located
branch offices. Each office has its own LAN and the three LANs are interconnected by routers
(R1, R2, and R3) over the three private WAN links leased from a telco (thus, they are not Internet
connections). Answer the following questions.

1. How many hosts does each LAN contain?
2. How many intermediary devices does each LAN contain?
3. How many access links and trunk links are in each LAN?
4. How many network nodes are in the enterprise network?
5. What intermediary devices are used for intra-networking in each LAN?
6. What intermediary device is used for inter-networking?
7. How many subnetworks are there in each LAN?
8. If PC1 in LAN1 sends a file to Printer1 in LAN1, is this inter-networking?
9. If PC1 in LAN1 sends a request message to Server1 in LAN3, is this inter-networking?
10. If PC1 in LAN1 connects to the IP Phone in LAN1, is this inter-networking?
11. If PC2 and Server1 in LAN3 exchange messages, is this inter-networking?

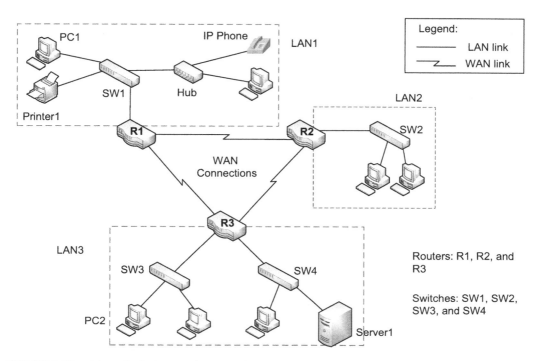

FIGURE 1.27   A hypothetical enterprise network

EXERCISE 1.3

Figure 1.23 is a small corporate network installed in a building. It has three switches connected to the border router with built-in firewall capability to prevent intrusions from the Internet. Disregarding the connection between the firewall router and the Internet:

1. How many LANs are there?
2. How many subnetworks are there?

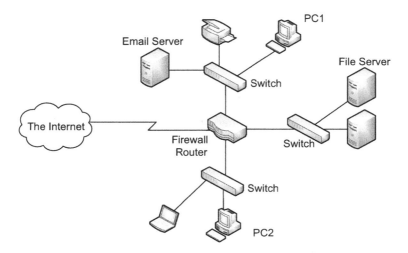

FIGURE 1.28   A hypothetical corporate network

3. If PC1 sends a message to the e-mail server, does this take inter-networking?
4. If PC1 sends a message to the file server, does this take inter-networking?
5. What is the intermediary device used for intra-networking?

EXERCISE 1.4

Let's assume that 8 Kbps is the data rate (for each direction) necessary to have a digitized telephone call. This means that a two-way full-duplex call between two parties takes 16 Kbps. How many telephone calls can be made concurrently with the data rate necessary to transport just one HDTV channel?

EXERCISE 1.5

1. Convert decimal values 38, 110, 192, and 255 to their 8-bit binary counterparts.
2. Translate the following 8-bit binary blocks to their corresponding decimal values.

   01100001   11110110   11100011   10100010

EXERCISE 1.6

1. Convert $0x$17AB to its binary counterpart.
2. Convert the following hex digits to binary bits. Each hex digit represents 4 binary bits.
   $0x$ABCDEF $0x$34A57 $0x$12DF01 $0x$78ADC
3. Convert the binary stream, '10110110100011100001' to hex, each representing 4 binary bits.
4. If the physical address of a computer's network card (NIC) is

00100110011110001010101101011100010010001101

what is its corresponding hexadecimal address?

EXERCISE 1.7

Conduct Internet search to locate OUIs of IT powerhouses including Cisco, Apple, Intel, and Microsoft. Observe how many different OUIs are owned by each company.

EXERCISE 1.8

1. Search the MAC and IP addresses of your smartphone. It might have two MACs: one for Wi-Fi and another for Bluetooth.
2. Smartphones come with a unique *International Mobile Equipment Identifier* (or IMEI). Search the IMEI of your smartphone. What is it and how is it different from the MAC and IP addresses?
3. List the MAC and IP addresses of your computer by issuing *ipconfig /all* for Windows and *ifconfig* for Linux/Unix at the command prompt. Today's computers are generally equipped with at least two MAC addresses, one for the Ethernet NIC and another for the Wi-Fi NIC. Observe that, at one point, only the MAC address in usage is associated with the host's IP address.

Exercise 1.9

Refer to Figure 1.24. If a signal state of a certain voltage strength is designed to carry 3 bits, how many different voltage states should be in the signaling system? How about 4 bits or 5 bits?

Exercise 1.10

Create a simple private P2P network and conduct file swapping. For this, form a team of two students each with his/her own computer. Then, create a P2P network by connecting the two computers on Wi-Fi. P2P requires additional configuration (e.g., creation of a workgroup on Windows). Once the configuration is complete, exchange files over the P2P network. If necessary, conduct an Internet search to learn the setup procedure.

2 Cybersecurity

Fundamentals

2.1 INTRODUCTION

Computer networks both small and large have become the backbone of society as valuable data are stored electronically and transported over the network. On the other hand, they have also become a fertile ground for serious cybersecurity threats to individuals, businesses, schools, and governments. It is no secret that computer networks have become the ideal conduit of numerous crimes.

Cyber threats are getting stealthier and more sophisticated, sustaining grave consequences on victims. Aggressors and organized crimes have launched serious cybersecurity attacks, and ill-prepared public and private organizations have suffered dearly. Amid the constant news of cyber-security breaches, adequate preparations including threat monitoring and prevention have become essential.

Cybersecurity is a broad and continuously changing field with numerous technical (e.g., net-works, computers) and non-technical (e.g., regulations, policy) issues entangled. Given the breadth, this book focuses on explaining fundamental concepts of cybersecurity largely from the technologi-cal perspective. This hardly means that non-technical subjects (e.g., security policy and regulations) are less important. In fact, they are equally, if not more, important in creating a successful cyberse-curity program at an organization.

2.1.1 LEARNING OBJECTIVES

The learning objectives of this chapter are:

- What are we trying to protect through the cybersecurity program?
- Three different entities through which a cybersecurity program is planned and implemented
- General terms and acronyms often used in the cybersecurity domain
- Different types of threat agents or actors
- A taxonomy scheme of cyber threat/attack types
- Categories of vulnerabilities that are exploited by threat actors
- Different strategies an organization can adopt to mitigate or manage cybersecurity risks
- Data protection requirements: confidentiality, integrity, and availability (CIA)
- Data protection requirements: authentication, authorization, and accounting (AAA)
- The principles of layering, limiting, simplicity, diversity, and obscurity in planning defense strategies and tactics
- Cyber kill chain as a general process model of cyberattacks
- World Wide Web, deep web, and dark web
- The search engine as a hacking tool
- Social engineering, which includes various phishing schemes and SPAM

2.2   WHAT ARE WE TRYING TO PROTECT?

2.2.1   MOTIVE OF THREAT ACTORS

Threat actors have many different motives and objectives in carrying out cyberattacks. Among them are financial gains through illegal means (e.g., sell stolen data, demand ransom, manipulate stock price); economic rewards by uncovering software vulnerabilities for vendors; a show of disgruntlement or retaliation by insiders (e.g., theft of intellectual property, sabotage); cyberterrorism; political influences; and even the disruption of enemy states. These days, the vast majority of cyberattacks are motivated by direct or indirect economic benefits.

2.2.2   ASSET TYPES

To achieve various objectives, threat actors mostly target valued assets of the targeted organization. Broadly, assets are any items that are valuable to the owner organization. They include intellectual properties, databases, software (e.g., internally developed business applications, off-the-shelf productivity tools, operating systems), client and server hardware, networks and networking devices, and even employee knowledge and know-how.

Some of them (e.g., off-the-shelf productivity tools) can be relatively easily replaced if lost or stolen. There are, however, assets that cannot be readily recovered from the loss. Especially, the most valued asset type these days is data/information such as intellectual properties, business secrets, and various databases on customers, products, financials, and internal business operations that have been accumulated over the years. That is, the center of an organization's security plan should evolve around deploying technical and non-technical measures to protect valued data/information.

2.2.3   DATA/INFORMATION PROTECTION

As explained, cyberattacks on a targeted organization are designed for gaining financial and non-financial benefits by stealing or damaging its valued data/information. Naturally, one of the very first risk management activities an organization needs to conduct is identifying and documenting data/information assets that need to be guarded. For that reason, *data/information security* has become the task of utmost importance. Data/information security is about protecting data in different states such as those stored on the storage, those being transferred over the network, or those being processed by the computer. In this book, thus, *cybersecurity* and *information security* are used interchangeably.

2.3   ENTITIES OF A CYBERSECURITY PROGRAM

Protecting valued information of an organization from cyber threats should be practiced through the combination of three entities: *people, products*, and *policies and procedures*.

2.3.1   PEOPLE

People are the most vulnerable element in cybersecurity, and thus continuous efforts should be made to prevent employees from falling victim to cyber threats. It takes only one mouse 'click' or a simple violation of an internal rule for an employee to intentionally or unintentionally drive an enterprise into staggering losses. Such risky behaviors may be the result of pure ignorance, complacency, emotions, or other psychological weaknesses. To counter the chance of human-side faults, such measures as user training, security awareness, and security practice assessment need to be in place and continuously practiced.

2.3.2 Products

An organization should deploy technologies including software programs and hardware products to reduce risks emanating from cyber threats. There are numerous attack points to which an organization is exposed, and many are tied to the organization's computer systems and network infrastructure. Besides, employees increasingly use their own personal devices (e.g., smartphones, tablets, smartwatches), connecting them to the organizational network. Frequently called BYOD (bring your own device), the personal devices employees bring in from outside form another front that threat actors can exploit these days. Facing the daunting task of defending numerous attack fronts (called threat/attack vectors), an organization should be adept at deploying counter systems such as the firewall, anti-virus, and intrusion detection.

2.3.3 Policies and Procedures

Protecting an organization from cyber threats should be facilitated through the institutional enforcement of formal security policies and procedures. People may falsely think that organizational security is not their responsibility but the work of IT professionals, and they may engage in improvised activities. Introducing formalized policies and procedures and preventing non-compliance reinforce the employees' mindset that they are also responsible for protecting the organization.

Examples of security-related policies include the acceptable IT and system usage, access control, change management, information security control, incident response, remote network access, email communications, disaster recovery, and business continuity plan (i.e., business operations in an emergency).

Among the security-related procedures are the security breach notification, request of access credentials, disposition of protected data and devices, report of policy violations, malware report, review of security technologies, and addition to or removal from the corporate network.

2.4 KEY TERMS OF CYBERSECURITY

Cybersecurity terms frequently used by researchers and industry practitioners are explained in this section.

2.4.1 Threat

Threats are dangers that may cause harm if acted upon an individual or organizational target. Among the numerous well-known cyber threats are malware, spam, and phishing (Chapter 8 introduces many of them). Threats can be technically intensive (e.g., malicious software) or less technical (e.g., scamming, social engineering). The threat source may be external (i.e., attackers from the cyberspace), internal (e.g., disgruntled insiders), or supply chain-related (e.g., a part supplier). When a threat is launched by the threat actor targeting an organization, this threat in action becomes an *attack*. Thus, there is a subtle difference between the threat as an intention or potential and the attack as an action although the two terms are frequently used interchangeably.

2.4.2 Threat/Attack Agent or Actor

Also called an adversary, the threat agent/actor is an individual (or software agent) who carries out a threat/attack, and she/he can be an external (e.g., cyber hacker) or internal (e.g., insider threat) entity. If the threat actor successfully achieves its goal, this results in *consequences/damages* on the victim company. Among the many possible consequences are data/information theft, financial losses, tarnished firm reputations, dropped share prices, unexpected lawsuits, loss of privacy, weakened customer confidence, and even loss of life. There are different types of threat actors (e.g., cybercriminals, hacktivists) to be explained shortly.

2.4.3 THREAT/ATTACK VECTOR

The threat vector is a *path*, *point of entry*, or *route* that a threat agent/actor exploits to activate the threat. That is, the vector itself is supposed to be benign by design, but attackers abuse it to deliver threats. For example, an adversary may send malware (i.e., a threat) to a business executive by attaching it to an email (i.e., threat vector). There are many other threat vectors including instant messages, text messages, webpages, browser pop-ups or plug-ins, cloud service (e.g., Amazon AWS), macros (e.g., Excel), remote access accounts, mobile devices, and mobile apps. Thus far, email remains the number one threat vector.

As can be seen, the threat vectors are not meant to be hazardous, but they just become a channel or conduit exploited by the threat actor to deliver threats, mounting an attack. Here, the *threat likelihood* represents the probability that a particular threat to an organization will come to fruition through a threat vector.

2.4.4 VULNERABILITY

In launching an attack targeting an organization, the threat actor takes advantage of its vulnerability, a form of weakness that can be exploited. Any organization inevitably has vulnerabilities. They may be defects related to installed software (e.g., business application) either developed in-house or purchased from a vendor. Weaknesses in human psychology and behaviors become the major source of vulnerability attackers can manipulate. Also, organizational vulnerabilities may stem from the lack of or missing organizational policies and/or procedures that enforce security-mindful practices.

It is not an overstatement to say that cyberattacks succeed because of vulnerabilities on the victim organization, largely created unintentionally or by mistake. For example, programming flaws in the installed operating system, server system misconfigurations, and the failure to mandate strong login credentials (e.g., passwords) are among them. As can be seen, cybersecurity is basically endless wrestling between the organization to find and remove its own vulnerabilities and adversaries who try to uncover and exploit the vulnerabilities.

2.4.5 RISK

Risk refers to the *potential for loss or damage* when a threat actor exploits one or more vulnerabilities of the target. The *damage* incurred to an organization may take many different forms. As an example, if a hospital is not ready to defend against the ravaging ransomware threat, it is taking the risks of financial losses (i.e., ransom payment) and also failure in patient care as their medical records are not available to the medical staff and doctors.

Generally, the risk level is measured as a function of *threats*, *vulnerabilities*, and *assets* (see Figure 2.1). That is, if there is a higher chance of an organization being exposed to threats, and if it has more vulnerabilities, it is subject to higher risks. Also, the more valued assets an organization needs to guard against threats and vulnerabilities, the associated risk gets higher. Naturally, the risk

FIGURE 2.1 Cybersecurity risk as a function of threats, vulnerabilities, and assets

assessment whose focus is identifying information assets that could be subject to cyberattacks is fundamental to any organization in order to better manage them.

2.5 THREAT AGENT/ACTOR TYPES

As stated, the threat agent/actor is either a person or a software agent that poses cyber threats or undertakes threat actions. Depending on the intent or motive, there are different threat actor types, and they are explained in terms of cybercriminals, script kiddies, insiders, hacktivists, and state-sponsored attackers. Remind that the categories are not exhaustive in representing all adversary types and also their acts are not necessarily exclusive from each other.

2.5.1 CYBERCRIMINALS

The cybercriminal's main motive is financial gains. For example, the ransomware attack is one of the frequented cyber incidents these days. In this crime, the attacker successfully blocks (e.g., encrypting data, crippling system booting) a victim organization from accessing its data assets. This way, an organization is held hostage by the attacker who demands ransom once the victim's (e.g., hospital, business, local government) internal data become unavailable.

2.5.2 SCRIPT KIDDIES

Script kiddies casually attempt to attack computer systems or networks with limited knowledge. They tend to rely on automated hacking software or scripts as there are so many free attack tools available in cyberspace these days.

2.5.3 HACTIVISTS

Hactivists, as a mix of 'hacking' and 'activism', direct their attacks at targets such as corporations, governments, religious groups, and other organizations for ideological reasons. Examples of such ideology are the freedom of speech, promotion of human rights, environmental protection, and objection of corporate power and government censorship.

2.5.4 INSIDERS

The insider is an employee, contractor, or business partner who has legitimate access to internal resources at an organization and the insider threat refers to harmful actions on its internal assets. Broadly, the insider threat can be caused malignantly or unintentionally. The malignant insider has reasons to inflict intentional damages on internal assets. Among them are the dissatisfaction with his/her treatment (e.g., receive a pink slip), personal financial troubles, need to conceal financial losses through fake transactions, coercion from an external party, or even bribes.

Also, a large share of security breaches occurring at organizations are unintentionally caused by their own employees, and there is an increasing trend of this type. This happens when employees are inadequately prepared. For example, the lack of education and training could make them more gullible or inattentive. Or, they may perform an act dangerous to the organization (e.g., opening a phishing email, bringing a malware-infected personal device to the work, inadvertently revealing private or confidential information).

2.5.5 STATE-SPONSORED ATTACKERS

The state-sponsored attacker is commissioned by a government. There could be various reasons for attacking a chosen target, such as crippling an enemy's computer system, stealing classified information (e.g., weapon design), paralyzing an industrial infrastructure (e.g., nuclear powerplant), launching a disinformation campaign for political gains, and stealing financial assets such as bitcoins. As the aggression is backed by a government, threat actors are well-resourced and highly trained.

One particular threat type is especially dangerous these days: *advanced persistent threat* (or *APT*). By definition, the APT is a prolonged, oftentimes multi-year persistent campaign to successfully intrude a selected target network or system to ultimately achieve the goal established by a state or government. Very often, the goal is successful penetration and access to highly confidential business or national security information. APT is especially dangerous because once a target is set, the adversaries direct their non-stop breach attempts only at the target. That is, no matter how well guarded a target organization is, it may ultimately succumb to the prolonged and enduring campaign.

2.6 THREAT TYPES

Bad actors take advantage of numerous techniques, tactics, and procedures to commit cyber aggressions. Although most of them are carried out over the computer network, they differ in their technical sophistication and malignancy as some attacks result in more severe consequences on the victim than others. Also, some attacks (e.g., malware development) are more technically demanding than others (e.g., port scanning).

The taxonomy scheme of threat types in Table 2.1 is based on the main threat mechanism employed. The categories are not necessarily mutually exclusive from each other as, more likely, an adversary combines multiple techniques to achieve his/her goal. Also, the categories in the taxonomy scheme are by no means exhaustive. Select threat methods of each category (except social engineering) are explained in Chapter 8.

2.7 VULNERABILITY TYPES

As stated, cyberattacks are successful because the targeted victim (whether an individual or an organization) has one or more vulnerabilities the threat actor can take advantage of. Vulnerabilities stem from different sources and they are largely classified into four types:

TABLE 2.1
Primary mechanisms of cyberattacks

Threat/attack mechanisms	Definition
Engage social engineering	Threat actors scam the victim into surrendering private information or visiting a malignant site.
Deliver or inject a malicious program	Threat actors deliver malware whose denotation will inflict intended damages.
Exploit weak- or mis-configuration in security settings	Threat actors exploit when a system's security setting is not configured, weakly configured, or misconfigured.
Abuse a network function or a protocol	Threat actors launch an attack by taking advantage of functional features built into a network protocol.
Exploit software design and/or development faults	Threat actors discover technical faults of a software program (e.g., browser, operating system) to exploit them.
Compromise cryptography-enabled protections	Threat actors attempt to neutralize the security technology (e.g., cryptography) or its protection (e.g., encrypted data in rest or in transit).

2.7.1 SOFTWARE VULNERABILITIES

These are defects in the operating system, business application, web browser and browser plug-in, smartphone app, video conferencing program, or other productivity or communication program. As a result of poor software design and/or development, the flaws allow cyber adversaries to exploit them (e.g., bypass security measures).

To improve the public awareness of particular software vulnerabilities and to encourage immediate remedial actions, there have been collective efforts to systematically document and share them. The most notable effort is the CVE (or Common Vulnerability Enumeration) database continuously updated by the US government (https://nvd.nist.gov).

2.7.2 WEAK OR MIS-CONFIGURATION

Some vulnerabilities are caused by the weak or mis-configuration of security settings. As an example, if a system's administrator uses simple or vendor-configured default credentials (e.g., default password) in deploying network nodes, this becomes an invitation for trouble. To assist IT professionals, there have been community efforts to share information on recommended security settings for commercial products (e.g., Windows server). In particular, CCE (Common Configuration Enumeration) is a notable effort that provides guidance in terms of preferred or required settings and configurations to achieve system security (visit nvd.nist.gov).

2.7.3 HARDWARE VULNERABILITIES

Limitations in the computer's hardware capacity could become a source of vulnerabilities. For example, think of a webserver computer that accepts and processes requests from clients (i.e., web browsers). If it has limited CPU or memory capacity, it won't be able to withstand DDOS (distributed denial of service) in which the attacker disrupts the web service by flooding the target with artificially generated bogus traffic. As a different type of example, imagine the situation in which server computers and/or intermediary devices are placed at a location that is not physically secured. This will make it easy for a threat agent (e.g., insider) to physically access hardware resources and data assets stored.

2.7.4 NON-TECHNICAL VULNERABILITIES

There can be many vulnerabilities at an organization which are not necessarily tied to a particular software, hardware, or network technology. They are more operational and risk management issues. Examples include vulnerable supply chain management (e.g., poor authentication of part suppliers), weakness in asset management (e.g., lack of documentation), flaws in risk management strategy, and missing or incomplete security policies and procedures. There are also human-side vulnerabilities stemming from employees' gullibility to phishing scams and their complacency against cyber threats due to their limited exposure to cybersecurity training and awareness initiatives.

2.8 RISK MITIGATION STRATEGIES

In Figure 2.1, it was shown that the cybersecurity risk is a function of *threat*s (or *threat likelihood*), *vulnerabilities*, and *assets*. The adequate management of the information security-related risk is fundamental for sustained business operations. An organization can manage the risk by taking one or more of the following strategies: *risk avoidance*, *risk mitigation*, *risk acceptance*, *risk deterrence*, and *risk transference*.

2.8.1 RISK AVOIDANCE

Risk avoidance is a strategy to eliminate the risk entirely simply by giving no chance to criminal activities. For example, to prevent any possibility of cyberattacks, an organization may decide not to have any website or internet connections. This will certainly cut the chance of cyber threats drastically. However, there is a heavy price to pay in exchange for avoiding risks that way. For example, the organization is unable to maintain effective communications with employees (e.g., no video conferencing). Also, it won't be able to run competitive business operations through such provisions as online transactions and seamless supply chain connectivity.

As can be seen, eliminating the risk entirely by embracing the avoidance approach is impractical because of the huge opportunity cost in most situations. However, it is certainly an option when an organization simply cannot take any chances. As a hypothetical example, a military unit handling top secrets may choose to completely sever its internal network from outside.

2.8.2 RISK MITIGATION (OR REDUCTION)

The strategy attempts to reduce risks to an acceptable or manageable level through technical and non-technical measures. An organization can decide the maximum level of risk it is willing to accept considering circumstantial factors such as regulatory requirements and assets that need to be protected from adversaries. Then, it can take measures (e.g., budget allocation, manpower hiring) to mitigate the risk to an acceptable level.

This practice is similar to buying car insurance, in which the owner can choose a liability option instead of the full coverage in order to reduce payment. With the decision, the owner is accepting the risk of other financial losses (e.g., damages on the car) resulting from a car accident as they are not covered by the liability insurance. Likewise, the risk level an organization is willing to live with certainly has financial and non-financial implications. A low-level risk acceptance demands a larger IT budget to protect the organization from potential internal and external threats through the additional deployment of countermeasures.

2.8.3 RISK ACCEPTANCE

An organization may decide to simply accept the existing cyber risk and potential losses resulting from it. Also known as 'risk retention', the strategy reflects the organizational decision that the return on financial investment designed to cut the cybersecurity risk is not justified. That is, the organization is willing to accept consequences if it falls victim to a cybercrime. Depending on the circumstance, this strategy can be practical to certain businesses. For instance, if a small business does not maintain assets critical enough to affect its business continuity even after they are stolen or damaged, it may not be worthwhile to invest in security products or services to protect the assets.

2.8.4 RISK DETERRENCE

Risk deterrence represents an attempt to discourage or prevent adversaries from mounting attacks by impressing upon them that the attack's high cost or risk outweighs its potential benefits. For example, the login screen of a website or a computer system can display a banner that warns legal consequences if any illegal activities are committed. Because it is inherently difficult to find and hold outside attackers accountable, deterrence approaches are expected to be effective for reducing the risk induced by internal threats (e.g., insiders) rather than those coming from outside the organization.

2.8.5 Risk Transference

With risk transference, an organization can transfer the risk to other alternatives that can compensate for losses if it is victimized. The transference typically takes the form of buying insurance, and this relatively new scheme has been growing in popularity because of the worsening cybersecurity problem. There are, however, challenges for an organization in adopting this way of risk transference. Most notably, if a firm suffers from a cyber incident, it is often difficult to quantify the loss (e.g., stolen business secrets) in terms of its corresponding monetary value.

2.9 DATA PROTECTION REQUIREMENTS: CIA

In planning to protect data/information assets, there are fundamental security requirements that need to be perfected. The requirements are frequently known as the CIA (*data confidentiality*, *data integrity*, and *data availability*) triad model.

2.9.1 Confidentiality (or Privacy)

Data confidentiality means that data should be readable only by the intended party and the content must be protected from eavesdropping and snooping. That is, even if data in storage or in transit over the network are stolen by an unauthorized party as a result of a cyber or insider attack, they should remain unreadable. To satisfy this condition, various encryption technologies are heavily used.

2.9.2 Integrity

Data integrity ensures that original data in storage, in process, or in transit are not changed (e.g., insertion, deletion, substitution) accidentally or not manipulated by unauthorized parties. If data are changed or tampered with, this should be detected. Another important aspect of data integrity is that the database prohibits the addition of invalid values (e.g., alphabets as a phone number) or values not complying with the required format (e.g., 12/3/2023 instead of 12-3-2023) to maintain their accuracy and consistency.

2.9.3 Availability

Data/information should be readily available to authorized users. The data/information availability principle applies to various situations. Among them are data/information availability for public viewers on a website and for internal employees who access a corporate database to carry out their duties. The principle is a critical condition for an organization to remain functional.

There are a number of threat types (e.g., denial of service, ransomware) that can severely restrict information availability directly and indirectly, and an organization should deploy countermeasures such as frequent data backups and a disaster recovery plan. Also, an organization's network should be fail-proof as its failure inevitably disrupts information availability.

2.10 DATA PROTECTION REQUIREMENTS: AAA

To protect data assets in their *confidentiality, data integrity,* and a*vailability (CIA), an organization needs to implement various technological and non-technological measures that* support *authentication, access control/authorization*, and *accounting* (AAA) requirements. That is, AAA represents core mechanisms through which data protections are achieved in CIA dimensions.

To visualize the relationship between CIA and AAA, imagine the situation that a malicious hacker is trying to access a valued corporate database of a company. If he/she gains access to the database, data can be stolen (compromising its confidentiality), manipulated (affecting its integrity), and erased or encrypted (limiting its availability). To mitigate the risk, the database access should be granted through the layers of authentication (i.e., only authenticated persons are eligible to access the system); access control/authorization (i.e., only authorized people are granted to change data); and accounting (e.g., data access and usage activities are logged to monitor and trace illegal activities).

2.10.1 AUTHENTICATION

Authentication means that the identity of an engaging party needs to be validated. The party can be a human or a software agent. There are numerous situations in which the party initiating communications or a system connection is subject to authentication. Among them are:

- An individual trying to access controlled resources such as protected online accounts and databases
- A client software (e.g., web browser, email program) initiating a connection with a server application (e.g., webserver, email server, database server)
- A website running an online store to sell products to individual and business customers
- An intermediary device (e.g., router) that forwards packets to another intermediary node and validates their authenticity
- Host devices (e.g., laptops, smartphones) joining a Wi-Fi network through wireless access points

To facilitate authentication, various solutions have been introduced, and they largely belong to five different types: *what you know*, *what you have*, *what you are*, *what you do*, and *where you are*.

2.10.1.1 Based on 'What You Know'

As the most prevalent form of authentication, pin numbers, passwords, and passphrases are good examples of 'what you know'. As another example, such questions as 'What is your pet's name?' and 'Where were you born?' are frequently used to recover a misplaced password or to undertake multi-factor authentication.

Here, the passphrase is longer, more complex, and more random than the password as it contains upper- and lowercase characters, digits, and special characters. The passphrase is generally easier to remember than the password, which may be a combination of known words and thus easier to forget. For example, if you make up a sentence based on a personally memorable event and combine the first or last letter of each word, the alphanumeric and special characters included in the combination become highly random and at the same time easy to remember.

2.10.1.2 Based on 'What You Have'

An individual can be authenticated through such items as a security device, security token, or verification card (see Figure 2.2). Examples include the smartcard that holds personal identification in its integrated chip and the security token that can produce verification information (e.g., one-time password) unique to its owner. Also, the cellphone is broadly used these days for personal authentication

FIGURE 2.2 Security token

using various authentication technologies including an app (e.g., Google's Duo Mobile) or short message service (SMS) that sends a verification code. The *digital signature* and the *digital certificate* (Chapter 10) that validate a particular person or a system (e.g., website) also belong to this type.

2.10.1.3 Based on 'What You Are'

Authentication can be based on biometric information unique to an individual, a highly reliable way of securing system or network access. Biometrics generally represent a person's physical features such as fingerprints, voice, face, and iris that are difficult to copy and reproduce. There are also cognitive biometrics unique to an individual, such as perceptions, memory, and a thought process. Although highly secure, biometrics are not necessarily guaranteed as a bulletproof technology as their signatures can be hacked or forged.

2.10.1.4 Based on 'What You Do'

This method authenticates a person based on the behavioral pattern or nuance he/she displays while using a device, thus often called behavioral biometrics. Examples are the characteristics of a person's computer keyboarding (e.g., typing pace and rhythm) and handwriting (e.g., signature match). This mode of authentication requires that authenticating devices need to learn the authorized user's behavioral characteristics mostly through machine learning, an artificial intelligence technique. This authentication technology is very hard to cheat.

2.10.1.5 Based on 'Where You Are'

A person (or a system) may be authenticated based on his/her location information such as the geolocation and IP address. This is similar to the situation in which your credit card usage will be blocked if you try to purchase a product far away from your residence without giving the credit card company a pre-notification. The location information may not identify the user but can be an indicator of abnormality. For example, any access attempt to the online banking site from an IP address or geolocation that does not make sense may be alerted or even blocked.

With rampant cyber incidents, an organization should use multi-factor authentication that combines at least two different authentication methods in tandem to verify a person's credentials and to allow the system or network access.

2.10.2 ACCESS CONTROL/AUTHORIZATION

Access control (or authorization) grants access permission to specific resources. In cyberspace, it is the process of allowing or denying access to (1) the network; (2) the computer system attached to a network; and (3) resources (e.g., data, files, programs) available on a computer system.

First, access to a network and its computer systems should be allowed only to authorized parties. For this, generally, a system's security setting applies authorization rules after an initiating party (an individual or system) is authenticated first. Also, access control measures (e.g., firewall, anti-virus, access control list) should be in place to thwart any malignant and stealthy attempts to penetrate the network.

Second, access rules of corporate assets should be in place at organizational, sub-organizational (e.g., department), and user group levels and enforced. A person or user group should be granted only minimum access to system resources (e.g., data, files) depending on his/her position and job qualification. This is a crucial element of user *identity management* that technically controls the accessibility of shared resources.

2.10.3 ACCOUNTING

The accounting function provides the access and usage records of system resources of a network node. For this, computers (especially servers) and other network nodes need to log events and activities performed on them by users and software agents. The gathering of information/data necessary for accounting is generally done through security or other types of logs. Practically, all network nodes (e.g., computers, intermediary devices, security devices) should keep logs for subsequent analysis and auditing of resource utilization and security controls.

Analyzing security or other log data obtained from network nodes can reveal rich information including:

- Have there been cyberattacks or intrusion attempts?
- Which corporate data have been requested and accessed?
- Which user performed what actions on which business data assets?
- What are the destination and source addresses of a particular request and accessed files?
- What events or login attempts have been successful or unsuccessful?

As can be seen, the analysis of accounting data is instrumental to improve threat mitigation, access control, and system and network capacity planning.

2.10.4 PROCEDURAL VIEWS

To illustrate the close relationship among AAA technologies in strengthening overall information security, let's take a look at the typical procedure in which a customer wants to order a product from an online store using her/his smartphone.

a. To order a product, the customer is required to log in to his/her online account first presenting the user/login name or email address for **identification**.
b. Then, the person needs to be validated through the **authentication** information such as the password or passphrase. The online site performs customer identification and authentication based on the user credentials submitted.
c. Once validated, the customer is granted to enter his/her account, a form of **authorization** to perform the transaction (e.g., place an order). Once authorized to enter his/her online account, the customer is granted *access* to specific resources (e.g., transaction history, items purchased in the past, shopping cart items) maintained by the vendor.
d. All customer activities on the online site are recorded for **accounting** so that the e-commerce business can review the activity details as needed.

Thus far, CIA and AAA principles are explained focusing on their important role in safeguarding data assets. In concluding this section, Figure 2.3 is presented to underscore that CIA and AAA principles are also crucial in protecting virtually all other corporate assets including applications, services (e.g., web service), client and server hosts, and network infrastructure.

CIA	Protection Layers		AAA
Confidentiality Integrity Availability	Applications	Services	Access Control/Authorization Accounting Authentication
	Data/Information Assets		
	Client and Server Hosts		
	Network Infrastructure		

FIGURE 2.3 Protecting an organization through CIA and AAA principles

2.11   PRINCIPLES OF CYBER DEFENSE

When it comes to defending an organization from cyber threats, there are general principles to follow in planning defense strategies and tactics. Key principles are explained in terms of *layering* (or *defense-in-depth*), *limiting*, *simplicity*, *diversity,* and *obscurity*.

2.11.1   LAYERING (DEFENSE-IN-DEPTH) PRINCIPLE

Security experts have been emphasizing the importance of the *defense-in-depth* principle in which attackers are forced to break multiple defense lines to access the protected asset.

2.11.1.1   Protection Layers

For this, not only should the entire enterprise network and its subnetworks be protected by several defense mechanisms, but also every host needs to be hardened by having frequent data backups and timely software patches, and by installing threat-mitigating technologies. More specifically, layered countermeasures need to be in place to bolster *physical security*, *perimeter security*, *internal network security*, *host security*, *application security*, and *data security*.

- **Physical security**: The entry to an organization's physical boundary needs to be secured and monitored through security guards, door locks, and video cameras.
- **Perimeter security**: The perimeter that connects an organization's network to the outside (e.g., the Internet, mobile phone network) need to be guarded by such technology as the firewall and intrusion detection system to form the frontline against external threats.
- **Internal network security**: An organization needs to deploy internal network security that will challenge attackers even if they successfully penetrated the perimeter defense. For example, the enterprise network can be segmented into subnetworks, each with a tailored defense in place. Also, intermediary devices (e.g., routers, switches, access points) need to be hardened for them to become an integral part of the defense line.
- **Host security**: To steal valued data, attackers need to gain an access to hosting computers. That is, user computers, servers, and mobile devices need to be protected through the host-based firewall, anti-virus, authentication and access control, and operating system updates. They become the next defense layer when an attacker successfully penetrates the perimeter and internal network protection.
- **Application/service security**: Many times, attackers attempt to remotely access and steal valued data through an application, most notably the web application that provides online services to users. The application is generally connected to the transactional or other databases in the back end. That is, any manipulation attempt of the web application should be controlled. Also, if a person has physical access to an enterprise application, its usage needs to be granted through the authentication and access control mechanisms built into the hosting system and the application itself.
- **Data/information security**: It is possible that an adversary was skilled, was able to penetrate all previous defense layers, and thus his/her hands are on the targeted data asset. However, this is where he/she will be forced to overcome an additional defense to finally own the data; that is, the direct protection of the data using such technology as file encryption or disk encryption.

2.11.1.2   Technical Measures and Organizational Initiatives

Widely used technical measures pertaining to each security layer are summarized in Table 2.2. The table also lists important organizational initiatives that lay the basis of and provides guidance in planning and deploying technical countermeasures to mitigate threats and remediate vulnerabilities. As can be seen, their planning details span all of the security layers from physical security through data security. The initiatives are briefly explained subsequently.

2.11.1.3 Security Policies and Procedures

Security policies and procedures (P&Ps) are documents that include *rules, baselines, standards, guidelines*, and *procedures* developed by an organization to reduce the risk emanating from cyber threats and internal vulnerabilities. They also provide guidelines on how to handle the situation and what remediation actions should be taken if an organization has been attacked or if it is exposed to threats. An organization can develop enforceable P&Ps at three different levels: *organizational-level, system-level*, and *issue-level*. To make P&Ps more systematic, policy elements related to three different levels can be captured in terms of each layer in Table 2.2.

As can be seen in Table 2.2, P&Ps cover a number of strategic, tactical, operational, and technical issues related to data/information security. Among the many issues are remote access, intermediary device configuration and operation, password and passphrase, email usage, handling sensitive data and data encryption, incidence/data breach response, Internet access, clean desk, ethics, and wireless communications. The technology landscape continues to evolve, making things more complicated and challenging, and thus P&Ps need to be revisited routinely (e.g., at least once a year) and also in an ad hoc manner (e.g., complying with a new regulation).

TABLE 2.2
Layers of defense-in-depth and protection measures

Security layers	Select technological measures	Covered chapters	Organizational initiatives
Data security	• Encryption of data in transit • Encryption of data at rest • Data backup	10 10	• Security policies and procedures
Application security	• Authentication • Access control	2, 10	
Host security	• Host-based firewall • Host intrusion detection system • Operating system patch management • Anti-virus/malware protection • Other host hardening measures (e.g., multi-factor authentication)	9 9	• Security awareness and training • Information security self-assessment
Internal network security	• Hardening intermediary devices • Wi-Fi network protections • Subnet segmentation and Virtual LANs for customized defense • Cyber Threat Intelligence (CTI) • Security information and event management (SIEM) • DNS infrastructure protection • Software defined network (SDN) • Perimeter security technologies can be selectively applied to internal network segments	5 6, 10 7 9 9 9 9 4,9,10	• Regulatory compliance self-assessment • Disaster recovery plan
Perimeter security	• Network address translation (NAT) • Perimeter (or border) firewall • Demilitarized zone (DMZ) • Proxy servers • Access control list (ACL) • Intrusion detection system (IDS) • Virtual private network (VPN)	4 9 9 9 9 9 10	
Physical security	• Guards, door locks, security cameras		

2.11.1.4 Security Awareness and Training

An organization needs to institute security awareness, training, and education programs for employees as they are always connected to the Internet and the threat landscape constantly changes. Such programs equip them with knowledge for informed decision-making against potential threats and vulnerabilities, as their small mistakes can result in crippling consequences to the employer.

It is safe to say that people are the most vulnerable element when it comes to cybersecurity. Especially, the vast majority (over 90%) of security breaches at an organization begin with a phishing attack. It is a favored form of social engineering by which cybercriminals skillfully exploit psychological weaknesses or cognitive limitations of humans (e.g., gullibility, fear, over-confidence, emotion). The human side-vulnerability is very difficult for technologies to effectively intervene, and thus offering routinized awareness and training programs for employees is crucial.

2.11.1.5 Information Security Self-Assessment

Through the information security self-assessment, an organization evaluates its current status in terms of its preparedness to defend its core information assets from known and unknown threats and plans for improvements. Thus, it is a process to identify problems and weaknesses of current security controls in protecting internal assets and to resolve them in a timely manner to avoid risks emanating from the lack of preparations. As can be seen in Table 2.2, the self-assessment effort to uncover possible threats and internal vulnerabilities needs to cut across many different aspects of all security layers.

2.11.1.6 Regulatory Compliance Assessment

Regulatory compliance is a fundamental requirement of an organization's security program. The self-assessment is about whether an organization complies with stated policies, standards, laws, and regulations related to the protection of data/information *at rest*, *in use*, or *in transit*. The rules continuously evolve and an organization is obligated to keep up with their changes to ensure data protection in terms of CIA (confidentiality, integrity, and accessibility) dimensions.

The evidence of regulatory compliance needs to be documented for auditing. An organization's failure to comply will not only amplify cyber risks considerably but also result in such negative consequences as reputational loss, penalties, and criminal or civil liabilities. Among the well-known regulations related to data privacy and security are the Health Insurance Portability and Accountability Act (or HIPPA) and the Sarbanes-Oxley Act (or SOX) from the US government, and the Payment Card Industry Data Security Standard (PCI DSS) introduced by credit card companies.

2.11.1.7 Disaster Recovery Plan

The disaster recovery plan is an organization's plan to restore its mission-critical functions from a disastrous event, which may be natural (e.g., earthquake, hurricane) or human-made (e.g., war, crippling ransomware attack). The plan requires identifying disasters to which an organization may be susceptible, assessing their risks, and developing a recovery plan for each disaster type. The recovery plan includes rules and protocols of data backup and regaining their access, and of the restoration of hardware, software application, networking equipment, power, and communication channels.

The quick recovery of mission-critical business functions is fundamental for business continuity and survival. As a case in point, a number of businesses (particularly small ones) at the World Trade Center in New York went bankrupt when the twin buildings were attacked on 9/11. The absence of an adequate disaster recovery plan such as the locational distribution of mission-critical data contributed to the failures.

Up to now, many issues related to the layering (defense-in-depth) principle have been explained.

2.11.2 LIMITING PRINCIPLE

With the limiting principle, a person should be able to access data and resources 'only' essential to conduct his/her organizational duties. As such, the principle is sometimes called the principle of least authority or least privilege as an employee is given the lowest level of clearance to access files, applications, systems and the network to perform assigned tasks.

As an example, if an employee needs only to 'read' customer records stored in a transactional database, there is no point in allowing him/her to create, update, or delete transaction records. This is because, if the employee's computer is infected with malware, it will automatically inherit his/her access privileges, potentially risking a massive data loss. Or, if the malware is ransomware, it will be able to encrypt all the files the employee is able to access using the inherited 'write' privilege.

As another example, imagine that a user is allowed to log in to a computer system with the IT administrator access privilege. This gives him/her a high-level authority (or privilege) in installing software, accessing system files and directories, changing security settings, and accessing other user accounts. This is a clear violation of the limiting principle as the user is given way more authority than what is necessary and, as a result, will expose the system to a much higher risk. If the user's credentials (e.g., password) are compromised by an adversary, the attacker inheriting the admin privilege can freely go deep into the system settings and wreak havoc. Figure 2.4 demonstrates the limiting principle in which the user is permitted to read, execute, and list contents of the Windows OS directory, but cannot 'modify' or 'write' in it.

2.11.3 SIMPLICITY PRINCIPLE

A security measure, whether it is technical or non-technical, should be as simple and transparent to the ordinary user as possible. The simplicity principle is closely associated with the ease-of-use

FIGURE 2.4　Limiting privileges for Windows OS directory

concept that has been repeatedly emphasized as one of the important critical success factors of an information system. When a security system is complex, its usage becomes more cumbersome due to the learning curve, its proper configuration becomes harder, and there is a higher chance of making mistakes in its usage.

In the meantime, when a security solution is easy to understand and can be implemented relatively effortlessly, it meets the principle of simplicity and has a great chance to succeed. This is because it is easy to use by internal people, but looks complex from outside, discouraging potential threat actors. Some examples that reflect the simplicity spirit are:

- Relying on a single sign-on password manager
- Enabling automatic full disk encryption to improve data confidentiality with no productivity sacrifice
- Automating data and file backup
- Using passphrases rather than passwords

2.11.4 DIVERSITY PRINCIPLE

The principle demands that an organization's defense be running on different technologies, configurations, or versions of the same technology, rather than the repetition of the same technology (thus creating redundancy). An example is using different operating systems for servers and deploying security products from different vendors to protect the network and data assets. This way, bad actors attempting to compromise the target will be forced to penetrate defense lines running technologies distinctively different from one another.

As an example, imagine that an organization uses the same operating system for all servers. If the adversary discovers an OS vulnerability and creates a back door to exploit the vulnerability in order to penetrate the system, he/she will be able to enter all servers facing little resistance. The risk can be curtailed if the organization uses operating systems from different vendors because the target space that can be exploited by the malware attack is significantly reduced. An organization may still want to streamline the product portfolio by using similar products to save IT costs. Then, one possible approach to reduce risks is to deploy different software versions as they may use modified algorithms to perform the same function.

As another example, think of the situation in which an organization uses a number of data servers. The IT admin has two options in configuring the password for authentication: all servers use one password versus all of them are given different passwords. If each server has a unique password, password management is more difficult; however, even if an attacker successfully penetrates one server, others are still protected.

There are clear tradeoffs in embracing the diversity principle. That is, creating the redundancy of using the same technology (e.g., identical software version) and the same system's setting is definitely cost-effective. It simply demands less operational (e.g., hiring of less IT staff) and maintenance efforts and budget. The uniform approach is, however, not a recommended practice from the cybersecurity perspective as it poses less challenge to threat actors.

2.11.5 OBSCURITY PRINCIPLE

With the obscurity principle, an organization attempts to improve information security by keeping the internal details hidden from outsiders. The obscurity or secrecy can apply to many different aspects of the IT infrastructure at an organization. They include the details of host systems and network implementations such as the type of computers, operating systems, and user applications used; the internal network architecture; and the IP address allocation scheme. If the details are unknown, this could make it difficult for perpetrators to devise an attack plan.

There are, however, debates about the benefits of this principle. The US National Institute of Standards and Technology (NIST), for example, suggested that obscurity not be the principal means of security due to its drawbacks. First, it could give a false sense of security. If an aggressor discovers the details, then the organization becomes vulnerable again. Second, adversaries can mount attacks without necessarily knowing the details. As an example, an attacker can send phishing emails to targeted people as long as he/she obtains their email addresses, and he/she doesn't need to know anything about either the internal network architecture or the platform of the email server.

2.12   CYBER KILL CHAIN – ATTACK PROCEDURE

This section explains the cyber kill chain, a popular framework introduced by Lockheed Martin Co. to depict the steps adversaries take to launch attacks on a target system and to incur intended damages. There are three attack phases in the cyber kill chain: *pre-compromise*, *compromise*, and *post-compromise*.

2.12.1   PRE-COMPROMISE PHASE

This is the phase in which the attacker conducts preparations necessary to mount an attack on a selected target, and they include activities of *reconnaissance*, *weaponization*, and *delivery*.

2.12.1.1   Reconnaissance

This is the first stage in which the adversary gathers information about the target organization. For this, the attacker may actively probe the target's defense system remotely over the Internet or passively gather information about the target without directly engaging with its defense line. The active engagement can expose the adversary's probing and thus skilled attackers take tactics not to leave traces while doing reconnaissance.

Passive reconnaissance activities are almost completely free from the risk of being detected by the targeted organization. Among the many different activities include Google search to find the target's system/network information (e.g., vendor, server OS); Wi-Fi packet sniffing outside the target's physical boundary; eavesdropping on employee conversations; scavenging dumpsters to recover sensitive information from scraped IT equipment; and even physical observation of the target's building.

Threat actors can also search for information on the target's employees of all ranks, especially those at the high post who may be compromised via social engineering. As we are living in an age with literally no privacy, so much personal information can be gained from cyberspace (e.g., social networks, websites, news publications, online yellow and white pages). That way, attackers can build a complete and accurate profile of a person, which includes such information as family, residence, phone numbers, email, social and professional networks, and preferred websites. Imagine that a hacker uses the profile information to build a perfect storyline to launch a social engineering attack. This is why security professionals agree that Google's search engine empowers more intrusion potentials than any other hacking technology.

2.12.1.2   Weaponization

Once vulnerabilities of the target system/network of an organization are determined through reconnaissance activities, the adversary creates an exploit (or program) and package it into a deliverable malware during the weaponization stage. The malware may be embedded into a benign-looking document to avoid its detection by the anti-virus or firewall.

The attacker may develop the malignant code from scratch; however, depending on the attack type, often she/he can recycle what is already available out there. That is, weaponization is getting easier these days as there are programs and source codes available freely or fee-based in cyberspace and adversaries can customize them. Ransomware that extorts ransom from victims is a good example. Security researchers reported that the infamous ransomware, WannaCry, had more than 12,000 variants in 2019.

2.12.1.3 Malware Delivery

In this stage, the adversary delivers malware to the targeted system/person through various 'infection' or attack vectors such as an email attachment, an email including a shady URL link, and posting on a compromised website. The delivery may be in the form of mass spamming, which may victimize random individuals or can be tailored to a particular individual (e.g., an executive). The customized message has a much higher chance of success and customization is possible as the attacker can build a storyline using the gathered information of the target.

2.12.2 COMPROMISE PHASE

In this phase, the attacker's malware successfully lands on the victim system, and the cyber kill chain models the process in two steps of *vulnerability exploitation* and *installation*.

2.12.2.1 Vulnerability Exploitation

Exploitation is the step in which the attacker's malware exploits the target's vulnerability to execute the code and to gain a foothold on the victim system. In the cyber kill chain model, the victim's vulnerability is primarily about the system's software vulnerability (e.g., unpatched operating system, database system, or web application that fails to validate input values). As explained, we can broaden the vulnerability scope to other types such as psychological gullibility due to the lack of training or the organizational failure to enforce security-bearing practices. The system- and human-side vulnerabilities become a fertile ground for adversaries to exploit.

2.12.2.2 Malware Installation

Once a target's vulnerability is successfully exploited, the attacker's malware is installed on the victim's system. Depending on the engineering details of installed malware, it very often activates the remote 'backdoor' capability through which an attacker can freely enter the system, bypassing the regular authentication and access control process. The traditional malware landing results in the virus code being stored in a file on the victim's computer. On installation, some malware may immediately begin its destructive routines, but others may keep a low key with no immediate actions until there is a triggering point.

As a relatively new type, file-less viruses are on the rise, which do not save the malware file on the computer's storage but hide in the volatile random access memory (RAM), making them difficult to trace. As file-less malware isn't installed on the disk as conventional malware is, its life generally ends when the system is rebooted. File-less malware is capable of abetting other benign applications that do malicious activities for it.

2.12.3 POST-COMPROMISE PHASE

In this phase, the attacker begins to take advantage of the compromised system's capability to execute various nefarious actions. To do so, this phase involves two-step processes: *command and control*, and *actions on objectives*.

2.12.3.1 Command and Control (C&C)

Very often, installed malware has the capability to connect back to the attacker (called C&C master) and report its successful landing on the target. From that point, the victim system (now called bot) can be remotely controlled by the C&C master. The victim computer now becomes a part of a large-scale botnet (or C&C network), a collection of many victimized computers. The details of the C&C network are explained in Chapter 8.

2.12.3.2 Actions on Objectives

Now, the attacker is ready to take nefarious actions. Again, the perpetrator's motivation varies greatly, ranging from vile actions such as stealing credit card information and sending spam to other computers, to simply exploiting the computer's CPU for crypto-currency (e.g., bitcoin) mining.

2.12.4 ADDITIONAL NOTES

As a cautionary note, although the cyber kill chain is intended to be a general model, not all attacks follow the same path. Also, included activities do not necessarily take place in a linear fashion as in Figure 2.5. Further, the model is grounded on the assumption that the victim is compromised by malware sent by an adversary despite that many cyberattacks do not necessarily involve malware. Also, a large share of malware infections does not necessarily turn the victim system into a member of a botnet. Nonetheless, the model is extremely useful for organizational defenders in understanding the malware-driven attack process and conceiving anti-malware strategies.

One more important lesson of the model is that if an organization is able to fend off the attack in the earlier stage (e.g., reconnaissance, delivery), it will be less costly to contain and remediate it. That is, the deeper malware penetrates into the advanced stage, the costlier it becomes to recover from the attack and resulting consequences.

2.13 WWW, DEEP WEB, AND DARK WEB

The Internet was born in the late 1960s; however, its usage exploded when the graphical browser similar to today's Chrome and Firefox was released in 1993 to allow effortless navigation of websites through URL links. Although the Internet has many different technology platforms, the WWW (or web for short) is the platform on which the vast majority of today's cybercrimes take place. It has literally become a jungle, crowded with scammers, criminals, and malicious hackers. Thus, having some fundamental understanding of the web's architecture is warranted. For this, the regular web (called surface web) is explained first, which is followed by how the deep web and the dark web differ from the regular web (see Figure 2.6)

2.13.1 WWW AND SURFACE WEB

The World Wide Web, or WWW (or simply web), represents a collection of information resources (e.g., texts, graphics, audios, videos) contained in public or private sites that are accessed through the Uniform Resource Locators or URL (e.g., http://www.whitehouse.gov). Simply speaking, the web is virtual cyberspace created by the billions of sites interconnected via URL links. The web's two enabling standards are HTML (Hypertext Markup Language) for webpage authoring and site development, and HTTP (Hypertext Transfer Protocol) that facilitates the exchange of webpage contents to display them on the browser.

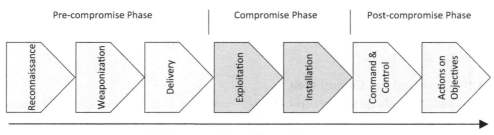

FIGURE 2.5 Phases and steps in the cyber kill chain

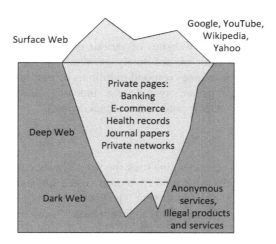

FIGURE 2.6   Surface web, deep web, and dark web

The surface web is a part of WWW whose contents can be downloaded using a regular web browser without restrictions (e.g., mandated login). For example, you can visit news sites to read articles, watch YouTube videos, issue queries to a search engine, and search homes on real estate sites.

2.13.2   DEEP WEB

There are also websites that are hidden or blocked from indexing by the search engine. They are collectively labeled as the deep web, and their access requires special software or user authentication/authorization. For example, if you visit a bank site, you are allowed to view the landing page and other webpages that provide general information about its banking services (e.g., checking and savings account options). These pages are a part of the regular, surface web.

If, however, you want to do financial transactions (e.g., deposit a check, move funds), you need to sign in to your personal account first. The webpages presented to you subsequently are a part of the deep web as they can be accessed only through the login process by a qualified account owner. As another deep web example, certain websites are protected by the HTML statement 'robots noindex meta tag', which prevents search engines from their indexing, and thus their contents are hidden from the public view. It is estimated that the deep webspace is much larger than that of the surface web.

2.13.3   DARK WEB

The dark web is another example of the deep web whose content cannot be readily accessed using a regular web browser such as Chrome and Firefox. As a relatively small segment of the deep web, the dark web is comprised of less than 30,000 'anonymized' websites, and their navigation requires the specialized 'Tor' browser (www.torproject.org).

Although much of the dark web is innocuous, there are definitely shady parts (e.g., black markets) that have gained their infamy by selling all kinds of illegal products (e.g., stolen goods, pornography, drugs) and services (e.g., hacking tools, financial fraud, illegal trades). There is even a service infrastructure such as ransomware-as-a-service (RaaS) through which ransomware tools are available to evil hackers to share the profit. The government continuously monitors and cracks down on illegal product/service vendors, but there are also practical difficulties as many sites are set up in countries with loose laws and regulations.

2.14   SEARCH ENGINE AS A HACKING TOOL

It is said that there are about 2 billion websites of various types in cyberspace. Naturally, search engines such as Google and MS Bing are absolutely essential for web surfers to locate a list of relevant websites. Powerful search engines respond to billions of user queries per day. To offer the service, search engines should find, gather, organize (e.g., indexing), and store site information, and they are explained here to highlight their potential as a hacking tool.

2.14.1   SPIDERS

To find and index websites, each search engine uses special software called robots or spiders. Web spiders crawl the webspace, gather information from each visited site and corresponding webpages, and send them back to home (e.g., Google server). The spider generally begins the journey from a popular website (e.g., web portal), collect its webpage data and send them back, and then moves on to another site following URL links. For instance, Google is said to use multiple spiders, each of which crawls over 100 pages per second, gathers around 600 kilobytes of data each second, and passes them back to Google.

2.14.2   GATHERING WEBPAGE INFORMATION

In gathering site information, spiders take different approaches in terms of how much data is gathered; how deeply it scours each website when it has a number of webpages; and how often the same site is revisited to obtain updated data. For example, in terms of how much data is gathered, some spiders may be designed to capture every significant word of a webpage, but other spiders may be instructed to collect only the words appearing in the title, subtitles, meta-tags, and particular positions of a webpage. Some spiders are programmed to copy the entire webpages of visited sites and send them back. For example, Google's search service has an option of viewing 'cached' pages. This is possible as the entire webpages of a visited site are copied and stored in Google's own server.

2.14.3   INDEXING

Information gathered and sent back by the spider is organized according to an indexing scheme, which enables fast search and retrieval of relevant sites. At this stage, website ranking is also calculated based on various weighting criteria including the word location, word frequency, distance between words, words included in meta tags, and labels in referring links.

Search sites use different formulas to assign weights to differing criteria for website indexing. This results in differences among search engines in their listings and rankings even when the same keywords are issued. When the indexing is complete, the resulting information is encoded and stored in a huge database to enable keyword searches of websites. This whole process including indexing is automated (see Figure 2.7).

2.14.4   SEARCH ENGINE AS A HACKING TOOL

Search engines are indispensable for web users. Unfortunately, they are also powerful weapons for malicious hackers. For example, Shodan (https://www.shodan.io/) is a specialized search engine designed to find devices connected to the Internet. Among them are servers, traffic lights, webcams, IoT devices, electronics, and industrial control systems. Shodan displays rich information of discovered devices including their IP address, device type, and location (e.g., country). Figure 2.8 displays the search result of 'refrigerator' on Shodan.

Also, it is not an overstatement when the Google search engine becomes the hackers' best friend as it can hunt sensitive but hard-to-find information scattered in cyberspace. Among the examples are mistakenly posted passwords and system vulnerabilities. To find such information, hackers use

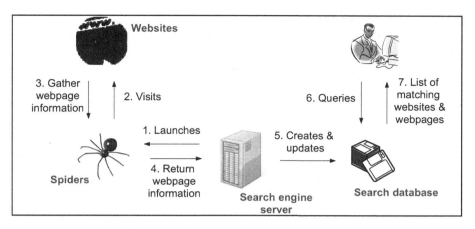

FIGURE 2.7 How search engines work

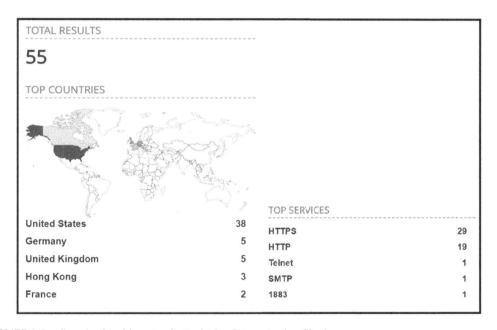

FIGURE 2.8 Search of 'refrigerators' attached to Internet using Shodan

the highly customized query technique called Google dorking. Besides, there are also other special-ized search engines designed for cybersecurity researchers and those optimized to search the dark web. Just like Shodan and Google, they are useful 'information gathering' or reconnaissance tools to bad actors.

2.15 SOCIAL ENGINEERING: LESS TECHNICAL BUT LETHAL

This section explains social engineering that has been a dominant method to launch cyberattacks. Social engineering represents a collection of non-technical tricks designed to manipulate people in an effort to obtain an unauthorized access to a target system or to steal private and oftentimes confi-dential information. For this, threat actors exploit weaknesses of human psychology (e.g., gullibility, intimidation) or cognitive ability (e.g., impersonation).

In initiating social engineering, threat actors use clever tactics rather than simply lying in an attempt to buy in or manipulate people's trust. For example, an attacker may cite direct or contextual information about the target system (e.g., server name) or a user (e.g., victim's name), or come up with a realistic scenario to trick a person into releasing sensitive information. Basically, it is much easier for attackers to cheat people to obtain protected information (e.g., passwords) than hack into a hardened system.

2.15.1 PHISHING

Among various social engineering tactics, the biggest threat has been phishing. It is an act of launching an e-mail or electronic communications in an attempt to scam users into surrendering private information (e.g., login credentials, or credit card numbers) for such evildoing as identity theft, financial extortion, and malware distribution. The majority of phishing emails carry one or more clickable links or web addresses, and it is safe to say that virtually all Internet users have been exposed to such phishing emails. Figure 2.9 illustrates clickable phishing emails sent to the author to steal the password of an email account. Not surprisingly, the sender's email and IP address were all spoofed.

2.15.1.1 Phishing Schemes

There are various phishing schemes.

a. **Spear phishing**: This attack targets a specific user, business, or organization with a message highly customized to the target. The customization significantly increases the chance of success (e.g., following a malicious URL link). As stated, this mode of attack is possible as so much information about the target is available in cyberspace, especially in social networks.

b. **Whaling**: It is a type of spear phishing in which an attacker targets 'big fish' (e.g., business executive or an important figure of an organization) to launch a criminal act, including extorting money, stealing sensitive information, or gaining access to a system.

c. **Vishing**: It is 'voice phishing' over the phone line to solicit sensitive information. To gain information, the attacker may just use the phone line (or leave a message) or combine vishing with other sources (e.g., texting or short messaging service) to further pretend that it is from a trusted source.

d. **Hoax**: It is a false warning that may be claimed to come from a trusted source such as the IT department of an organization to solicit sensitive information from unsuspecting users. For

FIGURE 2.9 Sample phishing email

example, the attacker may use a hoax to an employee of a company to change the configuration settings of its database system, making it vulnerable.

e. **Watering hole**: In the scheme, an attacker identifies a website frequented by the targeted individual or a group of individuals, and then plant malware after compromising it. For example, a manager of a manufacturing company may regularly visit a website of part suppliers. If the site is compromised by a malicious hacker, the visitor's computer is infected with malware – a form of the drive-by-download attack.

2.15.2 SPAM

2.15.2.1 Definition

Spam represents unsolicited commercial emails and more of a nuisance unless they hide harmful malware. Spam is different from emails computer users opt in to receive, oftentimes as a result of marketing promotions by advertisers. Spammers hide their source with email-address and IP-address spoofing. Also, spam is getting more tailored to selected targets, departing from the past practice of mass, indiscriminative flooding of identical messages. With the targeted personalization, spam has become more effective in trapping innocent victims.

2.15.2.2 Spam Bot and Anti-Spam

As a spam-related technology, the spam spider – also known as spam bot or harvesting bot – is a computer program. It can gather email addresses from various online sources including websites, mailing list archives, message boards, social networks, and online forums and bring them back to the evil master for spamming. A number of anti-spam measures have been applied by business organizations and internet service providers to battle spam. They include whitelisting (i.e., allow only those in the list of email addresses, domains, and/or IP addresses), blacklisting of spam senders, and spam hash filters (i.e., drop emails whose hash value matches one of the existing spam hashes). Nonetheless, spam continues to plague individuals and businesses.

2.15.2.3 Case: Spam's Global Supply Chain Network

Figure 2.10 demonstrates the global nature of the spam business, which shows a supply chain network of the illegal Viagra product. To reveal the network, the research team from the University of California in San Diego painstakingly gathered information by actually ordering the product. As it shows, selling an illegal product through spam involves various entities distributed globally. They include the marketing campaign network that distributes spam, manufacturer, merchant bank, customer banks, e-commerce affiliate programs, and other network service infrastructure.

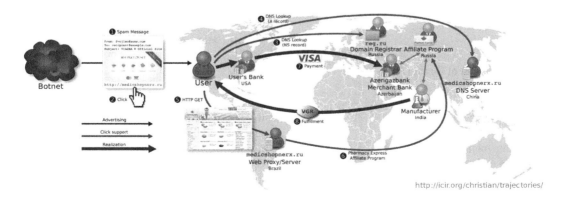

FIGURE 2.10 Global spam supply chain network (Source: http://icir.org/christian/trajectories)

CHAPTER SUMMARY

- The center of an organization's cyber defense plan should be on protecting valued data/information assets such as intellectual properties, business secrets, and various databases.
- Protecting valued information of an organization from cyber threats should be practiced through the combination of three entities: *people, products*, and *policies and procedures*.
- Some of the general terms often used in the cybersecurity domain include *threat, threat agent, threat actor, threat (or attack) vector, vulnerability*, and *risk*.
- There are different threat actor types, and *cybercriminals, script kiddies, insiders, hacktivists*, and *state-sponsored attackers* are among them.
- Cyberattacks are successful because the targeted organization has vulnerabilities in software, system configurations, hardware, and/or business operations and risk management, which a threat actor can take advantage of.
- An organization can manage the cybersecurity risk by taking one or more of the following strategies: *risk avoidance, risk mitigation, risk acceptance, risk deterrence*, and *risk transference*.
- In protecting data/information assets, *data confidentiality, data integrity*, and *data availability* (CIA) are fundamental security requirements that need to be perfected.
- For the protection of data/information in terms of CIA requirements, an organization needs to implement solutions that support *authentication, access control/authorization*, and *accounting* (AAA).
- General principles used to defend an organization from cybersecurity threats include *layering (or defense-in-depth), limiting, simplicity, diversity*, and *obscurity*.
- The cyber kill chain is a general framework that depicts steps adversaries take to launch attacks on a target system and is composed of three phases: *pre-compromise, compromise*, and *post-compromise*.
- The web is a virtual space in which the vast majority of today's cybercrimes take place, and there are three different types: surface web, deep web, and dark web.
- Search engines are very useful reconnaissance tools to malicious hackers as they can hunt sensitive but hard-to-find information such as system vulnerabilities.
- Social engineering represents a collection of non-technical tricks designed to manipulate people in an effort to gain unauthorized access to a target system or to steal private and oftentimes confidential information.
- Spam represents unsolicited commercial emails and more of a nuisance unless they hide harmful and executable malware. Its supply chain network is truly global.

KEY TERMS

access control
accounting
advanced persistent threat (APT)
asset
authentication
authorization
availability
bring-your-own-device (BYOD)
command and control
confidentiality
cybercriminal

cyber kill chain
dark web
deep web
defense-in-depth
disaster recovery
distributed denial of service (DDOS)
diversity principle
exploitation
Google dorking
hactivist
hoax

incident response	spam
information security	script kiddy
insider	Shodan
integrity	simplicity principle
layering principle	spear phishing
limiting principle	spider
obscurity principle	state sponsored attacker
phishing	surface web
reconnaissance	threat
risk	threat actor
risk avoidance	threat/attack vector
risk acceptance	vishing
risk deterrence	vulnerability
risk mitigation	watering hole
risk transference.	weaponization
search engine	whaling
social engineering	World Wide Web (WWW)

CHAPTER REVIEW QUESTIONS

1. The first step of the cyber kill chain, _____, is performed by an attacker to conduct a chain of activities subsequently.
   A) weaponization
   B) exploitation
   C) actions on objectives
   D) reconnaissance
   E) drive by download

2. Phishing is a type of the _____ attack.
   A) social engineering
   B) spam
   C) access control bypass
   D) fingerprinting
   E) weaponization

3. An organization that purchased different security products from different vendors is exercising which security principle?
   A) obscurity principle
   B) limiting principle
   C) layering principle
   D) complexity principle
   E) diversity principle

4. A malicious hacker is attempting to steal sensitive financial information from a company. For this, he chose its CEO as a specific target as she has complete access to sensitive data. Then the attacker tricks the CEO into revealing corporate data by engineering an elaborate website spoofing. This is an _____ attack.
   A) impersonation
   B) whaling
   C) vishing
   D) shoulder phishing
   E) insider

5. One of the key principles of cyber defense is to keep *simplicity* so that a security system should be easy to understand and use and does not disrupt routines. Which of these may NOT facilitate simplicity?
   A) Use a password manager to protect many passwords owned by an individual.
   B) Use automatic full disk encryption to protect data without sacrificing productivity.
   C) Use automatic data backup.
   D) Use passphrases that are more secure and easier to remember than typical passwords.
   E) Depend on the secrecy of system components as much as possible

6. The following represent available options an organization can take in dealing with security risks EXCEPT:
   A) *Avoidance* that fundamentally eliminates the creation of risks
   B) *Acceptance* that accepts risks as a part of life
   C) *Mitigation* that takes measures to reduce risks
   D) *Deterrence* that discourages threat attempts or attacks
   E) *Isolation* by transferring risks to other organizations

7. Which is CORRECTLY paired in managing the cybersecurity risk?
   A) Risk avoidance: All computer systems of an organization display a banner that warns of legal consequences if any illegal activities are committed.
   B) Risk mitigation: An organization decides to buy an insurance in preparation for cyber incidents.
   C) Risk deterrence: An organization decides the maximum level of risk it is willing to accept and plans a budget.
   D) Risk acceptance: A small business decides not to invest in security products or services to protect its assets.
   E) Risk transference: An organization decided not to have any website or internet connections.

8. What happens at the weaponization stage of the cyber kill chain?
   A) An exploit is transmitted to the target system.
   B) The attacker creates an exploit and packages it into a deliverable payload
   C) An exploit is installed on the victim's computer to create a remote *backdoor*.
   D) The victim system connects back to the attacker so that it can be remotely controlled.
   E) The attacker probes for any information about the target system.

9. Behavioral biometrics such as keystroke dynamics are the _____ type of authentication.
   A) what you have
   B) what you are
   C) what you know
   D) where you are
   E) what you do

10. Which is CORRECT in pairing an authentication method and its example?
    A) What you have – security token
    B) What you are – keyboarding
    C) What you know – fingerprint
    D) Where you are – behavioral attributes
    E) When you do – restricted in a military base

11. Figure Figure 2.11 must demonstrate the _____ principle in maintaining security.
    A) limiting
    B) simplicity
    C) layering
    D) defense-in-depth
    E) diversity

12. The cyber risk an organization should bear is a function of:
    A) authentication, authorization, and accounting
    B) confidentiality, integrity, and availability

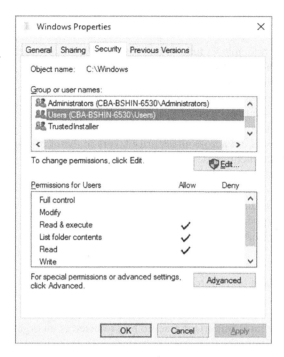

FIGURE 2.11   (Repeat of Figure 2.4)

    C) threat likelihood (or threats), vulnerabilities, and assets

    D) humans, products, and policies and procedures

    E) humans, vulnerabilities, and policies and procedures

13. Which of the following threat actors are more likely to carry out advanced persistent threats?

    A) insiders

    B) state-sponsored attackers

    C) cybercriminals

    D) script kiddies

    E) hactivists

14. Improving host security through anti-virus software and the host firewall results in _____.

    A) host firewalling

    B) host self-defense

    C) host hardening

    D) host patching

    E) host demilitarizion

15. Which of the following technologies is NOT designed for personal authentication?

    A) password and passphrase

    B) digital signature

    C) biometric solution

    D) security token

    E) access control list

16. Maintaining a reliable backup system of corporate database satisfies what aspect of security requirements?

    A) confidentiality

    B) integrity

    C) authentication

      D) authorization

      E) availability

17. The defense-in-depth principle includes measures of the following security layers EXCEPT the:

      A) application security layer

      B) intermediary device security layer

      C) host security layer

      D) internal network security layer

      E) perimeter security layer

18. The following initiatives cut across all security layers in their coverage EXCEPT the:

      A) plan to harden intermediary devices

      B) regulatory compliance self-assessment

      C) security policy and procedure

      D) security awareness and training

      E) disaster recovery plan

19. Which should be the LEAST exploited threat/attack vector?

      A) system users

      B) the network

      C) security policies and procedures

      D) web applications

      E) mobile devices

20. What is generally the most important asset to be protected at an organization?

      A) software/applications

      B) hosts (both clients and servers)

      C) the network

      D) data/information

      E) intermediary devices

21. Which of the following is a TRUE statement?

      A) Only the surface web uses web standard technologies including HTTP and HTML.

      B) The websites in the dark web can be accessed with a regular browser.

      C) The deep web and the dark web do not overlap.

      D) The surface webspace is larger than the deep webspace.

      E) The regular search engine indexes surface websites, but not the sites in the deep web.

22. The following lists phishing attacks EXCEPT:

      A) watering hole

      B) hoax

      C) whaling

      D) poisoning

      E) vishing

23. Imagine that the IT manager of a business organization decided to configure all enterprise servers with one complex password for authentication. This is a violation of the _____ security principle.

      A) obscurity

      B) diversity

      C) simplicity

      D) limiting

      E) defense-in-depth

24. An organization evaluates the current status in terms of its preparedness to defend core information assets from threats and subsequently plans for improvements. This is related to the:

      A) security policy and procedure

      B) security awareness and training

C) information security self-assessment

D) regulatory compliance self-assessment

E) disaster recovery plan

25. All network nodes (e.g., computers, intermediary devices, security devices) should record logs for subsequent analysis and the auditing of resource utilization and security controls. This describes the _____ requirement in information security.

A) accounting

B) authentication

C) data integrity

D) data availability

E) access control

HANDS-ON EXERCISES

EXERCISE 2.1

Experience cyberattacks crossing national boundaries by browsing real-time maps provided by cybersecurity firms. They are constructed using different technologies including the global deployment of sensors and honeypots, on-demand scan, on-access scan, and playback of recorded events. One of the most popular maps is Kaspersky's 'Cyberthreat Realtime Map'. Browse it here (https://cybermap.kaspersky.com/) and answer the following.

1. Use your mouse to point to a particular country of your interest and review its statistics related to the real-time detection of various threats (e.g., virus, intrusion detection, botnet, ransomware).
2. According to the site, what are the top five countries heavily infected with malware today?
3. Last week, what are the names of the most active malware in the US?
4. Click on the top three malware strains and read what nefarious activities they perform.

EXERCISE 2.2

Let's experience the power of Shodan, the search engine specialized to find IoT devices configured for 'remote access' over the Internet. This will give you an idea of what a powerful reconnaissance tool it can be to cyber adversaries.

1. Go to 'https://www.shodan.io' and create an account for an upgraded usage.
2. Once ready, search the keyword 'webcam' without the double quotes.
    a. On the side panel, narrow the search to webcams running Windows 7 or 8 OS.
    b. Click on the listed IPs and observe which ones allow remote access without a login and password.
    c. What information can be gathered by a bad actor to exploit a particular webcam?
3. Try the search keyword: 'OS:Windows XP' that is old and known for its vulnerabilities and has been subject to exploits.
4. Try the search keyword: 'port:22' to locate devices running on the SSH port.
5. Try the search keyword: 'port:3389' popular for remote desktop connections.
6. Try the search keyword of a product such as 'netgear' and explore the results.
7. Try the search keyword of a city such as 'city:San Diego' and explore the results.
8. Try the search keyword of the particular server version, Apache 2.2.3, that is a well-known webserver vulnerable to exploits.
9. Try other search keywords of your interest such as refrigerator and street lights.

EXERCISE 2.3

Distinguishing phishing emails from legitimate ones can be challenging. Visit the site www.sonic-wall.com and search 'SonicWALL Phishing IQ Test'. Go through the test questions that challenge you in detecting phishing emails.

EXERCISE 2.4

1. Individual and corporate email systems can adopt two different strategies in filtering spam: whitelisting vs. blacklisting. What are their pros and cons? (Perform an Internet search as needed.)
2. Greylisting is another approach to filter spam. Conduct an Internet search and explain how it works and how effective the solution is.

EXERCISE 2.5

CVE (Common Vulnerability Enumeration) is a national database to register (mostly software-related) vulnerabilities and their quantified severity. It is a highly important database for IT security professionals. At the same time, it is a very useful source for cyber adversaries in plotting attacks. Visit 'https://nvd.nist.gov/vuln/search' and answer the following questions.

1. How many vulnerabilities have been disclosed during the past three-month period?
2. How many vulnerabilities have been reported during the past three-year period?
3. How many vulnerabilities related to Windows OS or Mac OS have been found during the past three-month period?
4. How many vulnerabilities related to the 'authentication' of Android have been found during the past three-year period?

3 Essential Layers of Computer Networking

3.1 INTRODUCTION

This chapter explains the network architecture and its layers. The concepts are highly abstract and can pose a considerable challenge in their comprehension. Nonetheless, they are so fundamental to computer networking and thus they are introduced in the early part of this book. *You are encouraged to go through the entire chapter several times to better grasp the notions and their relationships.*

First of all, communications between network nodes demand precise execution of a number of predefined functions. If just one of the functions is not properly performed, nodes will either misunderstand or not be able to understand each other. These functions can be grouped in their similarities. The *standard architecture* in computer networking is a multi-layered framework (also known as a reference model) that broadly defines primary networking functions to be undertaken in each layer.

On the conceptual basis of general layer functions within a *standard architecture*, specific *standards* (many of which are protocols) running in each layer are explained. The layered framework of a standard architecture offers distinct benefits. Especially, changes of a particular software or hardware standard within a layer can be made independently of standards in other layers.

3.1.1 LEARNING OBJECTIVES

The objectives of this chapter are to understand:

- TCP/IP and OSI standard architectures
- Different types of the protocol data unit (PDU)
- The encapsulation and de-encapsulation process of PDUs
- Primary functions of the application, transport, internet, data link, and physical layers
- Key standards (including protocols) of each layer
- Details of IP and ICMP at the internet layer
- Details of TCP and UDP at the transport layer
- A host's software/hardware components that implement the layer functions

3.2 TCP/IP VS. OSI

3.2.1 STANDARD ARCHITECTURE

TCP/IP and OSI (Open Systems Interconnection) are two dominant standard architectures.

3.2.1.1 TCP/IP

The TCP/IP framework was introduced to facilitate the development of standards for the wildly popular Internet. The organization, *Internet Engineering Task Force* (or IETF), has been responsible for crafting the TCP/IP architecture and its standards. IETF is an international community of network designers, operators, vendors, and researchers. It maintains a number of working groups that develop the *Request for Comments* (or RFC), a formal publication on a particular TCP/IP-related project. Some RFCs become official TCP/IP standards after going through maturation stages and final ratifications by IETF. The list of working groups and RFCs are available on the IETF website (i.e., www.IETF.org).

3.2.1.2 OSI

OSI is another reference model from the *International Organization for Standardization* (or ISO), an international standard-setting body being represented by many national standard organizations including the *American National Standards Institute* (or ANSI) from the US. TCP/IP and OSI architecture models define network functions in terms of two slightly different multi-layer structures in which TCP/IP defines four functional layers and OSI has seven layers (see Table 3.1). Roughly, OSI further divides TCP/IP's application layer functions into those of application, presentation, and session layers. Also, you can observe that OSI separates the TCP/IP's subnet layer into data link and physical layers.

3.2.1.3 TCP/IP vs. OSI

In practice, standards introduced for OSI and TCP/IP complement each other rather than compete. The popular standards of the application, transport, and internet (or network) layers are from TCP/IP, and OSI standards dominate the data link and physical layers. As a result, the five-layer hybrid architecture composed of application, transport, internet, data link, and physical layers is widely used by practitioners. The hybrid structure also becomes the basis of my explanations throughout this book.

3.2.1.4 Layers and Core Functions

The primary layer functions are shown in Table 3.1.

- Application layer: This layer is responsible for application-to-application communications (e.g., web browser and webserver programs, email client and server programs). All user applications operate in this layer.
- Transport layer: This layer performs end-to-end (or host-to-host) handshaking and maintains reliability in data communications.
- Internet layer: This layer conducts inter-networking across two or more subnetworks.
- Data link layer: This layer is tasked to undertake intra-networking, which moves data within a subnetwork

TABLE 3.1
TCP/IP and OSI layers

TCP/IP	OSI	Hybrid	Layer	Key tasks
Application	Application	Application	5	Application-application communications
	Presentation			
	Session			
Transport	Transport	Transport	4	End-to-end logical connectivity
Internet	Network	Internet	3	Inter-networking across subnets
Network Access (or Subnet)	Data link	Data link	2	Intra-networking within a subnet
	Physical	Physical	1	Generation of signals and their physical delivery over the network

- Physical layer: This layer physically transports data/messages between network nodes.

Each network node (i.e., host and intermediary device) conducts many different layer functions internally. Whereas each host (e.g., PC, server, smartphone) implements all five layers internally, intermediary devices generally perform only a subset of five layers, as their primary mission is to transfer messages between hosts. For example, while traditional *switches* conduct data link and physical layer activities, *routers* mostly undertake internet, data link, and physical layer tasks (more details to follow).

3.2.2 STANDARD AND PROTOCOL

As said, each layer defines networking functions to be performed and they are formalized as *standards*. Certain layers (i.e., application and physical layers) have a lot more standards than other layers (i.e., internet and transport layers). Some of the well-known standards in each layer are listed in Table 3.2, and they are explained throughout the book. The standards are implemented in the form of software or hardware. Physical layer standards are hardware-related and standards of other layers are primarily implemented in software.

As a "subset" of *standards*, there are many *protocols* that are implemented in software. Each protocol contains a number of highly detailed communication rules to be followed by network nodes to exchange data (refer to Section 1.2.6). HTTP/HTTPS in the application layer, TCP in the transport layer, and IP in the internet layer are among the well-known protocols. As indicated, the physical layer includes numerous hardware-related standards, but they are not called protocols.

3.2.3 PROTOCOL DATA UNIT (PDU)

Host devices (e.g., computers, smartphones) perform all five layer functions. The layers except the physical layer produce discrete message units called *protocol data units* (PDUs) when two hosts communicate. Each PDU has a selective combination of *data*, *header*, and/or *trailer* fields. The data field (frequently called payload) is where the user data such as email, voice, or video are placed. To transport the user data, additional overhead information should be included in the header and/or trailer.

TABLE 3.2
Select standards in each layer

Layers	Select standards
Application	• Simple Mail Transfer Protocol (SMTP) – email delivery • Hypertext Transfer Protocol (HTTP/HTTPS) – web browsing
Transport	• TCP (Transmission Control Protocol) • UDP (User Datagram Protocol)
Internet	• IP (Internet Protocol) • ICMP (Internet Control Message Protocol)
Data link	• LAN: Ethernet, Wi-Fi • WAN/MAN: Carrier-Ethernet, Multi-Protocol Label Switching
Physical	• Cabling: twisted pair, optical fiber • Port/interface: RJ-45, serial port, parallel port • Transmission technology: modulation, multiplexing

---

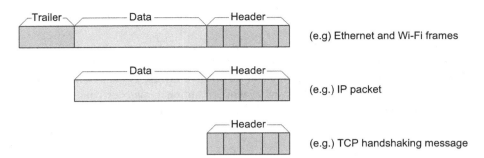

FIGURE 3.1   Three formats of protocol data units (PDUs)

A protocol (e.g., HTTPS, TCP) produces PDUs in one of three different formats (see Figure 3.1):

a. PDUs with a header, data field, and trailer
b. PDUs with a header and data field only
c. PDUs with a header only

The header and trailer added before and after the data field are further divided into several sub-fields to include information (e.g., source and destination addresses) required by a protocol.

There are application layer, transport layer, internet layer, and data link layer PDUs. Each layer's PDU has a distinctive name: *segment/datagram* for the transport layer PDU, *packet* for the internet layer PDU, and *frame* for the data link layer PDU (see Table 3.5). The application layer PDU, however, does not have a designated name, and thus we can just call it APDU.

In terms of the relationship between PDUs, once an APDU containing user data (e.g., email) is created on the application layer, this triggers the successive formation of a segment (or datagram), a packet, and a frame. Then, the frame that is still in 0s and 1s are turned into a signal (e.g., electronic, radio, or light signal) by a physical layer device for transmission. When the signal arrives at the destination host, there will be a reverse process (i.e., signal → frame → packet → segment (or datagram) → APDU). The layer processing that enables the exchange of application data between hosts is demonstrated in Figure 3.3 in terms of encapsulation and de-encapsulation.

3.3   LAYER FUNCTIONS: AN ANALOGY

Key layer functions are explained in this section. Comprehending primary responsibilities of each layer poses a considerable challenge when someone is exposed to this concept for the first time. To make it somewhat easier to visualize layer functions, they are explained through a real-life scenario in which a *business letter* (an analogy of the application PDU or APDU) is exchanged between Jayne and Brian living in two different cities (see Figure 3.2).

Assume that the following will take place sequentially:

1. Jayne writes a business letter in English.
2. Before mailing it, Jayne calls Brian to say that the business letter is going to be mailed and to ask Brian for a return call for its acknowledgement. Brian agrees to confirm the receipt.
3. The letter is sealed in an envelope with Jayne's and Brian's mailing addresses and placed in a mailbox.
4. Jayne's mail is transported to a local post office by a mailman's vehicle. At the local office, the mail is sorted out according to its destination address and shipped to a regional post office by a bigger postal truck. The same sorting is repeated a few times before the mail reaches the destination's local post office.

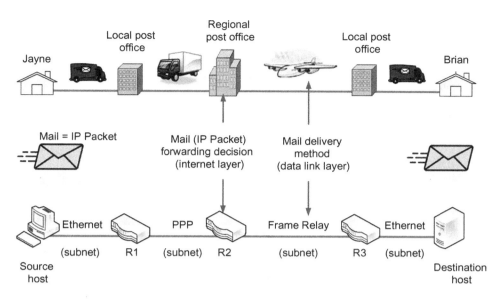

FIGURE 3.2 A real-life analogy of layer functions

5. At the local post office, a carrier delivers Jayne's mail to Brian in a delivery vehicle.

In that scenario, there is an equivalence between the delivery process of Jayne's mail and that of IP packets:

1. The business letter written by Jayne = application layer function (i.e., writing an email)
2. Jayne's call to Brian to notify the forthcoming mail and Brian's acknowledgement of its receipt = transport layer function (i.e., handshaking and acknowledgement)
3. Enveloping the letter with mailing addresses = internet layer function (i.e., IP packet creation)
4. Sorting Jayne's mail by post offices = internet layer function (i.e., IP packet routing)
5. Mail transportation by a 'vehicle' between two locations = data link layer function (i.e., actual delivery of IP packets)

Basically, the ultimate goal of a computer network is to safely deliver IP packets between communicating hosts. Again, always remember that modern computer networks exist to exchange IP packets (e.g., the 'envelope' containing Jayne's letter) between hosts. Then, data link layer technologies (e.g., Ethernet, Wi-Fi) are merely different transportation mechanisms (e.g., trucks, airplanes) used to deliver IP packets.

Going back to the difference between intra-networking and inter-networking, intra-networking represents the delivery process of IP packets by a data link-layer technology within a subnetwork boundary (step 5). Meanwhile, the construction of IP packets and their routing across subnetworks (steps 3 and 4) are key inter-networking activities. Pay close attention to the details of Figure 3.2 that includes much information.

3.4 LAYER PROCESSING

As stated previously, each layer – except the physical layer – produces its own PDUs, and each of them is passed onto either the upper or lower layer to become another PDU. For this, neighboring layers and their standards should work together to successfully transmit data. Passing PDUs between two neighboring layers results in continuous repetition of *encapsulation* and *de-encapsulation*, as in Figure 3.3. Whenever encapsulation is performed on a PDU coming down

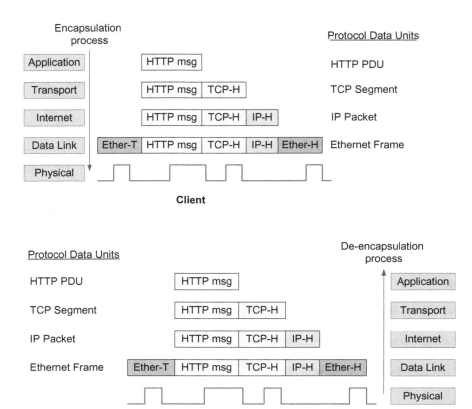

FIGURE 3.3   PDU encapsulation/de-encapsulation

from an upper layer, a new PDU is created (e.g., a packet becomes a frame). Whenever de-encapsulation is performed on a PDU coming up from the lower layer, a new PDU is created (e.g., a frame becomes a packet).

3.4.1   REPETITIVE ENCAPSULATIONS

The production of an application-layer PDU (APDU) triggers successive generation of the transport, internet, and data link layer PDUs. Figure 3.3 illustrates a scenario in which a request message is produced by a source host's web browser and processed through the layers to ultimately reach its target webserver program of the destination host. (Note: HTTP instead of the dominant HTTPS [HTTP over SSL/TLS] is used for easier demonstration.)

    a. Application layer: The HTTP request (as an APDU) is produced in the application layer. The APDU is, then, passed down to the transport layer.

    b. Transport layer: For encapsulation, a TCP header is added to the APDU, and the new entity becomes another PDU, a segment. The TCP segment, then, is moved to the internet layer.

    c. Internet layer: The TCP segment is added by an IP header as another form of encapsulation, resulting in a new PDU, an IP packet. The packet is then handed over to the data link layer.

    d. Data link layer: The IP packet becomes a data link PDU (frame) when a data link header and a trailer are added before and after the packet as another encapsulation process. Unlike the upper layer PDUs that have only a header, data link frames generally have both a header and a trailer. This is because data link is the last layer that creates PDUs before their release by the physical layer and thus the PDUs need boundary indicators.

e. Physical layer: The frame (still in 0s and 1s) coming down from the data link layer is encoded into an electronic, light, or radio signal and released to a wireless or wired network for propagation.

3.4.2 REPETITIVE DE-ENCAPSULATIONS

Once the data arrive at a destination host, a reverse, de-encapsulation process takes place in which the header and/or the trailer in each layer's PDU are removed and the remaining portion (i.e., payload) is pushed up to the next upper layer. As a result of the repeated de-encapsulation, the webserver program running in the application layer receives only the browser's original request message (i.e., APDU) and processes it.

With that understanding of the overall layer processing, the primary functions of each layer are explained in greater detail starting from the application layer.

3.5 APPLICATION LAYER (LAYER 5)

In this layer, following the user input (e.g., a mouse click), the client and server applications installed on host computers exchange data using a built-in communication protocol. For example, the web browser such as Chrome, as a client program, communicates with the webserver program (e.g., Microsoft IIS, Apache) using HTTP or HTTPS to download webpages.

3.5.1 HTTP DEMONSTRATION

Here is a simple demonstration of the browser–webserver communication based on HTTP. Again, although secure HTTPS is more than 90% of web traffic these days, HTTP is used for demonstration. When a web surfer enters http://www.sdsu.edu on a browser, it uses HTTP to produce an application PDU similar to:

```
--------------------------------------------------------------------------
Browser request:          GET / HTTP/1.1
Host: www.sdsu.edu
**** The rest is omitted ****
--------------------------------------------------------------------------
```

'GET' is a keyword for file request. 'HTTP/1.1' represents a HTTP version the browser wants to use to correspond with the *www.sdsu.edu* server program. On receiving the browser request, the webserver returns an HTTP response (as a PDU) that contains data (e.g., text, image) and a header similar to:

```
--------------------------------------------------------------------------
Server response:          HTTP/1.1·200·OK
Date:·Mon,·30·May·2016·21:41:33·GMT
Server:·Apache/2.4·(Unix)
Content-Length: 88
Content-Type: text/html
**** The rest is omitted ****
--------------------------------------------------------------------------
```

As can be seen, the response's header part contains such information as date, server program (e.g., Apache), and content type (e.g., text, image). The header is followed by the data field (e.g., image) requested by the browser. Figure 3.7 is an actual webpage composed of several text and image files.

3.5.2 SELECT APPLICATION-LAYER PROTOCOLS

Among numerous application-layer protocols being used, Table 3.3 lists some of them in terms of application types.

3.6 TRANSPORT LAYER (LAYER 4)

Once a PDU comes down from the application layer, the transport-layer immediately begins working to create its own PDU based on the APDU to perform predefined tasks. Broadly speaking, the primary responsibility of this layer is to establish a 'logical' end-to-end connection (or handshaking) between two communicating hosts/end nodes and to maintain the 'reliability' of data exchanges if necessary. As related, this layer is in charge of three functions:

a. Provision of data integrity
b. Session management
c. Port management

Transmission Control Protocol (TCP) and *User Datagram Protocol* (UDP) implement transport-layer functions. TCP is responsible for (a) and (b), and (c) is performed by both TCP and UDP.

TABLE 3.3
Standard application layer protocols

Application types	Standard protocols
Exchange emails	• Simple Mail Transfer Protocol (SMTP) • Internet Message Access Protocol (IMAP) • Post Office Protocol (POP, POP3)
Transfer files remotely	• File Transfer Protocol (FTP): Data not encrypted • FTP over SSL (FTPS): Secure version of FTP
Access accounts remotely	• Telnet: Data not encrypted • Secure Shell (SSH): Secure version of Telnet
Browse World Wide Web sites	• HTTP: Data not encrypted • HTTPS: Secure version of HTTP
Map between IP addresses and host names	• Domain Name System (DNS): Data not encrypted • DNS Security Extensions (DNSSEC): Secure version of DNS
Provide a temporary IP address to user stations	• Dynamic Host Configuration Protocol (DHCP)
Texting on wireless networks	• Short Messaging Service (SMS) Protocol
Exchange multimedia data on wireless networks	• Multimedia Messaging Service (MMS) Protocol

---

3.6.1 PROVISION OF DATA INTEGRITY

The transport layer is responsible for maintaining the integrity of APDU exchanged between end nodes, and this is achieved by two different mechanisms available through TCP, *error control* and *flow control*.

3.6.1.1 Error Control

The error control is intended to detect and correct transmission errors (e.g., change or loss of data), and TCP utilizes the *acknowledgement* mechanism for it (see Figure 3.4). To that end, a host station that receives an error-free APDU returns an acknowledgement to its sender. If there is no acknowledgement from the destination host, the source host retransmits the APDU presuming that there has been a transmission error. Although the working details of the acknowledgement-based error control is more complex, they are beyond the scope of this book.

3.6.1.2 Flow Control

The flow control is used to regulate the transmission speed between two engaging hosts so that one party is not overwhelmed by the other due to the mismatch in their data transmission capacity. The key mechanism of flow control is through the *window size* field (see Figure 3.4) that basically tells how many bytes of data can be sent before receiving an acknowledgement.

The window size shrinks whenever a party releases data, and if it reaches 0, then the sender should halt transmissions until an acknowledgement from the receiver node returns. The acknowledgement results in the expansion of the Window size, which allows the sender host to resume data transmissions. You can tell that the receiver host can intentionally hold the acknowledgement to slow down data flows.

3.6.1.3 TCP and Data Integrity

TCP mandates both error control and flow control between two hosts, and thus is ideal for user applications that need to exchange large files reliably. Among the application layer protocols that rely on TCP are SMTP, FTP, and HTTP. TCP is, therefore, called a *reliable protocol* as it makes use of the acknowledgement to improve the dependability of communications between hosts. Achieving such reliability, however, incurs significant overheads because of (1) the process burden for end nodes to produce acknowledgements and (2) the consumption of network bandwidth to deliver them.

Figure 3.4 displays the TCP segment's header fields. A segment is born when an APDU comes down to the transport layer and appended by a TCP header. For this, the APDU is placed in the data (or payload) field of the resulting segment, an *encapsulation* process.

Unlike the ordinary segment that has both a header and a data field, there is also a segment that contains only an acknowledgement. That segment has a header but no data field, as the acknowledgement information is contained in the header (see Figure 3.1).

Below are brief descriptions of the TCP header fields:

- The *source* and *destination ports* indicate the sending and receiving applications of the APDU contained in a segment.

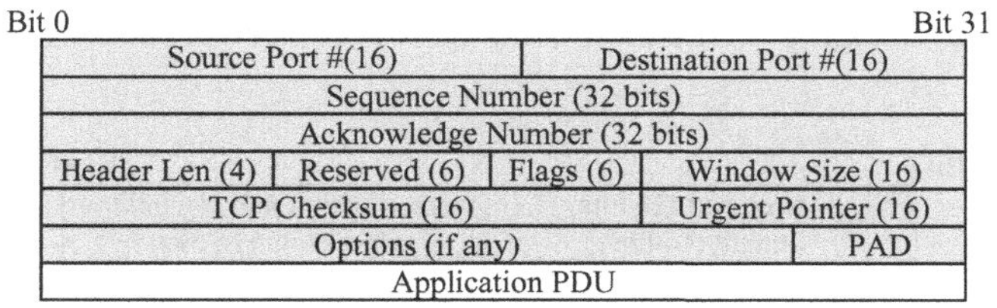

Bit 0   Bit 31

Source Port #(16)		Destination Port #(16)	
Sequence Number (32 bits)			
Acknowledge Number (32 bits)			
Header Len (4)	Reserved (6)	Flags (6)	Window Size (16)
TCP Checksum (16)		Urgent Pointer (16)	
Options (if any)			PAD
Application PDU			

FIGURE 3.4 TCP segment

- The *sequence number* is a unique identifier assigned to a segment to be transported. When multiple segments are released by a sending host, the receiving host recognizes their correct sequence based on the number. If segments arrive out of sequence, the receiving host performs their re-sequencing before presenting them to the user.
- The *acknowledgement number* is used to acknowledge one or more segments received.
- The *window size* is for flow control.
- The *flags* are for additional control functions such as session establishment (or handshaking) and session termination.
- The *checksum* is for detecting a possible transmission error within a segment and thus it is an error detection code.

3.6.1.4   UDP and Data Integrity

UDP is another transport layer protocol, an alternative to TCP. UDP's main concern is not in maintaining the integrity and reliability of application layer data as TCP does. UDP is, therefore, an *unreliable protocol* that does not perform the flow control and error control functions, and subsequently its header structure is simpler than the segment's. Figure 3.5 demonstrates the UDP's PDU (called *datagram*) and its header structure.

With the absence of *reliability* features, UDP significantly reduces the workload of source and destination hosts and also does not burden the network with acknowledgement traffic. This simplicity and efficiency make UDP an ideal transport protocol for real-time traffic produced by such applications as voice-over IP, video conferencing, online gaming, and multimedia streaming. These applications cannot afford delays resulting from TCP's handshaking and acknowledgement overheads. For them, avoiding latency is more important than ensuring the integrity of exchanged data. Besides, some application protocols including DNS and DHCP rely on UDP to deliver their messages as error control and flow control are not essential to them.

Just as with UDP, most protocols in other layers (e.g., IP, HTTP) are *unreliable*, as they have no built-in procedure to perform the detection and correction of transmission errors by themselves. This is fine because even if transmission errors (e.g., dropped IP packets) occur in other layers, TCP in the transport layer can find and fix them. But UDP does not.

3.6.2   Session Management

3.6.2.1   Session vs. No-Session

When two hosts try to exchange the APDU, two different options exist depending on the application type.

- Handshaking (for session establishment) should be done first between two hosts, which represents a mutual agreement to exchange data.
- Alternatively, the source host can simply dispatch the data to the destination host without handshaking. In this mode, there is no need for the source to seek an approval (or agreement) from the counterpart before releasing the data.

When handshaking is needed between two hosts, TCP is used. As it establishes a session through handshaking before exchanging application data, TCP becomes a *connection-oriented* protocol.

Bit 0		Bit 31
Source port (16 bits)		Destination port (16 bits)
Length (16 bits)		Checksum (16 bits)
Data (Application PDU)		

FIGURE 3.5   UDP datagram

Whereas, UDP is a *connection-less* protocol as application layer data relying on UDP are transmitted without having a formal handshaking process between the two engaging hosts. In summary, TCP is a connection-oriented and reliable protocol, whereas UDP is a connection-less and unreliable protocol.

3.6.2.2 Session Management by TCP

For the task of session management, TCP uses 3 bits (*SYN, ACK*, and *FIN* bits) in the *Flags* field (see Figure 3.4). The *SYN* bit is for a handshaking request, the *ACK* bit for an acknowledgement of session request, and the *FIN* bit for the termination of an existing session. By setting each of the three bits at either 0 or 1, two hosts can convey their intentions. For example, a source host sets SYN=1 when it wants handshaking with a target host. The *ACK* bit is used only for session management (e.g., handshaking, session termination), and thus should not be confused with the TCP header's *Acknowledge Number* field that is to confirm the arrival of APDUs.

Figure 3.6 demonstrates that exchanging application data between two hosts based on TCP is composed of:

1. *Session establishment* through the three-way handshaking of:

$$SYN \rightarrow SYN + ACK \rightarrow ACK$$

2. Exchange of application layer data or APDUs (e.g., webpages)
3. *Session termination* through the four-way correspondence of:

$$FIN \rightarrow ACK \rightarrow FIN \rightarrow ACK$$

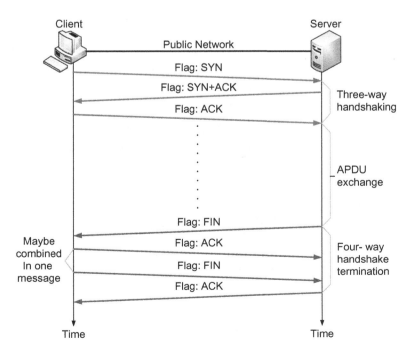

FIGURE 3.6 Session establishment and termination

3.6.2.3 TCP Session in Real Setting

To better relate the session management in Figure 3.6, a university webpage is demonstrated (see Figure 3.7). It shows that, to display the webpage on a browser, it has to download several objects including the main text page and several JPEG and GIF image files. To download an object, one TCP session is established. During a TCP session, sometimes just one TCP segment is enough to transport an object. Other times, multiple TCP segments are used to deliver one oversized object (e.g., object 2 in Figure 3.7) by fragmenting them.

There are at least four image files/objects in Figure 3.7 and their downloading takes at least four different TCP sessions. Although the TCP sessions are established in parallel to load the webpage faster, it is not difficult to see that there is a considerable overhead to be able to put together just one webpage. Because of the large TCP overhead of HTTP 1.1, the new standard HTTP 2.0 is designed to use just one TCP session to download all files needed to construct a webpage.

3.6.2.4 Application-Layer Protocols and TCP

Many application-layer protocols (e.g., HTTP, SMTP) require TCP-enabled handshaking. Once a logical connection (or session) is established through TCP handshaking, two hosts start to exchange APDUs (e.g., webpages, emails). Handshaking is not a guaranteed process, though. For example, when a server host is too tied up with handling existing sessions, it may not accept additional handshaking requests, or it may take too long to respond. The failure of handshaking results in the display of such error messages as in Figure 3.8.

3.6.3 PORT MANAGEMENT

Another important transport layer function is port management (Be careful; the port here has nothing to do with the switch or router port). TCP and UDP identify an 'application' through its unique 16-bit port number that is in the range of 0 through 65535 (see Figures 3.4 and 3.5). For example, when a TCP segment arriving at a host carries 80 in its destination port field, it is forwarded to the host's HTTP server application (see Table 3.4).

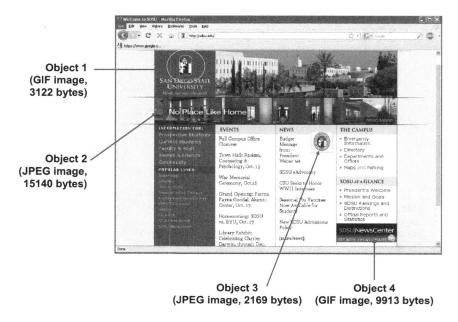

FIGURE 3.7   Objects of a webpage and TCP sessions (source: www.sdsu.edu)

FIGURE 3.8 Notification of failed TCP handshaking

TABLE 3.4
Well-known server ports

Protocols	Function	Server port
Telnet	Remote access	23
FTP	File transfer	20, 21
SMTP	Email delivery	25
DNS	Domain name service	53
DHCP	Dynamic IP address provision	67, 68
HTTP	Webserver access	80
HTTPS	Secure webserver access	443

3.6.3.1 Port Types and Ranges

Port numbers are divided into three groups: *well-known*, *registered*, and *private* ports.

- Well-known ports (0 through 1023): These ports are used to indicate *standard* server applications. Table 3.4 lists some of the well-known server ports.
- Registered ports (1024 through 49151): These ports are intended to identify proprietary applications such as MS SQL (1433) and MSN Messenger (1863).
- Private/dynamic ports (49152 through 65535): These ports are for ad hoc assignment of a "client" port.

3.6.3.2 Source vs. Destination Port

The source and destination port fields (see Figures 3.4 and 3.5) indicate the sender's and receiver's applications respectively. Generally, a client device connects to a server to use its resources (e.g., webpages, databases, files, emails), making the former a source and the latter a destination. For the connectivity, the client host randomly chooses a source port number (called an *ephemeral port*). Meanwhile, a well-known server port (see Table 3.4) is used to identify the destination application. Subsequently, the same port numbers will be reused throughout a session.

As for the ephemeral port number, although the IETF recommends that it be chosen from the private/dynamic port range, operating systems from different vendors are not necessarily programmed to conform to the guidance, sometimes selecting from the registered port range.

3.6.3.3 Socket

The IP packet arriving at a host station should be adequately handed over to the target application. As an example, imagine that a person's laptop is concurrently running multiple user programs including Firefox (for HTTP web browsing), MS Outlook (for SMTP email), and Zoom (for VoIP). When an IP packet containing an email message arrives at the laptop, how does it know that the email should be forwarded to MS Outlook, not Firefox or Zoom?

It uses *socket* information that combines an IP address and a port number assigned to an application. Therefore:

$$A \text{ socket} = An \text{ IP address} : A \text{ port number}$$

By combining an IP address and a port number, a host can direct incoming data to the right application. Figure 3.9 demonstrates a client socket (20.20.20.1:50000) and a server socket (30.30.30.1:80). The port number is simply a critical information piece to correctly forward data to a target program.

To be a little more specific, if TCP is used, a socket is assigned to 'each session' of an application to correctly forward exchanged data to the right session. This means that an application can be associated with multiple sockets, each assigned to a particular TCP session established. For example, referring back to Figure 3.7, the webpage results in at least four different TCP sessions and thus as many different combinations of source and destination sockets.

3.7 INTERNET LAYER (LAYER 3)

On receiving transport-layer PDUs (i.e., either TCP segments or UDP datagrams), the internet layer immediately undertakes its inter-networking functions. The internet layer's two key responsibilities are:

a. *Packet creation*: An IP packet is created by encapsulating the transport-layer PDU (i.e., either TCP segment or UDP datagram). The packet has a predefined structure including the data (or payload) and header fields as in Figure 3.10.
b. *Packet routing decision*: Assuming the existence of several delivery paths between the source and destination hosts, this layer makes the forwarding decision of an IP packet from one subnet to another subnet so that the packet can ultimately reach the destination host.

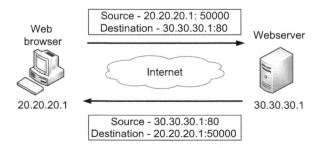

FIGURE 3.9 A demonstration of sockets

Bit 0				Bit 31
Version 4 (= 0100)	Header Length (4 bits)	Diff-Serv (8 bits)	Total Length in Octets (16 bits)	
Identification (16 bits)			Flags (3 bits)	Fragment Offset (13 bits)
Time to Live (8 bits)		Protocol in the Data field (8bits)	Header Checksum (16 bits)	
Source IP address (32 bits)				
Destination IP address (32 bits)				
Options (if any)				Padding
Data Field				

FIGURE 3.10 IPv4's packet structure

3.7.1 PACKET CREATION

There are currently two versions of the internet protocol (IP) standard: IPv4 and IPv6. Although IPv6 represents a significant enhancement over IPv4 in many aspects, the Internet is still dominated by the IPv4 standard for packet construction and transportation. Figure 3.10 shows the IPv4's packet structure; that of IPv6 is explained in Chapter 4. Each header field is briefly explained next.

As in Figure 3.1, field information is transmitted sequentially. For example, the *Identification* field follows the *Total Length in Octet* field. Their display in the multi-layers above is simply due to limited space. The header is 20 bytes in length excluding *Options* and *Padding*, and the data (or payload) field can be significantly longer (more than 65000 bytes) than the header although it is shown as a single row in the figure.

a. Version 4 (always 0100): It says that IPv4 is used to create the packet.
b. Header length (4 bits): It specifies header size.
c. Diff-Serv (8 bits): It indicates priority or urgency of a packet, thus intended to provide Quality of Service (QoS).
d. Total length in Octets (16 bits): It tells the size of an entire packet.
e. Identification (16 bits): It identifies a fragment of an IP packet if it is broken into smaller pieces prior to their transportation. These days, the fragmentation of an IP packet is avoided by host nodes during the initial negotiation process and thus usage of this field is limited.
f. Time to live (TTL) (8 bits): As a counter, its value (e.g., 64) is set by the source host's operating system to indicate the maximum number of routers a packet can pass through before reaching its destination host. Whenever a packet is forwarded by a router, the router decreases the packet's TTL value by one. If the packet still does not reach the destination network when the TTL counter becomes 0, it is removed by a router to prevent it from being 'lost' in cyberspace.
g. Protocol in the Data field (8 bits): It specifies the type of PDU contained in an IP packet's data field. For example, ICMP = 1, TCP = 6, and UDP = 17.
h. Header Checksum (16 bits): This field is used for detecting an error in the header (e.g., changed bits). Any IP packet with an error bit(s) in the header should be removed because it can affect network performance (e.g., confuse routers). The recovery of the dropped packet is handled by the transport layer's TCP.
i. Source and destination IP addresses: The fields include 32-bit IP address information necessary for packet forwarding.

3.7.2 Packet Routing Decision

The internet layer is also responsible for deciding a packet's *routing path* over an internetwork, thus inter-networking. For demonstration, a simple network in Figure 3.11 is used (Note: SW1 = switch, R = router, WAN links are frequently called serial lines).

In the figure, for example, communications between PC1 and Server1 can be through the R1–R3 or R1–R2–R3 route. When a packet from PC1 takes the R1–R3 route to reach Server1, the R1's *next-hop router* becomes R3. The routing decision by a router is, therefore, all about determining the next-hop router so that an IP packet ultimately reaches the destination host. The routing decision for an IP packet is made by each router along the way to its destination.

Bear in mind that the source and destination addresses of an IP packet stay unchanged all the way. For example, a packet issued by PC1 in Figure 3.11 carries the source IP address of PC1 and the destination IP address of Server1; and the IP addresses remain the same during the end-to-end journey through 3 (through R1–R3) or 4 (through R1–R2–R3). This is what makes IP addresses different from data link MAC addresses that *are used only within a subnetwork boundary*.

For packet routing, a router maps the destination IP address of an arriving packet to its routing table on its memory, finds the best path toward the destination network, and forwards the packet to the next-hop router (more in Chapter 11).

3.7.3 Perform Supervisory Functions

Although not as essential as the two tasks explained, the internet layer also performs utility functions through the exchange of *Internet Control Message Protocol* (ICMP) supervisory packets. There are

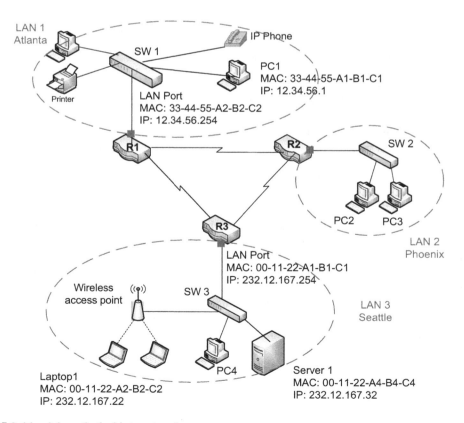

FIGURE 3.11 A hypothetical internetwork

many different usages of ICMP including the diagnosis of connectivity between two network nodes and the reporting of transmission errors (e.g., target host unreachable) back to the message source. ICMP produces its own PDU that is delivered to the destination node within the IP packet's data field to perform an intended supervisory task (see Figure 3.12).

Type, *Code*, and *Checksum* are three common fields included in all ICMP PDUs.

- The *Type* value indicates the supervisory function of a particular ICMP PDU. Among the heavily used are 0 (echo reply), 3 (destination unreachable), and 8 (echo request).
- The *Code* value provides additional information regarding the *Type* value. For example, if the Type value is 3 (destination unreachable), then the Code value explains the reason.
- The *checksum* is an error detection code of the ICMP PDU.

Among various supervisory functions, *Ping* is well-known and heavily used by IT professionals.

3.7.3.1 Ping Utility

Ping is an important utility in testing and troubleshooting network links and nodes. With it, a host station or router sends *echo requests* (type value = 8 in Figure 3.12) to a target node to check its availability and network connectivity. For example, entering *C:\>ping www.yahoo.com* at the command prompt produces ping requests destined to the Yahoo webserver. If the Yahoo server is active and is configured to respond to the echo request, it will reply back with *echo response* (type value = 0) ICMP messages. The response has two meanings: (1) the server is up and running, and (2) the link between the two communicating nodes works properly.

Although intermediary devices, especially routers, respond to pinging, most Internet servers are configured to ignore it these days out of cybersecurity concerns such as denial-of-service attacks. Figure 3.13 is a demonstration in which the Yahoo server (www.yahoo.com) is pinged four times from the author's residence. Below is a summary of key information elements in Figure 3.13:

- The Yahoo server's IPv6 address: 2001:4998:44:3507::8001
- The ICMP packet is 32 bytes long.
- The round-trip delay (latency) between the source and the destination is 48 milliseconds.

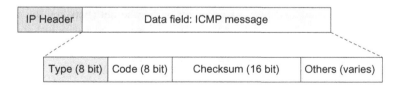

FIGURE 3.12 The structure of an ICMP packet

```
Command Prompt                                    —   □   ×

C:\Users\bshin>ping www.yahoo.com

Pinging new-fp-shed.wg1.b.yahoo.com [2001:4998:44:3507::8001] with 32 bytes of data:
Reply from 2001:4998:44:3507::8001: time=48ms
Reply from 2001:4998:44:3507::8001: time=48ms
Reply from 2001:4998:44:3507::8001: time=48ms
Reply from 2001:4998:44:3507::8001: time=48ms

Ping statistics for 2001:4998:44:3507::8001:
    Packets: Sent = 4, Received = 4, Lost = 0 (0% loss),
Approximate round trip times in milli-seconds:
    Minimum = 48ms, Maximum = 48ms, Average = 48ms

C:\Users\bshin>_
```

FIGURE 3.13 A demonstration of pinging

3.8　DATA LINK LAYER (LAYER 2)

When an IP packet comes down from the internet layer, the data link layer undertakes its predefined functions and develops its own PDU (i.e., frame) by encapsulating the IP packet. The data link layer standard (e.g., Ethernet, Wi-Fi) performs IP packet transportation between nodes 'within a subnetwork boundary'. In other words, this layer is responsible for intra-networking. In the following subsections, the data link concept is explained in the LAN and WAN contexts.

3.8.1　LAN Data Link

3.8.1.1　Frame and Switching

In Chapter 1, it was stated that intra-networking relies on one or more intra-networking devices such as switches and wireless access points. In other words, when the delivery of an IP packet between two nodes is done without going through a router, it becomes intra-networking (see Figure 1.4). For intra-networking, the IP packet produced on the internet layer is encapsulated within a frame and gets delivered (see Section 3.2.3; *frame* is the PDU name of the data link layer).

The delivery process of frames for intra-networking is called *switching*, and switching within a subnetwork is carried out purely based on MAC addresses. For this, each frame's header should contain 48-bit source and destination MAC addresses (refer to Figure 1.21).

3.8.1.2　Link Types

As an example, in Figure 3.14, PC1 is sending an IP packet (encapsulated within a frame) to Server1 and the SW1 switch relays the frame based on its destination MAC address. Then, the logical path between the two hosts (PC1 and Server1) via SW1 becomes one data link.

As a somewhat different example, think of a situation where PC1 sends an IP packet (again encapsulated within a frame) beyond the subnetwork boundary through the router (R1). The packet should first reach R1's LAN port (Fa0/1) before it is routed to another subnetwork via R1's other port. Then, the logical path from PC1 to R1's LAN port (Fa0/1) becomes a data link as well.

3.8.1.3　Technology Standard(s)

A data link relies on one LAN standard (e.g., Ethernet). There are also times when more than one LAN technology is used to form a data link for intra-networking. Using Figure 3.14 as an example, the data link between Laptop1 and Server1 relies on both Ethernet (between the wireless access point and Server1) and Wi-Fi (between Laptop1 and the wireless access point) standards. In this scenario, the wireless access point does the conversion between Ethernet and Wi-Fi frames. That

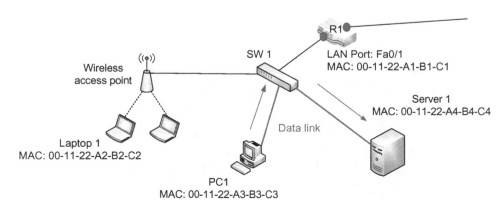

FIGURE 3.14　Use of MAC addressing for intra-networking

is, the data link between Laptop1 and Server1 produces two different frames, one for Ethernet and one for Wi-Fi.

3.8.1.4   Single Active Delivery Path

Remember that, within a subnetwork, only a single delivery path (therefore only a single data link) becomes active between any two nodes. This is true regardless of how many host stations and intermediary devices are in the subnetwork. Many subnetworks have more than one *physical* path available between two nodes to provide network redundancy and survivability. However, intermediary devices can figure out and disable redundant paths to ensure that there is only a single active path between any two stations at one point (more in Chapter 5). Using Figure 3.14 as an example, there should be only one active path delivering a frame from Laptop1 to Server1.

3.8.1.5   Frame's MAC Addresses

A frame's source and destination MAC addresses do not change within a subnetwork even if it may go through multiple intermediary devices. For instance, in Figure 3.14, when Laptop1 sends a frame to Server1, the frame's source MAC (00-11-22-A2-B2-C2) and destination MAC (00-11-22-A4-B4-C4) addresses remain the same while it passes through the wireless access point and SW1 switch.

Despite their differences in their frame structure, Ethernet and Wi-Fi – as two dominant LAN standards – use the same 48-bit MAC addressing. That is, regardless of whether a data link within a subnetwork is formed on one standard (e.g., Wi-Fi, Ethernet) or on two standards (i.e., Wi-Fi + Ethernet), the source and destination MAC addresses remain the same. The source and destination MAC addresses, however, change if the same packet is forwarded to another subnetwork through a router (see Figure 3.14's R1 as an example).

3.8.2   WAN Data Link

The same data link notion and principle apply to the "private" WAN connections that are *established through a proprietary telco network (e.g., AT&T), not through the public Internet.* As an illustration, refer to Figure 3.11 that is composed of LANs and WAN connections. Let's assume that a packet from PC1 to Server1 goes through R1 and R3. Then, the packet crosses three different data links separated by two border routers of R1 and R3.

- Data Link 1:   PC1 to R1 (LAN link)
- Data Link 2:   R1 to R3 (private WAN link)
- Data Link 3:   R3 to Server1 (LAN link)

Observe that Data Link 2 is a WAN connection. In Figure 3.11, therefore, each of the three WAN connections between routers becomes a data link. That between R1 (Atlanta) and R3 (Seattle) may be separated by a few thousand miles. Regardless of the distance, it is still a data link belonging to the enterprise network. Data links use different technologies for end-to-end connections (e.g., PC1 and Server1). For instance, while Data Links 1 and 3 may be on Ethernet, Data Link 2 may be on a leased line running the *Point-to-Point Protocol* (or PPP) WAN standard.

As explained, the data link address is for intra-networking only. Thus, when an IP packet from PC1 is dispatched to Server1, a first frame that encapsulates the IP packet is created only for the intra-networking of Data Link 1(PC1 to R1). In forwarding the same IP packet, R1 creates a new frame for the intra-networking of Data Link 2 (R1 to R3), and R3 creates another frame to deliver the IP packet to Server 1 on Data Link 3.

Creating a new frame with totally different source and destination addresses in each subnetwork encapsulating the same IP packet resembles the real-life scenario of Figure 3.2 in which the transportation vehicle (= frame) changes in each hop to ultimately deliver Jayne's mail (= IP packet) to Brian.

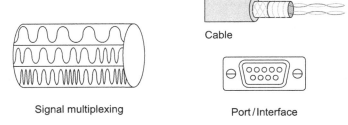

Signal multiplexing   Port / Interface

FIGURE 3.15   Select physical layer standards

3.9 PHYSICAL LAYER (LAYER 1)

On receiving a frame from the data link layer, the physical layer (layer 1) is responsible for physically transporting it through a wired (e.g., fiber optics, copper cables) or wireless (e.g., atmosphere) medium. The data link frame is a bitstream of 1s and 0s, and they should be 'encoded' into signals for delivery over the network. Fairly detailed explanations of the 'encoding' scheme are in Section 1.10 (Chapter 1). The physical layer functions are implemented in hardware devices such as network interface cards (or NICs) that convert data link layer frames into *electronic*, *radio*, or *light signals* for propagation.

Depending on the medium used to connect network nodes, electronic signals (for twisted pairs and coaxial cables), light signals (for optical fibers), or radio signals (for atmosphere) are produced and propagated. A number of conversion methods from bitstreams to signals and vice versa have been introduced as industry standards. As briefly stated in Section 1.10, sophisticated encoding technologies are used these days to transport bitstreams fast. Also, LAN and WAN links use different signal encoding standards.

For the reliable electronic, radio, or light signaling between two nodes, physical-layer technologies have to be standardized. Then, hardware products from different manufacturers remain compatible as long as they are compatible with the standards. Below are select physical layer details that require standardization (see Figure 3.15).

- Properties of signals (e.g., signal strengths, digital vs. analog signal encoding)
- Attributes of a physical port that processes signals (e.g., number of pins/holes, port speeds)

Although the correspondence of physical layer standards to the real-life scenario is not clear in Figure 3.2, the physical details of vehicle parts (e.g., size of tires) can be such examples.

3.10 LAYER IMPLEMENTATION

As stated, a host computer performs all five-layer functions internally. In this section, software and/or hardware elements responsible for conducting the layer functions are explained.

3.10.1 APPLICATION LAYER

Most protocols in this layer are built into 'user' applications. There are also application layer protocols such as DNS and DHCP that are not necessarily tied to a particular user application but play a critical role in computer networking. To observe all active applications in Windows, for example, pressing the *Ctr-Alt-Del* key combination will bring up the *Windows Task Manager* (see Figure 3.16). It shows the list of applications and processes. Processes are instances of an application program, and thus an application can have one or more associated processes. For example, as can be seen in Figure 3.16, there is one Chrome browser application active (left) but multiple processes running (right) due to tabbed browsing.

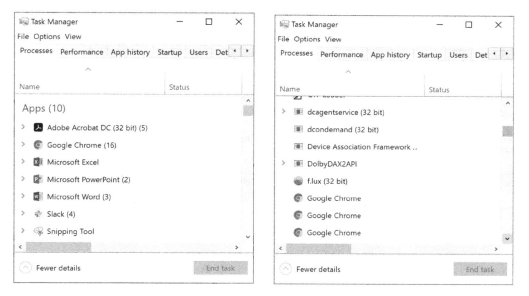

FIGURE 3.16 Applications (left) and their processes (right) in Windows Task Manager

3.10.2 TRANSPORT AND INTERNET LAYERS

The programs that execute transport and internet layer protocols including TCP, UDP, and IP are embedded in the operating system. As an example, Figure 3.17 demonstrates the TCP/IP configuration panel of Windows OS.

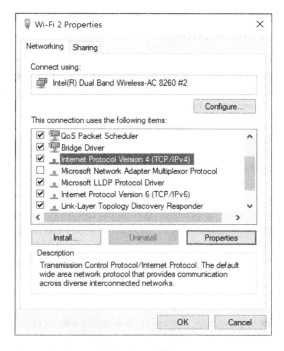

FIGURE 3.17 TCP/IP configuration through Windows OS

TABLE 3.5
Key layer functions and their implementation

Layers	Key functions	Implementation of layer functions	PDU name
Application	Application-to-application communication	Applications (e.g., browser)	No designated PDU name
Transport	Host-to-host (or end-to-end) handshaking, flow control/error control	Operating system	Segment (for TCP), Datagram (for UDP)
Internet	Packet creation and routing decision for inter-networking		Packet
Data link	Frame creation and switching for intra-networking	Network interface card (NIC)	Frame
Physical	Signal generation and delivery		No PDUs produced.

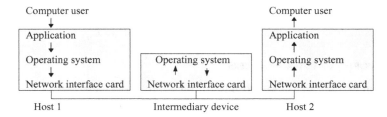

FIGURE 3.18 Hardware/software components of network nodes

3.10.3 DATA LINK AND PHYSICAL LAYERS

The data link and physical layer functions of a host are built into the *network interface card* (NIC). That is, the NIC implements a data link protocol, such as Ethernet or Wi-Fi, and interfaces with a transmission medium (e.g., twisted pair, optical fiber) through a physical port such as RJ-45. Wi-Fi does not need a connecting port. The host operating system communicates with the NIC through the device driver software.

In summary, exchanging application-layer data (e.g., email) entails connectivity of "user application <-> operating system <--> NIC" on a host. Table 3.5 summarizes key layer functions, their implementation places, and the name of PDUs produced in each layer. It is again highlighted that all five-layer functions are performed within a host computer, but only a subset of five layers are performed on intermediary devices.

Figure 3.18 summarizes the internal processing of application-layer data (e.g., email) initiated by a user on a host computer. Intermediary devices such as switches and routers have their own operating systems and NICs for networking. The intermediary device generally has no application-layer functions because its mission is to relay host-generated data through the network.

CHAPTER SUMMARY

- The standard network architecture represents a framework (or reference model) that broadly defines necessary network functions in a multi-layer structure. Among the well-known frameworks are Open Systems Interconnection (OSI) and TCP/IP.

- The protocol, as a standard, specifies rules of communication between software programs. There are syntactic (i.e., format of a message) and semantic (i.e., interpretation of a message) rules for a protocol.
- The protocol data unit (PDU) is a discrete message unit produced in each layer except the physical layer. The PDUs of data link, internet, and transport layers are called a frame, packet, and segment/datagram respectively.
- In the application layer, the client and server programs installed on host computers exchange data/messages using a built-in protocol.
- The transport layer is in charge of three functions: provision of data integrity, session management, and port management.
- The internet (or network) layer is responsible for inter-networking. For this, it creates IP packets and performs their routing across subnetworks conjoined by one or more routers. The routing of packets presumes that there are multiple delivery paths between any two communicating hosts.
- The data link layer transports IP packets between any two nodes within a subnetwork, which is also called intra-networking.
- The physical layer is responsible for transporting the data link layer's frames in electronic, radio, or light signals through wired (e.g., copper cables) or wireless (e.g., atmosphere) media.
- Application layer protocols are built into client and server programs. The transport and internet layer functions are embedded in the operating system. The data link and physical layer functions are handled by the network interface card (NIC).

KEY TERMS

application layer
acknowledgement (ACK)
checksum
connection-less
connection-oriented
data link layer
datagram
data integrity
de-encapsulation
destination port
Domain Name System (DNS)
Dynamic Host Control Protocol (DHCP)
encapsulation
error control
FIN
flags
flow control
frame
handshaking
header
Hyper Text Transfer Protocol (HTTP)
International Organization for
Standardization (ISO)
Internet Control Message Protocol (ICMP)
Internet Engineering Task Force (IETF)
internet layer
internet protocol (IP)

inter-networking
intra-networking
Open Systems Interconnection (OSI)
optical fiber
packet
physical layer
ping
port
private/dynamic port
process
protocol
protocol data unit (PDU)
registered port
reliable connection
reliable protocol
Request for Comments (RFC)
routing
segment
session
signal encoding
Simple Mail Transfer Protocol (SMTP)
socket
source port
standard architecture
standards
subnetwork
switching

SYN
TCP/IP
time to live (TTL)
trailer
Transmission Control Protocol (TCP)
transport layer

twisted pair
unreliable connection
unreliable protocol
User Datagram Protocol (UDP)
well-known port
window size field

CHAPTER REVIEW QUESTIONS

1. The standard _____ broadly depicts necessary functions of computer networking in terms of a layer structure.
   A) topology
   B) architecture
   C) platform
   D) reference
   E) protocol
2. All layers of a standard architecture have their own protocol data unit (PDU) except the _____ layer.
   A) application
   B) transport
   C) internet
   D) data link
   E) physical
3. An email message goes through encapsulations in the sequence of _____ before it is released to the network.
   A) segment–packet–frame
   B) segment–frame–packet
   C) frame–segment–packet
   D) packet–segment–packet
   E) packet–frame–segment
4. Which two layer functions are generally built into an operating system such as Windows and Linux?
   A) physical and transport layers
   B) transport and internet layers
   C) internet and data link layers
   D) physical and internet layers
   E) transport and data link layers
5. The socket is/represents:
   A) a group of applications providing similar services.
   B) used to indicate a range of available ports on a server.
   C) the combination of an IP address and a port number.
   D) the combination of an IP address and an application-layer protocol.
   E) the combination of an IP address and a session identification.
6. Which statement is true?
   A) IP is a connection-oriented protocol.
   B) UDP is a reliable protocol.
   C) IP is a reliable protocol.
   D) TCP is a reliable protocol.
   E) TCP is a connection-less protocol.

7. The TCP port is used to:
   A) prioritize a service request.
   B) forward a service request/response to a specific application.
   C) identify a sender's IP address.
   D) translate a domain name into an IP address.
   E) identify a sender's MAC address.

8. The _____ bit in the TCP header is used to request handshaking.
   A) FIN
   B) ACK
   C) SYN
   D) CON
   E) SEQ

9. Which is NOT accurate in terms of layer functions?
   A) application layer – to establish sessions (or handshaking)
   B) transport layer – to provide message (or data) integrity
   C) internet layer – to execute packet routing
   D) data link layer – to conduct frame switching
   E) physical layer – for the actual transportation of frames in signals

10. Which layer function(s) is/are implemented in the network interface card?
    A) physical layer only
    B) data link layer only
    C) physical layer and data link layer
    D) physical layer, data link layer, and internet layer
    E) physical layer, data link layer, internet layer, and transport layer

11. _____ most likely depend(s) on UDP in the transport layer.
    A) Emails
    B) Internet surfing with a web browser
    C) Online credit card authorization for Internet shopping
    D) File transfer using FTP (File Transfer Protocol)
    E) Three-way video conferencing over the Internet

12. Port numbers have to be included in the header of _____.
    A) packets only
    B) datagrams only
    C) segments only
    D) segments and datagrams
    E) packets, segments, and datagrams

13. TCP and UDP are compared. Which is CORRECT?

Protocol	TCP	UDP
A) Defined layer	transport	internet
B) Require handshaking	Yes	Yes
C) Require acknowledgement	Yes	Yes
D) Burden on communicating hosts	Low	Low
E) Burden on the network	High	Low

14. The TTL (time to live) value in the IP packet's header indicates a maximum number of _____ a packet can go through before reaching the destination:
    A) switches
    B) routers

    C) hosts

    D) networks

    E) circuits

15. Assume that an email should cross three subnetworks for its delivery to a destination host. How many different frames are produced along the way?

    A) 4

    B) 3

    C) 2

    D) 1

    E) not enough information to decide

16. Choose a CORRECT statement.

    A) A standard protocol should define either semantics or syntax, but not both.

    B) The term 'standard' is used interchangeably with 'architecture'.

    C) The semantics of a protocol is about how to interpret PDUs exchanged.

    D) A reliable protocol detects transmission errors but does not correct them.

    E) All standard protocols of the application layer are reliable protocols.

17. Assume that an email should cross three subnetworks for its delivery to a destination host. How many different packets are produced along the way?

    A) 0

    B) 1

    C) 2

    D) 3

    E) 4

18. The IP packet is encapsulated within the _____ to travel to the destination node.

    A) application message

    B) TCP segment

    C) UDP datagram

    D) frame

    E) ICMP packet

19. If a host computer develops a TCP segment with 80 as the source port and 54399 as the destination port, the host is most likely a(n) _____.

    A) client PC

    B) DHCP server

    C) webserver

    D) email server

    E) DNS server

20. Choose a CORRECT statement on port numbers.

    A) For a Windows host, 55953 becomes a well-known port number.

    B) Port numbers are divided into well-known and unknown ones.

    C) If a Linux machine sends a TCP segment with source port 45780 and destination port 7200, then the host must be an email server.

    D) Well-known port numbers are generally assigned to server applications.

    E) Well-known port numbers are also called ephemeral port numbers.

21. When the command "*C:\ping www.yahoo.com*" is issued by a client PC, the two hosts (the PC and Yahoo webserver) communicate based on _____ protocol in the internet layer:

    A) ICMP (Internet Control Message Protocol)

    B) UDP (User Datagram Protocol)

    C) ARP (Address Resolution Protocol)

    D) HTTP (Hypertext Transfer Protocol)

    E) SNMP (Simple Network Management Protocol)

22. The end-to-end error control and flow control are performed in the _____ layer.
    A) application
    B) internet
    C) transport
    D) data link
    E) session
23. Choose a mismatch between a standard and its corresponding layer.
    A) ICMP = internet layer
    B) Ethernet = data link layer
    C) Digital signal encoding = physical layer
    D) Domain Name System (DNS) = application layer
    E) Dynamic Host Configuration Protocol (DHCP) = internet layer
24. Which PDU type generally has a header and a trailer?
    A) data
    B) segment
    C) packet
    D) frame
    E) bit
25. When the command "*ping www.gmail.com*" is issued, at least two protocols are necessary to obtain the intended information. What are they?
    A) DHCP and UDP
    B) HTTP and DHCP
    C) DNS and ICMP
    D) DNS and HTTP
    E) ARP and HTTP

HANDS-ON EXERCISES

EXERCISE 3.1

You can observe HTTP request/response messages through a viewer site such as *http://www.rexswain.com/httpview.html* or a viewer program such as *http://www.httpwatch.com*. From *http://www.rexswain.com/httpview.html*, access a website of your choice and answer the following questions.

1. What are information items included in the request?
2. As for the server response:
    a. The response message is divided into two parts of _____ and _____
    b. What does the value 200 included in the first line mean? (search the Internet)
    c. What version of HTTP is used by both the browser and the server?
    d. What is the name of the webserver program?
    e. What is the size (in bytes) of the content (data)?
    f. What is the content type?

EXERCISE 3.2

1. Find out the IP address of a particular webserver using the *nslookup* command (e.g., C:\>*nslookup www.yahoo.com*). Assume that the IP of *www.yahoo.com* is 11.22.33.44. Try *http://11.22.33.44* and *http://11.22.33.44:80* (or *www.yahoo.com:80*). What happens?
2. What happens when you try http://11.22.33.44:70 (or *www.yahoo.com:70*) or any port other than 80? Explain the result.

EXERCISE 3.3

Operating systems let computer users view the list of TCP sessions and sockets. The command *C:\>netstat –n*, for example, displays active TCP connections.

1. Figure 3.19 displays TCP sessions and sockets of *C:\>netstat –n* after visiting a particular website with a browser. The output has four columns: protocol, source socket, destination socket, and status (e.g., established, syn_sent). Based only on the screenshot information:
   a. How many different sessions are established?
   b. How many different source sockets are used to establish the sessions?
   c. What is the port range assigned to source sockets?
   d. How many different destination sockets are shown in the sessions?
   e. What is the server port used by the destination socket? What is the protocol that uses the server port?

EXERCISE 3.4

Refer to Figure 3.14 and answer the following questions.

1. How many data links can be formed from Laptop 1 and list them? (Exclude the link to the wireless access point and the SW1 switch from the counting.)
2. How many data links can be formed from PC1 and list them? (Exclude the link to the wireless access point and the SW1 switch from the counting.)
3. How many of the data links identified in question 1 involve more than one intermediary device?
4. How many of the data links identified in question 2 involve more than one intermediary device?
5. If Server1 sends a frame to R1's LAN port (Fa0/1), what are its source and destination data link addresses? Does the MAC address change while the frame passes through the SW1 switch?
6. If Laptop1 sends a frame to the router R1's LAN port (Fa0/1), what are its source and destination data link addresses? Does the MAC address change while the frame goes through the wireless access point and the SW1 switch? *Hint*: Remember that both Ethernet and Wi-Fi use the comparable 48-bit MAC addressing scheme.

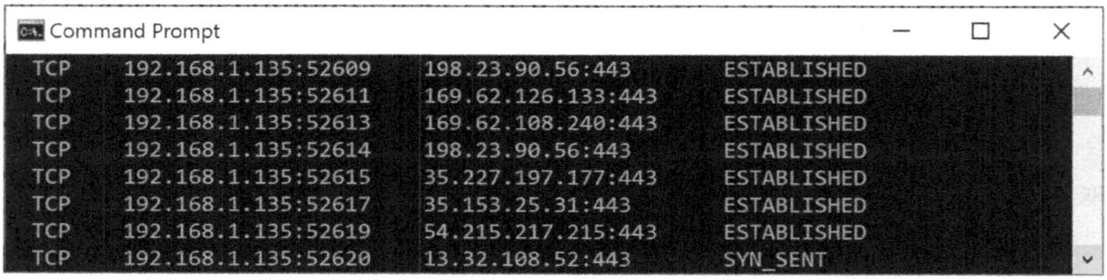

```
Command Prompt                                              —    □    ×
 TCP    192.168.1.135:52609    198.23.90.56:443        ESTABLISHED
 TCP    192.168.1.135:52611    169.62.126.133:443      ESTABLISHED
 TCP    192.168.1.135:52613    169.62.108.240:443      ESTABLISHED
 TCP    192.168.1.135:52614    198.23.90.56:443        ESTABLISHED
 TCP    192.168.1.135:52615    35.227.197.177:443      ESTABLISHED
 TCP    192.168.1.135:52617    35.153.25.31:443        ESTABLISHED
 TCP    192.168.1.135:52619    54.215.217.215:443      ESTABLISHED
 TCP    192.168.1.135:52620    13.32.108.52:443        SYN_SENT
```

FIGURE 3.19   Sample screenshot of TCP sessions and sockets

EXERCISE 3.5

Refer to Figure 3.11 that has three LANs and three WAN connections. Assume that WAN connections are lines leased from a private WAN provider such as AT&T (thus, not Internet links). Answer the following questions.

1. How many different data links can be formed from the IP Phone (on LAN1)? List them.
2. How many different data links can be formed from PC1 (on LAN1)? List them.
3. How many of the data links identified in question 1 involve more than one intermediary device?
4. How many of the data links identified in question 2 involve more than one intermediary device?
5. Assume that the IP Phone is requesting Laptop1 for a conference call, and the call connection is established via R1 and R3. How many data links are included in the end-to-end connectivity?
6. Assume that Laptop1 is connecting PC2 through the R3–R1–R2 route. How many data links are included in the end-to-end connectivity?
7. If PC1 sends an IP packet to Server1, what are the source and destination MAC addresses of the initial frame and the last frame that carry the IP packet? Does the data link address change on the way to Server1?
8. If an IP packet from PC1 travels to Server1 via R1 and R3, how many different frames are created during the trip?
9. If an IP packet from PC1 is dispatched to Laptop1 via R1 and R3, how many different frames are formed to complete the journey? Remember that Wi-Fi and Ethernet have different frame structures.

4 IP Address Planning and Management

4.1 INTRODUCTION

This chapter covers the fundamentals of IP addressing based on the IPv4 and IPv6 standards. Understanding IP addressing is fundamental for an IT professional to manage the network. The task of allocating IP addresses to network segments and nodes can be done relatively easily by depending on a software tool these days. Having theoretical knowledge, however, is important for effective planning and management of the network infrastructure and security measures at an organization.

Currently, IPv4 and IPv6 standards coexist. Drawbacks of IPv4 have been its limited address space due to its 32-bit structure, shortcomings in facilitating cybersecurity, and instability in supporting Quality of Service-demanding user applications. When it was first introduced, the IETF (*Internet Engineering Task Force*) didn't anticipate such an explosive growth of IP demands. This has been fueled by the addition of mobile devices such as smartphones and tablets to the Internet. Further, it is safe to say that sooner or later, most (if not all) computing and communication devices, mobile devices, sensors, home appliances, game consoles, IoT devices, and other consumer electronics will join the Internet, triggering the enormous consumption of IP addresses. Ultimately, we will witness a world where the Internet will interconnect them based on IPv6 addresses.

4.1.1 LEARNING OBJECTIVES

The objectives of this chapter are to learn:

- IP governance in terms of how IP space is allocated
- IPv4's address structure
- IPv4: classful IP allocation scheme
- IPv4: classless IP allocation scheme
- IPv4: IP address ranges assigned for special purposes
- IPv4: IP subnetting
- IPv4: subnet mask
- IPv4: IP supernetting
- IPv4: static vs. dynamic IP allocation
- IPv4: development of an IP assignment policy
- IPv6 (IP Next Generation): packet structure
- IPv6 addressing issues

4.2 GOVERNANCE OF IP ADDRESS SPACE

The IP address is composed of network identification (or network address) and host identification (or host address) parts. The network identification indicates a particular organization (e.g., firm, college, ISP). The host identification is assigned to a network node. Network addresses are allocated in a delegated manner by the *Internet Assigned Numbers Authority* or IANA (www.iana.org/). Being responsible for global coordination of IP space, IANA delegates available network address space to *Regional Internet Registries* (RIRs). There are currently five RIRs:

- AfriNIC for the Africa region   (www.afrinic.net/)

- ARIN for North America   (www.arin.net/)

- APNIC for the Asia Pacific Region   (www.apnic.net/)

- LACNIC for Latin America   (www.lacnic.net/en/)

- RIPE NCC for Europe, the Middle East, and Central Asia   (www.ripe.net/)

4.2.1 IP ALLOCATION PROCEDURE

In the past, the request for an IP address block was directly submitted to a registry by a client organization. Once obtained, the organization retained the virtual ownership of the granted IP block. All that has changed, and now Internet Service Providers (ISPs) play a central role in the management of IP address space and its allocation to requesting organizations. For this, large ISPs (e.g., AT&T) obtain IP blocks from Regional Internet Registries and divide them into smaller chunks for allocation to clients (e.g., small ISPs, business firms, schools). Individuals and small businesses, meanwhile, obtain a network address from their ISPs. Figure 4.1 demonstrates the top-down delegation of IP space. You can find the ownership of a particular network address on the RIR website.

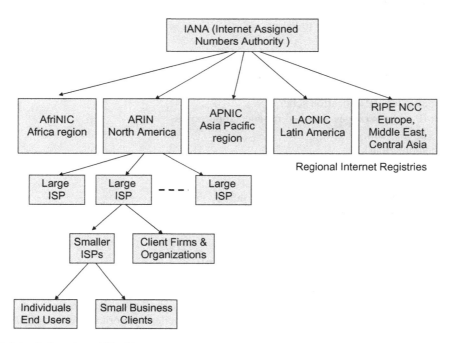

FIGURE 4.1 Delegation of IP address space

4.3 IPV4 ADDRESSING

The IPv4 standard uses a 32-bit address to uniquely identify a network node. Due to the lengthy nature of binary bits, we use the decimal format (e.g., 123.456.78.90) in which a dot-divided value is equivalent to 8 bits. With the 32-bit structure, the entire address space of IPv4 ranges between 0.0.0.0 (all 0s in binary) and 255.255.255.255 (all 1s in binary).

With only 32 bits, however, IPv4 is unable to create enough address space to accommodate growing global demands, especially due to the rapid growth of mobile and IoT devices. Already, IANA completed its allocation of the entire IPv4 space in 2011. Nonetheless, IPv4 addresses are still heavily used and will remain that way for years to come.

4.3.1 IPv4 ADDRESS STRUCTURE

An IP address is composed of at least two parts: network ID (or network address) and host ID (or host address) parts (see Figure 4.2). In this chapter, the term *network* is used as an identifier of an organization (e.g., company, university). For instance, if an organization's network ID is *195.112.36.x*, with *x* being any value for a host ID, the network address can also be expressed as *195.112.36.0*. So, as more bits are allocated for the network ID, fewer bits are available for the host ID.

Generally, an enterprise network is broken into smaller segments of subnetworks (or subnets). Subnets can be created according to physical (e.g., locations, buildings, floors) and/or logical (e.g., departments or workgroups of a business, colleges of a university) boundaries of an organization. The segmentation of a network into subnets requires that each subnet be uniquely identified. The network ID cannot be changed, as it represents an organization's official public address. Then, the only available option to create subnets in IPv4 is to split the host ID field into two parts: one for the host ID and the other for the subnet ID. This results in *borrowing* bits from the host ID field to create subnet IDs (see Figure 4.2). The creation of subnets adds more hierarchy to the structure of an IP address.

4.4 CLASSFUL IPV4 ADDRESS – LEGACY

The network ID under IPv4 can be either classful or classless. This section briefly explains the classful IP that was adopted in the early days of the Internet but is defunct now. Despite this, having a general idea is useful because classful network IDs are still owned by many organizations. Also, protocols (e.g., routing protocol) designed for the classful IP scheme are still out there. Under the classful scheme, the network ID allocated to an organization belongs to one of *class A*, *class B*, or *class C* types.

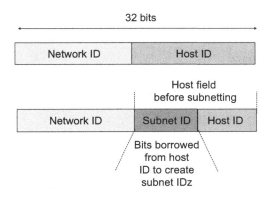

FIGURE 4.2 IPv4 address (without and with subnet ID)

4.4.1 Class A Network

In early days, very large firms were given a *class A* network status in which the first octet (8 bits) becomes a network ID and the remaining 3 octets (24 bits) constitute a host ID. When a company is given a class A network status, it can create about 16.7 million unique host IDs using the remaining 24 bits (2^{24} = 16.7 million). No organization in the world may need 16.7 million IP addresses to run its network, and this allocation resulted in much waste of IP space.

With the class A network, the first bit of 8-bit network ID is fixed at *0* and the next 7 bits uniquely determine a particular organization. It means that the first 8 bits of a class A network falls anywhere between 00000001 and 01111110 (00000000 and 01111111 are reserved for special occasions). This way, only 126 firms (1 through 126) in the world can belong to the class A network. If an organization owns the class A network ID of 125, for instance, the 32-bit IP addresses available for its network ranges from 125.0.0.0 through 125.255.255.255.

4.4.2 Class B Network

The Class B network was assigned to large public/private organizations. It uses the first 16 bits for the network ID and the remaining 16 bits for the host ID. With a 16-bit host ID, the class B network can create up to 2^{16} (about 65,500) host addresses. The first two bits of a network ID starts with *10* and the next 14 bits represent the unique network ID of an organization. In binary, thus, the first 16 bits of a class B network fall anywhere between 10000000.00000000 and 10111111.11111111 (or 128.0 ~ 191.255 in decimal). If an organization belongs to a class B network ID of 130.191, for instance, the 32-bit IP addresses available range from 130.191.0.0 through 130.191.255.255.

4.4.3 Class C Network

Class C network IDs were intended for small or mid-sized public/private organizations. The Class C network uses the first 24 bits for a network ID and the remaining 8 bits for a host ID. The Class C network starts with *110* bits, followed by 21 bits (total 24 bits) as a unique identifier of an organization. If an organization has a class C network ID of 192.10.10.x, for instance, IP addresses within the network ranges from 192.10.10.0 through 192.10.10.255.

There are also *class D* and *class E* addresses that were introduced for special functions such as multicasting. In Table 4.1, you can observe that the possible number of network nodes with an IP address is $2^n - 2$, where *n* = number of host bits. This is because the two (all 1s and all 0s) are excluded from counting as they are for special occasions such as packet broadcasting.

The classful IP system was designed when nobody expected such a spectacular growth of the Internet, and it turned out to waste too much available IP space. For example, there was a report that

TABLE 4.1
Classful allocation of IP space

Class	Initial bit(s)	Network ID	Host ID	Possible number of network nodes
A	0.........	8 bits	24 bits	$2^{24} - 2$ = 16.7 million
B	10........	16 bits	16 bits	$2^{16} - 2$ = 65,534
C	110.......	24 bits	8 bits	$2^8 - 2$ = 254
D (Multicast)	1110.....	N/A	N/A	N/A
E (Reserved)	1111.....	N/A	N/A	N/A

less than 5% of the classful IP space allocated has been actually used. Facing the depletion of IPv4 space, the *classful* IP scheme was replaced with the *classless* one.

4.5 CLASSLESS IPV4 ADDRESS – TODAY

In the classless scheme, the network ID is not necessarily a multiple of an octet (i.e., 8 bits, 16 bits, or 24 bits). For example, the first 13 bits can represent a network ID and the remaining 19 bits a host ID. The identification of a network address gets a little more complicated when it is not divided by an 8-bit block. In this case, it is better to work with binary digits to learn the network address.

Let's take 123.45.56.89 with the first 13 bits network ID as an example. The 32-bit binary of 123.45.56.89 is: '01111011. 00101101. 00111000. 01011001'. Here, the first 13 bits make up the network ID. Therefore, the 32-bit network address becomes: 01111011.00101000.00000000.000 00000 (thirteen bits of network ID + nineteen 0 bits of host ID). This translates into 123.40.0.0. Recall that, although the network ID is not a multiple of 8 bits, the conversion between the binary and decimal is always done in the 8-bit block. In the current IPv4 scheme, the network ID bits range anywhere between 13 and 27 bits.

4.6 SPECIAL IP ADDRESS RANGES

Within the entire IP space of 0.0.0.0 through 255.255.255.255, certain address ranges are designated for special functions, including *loopback*, *broadcasting and multicasting*, and *private IP*. They are explained in this section.

4.6.1 LOOPBACK

The loopback IP (127.0.0.0 ~ 127.255.255.255) is a special function a network node can use to send *packets addressed to itself*. The packet with a loopback destination address is, therefore, directed back to the source station before it is released to the network. The loopback IP has several utilities, and two of them are explained in terms of the (1) internal testing of the TCP/IP stack and (2) offline testing of an application.

4.6.1.1 Internal Testing of TCP/IP Stack

Loopback can be used to check if a host's own TCP/IP protocol stack is working properly and if its IP address is adequately tied to its network card (NIC) and MAC address. For instance, you can issue a ping request such as *c:\>ping 127.0.0.1* (or c:\>ping localhost). In this case, the ping packet does not physically leave your computer but is re-routed to the computer's receiving end of the TCP/IP stack by the NIC. Although the IP range 127.0.0.0 ~ 127.255.255.255 is reserved for the loopback function, 127.0.0.1 is primarily used. *Localhost* is the *domain name* of the loopback IP address and therefore has the same effect as 127.0.0.1.

4.6.1.2 Offline Testing of an Application

Loopback is also useful in testing a network application in the offline mode. For example, you can install a webserver program (e.g., Apache) in your local machine and then do test drives of webserver pages you created using the loopback function. With both the client (web browser) and server programs running on the same local machine, *http://127.0.0.1* or *http://localhost* is issued at the browser's (client) URL. Then, the browser generates a HTTP request message intended for the webserver and dispatches it.

With the loopback address, the browser's request will be directed back to the webserver after going through the lower layers. Remember that because HTTP is designed for correspondence between the web browser and webserver programs, *http://127.0.0.1* from a browser is delivered to the webserver running on the same machine. This request triggers a server response (i.e., webpage

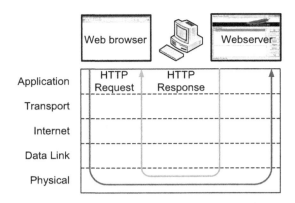

FIGURE 4.3 Internal client-server communications with a loopback IP

provision) to the browser, subsequently enabling browser request and server response cycles within the same machine, a convenient way to test webserver pages before putting them into production (see Figure 4.3).

4.6.2 BROADCASTING

Broadcasting results in the flooding of a packet from a node to all the other nodes of a subnetwork. There are protocols such as DHCP (to request a dynamic IP address) and ARP (to obtain a station's MAC address from its IP address) that rely on broadcasting to perform intended functions. The router is generally configured not to relay broadcasted packets for such reasons as network security and the prevention of *broadcast storms*. In other words, the effect of broadcasting is confined to the broadcast domain separated by a router port. There are two different types of packet broadcasting, *limited broadcasting* and *directed broadcasting*.

4.6.2.1 Limited Broadcasting

Limited broadcasting is when a node sends a packet to all other nodes within the same subnetwork. For example, when a computer broadcasts an IP packet with the destination address of 255.255.255.255 (all thirty-two 1s in binary), it is flooded to all nodes within the local network. However, the connecting router does not relay the broadcasting to other subnetworks. A packet's broadcasting IP address 255.255.255.255 is translated into the frame's MAC address of forty-eight 1s (FFFF.FFFF.FFFF) at the data link layer (see Figure 4.4).

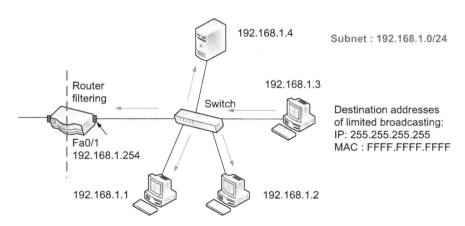

FIGURE 4.4 Limited broadcasting

4.6.2.2 Directed Broadcasting

With directed broadcasting, a packet is disseminated to all hosts of a subnetwork away from the sender's local subnetwork. For directed broadcasting, all 1s are used for the host ID part to flood a packet to a target subnetwork. When directed broadcasting is programmed in a router, it relays broadcasting packets to a target network just like unicasting packets. Directed broadcasting works in various conditions such as within a LAN or over the Internet. Directed broadcasting can be enabled on a router through a relatively simple command (e.g., 'ip directed-broadcast' for Cisco routers).

In Figure 4.5, for example, a host from the 192.168.100.0 subnet broadcasts an IP packet to 192.168.200.0 (a server farm subnetwork) for its concurrent delivery to all three servers. To that end, the sending host creates an IP packet with the destination address of 192.168.200.255/24 in which 255 (= 11111111) means packet broadcasting to the target subnetwork of 192.168.200.0 ('/24' represents the subnet identifier in prefix).

4.6.2.3 Security Risk of Directed Broadcasting

Directed broadcasting can pose security risks. Using the 192.168.200.255/24 example above, let's think of a scenario of how the function can be abused. Assume that there is a database server 192.168.200.10 on the 192.168.200.0/24 subnet. A hacker continuously sends 'inquiry' IP packets with the destination address of 192.168.200.255 and the 'forged' source address of 192.168.200.10. The forgery of an IP packet is relatively easy, as there are hacking tools. Remember that the hacker can send the packet from a remote location as routers forward it purely based on the destination address.

When the packet is delivered to all hosts of the target subnet, they will respond back to 192.168.200.10, the victim server, which will have to deal with the large volume of responses. Depending on the message type (e.g., ping request), this could badly affect the victim server's performance, resulting in *denial of service* (more in Chapter 8). This is frequently called the *smurf attack*. Due to such security risk, the router's default setup should turn off directed broadcasting. For example, the 'no ip directed-broadcast' command is used on the Cisco router. Also, the router's Access Control List (ACL) should specifically list the source and destination addresses allowed for directed broadcasting.

4.6.3 MULTICASTING

Multicasting results in packet delivery to a selected group of target nodes locally or remotely located (see Figure 4.6). For multicasting, the IP range of 224.0.0.0–239.255.255.255 has been reserved, which is the Class D range under the classful scheme. There are many existing and future applications for which multicasting makes much sense. The technology is effective in supporting communications through video on demand, audio streaming, and multi-party distributed video conferencing

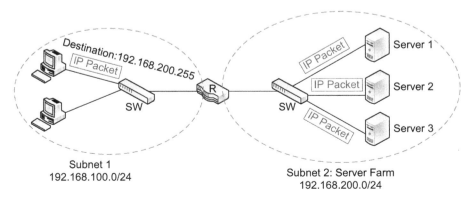

FIGURE 4.5   Directed broadcasting

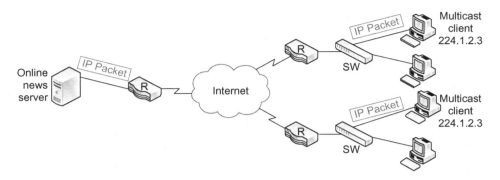

FIGURE 4.6   IP multicasting

or conference calls. It is also used widely for other applications such as stock trading, security surveillance, and online video gaming. It is not difficult to see the growing importance of the multicasting function.

One major benefit of multicasting is that it can significantly reduce network traffic in providing communication services. For instance, for the video on demand (VOD) service, the video streaming server sends just one packet to a number of clients. Without the multicasting technology, the server has to generate a unicast packet to each client and send it to possibly thousands of client computers one by one.

To listen to music or watch videos online, for instance, the client host dynamically associates or disassociates with a so-called *multicast group*. When client hosts join a multicast group, they are assigned the same multicast IP address (e.g., 224.1.2.3) for connectivity with the multicast server. At this point, the client hosts retain both the multicast IP and a regular unicast IP, and they accept packets destined to the two different IP addresses. IP multicasting primarily relies on UDP rather than TCP at the transport layer as UDP is faster. The *Internet Group Management Protocol* (IGMP) is a well-known internet layer protocol designed to manage the multicasting of packets. Multicasting over the Internet is possible when routers are multicasting enabled.

4.6.4   Private IP and NAT

Private IP addresses are intended for usage only within the boundary of an organization or home network, and thus border routers do not route packets with private IPs to the Internet. Three private IP address ranges are in use, one for classes A, B, and C reserved under the old classful scheme.

     a.   10.0.0.0 ~ 10.255.255.255
     b.   172.16.0.0 ~ 172.31.255.255
     c.   192.168.0.0 ~ 192.168.255.255

These days, companies heavily take advantage of private IPs for internal hosts and they are translated to one or more public IP addresses by the border router or firewall when packets are routed beyond the local boundary. The address conversion is called *network address translation* (NAT), *network masquerading*, or *IP-masquerading*. There are two different approaches for NAT: *one-to-one IP mapping* and *many-to-one IP mapping*. NAT shields internal computers and intermediary devices from casual snooping by outsiders. NAT is applied to the sender's IP address (source) but not the receiver's address (destination) of an outgoing packet.

4.6.4.1   NAT: One-to-One IP Mapping

With the one-to-one mapping, one private IP address is converted to one public IP address either statically or dynamically. With the static approach, one public IP is pre-assigned to a particular

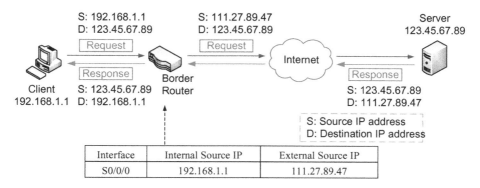

FIGURE 4.7 Router's one-to-one IP mapping and address conversion table

private IP and the pair is pre-programmed on the node (e.g., border router) that does the translation. With the dynamic approach, a range of public IPs are retained for NAT. On receiving a packet with a private source IP, the NAT node (e.g., border router) chooses a public IP from the public address pool and pairs it with the private IP. Then, the private IP is replaced by the public IP before the packet's release, and the mapping record is updated to the address conversion table. This dynamic choice of a public IP is more effective when there are many internal hosts. Figure 4.7 demonstrates the flow of packets through a corporate boundary when the one-to-one mapping (either static or dynamic) is used.

4.6.4.2 NAT: Many-to-One IP Mapping

The many-to-one mapping is when several internal hosts with different private IPs share a single public IP. To make this possible, the NAT node identifies each host computer by its *socket*, the combination of a private IP and a source port found in the transport layer's PDU (either segment or datagram). With the port number's inclusion in the mapping process, multiple private IPs can share one public IP. As a result, the source socket before and after the conversion becomes:

$$\text{Source private IP} + \text{source port} \rightarrow \text{Source public IP} + \text{source port}.$$

Generally, the mapping uses the same source port number for the conversion (e.g., from 192.168.1.1:4000 to 123.45.67.89:4000). When two source hosts are transmitting IP packets with the same source port, the NAT node (e.g., router, firewall) assigns two different port numbers from the available port pool to differentiate packets. The NAT approach that relies on sockets is known as *network address port translation* (NAPT) or *port address translation* (PAT). Figure 4.8 demonstrates a scenario in which three packets are sharing one public IP address (137.42.61.33) for NAPT.

4.6.4.3 Pros and Cons of NAT

Besides the improved security through the obscurity of internal nodes, NAT provides other benefits:

- **Flexibility in internal IP allocation**: By utilizing private IP addresses for internal nodes, more address space becomes available than when relying on public IPs. Recall that an organization can freely use any of the three private IP ranges to accommodate its needs. This makes network design, management, and expansion quite flexible when it comes to IP addressing. As a very simple example, several hosts with private IPs at a home network can share one public IP (instead of having three different public IPs) to access the Internet concurrently.
- **Consistency in internal IP allocation**: If internal network nodes rely on public IPs, an organization may face situations that require renumbering of node addresses, and this may not be a trivial task. If the internal network is on private IPs, existing IP assignment is less affected by

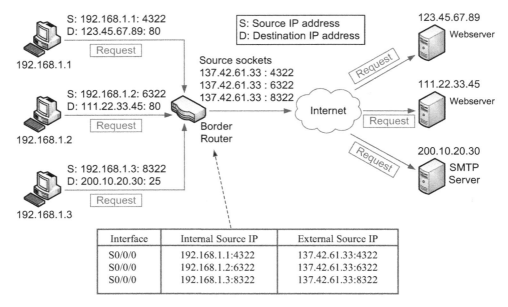

FIGURE 4.8   Router's many-to-one IP mapping and address conversion table

such circumstantial changes. For example, the change of an ISP by a business client does not affect the IP configuration of its internal nodes. Also, with the large address space available, IP allocation to each subnetwork can be more generous, expecting future business growth and other changes.

NAT has its share of drawbacks:

- **Potential performance degradation**: The border router or firewall has to conduct address translation for each inbound and outbound packet, and this can affect packet forwarding performance. As a result, deploying such time-sensitive applications as IP telephony and video streaming could be affected. In order to better serve these packets, the NAT node can implement such measures as priority-based routing.
- **Possible conflicts with some network applications**: Some network functions that rely on public IP address information, such as packet filtering, tunneling for *virtual private network* (VPN) (more in Chapter 10), TCP connections originated from outside, and communications based on the connection-less protocol (e.g., UDP), may be affected if NAT is not adequately set up.

4.7   SUBNETTING

This section explains the assignment of subnet addresses within an organization. Chances are that today's enterprise network is divided into subnets to accommodate the company's unique needs and circumstances. There are good reasons to segment an enterprise network into smaller subnets.

4.7.1   Main Benefits

a. **Security management**: Subnets allow customized planning and implementation of network security at different levels. For example, at a university's campus network, core academic systems that handle student records, human resources, and financials should be securely protected with additional layers of defense. By placing critical systems in a tightly protected subnet, they are separated from the remaining campus network including Wi-Fi that is more vulnerable to cyber threats.

b. **Customization of network segments**: Each subnet can be better customized in its design (e.g., choice of layer 2 devices and their physical connectivity) to serve the needs of information systems and systems users. For example, the subnetwork that supports a firm's data center is highly service-oriented and thus should provide fast and stable data access. That is, the design and implementation of the network segment should emphasize high network accessibility, reliability, and security.

c. **Limit broadcasting effect**: The negative effects of message broadcasting are contained at the subnet level. Unlike switches that relay broadcasted packets, routers block them by default and prevent a network from becoming a victim of excessive and unwarranted traffic.

4.7.2 SUBNETWORK ADDRESSING

4.7.2.1 Within a LAN

Creating subnetworks within an enterprise network results in IP addresses that contain three identifiers of the network, subnet, and host (see Figure 4.2). As an example, Figure 4.9 demonstrates a LAN with the network address of 192.168.0.0. The network is divided into three subnets (i.e., 192.168.1.0, 192.168.2.0, and 192.168.3.0), the third octet uniquely identifying a subnet within the LAN. You can observe that each LAN port of the router is also configured with an IP of a particular subnet.

4.7.2.2 LAN Meets WAN

An enterprise network comprised of multiple subnets may be just a LAN with one or more routers that join the subnets, as in Figure 4.9, or a combination of LANs and WAN links, as in Figure 4.10. As explained, each WAN link between two border routers is a subnet *if* it is running on the private infrastructure from a telco such as AT&T, which is an entity separated from the Internet. The client organization that leases the WAN link from a telco configures the link as a subnet giving a subnet ID. Figure 4.10 illustrates the assignment of subnet IDs when two LANs and a leased WAN connection form an enterprise network. That is, even if the physical WAN link is owned and maintained by the

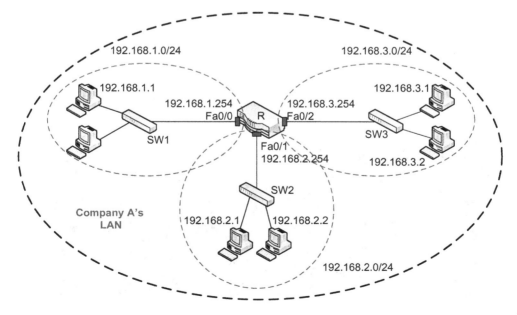

FIGURE 4.9 A firm's LAN with three subnetworks

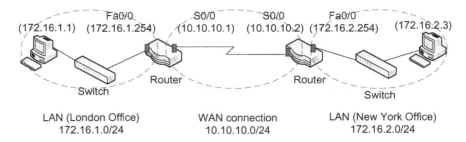

FIGURE 4.10   An organization's network with three subnets

telco, it becomes a logical part of the client's enterprise network. If the WAN link between London and New York is over the Internet, then it cannot be a subnet as there will be a number of routers between the two locations.

4.8   SUBNET MASK

4.8.1   DEFINITION

The *subnet mask* is a 32-bit combination used by a network node (e.g., host, router) to determine the subnet address of a particular IP address. More specifically, the *subnet mask* indicates the subnet address bits (network ID + subnet ID) of an IP address by 'masking' the host ID. Many industry practitioners use the two terms *network mask* and *subnet mask* interchangeably. This can cause much confusion to students, although it becomes less of an issue with practical experience.

The *subnet mask* uses either a *prefix* or a *combination of continuous 1s and 0s* in order to indicate the *network and subnet* combined portion of an IP address. Continuous 1s represent the 'network ID + subnet ID' part and continuous 0s indicate the host ID part of an IP address.

As a simple example, for the host address: 172.16.10.101

with network address:	172.0.0.0 (10101100.00000000.00000000.00000000)
with subnet address:	172.16.0.0 (10101100.00010000.00000000.00000000),

the subnet mask becomes 255.255.0.0 (11111111.11111111.00000000.00000000), or */16*. The prefix value (/16) represents the number of continuous 1s in the subnet mask.

The subnet mask is a critical piece of information because it is constantly referenced by routers and computers to determine the forwarding path of IP packets. For example, Figure 4.11 demonstrates

```
Command Prompt                                              —    □    ×

Wireless LAN adapter Wi-Fi 2:

   Connection-specific DNS Suffix  . : webpass.net
   IPv6 Address. . . . . . . . . . . : 2604:5500:5036:da00:f9d4:245:414b:e454
   Temporary IPv6 Address. . . . . . : 2604:5500:5036:da00:5cb6:aabe:e665:7b04
   Link-local IPv6 Address . . . . . : fe80::f9d4:245:414b:e454%5
   IPv4 Address. . . . . . . . . . . : 192.168.1.135
   Subnet Mask . . . . . . . . . . . : 255.255.255.0
   Default Gateway . . . . . . . . . : fe80::6238:e0ff:feb2:1f32%5
                                       192.168.1.1

Ethernet adapter Bluetooth Network Connection 3:
```

FIGURE 4.11   IP configuration of a host station

a subnet mask included in a host computer's IP configuration. The computer can determine its own subnet address based on the IP and subnet mask.

4.8.1.1 Examples

It is always a good idea to work with binary first and then translate the outcome into decimal to figure out the subnet mask and subnet address.

Example 1

Items	Decimal	Binary
Host address	176.20.38.4	10110000.00010100.00100110.00000100
Subnet mask (network ID + subnet ID)	255.255.255.0 or '/24' (prefix)	11111111.11111111.11111111.00000000
Subnet address	176.20.38.0	10110000.00010100.00100110.00000000
Host address with subnet mask	176.20.38.4/24	
Subnet address with subnet mask	176.20.38.0/24	

Example 2

Items	Decimal	Binary
Host address	192.168.1.51	11000000.10101000.00000001.00110011
Subnet mask	255.224.0.0 or '/11' (prefix)	11111111.11100000.00000000.00000000
Subnet address	192.160.0.0	11000000.10100000.00000000.00000000
Host address with subnet mask	192.168.1.51/11	
Subnet address with subnet mask	192.160.0.0/11	

4.8.2 SUBNETTING ADDRESS SPACE

An organization can create as many subnets as needed internally by borrowing bits from the host ID part (see Figure 4.2). For instance, let's think of a scenario in which an enterprise's network address is 130.191.0.0 and subnets are created by borrowing 2 bits from the host ID part. If 2 bits are borrowed, the subnet mask becomes 11111111.11111111.11000000.00000000; that is equivalent to 255.255.192.0 (or /18 in prefix). With 2 bits, four different subnets can be created within the enterprise network in which the 17th and 18th positions uniquely identify a subnet. *Yes, all 0s and all 1s are available to represent two different subnets.*

#	Subnet address (binary)	Subnet address (decimal)	Subnet mask
1	10000010.10111111.00000000.00000000	130.191.0.0	255.255.192.0
2	10000010.10111111.01000000.00000000	130.191.64.0	255.255.192.0
3	10000010.10111111.10000000.00000000	130.191.128.0	255.255.192.0
4	10000010.10111111.11000000.00000000	130.191.192.0	255.255.192.0

Then, 14 bits become available to create host IDs. The number of hosts that can own an IP address within each subnet becomes $2^{14} - 2 = 16,382$. Two (all 0s = 000000.00000000 and all 1s =

111111.11111111) are excluded from the counting because they are reserved for special functions. *So, the counting of possible subnets (2^n) and that of possible hosts ($2^n − 2$) based on available bits differ.* In the previous example, the first subnet (130.191.0.0) has a usable host address range of:

$$10000010.10111111.00000000.00000001 \sim 10000010.10111111.00111111.11111110$$
$$= 130.191.0.1 \sim 130.191.63.254 \left(\text{Remember to exclude all 0s and all 1s c.} \right)$$

4.8.3 BROADCASTING WITHIN A SUBNET

Previously, the broadcasting concept was explained in terms of limited – and directed – broadcasting. This section is an extension of the coverage. It was stated that, with all 1s for the host ID field of a packet, the packet is broadcasted to all nodes of a subnetwork.

EXAMPLE 1:
The host IP, 172.16.100.141, with the subnet mask, 255.255.0.0 (/16 in prefix), is translated into:

Host IP address:	10101100.00010000.01100100.10001101	(= 172.16.100.141)
Subnet mask:	11111111.11111111.00000000.00000000	(= 255.255.0.0)
Subnet address:	10101100.00010000.00000000.00000000	(= 172.16.0.0)

As the subnet is identified by the first 16 bits, broadcasting of a packet within a subnet uses all 1s for the remaining 16 host bits. The broadcast address, therefore, becomes

Broadcast address: 10101100.00010000.11111111.11111111   (= 172.16.255.255)

EXAMPLE 2:
The host IP, 192.168.10.141, with the subnet mask, 255.255.255.192 (/26 in prefix), is translated into:

Host IP address:	11000000.10101000.00001010.10001101	(= 192.168.10.141)
Subnet mask:	11111111.11111111.11111111.11000000	(= 255.255.255.192)
Subnet address:	11000000.10101000.00001010.10000000	(= 192.168.10.128)

With 26 bits of the subnet address, broadcasting of a packet within a subnet uses all 1s for the remaining 6 host bits. The broadcast address, therefore, becomes

Broadcast address: 11000000.10101000.00001010.10111111   (= 192.168.10.191).

4.9 SUPERNETTING

4.9.1 DEFINITION

Supernetting, also known as *classless inter-domain routing* (CIDR), is a concept opposite to *subnetting* that divides a network into smaller subnetworks. With supernetting, multiple subnetworks are combined (or summarized) into a larger subnet. Summarizing multiple subnets into a larger subnet

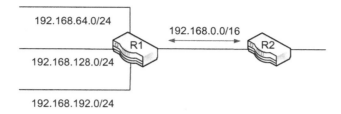

FIGURE 4.12   A supernet that summarizes three subnets

can make it easy to manage a network (e.g., router configuration) and boost network performance (e.g., faster routing decision).

As an example, imagine a hypothetical situation (see Figure 4.12) in which two routers R1 and R2 exchange packets and R1 is connected to three subnets each with a subnet address and subnet mask. Assume that 192.168.0.0/16 is the supernet address and mask that summarizes three subnets. The supernet is a higher abstraction that includes the three subnets. One main benefit of the summarization is that R2's router table adds only one entry instead of three subnet entries, making the overall list of R2's routing table smaller and subsequently facilitating faster routing decisions by R2.

Replacing three entries with one summarized entry in R2's routing table may not be that significant. However, if one supernet can substitute 1000 subnets, then R2's routing table becomes substantially smaller as it will have only one entry in place of 1000 entries. With the smaller routing table, R2 takes less time in determining the optimal routing path of a packet and improves packet forwarding performance. (More on the routing table are in Chapter 11.)

4.9.2   EXAMPLE 1

How does the supernetting (or IP summarization) work? In Figure 4.12, R1 is connected to three subnets:

Subnet address and mask (decimal)	Subnet address (binary)
192.168.64.0/24	11000000.10101000.01000000.00000000
192.168.128.0/24	11000000.10101000.10000000.00000000
192.168.192.0/24	11000000.10101000.11000000.00000000

The highlighted parts represent the subnet address. Their subnet mask (/24) becomes 11111111.11 111111.11111111.00000000 (or 255.255.255.0).

For supernetting, we need to come up with a common denominator of the three subnet addresses. You can observe that the first 16 digits '11000000.10101000' are shared by all three subnets, making them the longest common denominator. As a result, '11000000.10101000' becomes a supernet address. The new subnet address and subnet mask of the supernet becomes:

Supernet address:	11000000.10101000.00000000.00000000 = 192.168.0.0
Supernet's subnet mask:	11111111.11111111.00000000.00000000 = 255.255.0.0 (= /16)

4.9.3 EXAMPLE 2

Here is another example in which three subnets need to be summarized (the subnet addresses are in bold).

Subnet address and mask	Subnet address in binary	Subnet masks in decimal
172.16.35.0/24	**10101100.00010000.00100011**.00000000	255.255.255.0
172.16.39.0/24	**10101100.00010000.00100111**.00000000	255.255.255.0
172.16.31.0/24	**10101100.00010000.00011111**.00000000	255.255.255.0

To come up with the summarization, we need to decide a bitstream common to all three subnet addresses. It can be seen that the first 18 bits '*10101100.00010000.00*' become the common denominator. Therefore, the new summarized network in binary can be: **10101100.00010000.0000**0000.00000000 (or 172.16.0.0/18). Also, although not the longest, **10101100.00010000**.00000000.00000000 (or 172.16.0.0/16) is another 'conceptually easier' summarization as the first 16 bits are also common to all three subnets.

4.10 MANAGING IP ADDRESS SPACE

Allocating IP addresses to network nodes should be the result of a well-planned process. IP planning at an enterprise with multiple functional departments/business units and distributed geographical locations has implications on network management and security. Once IP addresses are allocated and configured on intermediary devices and host devices, reconfiguring them due to circumstantial changes such as organizational growth and restructuring can be painful. Accordingly, the management of IPs requires well-thought-out planning, anticipating such changes, and also the details of IP deployment should be thoroughly documented for future activities related to network planning, management, and updates. It is important to remind that the issues covered in this section apply to both IPv4 and IPv6, although the explanation is largely based on IPv4.

4.10.1 STATIC VS. DYNAMIC IP ALLOCATION

Given that there are many different node types that need an IP, the total number of nodes that need an IP address on a temporary (or dynamic) or permanent (or static) basis should be determined. Depending on the nature of intermediary devices and hosts, decisions can be made on the usage of static versus dynamic IP addresses. Categorically, user stations and other personal productivity tools such as mobile devices are assigned temporary IPs, as they don't have to be up and running all the time. Also, configuring user devices with a permanent IP becomes an administrative burden.

Network nodes other than user devices are generally given a static IP to provide various services (e.g., webpages, file storage, printing service, database transactions) on a permanent basis. Table 4.2 lists devices with a static IP in terms of (a) those offering various resources and services to user stations and (b) intermediary devices that facilitate link connectivity. Recall that, unlike the managed switch that needs an IP address only for its remote management over the network, the router needs a permanent IP for each port (or interface).

Assigning a permanent/static IP to a host computer requires the input of four information items: *IP address*, *subnet mask*, *default gateway* (the router port address that forwards IP packets beyond a subnet boundary), and *DNS server*(s) address that maps a domain name (e.g., www.facebook.com) to its corresponding IP address (see Figure 4.13).

TABLE 4.2

Network nodes and IP address assignment

Node categorization	Nodes	'Preferred' IP addressing
Resource/service consumers	End-user devices (e.g., workstations, smartphones, personal productivity tools)	Temporary/dynamic IPs
Resource or service provision	• Dedicated servers • Peripherals including printers, fax, and backup devices • Specialty devices including surveillance cameras, AC sensors, and alarms	Permanent/ static IPs
Intermediary devices	• Router LAN and WAN ports (interfaces) • Firewall • Managed switch (an IP address is assigned to remotely configure it over the network) • Managed wireless access point (an IP address is assigned to remotely configure it over the network)	Permanent/static IPs

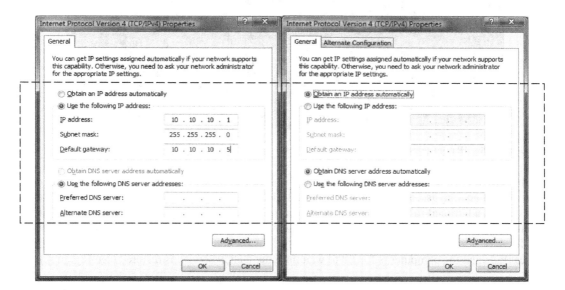

FIGURE 4.13 Static (left) versus dynamic (right) IP provision in MS Windows

4.10.2 Obtaining Dynamic IP through DHCP

End user devices are given a temporary IP through DHCP (Dynamic Host Configuration Protocol) as this curtails the management overhead considerably and also eliminates the chance of mistakes during manual configuration. In addition to a dynamic IP, the DHCP server also provides the *subnet mask*, *default gateway*, and *DNS server* information.

The DHCP server may be running on a dedicated computer or router. When a client station is powered on, its built-in procedure broadcasts an IP request to reach the DHCP server that maintains a range of temporary IP addresses. On receiving the request, the DHCP server leases an IP address for a limited time (e.g., 1 day). '*C:>ipconfig /all*' for Windows or '*C:>ifconfig /all*' for Unix/Linux displays the lease information including *Lease Obtained* and *Lease Expires*. After a client node is given a temporary IP address, the DHCP server passes the client's information to a DNS server for its dynamic database update (see Figure 4.14).

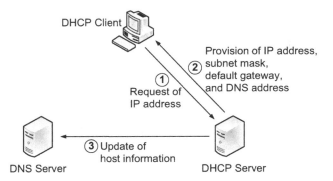

FIGURE 4.14   Temporary IP provision by DHCP

```
Connection-specific DNS Suffix  . :
Description . . . . . . . . . . . : Intel(R) Dual Band Wireless-AC 8260 #2
Physical Address. . . . . . . . . : F4-8C-50-28-29-EA
DHCP Enabled. . . . . . . . . . . : Yes
Autoconfiguration Enabled . . . . : Yes
Link-local IPv6 Address . . . . . : fe80::441e:e082:f579:ae21%5(Preferred)
IPv4 Address. . . . . . . . . . . : 10.0.0.6(Preferred)
Subnet Mask . . . . . . . . . . . : 255.255.255.0
Lease Obtained. . . . . . . . . . : Tuesday, August 25, 2020 9:30:55 AM
Lease Expires . . . . . . . . . . : Thursday, August 27, 2020 1:51:23 PM
Default Gateway . . . . . . . . . : 10.0.0.1
DHCP Server . . . . . . . . . . . : 10.0.0.1
DHCPv6 IAID . . . . . . . . . . . : 83135568
DHCPv6 Client DUID. . . . . . . . : 00-01-00-01-1F-E8-92-61-54-EE-75-BC-9A-6D
DNS Servers . . . . . . . . . . . : 10.0.0.1
NetBIOS over Tcpip. . . . . . . . : Enabled
```

FIGURE 4.15   IP configuration screenshot (Windows)

The leased IP is returned to the DHCP server if the host is shut down or taken off from the network. The client may issue a renew request to the DHCP server before its expiration. The DHCP standard defines additional rules of engagement when more than one IP address is offered to a client by different DHCP servers. Besides, with *Autoconfiguration Enabled*, the client can use a pre-assigned link-local IP address for *internal networking* only (not for Internet access) just in case the DHCP request fails and the computer is forced to wait until the DHCP service is restored (see Figure 4.15).

4.10.3   DETERMINING SUBNETS

A decision should be made on the number of subnetworks within a corporate network. The decision can be based on several technical and non-technical factors such as:

- Physical layout including the building location, occupied floors of a building, and geographical distribution of offices.
- Importance of limiting the scope of a broadcast domain so that possible broadcast storms do not impede network performance.
- Importance of defining functional boundaries of the corporate network to better serve business requirements. The logical boundaries of business functions include academic units (e.g., departments, colleges), business departments and units (e.g., marketing, accounting), and project workgroups.
- Importance of having different levels of **security control** for subnetworks. Network segmentation through subnetting is a fundamental element to improve security as each subnet divided by a router can have its own customized defense measures (e.g., firewall, access control list).

4.10.4 DEVELOPING IP ASSIGNMENT POLICY

An organization maintains an inventory of many network nodes whose subnets and IP addresses should be managed in a structured manner based on a formal policy. Otherwise, IT staff can face confusion and inefficiency in adding or deleting a node to/from the network, configuring IPs, network troubleshooting, and changing configurations. Moreover, inconsistency in IP configurations can have negative consequences on the integrity of network security and access control.

Because of unique functions performed by different node types, they can be grouped to define a consistent policy in IP provisioning, which will make network management less troublesome. For example, imagine that an IT specialist needs to troubleshoot a problem and should quickly locate the IP address of a particular router port on a subnet. If the policy requires that the router port be given the last available IP address of a subnet, she/he can guess the router port's IP without searching through the IP database. For demonstration, a hypothetical IP policy based on IPv4 is developed for a university network comprised of various functional units and network nodes (see Table 4.3). Table 4.3 is rather simplified, as the real policy has more structural details for a reasonably sized organization.

TABLE 4.3
A hypothetical policy for IPv4 allocation

IP range	Assignment
• Network address: 192.168.0.0	
• Subnet mask: 255.255.255.0 (/24)	
• Subnet range (third octet)	
192.168.1.0	DMZ (accessible from the Internet)
192.168.2.0 ~ 192.168.7.0	University administration
192.168.8.0 ~ 192.168.40.0	Academics (colleges and departments)
192.168.41.0 ~ 192.168.43.0	Library
192.168.44.0 ~ 192.168.50.0	Student labs
192.168.51.0	Campus storage area network
192.168.52.0	Campus operation and maintenance
192.168.53.0	Campus safety and security
192.168.54.0 ~ 192.168.55.0	Athletics
192.168.56.0 ~ 192.168.60.0	WAN links
192.168.61.0 ~ 192.168.62.0	Internet links
• Host range within a subnet (fourth octet)	
x.x.x.1 ~ x.x.x.2:	Router (gateway) and firewall interface(s)
x.x.x.3 ~ x.x.x.10:	Managed switches (core and workgroup switches)
x.x.x.11 ~ x.x.x.15:	Managed wireless devices (e.g., access points)
x.x.x.16 ~ x.x.x.25:	Servers
x.x.x.26 ~ x.x.x.40:	Peripherals (e.g., printers, fax, backup devices)
x.x.x.41 ~ x.x.x.250:	General user stations
x.x.x.251 ~ x.x.x.254:	Network technician/administrator stations

4.11   IPV6 ADDRESSING

4.11.1   BACKGROUND

IPv4 has limited address space due to the 32-bit address structure. Further, the classful IP scheme adopted in the early stage of the Internet contributed to the ineffective distribution and usage of the available IPv4 address space. A few measures have extended its life, which include the use of the classless (instead of classful) IP addressing scheme and private IPs that require network address translation (NAT). As numerous mobile and IoT devices are joining the Internet, there will be a gradual migration from IPv4 to IPv6. The adoption of IPv6 tends to be faster in Europe and Asia due to the shortage of IPv4 addresses in these regions.

4.11.2   IPV6 PACKET STRUCTURE

Before explaining the IP address, the IPv6 packet's header structure is briefly explained. Regular IPv6 packets contain a 40-byte header, significantly longer than 20 bytes of the IPv4 packet header (see Figure 4.16). IPv6 also allows the extended header longer than 40 bytes, but the explanation here focuses on the regular header structure. Although the header is longer than that of IPv4 largely because of the lengthy IP address bits, IPv6 has a simplified header structure with fewer fields, and this allows more efficient packet processing. IPv6 also allows the addition of a separate extension header to strengthen packet security in terms of integrity, authentication, and confidentiality.

The following is a summary of each field:

*   *Traffic Class* and *Flow Label* are designed to support Quality of Service (QoS). *Traffic Class* prioritizes traffic. The functional specs of *Flow Label* are still evolving.
*   *Payload length* indicates the length of the IPv6 payload (data field).
*   *Next header* indicates the type of PDU (e.g., protocol) in the data field.
*   *Hop limit* represents the maximum number of routers a packet is allowed to pass and is equivalent to *time to live* (TTL) of IPv4
*   *Source address* identifies the IPv6 address of a source node.
*   *Destination address* identifies the IPv6 address of a destination node.

4.11.3   IP ADDRESSING

The IPv6 address uses 128 bits or 32 hexadecimal digits (e.g., 0089:A0CD:0234:EF98:0000:000F: 0D0B:0F20) in which each represents 4 binary bits. Hexadecimal digits are not case sensitive (e.g., A0CD is equivalent to a0cd). With 128 bits, IPv6 affords enormous address space (literally a trillion times the IPv4 space), eclipsing the IP shortage problem for a long time to come. Out of 128 bits, the first 64 bits represent a subnetwork address, and the remaining 64 bits are for a host address within a particular subnetwork (see Figure 4.17).

Version 6 (= 0110)	Traffic Class (8 bits)	Flow Label (20 bits)	
Payload Length (16 bits)		Next Header (8bits)	Hop Limit (8 bits)
Source IP address (128 bits)			
Destination IP address (128 bits)			
Next Header or Payload (Data Field): Variable in size			

FIGURE 4.16   IPv6 Packet

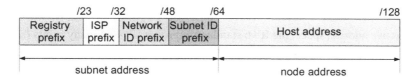

FIGURE 4.17 IPv6 address structure

4.11.3.1 Subnet Address Bits

IPv6 also adopts hierarchical IP addressing in which the 64 subnetwork address bits are further divided into:

- 23 bits for the regional registry prefix
- 9 bits for the ISP (Internet Service Provider) prefix
- 16 bits for the network ID prefix (also called site prefix)
- 16 bits for the subnet ID prefix

4.11.3.2 Host Address Bits

As for the 64-bit host address part, three options are available.

- The host address can be manually configured as a static IP.
- The host address can be dynamically provided by DHCPv6.
- Unique to IPv6, there is a third IP addressing option called EUI-64. EUI stands for *Extended Unique Identifier*. With EUI-64, the 64-bit host address of a computer can be automatically derived from its 48-bit MAC address. This approach, however, exposes a computer's MAC to the world, raising privacy concerns.

There are also private and loopback IP address ranges. For example, the loopback for IPv6 is 0:0:0:0:0:0:0:1 (or '::1' in abbreviation), equivalent to 127.0.0.1/8 for IPv4. If necessary, additional loopback addresses can be defined by an organization for internal usage.

4.11.4 ADDRESS ABBREVIATION

IPv6 addresses are long and can be shortened using two abbreviation rules.

Rule 1: *Leading zeros* within each block of hexadecimal values separated by colons (:) can be omitted. For example, the following two addresses are equivalent.
0089:A0CD:0234:EF98:0000:000F:0D0B:0000
89:A0CD:234:EF98:0:F:D0B:0

Rule 2: A group of consecutive zeros can be substituted by a double colon. For example, the following addresses are all equivalent.
0089:A0CD:0234:0000:0000:0000:0D0B:0F20
89:A0CD:234:0:0:0:D0B:F20
89:A0CD:234::D0B:F20

This trick of removing all 0s is allowed 'only once' to avoid confusion. For example,

0089::A0CD:0234::0D0B:0F20 can be interpreted as either
0089:0000:A0CD:0234:0000:0000:0D0B:0F20 or
0089:0000:0000:A0CD:0234:0000:0D0B:0F20.

4.11.5   IPv6 vs. IPv4 Standards

Besides the massive address space, the IPv6 standard improves IPv4 on many fronts (see Table 4.4). The protocol details of IPv6 are still evolving, and some of the key differences are highlighted here.

4.11.6   Transition from IPv4 to IPv6

The transition from IPv4 to IPv6 will be rather gradual. Currently, some networks and their nodes depend purely on IPv4, while many others support both IPv4 and IPv6. To ensure the coexistence of IPv4 and IPv6 for the foreseeable future, several technical solutions have been introduced. Among them are *dual IP stacks*, *packet tunneling*, and *direct address conversion*.

4.11.6.1   Dual IP Stacks within a Node

With the dual IP stack approach, the operating system of a network node supports both IPv4 and IPv6 concurrently. For example, Figure 4.18 demonstrates a scenario in which dual-stack routers (R4, R5, and R6) provide connectivity between IPv4 and IPv6 networks to enable the transition. Running dual IP stacks is a popular approach as operating systems of hosts and network nodes support them.

4.11.6.2   Direct Address Conversion

With this solution, IPv4 packets can be turned into IPv6 packets and vice versa. That is, IPv4 addresses of 32 bits can be directly converted into IPv6 addresses of 128 bits with a little bit of a

---

TABLE 4.4
Comparison: IPv4 vs. IPv6

Features	IPv4	IPv6 (IPng)
Network security	Using a security protocol is an option.	IPsec is expected to be mandatory for packet encryption, sender authentication, and data integrity.
Quality of Service	Relies on the *Diff-Serv* field	Provision of more refined QoS becomes available through the *Traffic Class* and *Flow Label* fields.
Packet size	Up to 64 KB in payload	Can be larger than 64 KB in payload using an extended header. Packets greater than 64 KB are called jumbograms. Jumbograms can be theoretically as large as 4 GB.
Methods of packet distribution	Unicasting, multicasting, and broadcasting are possible.	Broadcasting is not available. Instead, multicasting will be used extensively.
Network address translation (NAT)	Heavily used due to shortage of IP address space and weak security. Improving network security with NAT is losing its effectiveness as most security attacks are targeted at the application and transport layer functions. This makes the role of NAT in security increasingly marginal. Think of phishing through emails as an example.	By design, NAT is unnecessary, and this makes it easier to implement advanced network applications such as virtual private networks (VPNs). Despite this, there is also a possibility that NAT may return to IPv6 as vendors start to support it.

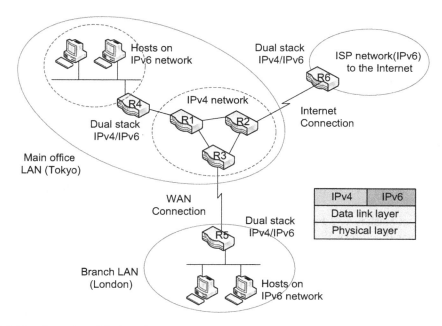

FIGURE 4.18 Scenarios of dual stack routers

| IPv6 Header | IPv4Header | IPv4 Data |

| IPv4 Header | IPv6Header | IPv6 Data |

FIGURE 4.19 Packet tunneling

trick. For the conversion, a 32-bit IPv4 address is preceded first by 80 zero bits and then 16 one bits. For example, the IP address of 123.45.67.89 can be translated into:

0000:0000:0000:0000:0000:ffff:123.45.67.89 or
0:0:0:0:0:ffff:123.45.67.89 or
::ffff:123.45.67.89.

4.11.6.3 Packet Tunneling

Tunneling has been introduced as well. For example, if a destination network is running on IPv6 but the local network is still on IPv4, then the local host can produce an IPv6 packet and encapsulate it within an IPv4 packet for delivery. Depending on the situation, the reverse can happen when an IPv4 packet is produced and encapsulated within an IPv6 packet for transportation.

As another scenario, tunneling can be used by dual stack routers (see Figure 4.18) for packet delivery. For example, if the source and destination hosts are all on IPv6 networks but a packet needs to pass through an IPv4 network, the dual-stack router can encapsulate/de-encapsulate the IPv6 packet by adding/dropping an IPv4 header (see Figure 4.19).

CHAPTER SUMMARY

- IANA delegates available network address space to Regional Internet Registries (RIRs). Large ISPs obtain IP blocks from RIPs and divide them into smaller chunks for allocation to clients. Individuals and small businesses obtain a network address from their ISPs.

- Provisioning of network IPv4 addresses can be either classful- or classless-based. With the now-defunct classful IP scheme, the network ID part is 8 bits (class A), 16 bits (class B), or 24 bits (class C). The network ID is no longer a multiple of an octet under the classless scheme.
- Certain IP ranges are designated for special functions including the loopback, broadcast, and multicast services.
- The loopback address is a special IP a host can use to send a message addressed to itself. Packets with a loopback addressed destination are, therefore, directed back to the sender before leaving the host.
- The private IP address is intended for internal use only as an organization's border router does not route packets to the Internet if they have a private IP. The border router or firewall should translate any private IP of a packet to a public IP through network address translation (or NAT).
- The subnet mask is a 32-bit combination used by network nodes to indicate the subnet part of a particular IP address. For this, it uses a prefix or a combination of continuous 1s and 0s.
- Supernetting is a concept opposite to subnetting. With supernetting, multiple subnets are combined (or summarized) into a larger subnet. It is an effective way of streamlining network address management and improving the router's packet forwarding performance.
- Some essential elements of planning IP allocation at an organization include deciding the number of nodes that need a dynamic or static IP address, determining subnetworks, and having a consistent IP assignment policy.
- IPv6 is distinctively different from IPv4 in many different ways including the IP addressing mechanism, packet structure, and Quality of Service (QoS) provision.
- For the coexistence of IPv4 and IPv6 into the foreseeable future, several solutions have been introduced, including *dual IP stacks*, *packet tunneling*, and *direct address conversion*.

KEY TERMS

1-to-1 IP address mapping
broadcast storm
broadcasting IP address
class A network
class B network
class C network
classful IP address
classless inter-domain routing (CIDR)
classless IP address
default gateway
default route
de-militarized zone (DMZ)
denial of service
directed broadcasting
dual IP stacks
Host identification
Internet Assigned Numbers Authority (IANA)
Internet Group Management Protocol (IGMP)
IP assignment policy

IP masquerading
IPv4
IPv6
jumbogram
limited broadcasting
localhost
loopback
m-to-1 IP address mapping
multicast group
multicasting IP address
network address port translation (NAPT)
network address translation (NAT)
network identification
network masquerading
packet tunneling
port address translation (PAT)
private IP address
Regional Internet Registry (RIR)
subnet mask
subnetting
supernetting

CHAPTER REVIEW QUESTIONS

1. Which organization allocates IP address blocks to large ISPs?
   A) Internet Assigned Numbers Authority
   B) Regional Internet Registry
   C) International Standard Organization
   D) Internet Engineering Task Force
   E) VeriSign

2. What is the largest decimal value of the 8-bit octet?
   A) 100
   B) 32
   C) 255
   D) 128
   E) 256

3. The IP address should have AT LEAST_____ part(s).
   A) network ID
   B) host ID
   C) network ID and subnet ID
   D) network ID and host ID
   E) network ID, subnet ID, and host ID

4. The transition from IPv4 to IPv6 will be gradual and one approach that allows their coexistence is direct address conversion. In that approach, 123.45.67.89 (IPv4) becomes _____ for IPv6:
   A) 0000:0000:0000:0000:0000:ffff:123.45.67.89
   B) 1111: 1111: 1111: 1111: 1111:ffff:123.45.67.89
   C) 123.45.67.89: 0000:0000:0000:0000:0000:0000
   D) 1111: 1111: 1111: 1111: 1111:0000:123.45.67.89
   E) 123.45.67.89:1111: 1111: 1111: 1111: 1111:ffff

5. When a packet is broadcasted to a target subnet that is different from the source host's subnet, it becomes _____ broadcasting.
   A) focused
   B) subset
   C) targeted
   D) directed
   E) limited

6. Which term represents IPs used only internally at an organization?
   A) private IPs
   B) campus IPs
   C) internal IPs
   D) encoded IPs
   E) reserved IPs

7. When the destination address of a packet is 255.255.255.255:
   A) The packet is delivered to all hosts on the Internet.
   B) The packet is delivered to all hosts of an enterprise network to which the source host belongs.
   C) The packet is delivered to all hosts of a multicasting network on the Internet.
   D) The packet is self-addressed and thus does not leave the source host.
   E) The packet is delivered to all hosts that are in the same subnet as the source host.

8. For a packet outgoing to the Internet, the *network address port translation* process changes its:
   A) source port number only.
   B) destination IP address only.
   C) destination and source IP addresses.

    D) source IP address and maybe source port number.

    E) destination IP address and maybe source port number.

9. Imagine a network (175.140.x.x) that uses 8 bits for the subnet ID. If a computer releases a packet with 175.140.115.255 as the destination IP, what should happen?

    A) The packet is delivered to the host, 175.140.115.255.

    B) The packet is delivered to the host, 175.140.115.0.

    C) The packet is delivered to all hosts within the subnet, 175.140.115.0.

    D) The packet is delivered to all hosts within the network, 175.140.0.0.

    E) The packet is delivered to the host, 175.140.0.255.

10. The network ID of an IP address, 10.7.12.6, is 10.7.0.0. The network plus subnet parts are:

    A) 10

    B) 10.7

    C) 10.7.12

    D) 10.7.12.6

    E) Not enough information to decide

11. When a firm uses 8 bits for its network identification (or ID), what does the subnet mask 255.255.255.0 tell you?

    A) Eight bits are assigned to the subnet identification.

    B) Sixteen bits are available to uniquely identify a host station.

    C) Four bits are assigned to the subnet identification.

    D) Eight bits are used to indicate the host identification.

    E) No bits are available to create subnets.

12. A firm has the network ID of 65.10.0.0 and the subnet mask of 255.255.0.0. What can be the destination address of a packet to be broadcasted to all nodes in the network? Assume that 255.255.255.255 is not used.

    A) 65.10.255.255

    B) 65.255.255.255

    C) 65.0.0.255

    D) 65.10.255.0

    E) 65.255.0.0

QUESTIONS 13–17:

Think of a network, 192.168.125.x, with the following requirements:

- Number of necessary subnets: 14
- Number of usable hosts per subnet: 14

Assuming that the minimum number of bits is borrowed from the host ID part.

13. What is the subnet mask of all subnets?

    A) 255.255.255.255

    B) 255.255.255.64

    C) 255.255.255.240

    D) 255.255.255.192

    E) 255.255.255.224

14. For the subnet 192.168.125.16, what is the first usable host IP?

    A) 192.168.125.16

    B) 192.168.125.17

    C) 192.168.125.32

    D) 192.168.125.20

    E) 192.168.125.64

15. For the subnet 192.168.125.32, what is the last usable host IP?
    A) 192.168.125.33
    B) 192.168.125.46
    C) 192.168.125.32
    D) 192.168.125.47
    E) 192.168.125.64
16. For the subnet 192.168.125.128, what is the broadcast IP?
    A) 192.168.125.129
    B) 192.168.125.240
    C) 192.168.125.255
    D) 192.168.125.15
    E) 192.168.125.143
17. How many (usable) IP addresses are available for a subnet?
    A) 6
    B) 10
    C) 14
    D) 15
    E) 16
18. Which host IPv4 address needs network address translation (NAT) to access the Internet?
    A) 123.7.86.215
    B) 127.0.0.1
    C) 192.168.0.1
    D) 255.255.255.255
    E) 127.127.127.1
19. Which information is NOT included in the first 64 network address bits of IPv6?
    A) regional registry prefix
    B) ISP prefix
    C) site prefix necessary for global routing
    D) subnet prefix
    E) time to live (TTL) prefix
20. Which statement is INCORRECT regarding network address translation (NAT)?
    A) It is implemented on layer 2 switches.
    B) It converts a private IP to a public IP.
    C) Routers or firewalls are used for its implementation.
    D) It can better protect the enterprise network.
    E) The port address translation allows several hosts to share a public IP.
21. An IPv4 address with the first octet of 127 can be used for
    A) classless IP assignment to a host.
    B) private IP assignment to a host.
    C) multicasting of packets to a subnet.
    D) testing connectivity to a router.
    E) offline testing of webserver pages.
22. Under the classful IP allocation scheme, Class B networks can use a maximum of _____ bits to indicate the host identification.
    A) 4
    B) 8
    C) 16
    D) 24
    E) 32

23. The subnet mask of a class B network is 255.255.255.0 at a firm. How many subnets can be created in that firm?
    A) 128
    B) 256
    C) 64
    D) 255
    E) 254

24. The following measures relieved the shortage problem of the IPv4's address space EXCEPT:
    A) Use of dynamic IPs assigned by the DHCP server
    B) Utilization of private IP addresses
    C) Reliance on more switches than routers for corporate networking
    D) Use of network address translation (NAT)
    E) Switching from the classful to the classless addressing scheme

25. Which of the following INCORRECTLY describes IPv6 addressing?
    A) An address is composed of two parts: 64-bit network ID and 64-bit host ID.
    B) The 64-bit host ID can be configured manually or auto-configured.
    C) IPv6 supports the broadcasting of IP packets just as IPv4 does.
    D) Host addresses can be dynamically provided through the DHCP service.
    E) The 64-bit host ID of a computer can be derived from its 48-bit MAC address.

HANDS-ON EXERCISES

Exercise 4.1

How many subnets do you see in the hypothetical enterprise network in Figure 4.20? Do not include the Internet connection in the counting. Assume that the WAN links are lines leased from a telco such as AT&T (not Internet connections).

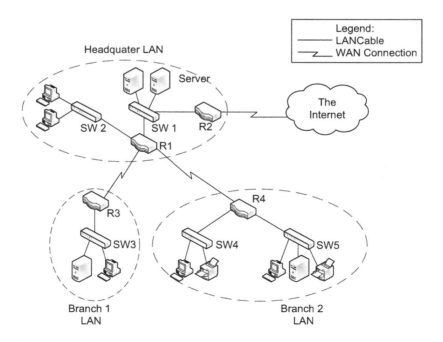

FIGURE 4.20 A hypothetical enterprise network

EXERCISE 4.2

1. For the host address, 195.112.36.59, where

Network ID: 195	Subnet ID: 112.36	Host ID: 59

   Decide the subnet address and subnet mask in both decimal and binary.
2. For the host address, 207.34.15.187, where

Network ID: 207.34	Subnet ID: 15	Host ID: 187

   Decide the subnet address and subnet mask in both decimal and binary.
3. For the following IP addresses, determine their subnet addresses and subnet masks in both decimal and binary.
   - 195.205.36.5/13
   - 192.168.36.5/21
   - 10.11.46.51/15
4. For the following IP addresses, determine their subnet addresses and subnet masks in decimal.

IP address of a host	Subnet address	Subnet masks
10.15.123.50/8		
17.100.222.15/13		
128.100.54.11/24		
141.131.75.162/13		
115.125.129.227/16		
162.15.115.2/21		
173.102.75.224/18		
192.168.124.31/20		
172.31.200.201/22		

EXERCISE 4.3

1. For the network address 130.190.0.0 (the first 16 bits as the network ID), 4 bits are borrowed from the host bits to create subnets.
   a. How many different subnets can be created?
   b. What is the subnet mask?
   c. List available subnet addresses.
2. Given the network address of 172.191.183.0 (the first 24 bits as the network ID), the firm decided to use 4 bits to create subnets.
   a. What is the subnet mask?
   b. List all possible subnet addresses.
   c. List usable host IPs of the first subnet (remember to exclude all 0s and all 1s).
3. Given the network address of 230.195.10.0 (the first 24 bits as the network ID), the firm's network administrator figures that 6 subnets are necessary.
   a. What is the minimum number of bits to be borrowed from the host ID part?
   b. Assuming that the minimum number of bits has been borrowed, what is the resulting subnet mask?
   c. List all possible subnet addresses.
   d. List usable host IPs of the last subnet.

EXERCISE 4.4

1. Determine the broadcast address of each subnet. Remember that working with binary is always easier. Assume directed (not limited) broadcasting.

Subnet address	Subnet mask	Broadcast address
130.191.0.0	255.255.192.0 (or /18)	
130.191.64.0	255.255.192.0	
130.191.128.0	255.255.192.0	
130.191.192.0	255.255.192.0	

2. Determine the broadcast address of each host assuming directed (not limited) broadcasting.

Host address	Subnet mask	Broadcast address
192.168.150.121	255.255.128.0 (or /17)	
172.57.237.200	255.248.0.0 (or /13)	

3. Given the following information:
   - Host IP address: 130.191.31.21
   - Network address: 130.191.31.0 (the first 24 bits as the network ID)
   - Subnet mask: 255.255.255.240 (/28)

   Determine:
   a. Total number of subnets possible
   b. Number of host bits in each subnet
   c. Number of host addresses possible in each subnet
   d. Subnet address of the host, 130.191.31.21
   e. Broadcast address of the host, 130.191.31.21
   f. First host address of the subnet, 130.191.31.16
   g. Last host address of the subnet, 130.191.31.16

4. A company has 192.10.10.0 as its network address (the first 24 bits as the network ID). It needs to have 14 subnets. Provide the following information:
   a. Minimum number of bits to borrow from the host ID part
   b. Subnet mask
   c. Total number of subnets possible
   d. List of all subnet addresses
   e. Number of usable host addresses per subnet
   f. Host IP range of the subnet, 192.10.10.16
   g. Broadcast address of the subnet, 192.10.10.16

5. A company has 192.168.3.0 as its network address (the first 24 bits as the network ID). It needs to have 6 subnets. Provide the following information:
   a. Minimum number of bits to borrow from the host ID part
   b. Subnet mask
   c. Total number of subnets possible
   d. List of all subnet addresses
   e. Number of usable host addresses per subnet
   f. Host IP range of the subnet, 192.168.3.32
   g. Broadcast address of the subnet, 192.168.3.32

EXERCISE **4.5**

Summarize the following subnet addresses into a supernet using the longest common denominator. Also, show their new subnet masks.

1.	192.168.1.0/24	192.168.2.0/24	192.168.4.0/24	
2.	192.168.129.0/24	192.168.130.0/24	192.168.132.0/24	192.168.145.0/24
3.	172.16.163.0/20	172.16.167.0/22	172.16.159.0/23	
4.	10.20.30.41/17	10.20.65.52/18	10.20.95.34/20	10.20.160.78/21

EXERCISE **4.6**

1) Use the address abbreviation rules to reduce the following IPv6 addresses to the smallest possible.
   a)   AD89:00C0:0204:0000:0000:ABC0:000B:0020
   b)   0000:0000:0000:0D89:0EC0:0204:00FB:0A20
   c)   0000:0D89:00C0:0204:0000:0000:000B:0000
2) Restore the following IPv6 addresses to their non-abbreviated ones.
   a)   89:CD:4::B:20
   b)   B:FD:3:F98:0::D0B:F20
   c)   B:1:3:8:0::B:0

5 Intermediary Devices

5.1 INTRODUCTION

There are many intermediary (or networking) device types designed to facilitate packet exchange between end nodes. Among them are the *bridge, switch, router, modem, firewall, multiplexer, channel service unit/data service unit* (CSU/DSU), and *Wi-Fi access point* (or AP). The primary responsibility of the bridge, switch, router, and access point is packet forwarding over LAN and WAN links. The others perform more specialized functions including the production and propagation of electronic and light signals over the WAN connection (e.g., modem, CSU/DSU), provision of network security (e.g., firewall), and bundling of data arriving from multiple transmission sources (e.g., multiplexer).

This chapter explains the *general-purpose* intermediary devices with more emphasis on the switch and router that dominate the wired network infrastructure. As another ubiquitous device type, the Wi-Fi access point is briefly mentioned but covered in depth on Chapter 6. Other specialty devices such as the firewall, modem, CSU/DSU, and multiplexer are covered in Chapters 9 and 13.

5.1.1 LEARNING OBJECTIVES

The primary objectives of this chapter are to learn:

- Intermediary devices and their operational layers
- The operating system of an intermediary device and its primary functions
- General properties of the bridge and wireless access point, switch, and router
- Differences between switching and routing
- Address Resolution Protocol (ARP)
- Collision domain
- Broadcast domain

5.2 GENERAL PROPERTIES

5.2.1 OPERATIONAL LAYERS

Intermediary devices usually implement functions below the transport layer (see Table 5.1). This means that they do not understand PDUs from the application and transport layers. For example, the router is an internet layer device and the ordinary switch runs in the data link layer. Table 5.1 summarizes popular intermediary devices in terms of the standard layers they operate. Among them, the technical details of layer 3 switches are largely beyond the scope of this book but will be briefly introduced in this chapter.

TABLE 5.1

Intermediary devices and their standard layers

Layers	Intermediary (or networking) devices
Internet	Router, Layer 3 switch
Data Link	Bridge, wireless access point, switch
Physical	Hub (or Multiport Repeater): No longer used, especially, in business organizations

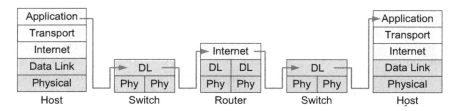

FIGURE 5.1   An illustration of layer processing by intermediary devices

5.2.2 Encapsulation and De-encapsulation

Like hosts, intermediary devices also conduct encapsulation and de-encapsulation to forward application-layer data (i.e., APDUs). Figure 5.1 demonstrates a scenario in which an application PDU from the source host goes through two switches (as layer 2 devices) and one router (as a layer 3 device) before it reaches the destination host. It indicates that whenever a message arrives at a switch or router, its de-encapsulation and re-encapsulation kicks in to perform functions defined in each of the data link and/or internet layers.

Figure 5.2 gives a closer look at encapsulation and de-encapsulation by a router based on a scenario in which the router interconnects Ethernet (as a LAN standard) and Point-to-Point/PPP (as a WAN standard). The two data link layer technologies are not compatible (e.g., different frame structures and data transmission methods), and the router provides necessary frame conversion through de-encapsulation and encapsulation. Remember that the IP packet stays the same during the end-to-end delivery.

When an Ethernet frame arrives at a LAN port, the router removes (i.e., de-encapsulates) the Ethernet frame's header and trailer and then moves the remaining IP packet to the internet layer. The router's internet layer, then, conducts such functions as the routing path decision of the packet and decreases the packet header's TTL (time to live) value by 1 (revisit Chapter 3). Then, the packet is handed over to the data link layer where the IP packet is encapsulated within a PPP frame for transfer over the WAN connection. As can be seen, routers should support popular LAN (e.g., Ethernet) and WAN (e.g., PPP) protocols to bridge the heterogeneity of data links.

5.2.3 System Components

Intermediary devices, except pure physical layer ones (e.g., hubs), have hardware and software components we see inside a computer. They include:

- Central processing unit (CPU)
- Memories: Read only memory (ROM), random access memory (RAM), non-volatile flash memory

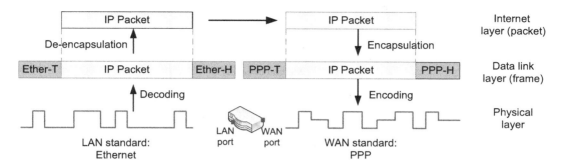

FIGURE 5.2 IP packet de-encapsulation/encapsulation by router

- Operating System: A vendor may choose to store OS in the non-volatile flash memory for faster access and transfer to RAM.
- System bus that moves data between system components
- Various ports (interfaces), including:
  - LAN ports mainly for Ethernet, including Fast Ethernet and Gigabit Ethernet
  - WAN ports for serial lines such as T-1 and DSL links.
  - Console port for direct access to the OS for system configuration and management

5.2.4 OPERATING SYSTEM

5.2.4.1 General Attributes

Intermediary devices except pure physical layer devices (e.g., hub) have an operating system that centrally controls devices' functions. The operating system allows a person to access it through the *command line interface* (CLI) and/or *graphical user interface* (GUI). As an example, Cisco's proprietary operating system is called the *Internetwork Operating System* (IOS), and the company uses IOS for both switches and routers.

The operating system has features to support specialized networking functions. Through CLI or GUI, one can change the system setting of a device. This includes the manual addition of switch/routing table entries, management of interfaces/ports (e.g., assign IPs, activate/deactivate ports), and configuration of device and port security (e.g., password protection). Because of its functional specialization, the operating system is relatively small in size. For example, Cisco's IOS is smaller than 100 megabytes, while Microsoft Windows 10 is almost 6 gigabytes.

With the compact size, the operating system of an intermediary device can be stored in the non-volatile *flash memory* that affords much faster access in reading files and also does not lose its content even if the device is turned off. When a switch or router is powered on, the operating system in the flash memory is copied into its *random access memory* (RAM) during the boot-up process.

5.2.4.2 Access to Operating System

To configure parameters of an intermediary device, its operating system needs to be accessed through the CLI or GUI. For instance, router manufacturers Cisco and Juniper Networks have their GUI tools called *Security Device Manager* and *J-Web* respectively. The GUI is more user-friendly as interactions with the operating system are primarily through a web browser, and thus it allows quick and intuitive configurations, monitoring, and troubleshooting of an intermediary device. The CLI is, however, preferred by many IT professionals in managing enterprise-class devices because of its flexibility. The operating system can be accessed through a console port or a LAN/WAN port (see Table 5.2 and Figure 5.3).

TABLE 5.2

Accessing the OS of an intermediary device

Port	Method of access
Console port	■ A host station directly connects to the console port using a console cable. The console port is dedicated for device management. ■ With no IP configuration initially, the intermediary device is not accessible through the network. At this point, the direct cabling from a host station to the console port is the only way to access its OS. ■ The host workstation uses a terminal program (e.g., HyperTerminal program for Windows) to access the OS. ■ Once in the OS, an IP address can be assigned to the intermediary device. No device is network enabled without an IP address. ■ Also, a login name and password should be set up so that only authorized people can access the OS.
LAN or WAN port	■ Once an intermediary device is configured with an IP address through the console port, the device is networking ready. ■ Then, such remote access program as Telnet, SSH (Secure Shell), or web browser can be used to access the device's OS over the network to change its configuration. Telnet uses plain text and is vulnerable to eavesdropping. SSH is the telnet's secure version that encrypts all communications. ■ In this mode, a host station can access the device's OS through its regular LAN or WAN port (not the console port) by signing in with the pre-configured login and password.

Note: Although a layer 2 device, the switch can be given an IP address for its remote access over the network. The IP address configured is, therefore, purely for device management and it has nothing to do with the switching function of layer 2 frames.

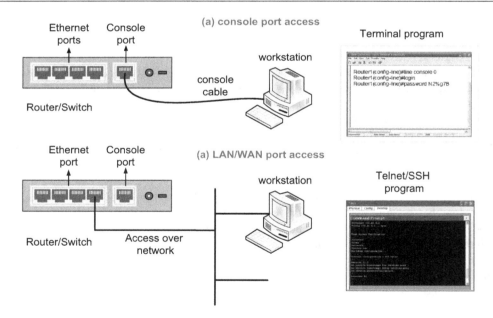

FIGURE 5.3   Operating system access through CLI

5.2.4.3   Example: Cisco's IOS and Access Protection

Cisco's router/switch uses the following commands to set up a password to protect it from unauthorized OS access (see Figure 5.4).

- *line console 0*: To set up an access privilege of the console port.
- *login*: Access to the OS requires login.
- *password N2%g7B*: The access password is *N2%g7B*.

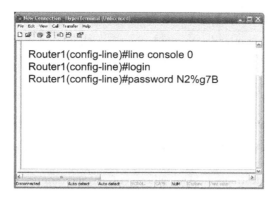

FIGURE 5.4   Protecting OS of an intermediary device

5.3   HUB (MULTI-PORT REPEATER)

5.3.1   PHYSICAL LAYER DEVICE

The hub is a purely physical layer device that accepts incoming signals that carry frames, regenerates the signal strength and shape, and repeats their propagation through all other connected ports. This device, therefore, does not need an operating system. On receiving a frame, the hub broadcasts it out to all connected ports except the entry port (see Figure 5.5). Then, the end node that has a matching destination MAC address copies the frame into its NIC memory and processes it, while the other hosts drop the frame because of the MAC address mismatch. Because of its mechanical relay function, the hub is also known as a *multiport repeater*.

5.3.2   DRAWBACKS

With the hub, the network becomes more vulnerable to data **collisions** when more than one host accidentally releases frames at the same time. When the hub is deployed, host NICs attached to it activate the *CSMA/CD* (Carrier Sense Multiple Access/Collision Detection) protocol to control network (or media) access and to remedy if collisions occur. As another major drawback, host stations are more exposed to **security risks** when the hub broadcasts their frames as it is relatively easy to eavesdrop. Due to obvious drawbacks, *hubs are rarely used these days* except for certain limited functions (e.g., multi-port extender).

FIGURE 5.5   A multi-port USB hub (Source: www.amazon.com)

5.4   BRIDGE AND WIRELESS ACCESS POINT

The bridge is a layer 2 device intended to divide the network into smaller segments. Network segmentation is to resolve growing pains of a network. Bridges, switches, and routers all can segment a network into more manageable sizes and control the flow of unnecessary traffic from one segment to another.

5.4.1   BRIDGE TABLE AND FRAME FILTERING

The bridge examines the MAC address of every frame arriving at its port and either passes or filters it by referring to its *bridge table* (see Figure 5.6). The bridging process is highly intuitive; that is, in the unicast mode, if the destination MAC address of an incoming frame is in the same network segment, then the frame is filtered (blocked). In Figure 5.6, for instance, if PC1 sends a frame to PC2 of the same network segment, the bridge also gets the frame as it is broadcasted by the hub. On receiving the frame, the bridge reads its bridge table and decides that the destination MAC address of PC2 connects to the same port Fa0/0 (belonging to the same segment) and thus filters the frame.

Such frame filtering has the effect of improving network response time by limiting unnecessary traffic flows. If a frame is broadcasted (instead of being unicasted) by the source host, the bridge relays the frame through all ports rather than blocking it. As a result, although the bridge does a good job of isolating unicast traffic, it is unable to contain the flow of host broadcasting to other segments. *The traditional bridge shown in Figure 5.6 is little used these days, as hubs are no longer used in a corporate environment and as switches dominate today's LANs.*

5.4.2   TRANSPARENT VS. TRANSLATIONAL BRIDGES

Bridges are either *transparent* or *non-transparent*. *Transparent bridges* interconnect network segments running the same LAN standard (e.g., Ethernet). The one in Figure 5.6 is an example of the transparent bridge. Being transparent means that the bridge simply relays frames as they are. When network segments running on different standards are bridged, the *non-transparent bridge* is used. It is also called the *translational bridge* as it performs frame conversion.

The *wireless access point* or *hotspot* is a translational bridge. In the corporate environment, access points provide connectivity between the Ethernet (wired segment) and Wi-Fi (wireless segment)

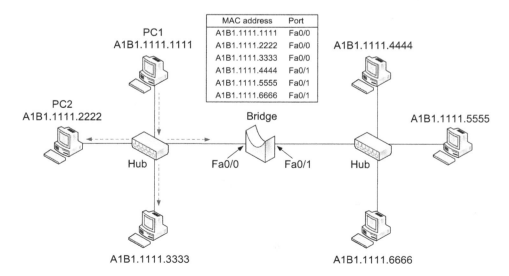

MAC address	Port
A1B1.1111.1111	Fa0/0
A1B1.1111.2222	Fa0/0
A1B1.1111.3333	Fa0/0
A1B1.1111.4444	Fa0/1
A1B1.1111.5555	Fa0/1
A1B1.1111.6666	Fa0/1

FIGURE 5.6   An example of bridge table

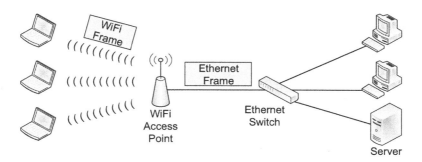

FIGURE 5.7   Wi-Fi access point as translational bridge

LANs (see Figure 5.7). Ethernet and Wi-Fi have their own frame structures with different information fields and, thus, the access point conducts frame conversion to bridge two different LANs. More details of the access point are explained in Chapter 6.

5.5 SWITCH

5.5.1 GENERAL FEATURES

The switch is one of the most popular intermediary devices used to form data links between host stations for 'intra-networking'. Although there are LAN and WAN switches, the focus here is the Ethernet switch that dominates wired LANs these days. The Ethernet LAN switch comes with a number of RJ-45 ports for twisted pair connectivity and, depending on the product model, has additional high-speed ports for fiber links. Each port comes with a permanent MAC address. The switch in Figure 5.8 has 24 RJ-45 ports, each supporting 10/100/1000 Mbps auto-sensing (adjusting to the host's NIC speed) and full-duplex transmission capacity.

5.5.2 ONE INPUT PORT-TO-ONE OUTPUT PORT

The switch forwards an incoming frame only to the port that directly or indirectly (via other switches) leads to its destination host. This one-to-one correspondence between input and output ports curtails network congestion considerably and eliminates frame collisions within a subnetwork. If two frames are heading to the same host concurrently, the switch places one frame in the waiting queue until the delivery of the other frame is completed. A switch can have a queue assigned to each port or alternatively have a common queue shared by all ports.

With *one input port-to-one output port* connectivity, the switch allows simultaneous formation of multiple data links with each link transmitting frames in the *full-duplex* mode between two host stations. For the full-duplex connectivity, a switch port keeps two separate circuits for two-way traffic. Also, neighboring switches can auto-negotiate to decide the link speed and duplex mode (either full-duplex or half-duplex). Although it relies on unicasting in the regular mode, the switch does broadcasting and multicasting as needed.

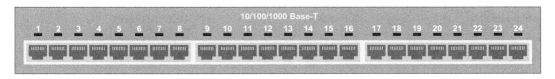

FIGURE 5.8   Ethernet switch – external view (not an actual product)

5.5.3 MEASURES OF SWITCH CAPACITY

There are several terms commonly used to indicate switch capacity.
a. *Port density*: The number of ports available on a switch (e.g., 24 ports)
b. *Wire speed*: The maximum data rate (speed) of a switch port (e.g., 100 Mbps, 1 Gbps)
c. *Forwarding rate*: The combined data rate of all switch ports. For instance, a switch with ten 100 Mbps ports has the forwarding rate of 1000 Mbps.
d. *Aggregate throughput*: This is an actual data rate that can be pushed through a switch at any moment. A majority of LAN switches have an aggregative throughput that is considerably lower than its corresponding forwarding rate because of their internal architecture. For instance, a switch with a forwarding rate of 1000 Mbps may have an aggregate throughput of 600 Mbps only.
e. *Non-blocking vs. blocking:* When the aggregate throughput of a switch can match its forwarding rate, the switch is called 'non-blocking' because all ports can concurrently achieve their highest transmission speeds without being constrained by the internal architecture. In reality, most switches are *blocking*. For example, a switch with forwarding rate of 1000 Mbps and aggregate throughput of 600 Mbps has 60% (600/1000) non-blocking capacity.

5.5.4 SWITCH PORT

5.5.4.1 Port Naming

The switched Ethernet is physically wired in a star topology where the switch is used as a central concentrator to which host stations are attached. The switch port is a part of the electronic circuit board, *LAN card*, which is similar to the host station's NIC. Each port comes with an identifying name, a MAC address, and wire speed. There is no universal convention of port naming, and vendors have their own way of doing it.

As an example, Table 5.3 shows one naming approach for a switch with 24 Fast Ethernet ports and 2 Gigabit Ethernet ports. Here, 0/3 means that 0 is a bay number and 3 is a port number recognized by its operating system. As can be seen, each switch port is given a unique data link layer MAC address. The switch's operating system understands both full and abbreviated port names in Table 5.3 and thus can be used interchangeably for configuration.

TABLE 5.3
Switch port naming (a hypothetical example)

Port full name	Abbreviation	MAC address
FastEthernet0/1	Fa0/1	0005.B119.6A01
FastEthernet0/2	Fa0/2	0005.B119.6A02
----	----	-----
----	----	-----
FastEthernet0/23	Fa0/23	0005.B119.6A03
FastEthernet0/24	Fa0/24	0005.B119.6A04
GigabitEthernet1/1	Gi1/1	0005.B119.7C03
GigabitEthernet1/2	Gi1/2	0005.B119.7C04

5.5.4.2   Port Speed

Switch ports come in several speeds including Ethernet (10Mbps), Fast Ethernet (100 Mbps), and Gigabit Ethernet (1000 Mbps). Some switches have ports that support only a single speed, while others come with mixed port speeds (e.g., 100 Mbps Fast Ethernet + 1 Gbps Gigabit Ethernet).

Many switches come with ports that can dynamically adjust their transmission speeds (e.g., 10/100/1000 Mbps) matching those of connecting hosts. For the matching, the host's Ethernet NIC and the switch port negotiate the highest speed that both parties can support by exchanging a set of bits (not an ordinary frame) in advance. This auto-negotiation process is defined by an IEEE standard. As stated, some switches support only twisted pair connectivity and others support more than one cabling option (e.g., twisted pair and optical fiber).

5.5.5   SWITCH TABLE

5.5.5.1   Switch Table Entries

The switch forwards incoming frames referring to entries in its *switch table*. The switch table stores MAC addresses of directly and indirectly connected *hosts* (shown as MAC addresses) and their *exit ports* (see Table 5.4). Besides, the switch table maintains additional information of the *address type* and *Virtual LAN* (VLAN). The address type field indicates whether an entry is *static* (i.e., manually entered) or *dynamic* (i.e., automatically obtained through its own learning process).

Using the static entry method, a network administrator can maintain more control (e.g., security) by deciding which hosts can be attached to the network. Static entries stay in the switch table until they are manually removed. Despite the advantages, the manual addition/removal is a time-consuming process and poses difficulties in network management, especially when the network gets bigger. On the contrary, the automatic creation of entries through the switch's dynamic self-learning lacks the benefits of better control and security but becomes more accurate (i.e., no human errors) and cost effective (e.g., less human intervention).

As for the VLAN field, all switch table entries belong to what they call *default VLAN* (with VLAN ID = 1), initially. The VLAN concept is extremely important and explained in Chapter 7. Among the fields, the MAC address and exit port columns are fundamental in understanding the concept of frame switching.

5.5.5.2   Switch Learning

As stated, entries can be dynamically added to the table through *switch learning*. Here is how it works using the hypothetical network in Figure 5.9.

   a. When an Ethernet frame (let's say, source: A1B1.1111.1111 and destination: A1B1.1111.2222) arrives at the port, Fa0/2, SW1 searches its switch table to find an entry that matches A1B1.1111.2222.
   b. If the entry is found, then SW1 releases the frame through the entry's exit port.
   c. If the entry is not found, then SW1 broadcasts the frame to all ports except the source port, Fa0/2.

TABLE 5.4
Demonstration of a switch table

Destination MAC address	Exit port	Address type	VLAN
0002.584B.16E0	FastEthernet0/1	Static	1
00B0.D0F3.47AC	FastEthernet0/2	Static	1
00C1.4AC7.23D2	FastEthernet0/3	Dynamic	1
00B0.D045.963A	FastEthernet0/3	Dynamic	1

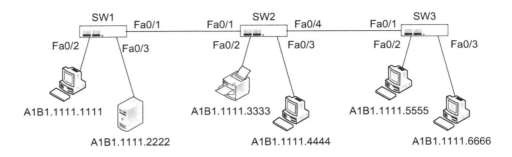

FIGURE 5.9 Switch learning

d. In doing step (c), SW1 learns that the source MAC address, A1B1.1111.1111, is either *directly* or *indirectly* connected to its Fa0/2, and updates the pairing information (A1B1.1111.1111 and Fa0/10) to its switch table.

e. This learning and updating of table entries continues until the table is complete with all host information.

In many subnetworks, several switches are interlinked. In this situation, the switch table lists only host *MAC address* and *exit port* pairs. As a result, depending on network topology, one exit port can be paired with one or more host MAC addresses. As an example of the *one port-to-one MAC address* pairing, SW1's switch table links its Fa0/2 with A1B1.1111.1111.

As for the *one port-to-multiple MAC addresses* pairing, SW1's Fa0/1 is ultimately connected to four different hosts (i.e., A1B1.1111.3333, A1B1.1111.4444, A1B1.1111.5555, and A1B1.1111.6666). Observe that SW1's switch table does not contain any information of SW2 and SW3, though. This is because SW1 is concerned only about the hosts (end nodes) ultimately connected through SW2 and SW3.

5.5.5.3 Aging of Switch Table Entries

The entries *dynamically* added to a switch table have aging time (e.g., 300 seconds) that they can stay in the table without being referenced. When the aging time of an entry expires, the switch considers that the end node's MAC address is inactive and removes the record from the switch table.

Aging time can be manually specified on a switch. In configuring aging time, if it is set too short, this will result in premature removal of MAC addresses (including legitimate ones) from the switch table. This premature dropping can result in more broadcasting of frames by the switch, negatively affecting network performance.

With longer aging time, on the other hand, the switch table can retain more inactive MAC entries (e.g., turned-off computers) and this can adversely affect the learning and updating process of the switch table. As stated, the static entry remains in the switch table permanently unless manually dropped and is therefore not affected by aging.

5.5.6   Switch Types

5.5.6.1   Non-Managed vs. Managed Switches

Switches are either non-managed or managed. The non-managed switch is a relatively simple and inexpensive device that does not allow any modification of its configuration and is literally put into production as it is. It therefore has only limited features, such as the auto-negotiation of data transfer speed and transmission mode (e.g., half-duplex vs. full-duplex).

In contrast, the managed switch allows the manual configuration of switch functions by interfacing with its operating system. Among available functions are the login and password setup to control device accessibility, configuration of port security, activation of built-in supervisory protocols, creation of virtual LANs, and management of other functions (e.g., backup of system files). Deploying the managed switch on a LAN, therefore, requires knowledge for its initial setup and continuous management.

As stated, switches are layer 2 devices that use only MAC addresses to make forwarding decisions of frames. However, the managed switch is generally assigned an IP address so that it can be remotely accessed through the web browser, telnet (remote access utility), and/or SSH (telnet's secure version) (see Table 5.2 and Figure 5.3). When a switch is given an IP address, thus, it has nothing to do with the switch's frame forwarding function, which relies only on the destination MAC address. Recall that the switch is a layer 2 device.

5.5.6.2   Store-and-Forward vs. Cut-Through Switches

In terms of frame forwarding, a switch uses either the *store-and-forward switching* or *cut-through switching* method.

Store-and-Forward Switching: When a frame begins to arrive at a port, the switch waits until the entire frame becomes available for forwarding (or switching). During the waiting, the frame is temporarily stored in a queue. Once the entire frame becomes available, it conducts such routines as error detection using the frame's *frame check sequence* (FCS) and the validation of frame length. If a transmission error is found, the frame is dropped. Otherwise, the switch forwards the frame according to switch table information.

Cut-Through Switching: When a frame begins to arrive at a port, the switch does not wait until the entire frame becomes available. Instead, the switch begins forwarding as soon as information (e.g., destination MAC address) necessary for the switching decision becomes available. This approach reduces latency (or delay) in its delivery; however, the switch is unable to perform such routine functions as the detection of transmission errors and frame length validation. In this mode, therefore, defective frames could be relayed to destination hosts where their NICs conduct their error detection. When a faulty frame is dropped by the destination node, the sender's TCP learns the frame error as there is no acknowledgement and thus retransmits it.

Some switches are designed to change between the two alternative modes in which they use cut-through switching when the transmission error rate remains below a threshold level, but shift to the store-and-forward mode otherwise.

5.5.6.3   Symmetric vs. Asymmetric Switches

The speeds of switch ports can be either symmetric or asymmetric. With symmetric switching, all ports use the same speed such as 100 Mbps. When traffic is more evenly distributed throughout a network, symmetric switching makes sense. For instance, a small network may be running on the peer-to-peer relationship in which the host computer acts as a client and a server simultaneously. With no dedicated servers, traffic flows are not concentrated on particular hosts. Peer-to-peer computing, though, is not a popular choice in enterprise computing these days.

In asymmetric switching, switch ports take advantage of different transmission speeds. For example, a switch can have a combination of 100 Mbps Fast Ethernet and 1 Gbps Gigabit Ethernet ports, or it can have 10/100/1000 Mbps auto-sensing ports. Asymmetric switching is necessary when network traffic is centered on one or more ports.

For instance, in the client-server computing environment, client nodes access resources available from dedicated servers such as email, web, database, and collaboration servers. Naturally, much network traffic is directed at servers, and the switch ports that link servers should be able to relay data at a faster rate than those connecting clients. Otherwise, the server links can become bottlenecks that negatively affect overall network performance. Most enterprise-class switches use asymmetric switching because of their flexibility in handling concentrated traffic (see Figure 5.10).

Besides using the asymmetric switch, the *link aggregation* is another solution to augment network throughputs. The link aggregation (also known as *bonding* or *trunking*) enables the bundling of two or more physical links between switches or between a switch and a host (primarily server) (see Figure 5.11). More explanations are provided in Chapter 7.

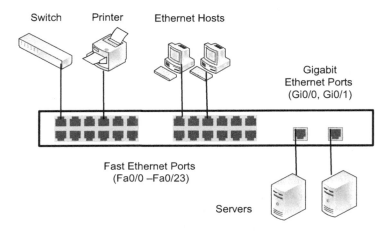

FIGURE 5.10   Demonstration of an asymmetric switch

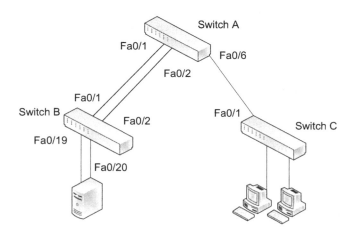

FIGURE 5.11   A switched network with link aggregations

5.5.6.4 Layer 2 vs. Layer 3 Switches

Traditional switches operate in layer 2 (data link layer), performing frame forwarding based only on MAC addresses. The layer 3 switch (or multi-layer switch) behaves differently from its layer 2 counterpart. Its port (or interface) can be flexibly configured either as a switch port (with only a MAC address associated) or as a router port (with a MAC and an IP address paired). With an IP address activated on a port, the layer 3 switch basically acts just like a router. For instance, multiple subnetworks can be joined by the layer 3 switch for inter-networking.

As another unique feature, the layer 3 functions are implemented in hardware and thus the switch processes packets faster than the traditional router whose layer 3 functions are software-based. Hardware-based processing is simply quicker than that based on software and this explains the popularity of layer 3 switches for internetworking within an enterprise or campus.

The layer 3 switch, however, is not designed to substitute the router because it is optimized for the enterprise network and thus lacks certain router functions. Most notably, its support for WAN connections and advanced routing protocols is considerably weaker than the regular router. For example, you can observe that there is no WAN serial port in Figure 5.12. Layer 3 switches are widely used in place of pure routers within the boundary of an enterprise or campus network. Bear in mind that, unless the term *layer 3 switch* is used, a switch is a layer 2 device.

5.5.6.5 Fixed, Stackable, and Modular Switches

There are several switch types in terms of their structural design:

a. With the *fixed port switch*, what you see is what you get because ports cannot be added or changed.
b. With the *stackable switch*, multiple switches can be stacked on top of the other and they, as a whole, function as one oversized switch with many ports. The stacked switches are conjoined by high-speed cables in a daisy chain fashion.
c. The *modular switch* comes with one or more slots that can accept a line card (or module) with multiple ports. Figure 5.13 demonstrates a switch with several modules, each with multiple ports.

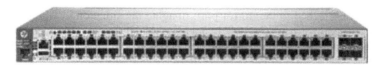

FIGURE 5.12 Ethernet layer 3 switch (Source: www.amazon.com)

FIGURE 5.13 A modular switch and multi-port switch card

5.5.6.6   Power over Ethernet (PoE)

Many switches offer *power over Ethernet* (PoE) capability. With its technology details standardized by IEEE 802.3, PoE enables a switch to use Ethernet LAN cables not only to transmit data but also to supply electric power to connecting nodes such as wireless access points (APs), VoIP phones, and web cameras (see Figure 5.14). Using PoE-enabled switches, the planning and deployment of network nodes becomes more flexible without being constrained by accessibility to power sources. The PoE-enabled switches are costlier than the ones with no PoE capability.

5.5.7   Security Issues

5.5.7.1   Safeguarding Switch Ports

It is essential that only qualified computers are allowed to join intermediary devices to secure a network. Given the dominance of Ethernet switches for wired LANs, allowing uncontrolled access to switch ports by any computer can pose a grave security threat to an enterprise. To neutralize such risks, IT staff should use managed switches to block unauthorized access to the network.

a. Above all, there are fundamental steps to protect the switch through such measures as the authentication and access control, and the use of secure remote access protocols (e.g., SSH).
b. The switch can be instructed to allow only one or two legitimate MAC addresses on a particular port and automatically shut down the port if an unauthorized computer attempts to join. This will prevent a network from such risks as *footprinting* and *reconnaissance*, stealth access to other computers, and direct attacks such as *MAC address flooding* (more details in Chapter 8) by an intruder.
c. It is a good practice to manually shut down all unused ports of a switch. This can be done by issuing simple commands. For example, the port Fa0/1 of a Cisco switch is manually turned off by issuing '*interface fa0/1*' and '*shut*' consecutively at the command prompt. Such a switch setup to safeguard a network from potential hostile threats is only possible with managed switches.

5.5.7.2   Port Mirroring

Managed switches come with a *mirror port* for network management. Frames going through some or all regular ports of a switch can be copied to its mirror port so that network traffic can be monitored by the computer attached to the mirror port. Imagine the situation in which an attacker finds a way to connect to the mirror port of a switch and observes all frames (and inside packets) passing by. It highlights the importance of securing physical access to switches and switch ports.

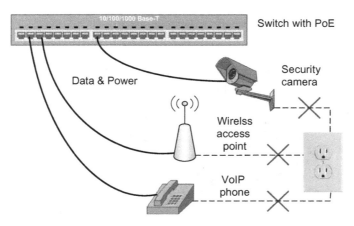

FIGURE 5.14   Power over Ethernet

5.6 ROUTERS

5.6.1 TWO PRIMARY FUNCTIONS

5.6.1.1 Routing Table Development and Update

The router develops and maintains a routing table as the reference table for packet forwarding decisions. Just as with the switch table, entries of the routing table can be manually added and also automatically created by the router based on the information obtained from other routers. For automatic updates of routing table entries, a router periodically shares its own status information with other routers using a protocol such as *Open Shortest Path First* or OSPF.

An example of the routing table is shown in Table 5.5. Using a simplified structure, it shows only three columns of the *destination subnet, subnet mask*, and *router's exit port* that are essential for the routing decision of arriving packets and their subsequent forwarding through an exit port. Basically, each entry of the routing table tells which exit port is used by the router to send a packet to a particular subnet address. For example, if an arriving packet has a destination address that matches the subnet, 192.168.30.0/16, then the router will release the packet through its FastEthernet0/2 port. More details of the routing table in its complete structure and the mechanism of packet routing decisions are explained in Chapter 11.

5.6.1.2 Packet Forwarding

The ultimate task of a router is IP packet routing (or forwarding). On receiving an IP packet, the router examines its routing table entries to determine the optimal delivery path and forwards the packet to the *next hop* (see Section 3.7.2) that ultimately leads to the destination. Routers interconnect subnetworks when each subnetwork uses a particular LAN (e.g., Ethernet, Wi-Fi) or WAN (e.g., PPP) standard (revisit Section 1.6). Depending on the size, each subnetwork may include multiple layer 2 switches with a number of hosts (end nodes) attached. The subnetwork separated from other subnetworks by a router becomes a *broadcast domain*, a boundary of packet broadcasting. That is, the router does not relay broadcasted IP packets unless specifically configured (see Section 4.6.2).

5.6.2 ROUTER PORTS

Physically, the router is a computer specialized in IP packet forwarding across subnetworks. Figure 5.15 demonstrates a router with Fast Ethernet LAN ports and serial WAN ports. Similar to the Ethernet switch port, the router's LAN ports generally require the RJ-45 connector for cabling. Although not included in the figure, a router can have high-speed LAN ports for optical fibers. Several standards are available for WAN serial ports and Figure 5.15 demonstrates two of them. Many routers marketed for home and small business networks also use the RJ-45 port (instead of serial ports) for Internet access through the ISP router.

TABLE 5.5
Routing table entries (a simplified structural view)

Destination subnet/subnet mask	Exit port (interface)
192.168.10.0/24	FastEthernet0/0
192.168.20.0/24	FastEthernet0/1
192.168.30.0/16	FastEthernet0/2
...	....

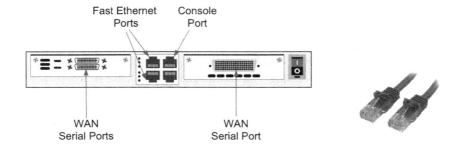

Fast Ethernet   Console
Ports   Port

WAN   WAN
Serial Ports   Serial Port

FIGURE 5.15   Router ports (left) and RJ-45 LAN connector (right) (not an actual product)

5.6.3   ROUTER PORT NAMING

Many routers are modular in which, besides the built-in LAN and WAN ports, additional modules can be installed in the expansion slot(s). The modules are LAN or WAN interface cards, each with one or more attached ports. Each router port connects to a subnetwork and thus no two ports of a router should be on the same subnetwork. There is no universal convention in naming router ports (interfaces), and vendors have their own way of port naming.

5.6.3.1   Example: Cisco Router's Port Naming

Just as with Cisco switches, Cisco routers use the naming approach of '*media_type slot#/port#*' in which Ethernet LAN and serial WAN are representative media types. Assuming that a router comes with built-in (fixed) ports and additional expansion slots, the built-in ports are in slot 0 (rather than 1). The LAN or WAN card installed in an expansion slot has one or more ports and a particular port of a slot is identified with a '*slot#/port#*' combination (see Figure 5.16).

For instance, the first port of slot 0 becomes Serial0/0 or FastEthernet0/0, and the second port of slot 0 is Serial0/1 or FastEthernet0/1. As another example, FastEthernet1/0 and FastEthernet1/1 reflect the first and second Fast Ethernet ports in slot 1. Depending on the router model, the port naming is further extended to represent a combination of '*slot#/subslot#/port#*' (e.g., Serial0/0/0). The Cisco operating system, IOS, recognizes the pre-assigned port names and numbers.

5.6.4   ROUTER PORT ADDRESSING

The router's LAN port such as FastEthernet0/1 or GigabitEthernet1/1 should be configured with a pair of MAC and IP addresses for it to be operational. It is because the LAN is a *point-to-multipoint* environment in which a computer's message can have multiple destinations within a subnetwork, making it necessary to use unique MAC addresses for intra-networking.

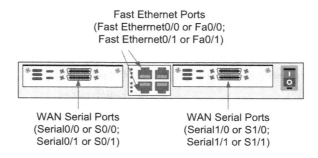

Fast Ethernet Ports
(Fast Etherrnet0/0 or Fa0/0;
Fast Ethernet0/1 or Fa0/1)

WAN Serial Ports   WAN Serial Ports
(Serial0/0 or S0/0;   (Serial1/0 or S1/0;
Serial0/1 or S0/1)   Serial1/1 or S1/1)

FIGURE 5.16   Cisco's LAN and WAN port naming (not an actual model)

Meanwhile, the serial WAN port needs to have an IP address but not a unique source MAC address because of the *point-to-point* nature of WAN communications. As a simple example, imagine the Internet WAN link between a residence and an ISP, which has only a single possible destination from a source. For this reason, the pairing between an IP address and a MAC address applies only to the LAN port, but not to the WAN port. The WAN frame also has data link address fields, but they are literally space fillers, containing values (e.g., all ones) of little meaning.

The router port may be in the 'up' or 'down' state, and the former is an indication that the port is ready for packet exchanges. For a LAN/WAN port to be in the 'up' state, it should be given a unique IP address and then be activated. Besides, the router connects to a WAN link through the external device called CSU/DSU unless the CSU/DSU function is built into the router. In the WAN link, the CSU/DSU converts digital signals from a router to another digital signal format required by the particular link (e.g., T-1 line) in the physical layer.

5.6.5   ROUTER CONFIGURATION

Besides IP packet routing (i.e., inter-networking across multiple subnetworks), the router supports a variety of other functions for adequate network management and protection. They are conveniently divided into basic and advanced features.

5.6.5.1   Basic Configuration Features

Basic features available from a router include:

a. Labeling the router (e.g., R1)
b. Setting up a password for user authentication and access control of the router
c. Setting up the remote access to the router for its administration
d. Configuring an IP for each of the router's LAN/WAN ports/interfaces and their activation
e. Manual addition of static routing paths to the routing table
f. Enabling the dynamic construction and update of the routing table entries

5.6.5.2   Advanced Configuration Features

Depending on the product, a router also supports other advanced functions primarily designed to enhance the security of the computer network. Among them are:

a. An *access control list* to control inbound and outbound traffic flows by filtering IP packets based on such information as IP addresses and TCP/UDP ports (more in Chapter 9)
b. *Network address translation* (NAT) that performs conversion between internally used *private* IP addresses and externally shown *public* IP addresses to shield internal hosts from public views (more in Chapter 4)
c. Provision of *dynamic (or temporary) IP addresses* to requesting stations through the DHCP server function (more in Chapter 4)
d. A *virtual private network* (VPN) to support secure WAN connections between two remote locations over the Internet (more in Chapter 10)
e. *Anti-virus*, *firewall*, and/or *intrusion detection* to protect a network from various threat vectors (more in Chapter 9)
f. *Security auditing* that examines current router setup, detects potential threats to the router and associated networks, and recommends configuration changes to neutralize related risks.

5.7   SWITCHING VS. ROUTING

In this section, differences between *switching* (by switches) and *routing* (by routers) are revisited in more detail. Again, relating switching to intra-networking and routing to inter-networking makes their conceptual and technical differences easier to comprehend. Both switching and routing are intended to move application data (i.e., APDUs) from the source to the destination, more likely through multiple intermediary devices and trunk links.

The fundamental reason for conducting switching and routing is that creating a full mesh network that directly interconnects all host nodes is neither practical nor feasible. With that said, the key differences between switching and routing are recapped in terms of:

a. Data link layer vs. internet layer operations
b. Connection-oriented vs. connection-less data transmissions
c. Single delivery path vs. multiple delivery paths

5.7.1 DATA LINK LAYER VS. INTERNET LAYER

As explained, while the data link layer is responsible for frame *switching* within a single subnetwork (thus intra-networking) based on MAC addresses, the internet layer is responsible for a packet *routing* decision relying on IP addresses to move packets across subnetworks (thus inter-networking) joined by routers. The routing performed in the internet layer is therefore conceptually distinct from the switching of the data link layer. Here, the route can be understood as the *end-to-end delivery path of an IP packet formed through multiple data links*.

5.7.2 CONNECTION-ORIENTED VS. CONNECTION-LESS

With switching within a subnet, the logical delivery path between two end nodes is pre-determined no matter how many intermediary devices are involved to form the path. The switch table entries reflect logical paths between any two host nodes within a subnet. Once decided, the logical switching path between any two hosts does not change unless there is an inordinate development (e.g., switch failure) that makes it difficult to use the same path. Keeping the same delivery path between two hosts makes switching a connection-oriented undertaking.

Meanwhile, the routing path of a packet between two host nodes situated in different networks is not necessarily pre-determined but can be dynamically decided by each router. For the forwarding decision of an arriving packet, the router refers to its routing table that periodically updates the network's changed conditions (e.g., traffic congestion in an area). This makes the packet routing decision a connection-less process (more in Chapter 11).

5.7.3 SINGLE DELIVERY VS. MULTIPLE DELIVERY PATHS

There should be only a single *active* delivery path at a time between any two hosts when it comes to switching. In fact, many organizations maintain the redundancy of physical links between two nodes for intra-networking. Having a partial mesh topology through link redundancy among intermediary devices within a subnetwork is fundamental to improve network availability. However, switches have a built-in routine called *spanning tree protocol* that figures out the path redundancy and erases it, allowing only a single data link to be active between any two nodes at a time.

As for routing, there is no such requirement of a single *active* delivery path at a time between two hosts. That is, it assumes the availability of multiple end-to-end active paths between two hosts for inter-networking. Naturally, it requires a process to determine an optimal delivery route of the packet. For this, the router makes a forwarding decision for each arriving packet by mapping its destination IP address to the routing table. Relatively speaking, the simplicity of switching decisions (because there is only one active delivery path) makes it significantly faster than routing decisions.

5.8   ADDRESS RESOLUTION PROTOCOL (ARP)

5.8.1   BACKGROUND

Transporting application data (i.e., APDUs) across subnetworks requires that switching (based on MAC address information) and routing (based on IP address information) go hand in hand. For this, the host's LAN port should have MAC and IP addresses coupled. This way, the destination IP address becomes a vehicle to forward packets between subnetworks (inter-networking), and the destination MAC address is used to move frames within a subnetwork (intra-networking). However, the binding information between an IP and a MAC is not always available to the network and thus there should a mechanism to provide it. This is the mission of the *Address Resolution Protocol* (ARP).

The ARP request is issued when the MAC address of a node (e.g., a host station, a router port) needs to be obtained based on its IP address. For instance, assume that a source host (192.168.10.1) has to deliver a frame to a target host (192.168.10.2) within a subnetwork (192.168.10.x). In this situation of intra-networking, the *frame* should include the target host's MAC address in the frame header. If the source host finds the target host's IP and corresponding MAC addresses in its own ARP table (or ARP cache), the mapping between them becomes straightforward. If the entry is not in the local ARP table, then an ARP request message is broadcasted by the source node.

5.8.2   ARP TABLE

Figure 5.17a shows the ARP table of a host obtained by issuing the *C:\>arp –a* command. It can be observed that the host computer's ARP table contains only IP addresses and corresponding MAC (or physical) addresses. The router's ARP table (see Figure 5.17b) has one more column that indicates the exit port (interface) of a target MAC address. This additional exit port information is required because, unlike the host station that belongs to only one subnetwork, the router is designed to connect several subnetworks simultaneously.

5.8.3   ARP USAGE SCENARIOS

There are different situations in which ARP is utilized by a source node (a host station or router) to learn the MAC address of a target node.

   a. The source and destination hosts are in the same subnetwork (see Figure 5.18): The source host learns from a packet's destination IP address that the target host is in the same subnetwork.

```
Command Prompt                               —    □    ×

Interface: 169.254.70.11 --- 0x12
  Internet Address        Physical Address        Type
  169.254.255.255         ff-ff-ff-ff-ff-ff       static
  224.0.0.2               01-00-5e-00-00-02       static
  224.0.0.22              01-00-5e-00-00-16       static
  224.0.0.251             01-00-5e-00-00-fb       static
  224.0.0.252             01-00-5e-00-00-fc       static
  239.255.255.250         01-00-5e-7f-ff-fa       static
  255.255.255.255         ff-ff-ff-ff-ff-ff       static
```

(a)

Internet address	Physical address	Interface(port)
172.16.10.1	00-23-4C-6A-64-29	FastEthernet0/0
172.16.5.1	00-23-4C-6D-7B-EF	FastEthernet0/1
172.16.7.1	00-23-4C-2C-8A-DE	FastEthernet0/2

(b)

FIGURE 5.17   Sample host (a) and router (b) ARP tables

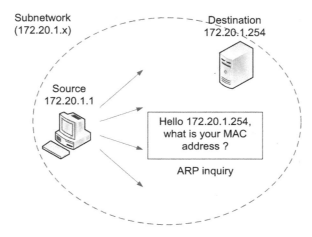

FIGURE 5.18 Scenario 1: Host-to-host ARP inquiry

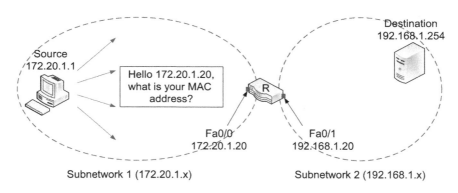

FIGURE 5.19 Scenario 2: Host-to-router ARP inquiry

An ARP inquiry is broadcasted by the source when it does not know the target's MAC address, and the source uses the returned MAC address to create a layer 2 frame.

b. The source and destination hosts are in two different subnetworks joined by a router (see Figure 5.19): The source host learns from a packet's destination IP address that the target host is not in the same subnetwork and the packet is directed to the router R for forwarding. The source broadcasts an ARP inquiry to learn the MAC address of the router's LAN port, Fa0/0, and uses the returned MAC address to create a layer 2 frame.

c. A router forwards a packet to another router when the source and destination hosts are not in neighboring subnetworks (see Figure 5.20): R1 learns from a packet's destination IP address that the target host is not in the same subnetwork and the packet has to be directed to R2 for further routing. R1 broadcasts an ARP request to obtain the MAC address of R2's Fa0/0 and uses the returned MAC address to create a layer 2 frame.

d. A router sends a packet to its destination host when they are in the same subnetwork (see Figure 5.21): Router R learns from a packet's destination IP address that the target host is in the same subnetwork as its port Fa0/1. Router R broadcasts an ARP request to obtain the MAC address of the destination host and uses the returned MAC address to create a layer 2 frame for delivery.

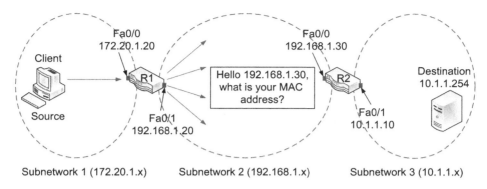

FIGURE 5.20 Scenario 3: Router-to-router ARP inquiry

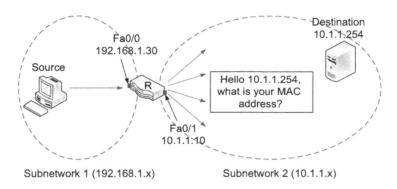

FIGURE 5.21 Scenario 4: Router-to-host ARP inquiry

5.9 COLLISION VS. BROADCAST DOMAINS

The concepts of collision domain and broadcast domain are explained in this section. Understanding their definitions and differences is important because they have implications on the choice of intermediary devices and architecting an adequately performing enterprise network.

5.9.1 COLLISION DOMAIN

5.9.1.1 Definition

The *collision domain* represents a network segment within which only a single node is allowed to transmit data at a time because multiple outstanding frames from different sources result in collisions. The collision occurs because all hosts within a collision domain share the hardwired or wireless medium.

Within a subnetwork, the switch performs the role of dividing collision domains. In other words, the switch is able to contain frame collisions to a collision domain and prevent them from triggering collisions in other collision domains. The switch uses *buffering* to prevent collisions. As an example of buffering, when the three PCs (PC1, PC2, and PC3) concurrently release frames destined to the printer in Figure 5.22, the switch allows the flow of a frame from a PC while buffering the other two PCs' frames in its memory to avoid collisions.

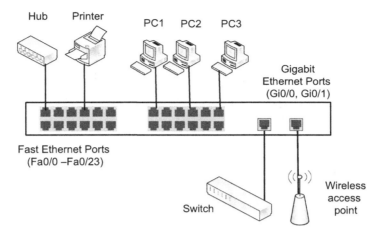

FIGURE 5.22   Switch as a collision domain divider

5.9.1.2   Collision Domain Types

Figure 5.23 demonstrates that a switch can create multiple collision domains of different types.

- **Collision Domain 1** is formed by the direct connection between an end node (e.g., printer) and a switch port. It is a simple but prevalent collision domain type. In this domain, only one bitstream (e.g., between PC1 and Printer1) is allowed to flow at a time and those from other sources (e.g., from LT1 to Printer1) are buffered by the switch to avoid collisions.
- **Collision Domains 2 and 3** are formed by the direct link between two switch ports or between a switch port and a router port. As is the case with Collision Domain 1, only one bitstream is allowed to flow through the link at a time, and those from other sources (e.g., from LT1 to Server1) are buffered to avoid collisions.
- **Collision Domain 4** is formed by the Wi-Fi access point (AP), its associated hosts, and its connection link to a switch port. Hosts can access the network through wireless connections. The AP allows only a single host to transmit data at a time regardless of how many host stations are within the domain. This is because wireless communications result in broadcasting

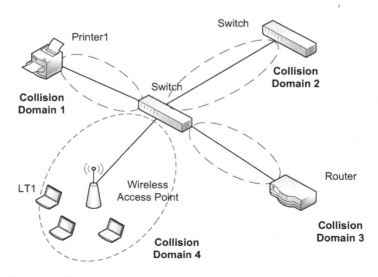

FIGURE 5.23   Types of collision domain

and concurrent signal propagations by more than one host result in frame collisions. To prevent collisions, Wi-Fi devices rely on the media access control protocol called CSMA/CA (more in Chapter 6). Note that new Wi-Fi standards (e.g., Wi-Fi 5, Wi-Fi 6) are making things a little more complicated to improve network performance.

5.9.2   BROADCAST DOMAIN

The broadcast domain represents the scope that a network node's broadcasted messages can reach and is created by the router. Hubs, bridges, access points, and switches relay broadcasted frames to all nodes attached. That is, whenever a device of the types is added to an existing network, the broadcast domain's scope grows. The layer 1 devices (e.g., repeaters, hubs) do not even know that broadcasting is in progress because it mechanically relays frames to all connected ports. Layer 2 devices (e.g., switches, access points) can tell broadcasting as they understand the meaning of a frame carrying all 1s (48 bits) as the destination MAC address. Unlike layer 1 and layer 2 devices, routers do not relay broadcasted messages and thus each *router port* becomes the boundary of a broadcast domain (see Figure 5.24). In other words, the subnetwork itself becomes a broadcast domain.

There is, however, an exception of the definition. As stated, the layer 2 switch does not create broadcast domains in its default mode. However, by configuring so-called *virtual LANs* (or VLANs) on it, a switch can segment a subnetwork into smaller broadcast domains. That is, when VLANs are defined on a switch, each VLAN itself can become a broadcast domain. This means that, by defining VLANs, several broadcast domains can be formed within Broadcast Domain 1 and also within Broadcast Domain 2 in Figure 5.24. The VLAN is explained in Chapter 7.

5.9.3   COLLISON VS. BROADCAST DOMAINS

When a network node broadcasts a message, the host's NIC that receives the message generally does not have capability to process it and thus forwards it to the computer's CPU (central processing unit) for processing. Remember that the NIC performs only layer 1 (physical layer) and layer 2 (data link

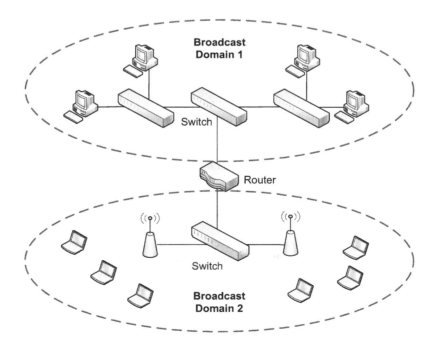

FIGURE 5.24   Two broadcast domains formed by a router

TABLE 5.6

Dividers of collision and broadcast domains

Intermediary devices	Layer	Collision domain divider?	Broadcast domain divider?
Wireless access points	2	No	No
Switches	2	Yes	No (Yes with VLANs)
Routers	3	Yes	Yes

layer) functions (see Chapter 3). Protocols that rely on broadcasting to convey their messages are generally defined above the data link layer, and thus they are beyond the NIC's handling.

For example, DHCP (Dynamic Host Configuration Protocol) and ARP (Address Resolution Protocol) rely on broadcasting. Broadcasting, therefore, not only multiplies the traffic volume but also becomes a processing burden on the host's CPU.

In sum, depending on the choice of intermediary devices, the scope of the collision domain and of the broadcast domain is determined, which has varying implications on network performance. Generally, reducing the size of each collision and broadcast domain improves overall network performance and allows more customized deployment of security protections. Table 5.6 summarizes intermediary devices in their capacity to define the collision and broadcast domains.

CHAPTER SUMMARY

- Intermediary devices relay IP packets and thus generally implement functions below the transport layer. For example, the router is an internet layer device, and the ordinary switch runs in the data link layer, and thus they do not understand the application and transport layer PDUs.
- Like hosts, intermediary devices also conduct encapsulation and de-encapsulation to forward application-layer data (i.e., APDUs).
- Intermediary devices except pure physical layer devices (e.g., hub) have an operating system that centrally controls devices' functions. The operating system allows a person to access it through the *command line interface* (CLI) and/or *graphical user interface* (GUI).
- The hub is a purely physical layer device that accepts incoming signals that carry frames, regenerates the signal strength and shape, and repeats their propagation through all other connected ports. It is rarely used these days in the business network.
- The bridge is a layer 2 device designed to divide a subnetwork into smaller, manageable segments and to control traffic flow between them. The bridge is either a transparent or non-transparent (translational) type.
- The Wi-Fi access point is a non-transparent bridge and is equipped with a WNIC and bridging software to enable packet forwarding between two different LAN standards, mainly between Ethernet and Wi-Fi.
- The switch is used to form data links between host stations for intra-networking. It supports the concurrent formation of multiple data links, each link moving data in the full-duplex mode. The switch table becomes the reference source for switching decisions.
- Switches can be categorized from different angles: non-managed vs. managed; store-and-forward vs. cut-through; symmetric vs. asymmetric; layer 2 vs. layer 3; and structural design (i.e., fixed, stackable, and modular).
- The router conducts routing of IP packets for inter-networking. For this, it generally comes with both LAN and WAN ports. Whereas the LAN port needs a pair of MAC and IP addresses,

the WAN port needs only an IP address. The router may also support advanced functions, especially those necessary to protect corporate networks.

- The differences between *switching* by switches and *routing* by routers can be understood in terms of data link layer (for intra-networking) vs. internet layer (for inter-networking); connection-oriented vs. connection-less; and single delivery path vs. multiple delivery paths.
- Address Resolution Protocol (ARP) is used to obtain the MAC address of a network node based on its IP address. ARP is an important protocol because moving data across sub-networks requires both switching (based on MAC addresses) and routing (based on IP addresses).
- The collision domain is a network segment where only one host is allowed to transmit data at a time to avoid collisions in data transmissions. The switch becomes a divider between collision domains.
- The broadcast domain defines the boundary of data/message broadcasting. The router does not relay broadcasted messages unless its default setting is changed and thus becomes a divider between broadcast domains.

KEY TERMS

access control list (ACL)
address resolution protocol
aggregate throughput
aging time
asymmetric switch
blocking switch
bonding
bridge
bridge table
broadcast domain
collision
collision domain
command line interface (CLI)
connection-less
connection-oriented
console port
CSU/DSU
cut-through switch
denial of service (DOS)
exit port
fixed switch
flash memory
forwarding rate
frame check sequence
graphical user interface (GUI)
hub
hyperterminal
layer 2 switch
layer 3 switch
link aggregation
MAC address flooding

managed switch
media access control
mirror port
modular switch
multiport repeater
multilayer switch (MLS)
network address translation
non-blocking switch
non-managed switch
port density
power over Ethernet (PoE)
random access memory
RJ-45 port and connector
router
secure shell (SSH)
security auditing
stackable switch
store-and-forward switch
switch learning
switch table
switch
symmetric switch
telnet
translational bridge
transparent bridge
trunking
virtual LAN (VLAN)
virtual private network
WAN interface card (WIC)
wire speed

CHAPTER REVIEW QUESTIONS

1. The Wi-Fi access point connects two different LAN standards, generally Ethernet and Wi-Fi. Then, it must be a _____ device.
   A) router
   B) hub
   C) bridge
   D) gateway
   E) switch

2. When a host station's NIC is connected to a hub, the link should use ___ transmission.
   A) half-duplex
   B) full-duplex
   C) partial duplex
   D) simplex
   E) partial simplex

3. Which is correctly pairing an intermediary device with its standard layer?
   A) access point: layer 3 device
   B) switch: layer 3 device
   C) bridge: layer 2 device
   D) router: layer 2 device
   E) repeater: layer 2 device

4. What protocol is used to find the MAC address of a computer based on its IP address?
   A) Hypertext Transfer Protocol (HTTP)
   B) Transmission Control Protocol (TCP)
   C) Address Resolution Protocol (ARP)
   D) Internet Protocol (IP)
   E) CSMA/CD Protocol

5. Which may NOT be an advanced router function?
   A) Access control list for packet filtering
   B) Network address translation between the private and public IP addresses
   C) Provision of dynamic IPs to requesting host stations using DHCP
   D) Firewall and intrusion detection
   E) Automatic configuration of an IP address on the router port/interface

6. Which of these may be an adequate naming of a router's WAN port?
   A) FastEthernet0/0
   B) Console port
   C) Auxiliary port
   D) Serial0/0
   E) Fiber0/1

7. Choose a CORRECT statement about the switch.
   A) The switch cannot be given an IP address.
   B) The switch is also known as a multi-port repeater.
   C) The switch port operates in the full-duplex mode.
   D) The risk of frame collisions gets higher as the number of hosts attached to a switch increases.
   E) CSMA/CD is used to avoid frame collisions when a network is running on switches.

8. Which is NOT a possible scenario in which ARP is used by the source?
   A) Source: PC, Destination: server
   B) Source: PC, Destination: router
   C) Source: router, Destination: router

  D) Source: switch, Destination: router
  E) Source: router, Destination: server
 9. Which statement describes the switch table?
  A) All switch table entries should be manually configured by the network administrator.
  B) The switch broadcasts a frame whose destination address is not in the switch table.
  C) All switch table entries should be constructed through the switch's learning process.
  D) IP addresses and exit ports are among the entry information of the switch table.
  E) The switch drops a frame when its source address is not in the switch table.
10. The following summarize differences between 'switching' and 'routing' EXCEPT:

		Switching	Routing
A)	Layer defined	data link layer	internet layer
B)	Connection-orientation	connection-less	connection-oriented
C)	Networking type	intra-networking	inter-networking
D)	Delivery paths	single path	multiple paths
E)	Name of PDUs	frame	Packet

11. A switch has eight Gbps LAN ports. What is the aggregate throughput necessary to give the switch 100% non-blocking capacity?
  A) 6.4 Gbps
  B) 8.0 Gbps
  C) 8.4 Gbps
  D) 4.0 Gbps
  E) 3.2 Gbps
12. Figure 5.25 must be a partial view of _____.
  A) a host's ARP table
  B) a routing table
  C) a DNS table
  D) a host's routing table
  E) a switch table
13. Which protocol uses broadcasting?
  A) Simple Mail Transfer Protocol (SMTP)
  B) Hypertext Transfer Protocol (HTTP)
  C) Transfer Control Protocol (TCP)
  D) Address Resolution Protocol (ARP)
  E) Internet Control Message Protocol (ICMP)
14. The router uses ARP _____.
  A) to notify its presence when it becomes active
  B) to notify that it will become inactive soon

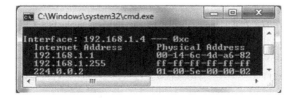

FIGURE 5.25 A sample screenshot

C) every time it forwards an IP packet to a host (e.g., webserver)

D) whenever it has to broadcast an IP packet

E) when it needs to forward an IP packet to another router whose MAC address is not available

15. A switch has eight Gbps LAN ports. What are its *wire speed* and *forwarding rate*? Also, what *aggregate throughput* is needed to give the switch 80% non-blocking capacity?

A) 1 Gbps, 8 Gbps, 6.4 Gbps

B) 1 Gbps, 1 Gbps, 8 Gbps

C) 1 Gbps, 16 Gbps, 1.6Gbps

D) 2 Gbps, 16 Gbps, 6.4 Gbps

E) 2 Gbps, 8 Gbps, 8 Gbps

16. Cut-through switching is when _____.

A) all switch ports use the same wire speed for switching.

B) switch ports have different wire speeds.

C) a switch begins forwarding a frame as soon as information necessary for the switching decision becomes available.

D) there is no switch learning or aging of switch table entries.

E) frames going through the regular ports of a switch are copied to its mirror port

17. Symmetric and asymmetric switches differ in terms of _____.

A) whether a switch supports both the switch and router modes

B) whether available ports have the same speed or allow different transmission speeds

C) whether a switch allows changes in configurations

D) whether a switch allows the change between the store-and-forward and cut-through modes

E) whether a switch allows the change between the error detection and non-detection modes

18. The network relying on _____ devices restricts the frame delivery between any two host stations to a single path.

A) modem

B) switch

C) router

D) layer 3 switch

E) CSU/DSU

19. Imagine a hypothetical network on which a wireless bridge with two ports (say, Fa0 and Fa1) connects two hubs (Hub A to Fa0 and Hub B to Fa1). The connectivity of five host computers to the bridge ports is summarized in the following table. Remember that the MAC addresses are hexadecimal.

End Stations	MAC Address	Port
1	1100.0000.1111	Fa0
2	1100.0000.2222	Fa0
3	1100.0000.3333	Fa0
4	1100.0000.4444	Fa1
5	1100.0000.5555	Fa1

Which entry in the *Filter* or *Forward* column of the bridge table is CORRECT?

Source MAC Address	Destination MAC Address	Filter or Forward
1100.0000.1111	1100.0000.2222	A) Forward
1100.0000.1111	1100.0000.4444	B) Filter

Source MAC Address	Destination MAC Address	Filter or Forward
1100.0000.5555	1100.0000.4444	C) Forward
1100.0000.3333	FFFF.FFFF.FFFF	D) Filter
1100.0000.2222	1100.0000.4444	E) Forward

20–21: A system administrator issued a command to a network node and it displayed summary information shown in the following table.

Interface	IP Address	MAC Address
Fa 0/0	192.168.2.10/24	0001.34AB.1234
Fa 0/1	<not set>	0001.3464.A23C
Fa 0/2	<not set>	0001.3486.B18A
Serial 0/0	192.168.5.10/24	0001.3412.B23A
Serial 0/1	<not set>	

20. What kind of network node is it?
    A) router
    B) switch
    C) bridge
    D) hub
    E) server
21. Among the highlighted items in the table, which entry must be an INCORRECT one?
    A) FastEthernet 0/0
    B) 192.168.2.10/24
    C) 0001.3464.A23C
    D) 0001.3412.B23A
    E) Serial 0/1
22. Choose a CORRECT statement about the operating system of an intermediary device.
    A) Hubs and repeaters need an OS to function.
    B) The switch's OS does not allow the modification of its port security.
    C) The router's OS is about the same size as Windows or Linux OS developed for personal computers.
    D) The router's OS is generally stored in the non-volatile flash memory.
    E) When the router is powered on, the OS stored in its hard disk drive is copied into the RAM.
23. Which is an ideal intermediary device to divide a network into smaller broadcast domains?
    A) Switch
    B) Bridge
    C) Access point
    D) Router
    E) Multiport repeaters
24. When the layer 2 and layer 3 switches are compared:
    A) The layer 3 switch has more ports than the layer 2 switch.
    B) The layer 3 switch has more throughput than the layer 2 switch.
    C) The layer 3 switch has fewer collisions than the layer 2 switch.
    D) The layer 3 switch port can be either a switch port or a router port.
    E) The layer 3 switch port offers higher security than the layer 2 switch port.

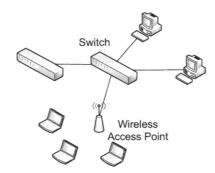

FIGURE 5.26   A hypothetical network

25. How many collision domains do you see in Figure 5.26?
    A) 2
    B) 3
    C) 4
    D) 5
    E) 6

HANDS-ON EXERCISES

EXERCISE 5.1

Imagine a hypothetical network in which a bridge with two ports (say, Fa0/0 and Fa0/1) connects to two hubs (Hub A to Fa0/0 and Hub B to Fa0/1) and the bridge table is shown as follows. Remember that the MAC addresses are hexadecimal numbers.

End stations	MAC address	Port
1	1100.0000.1111	Fa0/0
2	1100.0000.2222	Fa0/0
3	1100.0000.3333	Fa0/0
4	1100.0000.4444	Fa0/1
5	1100.0000.5555	Fa0/1

Decide what the bridge does to incoming frames by completing the following table. The following is the description of each column:

- Filter/Forward: Decide if a frame is going to be filtered or forwarded by the bridge.
- Output port: What is the port through which a frame will be forwarded?
- Receiving hosts: Which host(s) gets the frame, although it may not be picked up and processed?

Hint: When a frame's destination address is composed of all 1s (in other words, 48 ones) or is not found on the bridge table, the frame is broadcasted.

Source MAC address	Destination MAC address	Filter or forward	Output port	Hosts receiving the frame
1100.0000.1111	1100.0000.2222			
1100.0000.1111	1100.0000.4444			
1100.0000.5555	1100.0000.4444			
1100.0000.3333	FFFF.FFFF.FFFF			
1100.0000.4444	1100.2B22.4A4C			
1100.0000.5555	FFFF.FFFF.FFFF			

EXERCISE 5.2

Refer to the switch in Figure 5.8.

1. What is the switch's port density?
2. What is the switch's wire speed?
3. What is the switch's forwarding rate?
4. Assume that the switch can attain aggregate throughput equivalent to 80% of its forwarding rate. What is its aggregate throughput? Is this switch non-blocking?
5. Can the aggregate throughput of a switch be higher than its forwarding rate? Why or why not?

EXERCISE 5.3

Complete SW3's switch table in Figure 5.9.

EXERCISE 5.4

Refer to the hypothetical network in Figure 5.25. Assume that each switch has Fast Ethernet (100 Mbps) ports and all entries of the switch table are dynamically added.

Then:

1. Assign a MAC address of your choice to each host station.
2. For each switch, determine the name of switch ports that connect hosts or other switches.
3. Assign a MAC address to each LAN port named (refer to Table 5.3).
4. Develop a complete switch table for each of the five switches. The switch table should list MAC address-exit port pairs.

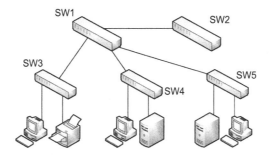

FIGURE 5.27 A hypothetical switched Ethernet

Exercise 5.5

A command is issued to a router and it displayed summary information of port status as in the table (it is not a routing table). Answer the following questions.

Interface (Port)	Link Status	IP Address	MAC Address
FastEthernet 0/0	Up	192.168.2.10/24	0001.34AB.1234
FastEthernet 0/1	Down	<not set>	0001.3464.A23C
FastEthernet 0/2	Down	<not set>	0001.3486.B18A
Serial 0/0	Up	192.168.5.10/24	
Serial 0/1	Down	<not set>	

1. How many LAN ports are on the router and what is their speed?
2. How many WAN ports are on the router?
3. How many LAN and WAN ports are ready for networking?
4. Why does the serial port have no MAC address?
5. Can FastEthernet 0/1 have an IP address, 192.168.2.1/24?
6. Can FastEthernet 0/2 have an IP address, 192.168.4.1/24?
7. How many different subnetworks are currently interconnected by the router?
8. Up to how many different subnetworks can be interconnected by the router?

Exercise 5.6

1. Refer to Figure 5.17. What is a key difference between the host's and router's ARP tables?
2. Refer to Figure 5.17a. Assuming that the subnetwork address is 169.254.x.x, explain the entries "169.254.255.255 ff-ff-ff-ff-ff-ff" and "255.255.255.255 ff-ff-ff-ff-ff-ff" in their meanings.
3. Refer to Figure 5.17b and answer the following questions.
   (a) How many different subnetworks is the router interconnecting?
   (b) Can we tell from the ARP table if the router has a WAN connection? Why or why not?
4. Does the layer 2 switch need to maintain an ARP table for frame switching? Why or why not?

Exercise 5.7

DNS and ARP work together to deliver packets successfully. To understand the procedure, assume that the browser of a PC (192.168.1.1 with 192.168.1.x as the subnet address) is trying to send an HTTP request to the webserver, *www.whitehouse.gov* (let's say 123.45.67.89). Then, the following activities take place in succession for the PC to successfully release the HTTP request. Think logically and fill in the blanks.

1. The PC's browser produces a HTTP request destined to the webserver (*www.whitehouse.gov*) on receiving the user input, but the PC does not know the webserver's _____ initially.
2. The PC sends an inquiry to a designated _____ server to learn *www.whitehouse.gov*'s IP address.
3. The _____ server returns the IP address of the _____ server to the PC.
4. The PC creates a packet with the sender's IP address (_____) and the receiver's IP address (_____).

5. From *www.whitehouse.gov*'s IP address, the PC realizes that the target server is not in the PC's _____ and, therefore, the packet should travel beyond the local subnetwork boundary.
6. The PC already knows the default gateway (see Section 4.10.1), the router port that leads to other networks. Assume that the default gateway is (192.168.1.250). The PC (192.168.1.1) and the default gateway (192.168.1.250) are in the same subnetwork and therefore the packet delivery between them becomes a/an _____ activity.
7. For the delivery of the packet containing the HTTP request, the PC should use the _____ address of the default gateway (192.168.1.250) in the frame that encapsulates the packet.
8. The PC already knows the default gateway's IP address (provided by a DHCP server during its booting), but the PC does not know the default gateway's _____. This triggers the broadcasting of a(n) _____ inquiry by the PC.
9. On receiving the _____ inquiry, the default gateway (192.168.1.250) responds by sending its _____ address to the PC.
10. The PC updates the default gateway's IP and MAC address pairing to its _____ table. Then, it creates a data link layer PDU called _____ and sends it directly to the default gateway to embark a long journey to the *www.whitehouse.gov* server.

EXERCISE 5.8

Identify collision domains and broadcast domains in each of four hypothetical networks (Figure 5.28).

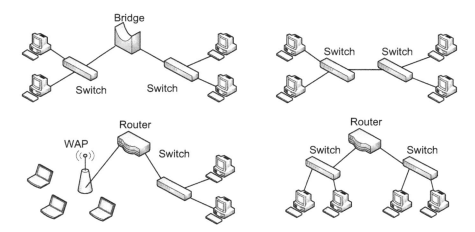

FIGURE 5.28   Four hypothetical networks

6 Wi-Fi and Cellular Network

6.1 INTRODUCTION

Various wireless technologies have been introduced and are currently in use. They can be classified into PAN, LAN, MAN, and WAN types in terms of the general coverage scope (see Figure 6.1). IEEE (the Institute of Electrical and Electronics Engineers) is mainly responsible for developing their standards, except those of satellite and cellular networks. IEEE is a non-profit and probably one of the largest professional associations in the world, working toward the advancement of information technologies.

6.1.1 WIRELESS NETWORK STANDARDS

Among the well-known wireless standards are:

1. Personal area network (PAN): The IEEE 802.15 standard was designed to cover a relatively small area, typically less than 10 meters in diameter. Because of the historical background, IEEE 802.15 is better known as Bluetooth. Its connection speed is generally less than 2 Mbps, substantially slower than popular Wi-Fi standards. For data transmissions, it relies on the 2.45 GHz radio frequency band, available license-free to software and hardware manufacturers. IEEE 802.15 is not suitable for high-speed networking. *Wi-Fi Direct* is another standard that enables direct communications between Wi-Fi devices without the wireless access point.
2. Local area network (LAN): IEEE 802.11 (or Wi-Fi) represents a collection of wireless LAN standards including IEEE 802.11n, IEEE 802.11ac, and IEEE 802.11ax, designed to support home/SOHO networks and organizational LANs.
3. Metropolitan area network (MAN): IEEE 802.16 (WiMax or WirelessMAN) is designed to cover a longer distance than IEEE 802.11 standards (e.g., the last mile link between an ISP and its residential/business clients). IEEE 802.16 is primarily intended to offer wireless broadband services comparable to DSL or Cable. There are also MAN standards intended for network access in fast-moving vehicles. Besides, IEEE 802.11 (Wi-Fi), most notably IEEE 802.11s (Wi-Fi Mesh), is being adopted for MAN services.
4. Wide area network (WAN): As the most popular wireless WAN platform, cellular networks are everywhere providing subscribers with voice and high-speed data service. Although cellular networks operated by telecommunications carriers (or telcos) were originally introduced mainly for voice, they are now widely utilized to access the Internet with smartphones, tablet computers, and other mobile devices. As another wireless WAN, the satellite network has been in use for TV/radio broadcasting and long-distance voice/data service.

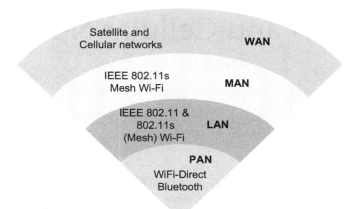

FIGURE 6.1   Select wireless networking technologies

6.1.2 Leaning Objectives

With the prevalence of Wi-Fi standards, today's computer operating systems, including Windows, Apple, Android, and Linux, all support the technology. This chapter focuses mostly on explaining Wi-Fi (IEEE 802.11) standards in their technical details and implementation issues. Then, the fundamentals of cellular networks are briefly explained.

The key learning objectives include:

- Standard layers of Wi-Fi
- Wi-Fi setup modes (Ad hoc vs. Infrastructure Modes)
- Wireless access point and its operational modes
- Service set identifier, basic service set, and extended service set
- Methods of media access control
- Wi-Fi frame types
- Radio frequency and channel usage by Wi-Fi
- Authentication and association in Wi-Fi network
- Various Wi-Fi standards currently available
- Wi-Fi Mesh network (IEEE 802.11s)
- Wi-Fi home and SOHO (small office and home office) networks
- Mobile cellular wide area networks

6.2 STANDARD LAYERS AND WI-FI CARDS

As a dominant LAN standard, Wi-Fi operates in the data link and physical layers, and its technical functions are implemented in the *wireless network interface card* (or wireless controller).

6.2.1 Data Link Layer

Wi-Fi's data link layer performs the following functions:
  a. Creation of Wi-Fi frames that encapsulate an IP packet
  b. Implementation of measures to improve the reliability of data transmissions to compensate for uncertainties of the wireless communication environment
  c. Authentication and association between Wi-Fi nodes (i.e., clients, access points)

d. Protection of data in transit with encryption technologies
e. Provision of the translational bridge function to join different LAN standards (e.g., Wi-Fi and Ethernet)
f. Media access control based on the *Carrier Sense Multiple Access/Collision Avoidance* (CSMA/CA) and *Request to Send/Clear to Send* (RTS/CTS) protocols to avoid transmission collisions between Wi-Fi clients.

6.2.2 PHYSICAL LAYER

At the physical layer, Wi-Fi uses radio waves/signals for message transmissions. For this, the layer specifies technical details of signal encoding including frequency bands and modulation methods (revisit Chapter 1 for *frequency* and *modulation* concepts). Just as other wireless communication systems (e.g., cellular networks), Wi-Fi uses spread spectrum technologies (e.g., OFDM – Orthogonal Frequency Division Multiplexing, OFDMA – Orthogonal Frequency Division Multiple Access) to encode digital data. The spectrum technologies are designed to reduce radio signal propagation problems (e.g., interference between nearby wireless nodes) and utilize available bandwidth more efficiently.

6.3 WI-FI SETUP MODES

Two different approaches are used to set up the Wi-Fi network: *ad hoc mode* and *infrastructure mode*.

6.3.1 AD HOC MODE

With the *ad hoc mode* (or peer-to-peer mode), two or more wireless stations can directly exchange frames without relying on a wireless access point (see Figure 6.2). This mode is easier to set up and dismantle, and thus adequate to arrange a relatively small temporary Wi-Fi network.

6.3.2 INFRASTRUCTURE MODE

With the *infrastructure mode*, Wi-Fi and the wired network (mostly Ethernet) coexist, and access points provide connectivity between them, thus conducting the bridge function (revisit Chapter 5). In Figure 6.3, for example, two access points are deployed within the corporate boundary. Most corporate and campus Wi-Fi networks are in the infrastructure mode because the key resources, including servers and network printers, are attached to the high-speed Ethernet, and Wi-Fi enables laptops, tablets, and other mobile devices to access the resources available through the Ethernet LAN.

FIGURE 6.2   Wi-Fi in ad hoc mode

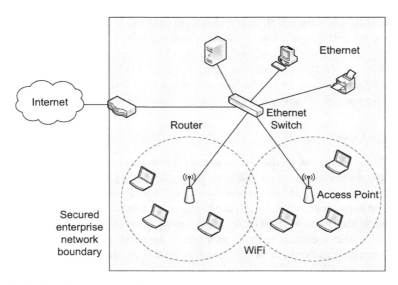

FIGURE 6.3   Wi-Fi in infrastructure mode

6.4   WIRELESS ACCESS POINTS (APS)

6.4.1   AP in Infrastructure Mode

The AP can be a dedicated device (see Figure 6.4) or software running on a computer or any other device. For instance, smartphones running Android or other operating systems have built-in capability to turn themselves into an AP after a simple setup. The AP device used in a corporate network (not the smartphone-enabled AP intended for personal usage) can associate a number of Wi-Fi clients, usually 15–50 host stations including laptops and mobile devices. It is equipped with its own wireless NIC (or WNIC) and bridging capability to facilitate data flows between different LAN standards. In fact, one of its primary roles is to provide interconnectivity between Ethernet and Wi-Fi network segments through the translation of their frames (revisit Chapter 5).

The AP is therefore a layer 2 device, and the switch and all host stations attached to the AP belong to the same subnet. Although a layer 2 device, the AP may be configured with an IP address for remote access and management, but not for frame deliveries. Besides bridging, the AP in the

FIGURE 6.4   Wireless access point (Source: www.amazon.com)

infrastructure mode conducts other functions crucial to the Wi-Fi network, as summarized in Table 6.1. As can be seen, the AP plays a central role in carrying out most of the Wi-Fi's data link layer functions listed in Section 6.2.1, although Wi-Fi clients also undertake some of them. More details are explained throughout the chapter.

Each AP is able to cover limited space in offering Wi-Fi connectivity, and the invisible boundary around an AP becomes a cell or basic service set (BSS). The size of each cell is limited because the distance between the AP and associated stations adversely affects effective *throughput* due to signal attenuation (or weakening). For example, it is said that the effective indoor range of APs is less than 50 meters. With the distance limit, a corporate LAN of reasonable size needs to deploy multiple APs. A university campus network may need hundreds or thousands of APs for its coverage. Also, there should be overlapping between neighboring cells in order to allow handoffs when a mobile host moves from one cell to another. In general, neighboring cells are required to have 10–15% overlap to facilitate roaming by Wi-Fi clients.

A client station should associate (or bind) itself to an AP before exchanging frames. The AP maintains an association table that lists associated/authenticated wireless nodes. The association table includes host information such as hostnames, IP addresses, and MAC addresses (see Figure 6.5 for a sample table). As host stations continuously associate and de-associate with an AP, its association table is updated dynamically.

With the growing complexity of the Wi-Fi network in the infrastructure mode, APs have evolved into two types of *thick* and *thin* APs. The thick AP is a traditional AP that conducts key functions listed in Table 6.1. Meanwhile, the thin AP acts as a communication post, delegating the traditional AP functions to a master AP controller. For instance, in Figure 6.3, the Ethernet switch can become an AP controller that can reconfigure the parameters of multiple thin APs remotely. By deploying thin APs, their management becomes less labor-intensive and thus can lower maintenance and operational costs. Some AP controllers come with additional functions such as a firewall between the wired and wireless networks, intrusion detection/prevention, and traffic monitoring.

TABLE 6.1
Key functions of wireless access point (AP)

AP functions	Description
Bridging	Conducts bridging in the form of frame conversion between Wi-Fi (IEEE 802.11) and Ethernet (IEEE 802.3).
Authentication	Authenticates host stations attempting to join a Wi-Fi network and allows association (a form of binding) once they are authenticated.
Media access control	Conducts media access control so that, regardless of the number of hosts associated with an AP, only a single host is allowed to transmit frames to the AP at a time to prevent frame collisions.
Data security	Utilizes data encryptions for secure communications with host stations.
Frame routing	Some APs (called mesh points) can relay frames to the destination host purely on the Wi-Fi segment only (see Section 6.10).

Host name	IP address	MAC address	State
Shin09	172.26.10.1	0203.23AB.D051	Associated
Jmon	172.26.10.12	0203.23A3.D591	Authenticated
Glan7	172.26.10.14	0203.236B.A031	Associated

FIGURE 6.5   Sample association table

6.4.2 AP in Non-Infrastructure Modes

Some APs are able to switch between the infrastructure mode and other non-infrastructure modes (e.g., repeater, bridge, wireless router). Although it could be confusing, remember that this explanation is about the AP's operational modes, and thus do not confuse them with the Wi-Fi network's setup modes (i.e., ad hoc and infrastructure modes). Among the AP's non-infrastructure modes, the repeater and bridge modes are explained (see Figure 6.6).

6.4.2.1 Repeater Mode

In the repeater mode, an AP relays (or rebroadcasts) radio transmissions to another AP in order to extend the range of a Wi-Fi network or to overcome the signal blockage. When it becomes a repeater, the AP does not need to be physically tied to an Ethernet LAN. Its drawback is that the relay of frames between two neighboring APs can result in a considerable loss of throughputs or actual transmission speeds.

6.4.2.2 Bridge Mode

This mode of operation is useful in places where network traffic needs to be separated between user groups. Figure 6.6 demonstrates a scenario in which APs serve two different user groups (i.e., staff and guests) to share Internet access. In this setting, the AP assigned to guests is given a different SSID in order to protect the corporate network's security. As another example, think of a coffee shop that installs an AP in the bridge mode to provide free Internet access to customers while the staff is on a different, password-protected AP.

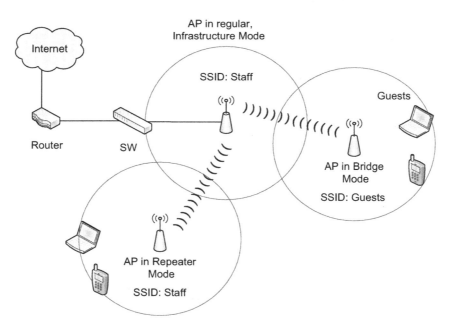

FIGURE 6.6   Access point in repeater vs. bridge mode

6.5 SSID, BSS, AND ESS

6.5.1 SERVICE SET IDENTIFIER (SSID)

The service set identifier (SSID) is a unique identifier or name of a Wi-Fi LAN and is configured on the AP. On a LAN, while multiple APs may belong to the same SSID (see Figure 6.8), it is also possible that two or more SSIDs coexist to provide network access to different user groups as in Figure 6.6. The screenshot in Figure 6.7 demonstrates a partial list of Wi-Fi networks and their SSIDs detected at the author's residence. The AP periodically broadcasts beacon frames containing its SSID so that nearby client hosts can associate with it after authentication. Clients are required to include the case-sensitive SSID in the association-requesting frame. In public Wi-Fi zones (e.g., airports and coffee shops), APs are set up with guest SSIDs to invite mobile clients without their authentication.

Alternately, an AP can be configured not to broadcast its SSID. In this case, the beacon frame includes a null value in the SSID field. In this non-broadcast mode, SSID can be used to authenticate client stations that attempt to associate with an AP. This requires that clients be pre-programmed with the same SSID. When an SSID is used for authentication, it may be exchanged with or without encryption. Using the non-encrypted SSID to authenticate host stations is not safe at all because the plain-text SSID can be easily intercepted.

Notes:

- The RSSI (Received Signal Strength Indication) is a negative value, and thus the lower, the better.
- CCMP is WPA2 with AES encryption.
- Wi-Fi security gets stronger in the sequence of 'Open Authentication < WEP < WPA < WPA2 < WPA3' (more in Chapter 10).

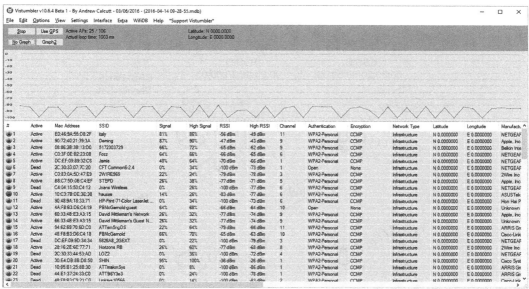

Notes:
- The RSSI (Received Signal Strength Indication) is a negative value, and thus the lower, the better.
- CCMP is WPA2 with AES encryption.
- Wi-Fi security gets stronger in the sequence of "Open Authentication <WEP <WPA <WPA2 < WPA3" (more in Chapter 10).

FIGURE 6.7 SSIDs on a neighborhood (Demo: Vistumbler 10.6)

6.5.2 BSS vs. ESS

The Wi-Fi network is divided into two building blocks in its coverage scope: *basic service set* (BSS) and *extended service set* (ESS).

6.5.2.1 Basic Service Set (BSS)

The BSS is the smallest building block in the ad hoc and infrastructure modes. In the ad hoc mode, the BSS is composed of at least two hosts. In the infrastructure mode, the BSS needs at least one host station and one AP. In general, a BSS contains an AP and multiple user devices associated with it. Each BSS has a 48-bit *basic service set identifier* (BSSID) used to uniquely distinguish one from the others. This means that a Wi-Fi network can have as many BSSIDs as the number of basic service sets.

The BSSID of a BSS is the AP's MAC address. For example, you can observe a MAC address (as BSSID) associated with each SSID in Figure 6.7. It is important not to confuse BSSID and SSID. One SSID can have one or more BSS and therefore one or more BSSIDs. At home networks, in general, one AP (thus, one BSS) is enough to cover the entire residence, and thus only one BSSID is shown.

6.5.2.2 Extended Service Set (ESS)

When multiple basic service sets are formed to cover a larger area and more user devices, they as a whole become an *extended service set* (ESS). The ESS, therefore, contains multiple cells each with an AP and one or more user devices (hosts). A user device's wireless NIC is associated with a single AP and deploying multiple APs (thus, multiple basic service sets) to form an ESS grows the scope of a Wi-Fi network. Neighboring basic service sets overlap to allow handoffs. Roaming between two basic service sets requires that a user station associates, de-associates, and re-associates with different APs.

For example, imagine a company's Wi-Fi LAN (SSID = My_Wireless) that covers four large rooms in which each room, as a BSS, has an AP and multiple user devices associated with it (see Figure 6.8). If the four basic service sets are interconnected by an Ethernet switch located in a wiring

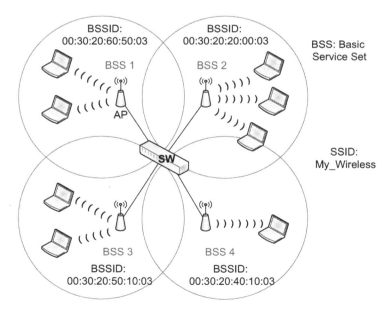

Extended Service Set (ESS) = BSS1 + BSS2 + BSS3 + BSS4

FIGURE 6.8 Basic service set vs. extended service set

closet, the entire Wi-Fi network results in an ESS. In terms of IP address allocation, all nodes including APs and user stations within the ESS belong to the same subnet and, therefore, only a single frame delivery path (as a data link) becomes active between any two user nodes.

6.6 MEDIA ACCESS CONTROL

Due to message broadcasting, Wi-Fi should enforce a mechanism to control network access and to avoid frame collisions within the BSS. This means that each BSS becomes *a collision domain* in which only a single station is allowed to release data at a time to avoid collisions. The transmission collisions and subsequent process to restore normalcy degrade network throughput.

The process of granting network access only to a single station is handled by the *media access control* (MAC) protocol. The MAC protocol defines rules that hosts (more specifically, their wireless NICs) comply to ensure that only one station releases data at a time within the BSS. In Wi-Fi, two different MAC standards have been in use: *Carrier Sense Multiple Access – Collision Avoidance* (CSMA/CA) and *Request to Send/Clear to Send* (RTS/CTS). In the regular mode, CSMA/CA is activated, and RTS/CTS becomes available as an option.

6.6.1 CSMA/CA

CSMA/CA's mechanism for preventing collisions beforehand and for maintaining communication reliability through an *acknowledgement* (or ACK) is summarized as follows:

CSMA/CA:

1. A host station's wireless NIC listens to Wi-Fi activities.
2. When the 'channel' of a BSS is clear (meaning no ongoing traffic), a user device may send frames to the AP. This first-come-first-served principle represents the *Carrier Sense Multiple Access* (CSMA) part of the protocol.
3. Before releasing frames, however, the user device must wait for a random amount of time (or random back-off time). This is for the *collision avoidance* (CA) part of the protocol. The user node, however, may transmit frames without waiting if there has been no network traffic beyond a certain time period.
4. After the random waiting, the user device begins frame transmissions to the AP if the network is still clear.

ACK (Acknowledgment):
5. The AP immediately returns an acknowledgment (ACK) for each frame it receives from the client station. If there is no ACK from the AP within a predetermined time limit, the source node retransmits the frame.

Wi-Fi's CSMA/CA has its limitations, and three stand out:
a. If several hosts within a BSS try to transmit frames concurrently, collisions still can occur due to such a reason as blind spots.
b. With CSMA/CA, all nodes within a BSS have an equal chance (i.e., first-come-first-served) of accessing the network. That is, no priority scheme is applied to frames so that urgent or real-time ones (e.g., voice-over IP) can be delivered ahead of the others.
c. One transmitting node may monopolize the channel as long as it needs. As a result, the lack of equity in network access and capacity sharing can result.

6.6.2 RTS/CTS

RTS/CTS (request to send/clear to send) is another media access control protocol designed to provide higher assurance in collision avoidance than CSMA/CA. The protocol has been introduced mainly to resolve the 'hidden node' problem in which two user stations associated with an AP are at opposite sites or are located at each other's blind spots (see Figure 6.9). When user nodes are unable to sense each other, they may release data simultaneously, resulting in collisions. The RTS/CTS protocol is used to keep such incidents from happening.

The process of RTS/CTS is depicted in Figure 6.10. When RTS/CTS is activated on a user node's wireless NIC, the station sends RTS to its associated AP. Then, the AP broadcasts the CTS frame to grant the requesting client the right to transmit data and also to alert others to hold off on their transmissions. Once this handshaking based on RTS/CTS is complete, the user node starts sending data frames. The activation of RTS/CTS, however, increases network overheads because of additional RTS/CTS frames exchanged and thus can negatively affect Wi-Fi performance. This is especially so when the activation of RTS/CTS is unnecessary, as there is little chance of transmission collisions.

When a Wi-Fi network with CSMA/CA experiences many collisions, RTP/CTS built into the host's wireless NIC may be activated. APs are programmed to automatically broadcast CTS in response to a client's RTS message. As an optional feature, the RTS/CTS function is generally offered in more costly, high-end wireless NICs. Thus, chances are that home or SOHO (small office and home office) products may not come with the RTS/CTS capability.

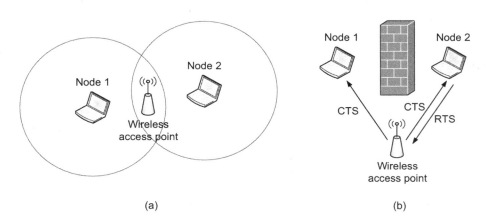

(a)   (b)

FIGURE 6.9   Hidden node problems

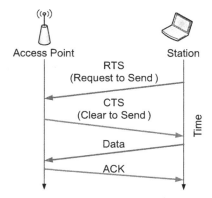

FIGURE 6.10   Four-way handshake with RTS/CTS

6.6.3 DRAWBACKS OF CSMA/CA AND RTS/CTS

The access control mechanism based on CSMA/CA or RTS/CTS has one common drawback – frames are permitted to transmit data on the 'first-come-first-served' basis. Under the access scheme, emails are given the same priority as voice calls, a clear problem. The IEEE 802.11e standard complements the MAC protocols by offering Quality of Service (QoS) for the Wi-Fi network so that frames are processed according to their urgency level. This QoS affords much better throughput for time-sensitive applications such as voice-over IP, audio/video streaming, and video conferencing. The IEEE 802.11n and newer Wi-Fi standards support IEEE 802.11e for the QoS-based frame prioritization.

6.7 WI-FI FRAMES

When frames are broadcasted through the unguided medium (air), things are more complicated than when they are propagated through a guided (wired) medium such as the twisted pair and fiber-optic cable. For instance, wireless links are subject to disruptions caused by such conditions as the interference, data stream collision, signal attenuation, and handoff. Also, with frame broadcasting, Wi-Fi nodes become much more vulnerable to security threats.

This hostile environment demands that more coordination and control functions be in place for wireless networking. Facing such challenges, Wi-Fi uses three different frame types in order to exchange user-produced data and conduct supervisory functions. They are the *data-*, *management-*, and *control frames.*

6.7.1 DATA FRAME

Data frames carry actual user data (e.g., emails). Figure 6.11 demonstrates the data frame's structure – composed of the header, data, and trailer fields. As can be seen, the header is quite complex. When an AP is linked to an Ethernet switch, the Wi-Fi frame's complex header/trailer is converted into the Ethernet frame's header/trailer (or vice versa) by the AP for frame transportation across the two different platforms. Figure 6.11 is for demonstration only and thus the details are not explained.

6.7.2 MANAGEMENT FRAME

The management frame's primary role is to establish/handshake and maintain connections between Wi-Fi nodes (e.g., AP and client stations) through the *authentication* and *association* procedure. For this, management frames include authentication frames, association/de-association frames, and beacon frames.

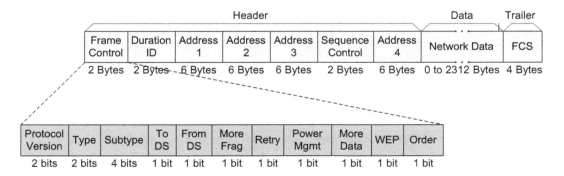

FIGURE 6.11 Wi-Fi data frame structure (for information only)

Above all, only qualified stations should be allowed to join an AP. For this, a host station authenticates itself to the target AP by sending an authentication frame. Also, they exchange the association and de-association frames to establish an association (or binding) and to terminate it. Additionally, beacon frames are periodically broadcasted by the AP to announce its presence. The beacon frame includes the AP's MAC address and SSID. The wireless NIC of a host node continually scans all Wi-Fi frequency channels and listens to beacons to choose the best AP to associate with.

6.7.3 CONTROL FRAME

Control frames are used to aid the delivery of data frames. For example, the acknowledgement (ACK) frame that confirms the receipt of a data frame is an example of the control frame. Frames carrying RTS (Request to Send) and CTS (Clear to Send) messages are also this type.

6.8 WI-FI AND RADIO FREQUENCY

6.8.1 RADIO SPECTRUM

In this section, the *radio wave* (radio) used for the delivery of Wi-Fi frames is explained. Radio waves are heavily used to offer various traditional (e.g., AM and FM radios) and advanced (e.g., Wi-Fi and cellular networks) services in which communicating nodes can be either fixed or mobile.

As in Table 6.2, the radio spectrum consists of a number of frequency ranges starting from *very low frequencies* all the way to *extremely high frequencies*. Radio waves that cover the *ultra-high* (UHF), *super high* (SHF), and *extremely high* (EHF) frequency ranges of the radio spectrum are called *microwaves*. Recent development of advanced communication technologies including Wi-Fi, Bluetooth, WiMax, satellite broadcasting, GPS (global positioning system), and cellular phone systems all take advantage of microwaves.

6.8.2 LOW VS. HIGH RADIO FREQUENCY

What are the implications of relying on low versus high radio frequencies in wireless networking? Most notably, high frequency channels use more power (therefore, higher signal strength) than low frequency ones, and this results in the delivery of higher data quality. The tradeoff is that radio waves in higher frequency ranges lack flexibility in transmissions, making them more susceptible to interferences and subsequently limiting their effective distance. That is, low-frequency signals are

---

TABLE 6.2

Radio frequency spectrum and microwave ranges

Radiowave Frequency Ranges		
Name	**Frequency ranges**	
Extremely Low Frequencies (ELF)	30 – 300 Hz	
Voice Frequencies (VF)	0.3 – 3 kHz	
Very Low Frequencies (VLF)	3 – 30 kHz	
Low Frequencies (LF)	30 – 300 kHz	
Medium Frequencies (MF)	0.3 – 3 MHz	→ AM Radio
High Frequencies (HF)	3 – 30 MHz	
Very High Frequencies (VHF)	30 – 300 MHz	→ FM Radio
Ultra High Frequencies (UHF)	0.3 – 3 GHz	TV, GPS,
Super High Frequencies (SHF)	3 – 30 GHz	Wi-Fi, 3G,
Extremely High Frequencies (EHF)	30 – 300 GHz	4G, Satellite

more flexible in getting around barriers (e.g., mountains) and thus can propagate farther than high-frequency ones. Referring to Table 6.2, we are able to see why AM radio travels farther than FM radio, but FM's sound quality is significantly better than AM's.

6.8.3 GOVERNANCE

The usage of the radio frequency spectrum is generally regulated by the government. In the United States, for example, the *Federal Communications Commission* (FCC) oversees the non-federal government usage of radio (e.g., cellular phone service by Verizon). Also, the *National Telecommunication and Information Administration* (NTIA) is responsible for the management of radio ranges utilized by the government for national defense, law enforcement and security, transportation, emergencies, and others. Through an advisory committee, FCC and NTIA coordinate to manage the radio frequency spectrum.

6.8.4 LICENSED VS. UNLICENSED RADIO

The radio spectrum includes both licensed (i.e., license required) and unlicensed (i.e., license-free) frequency bands. At present, a large share of the radio spectrum is regulated; thus, licensing is required for its exclusive usage. There are also unlicensed bands, frequently known as *industry, scientific, and medical* (ISM) bands. Vendors use ISM bands to develop software and hardware products ranging from traditional home appliances and electronics (e.g., microwave ovens, cordless phones) to networking devices for Wi-Fi and Bluetooth. The license-free ISM bands include 900 MHz, 2.4 GHz, and 5.0 GHz bands whose frequency ranges in North America are summarized in Table 6.3.

6.8.5 WI-FI CHANNELS

This section explains how the frequency range of the 2.4 GHz ISM band is further divided into Wi-Fi channels used by various IEEE 802.11 Wi-Fi standards. In North America, including the US and Canada, there are 11 frequency channels in the 2.4 GHz band with a channel capacity (or bandwidth) of 22 MHz. Countries vary in the number of frequency channels available, as many countries support 13 channels in the 2.4 GHz band.

In North America, the frequency ranges of 11 neighboring channels are overlapped (see Figure 6.12). For example, Channel 1's frequency range (2.401~2.423 GHz) overlaps with those of Channels 2, 3, 4, and 5. This makes only 3 (Channels 1, 6, and 11) out of 11 channels *non-overlapping* from each other. Even if the bandwidth of each channel is 22 MHz, 20 MHz are available for data transmissions, and the remaining 2 MHz is used as a 'guard' band to prevent signal interference between neighboring channels.

Things are a little bit more complicated with the 5.0 GHz ISM band. In the US, for example, there are 25 non-overlapping channels (e.g., 36, 40, 44, 100, 132, and 165), each with 20 MHz bandwidth.

TABLE 6.3
ISM bands (North America)

ISM bands	Frequency range
900 MHz	902–928 MHz
2.4 GHz	2.4–2.4835 GHz
5.0 GHz	5.180–5.825 GHz

Channel	Lower Frequency	Upper Frequency
1	2.401	2.423
2	2.406	2.428
3	2.411	2.433
4	2.416	2.438
5	2.421	2.443
6	2.426	2.448
7	2.431	2.453
8	2.436	2.458
9	2.441	2.463
10	2.446	2.468
11	2.451	2.473

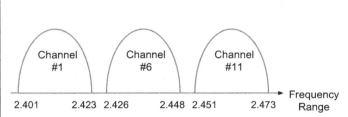

FIGURE 6.12   2.4 GHz non-overlapping channels (in the US and Canada)

Just as in the 2.4 GHz band case, countries differ in allocating channels for the 5.0 GHz band. *Remember that each 20 MHz channel capacity of 2.4 GHz and 5.0 GHz bands becomes a building block of Wi-Fi link capacity.*

6.8.6   PLANNING BASIC SERVICE SETS

Why are frequency channels overlapped as explained in the previous section? The short answer is to capitalize available bandwidth more effectively through channel reuse. Let us see how it works. When neighboring APs operate in non-overlapping channels, this reduces signal interferences and improves transmission speeds. That is, when multiple APs are deployed to cover an area using the 2.4 GHz band, they should use the three non-overlapping channels to minimize signal interferences.

Figure 6.13 demonstrates a case in which APs of neighboring cells are instructed to use non-overlapping channels. It also shows that the same frequency channels are reused when they are separated. The five APs represent five different cells or basic service sets (BSS), and all five of them as a whole become one extended service set (ESS). Remember that no matter how many client nodes are associated with an AP *on a single channel*, CSMA/CA – the Wi-Fi's *media access control* protocol – allows only one client to exchange data with the AP at a time.

When there is only one AP in an area (e.g., home), you can choose any of 11 channels, as you don't have to worry about channel reuse by adjacent cells. However, if your and your neighbors' APs are configured to use the same channel, your Wi-Fi LAN's performance may be affected by potential interference. As shown in Table 6.3, the 5.0 GHz band has a much larger capacity than the 2.4 GHz

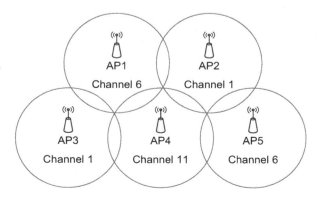

FIGURE 6.13   Wi-Fi channel selection in an area

TABLE 6.4
Wi-Fi standards

Status	IEEE standards	Rated speeds
Legacy	802.11b	11 Mbps
	802.11a	54 Mbps
	802.11g	54 Mbps
Current		
	802.11n (or Wi-Fi 4)	100–600 Mbps
	802.11ac (or Wi-Fi 5)	Up to 1.3 Gbps
	802.11ax (or Wi-Fi 6)	Up to 1.2 Gbps per stream Up to 4.8 Gbps for quad-stream

band and thus supports more transmission channels (e.g., 25 non-overlapping channels of 20 MHz bandwidth). The larger bandwidth allows the creation of more basic service sets, making the 5.0 GHz band much more flexible than the 2.4 GHz band in channel allocation.

Lastly, the relationship of the three terms (i.e., *spectrum, bands*, and *channels*) that have been introduced thus far is further clarified.

- The radio wave *spectrum,* as the entire frequency range of radio (see Table 6.2), is divided into a number of *service bands* for various communication services. For instance, the service band of AM radio is 500–1500 kHz in the US.
- A particular service band is, then, further divided into multiple *service channels*. For example, the service band of AM radio is divided into many 10 kHz channels, with each channel to be used by an AM radio station (see Figure 6.12 for another example).

6.9 WI-FI STANDARDS

Several Wi-Fi standards have been introduced by IEEE and they are summarized in Table 6.4, including legacy ones (i.e., 802.11a, 802.11b, and 802.11g). Currently, the 802.11n, 802.11ac, and 802.11ax standards dominate Wi-Fi networks. Wi-Fi standards have different *rated speeds*, maximum speeds that can be theoretically achieved under ideal conditions.

There is, however, a considerable gap between rated speeds and actual *throughputs* that we experience. For example, although 802.11n's rated speed is more than 100 Mbps, its actual throughput is typically less than 50 Mbps, varying greatly depending on the setup. Various factors contribute to the significant gap:

- Distance between an AP and associated hosts
- Number of client hosts associated with an AP
- Signal attenuation (or weakening)
- Waiting time necessary to prevent transmission collisions (see CSMA/CA)
- Required acknowledgements of delivered frames

6.9.1 IEEE 802.11N (OR WI-FI 4)

IEEE 802.11n is intended to offer wired LAN-like performance as high data rates are critical for transporting multimedia data such as high-quality videos. IEEE 802.11n builds on the legacy 802.11 standards and this backward compatibility allows their coexistence. Some of the key features that differentiate 802.11n from the legacy standards are summarized here.

6.9.1.1 Throughput Modes

Unlike the legacy standards in which each link between an AP and a client gets 20 MHz channel bandwidth, 802.11n supports two throughput modes: 20 MHz and 40 MHz. Designed to further enhance Wi-Fi speeds, the 40 MHz mode uses *channel bonding* for which two neighboring 20 MHz channels are combined to create a bigger pipe. In developing hardware/software for 802.11n, the vendor support for the 20MHz throughput mode is mandatory, but that for 40 MHz remains optional.

6.9.1.2 2.4/5.0 GHz Bands

While the legacy standards utilize one frequency band (i.e., 2.4 GHz or 5.0 GHz band), 802.11n supports both 2.4 GHz and 5.0 GHz bands either concurrently or non-concurrently. Assuming that there are two antennas on a user device, the dual-band technology allows that one antenna transmits data on a 2.4 GHz frequency channel and the other on a 5.0 GHz channel.

If two 2.4 GHz and 5.0 GHz frequency channels can be used concurrently, it is *concurrent dual-band transmissions*. If two antennas alternate 2.4 GHz and 5.0 GHz channel usage, then it becomes *non-concurrent dual-band transmissions*. The 5.0 GHz band is much less crowded than the 2.4 GHz band and thus subject to less signal interference.

6.9.1.3 Single-User MIMO (or SU-MIMO)

The legacy standards (i.e., 802.11a, b, and g) rely on '*single input, single output*' (or SISO) technology, in which there is only one data stream between two nodes (e.g., user node and AP) through a 20 MHz channel of either 2.4 GHz or 5.0 GHz band.

On the other hand, 802.11n supports both SISO and '*multiple inputs, multiple outputs*' (or MIMO) transmissions. As a radical shift from the SISO paradigm, 802.11n's MIMO supports up to four simultaneous data streams between two network nodes (e.g., AP and laptop). As multiple data streams (also called spatial streams) are established between two nodes, it is also known as *single-user MIMO*. The multi-path propagation of data streams considerably increases the overall bandwidth.

Currently, the majority of 802.11n-ready APs and computers sold in the marketplace have two or three antennas, supporting fewer data streams and lower speeds than the maximum capacity possible. *Remember that 802.11n supports only single-user MIMO. That is, within a basic service set, only one client is allowed to exchange data (through multiple data streams) with the AP at a time.*

6.9.2 IEEE 802.11ac (or Wi-Fi 5)

Wi-Fi 5 is the most widely deployed Wi-Fi standard currently, and vendor products support rated speeds anywhere from 500 Mbps up to 1.3 Gbps.

6.9.2.1 5.0 GHz Band

802.11ac utilizes only the 5.0 GHz band, which is less crowded and thus risks less interference than the 2.4 GHz band. The 5.0 GHz band also supports more non-overlapping 20MHz channels (e.g., 25 in the US) than 2.4 GHz (e.g., 3 in the US; see Figure 6.12) rendering much flexibility in Wi-Fi network design and improved performance. 802.11ac is backward compatible and thus can coexist with other 802.11 devices running on the 5.0GHz unlicensed band.

6.9.2.2 Channel Throughput Modes

802.11ac supports 20 MHz, 40 MHz, 80 MHz, and 160 MHz channel modes for faster throughputs than 802.11n. 802.11ac-compliant devices are required to support 20 MHz, 40 MHz, and 80 MHz throughput modes, but support for 160 MHz remains optional. The formation of larger pipes is done by aggregating multiple 20 MHz basic channels (channel bonding).

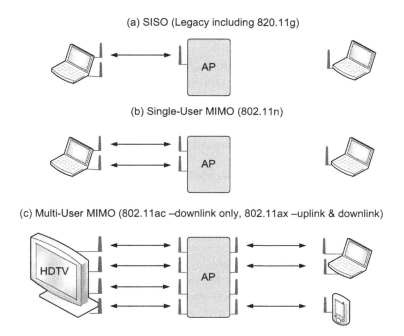

FIGURE 6.14 SISO, single-user MIMO, and multi-user MIMO

Capitalizing on the several channel options, 802.11ac-enabled APs can switch the channel capacity dynamically on a frame-by-frame basis in order to utilize available network capacity more efficiently. For example, the AP exchanging frames with a client node based on a 20 MHz channel can add the next idle 20 MHz channel to form a 40 MHz channel and grow bandwidth. The 40 MHz channel can dynamically grow to 80 MHz through the bonding with the next idle channel of 40 MHz.

6.9.2.3 Multi-User MIMO (or MU-MIMO)

Wi-Fi 5 uses *multi-user MIMO* for the first time. In MU-MIMO, multiple nodes transmit and receive data streams concurrently (see Figure 6.14c). MU-MIMO is a significant departure from previous standards that the AP can exchange data with only a single device at a time through the single-user MIMO (802.11n) or single-user SISO (single input, single output) mode.

Wi-Fi 5 supports up to eight simultaneous data streams for the 'downlink' from an AP to client devices. Using the downlink of eight data streams, an AP can transmit frames up to four different client nodes *concurrently*. As for the uplink (from clients to an AP), Wi-Fi 5 allows that only a single device can transmit data to an AP within a basic service set. With the AP sending eight data streams at the same time for the downlink, the Wi-Fi network performance is still improved considerably over 802.11n.

6.9.3 IEEE 802.11ax (or Wi-Fi 6)

Wi-Fi 6 released in 2019 is the next generation Wi-Fi standard. Similar to Wi-Fi 5, Wi-Fi 6 uses MU-MIMO of eight data streams, but in a more effective way. The standard improves network performance markedly over Wi-Fi 5 by using the following technology elements:

a. While Wi-Fi 5 takes advantage of the 5 GHz band, Wi-Fi 6 supports both 2.4 GHz and 5 GHz ranges, as the 2.4 GHz signals are better in penetrating hard walls. The future Wi-Fi 6 is expected to support the 6 GHz band as well.

b. While Wi-Fi 5 supports MU-MIMO only from an AP to client devices (i.e., downlink only), Wi-Fi 6 allows multiple user devices to send data to an AP concurrently, realizing MU-MIMO in both the downlink and uplink.

c. Wi-Fi 6 uses the OFDMA standard to allow several users to transmit data to an AP (uplink) at the same time. Wi-Fi 4 and Wi-Fi 5 use OFDM and thus are unable to support multiple access for the uplink (see Section 6.12.2).

d. Wi-Fi 6 improves data rates using an advanced encoding (or modulation) technology (see Chapter 1). Remind that *encoding* and *multiple access* are different technology notions, as the former is about converting data to signals and the latter is about granting multiple signal transmissions concurrently.

e. Two access points (APs) can be located closely to coordinate network load sharing in a congested area.

f. As a unique function, Wi-Fi 6 supports cellular data offloading in which the cellular network including 5G offloads its traffic to a complementary Wi-Fi network if the cellular network experiences an issue such as poor receptions and overloads.

With the extremely fast speed, Wi-Fi 6 is able to support high-density public areas such as train stations and high-throughput applications that demand greater bandwidth, such as 4K/8K videos and augmented reality. IoT (Internet of Things) is another environment in which hundreds or thousands of mobile devices, electronic devices, and sensors may need to exchange data in a secure manner and without delays.

6.9.4 COMMON FEATURES AND COMPARISON

QoS support: All Wi-Fi 4, 5, and 6 support the Quality of Service (QoS) standard (IEEE 802.11e) so that client stations with time-sensitive data are given a higher priority in network access to relieve transmission delays.

Media access control: As the new standards use more complex technologies to achieve higher throughput, a question remains as to 'Does the traditional media access control of CSMA/CA and RTS/CTS apply to standards that support MU-MIMO?' The answer is yes. Basically, MAC works at the basic 20 MHz channel level. That is, when 802.11n/ac/ax dynamically grows its transmission capacity by merging with the next idle channels (e.g., 20 MHz to 40 MHz), the MAC mechanism applies to each 20 MHz channel to detect its availability.

Some key features of Wi-Fi 4, 5, and 6 standards are compared in Table 6.5.

TABLE 6.5
Comparison of 802.11n, 802.11ac, and 802.11ax standards

Features	802.11n	802.11ac	802.11ax
Frequency bands (unlicensed)	2.4 and 5.0 GHz	5.0 GHz	2.4 and 5.0 GHz
Channel bandwidth options (in MHz)	20, 40	20, 40, 80, 160	20, 40, 80, 160
MIMO-support	Single User-MIMO or SU-MIMO	MU-MIMO (downlink only)	MU-MIMO (Both uplink and downlink)
No. of client hosts concurrently supported by an AP	1	Up to 4	Up to 8

6.10   WI-FI MESH NETWORK (IEEE 802.11S)

The *Wi-Fi Mesh* or *Mesh Wi-Fi* network uses the same Wi-Fi standards, but it is different from the traditional Wi-Fi network where APs are connected to the Ethernet switch or router of a wired network. Thus, Wi-Fi Mesh can be a cost-effective alternative for quickly creating a new network if there is no existing network infrastructure at a place. Wi-Fi Mesh uses the mesh networking of APs, called *mesh points* (see Figure 6.15).

The Wi-Fi Mesh network is unique, as mesh points can route Wi-Fi frames among themselves without depending on the wired LAN (typically Ethernet) in the infrastructure mode (see Figure 6.3). With the relay function among mesh points, only one or a few mesh points need to be connected to a wired network to allow user devices to access the Internet. The Wi-Fi Mesh network may use the full or partial mesh topology.

Mesh points use their own routing capacity – a mechanism similar to switching – to relay frames to a particular mesh point attached to a wired network. Depending on the circumstance, mesh points intelligently figure out the best possible route to avoid slow or troubled mesh points. The default routing protocol used by Wi-Fi Mesh is called Hybrid Wireless Mesh Protocol and it uses license-free 2.4 GHz and 5 GHz bands.

Wi-Fi Mesh is, thus, a good technology choice when a place lacks wired network infrastructure, which can be a building, campus, trolley or subway, community, or metropolitan area. As it does not require hardwire connectivity to every mesh point, Wi-Fi Mesh is a highly flexible and easily deployable technology to create organizational LANs, MANs, or municipal networks, and home networks. A number of cities have deployed the free Wi-Fi municipal network using the Wi-Fi Mesh standard. Also, the popularity of Wi-Fi Mesh is growing for home networks as more vendors are introducing products.

6.11   WI-FI HOME/SOHO NETWORK

In this section, the implementation details of Wi-Fi at home and SOHO (Small Office and Home Office) are explained. These days, most home networks are using Wi-Fi as computers come with a built-in wireless NIC. The Wi-Fi home/SOHO network is generally composed of a broadband modem (e.g., DSL or Cable modem), a wireless access router as an intermediary device, and end nodes such as laptops, tablet computers, and smartphones. Figure 6.16 demonstrates a general arrangement of the Wi-Fi network and structural details of the wireless access router.

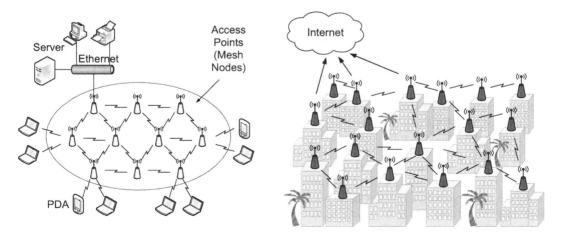

FIGURE 6.15   Wi-Fi Mesh at an enterprise and in a city

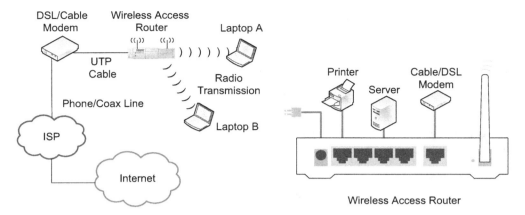

FIGURE 6.16 Wi-Fi home/SOHO network (left) and wireless access router (right)

6.11.1 DSL/CABLE MODEM

The DSL/Cable modem, as a physical layer device, is similar to the traditional dial-up modem in its functionality as it performs conversion between digital and analog signals (Chapter 13). More specifically, it translates computer/router-generated digital signals to analog signals for transmissions over the phone (for DSL) or coaxial (for Cable) line. The modem also converts analog signals coming from the ISP circuit back into the digital signal format that the wireless router understands.

6.11.2 WIRELESS ACCESS ROUTER

The majority of wireless access routers manufactured for the home/SOHO network combine the switch, router, and AP functions altogether. The particular product – not an actual model – in Figure 6.16 has four Ethernet switch ports and a WAN port to link the Cable/DSL modem. Key functions commonly incorporated into the wireless access router are:

a. *Router function* to access the Internet through an ISP network. The router connects two different subnets: (1) a home network and (2) a WAN subnet that links the home router to an ISP's router. The ISP's DHCP server provides a dynamic, public IP address to the home network, thus becoming the IP address of the WAN router port.
b. *Ethernet switch function* to provide hosts with a cabling option to connect to the home network.
c. *Wireless access point (AP)* that supports the configuration of radio channels, channel bandwidth options, SSID naming, and network security.
d. *Internal DHCP server function* to provide private IP addresses to the home network's internal nodes.
e. *Network address translation (NAT) function* for internal nodes to share a single public IP address offered by the ISP's DHCP server.
f. Other optional functions including the firewall, VPN, and DNS services.

Figure 6.17 demonstrates logical relationships among the technical components of the wireless access router. Implementing several intermediary device functions (i.e., AP, Ethernet switch, and router) in one physical unit makes sense because, unlike the corporate network that contains a large number of client and server hosts and handles much network traffic, the home/SOHO network is much smaller in scale, generally composed of only a few host stations, and thus does not justify the separation of device functions.

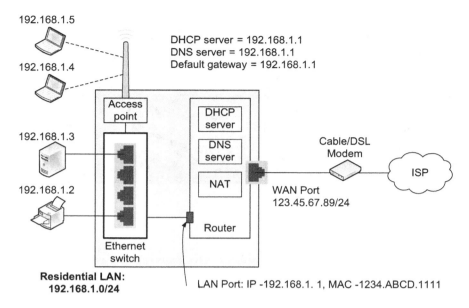

FIGURE 6.17 Wireless access router – logical view

6.11.3 IP CONFIGURATION

Figure 6.17 also demonstrates a scenario of IP address configuration:

- The home network is given a network address of 192.166.1.0/24. All node addresses on the 192.166.1.0/24 network are therefore private IPs that cannot be used for packet routing over the Internet.
- The WAN port is on a different subnet (123.45.67.0/24) and is given an IP address of 123.45.67.89.
- The wireless access router has an internal LAN port with an IP address of 192.168.1.1 and a MAC address of 1234.ABCD.1111. The LAN port is invisible to us, but it internally links the router to the Ethernet switch. The router's LAN port (192.168.1.1) therefore becomes the default gateway of hosts at the home network.
- The router has a DHCP server that allocates private IPs to internal nodes. The IP address (123.45.67.89) that publicly represents the home network is provided by the ISP's DHCP server.
- The router has a DNS server that stores hostnames in the home network and their corresponding IP addresses.
- The router has a network address translation (NAT) function that translates non-routable private IPs to the public IP address (123.45.67.89).

The screenshot of the laptop (192.166.1.4) in Figure 6.18 summarizes the IP assignment in which the router's LAN port (192.166.1.1) becomes the default gateway and, at the same time, the same IP address is shared by the DHCP and DNS servers.

6.12 CELLULAR NETWORK

This section explains the cellular WAN technology, arguably one of the most important developments in telecommunications. Broadly speaking, its technology fits into the layer architecture covered in Chapter 3, although the relationship is a little nebulous. Despite that much of the technical detail belongs to the physical and data link layers, there are elements crossing to higher layers. Emphasis here is on introducing the fundamentals without relating them to standard layers.

```
C:\Windows\system32\cmd.exe                                    _  □  x

   Physical Address. . . . . . . . . : 00-1B-9E-20-A9-71
   DHCP Enabled. . . . . . . . . . . : Yes
   Autoconfiguration Enabled . . . . : Yes
   Link-local IPv6 Address . . . . . : fe80::20ed:834d:a8e8:c7e5%9(Preferred)
   IPv4 Address. . . . . . . . . . . : 192.168.1.4(Preferred)
   Subnet Mask . . . . . . . . . . . : 255.255.255.0
   Lease Obtained. . . . . . . . . . : Thursday, February 05, 2009 10:55:58 PM
   Lease Expires . . . . . . . . . . : Monday, February 09, 2009 2:21:04 PM
   Default Gateway . . . . . . . . . : 192.168.1.1
   DHCP Server . . . . . . . . . . . : 192.168.1.1
   DNS Servers . . . . . . . . . . . : 192.168.1.1
   NetBIOS over Tcpip. . . . . . . . : Enabled
```

FIGURE 6.18   IP configuration of home network

6.12.1   GENERAL ARCHITECTURE

The cellular network's general architecture includes cells, base stations, and the mobile terminal switching office (MTSO), as in Figure 6.19.

6.12.1.1   Cell

The cellular network is constructed by a carrier (e.g., Verizon, AT&T) to provide wireless WAN service for both voice and data through high radio frequency ranges (e.g., UHF, SHF, and EHF). For this, the carrier divides operating areas into cells, conceptually similar to Wi-Fi's basic service sets. Each cell, spanning around 100 meters within a city but larger in suburban and rural areas, is allocated a certain number of radio frequency channels, which limits the number of users that can be served at once. Although cells may be hexagonal, square, or circular, the hexagonal shape remains a popular choice. Adjacent cells use different frequency ranges to avoid interferences or crosstalk and to allow frequency reuse by other, sufficiently separated cells.

6.12.1.2   Base Station

The cell has a base station that communicates with mobile hosts using high-frequency radio signals. The base station houses various devices such as the antenna, transmitter, receiver, and controllers. The controller controls the transmitter and receiver devices and provides the interface between a cell site and MTSO. Generally, the base station is mounted on a cell tower and connected to a MTSO through a fixed line. Each MTSO serves multiple base stations.

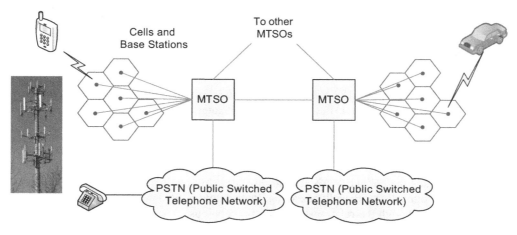

FIGURE 6.19   Mobile cellular network architecture

6.12.1.3 Mobile Terminal Switching Office (MTSO)

The MTSO, similar to the Central Office (CO) of PSTN (Public Switched Telephone Network), performs fully automated functions essential for mobile service provisions including call setup and termination, call routing, handoffs, roaming, and monitoring calls for billing. A MTSO connects to other MTSOs for wireless communications and to the traditional telephone network (PSTN) for landline connectivity.

6.12.1.4 Call Channels

There are two types of communication channels between mobile devices and a base station: traffic and control channels. The traffic channel transports voice and data. In each cell, one channel is set aside as a control channel to exchange signaling information (e.g., host location, call setup, caller ID) and to perform such functions as domestic/international roaming and handoff/handover that allows a mobile host to move between cells while communicating.

6.12.2 MULTIPLE ACCESS TECHNOLOGIES

Cellular systems use *random access* technologies that pack multiple phone calls and Internet data traffic into a limited frequency band. For this, different *multiple access* technologies have been introduced over the years. Starting with FDMA, they evolved into TDMA, CDMA, OFDM, and subsequently OFDMA. All technologies described here are physical layer concepts (see Chapter 13). The details are highly complex, and Figure 6.20 visually simplifies their differences in using available network bandwidth.

6.12.2.1 FDMA (Frequency Division Multiple Access)

The *multiple access* technology divides an available frequency band into smaller frequency channels, each of which is allocated to an individual. It was used by the analog-based AMPS (Advanced

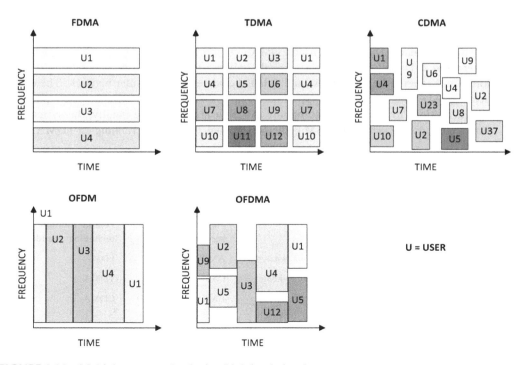

FIGURE 6.20 Multiple access technologies (high-level views)

Mobile Phone Service) standard, the first-generation cellular service. This conceptually resembles Frequency Division Multiplexing (Chapter 13).

6.12.2.2 TDMA (Time Division Multiple Access)

This standard further divides each frequency channel resulting from FDMA into several time slots (e.g., three slots) and each time slot is allocated to an individual, resulting in the usage of one channel by multiple calls. It was used by the GSM (Global System for Mobile communications) system that dominated the second generation of cellular service. This technology resembles to Time Division Multiplexing (Chapter 13).

6.12.2.3 CDMA (Code Division Multiple Access)

In CDMA, a frequency band available is not subdivided as in FDMA and TDMA; instead, radio signals carrying voice/data are scattered across the frequency range using the 'spread spectrum' technology. Several spread spectrum methods that dynamically spread a signal over a large frequency band have been introduced. Frequency hopping spread spectrum (FHSS), direct sequence spread spectrum (DSSS), and time hopping spread spectrum (THSS) are among them. With spread spectrum, a unique key is appended to each digitized voice/data for identification by the receiver device. It was used by second- and third-generation services such as CDMA2000.

6.12.2.4 OFDMA (Orthogonal Frequency Division Multiple Access)

OFDMA is the multi-user version of OFDM (Orthogonal Frequency Division Multiplexing), which itself is an advancement of FDM (Frequency Division Multiplexing). The 4G and 5G cellular network standards use OFDMA. The newest Wi-Fi 6 standard also uses OFDMA.

6.12.3 CELLULAR NETWORK GENERATIONS

Cellular networks have evolved through five generations. As of this writing, they are currently in the fifth generation (see Table 6.6).

a. **Generation 1**: The first generation (1G) cellular network was purely analog and introduced primarily for voice communications. AMPS (Advanced Mobile Phone Service) was a well-known 1G standard. The network used FDMA.

b. **Generation 2**: Digital phones replaced analog phones from the second generation (2G) and more people started Internet access and email exchange on the cellular network. The downstream speed of digital data was approximately up to 200 Kbps. The cellular system provided data encryptions to prevent eavesdropping. Also, to improve voice quality, the system had error detection and correction. GSM is the best-known 2G standard running on TDMA.

TABLE 6.6
Generations of cellular service

Generation	Period	Network features	Popular systems/ services	Popular multiple access technology standard
1G	1980s	Voice-centric analog, circuit switching	AMPS	FDMA
2G	1990s	Voice and slow data, circuit switching	GSM	TDMA
3G	2000s	Voice and faster data, circuit switching networks	UMTS, CDMA2000	CDMA
4G	2010s	IP-based packet switching	LTE	OFDMA
5G	2020s	IP-based packet switching	5G-NR (New Radio)	OFDMA

c. **Generation 3**: The arrival of 3G service improved access to the Internet significantly with downloading speeds up to 2 Mbps through such standards as UMTS (Universal Mobile Telecommunications Systems) and CDMA 2000. Their technology basis is CDMA. With 3G, worldwide roaming for travelers became available. 1G, 2G, and 3G technologies rely on the *circuit switching* technology that dedicates fixed network capacity to a user (Chapter 13).

d. **Generation 4**: Although there are several 4G technologies, Long-Term Evolution (LTE) has received global acceptance, which includes support from all US carriers. As a wireless broadband data service, it supports only IP-based *packet switching* as opposed to 1G/2G/3G's *circuit switching*. With *packet switching,* available network capacity is dynamically reassigned to different users to maximize its usage and also provides higher connection speeds to each user.

e. **Generation 5**: One of 5G's greatest achievements is its superfast data rate; it thus can download a high-resolution movie in seconds. It takes advantage of 20–60 GHz high frequency wavebands to achieve such data rates (current 4G LTE generally depends on frequency bands below 2 GHz). The 5G network offers an ideal platform for the Internet of Things (IoT), self-driving cars, augmented virtual reality, and three-dimensional holograms. These applications generate an enormous amount of data that need to be moved, oftentimes in near real-time. As a simple example, the 3D hologram will allow mobile-commerce customers to try on newly arrived clothes on their smartphones.

CHAPTER SUMMARY

- Wireless networks use PAN (e.g., Bluetooth, Wi-Fi Direct), LAN (e.g., Wi-Fi), MAN (e.g., WiMax, Wi-Fi Mesh), and WAN (e.g., satellite, cellular) technologies.
- Just as other LAN standards (e.g., Ethernet), Wi-Fi runs in the data link and physical layers. The Wi-Fi functions of a host are implemented in the *wireless network interface card.*
- Two different approaches are used to set up the Wi-Fi network: *ad hoc mode* and *infrastructure mode*.
- The access point plays a central role in carrying out most of Wi-Fi's data link layer functions.
- Some access points are able to switch between the infrastructure mode and non-infrastructure modes (e.g., repeater mode, bridge mode).
- The service set identifier (SSID) is a unique name of a Wi-Fi LAN and is configured on APs.
- The basic service set (BSS) is the smallest building block of a Wi-Fi LAN. In the ad hoc mode, it takes a minimum of two stations. In the infrastructure mode, it needs at least one host station and one access point.
- The extended service set (ESS) consists of multiple basic service sets, each with an access point and associated host stations.
- CSMA/CA and RTS/CTS are two media access control (MAC) standards used to avoid collisions during data transmissions.
- Wi-Fi uses three different frame types in order to exchange user data and conduct supervisory/control functions: data frames, management frames, and control frames.
- Several Wi-Fi standards have been introduced by IEEE, including legacy ones (i.e., 802.11a, 802.11b, 802.11g). Currently, the 802.11n, 802.11ac, and 802.11ax products dominate the marketplace.
- The recent development of advanced communication technologies including Wi-Fi, Bluetooth, WiMax, satellite broadcasting, GPS (global positioning system), and cellular phone systems all take advantage of microwaves.
- MIMO (Multiple inputs, multiple outputs) is a Wi-Fi technology that allows concurrent delivery of several bit-streams within a BSS while SISO (or single input, single output), used by 802.11a, 802.11b, and 802.11g, allows only one bit-stream.
- The radio spectrum includes both licensed and unlicensed frequency bands.

- Currently, the 802.11n (Wi-Fi 4), 802.11ac (Wi-Fi 5), and 802.11ax (Wi-Fi 6) standards dominate Wi-Fi networks.
- Depending on the IEEE standard, the access point can support MIMO in either single-user mode (IEEE 802.11n) or multi-user mode (IEEE 802.11ac and IEEE 802.11ax).
- The Wi-Fi Mesh network uses Wi-Fi standards, but it can cover considerably larger territories (e.g., metropolitan area) using mesh networking of APs – frequently called mesh points. Mesh points can 'route' frames, and thus they do not need to depend on the wired LAN for packet propagation.
- The Wi-Fi home/SOHO network is generally composed of a broadband modem (e.g., DSL/Cable modem), host stations, and a wireless access router that bundles the router, switch, and access point functions.
- The cellular network's general architecture includes cells, base stations, and mobile terminal switching offices (MTSO).
- Cellular systems use *random access* technologies that can pack multiple phone calls and Internet data traffic into a limited frequency band. FDMA, TDMA, CDMA, OFDM, and OFDMA are among the technology standards.
- Cellular networks dominate the wireless WAN, and their technologies have evolved through five generations and are currently in the fifth generation.

KEY TERMS

ad hoc mode
base station
basic service set (BSS)
basic service set identifier (BSSID)
Bluetooth
bridge mode
broadband modem
Carrier Sense Multiple Access/Collision
Avoidance (CSMA/CA)
cell
cellular network
channel
channel bonding
circuit switching
clear to send (CTS)
Code Division Multiple Access (CDMA)
dual-band transmission
control frame
data frame
extended service set (ESS)
Federal Communications Commission
(FCC)
Frequency Division Multiple Access
(FDMA)
frequency band
Frequency Hopping Spread Spectrum
(FHSS)
Global System for Mobile Communications
(GSM)

IEEE 802.11
IEEE 802.11n (Wi-Fi 4)
IEEE 802.11ac (Wi-Fi 5)
IEEE 802.11ax (Wi-Fi 6)
IEEE 802.11e
IEEE 802.11s
IEEE 802.15
IEEE 802.16
Industry, scientific, and medical (ISM) band
infrastructure mode
licensed radio
Long-Term Evolution (LTE)
management frame
master controller
mesh point
microwave
mobile terminal switching office (MTSO)
Multi-input-multi-output (MIMO)
multi-user MIMO (MU-MIMO)
non-overlapping channel
Orthogonal Frequency Division
Multiplexing (OFDM)
Orthogonal Frequency Division Multiple
Access (OFDMA)
packet switching
peer-to-peer mode
radio spectrum
radio wave
repeater mode

request to send (RTS)
service band
service channel
service set identifier (SSID)
single-input-single-output (SISO)
single-user MIMO (SU-MIMO)
spread spectrum
Time Division Multiple Access (TDMA)

thick access point (AP)
thin access point (AP)
unlicensed radio
Wi-Fi Direct
Wi-Fi Mesh
wireless access point (AP)
wireless access router

CHAPTER REVIEW QUESTIONS

1. Which statement describes the IEEE 802.11n (Wi-Fi 4) standard?
   A) Its rated speed is less than 10Mbps.
   B) With channel bonding, a 2.4GHz channel and a 5.0GHz channel can be combined to create a larger channel.
   C) It uses a single antenna to achieve the multiple inputs and multiple outputs (MIMO) mode.
   D) It is unable to support Quality of Service (QoS), as all Wi-Fi frames receive the same priority.
   E) The dual-band transmission can use both 2.4 GHz and 5.0 GHz concurrently.
2. What is a difference between the basic service set (BSS) and the extended service set (ESS)?
   A) number of clients
   B) number of servers
   C) number of overlapping channels available
   D) number of wireless access points (APs)
   E) number of wireless switches
3. An AP may be in the regular AP mode or in the _____ mode.
   A) firewall
   B) modem
   C) peer-to-peer
   D) repeater
   E) switch
4. With the _____ protocol activated, when a user station wishes to transmit data, it has to obtain the AP's permission.
   A) Carrier Sense Multiple Access/Collision Avoidance + Acknowledgement
   B) Carrier Sense Multiple Access/Collision Avoidance
   C) Carrier Sense Multiple Access/Collision Detection
   D) Request to Send/Clear to Send
   E) Carrier Sense Multiple Access/Collision Detection + Acknowledgement
5. When an AP issues the acknowledgement of a frame it receives, it is delivered in a ___ frame.
   A) control
   B) data
   C) beacon
   D) supervisory
   E) management
6. Which function is generally NOT built into the wireless access router sold for home networking?
   A) wireless access point
   B) Ethernet switch
   C) DHCP server
   D) network address translation
   E) CSU/DSU

7. The 2.4 GHz band supports _____ non-overlapping channels in North America.
   A) 1
   B) 3
   C) 7
   D) 11
   E) 2

8. A corporate network has a number of switches and APs interconnected. The network is closely guarded through several security measures. The network administrator, however, wants to provide Internet access to its visitors during business meetings at the conference room. For this, she can configure the conference room's AP in the _____ mode.
   A) virtual LAN
   B) repeater
   C) infrastructure
   D) bridge
   E) client

9. Which can be a legitimate identifier of a basic service set of a Wi-Fi network?
   A) 00:30:20:20:00:13
   B) 00:30:20
   C) 0..172
   D) 10010101
   E) 192.168.13.34

10. Bluetooth is a popular wireless standard for the _____.
    A) metropolitan area network (MAN)
    B) personal area network (PAN)
    C) wide area network (WAN)
    D) local area network (LAN)
    E) enterprise network

11. There are two unlicensed bands used for Wi-Fi: 2.4 GHz (range of 2.4–2.48 GHz) and 5.0 GHz (range of 5.20–5.85). Which statement is CORRECT?
    A) The bandwidth of the 5.0 GHz band is roughly 4 times larger than that of 2.4 GHz.
    B) The bandwidth of the 2.4 GHz band is roughly 8 times larger than that of 5.0 GHz.
    C) The bandwidth of the 2.4 GHz band is roughly 4 times larger than that of 5.0 GHz.
    D) The bandwidth of the 5.0 GHz band is roughly 8 times larger than that of 2.4 GHz.
    E) The bandwidth of the 2.4 GHz band is roughly equal to that of 5.0 GHz.

12. How can laptops associated with an AP avoid transmission collisions?
    A) Using electronic tokens
    B) Using the spread spectrum technology
    C) Using random back-off time even when the network is quiet
    D) Using a collision detection mechanism
    E) Using the first-come-last-served approach

13. The following are key functions of the AP EXCEPT:
    A) It undertakes frame conversion primarily between Wi-Fi and Ethernet.
    B) It authenticates host stations attempting to join a Wi-Fi network.
    C) It dynamically allocates radio transmission channels to neighboring APs.
    D) It performs media access control to prevent transmission collisions.
    E) It encrypts data for secure communications with clients.

14. Which is ACCURATE?
    A) authentication request – control frame
    B) association request – management frame
    C) acknowledgement – data frame

D) RTS/CTS – management frame

E) beacons – data frame

15. Which of the following describes Wi-Fi technology?

   A) The Wi-Fi Mesh network uses routers for frame routing.

   B) The wavelength of radio waves as the Wi-Fi medium is measured in GHz.

   C) Radio waves used for Wi-Fi are in the frequency range of microwaves.

   D) Wi-Fi uses the ring topology to deploy APs.

   E) Wi-Fi uses licensed frequency ranges of the radio spectrum.

16. Which is FALSE regarding the IEEE 802.11 standard?

   A) In North America, 11 channels are defined within the 2.4 GHz frequency band.

   B) In North America, channel 1, 6, and 11 are non-overlapping channels of the 2.4 GHz frequency band.

   C) An AP may periodically broadcast the beacon frame to announce its presence, and it may include SSID.

   D) The ad hoc mode is more popular than the infrastructure mode in creating Wi-Fi networks at the university campus.

   E) Binding between a user device and an AP requires the client's authentication and association.

17. The 4G and 5G cellular networks rely on the _____ standard technology to facilitate concurrent network access by more people.

   A) TDMA

   B) FDMA

   C) CDMA

   D) OFDMA

   E) OFDM

18. What is the baseline channel capacity/bandwidth of all Wi-Fi standards including 802.11ax?

   A) 40 MHz

   B) 15 MHz

   C) 10 MHz

   D) 5 MHz

   E) 20 MHz

19. Which function is performed in the physical layer of the Wi-Fi 5 and Wi-Fi 6 standards?

   A) Facilitate the reliability of data transmissions by creating the acknowledgement frame.

   B) Authentication and association of client hosts by the AP.

   C) Ensures data confidentiality through encryptions.

   D) Controls media access with CSMA/CA and RTS/CTS protocols.

   E) Uses a spread spectrum technology for frame propagations.

20. The technical details of Wi-Fi standards are defined in the_____.

   A) physical layer only

   B) physical and data link layers only

   C) physical, data link, and internet layers only

   D) physical, data link, internet, and transport layers only

   E) physical, data link, internet, transport, and application layers

21. One of the key differences between 4G/5G and 2G/3G cellular systems is:

   A) While 4G and 5G use packet switching, 2G and 3G depend on circuit switching to deliver voice/data.

   B) 4G and 5G support handovers (or handoffs) and roaming that are not available for 2G and 3G.

   C) 4G and 5G support both voice and data, but 2G and 3G support only voice.

   D) Whereas 2G and 3G rely on FDMA, 4G and 5G take advantage of OFDM.

   E) Unlike 2G and 3G that are analog, 4G and 5G are pure digital systems.

22. Which describes the cellular network's general architecture?
    A) The base station is mainly responsible for the handoff and roaming functions.
    B) The cellular network takes advantage of high radio frequency ranges such as UHF and SHF.
    C) Each cell has a MTSO that directly communicates with mobile hosts (e.g., smartphones).
    D) MTSO is mounted on a cell tower.
    E) The base station is a connecting point to the traditional landline phone.
23. Which states the IEEE 802.11ax (or Wi-Fi 6) standard?
    A) It uses the Single User-MIMO (or SU-MIMO) technology.
    B) Both the uplink and downlink can support the concurrent transmissions of multiple data streams between an AP and three user devices.
    C) It supports only two channel bandwidth options of 20 MHz and 40 MHz.
    D) For backward compatibility, it uses only the 2.4 GHz radio band.
    E) It became 'the' standard technology for Wi-Fi Mesh networks.
24. The Wi-Fi Mesh network standard:
    A) Requires that mesh points are attached to an Ethernet switch.
    B) Requires the full mesh topology in creating the network of Wi-Fi mesh points
    C) Uses the frame structure different from regular Wi-Fi standards (e.g., Wi-Fi 5).
    D) Uses the default routing protocol called Hybrid Wireless Mesh Protocol.
    E) Is exclusively used for local area networks.
25. Which describes the cell of a cellular network?
    A) The control channel of a cell transports signaling information necessary for call setup.
    B) The cell is equally sized regardless of its location (e.g., city, suburban, rural).
    C) Neighboring cells use the same frequency range as long as there is no interference.
    D) The cell may or may not have a base station that communicates with mobile hosts.
    E) All cells are designed to have the hexagonal shape.

HANDS-ON EXERCISES

EXERCISE 6.1

Refer to Table 6.3:

1. What is the bandwidth of each ISM band in North America?
2. When the bandwidths of three ISM bands are compared, what can you say in terms of their relative capacity?
3. The bandwidth necessary for voice communication is about 4 kHz for one direction. How many voice calls can be accommodated within the 2.4 GHz band? Remember that each call needs two separate channels for two-way talks.

EXERCISE 6.2

Figure 6.21 is a hypothetical corporate network with several APs. It indicates that at least one laptop computer is associated with each AP. Answer the following questions.

1. How many basic service sets do you see in the network?
2. How many BSSIDs should the network have?
3. How many extended service sets do you see in the network?
4. Which AP can be in the repeater mode?
5. Can AP4 and AP5 use 802.11ac and 802.11ax concurrently? Why or why not?
6. How many subnets do you see in the enterprise network?

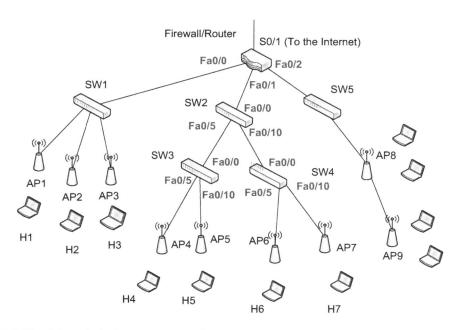

FIGURE 6.21 A hypothetical corporate network

7. The company decides to use private IPs with 172.16.0.0/16 as the network ID. Assuming that it uses the third octet to create subnets, assign subnet addresses and allocate the last available IP address of each subnet to the router port. What are the IP addresses of router ports Fa0/0, Fa0/1, and Fa0/2?

8. Assign an IP address to H4 through H7 based on the subnet address. What are they?

9. Assign a MAC address to H4 through H7, and also to the router's LAN port Fa0/1. What are they?

10. Based on the results so far, develop a correct switch table for S2, S3, and S4. Include two columns of MAC addresses and exit ports in the switch table.

11. Assuming that the switch table for S2, S3, and S4 are completed, what happens if H4 broadcasts an IP packet?

Exercise 6.3

There are various tools that can find Wi-Fi LANs around your place. In this exercise, we use two programs: Vistumbler (www.vistumbler.net), as an open-source program; and the command mode utility program *netsh*, available on Windows.

1. Download a recent version of Vistumbler (as in Figure 6.7) and launch it. Search hotspots around your place and answer questions. You can sort data in ascending or descending order by clicking on a column label.
   a.   What are the radio frequency channels used?
   b.   How many BSSIDs do you see?
   c.   What are popular security (or privacy) standards for authentication and encryption?
   d.   Which 802.11 standards can you observe?
   e.   Is any Wi-Fi network in the *ad hoc* mode?
   f.   Among the different types of information captured by Vistumbler, which may be particularly useful to an attacker and why?

2. This time, you are to use the command mode utility program, *netsh*, on Windows. Among its available commands are:
C:\netsh
C:\netsh>wlan
C:\netsh wlan>show interfaces
C:\netsh wlan>show networks
C:\netsh wlan>show networks mode=bssid

Using the netsh commands, answer the Vistumbler questions above to the extent possible.

EXERCISE 6.4

Certain ISPs offer a router bundled with a DSL/Cable modem. Then, there are two intermediary devices at a home network: (1) a router with a built-in DSL/Cable modem, and (2) a wireless access point with an Ethernet switch. Using this scenario, try to redraw Figure 6.17 (logical diagram) to reflect the changed setup and reassign IP addresses to the router's LAN and WAN ports.

EXERCISE 6.5

The screenshot in Figure 6.22 summarizes the status of a wireless access router of a home network. It shows three sections: Internet port, LAN port, and wireless port. Each part represents the status of the router, switch, and access point although they are all combined. That is, the *Internet port* is the router's WAN port connected to an ISP router remotely. Answer the following questions, referring to Section 6.11.

1. What is the router's public IP address that represents the home network to the Internet?
2. Who provides the public IP address of the WAN port?

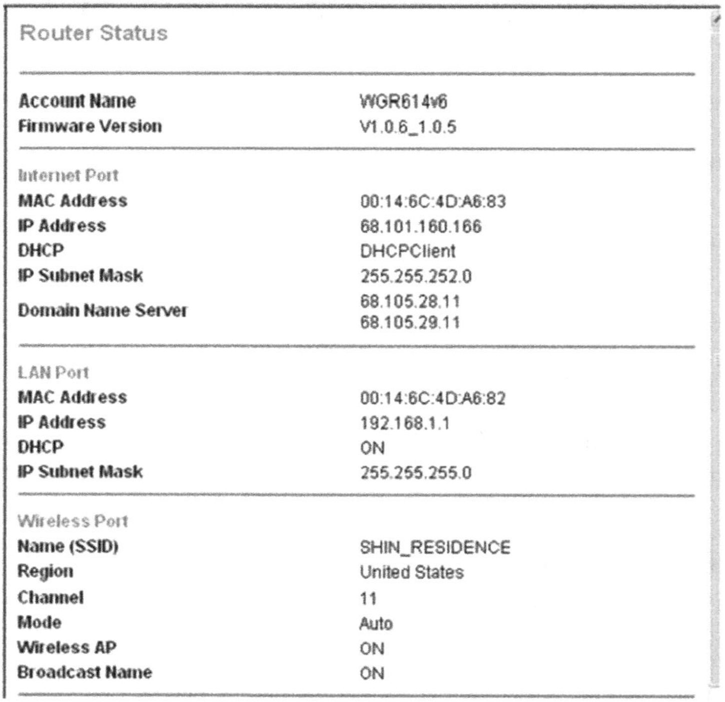

Router Status

| Account Name | WGR614v6 |
| Firmware Version | V1.0.6_1.0.5 |

Internet Port

MAC Address	00:14:6C:4D:A6:83
IP Address	68.101.160.166
DHCP	DHCPClient
IP Subnet Mask	255.255.252.0
Domain Name Server	68.105.28.11
	68.105.29.11

LAN Port

MAC Address	00:14:6C:4D:A6:82
IP Address	192.168.1.1
DHCP	ON
IP Subnet Mask	255.255.255.0

Wireless Port

Name (SSID)	SHIN_RESIDENCE
Region	United States
Channel	11
Mode	Auto
Wireless AP	ON
Broadcast Name	ON

FIGURE 6.22   Router configuration

3. What is the subnet address of the public IP address?
4. Can you find out the address of the ISP's DHCP server(s)?
5. What are the addresses of the ISP's DNS servers?
6. What is the subnet address of the home network?
7. What should be the default gateway address of home computers?
8. Given the subnet address of the home network, how many hosts can be assigned an IP address?
9. Does the access router rely on network address translation (NAT)? Why or why not?
10. Does the access router have an internal DHCP server?
11. What is the frequency band (e.g., 2.4 GHz or 5 GHz) the access point is using?
12. The Internet WAN port has its own MAC address in addition to the IP address. This deviates from our understanding that, in general, a WAN port does not need a unique MAC address because of the point-to-point link between the home and ISP routers. You can guess that, when the MAC address is included in each frame, the ISP can determine where particular packets are coming from even if their source IP addresses are spoofed.

EXERCISE 6.6

Think of the following small business network with wireless and wired network segments (see Figure 6.23). The IT administrator wants that business guests can access the Internet, but not the workstations and server on the wired LAN. Discuss what the IT administrator can do assuming that all options are open. There could be multiple solutions. *Hint*: Think of solutions in terms of deploying additional routers to further segment the network, planning a new subnet scheme, configuring the routing table, adding additional Internet lines, and others.

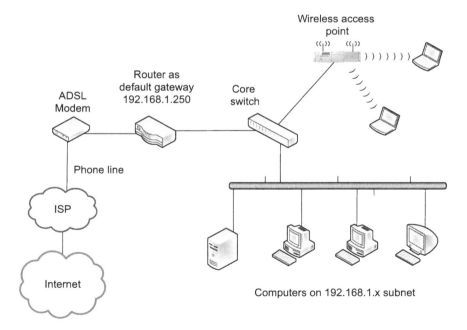

FIGURE 6.23 A hypothetical small business network

7 Ethernet LAN

7.1 INTRODUCTION

Ethernet has been the dominant land-based (or wired) LAN, and its technology has been continuously evolving to provide higher network speeds and reliability. Although there have been technologically more advanced challengers such as Token Ring and Fiber Distributed Data Interface (FDDI), Ethernet has prevailed, demonstrating its enormous popularity and staying power. Since its introduction by Xerox in 1975 by the name of Ethernet, it has become the IEEE's 802.3 LAN standard.

Ethernet and Wi-Fi coexist supplementing each other. Although the official name of Ethernet is IEEE 802.3, people are used to the original name. With the extensive usage of switches for Ethernet LANs, the emphasis of this chapter is on various technical issues associated with the *switched Ethernet* (i.e., the Ethernet LAN running on switches).

7.1.1 LEARNING OBJECTIVES

This chapter explains the switched Ethernet focusing on the following:

- Standard layers covered by Ethernet
- Structure of the Ethernet frame
- Design approaches of the Ethernet LAN: flat design vs. hierarchical design
- Spanning Tree Protocol (STP)
- Link aggregation (or bonding) technology
- Benefits of creating virtual LANs (VLANs)
- VLAN tagging and trunking
- VLAN types
- Inter-VLAN routing

7.2 STANDARD LAYERS

Just as with other LAN and WAN standards, Ethernet's technical specifications are defined in the data link and physical layers. In fact, the data link layer is divided into two sub-layers of *logical link control* (LLC) and *media access control* (MAC) for LAN standards (see Figure 7.1). The standard details of Ethernet and Wi-Fi are defined in the MAC sub-layer. The LLC sub-layer (as the IEEE 802.2 standard) provides the interface between the internet layer and the MAC sub-layer. A key function of LLC is to identify the upper (i.e., internet) layer protocol such as IP included in the frame. The technical specifications of Ethernet are, therefore, covered by the MAC sub-layer and the physical layer.

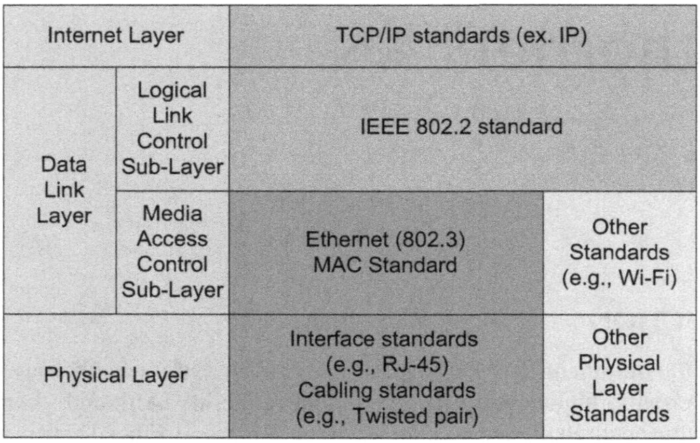

Internet Layer		TCP/IP standards (ex. IP)	
Data Link Layer	Logical Link Control Sub-Layer	IEEE 802.2 standard	
	Media Access Control Sub-Layer	Ethernet (802.3) MAC Standard	Other Standards (e.g., Wi-Fi)
Physical Layer		Interface standards (e.g., RJ-45) Cabling standards (e.g., Twisted pair)	Other Physical Layer Standards

FIGURE 7.1   Layers of Ethernet (IEEE 802.3) standard

Among important responsibilities of the Ethernet's MAC sub-layer are:

- Creating Ethernet frames encapsulating a packet in the data field
- Access control to shared media in hub-based Ethernet (not switched Ethernet) in which only a single station is allowed to transmit data at a time to avoid collisions.
- Switching decisions on arriving frames referring to the switch table
- Managing virtual LANs (VLANs) and handling VLAN traffic

The physical layer standards of Ethernet are explained in Chapter 13. This chapter focuses on the data link layer functions of switched Ethernet that uses layer 2 switches (not layer 1 hubs) to connect host stations.

7.3   ETHERNET FRAME

7.3.1   FRAME STRUCTURE

Ethernet has its own frame structure. The Ethernet frame carries the internet layer packet (primarily IP packet) in its data field. The frame contains a header and a trailer added before and after the data field (see Figure 7.2). The responsibility of each field in the header and trailer is summarized next.

Preamble	7 bytes
Start-of-Frame Delimiter	1 byte
Destination Address	6 bytes
Source Address	6 bytes
Length (46~1500 bytes) or Type of Payload	2 bytes
Payload (Data)	variable
Pad (if necessary)	
Frame Check Sequence	4 bytes

FIGURE 7.2   Ethernet frame

- The *Preamble* is used for the synchronization of clock rates between communicating nodes. The nodes should be exactly aligned in their process timing and preamble bits, repetition of 1010 ... 1010, are used to achieve that synchronicity.
- The bit combination (10101011) in the *Start Frame Delimiter* field indicates the beginning point of a frame.
- The *Source/Destination MAC Address* field contains 48-bit MAC addresses of the source and destination nodes.
- The *Length/Type* field includes information on either the length of a frame's data field in hexadecimal (the value is less than $0x0600$) or the type of the upper layer protocol (e.g., IP).
- The *Data* field includes the payload (or data) ranging from 46 through 1500 Octets. The field primarily contains an IP packet. As the data field is limited in size, an IP packet can be fragmented to fit into the data field. However, such fragmentation of an IP packet can be problematic (e.g., additional process burden on routers) and is generally avoided. To prevent packet fragmentations, two hosts pre-negotiate the maximum size of the transport layer PDU (i.e., TCP segment, UDP datagram).
- The *PAD* field is added if the data field is too small to meet the required size of at least 46 bytes.
- The *Frame Check Sequence* (FCS) field contains an error detection code used by the destination host to discover any transmission errors (e.g., bit change) in the frame. If the host's NIC detects an error, the frame is discarded. The removed message is subsequently detected by TCP of the source host and retransmitted. If UDP was used, the source host doesn't take the recovery action.

The following describes the error detection procedure based on the FCS value.

Source host:

1. Frame value (bitstream) = X
2. Cyclic Redundancy Check (CRC) code = Y (a standardized value)
3. Division = Frame value/CRC code = X/Y
4. Remainder value of X/Y = R1
5. The frame with R1 in the FCS field is released to the network.

Destination host:

6. On receiving the frame, the host repeats the steps 1 through 4 and computes its own remainder value, R2.
7. If R1 = R2, then there is no error in the frame, ELSE drop the frame

7.3.2 ADDRESSING MODES

Ethernet frames are in three different addressing modes: unicasting, multicasting, and broadcasting. In broadcasting, the frame's destination address field contains FF-FF-FF-FF-FF-FF (1 bit repeating 48 times). This is similar to IP broadcasting for which the destination address field of an IP packet is filled with all 1s (i.e., 255.255.255.255).

The multicasting address in hexadecimal ranges between 01-00-5E-00-00-00 and 01-00-5E-7F-FF-FF. Multicasting is used for different applications such as the exchange of routing table information, video streaming, and multimedia conference calls. Just as unicasting relies on the mapping between the IP and MAC addresses to deliver an IP packet within a frame (revisit ARP in Section 5.8), multicasting and broadcasting also need the mapping between the two addressing schemes. For example, the destination address of 255.255.255.255 is translated into FF-FF-FF-FF-FF-FF when a frame encapsulates the packet.

7.4   ETHERNET LAN DESIGN

Switched Ethernet dominates wired LANs. When switches are used to create an Ethernet LAN, there is no limit to the number of switches that can be attached to it and therefore no limit to its maximum span at least in theory. To give a perspective, the Ethernet standard recommends that the maximum segment length between any two switches directly joined by the twisted pair be up to 100 meters in order to maintain the integrity of data transmissions. When optical fibers are utilized, their maximum segment distance increases considerably (e.g., at least 300 meters) due to their reliability of signal propagations (e.g., low signal attenuation and high noise resistance).

7.4.1   FLAT VS. HIERARCHICAL DESIGN

7.4.1.1   Flat Design

In creating a switched LAN, it can take a flat or hierarchical structure in terms of the relationship between switches. As illustrated in Figure 7.3, the flat design is mainly for a small LAN in which one or more switches are directly cabled with no apparent layered or tiered relationship between them. This approach is easy to implement and manage when the LAN size stays relatively modest.

7.4.1.2   Hierarchical Design

When the number of attached switches grows, the flat design approach becomes difficult in managing (e.g., troubleshooting), maintaining performance, and ensuring network reliability. For example, the campus network as an oversized LAN is formed by a number of smaller LANs and thus poses challenges in its management and operations. Imagine a university campus LAN that provides connectivity to thousands of servers, PCs, laptops, and mobile devices scattered in 40 building LANs through 800 switches of various speeds, 3000 wireless access points, and 100 routers (including layer 3 switches). The campus LAN is simply too big to adopt the flat design.

(a) **Three-tier architecture**: If a large LAN consists of a number of smaller LANs, each with a number of network nodes, the three-tier hierarchical design (or topology) can be adopted. In this scheme, intermediary devices (e.g., layer 2 or 3 switches, routers) are assigned to the *access*, *distribution*, or *core* layers. As an example, imagine that the campus LAN in our example consists of 40 building LANs. Then, in each building, a distribution switch connects to access (or workgroup) switches in the wiring closet(s) of each floor forming the two-tier relationship. Then, the distribution switches of 40 different buildings can be coupled by the third-tier, core layer switches to complete the campus LAN.

(b) **Two-tier architecture**: Alternatively, when the LAN of a company is not large enough to justify the three-layer structure (e.g., a building of modest size), the firm may opt for the two-tier architecture in which the core and distribution layers are combined to become one layer. In the two-tier approach, therefore, the core layer switch provides interconnectivity of access layer devices.

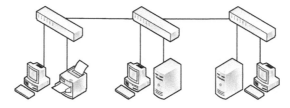

FIGURE 7.3   Ethernet with flat structure (logical view)

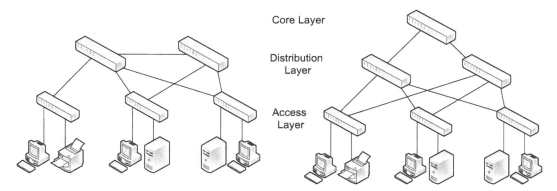

FIGURE 7.4   Two-tier (left) vs. three-tier (right) design of Ethernet LANs (logical view)

Figure 7.4 demonstrates a logical view of the two-tier versus three-tier structures of a LAN. The figures are labeled as 'logical' to highlight the association relationship of switches placed in different layers. In fact, their corresponding physical layout is quite different from the logical view because switches from different tiers may be co-located. For instance, imagine the situation where a distribution layer and core layer switches are co-located in the main equipment room of a building. The physical layout of intermediary devices is explained in terms of the *structured cabling system* concept in Chapter 13 (see Section 13.4.2).

7.4.2 ACCESS LAYER IN HIERARCHICAL DESIGN

In the access layer, computers, network printers, IP phones, and other end nodes are connected to the LAN via such intermediary devices as access (or workgroup) switches and wireless access points. Generally, layer 2 devices are popular choices to link user stations and servers to the network. Ethernet switches in the access layer are primarily equipped with Fast Ethernet (100 Mbps), Gigabit (1000 Mbps), or 10 Gigabit Ethernet ports these days.

7.4.2.1 Access Layer Switches

Access layer switches support various management functions. For example, switches can be configured for controlled access to prevent unauthorized computers from joining the network. For example, a switch port can grant only one or two pre-assigned MAC addresses to physically connect. Also, they allow the formation of *virtual LANs* (or VLANs) so that hosts attached to a network can be logically divided into groups. More on VLANs in terms of their implementation and ensuing benefits are explained shortly. Besides, many access switches are *Power over Ethernet* (PoE) enabled so that the Ethernet cable can supply electrical power along with data to connecting nodes such as wireless access points, IP phones, and security cameras. With the PoE support, these devices can be flexibly placed in convenient or strategic locations not constrained by the availability of power sources (refer to Section 5.5.6.6).

7.4.3 DISTRIBUTION AND CORE LAYERS IN HIERARCHICAL DESIGN

The distribution layer mediates traffic between the access and core layers. The core layer's intermediary devices tie network segments of the access layer. Because of the hierarchical relationship among network nodes, much traffic is handled by the top two tiers, and the planning of these layers should facilitate rapid packet forwarding to prevent congestions. To ensure this, layer 2 or 3 switches or routers in these layers are generally faster (e.g., Gigabit, 10 Gigabit) than access layer switches.

7.4.3.1   Full Mesh vs. Partial Mesh

Whether a hierarchical network is two-tiered or three-tiered, its designer has choices of interconnecting intermediary devices of the core and distribution layers in either *full mesh* or *partial mesh*. Having redundant paths in the two layers through full or partial mesh is critical to prevent the formation of a single point of failure and to minimize the risk of LAN downtime due to device or link failures.

There has been an increasing popularity of the non-traditional Ethernet topology called Leaf-Spine, which adopts the two-layer architecture similar to Figure 7.4. Thus, it is composed of access (or leaf) and core (or spine) switches but they are connected in the full mesh, instead of the partial mesh, topology. The 'full mesh' is intended to improve the handling of 'lateral traffic' (also called east-west traffic) between servers and virtual machines attached to access layer switches. The lateral traffic has been growing as more applications are time-sensitive and/or data-intensive.

7.4.3.2   Device Types

The core and distribution layer devices may be layer 2 switches, layer 3 switches, or routers. Unlike layer 3 switches and routers, layer 2 switches cannot *route* IP packets, but they offer faster and more cost-effective network services. In today's campus LAN, layer 3 switches are used widely in the distribution and core layers because they can also do IP packet routing faster than ordinary routers (see Section 5.5.6.4). Although they may not be as versatile as routers in performing packet routing, layer 3 switches can handle relatively simple routing faster within an enterprise network.

Lastly, the core and distribution layers are primarily responsible for interconnecting *virtual LANs* (VLANs) configured on access layer switches. The process of coupling VLANs is called inter-VLAN routing (to be explained).

7.4.4   Benefits of Hierarchical Design

The hierarchical network design offers several benefits to an organization including its flexibility in adding a large number of hosts, managing the network, sustaining network performance, and ensuring network reliability.
   a. The network becomes more modular and the modularity makes it easy to manage (e.g., configuration), maintain (e.g., troubleshoot), and grow (i.e., scalability) the network as needed.
   b. With the layer approach, the access-level local traffic and the enterprise-level traffic at the distribution/core layers are separated, and the separation contributes to the better usage of network capacity.
   c. Optimizing network performance through such measures as *link aggregation* (see Section 7.6) becomes less complicated.
   d. It is easy to add link redundancy between intermediary nodes to improve network availability. During normal operations, however, only a single path (or data link) is activated between any two switch nodes and redundant paths are disabled to avoid loops (revisit Section 5.7.3). The function of maintaining only a single active delivery path between any two switches is performed by the *Spanning Tree Protocol* running on switches (to be explained).

7.5   SPANNING TREE PROTOCOL (STP)

7.5.1   Link Redundancy

7.5.1.1   Importance of Having Link Redundancy

It was explained that, when multiple switches are joined, redundant physical links are added to prevent a single point of device or cabling failure from crippling the network. Take Figure 7.5 as an example, the three access layer switches (D, E, and F) can be directly connected to each other without the help of additional switches (A, B, and C). However, when the switches D, E, and F are

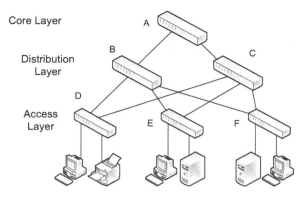

FIGURE 7.5   Availability of redundant paths (logical view)

directly cabled in the flat design, the disruption of any trunk link affects the integrity of the entire network, and thus it becomes a single point of failure. Meanwhile, Figure 7.5 shows that with the addition of A, B, and C switches, redundant paths are created between nodes. For example, the packet delivery from switch D to switch F can take the path: (1) D → C → F; (2) D → B → F; or (3) D → B → A → C → F. This redundancy is important to have improved accessibility and availability of a switched LAN even when a part of it goes down.

7.5.1.2   Unintended Creation of Link Redundancy

Configuration mistakes: Although link redundancy is intentionally introduced to increase network availability and survivability through backup paths, there are also situations in which such redundancy is formed unexpectedly. For example, due to the complexity of a large switched network, its network administrator may make mistakes in connecting and configuring switch ports resulting in link redundancy. The chance of making such configuration mistakes gets higher when an IT person deals with switches distributed in several wiring closets on different floors. In this situation, many cables coming from different rooms and floors can confuse him/her in cabling.

Rogue devices: Unintended redundancy can be introduced by non-IT staff (e.g., computer end-users) when they add their own intermediary devices such as hubs to their workplace in order to attach additional end nodes. As a scenario, Figure 7.6 demonstrates a network in which two hubs are locally installed by office workers to connect more computers. When the two hubs are directly linked, this results in link redundancy.

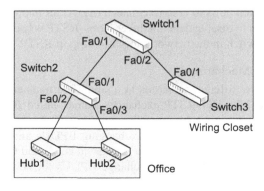

FIGURE 7.6   Network redundancy created at a work area

7.5.1.3 Consequence of Link Redundancy

Then, what is wrong with having additional links on a switched Ethernet, allowing multiple paths between nodes? As explained previously, switches are data link devices relying on the switch table to forward frames. With layer 2 switching, there should be only a single active path (or data link) between any two hosts, making it different from the layer 3 routing that allows multiple delivery paths at one point (revisit Section 5.7.3).

When there exists more than one active path to traverse between any two points in a switched network, this forms a loop. One or more loops in a switched Ethernet can be highly detrimental to its normal operations because the loop allows the perpetual circulation of certain frames (e.g., broadcasted frames) in the network.

In layer 3 packet routing, the gradual decrement of the *time to live* (TTL) field value of an IP packet fundamentally prevents it from going astray on the Internet endlessly (refer to Section 3.7.1). The Ethernet frame, however, does not contain such TTL value that automatically disqualifies it. For instance, assume that the redundant links in Figure 7.5 are all active and that a station broadcasts an ARP (Address Resolution Protocol) packet to switch D. This triggers a continuous reproduction of ARP packets flooding the network. This risk becomes one important reason (besides security concerns) that the unauthorized installation of intermediary devices by end users should be banned.

To summarize, the Ethernet LAN may have redundant links between any two switch nodes to restore connectivity when there is a link or switch node failure. However, only a single path should be active at a time to prevent the formation of a loop that can trigger broadcast storms and deteriorate network performance. The reproduction of broadcasting also results in repeated arrivals of the same frame at a host computer, resulting in frame duplications.

7.5.2 LOOP DETECTION WITH STP

Then, how to detect and resolve the formation of redundant links and resulting loops on a switched Ethernet?

7.5.2.1 Loop Detection Protocol

Ethernet switches are equipped with a protocol that can automatically recognize a loop between any two switch nodes and selectively block switch ports to sever the loop. For this, the protocol elects a switch as the *root switch*, and then redundant paths to the root switch are identified and blocked. The loop detection process itself is beyond the scope of this book. Here, the loop-forming switch ports are not physically shut down but just blocked (similar to the sleep mode) so that they can be awakened as needed (e.g., changes in the network topology).

The IEEE standard protocol that identifies redundant paths and performs their de-activation and re-activation is the *Spanning Tree Protocol* (STP). The newer version, the *Rapid Spanning Tree Protocol* (RSTP), performs much faster convergence than STP in identifying and removing loops or reactivating blocked switch ports to restore connectivity. As an improvement of STP, RSTP has become a preferred protocol to disable data link layer loops. RSTP is backward compatible and thus rolled back to STP if any switch in the network does not support RSTP.

7.5.2.2 Loop Detection Mechanism

Figure 7.7 demonstrates two different scenarios in a simplified manner. During the normal mode of operations as in Figure 7.7a, STP/RSTP exchanges frames called *Bridge Protocol Data Units* (BPDUs) that contain information used by switches to ultimately locate redundant paths based on the built-in algorithm. Let's assume that after exchanging BPDUs and executing the STP/RSTP algorithm, it is determined that the direct link between switches B and C should be disabled to cut the loop. To do this, Switch B and Switch C exchange BPDUs for necessary coordination. Then, one port (either Fa0/2 of Switch B or Fa0/2 of Switch C) turns into the *blocking state* that does not accept regular frames.

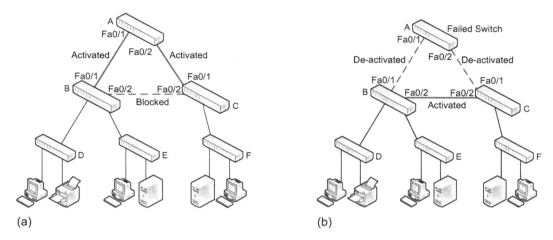

FIGURE 7.7 Demonstration of STP/RSTP (logical view)

Meanwhile, when there is a change in the network topology such as Switch A's failure as in Figure 7.7b, Switch B and Switch C exchange BPDUs and the blocked port is rolled back from the *blocking* to *forwarding* mode to reinstate the link. To make that happen, the switch port processes BPDUs even when it is in the blocking (or sleep) mode. STP/RSTP of a switch is automatically activated when the device is put into production.

7.6 LINK AGGREGATION

This section explains the *link aggregation* (also known as *port trunking* or *port bonding*) technology used by Ethernet. With this technology, two or more physical links between any two network nodes (e.g., a server and a switch) are combined to become one logical link with a bigger capacity. With link aggregation, therefore, bandwidth between two devices is multiplied by the number of concurrent links. Figure 7.8 demonstrates two different scenarios of link aggregation.

7.6.1 LINK AGGREGATION: SCENARIO 1

In Figure 7.8a, the bonding of two Fast Ethernet ports (Fa0/0 and Fa0/1) between two switches increases bandwidth to 200 Mbps in both directions (full-duplex) when each link has a speed of 100 Mbps. This allows the two workstations connected to a switch to transmit at their full speed (100 Mbps) without delays. Also, with the bonding, there is no need for upgrading the switches with a faster port speed (e.g., gigabit Ethernet). In Figure 7.8b, two Fast Ethernet ports (Fa0/1 and Fa0/2) are linked to two NICs (or a multiport NIC) of a server, effectively augmenting throughput to 200 Mbps in full-duplex.

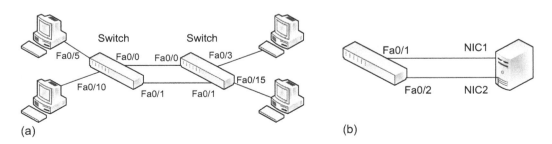

FIGURE 7.8 Link aggregation: Scenario 1

7.6.2   LINK AGGREGATION: SCENARIO 2

Think of another scenario in Figure 7.9. There are three core/distribution Gigabit Ethernet switches connecting three workgroup (or access) switches. All core/distribution switches have Gigabit Ethernet ports and workgroup switches have both Gigabit and Fast Ethernet ports. Access switches attach a number of hosts including servers via their Fast Ethernet ports. Servers use link aggregation to cut their response time. In this situation, if each of the trunk lines between A and B, and between A and C, relies on a single Gigabit link, it can become a bottleneck when the aggregated traffic to switch A surpasses its link capacity. In that situation, the aggregation of two or more links between A and B, and between A and C, mitigates the bottleneck risk.

7.6.3   LINK AGGREGATION CONTROL PROTOCOL

The link aggregation can be done by issuing relatively simple commands to managed switches. The technology standard from IEEE is *Link Aggregation Control Protocol* (LACP). LACP allows bundling of up to 8 ports, although some switch products may support fewer than that. The LACP-based link aggregation on a switch is implemented by issuing commands similar to (somewhat different depending on the device manufacturer):

#lacp	(Note: Activate LACP protocol)
#add port=1,3	(Note: Port 1 and 3 are bonded)

In summary, using link aggregation offers several obvious benefits:

- It multiplies the bandwidth of a network path, contributing to better network performance through load balancing.
- It is a cost-effective way of augmenting link capacity without upgrading current hardware (e.g., intermediary devices, cabling). With the advancement of Ethernet standard speeds (i.e., 100 Mbps → 1,000 Mbps → 10,000 Mbps), replacing existing switches with faster ones can be costly.
- The bonding of switch ports has the effect of creating a backup link between two nodes and thus enhances a network's availability and accessibility.

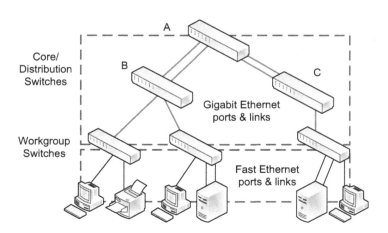

FIGURE 7.9   Link aggregation: Scenario 2

7.7 VIRTUAL LANS (VLANS)

7.7.1 BACKGROUND: WITHOUT VLANs

Imagine a firm's hypothetical LAN with several switches that attach many user stations and servers as in Figure 7.10. It shows that the computers belong to three different departments/groups: IT, Marketing, and Accounting. To be more realistic, you can assume that each computer represents a collection of hosts.

Assume that these computers are located on three different floors of a building interconnected by workgroup and core switches. As the company is relatively small, the two-tier hierarchical solution with one subnet of the production network makes it easy to set up, maintain, and operate the LAN. However, when the company's network gets larger, with many more user stations and servers, the single subnet approach is no longer effective because all nodes are in one large broadcast domain (revisit Section 5.9).

7.7.1.1 Effects of Message Broadcasting

Network nodes, including switches, workstations, and servers, routinely broadcast (or multicast) packets to conduct network functions and the broadcast reaches all nodes of a subnet. For instance, the *Spanning Tree Protocol* (STP) installed in switches periodically releases multicasting messages to find redundant paths between any two network nodes. Also, the *Address Resolution Protocol* (ARP) is a busy protocol that broadcasts an inquiry to obtain the MAC address of an IP address. As another example, the *Dynamic Host Configuration Protocol* (DHCP) request is broadcasted by host stations (e.g., laptops, tablets, smartphones) to obtain a dynamic IP address.

More often than not, such broadcasting should be limited to a sub-section or a sub-group (e.g., business department, project group) of the entire broadcast domain. In this situation, packets unnecessarily crossing the sub-section or sub-group boundaries (e.g., across business units) not only negatively affect overall network performance but also have security implications. The side effects become more evident and serious when the network gets larger by adding more hosts and covers functionally diverse business units/groups. A clear solution for such a problem is *modularization*, for which a network is segmented and managed as a collection of modules (or segments).

7.7.1.2 Network Segmentation with Routers

Then, what solutions exist to divide the network into smaller segments? One approach is to place routers to create smaller subnetworks because the router filters broadcasting (revisit Section 5.9.2).

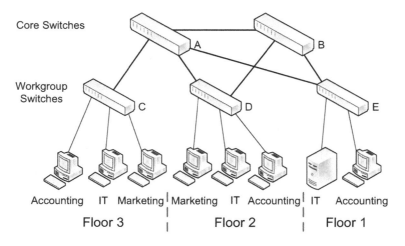

FIGURE 7.10 Logical layout of a LAN

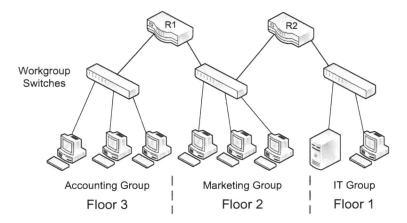

FIGURE 7.11   Router-based segmentation of a LAN

This solution makes sense when all hosts attached to a particular switch belong to the same functional group (e.g., accounting) as in Figure 7.11. In this case, a router port (interface) can be dedicated to the hosts of a particular unit/group. This works neatly because the subnetwork boundary defined by a router port and the boundary of a business unit coincide.

However, using routers poses practical challenges when the ports of a switch are assigned to multiple groups/units that may share offices on the same floor, as in Figure 7.10. This arrangement rather reflects the reality of most organizations these days, making it difficult to utilize routers to limit traffic flows (especially broadcasted traffic) to a group. Then, is there a way that a switched Ethernet can be conveniently divided into logical segments as needed without relying on the router(s) while allowing the flexible addition of hosts from different departments/groups to switches regardless of their physical locations? This is where the VLAN technology comes in.

7.7.2 VLAN CONCEPT

With the creation of VLANs on switches, a switched LAN normally as one broadcast domain can be further segmented into multiple broadcast domains according to certain logical boundaries such as workgroups, project teams, and departments. Figure 7.12 demonstrates what happens when a message is broadcasted to the network with two VLANs, as the message reaches only stations and servers belonging to the same VLAN.

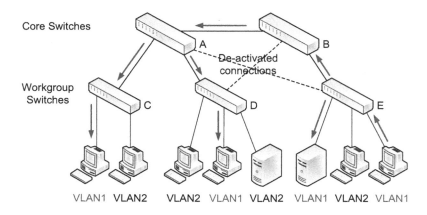

FIGURE 7.12   Limiting broadcasting effects with VLANs

7.8   VLAN SCENARIOS

7.8.1   WITHOUT VLANs

For a more in-depth explanation of VLANs and their relationship with IP configurations, think of a simple network in which all six computers from three business departments (IT, Marketing, and Accounting) and three switches belong to the same subnet of 192.168.10.0/24 (see Figure 7.13). As all end nodes belong to the same subnet, a broadcasted message will reach all connected switch ports, except the source port. Again, to be more realistic, you can assume that each computer represents a group of host stations.

In Figure 7.13, all hosts belong to the *default VLAN* (VLAN ID = 1) when there are no specific VLANs configured on the switches. In other words, all hosts in Figure 7.13 belong to the same VLAN of VLAN ID = 1, and this means that any host can send data link frames to any other host without restrictions. With no particular VLANs defined, the switch table for Switch B reads like Table 7.1. The table allows direct mapping between a destination MAC address and its exit port, and all exit ports belong to the same default VLAN of VLAN ID = 1. It is a traditional switch table explained in Chapter 5 (see Table 5.4).

7.8.2   WITH VLANs

Is there a way to divide a switched Ethernet LAN into segments (i.e., broadcast domains) without relying on routers? Creating virtual LANs (or VLANs) is the answer. VLANs are formed by adequately configuring switch ports. VLANs can be created in a static or dynamic manner. With the dynamic approach, switch ports are dynamically assigned to VLANs by a dedicated server based on such information as the MAC address of a computer attached to a switch port. This dynamic allocation, however, has not been a widely accepted practice.

In the rest of this chapter, the explanation focuses on creating static VLANs on Ethernet switches. Once VLANs are deployed, computers belonging to different VLANs cannot exchange frames directly through the switches and also a frame broadcasted by a computer only reaches to other

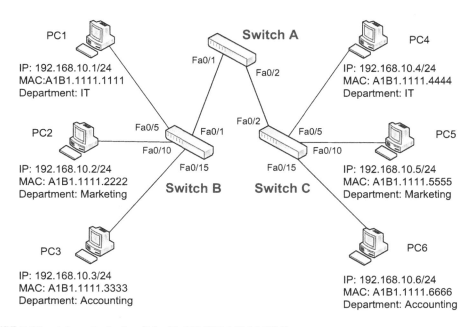

FIGURE 7.13   A hypothetical switched LAN (192.168.10.0/24)

TABLE 7.1
Switch B's switch table with default VLAN ID

MAC adress	Exit port	VLAN ID
A1B1.1111.1111	FastEthernet 0/5	1
A1B1.1111.2222	FastEthernet 0/10	1
A1B1.1111.3333	FastEthernet 0/15	1
A1B1.1111.4444	FastEthernet 0/1	1
A1B1.1111.5555	FastEthernet 0/1	1
A1B1.1111.6666	FastEthernet 0/1	1

computers within the same VLAN. To establish static VLANs, a network administrator conducts the following steps that involve both planning and actual configurations:

1. Define VLANs on switches (Planning/Switch configuration)
2. Decide the overall range of trunk and access ports (Planning)
3. Decide a specific range of access ports for each VLAN (Planning)
4. Configure access and trunk ports on switches (Switch configuration)

7.8.2.1 Define VLANs on Switches

In this stage, VLANs (VLAN IDs and VLAN names) are created on switches from Cisco. For demonstration, let's assume that there are 24 Fast Ethernet ports on each of the three switches in Figure 7.13, and it is decided to develop one VLAN for each business unit. An example is presented next, where VLAN IDs of 10, 20, and 30 are assigned to the IT, Marketing, and Accounting departments respectively. (It is unnecessary to memorize the commands.)

Example: Defining three VLANs on a Cisco switch

```
# vlan 10
# name IT
# vlan 20
# name Marketing
# vlan 30
# name Accounting
```

7.8.2.2 Decide Overall Range of Trunk and Access Ports

A switch port becomes either an *access port* or a *trunk port* (recall the definition of the access and trunks links in Chapter 1). In this stage, the ranges of trunk and access switch ports are pre-planned for subsequent configuration in the third stage. For instance, given 24 ports in each switch, we may decide that the first 3 (Fa0/1 ~ Fa0/3) are for trunk ports and the remaining 21 (Fa0/4 ~ Fa0/21) are for access ports.

Access port: The switch port that directly links a host (e.g., workstation, server) is set up as an *access* port, and therefore, the access port provides the host with physical connectivity to the network. In Figure 7.14, as an example, Switch B uses three access ports (Fa0/5, Fa0/10, and Fa0/15) for PC1, PC2, and PC3 respectively. Each *access link* connects a computer's NIC port (mostly RJ-45 port) to an access port of Switch B.

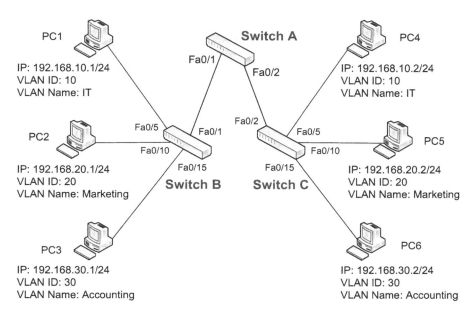

FIGURE 7.14 A switched LAN with three VLANs

An access port belongs to a particular VLAN, and it forwards frames only when the source and destinations computers are on the same VLAN. That is, computers attached to the access ports of VLAN 10 cannot communicate directly with computers attached to the access ports of VLAN 20 or VLAN 30, despite that the host computers are all hardwired to the same switch.

Trunk port: The switch port designated to connect another switch is configured as a *trunk* port and the cabling itself becomes a *trunk* link. Unlike the access port that belongs to a single VLAN, the *trunk port* transports frames of any VLAN. The trunk link, therefore, is a point-to-point link that interconnects trunk ports of two different switches and transports the traffic of all VLANs.

In Figure 7.14, as an example, Switch B's Fa0/1 is a trunk port that forwards frames from VLAN 10, VLAN 20, and VLAN 30 to Switch A's trunk port Fa0/1 over the trunk link. You can also observe another trunk link between Switch A's trunk port Fa0/2 and Switch C's trunk port Fa0/2.

7.8.2.3 Decide Specific Range of Access Ports for Each VLAN

In this stage, each 'access' port is assigned to one VLAN in a non-overlapping manner. (Although multiple VLANs can be assigned to a switch port, the technical details are beyond the scope of this book.) For example, let's assume that, in the planning stage, it was decided that the first 3 (Fa0/1 ~ Fa0/3) are for trunk ports and the remaining 21 (Fa0/4 ~ Fa0/21) are for access ports.

Then, in one scenario, the 21 access ports available can be assigned to VLANs, as in Table 7.2. According to the allocation plan, ports Fa0/4 though Fa0/8 are exclusively used for VLAN 10 on each switch. With that allocation, a computer connected to any switch port between Fa0/4 and Fa0/8 belongs to the IT department. The same applies to VLAN 20 and VLAN 30. Meanwhile, three switch ports (i.e., Fa0/1, Fa0/2, and Fa0/3) have been dedicated as trunk ports and therefore cannot be assigned to a particular VLAN ID.

7.8.2.4 Configure Access and Trunk Ports on Switches

In this stage, based on the previous planning (Sections 7.8.2.2 and 7.8.2.3), access ports are assigned to VLANs, and trunk ports are defined manually. For this, we apply the same configuration to all switches. In practice, the 'manual' configuration on a switch can be automatically replicated to all other switches using a standard protocol. Using the protocol saves much work and also prevents human mistakes in setting up VLANs when many switches are attached to a network.

Once the necessary VLANs are programmed, the switch forwards Ethernet frames only when the source and destination hosts belong to the same VLAN. To demonstrate how a switch port becomes an access port or a trunk port, the necessary commands are shown as follows based on the Cisco product.

Example: Cisco switch

Assigning the access port range (Fa0/4~Fa0/8) to VLAN 10 takes three commands entered successively into the command prompt.

# *interface range* Fa0/4–8	Note: Fa0/4~Fa0/8 are to be configured
# *switchport mode* access	Note: Fa0/4~Fa0/8 are access ports
# *switchport* access vlan 10	Note: Assign Fa0/4~Fa0/8 to VLAN 10

Setting up switch ports (Fa0/1~Fa0/3) as trunk ports takes three commands entered in succession into the command prompt.

# *interface range* Fa0/1–3	Note: Fa0/1~Fa0/3 are to be configured
# *switchport trunk encapsulation dot1q*	Note: Use 802.1Q tagging protocol
# *switchport mode* trunk	Note: Fa0/1~Fa0/3 are trunk ports

• Comment: The 802.1Q tagging protocol is explained in Section 7.9.

7.8.3 SEGMENTED BROADCAST DOMAINS

Once VLANs are created on the switches, only computers attached to the same VLAN ports (e.g., PC1 and PC4) can directly exchange frames through switches. Also, each VLAN becomes a broadcast domain, meaning that when a switch port receives a frame to broadcast, it is relayed only to other access ports sharing the same VLAN ID. That way, the switched Ethernet LAN in Figure 7.14 is divided into three broadcast domains, each pertaining to a business function.

Once the VLANs are configured and when enough frames are exchanged over the network (refer to Section 5.5.5.2), each switch will complete its own switch table. The completed switch table of Switch B is shown in Table 7.3. Notice the VLAN IDs changed from the default VLAN ID = 1.

TABLE 7.2

Sample allocation plan of switch ports to VLANs

Port type	Port ranges	VLAN IDs	VLAN names
Trunk ports	Fa0/1~Fa0/3		
Access ports	Fa0/4~Fa0/8	VLAN 10	IT
	Fa0/9~Fa0/14	VLAN 20	Marketing
	Fa0/15~Fa0/24	VLAN 30	Accounting

TABLE 7.3
Switch B's switch table with three VLANs

MAC address	Exit port	VLAN ID
A1B1.1111.1111	FastEthernet 0/5	10
A1B1.1111.2222	FastEthernet 0/10	20
A1B1.1111.3333	FastEthernet 0/15	30
A1B1.1111.4444	FastEthernet 0/1	10
A1B1.1111.5555	FastEthernet 0/1	20
A1B1.1111.6666	FastEthernet 0/1	30

7.8.4 VLAN ID vs. Subnet Addressing

There is an important question on what should be the relationship between the VLAN and the subnet address. Generally, one-to-one mapping between the VLAN ID and the subnet IP address (see Figure 7.14) is a popular practice, although one VLAN can include multiple subnets and multiple VLANs can belong to one subnet. The one-to-one pairing between the VLAN and the subnet address simplifies network administration. This also means that the VLAN and subnetwork boundaries are identical on a switched Ethernet LAN (without using a router!).

Pairing a VLAN and a subnet can be confusing because it contradicts the early explanation that the subnet boundary is defined by a router port. With VLANs, however, you can observe that the traditional subnet boundary is further divided into multiple subnets on a *switched network* without relying on the router. The one-to-one mapping relationship in Figure 7.14 is summarized as:

VLAN name	VLAN ID	Subnet IP
IT	10	192.168.10.0/24
Marketing	20	192.168.20.0/24
Accounting	30	192.168.30.0/24

7.9 VLAN TAGGING/TRUNKING (IEEE 802.1Q)

7.9.1 Background

Going back to Figure 7.14, assume that PC1 and PC3 are on the same VLAN, let's say VLAN 10. In this situation, if PC1 sends a frame to PC3, switch B will directly forward the Ethernet frame to PC3 after referring to its own switch table and confirming that both PCs are on the same VLAN 10.

When two PCs on the same VLAN are not directly connected to the same switch, delivering an Ethernet frame between them becomes a little tricky. For example, assume that an Ethernet frame needs to be delivered from PC1 to PC4 in Figure 7.14. The two PCs are attached to two different switches, Switch B and Switch C. This means that the Ethernet frame needs to travel through two trunk links (i.e., the first one between Switch B and Switch A, and the second one between Switch A and Switch C).

As trunk links transport frames from all VLANs, there should be a mechanism that identifies the VLAN ID of a particular Ethernet frame. The delivery process of Ethernet frames from different VLANs over the trunk link is termed *trunking* (see Figure 7.15). So, VLAN trunking takes place between switches, but not between hosts and switches. The mechanism for implementing VLAN trunking is standardized by the IEEE 802.1Q standard (revisit Section 7.8.2.4 to make sense of the tagging statement).

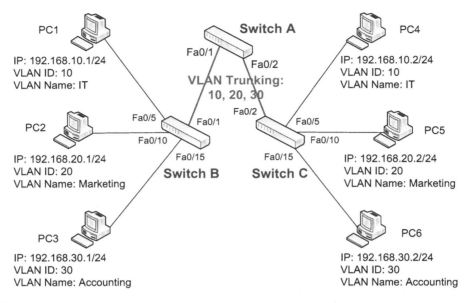

FIGURE 7.15   VLAN trunking/tagging

7.9.2   VLAN TAGGING

To implement VLAN trunking, IEEE 802.1Q uses *tagging* for which a switch inserts VLAN-related information into the regular Ethernet frame arriving from an attached host and then releases the tagged frame through a trunk port. In other words, regular frames are produced by hosts, and they are transformed into VLAN tagged frames by switches. Figure 7.16 compares the regular frame with the VLAN tagged frame that has two additional fields intended to convey VLAN information: *Tag Protocol Identifier* (TPID) and *Tag Control Information* (TCI).

The TPID field has a decimal value of 33024, which signals VLAN presence within an Ethernet frame. The length field of a regular frame can have only up to 1500 in decimal and, thus, a switch

Regular Ethernet Frame		Frame with VLAN Tag	
Preamble	7 bytes	Preamble	
Start-of-Frame Delimiter	1 byte	Start-of-Frame Delimiter	
Destination Address	6 bytes	Destination Address	
Source Address	6 bytes	Source Address	
Length (46~1500 bytes) or Type of Payload		Tag Protocol Identifier Value (TPID) = 33,024	2 bytes
Payload (Data)	2 bytes	Tag Control Info: Priority (3 bits); VLAN ID (12 bits)	2 bytes
Pad (if necessary)	variable	Length (46~1500 bytes) or Type of Payload	
Frame Check Sequence		Payload (Data)	
	4 bytes	Pad (if necessary)	
		Frame Check Sequence	

FIGURE 7.16   Ethernet frames: Regular vs. VLAN tagged

can tell the tagged frame. The TCI field is composed of *Priority* (3) and *VLAN ID* (12) bits. With the priority bits, an Ethernet frame is able to indicate its urgency in delivery. The priority bits are important because the frames of certain VLANs (e.g., voice-over IP) cannot afford delays. The VLAN ID bits identify the VLAN an Ethernet frame belongs to.

7.9.3 VLAN Tagging/Untagging Process

To demonstrate how the VLAN tagging works, let's assume that an Ethernet frame is delivered from PC3 to PC6 in Figure 7.17. It is also assumed that VLANs have already been fully configured on the switches according to Table 7.2's allocation plan. Also, presume that all three switches have their completed switch tables as in Table 7.3 for Switch B.

The delivery of a frame from PC3 to PC6 takes the following steps:

a. Initially, PC3's NIC constructs a regular Ethernet frame (see Figure 7.16) and dispatches it to Switch B's Fa0/15.
b. On receiving the frame, Switch B recognizes the VLAN configuration of its Fa0/15 port and adds a VLAN tag of TPID and TCI (see Figure 7.16) to the regular frame. Here, the VLAN ID becomes 30.
c. Once the VLAN tag is added by Switch B, it refers to the switch table to identify the exit port for PC6's MAC address and confirms that PC6 belongs to the same VLAN 30. Switch B releases the tagged frame through the trunk port, Fa0/1.
d. Switch A receives the tagged frame. It checks its switch table to determine the exit port for PC6's MAC address, confirms that PC6 belongs to the same VLAN 30, and forwards the tagged frame to Switch C through its trunk port, Fa0/2.
e. Switch C, on receiving the tagged frame, checks its own switch table to determine the exit port for PC6's MAC address and confirms that PC6 belongs to the same VLAN 30. It then removes the VLAN tag from the frame and dispatches the original regular frame to PC6 via its access port Fa0/15.

The tagging and untagging procedure between PC3 and PC6 is summarized in Figure 7.17.

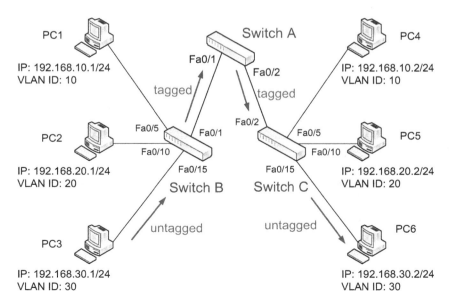

FIGURE 7.17 VLAN tagging and untagging

7.10 VLAN TYPES

Various VLAN types can be defined on a switched LAN, and Default VLAN, Data VLAN, and Voice VLAN are explained as popular VLAN types.

7.10.1 DEFAULT VLAN

As explained, all switch ports automatically belong to the *Default VLAN* when a switch is in out-of-the-box condition and not configured with any other specific VLAN(s). In other words, all host stations attached to the switch belong to one broadcast domain of the default VLAN (see Table 7.1). Thus, all computers in Figure 7.13 are not segmented by additional VLANs, and therefore they all belong to the default VLAN. In this mode, the regular frame produced by a source host is relayed by switches without VLAN tagging.

7.10.1.1 Example: Default VLAN on Cisco Switch

The Cisco switch stores its VLAN information in the *vlan.data* file kept in its flash memory and it can be displayed by issuing '*show vlan*' at the command prompt. Figure 7.18 indicates that the switch has 24 Fast Ethernet ports, and all belong to the default VLAN. In other words, all 24 ports belong to the same broadcast domain with no restriction in communications between any two computers attached to the switch.

7.10.2 DATA VLAN

Data VLANs are designed to transport computer-generated data traffic and the majority of VLANs belong to this type. As an example, Figure 7.17 demonstrates three different data VLANs assigned to IT (VLAN 10), Marketing (VLAN 20), and Accounting (VLAN 30) units to segment the *switched* Ethernet into three logical boundaries (and three broadcast domains).

7.10.2.1 Example: Data VLANs on Cisco Switch

Figure 7.19 displays switch ports assigned to VLAN 10, 20, and 30 according to the allocation plan in Table 7.2. In that plan, the ports ranging from Fa0/4 through Fa0/24 are access ports. Meanwhile,

```
SwitchB# show vlan

VLAN    Name        Status       Ports
-------  ----------  ----------   -------------------------------------
1        default     active       Fa0/1, Fa0/2, Fa0/3, Fa0/4, Fa0/5
                                  Fa0/6, Fa0/7, Fa0/8, Fa0/9, Fa0/10
                                  Fa0/11, Fa0/12, Fa0/13, Fa0/14, Fa0/15
                                  Fa0/16, Fa0/17, Fa0/18, Fa0/19, Fa0/20
                                  Fa0/21, Fa0/22, Fa0/23, Fa0/24
```

FIGURE 7.18 Default VLAN (Cisco switch)

```
SwitchB#show vlan

VLAN    Name        Status       Ports
-------  ----------  ----------   -------------------------------------
10       IT          active       Fa0/4, Fa0/5, Fa0/6, Fa0/7, Fa0/8
20       Marketing   active       Fa0/9, Fa0/10, Fa0/11, Fa0/12, Fa0/13, Fa0/14
30       Accounting  active       Fa0/15, Fa0/16, Fa0/17, Fa0/18, Fa0/19,
                                  Fa0/20, Fa0/21, Fa0/22, Fa0/23, Fa0/24
```

FIGURE 7.19 Data VLANs (Cisco switch)

the first three ports (i.e., Fa0/1~Fa0/3) were planned as trunk ports. As they were not assigned to any particular VLAN, the three ports are not listed in the VLAN summary.

7.10.2.2 Data VLAN and Network Security

Data VLANs with more specific objectives can be created to serve organizational needs. For example, imagine the following two scenarios in which VLANs aim to enhance network and data security (see Figure 7.20).

- **Scenario 1**: A firm's conference room is frequently occupied by guests and business clients. The room does not provide access to the corporate network for security reasons but offers Internet connectivity through a Wi-Fi access point (AP). Then, the AP can be assigned to a dedicated VLAN so that Wi-Fi traffic is separated from other internal traffic in order to safeguard the corporate network from potential threats.
- **Scenario 2**: A firm's data center holds a number of networked servers that store and process large amounts of corporate data. Imagine that the servers are not logically or physically detached from the rest of the corporate network, thus belonging to a larger broadcast domain. Then, attackers can find the servers (i.e., their IP addresses) easily by broadcasting Address Resolution Protocol (ARP) requests. However, if the data center belongs to a particular VLAN having its own broadcast domain, such an IP probe is prevented.

7.10.3 Voice VLAN

Voice VLAN is the one dedicated to voice traffic. The computer network has emerged as a cost-effective alternative to the traditional telephone system. Traditional voice communications require that an organization maintain a voice network separate from the data network. This incurs substantial maintenance and operational costs to the organization.

When the voice and data services are merged on the same network platform (see Figure 7.21), this convergence results in considerable cost savings in equipment purchase, operations, and management. For example, with the consolidation of voice and data, there is no need for additional purchase of telephone equipment, for hiring telephone network experts, and for separate maintenance of voice and data networks. In order to combine voice and data services without sacrificing call quality (e.g., call delays, call dropping), a VLAN can be dedicated to voice traffic. The voice VLAN transports digitized voice calls and also necessary signaling information (e.g., call setup, dial tones, caller IDs).

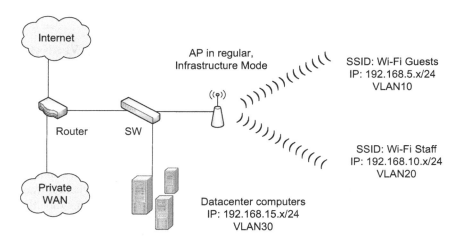

FIGURE 7.20 Improving network security with VLANs

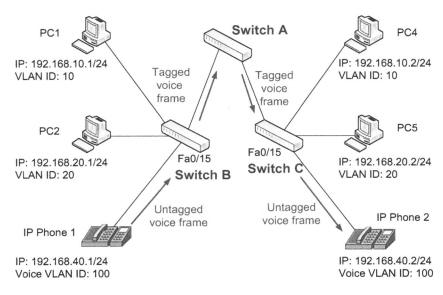

FIGURE 7.21 Demonstration of voice VLAN

7.10.3.1 Practical Implementation

- **High priority to voice VLAN traffic**: Given the time-sensitivity of voice traffic, calls should experience little transmission delays. To that end, the voice VLAN should be given a higher priority than the data VLAN in transporting frames over the trunk link (Recall the priority bits of Tag Control Information in Figure 7.16). Figure 7.21 demonstrates two Data VLANs (VLAN 10 and VLAN 20) and one Voice VLAN (VLAN100). To implement the differentiated priority scheme, both Switch B and Switch C are instructed to give a higher priority bit to frames arriving at the switch port (Fa0/15) that processes voice-related frames.

- **Access port with two VLAN IDs**: In fact, the reality of setting up the voice VLAN is a little more complicated than the simplified view in Figure 7.21. In practice, the port Fa0/15 of Switch B and Switch C can be given two VLAN IDs: one for Data VLAN and one for Voice VLAN. By doing that, one cable is shared by the two VLANs connecting both a VoIP phone and a computer to the Fa0/15 switch port. This makes sense because a worker's desk needs both a phone and a computer, and having separate cabling for each device is simply not an attractive solution.

Generalizing it, a switch port of an access link can be assigned to two or more VLANs for practical reasons (e.g., an employee who works for both Marketing and Accounting departments; an executive who heads both Accounting and IT departments; an engineer who is involved in multiple projects when a VLAN is created for each project team). Then, the switch port is configured as a trunk port, although it connects to an access link.

7.11 INTER-VLAN ROUTING (ADVANCED: OPTIONAL READING)

This section explains solutions available to exchange frames between VLANs, commonly known as inter-VLAN routing. It was shown that when a LAN has only Ethernet switches, frames cannot cross different VLANs directly. For instance, PC1 and PC5 in Figure 7.17 cannot directly exchange frames as they belong to VLAN 10 and VLAN 20 respectively. Then, what solutions are available to forward a frame from one VLAN to another? Generally, the inter-VLAN communication relies on the router. Alternatively, the layer-3 capable switch (or multi-layer switch) can be used instead of the router. It was previously explained that layer 3 switches perform basic router functions and thus are used much in the enterprise LAN.

Two different approaches to inter-VLAN routing are explained:

a. Assign a physical router port (interface) per subnet
b. Assign *sub-interfaces* to a physical router port to bridge multiple subnets

7.11.1   A ROUTER INTERFACE PER VLAN

In this solution, a router's physical port is dedicated to a VLAN (i.e., a subnet); thus, interconnecting several VLANs by a router needs as many designated physical ports. This is consistent with the principle that the network segment linked to a particular router port becomes a subnet.

7.11.1.1   Scenario 1

Figure 7.22 demonstrates a simple network with the inter-VLAN routing implemented based on *one physical port per VLAN* (thus, per subnet). There are two VLANs (VLAN 10 and VLAN 20) with corresponding two subnets. For IP packets to cross VLANs, the router connects the switch via two separate ports (Fa0/0 and Fa0/1), each port assigned to a subnet (thus a VLAN). VLAN 10 has a subnet address of 192.168.10.0/24 and the router's Fa0/0 with an IP address of 192.168.10.250 belongs to VLAN 10. Meanwhile, VLAN 20's subnet address is 192.168.20.0/24 and the router port Fa0/1 with 192.168.20.250 belongs to VLAN 20.

In this setup, although the switch cannot directly relay frames between VLAN 10 and VLAN 20, the router is able to bridge them with its routing capability. For the router to enable the inter-VLAN crossing, the router port's IP of a subnet is configured as the default gateway of computers in the subnet. Therefore:

PC1 and PC2 (VLAN 10) have the default gateway of 192.168.10.250
PC3 and PC4 (VLAN 20) have the default gateway of 192.168.20.250

Furthermore, each switch port (Fa0/4 for VLAN 10 and Fa0/11 for VLAN 20) that links to the router port becomes an access port, not as a trunk port, because each link transports frames of a single VLAN (or single subnet). This is in conflict with the definition in Chapter 1 in which any link between intermediary nodes is considered a trunk link. This is where the general definition of trunk links does not hold up.

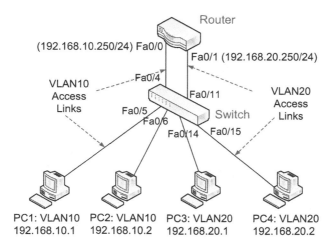

FIGURE 7.22   Assigning a router port per VLAN

7.11.1.2 Scenario 2

Let us take a look at another complicated scenario in which three switches connect two VLANs (see Figure 7.23). Here, the ports linking Switch 1 (Fa0/1) and Switch 2 (Fa0/1) and linking Switch 1 (Fa0/2) and Switch 3 (Fa0/1) are configured as trunk ports because they have to carry both VLAN 10 and VLAN 20 frames. Meanwhile, all the other switch ports including those (Fa0/3 and Fa0/24) between the Router and Switch 1 become access ports as they transport frames pertaining to only a particular VLAN (or a subnet). In other words, the router port Fa0/1 connects to 192.168.10.0/24 (VLAN 10), while the router port Fa0/2 becomes a default gateway for the subnet 192.168.20.0/24 (VLAN 20).

In this setup, the frames traveling between Switch 1 and Switch 2, and between Switch 1 and Switch 3, are tagged with VLAN information (i.e., TPID and TCI). However, Switch 1 untags the VLAN information when the frame is passed to the router for inter-VLAN routing. This approach of having one physical link to the router per subnet (thus VLAN) is relatively an easy solution when the VLAN structure is simple. However, if the number of VLANs increases, the solution is not sustainable, as more router ports and switch ports should be dedicated for inter-VLAN routing and this also requires more cabling.

7.11.2 SUB-INTERFACES/PORTS

The more widely used solution of inter-VLAN routing is to create multiple *virtual interfaces* (called sub-interfaces) tied to one *physical interface* (e.g., Fa0/1) and then assign a sub-interface to a VLAN. This means that the router can use just one physical interface to link multiple VLANs (thus, multiple subnets). With the use of virtual interfaces (or ports), the router does not need to have as many physical links as VLANs. This makes it fundamentally different from the dedication of a physical interface (or port) per VLAN as in Figures 7.22 and 7.23, making the network topology simpler with reduced physical links.

For example, Figure 7.24 shows the same network topology as Figure 7.23, except that there is only one physical link between the Router and Switch 1. For this, the router's physical interface

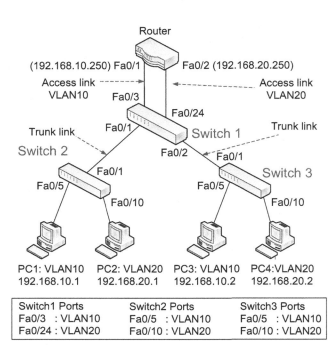

Switch1 Ports	Switch2 Ports	Switch3 Ports
Fa0/3 : VLAN10	Fa0/5 : VLAN10	Fa0/5 : VLAN10
Fa0/24 : VLAN20	Fa0/10 : VLAN20	Fa0/10 : VLAN20

FIGURE 7.23 Assigning a router port per VLAN

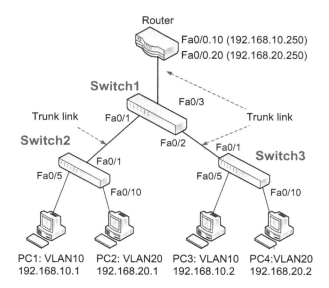

FIGURE 7.24 Inter-VLAN routing with sub-interfaces

TABLE 7.4

Relationships between physical interface, virtual interfaces, VLAN IDs, and IP addresses (this is not a routing table)

Physical interface	Virtual interfaces (sub-interfaces)	VLAN ID	IP address
Fa0/0	Fa0/0.10	10	192.168.10.250
	Fa0/0.20	20	192.168.20.250

Fa0/0 can have two logical/virtual interfaces (let's say Fa0/0.10 for VLAN 10 and Fa0/0.20 for VLAN 20). The creation of logical/virtual interfaces is done through the configuration of a router's operating system. As each VLAN has its own subnet address, the router's physical interface Fa0/0 ends up with two IP addresses (192.168.10.250 and 192.168.20.250) tied to two different virtual interfaces (Fa0/0.10 and Fa0/0.20) respectively. The relationship is summarized in Table 7.4.

With the use of virtual sub-interfaces, the mechanism of inter-VLAN routing by the router is identical to that of Figure 7.23, except that the router link now becomes a trunk link to transport two different kinds of VLAN traffic. In that setup, PC1 and PC3 should have 192.168.10.250 as their default gateway, and that of PC2 and PC 4 becomes 192.168.20.250.

7.12 VLANS AND NETWORK MANAGEMENT

VLANs are prevalent and fundamental in enterprise networks. There are significant benefits of deploying VLANs, and some of them were explained earlier. The main benefits are summarized before concluding the chapter.

a. **Network performance**: Above all, VLANs improve network performance by reducing traffic congestion. They protect a network from having broadcast storms because the broadcasting effect is confined to a VLAN and inter-VLAN routing does not relay broadcasted messages. When there are hundreds or thousands of computers, the effect of controlled broadcasting on overall network performance is significant. Also, the priority scheme allows that messages from time-sensitive VLANs (e.g. voice VLAN) are transported ahead of others.

b. **Flexibility**: With VLANs, network management to dynamically reflect organizational changes (e.g., relocations of office space, job reassignments of employees) becomes more transparent and flexible. For example, imagine the internal transfer of an employee from accounting to marketing in Figure 7.14. The employee's computer can be easily reassigned by hooking up it to a switch port pre-allocated to the marketing department's VLAN. That is, an employee's physical location (e.g., building floor) does not affect his/her re-association with a particular VLAN (and therefore subnet).

c. **Network security**: VLANs improve network security. Computers belonging to a VLAN cannot directly reach those in other VLANs without relying on inter-VLAN routing, even when they are attached to the same switch. Also, the broadcasting effect is confined to a VLAN protecting the data from eavesdropping by someone outside of the VLAN boundary. Besides, each VLAN can be customized with its own access and security policies.

CHAPTER SUMMARY

- Ethernet's technical specifications are defined in the data link and physical layers. The data link layer is divided into two sub-layers of *logical link control* (LLC) and *media access control* (MAC) for LAN standards. The standard details of Ethernet are defined in the MAC sub-layer.

- Ethernet frames have their own frame structure with the header, data, and trailer fields. The header includes the preamble, start frame delimiter, source MAC address, destination MAC address, and length/type sub-fields.

- A switched Ethernet LAN can take a flat or hierarchical structure in terms of the relationship between switches. The flat design is for a small LAN. When the number of attached switches grows, a two-tier or three-tier hierarchical architecture is used.

- Whether a hierarchical network is two-tiered or three-tiered, its designer has choices of interconnecting intermediary devices of the core and distribution layers in either *full mesh* or *partial mesh*.

- The core and distribution layer devices may be layer 2 switches, layer 3 switches, or routers.

- The Spanning Tree Protocol (STP) and Rapid Spanning Tree Protocol (RSTP) detect redundant paths between any two end points (or hosts) within a switched network and performs their de-activation and re-activation as needed.

- With link aggregation, two or more physical links between two network nodes can be combined to multiply transmission capacity as one logical link. The technical details are standardized as IEEE 802.1AX (called Link Aggregation Control Protocol).

- With virtual LAN (VLAN), hosts on a switched Ethernet are logically divided into smaller segments, each becoming a broadcast domain.

- VLANs are implemented on LAN switches through the following procedure: define VLANs on switches; decide the overall range of trunk and access ports; decide the specific range of access ports for each VLAN; and configure access and trunk ports on switches.

- When it comes to the relationship between the VLAN and the subnet address, generally, the one-to-one mapping between them is a popular practice,

- VLAN tagging is a process of adding VLAN information to regular Ethernet frames. On arriving at a switch port from a user station, an Ethernet frame is 'tagged' to track the frame's VLAN identity while in transit over trunk links.

- Various VLAN types can be defined on a switched LAN, and *Default VLAN*, Data VLAN and *Voice VLAN* are popular VLAN types.

- Inter-VLAN routing refers to the process of forwarding data between different VLANs through a router.

- Among the inter-VLAN routing approaches are (1) assign a router port (interface) to each sub-net (thus a VLAN); and (2) create logical sub-interfaces on a physical router port and assign a sub-interface to a subnet (thus a VLAN).

KEY TERMS

access layer
access port
blocking state
bridge protocol data unit (BPDU)
core layer
cyclic redundancy check (CRC)
data VLAN
default VLAN
distribution layer
forwarding state
frame check sequence
full mesh
IEEE 802.1Q
inter-VLAN routing
link aggregation
Link Aggregation Control Protocol (LACP)
link redundancy
logical link control (LLC)
media access control (MAC)

partial mesh
port bonding
port trunking
Power over Ethernet (PoE)
Preamble
Rapid Spanning Tree Protocol (RSTP)
Spanning Tree Protocol (STP)
start frame delimiter
sub-interface
switched Ethernet
Tag Control Information (TCI)
Tag Protocol Identifier (TPID)
trunk port
virtual interface
virtual LAN (VLAN)
VLAN tagging
VLAN trunking
voice VLAN

CHAPTER REVIEW QUESTIONS

1. When two or more lines are concurrently used between a pair of switches or between a host and a switch to increase throughput, it is termed _____.
   A) link aggregation
   B) tunnel aggregation
   C) virtual aggregation
   D) trunk aggregation
   E) bandwidth augmentation
2. The Spanning Tree Protocol (STP) _____
   A) disables redundant paths in a switched Ethernet LAN, and re-activates them as needed.
   B) is a protocol designed to exchange information necessary to develop the switch table.
   C) is a protocol that automatically creates VLANs.
   D) is a protocol that synchronizes the clock speed between switches.
   E) is a protocol that allows bonding of two or more links to multiply throughput.
3. The Ethernet VLAN _____.
   A) facilitates the recovery of transmission errors
   B) creates smaller segments of a network
   C) prevents message broadcasting
   D) generates redundant delivery paths between two hosts
   E) widens available bandwidth between two network nodes
4. Ethernet standards are defined in the _____.
   A) physical layer only
   B) data link layer only

    C) internet layer only

    D) physical and data link layers

    E) physical, data link, and internet layers

5. Ethernet synchronizes the transmission speed between network nodes using the frame's _____ field.

    A) preamble

    B) frame check sequence

    C) trailer

    D) Tag Control Information

    E) flow control

6. On the switched Ethernet with VLANs, the priority (or urgency) level of a frame in transit can be indicated using _____ information.

    A) Rapid Spanning Tree Protocol

    B) Tag Control Information

    C) Link Aggregation Control Protocol

    D) Cyclic Redundancy Check

    E) Tag Protocol Identifier

7. One of the benefits of having VLANs is _____.

    A) higher network survivability

    B) reduced delays for real-time traffic

    C) prevention of network loops

    D) lower transmission errors

    E) reduced errors in network cabling

8. VLANs in Ethernet are configured on _____.

    A) hubs

    B) switches

    C) routers

    D) wireless access points

    E) user hosts

9. When particular VLANs are not created on a switched Ethernet LAN, all host computers belong to the ____ VLAN.

    A) data

    B) management

    C) voice

    D) default

    E) supervisory

10. Sub-interfaces can be created on the _____ for inter-VLAN routing.

    A) bridge port

    B) switch port

    C) router port

    D) repeater port

    E) wireless access point

11. Corporations may introduce VLANs _____.

    A) to better manage changes (e.g., reassignment of a worker)

    B) to avoid network maintenance

    C) to better interconnect wireless and wired LAN segments

    D) to extend the scope of a LAN without compromising network performance

    E) to effectively link wide area networks

12. Which is NOT true regarding the VLAN?

    A) Creating VLANs on a switch requires the configuration of both access and trunk ports.

    B) A switch's access port can be given more than one VLAN ID.

C) VLANs can improve security through network fragmentation.

D) Users of a VLAN can share the same IP subnet, regardless of their physical locations.

E) To develop VLANs, the network needs to have the access and core layer switches.

13. Choose an INCORRECT statement regarding VLANs.

A) VLANs can divide a network into logical segments such as workgroups.

B) VLANs are configured on switches but not on host computers.

C) The layer 2 switch can be used to exchange frames between two different VLANs.

D) The VLAN itself becomes a broadcast domain.

E) Oftentimes, an IP subnet and a VLAN are paired.

14. The Ethernet switch determines the VLAN ID of a frame coming from a neighboring switch based on the _____.

A) destination address

B) source address

C) tag control information (TCI)

D) tag protocol identifier (TPID)

E) frame check sequence

15. Which statement is CORRECT?

A) The data link layer is divided into the LLC (logical link control) and MAC (media access control) sub-layers.

B) Ethernet has only one cabling standard in the physical layer.

C) The LLC layer is responsible for frame construction and switch operations.

D) The Ethernet frame's Frame Check Sequence ensures synchronization of data transmission speeds between two network nodes.

E) Ethernet frames without VLAN tagging can carry information on frame priority.

16. Sub-interfaces of a router port (interface) can be used in order to _____

1) relay packets between VLANs.

2) make Ethernet switches obsolete.

3) enable link aggregation.

4) remove packets from unknown source hosts.

5) fragment a VLAN into smaller VLANs.

17. Switches in this layer may be *Power over Ethernet (PoE)* enabled so that the cabling not only transports frames but also supplies power to end nodes such as access points and security cameras.

A) trunk layer

B) core layer

C) distribution layer

D) root layer

E) access layer

18. The CRC (Cyclic Redundancy Check) code of the Ethernet frame is used to _____.

A) detect data redundancy

B) detect transmission errors

C) perform flow control

D) synchronize the clock cycle between two computers

E) indicate the beginning of a frame

19. Choose an ACCURATE statement on Ethernet.

A) A loop between two hosts is allowed.

B) In general, switches are interconnected in the full mesh topology.

C) The RSTP is faster than the STP in forwarding VLAN frames.

D) The STP was developed to detect overloaded links.

E) Layer 2 or layer 3 switches can be used in the core layer.

20. See the switch table that follows. How many broadcast domains are defined in the switch?
    A) 8
    B) 4
    C) 3
    D) 5
    E) Unable to decide.

MAC address	Exit port	VLAN ID
A1B1.1111.1111	FastEthernet 0/5	10
A1B1.1111.2222	FastEthernet 0/10	20
A1B1.1111.3333	FastEthernet 0/15	30
A1B1.1111.4444	FastEthernet 0/1	10
A1B1.1111.5555	FastEthernet 0/1	20
A1B1.1111.6666	FastEthernet 0/1	30
A1B1.1111.7777	FastEthernet 0/2	40
A1B1.1111.8888	FastEthernet 0/2	40

21. The Ethernet frame's length field represents length information of the _____.
    A) data field
    B) entire frame
    C) address field
    D) frame minus data field
    E) frame check sequence field

22. Ethernet switches that cover a large campus network of 10 buildings may be organized in a _____ topology to handle its high traffic volume.
    A) bus
    B) ring
    C) hierarchy
    D) point-to-point
    E) star

23. The Bridge Protocol Data Unit (BPDU) contains information related to _____.
    A) link aggregation
    B) VLAN configuration
    C) VLAN tagging
    D) inter-VLAN routing
    E) redundant path identification

24. Refer to the figure below. On switch B, four ports are currently physically linked to other nodes. How many of them are configured as access ports if there are VLANs?
    A) 0
    B) 1
    C) 2
    D) 3
    E) 4

25. Refer to Figure 7.25. If the computer H sends a document to the printer G, which link(s) should be transporting the VLAN tagged frame?
    A) H → F, F → C, and C → A
    B) H → F and D → G

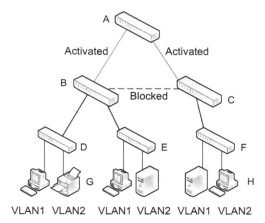

VLAN1 VLAN2   VLAN1 VLAN2 VLAN1 VLAN2

FIGURE 7.25 A hypothetical switched Ethernet

C) F → C, C → A, A → B, B → D
D) C → A and A → B
E) all links from H through G

HANDS-ON EXERCISES

EXERCISE 7.1

This case in Figure 7.26 is constructed from the actual network of a manufacturing firm. With about 100 employees, it is a mid-sized company and occupies a three-story building. The *Main Equipment Room* is located on the building's first floor and houses main intermediary devices (e.g., core switches and router) and all servers. The wiring closets on the second and third floors house access (or workgroup) switches to connect end nodes, mainly user stations and IP surveillance cameras.

The enterprise network is divided into two subnets: the production network (172.16.10.0/24) that includes user stations and various servers, and the surveillance network (172.16.20.0/24) of video cameras installed to monitor the facility. The surveillance camera has an IP address and connects to an access switch. The router separates the surveillance network from the production network. All switches are given an IP address just for remote configuration and management. The cabling and transmission speeds of network links are summarized as follows:

- Trunk links between intermediary devices (switches and router): 1 Gbps CAT6; all trunk links of the production network are running link aggregation effectively achieving 2 Gbps bandwidth.
- Access links for user stations and surveillance cameras: 100 Mbps CAT6
- Access links for servers: 1 Gbps CAT6

Questions:

1. What cable is used for the trunk and access lines?
2. What is the connection speed of each trunk and access link?
3. What are connection speeds of internal servers and client stations to switches?
4. What measure is taken to double the link capacity?
5. Why do layer 2 switches have an IP address?
6. How many subnetworks are there, and what could be the reason(s) for dividing the enterprise LAN?

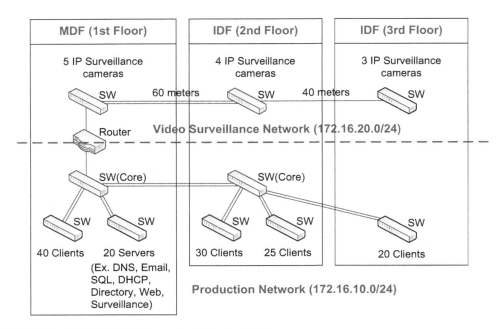

FIGURE 7.26   EQUIP Co.'s Ethernet LAN (logical view)

7. How many broadcast domains exist in the network?
8. What approach is taken in the design of the surveillance network: flat or hierarchical design? How many layers (tiers) do you see?
9. What approach is taken in the design of the production network: flat or hierarchical design? How many layers (tiers) do you see?

Exercise 7.2

Based on Figure 7.13 and Table 7.1, answer the following questions assuming that creating additional VLANs is not an option.

1. What is the VLAN ID assigned to hosts at the IT, Marketing, and Accounting departments?
2. How many subnet addresses do you see in the network?
3. If the computer (192.168.10.1) broadcasts a frame to Switch B, which ports will relay the frame?
4. If the computer (192.168.10.1) broadcasts a frame to Switch B, which computers will receive the frame?
5. If the computer (192.168.10.1) broadcasts a frame to Switch B, what will be the destination IP (for packet) and MAC (for frame) addresses?
6. Construct the switch table of Switch A and Switch C (include VLAN ID).
7. What problem(s) do you see with this switched Ethernet?
8. Without changing the switch and host configurations, can Switch A be replaced by a router to create network segments corresponding to three business functions? Why or why not?
9. If the answer to Question 8 is no, what change (e.g., network cabling, computer relocation) can be made to use a router(s) to create network segments pertaining to three business functions? (Assume that all three switches are re-used.)
10. Let's consider Question 9 in the context that the network is implemented within a three-story building and the location of each switch is as follows:
    Switch A (core switch): Main equipment room, first floor

Switch B (workgroup switch): Wiring closet, second floor

Switch C (workgroup switch): Wiring closet, third floor

Assume that each of the second and third floors has several rooms occupied by the three different business units and all computers on a floor are connected to the same switch located in the wiring closet. In this situation, what can to be done to create three network segments for the three different business units if routers have to be used? Is it an effective solution?

EXERCISE 7.3

Refer to Figure 7.14 and answer the following questions.

1. What are access ports currently used by Switch A?
2. What are access ports currently used by Switch C?
3. How many trunk ports are used on Switch A and Switch C, and what are they?
4. Can Switch A's Fa0/1 and/or Fa0/2 be configured as access ports?
5. If Switch B's Fa0/1 is configured as an access port, what could be the effect?
6. Given the port range of each VLAN in Table 7.2, how many hosts can be attached to VLAN10, VLAN20, and VLAN30 respectively?
7. If PC1 broadcasts a frame, which switch(es) and which PC(s) should receive the frame?
8. If PC1 pings PC2 (C:\ping 192.168.20.1), would it reach PC2? If not, what is the reason? *Hint*: The switch is a layer 2 device and cannot perform packet routing.
9. If PC1 pings PC4, would the ping request reach PC4? Why or why not?
10. Now, let's assume that VLANs are removed from all three switches. However, IP addresses and subnet masks of 6 PCs remain the same.
    a. If PC1 pings PC4, would the message reach PC4? Why or why not?
    b. If PC1 pings PC5, would the message reach PC5? Why or why not?
    c. If PC1 pings PC2, would the message reach PC2? Why or why not?

EXERCISE 7.4

Referring to Figure 7.17, describe step-by-step what happens when the following Ping packets are issued (assume that the construction of all switch tables has been completed).

1. PC1 pings PC4
2. PC1 pings PC6
3. PC1 pings 255.255.255.255
4. PC1 pings 192.168.20.255

EXERCISE 7.5

Perform the following activities based on Figure 7.22.

1. Assign MAC addresses to four PCs and also two router LAN ports (Fa0/0 and Fa0/1).
2. Assume that the switch has 24 ports. Develop a summary table similar to Table 7.2 by assigning its first three ports as trunk ports and the remaining ports as access ports to VLAN10 (Fa0/4 ~ Fa0/13) and VLAN20 (Fa0/14 ~ Fa0/24). Recall that, in practice, this port assignment should be programmed to the switch.

3. Now, configure the IP address, subnet mask, and default gateway on each PC consistent with Figure 7.22 by completing the following table.

	PC1	PC2	PC3	PC4
IP address	192.168.10.1			
Subnet mask				
Default gateway				

4. The switch table is blank initially. The switch will, therefore, be forced to broadcast arriving frames whenever necessary. When enough frames are exchanged, the switch will be able to complete switch table entries based on the information of frames it relayed and the VLAN information manually programmed in step 2. Develop the switch's switch table that contains columns of exit ports, MAC addresses, and VLAN IDs.

5. Now, explain step by step what happens when the following commands are issued.
   a. PC1>ping 192.168.10.2
   b. PC1>ping 192.168.20.2
   c. PC1>ping 255.255.255.255

6. If the VLAN option is not available, what alternative design approach can be applied to create a network that is functionally identical to the one in Figure 7.22? What are the advantages and disadvantages of the alternative network design?

8 Cybersecurity

Threats

8.1 INTRODUCTION

This chapter explains malicious software tools, techniques, tactics, and procedures used by threat actors. They are conveniently organized in terms of the taxonomy scheme of attack mechanisms introduced in Chapter 2 (see Table 2.1). Cyber adversaries more likely use a combination of threat mechanisms in launching a cyberattack rather than relying upon just one of them. As a simple example, chances are that a bad actor uses phishing or spam to infect the targeted computer with malware.

As social engineering exploits the cognitive, psychological, and/or behavioral vulnerabilities of a targeted individual, it differs from other threat mechanisms that mobilize significant technical elements. Thus, social engineering was separately explained in Chapter 2, and this chapter focuses on other threat types.

The objectives of this chapter are to learn malignant software tools, techniques, tactics, and procedures pertaining to each threat mechanism, as summarized in Table 8.1. Readers are, however, cautioned that numerous attack methods been documented, and thus the table list represents just a well-known subset of them.

8.2 DELIVER OR INJECT A MALICIOUS PROGRAM

Malware represents a type of software designed to cause destructive damages to the infected system and subsequently to the system owner or user (e.g., financial losses). The damages are inflicted on data assets (e.g., data destruction, data theft, data encryption) and applications installed (e.g., file corruptions). Also, the hardware operation of network nodes and even hardware itself can be affected (e.g., disable an industrial system, overheat CPUs, corrupt data on the BIOS chip of the motherboard).

There are a number of malware infection vectors. Among them are design flaws in operating systems; an email attachment disguised as an innocuous file; phishing or spam email with a malicious link to a compromised website; a browser plug-in or third-party application hiding malware; and a legitimate online advertisement with a URL link to the second website containing an exploit pack.

Among prevalent and well-known malware types are the *virus, worm, Trojan, bot, rootkit, and logic bomb.* In fact, it is difficult to clearly characterize and categorize the nature and properties of each malware type because they continuously morph into new directions. To some people, for instance, the virus is a type of malware with its own unique functional features and thus is different from other malware types. To others, the virus broadly refers to any evil code designed to disrupt the target network, system, or system usage. In this chapter, the malware types are explained based on their narrower definitions.

8.2.1 Virus

The virus is an executable program, and an infected system produces a multitude of symptoms ranging from mild annoyance to more severe damages. Among the select are: the system can crash or be locked up, leading to the denial of system service; files and directories can be manipulated (e.g.,

TABLE 8.1

Select malicious software tools, techniques, and tactics as learning objectives

Covered sections	Threat/attack mechanisms	Malignant software tools, techniques, tactics, and procedures (learning objectives)
8.2	Deliver or inject a malicious program	virus, ransomware, worm, trojan, bot, rootkit, logic bomb, spyware, adware
8.3	Exploit weak- or mis-configuration of security settings	weak/default password, rogue access point
8.4	Abuse a network protocol and its embedded functions	spoofing, denial of service, packet sniffing, port scanning, man-in-the-middle/session hijacking, poisoning, Wi-Fi wardriving
8.5	Exploit software design- and/or development faults	zero-day, cross-site scripting, SQL injection

erased, encrypted); the computer's security settings may be turned off; data may be stolen over the network; and the system can behave erratically or slow down significantly. There are generally two virus *carriers*: an infected file, and a human actor who transports the file manually or electronically. The virus is divided into the *program* and *data* virus types.

Program Virus: The program virus is an executable malicious code and spreads by attaching itself to a benign software program, called a host program. When the host program is executed, the virus code (or payload) is executed as well, infecting the system and beginning its nefarious actions. System users, however, fail to notice the infection because generally, the host program behaves normally after its execution.

Certain viruses are designed to destroy the original benign program or overwrite the program code on its infection, which can destroy specific functions of the benign application, resulting in data corruptions and/or providing additional malicious features. Many virus developers go extra miles to avoid the detection of changes in the virus-tainted execution file. For example, the virus-carrying executable code is digitally signed using a stolen private key to fool the anti-virus program.

Data Virus: The data virus infects a data/document file (rather than the executable program), and the most common type is the macro virus. A macro is a predefined sequence of instructions written in a script and grouped together for them to run like a single command. The macro function is supported by user applications including productivity tools to expedite tedious and many times routine tasks. Among tools that support the macro function are the database (e.g., MS Access), spreadsheet (e.g., MS Excel), presentation (e.g., MS PowerPoint), and word processor (e.g., MS Word). The data virus is dangerous, as people don't normally take its risks seriously as is it embedded within a non-executable file. Currently, the harmful macro can be detected by an anti-virus program.

8.2.2 Ransomware

One of the deadly virus types these days is ransomware, and thus its separate explanation is warranted. Ransomware can be either *locker* or *crypto* type.

8.2.2.1 Locker Ransomware

The locker type limits access to a system or its data files by either denying input to the graphical user interface (GUI) or restricting computing resources (e.g., lock user files) until a ransom is paid. Locker ransomware usually does not cripple the affected system or damage data assets as it does not encrypt them. Rather, it intends to cause psychological panicking on the part of the user so that he/

FIGURE 8.1 Locker ransomware sample screenshot (Source: www.knowbe4.com)

she rushes into certain irrational actions (e.g., call the provided telephone number disguised as tech support) (see Figure 8.1).

8.2.2.2 Crypto Ransomware

Crypto ransomware is a fundamentally different beast as it encrypts data assets or paralyzes client/server computers, holding an organization hostage for ransom in exchange for their recovery. Cyber criminals use various insidious techniques to demand ransom, and they keep evolving. The most prevalent technique is to encrypt data assets (i.e., file-level encryptions) of the compromised system. Another technique is to encrypt the master boot sector so that the infected computer system cannot boot. Some ransomware strains also steal data files before their encryption. Adding more grief to victims, some strains not only request a payment to reverse the encryption but also include a countdown timer (see Figure 8.2) that will permanently delete files until victims comply.

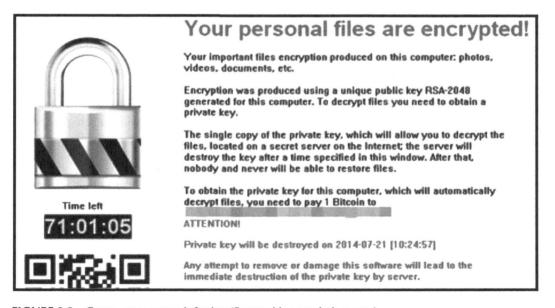

FIGURE 8.2 Crypto ransomware infection (Source: blog.trendmicro.com)

Crypto ransomware does not infect operating system files, as the OS needs full functionality if the virus distributor is expected to be compensated. As in Figure 8.2, typical ransomware uses asymmetric cryptography (e.g., RSA 2048) of public and private keys to encrypt files. It may use a *command and control* (C&C) botnet server that sends a public key only to the affected machine, making it practically impossible to decode encrypted data files. The vast majority of ransomware attacks have been on computers running Windows OS. However, attacks on mobile devices and industrial control systems are going to grow.

The financial extortion of victim organizations is the threat model. There is no shortage of alarming statistics on how malignant hackers are using ransomware to hold companies, hospitals, and non-profit organizations hostage. As a new development, cybercriminals have launched Ransomware-as-a-Service (RaaS), a dark web platform in which service providers and ransomware distributors share the profit. At the moment, the best protection is to make frequent backups of data files and then take the backup device 'offline', as ransomware can follow the network to find all network-attached devices.

8.2.3 WORM

The worm is a malware program designed to replicate itself and spread to other computers over the network without human interventions. The self-replication capability without being attached to another program is what makes it different from the virus. That is, the worm becomes a stand-alone, self-sustaining code that propagates by itself. To do that, it frequently takes advantage of known/unknown vulnerabilities of a target operating system or relies on social engineering (e.g., a benign-looking email with a worm attached) to trick system users into its execution.

Just as with viruses, worms can inflict nefarious damages if infected. Some worms are not necessarily designed to harm the infected system. Because of its self-replication ability and resulting bandwidth consumptions, one of their destructive effects is disrupted network performance.

8.2.3.1 Case: Sobig Worm

Sobig was a worm architected to replicate by itself and also included a malware function designed to execute a Trojan function. Sobig was initially sent to numerous email accounts as an attachment from a spam network. It used various subject lines such as *Re: Approved* and *Re: Thank you!* When a gullible user clicked on the attachment with such filenames as *details.pif* and *application.pif*, the program was executed. The worm was designed to search the infected machine to find email addresses. Then, it relayed the worm program to all email addresses recovered from the victim machine, resulting in a large-scale replication and the spread of automatically generated emails.

Also, the worm planted malicious code in the affected computers to initiate contacts with shadowy servers to obtain the URL of a Trojan webserver. Once the URL was obtained, the victim computer visited the webserver and downloaded a Trojan program. When it was secretly installed, the infected computer became a proxy server through which spammers could send spam without being traced.

8.2.4 TROJAN

A Trojan, named after the mythological Trojan horse, is a malignant code hidden behind a program or webpage that looks legitimate but does something other than advertised. The benign program performs functions as advertised (e.g., calendar, video play) but the secretly hidden Trojan code performs a vile operation. One popular approach executed by bad actors is to compromise a company's site that sells software products online, and manipulate a downloadable program to plant a malicious code. Or, on compromising a company, a Trojan can be planted inside a software patch that will be automatically pushed to existing clients for routine security updates.

Whether downloaded from a website, pushed remotely for routine security updates, or sent in an email attachment, the delivered evil code is triggered when the benign host program is executed or when a downloaded webpage is displayed on the browser. It is also possible that Trojan stays dormant for a while to avoid anti-virus or any other threat detection technology before it launches vile activities. The 'attachment of an evil code' to an innocent program gives resemblance to the virus. Trojans, however, differ from the virus or worm as they are not designed to infect other files/programs or self-replicate.

The majority of Trojans are programmed to create a covert backdoor that allows attackers to gain sneak access to a target system locally or remotely by bypassing the normal authentication and login procedure. Then, the attacker can literally turn an infected computer into a stealth server that gives almost complete control to him/her through such a session as HTTPS. Now, the attacker can exercise a host of harmful activities. Among them are the uploading and downloading of valued assets, planting malware for subsequent distributed-denial-of-service (DDOS) attacks to a target victim, stealing passwords and other sensitive information, installing spyware for keystroke monitoring, and gathering email addresses for spam distribution.

8.2.4.1 Case: FreeVideo Player Trojan

There was once a website whose visitors were asked to install a FreeVideo player *codec* to view certain videos. As a computer program, the codec compresses and decompresses audio and video files. It shrinks large movie, video, or music files to transfer quickly over the Internet. When clicked for downloading, this installed the FreeVideo player, benign-looking but with a Trojan hidden. One of the things the Trojan did was to change the IP address of the victim computer's DNS setup so that DNS inquiries could be sent to the rogue DNS server controlled by the attacker(s) located in a third country. The name resolution by the rogue DNS server re-directed system users to dangerous websites infested with malware.

Although the FreeVideo player could be removed through the regular un-installation procedure, this did not roll back the DNS setting. A learned lesson is that the border firewall of an organization should filter all DNS queries not directed to the official DNS server internally arranged. Also, computer users should beware of software downloading from questionable sites, and they need to check DNS entries to ensure that the inquiries of name resolution are sent to the local DNS server.

8.2.5 BOT AND BOTNET

The *bot* is a secret program planted by a cybercriminal to turn innocent computers into zombies. The bot program, once it successfully finds a 'home' on a victim computer, has the capability to report back to the criminal master and listen to his/her commands. The bot also has a built-in program logic that goes to other computers (as spiders) over the network, finds their weak spots, infects and turns them into zombies, and reports the 'successful landing' back to their evil master.

The collection of zombies thus formed is called a *botnet*, and they can be collectively 'remote controlled' by an evil master (see Figure 8.3). That is, the bots of a botnet can act in a coordinated manner, executing routines according to commands coming from the master. For large-scale coordination, the attacker sets up one or more command and control (C&C) servers. Also called *handlers*, they are generally harbored in compromised computers, and the attacker remotely controls them through such protocols as *Internet Relay Chat* (IRC), *HTTPS*, and *P2P*. The remote-control capability through the C&C server is what differentiates the bot from other malware types.

Architecture-wise, a botnet can be client/server or peer-to-peer. With the client/server mode, a botnet has a dedicated C&C server(s) and thus it is easier for the attacker to get caught. In the peer-to-peer mode, the C&C servers are distributed, making them harder to track. For this reason, it is reported that the peer-to-peer architecture is more popular these days.

Through the botnet, an attacker can unleash evil activities such as distributing spam emails, stealing data and personal information, triggering DDOS attacks, attempting phishing, spreading new malware, and hacking websites. In particular, the botnet has become a perfect channel for spam dissemination. It is said that there are thousands of botnets in cyberspace. Well-known examples

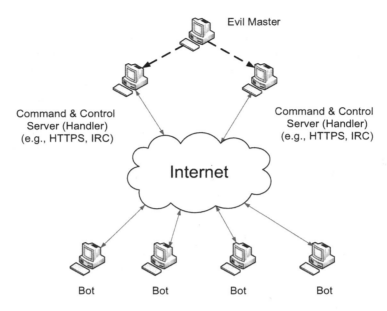

FIGURE 8.3   Client/server botnet architecture

include Grum, Bobax, Rustock, Cutwail, and Bagle. Taking down a botnet is difficult and has only short-term effects because getting it back up again is relatively easy, thanks to such programs as pay-per-install and botnet renting available in the underground marketplace.

8.2.5.1 Case: Cutwail Botnet

As a case in point, Cutwail is considered one of the largest botnets in terms of the number of compromised hosts. It was estimated that somewhere around 1.5–2 million personal computers were infected and had 30 different C&C servers. The botnet had a capacity of flooding the Internet with over 7 billion spam emails a day. The bots were able to report back to the evil master the statistics of how many spam emails were delivered. It was also used to launch DDOS attacks on different organizations including Twitter. IT security researchers found that the Cutwail's engine and its botnet were rented to spam advertisers willing to pay for mass emailing.

8.2.6 ROOTKIT

The rootkit is a malware program used by an adversary to hide the presence of other malware on a computer system and thus regular anti-virus software may not detect it. For this, it secures the admin-level access privilege on a victim system and may alter or replace its operating system files so that malicious activities are ignored or other malware is concealed.

For example, before the rootkit infection, all active applications and their processes including a malware-triggered process can be shown (see Figure 8.4). Recall that a process is an instance of an application and one application can hatch multiple processes. For the visualization of their relationship, think of a browser application that opens multiple webpages through tabbed browsing. After the rootkit infection, however, the 'evil' process becomes invisible as the malware has tampered with the related operating system function. To prevent the rootkit attack, the operating system should be designed to make it difficult to modify its core functions (generally implemented as a part of the OS kernel).

A rootkit may be delivered to a computer through a Trojan or any other malware infection vectors including phishing. As the integrity of an operating system is affected, the rootkit infection could

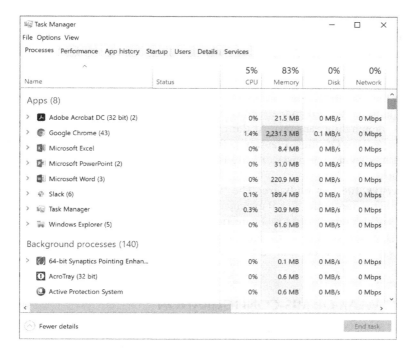

FIGURE 8.4 List of visible applications and processes running (Windows task manager)

trigger some abnormal behaviors. For example, the host computer's anti-virus may stop functioning, OS settings may change independently, background images may change, items pinned to the taskbar may disappear for no reason, and/or there may be slowed system performance.

8.2.7 Logic Bomb and Other Malware Types

The *logic bomb* is time bomb-style malware that lies dormant until a specific logical event or condition is met to trigger its pre-programmed activities. Some examples of the event or condition are system rebooting, a particular day and time, and a number of database transactions processed by the targeted system. The logic bomb is mainly designed to inflect damages by corrupting or destroying things (e.g., database, files, hard drive), a clear form of sabotage. Its typical case is an insider attack by a disgruntled or terminated employee.

If a logic bomb is secretly planted on a system by an insider, its payload might be just a few lines of code (e.g., script) inserted into a large computer program. Then, chances are that the traditional anti-virus tool cannot detect it because the code is customized and thus it does not match existing malware signatures. To make it even more difficult to detect, the 'bomb' may be installed by someone with privileged access to the target system and who is familiar with system controls. Numerous logic bomb cases have been reported.

Besides, *spyware* steals personal information (e.g., keystroke loggers) and monitors/tracks the usage of a victim system. *Adware* displays uninvited advertisements on a user's computer screen.

8.2.8 Malware Features

It is worth it to characterize common features or trends found in many malware programs.

    a. **Multiple payload functions**: Chances are that malware combines more than one functional element in its payload, a software code embedded in malware designed to cause damages to the infected system on its execution. Such functional combinations have two implications on defenders. First, its execution is designed to cause maximum damages, making the attack more effective to the perpetrator but costlier to victims. Second, by embedding a technique to evade anti-virus/malware, it can increase the chance of fooling the defender's countermeasures.

b. **Application- vs. OS-level infection**: Malware attacks user systems both at the application level and the operating system level. At the application level, the most prevalent attack is the installation of an evil code to inflict damages on the victim (e.g., deleting files, stealing user data, demanding ransom). At the OS level, as is the case of the rootkit, attacks can modify or replace OS files. Planting a Trojan to open a backdoor, changing the DNS setting, and modifying the password file to gain a stealthy access to a target computer are among those.

c. **File-based vs. file-less malware**: The 'file-less' malware is rising. Unlike the traditional malware that writes to the disk if executed, staying in the file system and making the executable file visible, the file-less malware runs only in the random access memory (RAM) if infected. This makes it more difficult for anti-malware to detect and remove. The attacker also finds a way to keep it alive even when the system is rebooted, which erases RAM contents.

8.3 EXPLOIT WEAK OR MIS-CONFIGURATION

As a widespread problem, when the security control of a system, an application, or a network device is weakly configured or simply misconfigured, this opens up an opportunity for cyber adversaries to exploit. There are many different scenarios of weak or mis-configuration. Examples are:

- Using default configurations that were set by the vendor
- Forgetting to change configurations meant for a temporary usage (e.g., testing)
- Leaving unused TCP/UDP ports open, exposing them to remote attacks
- Using loosely defined or incomplete firewall rules
- Failing to implement multi-factor authentication

The rest of this section explains two additional examples related to weak security setting: failure to enforce strong passwords/passphrases and the installation of a rogue access point.

8.3.1 Failure to Enforce Strong Passwords

As we know, the password is the most prevalent form of user authentication. An individual typically uses a large number of passwords to access different websites these days, and their safe maintenance and usage has become a challenge. The password can be stolen in many different ways including the trial and error, social engineering, phishing, login spoofing, keystroke logging with malware, hacking of a password database, and password cracking.

If a system fails to enforce strong user passwords, this becomes a source of vulnerability. As a related threat type, password cracking is explained. For an attacker to obtain or steal user passwords, he/she can use one or more software tools and the computer's brute processing capacity.

For example, the operating system stores user passwords encrypted by such standards as DES (Data Encryption Standard) or hashed by such hash functions as MD5 and SHA-256. Linux, for instance, keeps encrypted passwords and their related information (e.g., password expiration) in the '*/etc/shadow*' file that is readable only with the root access privilege. In Windows OS, passwords are hashed and stored in the *C:\Windows\System32\Config\SAM* file that remains invisible to users. Also, billions of passwords stolen from compromised password databases are being sold on the dark web's black market. More likely, the stolen passwords were encrypted before their storage.

Bad actors may acquire encrypted passwords from the dark web or access a target computer and copy the password file so that they can work on their own terms using password-cracking software. There are a number of open-source or proprietary password recovery tools. The hacking tools are necessary evils as system administrators also rely on them to recover passwords that might have been misplaced. They support various techniques designed to break the ciphertext (encrypted plaintext), and *brute force-* and *dictionary attacks* are among two well-known techniques.

8.3.1.1 Brute Force Method

It breaks an encrypted or hashed password by trying every possible alphanumeric combination exhaustively in an automated fashion using a computer's brute force. For example, if the password size is 64-bit (or 8 characters) or less, there are 2^{64} possible binary combinations, as computers only understand 0s and 1s. The brute force software encrypts/hashes each combination and compares the resulting value with the one obtained. The recovery time of a password using an ordinary computer that can process half a million passwords per second is summarized in Table 8.2.

8.3.1.2 Dictionary Method

The *dictionary* method attempts to retrieve a password by linking an electronic dictionary file that contains a very large volume of vocabulary (see Figure 8.5) to a password recovery program.

TABLE 8.2

Password cracking with brute force (Source: businessweek.com)

Characters included	Password length		
	6 Characters (48 bits)	7 Characters (56 bits)	9 Characters (72 bits)
Lowercase letters only	10 minutes	4 hours	4 months
Lowercase and uppercase letters	10 hours	23 days	178 years
All ASCII characters – letters, numbers, and special characters	18 days	4 years	44,530 years

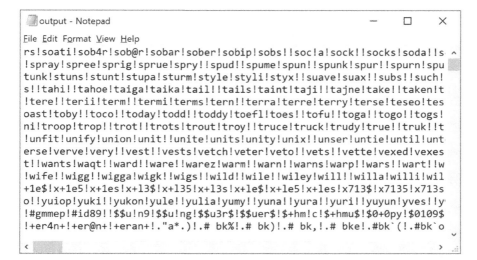

FIGURE 8.5   Sample vocabulary in dictionary file

This way, the software applies dictionary words to the decipher engine. This technique is effective because people tend to create passwords made up of certain dictionary terms that are easy to remember. To recover a password, the software program encrypts/hashes each word or combined words in the dictionary, and compares the result with an encrypted/hashed password. To have a better chance, the software can subject each word or a combined word to a list of altering rules such as alternating uppercase and lowercase letters.

8.3.2 INSTALLATION OF A ROGUE ACCESS POINT (AP)

The rogue AP generally means an AP installed by an organization's employee for personal usage without obtaining formal permission. The rogue AP installed by a non-IT professional can result in a vulnerable security setting, a case of weak or mis-configuration. This becomes an invitation for trouble when it can allow a malicious attacker to access the enterprise network, bypassing its network defense, and ultimately to internal resources (see Figure 8.6). Due to the risk, an organization should adopt a policy that restricts unauthorized employees from installing an AP (and other intermediary devices) at their own discretion. Also, an organization needs to deploy a monitoring system that detects such rogue APs and intermediary devices.

8.4 ABUSE NETWORKING PROTOCOL AND EMBEDDED FUNCTIONS

There are numerous standardized or proprietary networking protocols, and each protocol comes with various functional features. Some of the functions are controlled by flipping just one bit in the message. For example, think of the SYN, ACK, and FIN bits used for TCP-based session management (see Section 3.6.2.2). No matter how small or trivial the bits may look, they are so fundamental to sustain normal network operations. Cyber attackers, however, view them differently, mainly from the perspective of exploiting them to their advantages and to serve their wicked motives. This section introduces some of the techniques used by bad actors to abuse ordinary network protocols and their functional elements.

8.4.1 SPOOFING

Spoofing, synonymous with *masquerading* and *impersonation*, is defined as pretending (or faking) to be someone or something. There are many different spoofing techniques, and some of them are explained here.

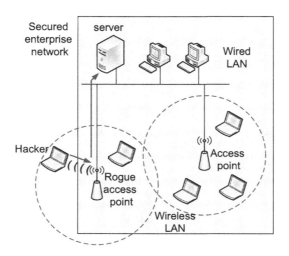

FIGURE 8.6   Dangers of rogue AP installed by an employee

8.4.1.1 IP Spoofing

IP spoofing is one of the most common types of online camouflage in which a packet's source IP address is replaced with another one to mask the sender's true identity. Not surprisingly, IP spoofing has been heavily utilized by cyber criminals to execute *denial of service*, to spread spam, to initiate phishing, or to launch other types of cyberattacks.

There are at least three techniques available – virtual private network (VPN), IP spoofing software, and IP proxy server – to hide the source IP for both malicious and legitimate reasons. How the VPN technology, especially in the tunnel mode, can shield the source IP from prying eyes is explained in Chapter 10. The proxy server system is explained in Chapter 9. Also, there are software tools that can manipulate a packet's source address, and some of them are freely available.

8.4.1.2 MAC Spoofing

The MAC address, although permanently printed on the network interface card (NIC or adapter), can also be spoofed relatively easily, sometimes by directly changing it through the operating system. For example, if the NIC's driver supports it, the MAC address spoofing can be done through the *device manager* on the Windows OS (see Figure 8.7). MAC spoofing can also be done with a software tool that does address translation. MAC spoofing is generally not as damaging as IP spoofing because its usage is restricted to a particular subnet.

MAC spoofing, however, can disrupt a network or degrade network performance. For example, a hacker's computer can hide itself on a network, or MAC spoofing can be used to impersonate another legitimate device on a subnet. Many internet service providers (ISPs) track the MAC address of their clients' router port in providing Internet access. Certainly, a hacker can try to use the ISP service by spoofing the MAC address of its client. Besides, to provide device anonymity in accessing Wi-Fi networks and to make it difficult for ISPs to track Internet users, today's operating systems, including Android and iOS, support MAC address randomization, a form of MAC spoofing.

FIGURE 8.7 Changing MAC address on Windows OS

8.4.1.3   Email Address Spoofing

With email spoofing, an email sender can falsify its originating email address and header information. This is relatively easy because the dominant email standard SMTP (Simple Mail Transfer Protocol) was not designed with security in mind. For example, there is no built-in mechanism for source address authentication in SMTP. Also, even though email authentication protocols/frameworks (e.g., sender policy framework) have been developed, they are not widely used.

Not surprisingly, spammers rely heavily on email spoofing to mask spam sources. Also, virtually all phishing emails use the spoofed source address to mislead recipients by giving the impression that they are from a trusted source. Technically, changing the source email address or using a deceptive domain name (e.g., yahoo.com vs. yohoo.com) is not difficult.

Email spoofing can have serious consequences on legitimate email users. For example, imagine a situation in which a spammer floods the Internet with spoofed emails using an innocent person's email address as the sender. Then, the victim's email inbox will be filled with *undeliverable* emails. Also, the victim may receive angry emails from spam recipients, or the internet service provider may terminate his/her email account.

8.4.1.4   Web (or HTTP/HTTPS) Spoofing

Web spoofing happens when a person is tricked into a copycat site. The bogus website can be infested with malware that may steal personal login credentials or perpetrate other evil activities. The fake website closely resembles the original site in design and oftentimes uses a similar URL address, making it difficult to tell the difference. As a matter of fact, replicating a genuine website has become so easy these days because of software tools.

Different tricks are used to entice people to spoofed websites. Most notably, spoofed spam or phishing email that contains a hyperlink to the spoofed site can be sent to potential victims. As explained, phishing emails are increasingly customized to a target because the bad actors can find much personal information from cyberspace, especially through social networking sites. There are other ways to trick computer users into a spoofed website:

- The DNS setup of a user computer can be changed when it is infected with malware.
- The database of a DNS server can be changed to link a legitimate domain name to the IP address of a spoofed website.
- A URL included in a regular webpage is changed to the URL of a spoofed webpage.

8.4.2   Denial of Service

Denial-of-service (DOS) is one of the frequented cyberattacks. With DOS, the attacker generates enough traffic targeting a particular server – primarily a webserver – so that either the overwhelmed system becomes unavailable to ordinary users or its service response slows to a crawl. Oftentimes, DOS attacks are politically or ideologically charged these days. With much consumption of the network bandwidth, the DOS attack can also debilitate the performance of target networks. For example, there was a report that the average bandwidth consumed by DOS was about 5 Gbps, sometimes exceeding 10 Gbps.

8.4.2.1   DOS with Pinging

This floods a target server with auto-generated ICMP requests for communication (see Section 3.7.3). When the server's CPU time is spent on responding to the fraudulent ICMP inquiries, this can significantly undermine the server's capacity to react to other legitimate communications. Due to this risk, the majority of servers on the Internet disable the ping response function these days.

8.4.2.2 DOS with SYN Requests

Flooding the target server with bogus SYN requests to pretend handshaking attempts is another popular technique. An attacker can use a software tool or a network of compromised computers to rapidly produce SYN messages, each carrying a spoofed source IP address, targeting a victim server. The victim responds with an SYN/ACK and waits for the return of an ACK from the spoofed IP address (see Figure 3.6), which is not going to happen. This results in the consumption of server resources and limits other regular connections.

8.4.2.3 Distributed DOS

Generally, DOS does not physically harm or infect the target system or network. However, when it takes advantage of flaws in system design (e.g., defects in the server operating system), the consequence can be more severe (e.g., server crash). To produce enough traffic and to camouflage attack sources, most DOS attacks are executed in the form of distributed DOS (or DDOS).

For DDOS, evil programs are planted in a number of compromised computers and they launch attacks to a target server at once. The *botnet* explained earlier becomes a perfect platform for the large-scale DDOS, as the attacker uses one or more *command and control* hosts (or *handlers*) to coordinate attacks on a target. Chances are that the handlers themselves are also victimized computers. This makes it difficult to pinpoint the original source of DDOS.

8.4.2.4 MAC Address Flooding

It is a form of DOS on switches, which disrupts normal switch operations. This attack is not prevalent but can pose a serious threat to the integrity of an enterprise network. An attacker can use a tool that generates a large volume of Ethernet frames with bogus source and destination MAC addresses and release them to a connected switch. On receiving them, the switch surely has no entries of them in its switch table. Thus, the bogus MAC addresses and their connecting ports are updated in its switch table while the frames are broadcasted to all ports.

The bogus MAC addresses are continuously updated into the switch table and, sooner or later, it will be filled to capacity. The maxed-out table prevents the switch from updating other legitimate entries. Also, all aged-out legitimate MAC entries will be continuously replaced with spoofed MAC entries. From that moment, whenever a frame arrives with a destination MAC address not listed in the switch table, the switch broadcasts the frame.

When multiple switches are interconnected, other switches will soon follow suit, triggering domino effects on the switched LAN. This form of attack imposes a heavy process burden on the switches and also the excessive broadcasting degenerates network throughput. Besides, the attacker can capture legitimate frames broadcasted by switches.

To reduce such risks, it was emphasized that an organization should take preventive measures to lower the chance of such attacks. These include (1) allowing only one or more legitimate MAC addresses of user stations on a switch port; (2) automatic shutdown of a switch port if an unauthorized computer attempts to connect to it; and (3) shutting off all unused switch ports.

8.4.2.5 DOS on Wi-Fi

Wi-Fi is also an environment highly conducive to DOS due to the open nature of wireless communications. In Wi-Fi, the source of DOS can be both intentional (e.g., a hacker's malicious moves) and incidental (e.g., signal interferences, transmission collisions). For example, a bad actor can flood the radio frequency spectrum with enough interference (or signal 'noise') to prevent Wi-Fi clients from communicating with the access point. He/she can inject fictitious frames into a Wi-Fi network to keep legitimate users from accessing it. He/she can set up his/her wireless NIC to release a continuous stream of *clear-to-send* (CTS) frames pretending to be an AP. CTS frames force all client nodes to wait, denying their network access and resulting in DOS. To execute this attack, however, the threat actor needs to gain Wi-Fi access one way or another through such a trick as the evil twin access point (see Figure 8.11).

8.4.2.6   DOS Case: MyDoom

MyDoom was probably one of the most destructive computer worms, affecting computers running Windows OS. It was designed to propagate mainly through email attachments with a deceptive transmission error message on the subject line such as *Mail Delivery System* or *Mail Transaction Failed*. According to a report, about one in five emails was attributable to MyDoom when it was most active. Its payload triggered three different attacks if activated – worm, DDOS, and Trojan.

- It was a worm that generated mass emails. When the mail attachment was activated by a susceptible system user, it located email addresses stored in the infected system and re-sent the worm to recovered email addresses. This resulted in the worm's effective replications. The warm was also known to copy itself to the file-sharing folder of a popular P2P application for mass spreading.
- The infected computer systems were instructed to mount a DDOS attack on a particular target website.
- It also created backdoors on the victim computer by opening a range of TCP ports, which allowed it to be remotely accessed and controlled.

8.4.3   PACKET SNIFFING

As an attempt to steal information contained in packets, packet sniffing is equivalent to the wiretapping of telephone lines. Packet sniffing can be especially problematic in wireless networks that broadcast packets. The old-fashioned hub-based Ethernet that broadcasts packets is highly vulnerable to packet sniffing as well. On the Ethernet LAN relying on switches (switched Ethernet), packets are better protected from sniffing because of the point-to-point communication mode between hosts, and message broadcasting is used only when it is specifically requested or inevitable. As an exception, if a threat actor finds a way to connect to the 'mirror port' of an Ethernet switch, all packets can be ransacked, and thus the mirror port should be closely guarded.

Many network protocols produce data in clear text, making them vulnerable to snooping. For example, FTP (port 20, 21), Telnet (port 23), SMTP (port 25), POP3 (port 110), IMAP (port 143), and HTTP (port 80) all transmit data and authentication information in plain text and thus should be avoided. More secure siblings that add SSL/TLS (e.g., FTPS for FTP, HTTPS for HTTP, SSH for Telnet) are available to replace insecure protocols. Simply put, exchanging sensitive data in clear text is an invitation for trouble.

8.4.3.1   Packet Sniffing with Wireshark

Various packet sniffing tools are used by practitioners for the diagnosis and analysis of network traffic. Among the well-known applications is Wireshark, that can sniff PDUs of popular protocols such as Ethernet and Wi-Fi. Figure 8.8 illustrates Wireshark, whose GUI has three layers or panes. The top layer lists captured *packets* (both requests and responses) and their attributes that include the timestamp, source and destination IP addresses, packet-triggering protocol, and frame length. The middle layer displays PDUs associated with each *packet*. The bottom layer shows the actual content of a PDU in both hex and plain text.

Currently in Figure 8.8, the top layer highlights message #15, indicating the particular packet was triggered by an HTTP message (i.e., request to *www.cnn.com*). The second layer lists PDUs associated with the particular *packet* #15 (i.e., Ethernet frame, IP packet, TCP segment, and HTTP PDU). Given that HTTP is highlighted in the second layer, the third layer displays its corresponding HTTP request message.

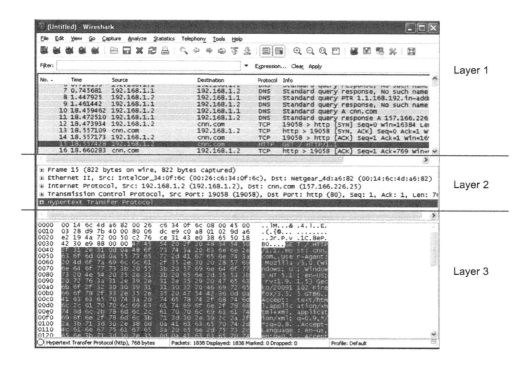

FIGURE 8.8   Packet sniffing with Wireshark

8.4.4   PORT SCANNING

The TCP/UDP port is an entrance through which application messages leave and arrive (revisit Section 3.6.3). Attackers want to know which entrance is open for business and can become a target. Some of the well-known server ports are listed in Table 3.4. Port scanning is a reconnaissance act of surveying the ports of a potential target generally in an automated fashion to obtain information, including:

- Open (or listening) ports waiting for a connection
- Service/program currently running on a particular port
- Port accessibility (e.g., the possibility of anonymous login)
- Authentication requirement for a network service
- Target computer's operating system

As a key reconnaissance activity, port scanning often takes place at the early stage of an attack in order to determine a target system or to gather preliminary information and probe ways into it. For instance, a port scanner can send SYN packets to a system and watch SYN-ACK responses to determine its *listening* ports and thus the system's vulnerability to hacking. Port scanning tools can scan both connection-oriented TCP and connection-less UDP ports.

8.4.4.1   Port Scanning with Zenmap

As a popular utility program, Zenmap (formerly Nmap) helps network professionals in exploring, tracking, and securing networks. Zenmap is able to scan a particular target host or an entire network

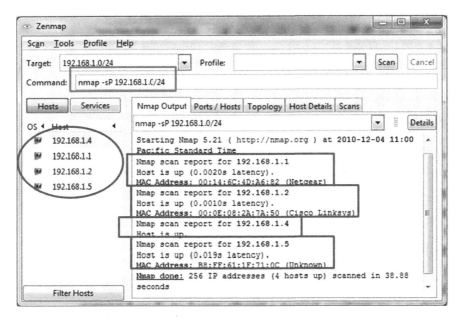

FIGURE 8.9   Scanning a network with Zenmap

via its command line interface (CLI) or graphical user interface (GUI). It can sweep one or more networks entirely to search hosts that are currently up and determine their system details such as open ports and the operating system. As a powerful utility program for network management and security auditing, it is also abused by the wrong hands when they try to learn about target systems or networks and to locate their vulnerabilities.

As an example, Figure 8.9 demonstrates a home network (192.168.1.0/24) and its scanning results using the Zenmap's *ping scan* function. The screenshot shows the command issued (*Nmap – sP 192.168.1.0/24*) and a summary of search results in terms of host addresses and their MAC addresses. The home network's nodes at the time of scanning include:

- 192.168.1.1: The home network's default gateway
- 192.168.1.2: A phone adaptor for VoIP over the Internet
- 192.168.1.4: A laptop with Zenmap installed
- 192.168.1.5: Apple's iPad

The figure does not list open ports, whose information comes with more in-depth scanning.

8.4.5   Man-in-the-Middle/Session Hijacking

Man-in-the-middle (MITM) is when an attacker intercepts IP packets exchanged between two hosts and relays or substitutes them as a middle man. It is the act of hijacking a session already established (or to be established) between network nodes. The two communicating nodes have no idea of the session hijacking and believe that they are talking to a trusted partner. The attacker may perpetrate it to steal sensitive data or to obtain access credentials (e.g., password) in order to intrude into a protected network. Among various techniques of MITM, those using a bogus DHCP server and an evil twin in Wi-Fi are demonstrated. ARP poisoning, explained in Section 8.4.6.1, is another example of MITM.

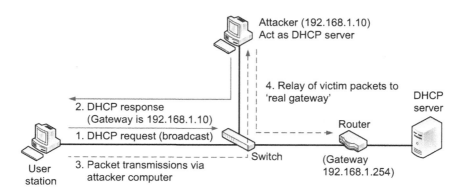

FIGURE 8.10 DHCP spoofing and MITM

8.4.5.1 MITM with Bogus DHCP Server

A rogue computer on a subnet can act as a DHCP server providing temporary IP addresses to requesting clients (see Figure 8.10). When the 'real' DHCP server is not on the same subnet as clients, the DHCP request for a dynamic IP has to be relayed to another subnet by a router. Or the DHCP server may be running on the router. In this situation, the response from the 'real' DHCP server can take longer than the response from the rogue server, and subsequently, the requesting client can choose the IP address and other additional information (e.g., DNS address, subnet mask, and default gateway) the rogue server provides.

Now, imagine that the default gateway offered by the rogue DHCP server is actually its own IP address. Then, all out-bounding packets from the victim station will be directed to the rogue computer disguised as a legitimate gateway to the external network. The attacker can view, copy, or modify packet contents before forwarding them to the real default gateway. This is a form of MITM and, at the same time, another example of spoofing, thus DHCP spoofing.

8.4.5.2 MITM with Evil Twin

MITM is also used by intruders to break into a Wi-Fi network by 'hijacking' a wireless connection. For this, a hacker can use a packet sniffing tool to monitor frames passed between the employee computers and an AP of a company to capture such information as IP addresses and SSID. Then, the hacker can set up a fake AP that operates at a higher power outside the target organization's physical boundary, but close enough so that the fake AP's signals are picked up by the computers inside.

The fake AP becomes a different type of rouge AP known as the *evil twin* AP (see Figure 8.11). With the close proximity between the evil twin AP and internal stations, they can re-associate themselves with the malicious evil twin. This way, although it appears that the corporate AP and host are communicating directly, they are actually sending and receiving data through the evil twin AP.

With the re-association, the evil twin is able to do either an *active* or *passive* replay. With the active replay, the intercepted messages are altered before their forwarding. In the passive mode, the attacker just captures frames, steals their contents, and forwards them without alterations. For example, the victim's access credentials, such as the user name and password, can be stolen to access the corporate network and do damages.

8.4.6 POISONING

Poisoning is an act of enlisting or injecting bogus information into a target system(s) in order to stage subsequent attacks (e.g., steal data, denial of service, malware distribution). ARP poisoning

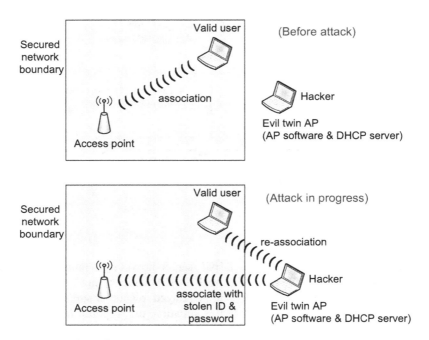

FIGURE 8.11 MITM with evil twin AP

and DNS poisoning are well known. Explaining DNS poisoning requires general understanding of the DNS infrastructure, and thus it is explained in Chapter 9.

8.4.6.1 ARP Poisoning (also ARP Spoofing)

ARP provides the mapping between IP and MAP addresses in IPv4 (revisit Section 5.8). Now, think of a scenario as in Figure 8.12. Initially, the attacker continuously sends ARP replies (not requests) to PC1 to tell that the MAC address of its default gateway (R1) is the attacker's own MAC address. After some time, PC1 buys the attacker's information and makes a wrong entry into its ARP cache, effectively becoming a victim. Then, the attacker sends ARP messages to R1 to tell that the MAC address corresponding to PC1's IP is the attacker's own MAC address. Now, both the PC1's and

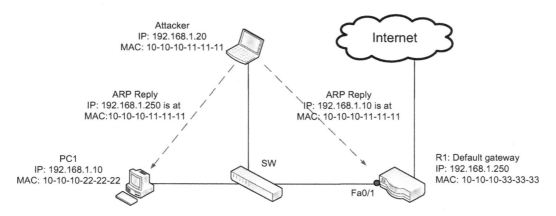

FIGURE 8.12 ARP poisoning

R1's ARP cache is poisoned. Once poisoned, the ARP cache of R1 will include yellow-highlighted, poisoned entries:

IP address	MAC address	Interface/port
192.168.1.250	10-10-10-33-33-33	Fa0/1
192.168.1.10	10-10-10-11-11-11	Fa0/1
192.168.1.20	10-10-10-11-11-11	Fa0/1

From this point, traffic flows between PC1 and R1 are through the attacker's computer, another man-in-the-middle (MITM) attack resulting from ARP poisoning. Also, think of the scenario where the attacker machine simply drops all IP packets between the two victims. This will result in the denial of service that blocks PC1's Internet access. As can be seen, ARP poisoning is a conduit to other threats. The fundamental weakness of ARP is that it works passively, so a computer updates its ARP table purely based on ARP replies. Because of ARP's venerabilities (e.g., ARP poisoning, MAC spoofing, MAC duplicating), it has been replaced by the more secure NDP (Neighbour Discovery Protocol) in IPv6.

8.4.7 Wi-Fi Threat: Wardriving

Wi-Fi networks are easily exposed to various security threats as data are transmitted in the open space. For example, with a utility tool, anyone can capture broadcasted Wi-Fi frames while driving or walking around areas with Wi-Fi signals. Such practice has been popularized in the name of wardriving. Information obtained through wardriving can be exploited (e.g., free Internet access). When the wardriving tool is in the wrong hands (e.g., drive-by attackers), this poses security risks.

8.5 EXPLOIT SOFTWARE DESIGN/DEVELOPMENT FAULTS

Chances are that a software program has faults or defects in its coding, which makes it vulnerable to cyberattacks. The software bugs are the results of human errors during the software design or development stage. The human errors may be caused by such conditions as the shortage of allocated resources, an unrealistic development schedule, an erroneous design logic, bad programming practices, and the lack of skilled testing. This section explains some of the cyber threats related to software design or development flaws.

8.5.1 Zero-Day Attack

When a software program with bugs is released, chances are that its developers or testers are simply unaware of them. Realistically, due to the complex nature of software engineering, it is very difficult to develop a large-scale program with no faults. In the past, security-related defects were reported in numerous applications including web browsers, database programs, multimedia players, mobile apps, and operating systems. The flaws make it much easier for malignant hackers to exploit the program (e.g., plant malware on the target system, bypass input value screening).

The zero-day attack is, therefore, an act of exploiting software bugs that have not been patched by its vendor. If a malignant hacker learns a programming flaw, he/she can develop malware to exploit it and launch attacks on identified targets before the software company discovers the defect and distributes a patch. Not surprisingly, when a software program is released, bad actors are energized to uncover its defects before the vendor finds them. As threat actors do not disclose the discovery of security bugs in software, determining how long they have been exploited is difficult. For example, on one occasion, a popular web browser had a fault that was not discovered for more than five years after its release.

8.5.2 Cross-Site Scripting

Cross-site scripting (XSS) is a very common attack mechanism. It is designed to execute a malicious script (e.g., javascript) in the browser of the victim computer. Here, rather than sending the script directly to the victim computer, the attacker uses an indirect approach. That is, the harmful script is injected into the website that accepts and stores the submission *without validating the content*. A user who visits the website could retrieve the evil script stored and download it, which will be automatically executed by the browser (see Figure 8.13).

These days, the majority of websites are designed to dynamically accept user inputs (e.g., blogs, surveys, comments, new rent postings) for improved interactivity with site visitors. A sample screenshot is shown in Figure 8.14 in which the input window is supposed to accept plain texts and store

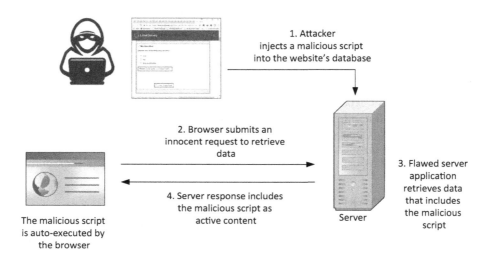

FIGURE 8.13   How XSS attack works

FIGURE 8.14   Sample website that accepts user inputs

them. Bad actors, however, can submit a malignant script instead and observe the site's reaction. If the website accepts the script and stores it in its database (rather than detects and filters it as a script), this indicates that there are faults in the site's application programming.

Now, imagine a site visitor retrieves the malignant script saved in the server site's database as part of his/her routine activities to read blogs, comments, or other stored information. If the script is retrieved and downloaded, the browser automatically executes it, triggering its evil actions such as stealing browser cookies and redirecting to another malware-infested website.

8.5.2.1 XSS Success Conditions

The success of an XSS attack, thus, requires that a website meet two conditions. First, the site's programming is flawed to accept a user's input (including a malicious script) without its validation. Second, once the script is stored in the site's database, the server site includes it in its response to a browser request. This mode of attack becomes successful because the program on the server site doesn't include the routine of filtering disqualified information submitted to the website.

8.5.3 SQL INJECTION

8.5.3.1 SQL Basics

SQL (Structured Query Language) is a standard language ubiquitously used to execute queries against relational databases. SQL's three most important keywords used to query a database are 'SELECT', 'FROM', and 'WHERE', that allow the selective retrieval of data records that meet filtering criteria. So, a simple query takes the form of 'SELECT *attribute(s)* FROM *table* WHERE *selection criteria*'. SQL is highly intuitive, and you can guess what will be the result of the following SQL query submitted to a database 'SELECT *first name and last name* FROM *client table* WHERE *zip code=92182*'.

8.5.3.2 Web Entry and Its SQL Translation

Based on the basics of SQL, let's take a step further. The input fields, as in Figure 8.15, are pretty much every website you visit if the site maintains a login account. Let's assume that you submitted your user name (e.g., happydog) and password (e.g., mypassword) to order a product from the site. Then, they are translated into a SQL query and processed by the site's database to find a match with your credentials already stored. The translated SQL query is something like: [SELECT *user_info* FROM *customer_table* WHERE *username* = *'happydog' and password* = *'mypassword'*]. If the submitted credentials match a customer record stored in the website's database, then you are allowed to sign in and the site retrieves your personal information such as your profile and past transactions.

8.5.3.3 SQL Injection

As can be seen, the entry fields are supposed to accept plain user credentials. Bad actors, however, can inject a malicious code (a SQL command) instead and observe the site's reaction. If the website accepts the malicious SQL command and processes it (rather than filtering it), this reflects a flaw in the site's program, posing a serious security threat to the online business. A well-known example of the dangerous SQL statement is: [SELECT * FROM *customer_table* WHERE *first_name*

```
Please enter your username and password.

Username:                              Password:
                                       (case sensitive)
[                    ]                  [                    ]
```

FIGURE 8.15 A login field that accepts user credentials

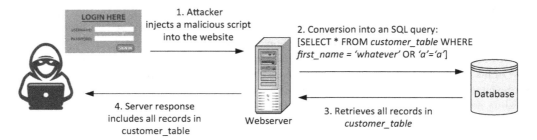

FIGURE 8.16   How SQL injection attack works

= *'whatever' or 'a'='a'*]. If the statement is not filtered, then the SQL processing will retrieve all records in the customer_table and send them to the attacker's browser (see Figure 8.16).

Depending on the malicious SQL query, its processing may result in the removal of database records or dumping of the entire database to the client browser and subsequent data theft. Chances are that the large-scale data theft (e.g., customer data, tax records, passwords) incidents reported on news outlets are the consequences of the SQL injection attack. Again, a classic case of defective web programming that fails to block erroneous or forged SQL commands.

CHAPTER SUMMARY

- Malware is a hostile computer code designed to cause malicious damages to infected systems and/or to harm system users. Among them are the virus (e.g., ransomware), worm, Trojan, bot, rootkit, logic bomb, adware, and spyware.
- The examples of weak or mis-configuration in security settings include the failure to enforce strong passwords, making them vulnerable to password cracking attacks and the installation of a weakly protected rogue access point.
- The brute force attack (in password cracking) breaks an encrypted or hashed password by trying every possible key/password combination exhaustively in an automated fashion using a computer's brute force.
- The dictionary method (in password cracking) cracks an encrypted or hashed password by automatically trying various combinations of dictionary terms. For this, an electronic file that contains dictionary words is linked to a password-cracking software engine.
- Spoofing, also called masquerading, is an act of faking to be someone or something to hide the real identity. Among many techniques are IP and MAC address spoofing, email address spoofing, and web spoofing.
- Denial-of-Service (DOS) refers to the aggression that one or more attackers generate enough bogus traffic targeting a server of an organization so that either the overwhelmed system becomes unavailable to ordinary users or its service response slows to a crawl.
- Packet sniffing is equivalent to the wiretapping of telephone lines in an attempt to steal information. The packet sniffing can be especially problematic in wireless networks that broadcast data.
- Port scanning is an act of probing the ports of a target host in an automated fashion using a software tool to obtain information (e.g., open ports) about the host. To attackers, it constitutes a key reconnaissance step to find a way into a target system.
- Man-in-the-middle (MITM) is a form of attack in which an attacker is able to hijack a session and relay (or substitute) data as a middle man. This way, an attacker can steal sensitive data or

obtain credentials (e.g., password) in order to intrude into a protected network. Examples of MITM include using a bogus DHCP server, an evil twin access point, and ARP poisoning.

- Poisoning, such as ARP and DNS poisoning, is an act of enlisting or injecting bogus information into a target system(s) in order to stage subsequent attacks (e.g., steal data, denial of service, malware distribution).

- Attackers exploit software design or development faults. Among the many techniques of this type are the zero-day, cross-site scripting, and SQL injection.

KEY TERMS

Adware	masquerading
ARP poisoning	logic bomb
bot	packet sniffing
botnet	password cracking
brute force attack	payload
cross-site scripting (XSS)	poisoning
denial of service (DOS)	port scanning
DHCP spoofing	ransomware
dictionary attack	rogue access point
distributed denial of service (DDOS)	rootkit
email spoofing	session hijacking
evil twin access point	spoofing
file-based malware	spyware
fileless malware	SQL injection
fingerprinting	Trojan
HTTP spoofing	virus
IP spoofing	wardriving
keystroke logger	web spoofing
MAC address flooding	Wireshark
MAC spoofing	worm
malware	Zenmap
man-in-the-middle (MITM)	zero-day attack

CHAPTER REVIEW QUESTIONS

1. A video player infected with _____ malware was downloaded. When the player was installed, the malware was activated and changed my computer's default DNS setup to direct all DNS inquires to the rogue DNS server maintained by a criminal group.
   A) worm
   B) Trojan
   C) macro
   D) rootkit
   E) backdoor

2. A hacker sends an email with an attachment that, if activated by an unsuspecting user, searches up to 50 other email addresses stored in the victim's system and relays the same infection code to the email addresses. This must be a _____.
   A) worm
   B) Trojan horse
   C) zombie

    D) virus

    E) spam

3. Flooding the _____ is a popular approach to trigger the denial of service on a target server. Assume that the ICMP protocol on the target server has been disabled.

    A) ARP request

    B) traceroute message

    C) SYN request

    D) telnet message

    E) DNS request

4. Which attack or pre-attack can be done without planting malware or gaining access to a target computer or network?

    A) worm

    B) Trojan

    C) denial-of-service

    D) port scanning

    E) MAC address flooding

5. When an IP packet with a spurious source IP address is crafted in an attempt to bypass a firm's firewall, it is a form of _____.

    A) phishing

    B) sniffing

    C) spoofing

    D) fingerprinting

    E) backdooring

6. Which of the following threats resembles session hijacking in its operational mechanism?

    A) denial of service

    B) wardriving

    C) cross-site scripting

    D) man-in-the-middle

    E) SQL injection

7. Denial of Service (DOS) attacks are intended to compromise a system's _____.

    A) confidentiality

    B) availability

    C) integrity

    D) privacy

    E) authenticity

8. Every possible combination of alphanumeric characters can be applied to crack the password of a system. This is a form of _____.

    A) brute force attack

    B) backdooring

    C) dictionary attack

    D) packet sniffing

    E) hash attack

9. The following is a type of 'program virus' EXCEPT _____:

    A) macro

    B) Trojan

    C) logic bomb

    D) rootkit

    E) ransomware

10. The evil twin AP is a form of _____.
    A) man-in-the-middle attack
    B) war-driving attack
    C) zombie AP attack
    D) denial of service attack
    E) port scanning attack
11. Which represents a security hazard a corporate employee can create unintentionally?
    A) evil twin AP
    B) rogue AP
    C) master AP
    D) war driving AP
    E) drive-by hacker AP
12. Wireshark is probably the most popular tool for _____?
    A) port scanning
    B) packet sniffing
    C) man-in-the-middle attack
    D) social engineering
    E) spam generating
13. Which may be the LEAST relevant approach to directly steal or recover someone's password?
    A) social engineering
    B) port scanning
    C) phishing
    D) brute force attack
    E) keystroke logging
14. A file that contains macro instructions that remove user files on a victim computer is considered as a:
    A) data virus
    B) ransomware virus
    C) rootkit virus
    D) armored virus
    E) It is not a virus file.
15. Which is NOT a well-known security threat for the Wi-Fi LAN?
    A) rogue access point
    B) evil twin
    C) wardriving
    D) denial of service
    E) fingerprinting
16. The _____ is a password cracking method that relies on a computer's powerful processing capability.
    A) worm
    B) social engineering
    C) dictionary attack
    D) packet sniffing
    E) port scanning
17. When an attacker sets up his/her wireless NIC to broadcast a continuous stream of CTS (clear-to-send) frames, this should result in _____.
    A) man-in-the-middle
    B) wardriving

    C) zombie AP

    D) denial of service

    E) port scanning

18. Which correctly describes ARP poisoning?

    A) An attacker sends 'ARP replies' to a target computer to tell that the MAC address of its default gateway is the attacker's own MAC address.

    B) An attacker sends 'ARP requests' to a target computer to tell that the MAC address of its default gateway is the attacker's own MAC address.

    C) An attacker sends 'ARP requests' to the default gateway to tell that the IP address of its victim computer is the attacker's own IP address.

    D) An attacker sends 'ARP requests' to the default gateway to tell that the MAC address of its victim computer is the attacker's own MAC address.

    E) An attacker sends 'ARP replies' to a target computer to tell that the IP address of its default gateway is the attacker's own IP address.

19. Choose an INCORRECT statement regarding spoofing.

    A) Spoofing and masquerading are synonymous.

    B) MAC spoofing is damaging because it shuts down wireless NICs.

    C) IP spoofing is used to conceal the sources of *denial of service* attacks.

    D) Email spoofing is used much by spammers.

    E) Phishing is used much to draw traffic to spoofed websites.

20. When an attacker sets up a DHCP server to steal user information (e.g., password), it is a type of _____ security threat.

    A) man-in-the-middle

    B) rogue access point

    C) evil twin

    D) wardriving

    E) denial of service

21. Ransomware is a type of malware that can negatively affect the data _____ of a system. (Revisit the types of damages ransomware can cause.)

    A) confidentiality

    B) integrity

    C) authentication and integrity

    D) authorization and confidentiality

    E) confidentiality, integrity, and availability

22. MAC address flooding by an attacker is a form of the _____ attack.

    A) denial of service

    B) spoofing

    C) scanning

    D) network reconnaissance

    E) command and control

23. The 'backdoor' is often created when a system is infected with ____.

    A) a virus

    B) ransomware

    C) a keyboard logger

    D) a logic bomb

    E) a Trojan

24. An attacker submitted an email bshin@sdsu.edu' (note ' at the end) to an online site that requires registration in order to test whether emails are being validated by the website system. This may be a precursor to the _____.

    A) spoofing attack

    B) SQL injection attack

C) session hijacking attack
D) packet sniffing attack
E) email spoofing attack

25. The _____ attack occurs when an attacker takes advantage of the flawed web application that accepts a user input *without* its validation (or filtering) and then present it back to users.
    A) SQL injection
    B) cross-site scripting
    C) session hijacking
    D) man-in-the-browser
    E) spoofing

HANDS-ON EXERCISES

EXERCISE 8.1

Search 'Digital Attack Map' that monitors DDOS attacks here (https://www.digitalattackmap.com/) and answer the following questions. Move the mouse over the map to see more details of a particular DDOS.

1. What are destination ports used much for DDOS?
2. What is the reported bandwidth (Gbps) of DDOS attacks related to the United States (either as a source or a destination)?
3. What are technologies or protocols (e.g., TCP connection, ICMP) used for DDOS attacks?
4. How long do they last? What is the shortest and the longest durations of DDOS you found?

EXERCISE 8.2

Visit 'https://www.spamhaus.com/threat-map/' to watch botnet activities. If the site's URL changes, search 'Live botnet threats worldwide'. Browse the site and answer the following questions.

1. What is the number of active bots detected in the last 24 hours?
2. What are the worst botnet countries?
3. What are the worst internet service providers (ISPs) that have active botnets?
4. Where on the global map do you see more command and control servers?

EXERCISE 8.3

Google Dorking, also called Google Hacking, represents a technique to find sensitive information that is difficult to find with ordinary search queries. For this, Google Dorking uses advanced queries that are designed to comb through the massive database of internet sites maintained by Google (refer to Section 2.14). Although illegal if used for cybercrimes, it becomes a powerful tool for bad actors to find potential preys, vulnerable systems, information accidentally leaked, or soft spots of their target. Let's try some queries to find information of such nature. Although there is no guarantee of recovering such sensitive information, the sample queries should give you an idea of what the power search can come up with.

1. Issue the following queries to find passwords accidently released or posted:
   • filetype:txt username password
   • login * password =* filetype txt
   • password filetype:xls site:*.*

- filetype txt username password @facebook.com
- filetype txt @gmail.com username password

2. Issue the following queries to find other types of sensitive or private information
   - To find email list: filetype:xls inurl:'email.xls'
   - To fine live cameras: inurl:top.htm inurl:currenttime
   - inurl:'lvappl.htm'
   - To find open FTP servers: intitle:'index of' inurl:ftp
   - To find SSH private keys: intitle:index.of id_rsa -id_rsa.pub

Exercise 8.4

In this exercise, you are going to experience MAC address spoofing using the function available on Windows as in Figure 8.7. For this, open *Device Manager* in Windows, then *Network Adapters*, and then choose an adapter you want to change its MAC address. Go to *Advanced* and observe if you are allowed to change its properties. Depending on the adapter, its driver may or may not allow you to change its MAC address. If the change is not allowed, try other adapters and repeat the process.

Exercise 8.5

The following exercise provides a glimpse of how the brute force attack can break passwords.

1. Visit a site that performs hash value calculations based on MD5, SHA-1, and other hash functions. Alternatively, you can install a free command-line hash generator (e.g., md5deep.sourceforge.net).
2. Come up with passwords of different lengths and complexities (e.g., ones with pure uppercase or lowercase letters, ones with upper- and lowercase letters mixed, ones with numbers and special characters). Obtain their corresponding hash values. As explained, major operating systems store hashed passwords for their protection. However, let's assume that the password file of a computer was stolen and the attacker was able to obtain hashed passwords.
3. Now, visit the online site *https://crackstation.net* that can decipher hash values using its massive database of words and sentences. Pretending to be the attacker, enter the hash values derived in (2) in order to crack them. What do you learn in terms of recovering passwords of different lengths and complexities?

Exercise 8.6

Through this exercise, you are using Zenmap's reconnaissance functions to scan a network.

1. Set up a network for an experiment: Use your home network that has at least one router (e.g., a wireless access router that bundles the switch, access point, and router functions) and two hosts. If necessary, two or more students can team up to do the project.
2. Find out the following information:
   - IPv4 address of the hosts:
   - Physical (MAC) address of the hosts:
   - Subnet mask:
   - IP address of the default gateway:
   - IP address of the local DNS server:
   - IP address of the local DHCP server:
3. Download Zenmap from http://nmap.org/ and install it on your computer. Zenmap accepts various *profiles* (or scan options) in addition to receiving text commands (see Figure 8.9).

4. **Survey the home network using** *Ping scan*: The Ping scan sends an ICMP echo request to every host address of a subnet and any responding host is considered up and running. Assuming that your home network is 192.168.1.0/24, issue '*Nmap –sP 192.168.1.0/24*' (*s* and *P* in the '*-sP*' flag mean *scan* and *Ping* respectively). Then, answer the following questions:

   a. How many IP addresses are scanned by the Ping scan? Explain why.
   b. What IP addresses are found 'up' and what are their corresponding MAC addresses?

   Oftentimes, hosts are instructed to ignore ICMP pinging to prevent probing. In this case, probing packets can be sent to a particular port (e.g., 80 for HTTP) of every possible host IP address. With the probing packets destined to reach TCP port 80, chances are that the border router/firewall is instructed not to filter them. Meanwhile, on receiving the probing packets, computers respond with the TCP's RST (reset the connection) flag as the socket does not exist or closed. Assuming that the home network is 192.168.1.0/24, the command to issue packets to port 80 of all possible hosts in the network is '*Nmap -sP -PT80 192.168.1.0/24*'.

   a. Does it end up with identical results as the ordinary Ping scan earlier?

5. **Surveying host ports with** *TCP SYN port scan*: An intruder can find potential target hosts with the Ping scan. Once a target host is determined, the attacker's next move is to identify its vulnerable port(s) through port scanning. Among many different options of port scanning available on Zenmap, *TCP SYN scan* is attempted. With the option, Zenmap sends a SYN packet to each port – the first step in the three-way TCP handshaking process (review Chapter 3).

   An 'open' port of the target host may respond with SYN/ACK bits flagged. On receiving the SYN/ACK packet, Zenmap returns RST (for reset) rather than ACK to abruptly terminate the three-way handshaking, but learns that the particular port is listening and open for business. If a SYN packet is sent to a 'closed' port, then the target host responds back with RST, indicating Zenmap that the target is not listening on the particular port. This port scan based on a SYN packet is also called *stealth scan* as the three-way handshaking with open ports is never completed because of the abrupt termination by the attacker but enables him/her to survey open ports without leaving a trace.

   Assuming that the target host's IP is 192.168.1.1, issue the command '*Nmap -sS 192.168.1.1*' for *TCP SYN port scan* (or *stealth scan*).

   a. What information is obtained about the target host?
   b. Zenmap categorizes port status into several types. How many ports are *open* (i.e., inviting for a connection) and *closed* (i.e., rejecting a connection)?

6. Among the various *profiles* (or scan options) available, the ***intense scan*** option tries to capture every possible information of the target by issuing different types of requests. Enter the targeted IP address into the *Target* field and then choose *intense scan* from *Profile* options. Observe the automatic formation of the corresponding text command in the *Command* field. Summarize what additional information is gathered.

9 Cybersecurity

Network and Host Protection

9.1 INTRODUCTION

The previous chapter explained some of the common cybersecurity threats faced by an organization. In this chapter, various technologies available to counter the threats and to protect workplaces are explained. In fact, when it comes to cybersecurity, there is no silver bullet that deters or prevents attacks, and both technological and non-technological (e.g., education and training, information assurance) countermeasures need to be in place to mitigate threats and curtail risks (revisit Section 2.11.1). This chapter focuses more on technological solutions widely used to defend networks and computer systems.

9.1.1 LEARNING OBJECTIVES

Many technology solutions in Table 2.2 that strengthen cyber defense have been explained in previous chapters. They include authentication technologies (Chapter 2), network address translation (Chapter 4), hardening intermediary devices (Chapter 5), Wi-Fi network protections (Chapter 6), and subnet segmentations and VLANs (Chapter 7).

The objectives of this chapter are to learn technology-enabled defense solutions largely pertaining to perimeter security, internal network security, and host security layers (Table 9.1). Recall that they represent just some of the important anti-threat measures being used and thus are nowhere close to the exhaustive list.

9.2 ACCESS CONTROL LIST (ROUTERS)

Ordinary routers come with the capacity to create and maintain an *access control list* (ACL) that includes a collection of inbound or outbound packet filtering rules. With the ACL, the router grants or denies IP packets based on the header information of the transport and internet layer PDUs. The ACL-based filtering decision primarily relies on:

- Source and destination IP addresses
- Source and destination TCP/UDP port numbers
- Protocol type (e.g., ICMP, UDP)
- ICMP message types (e.g., ping, traceroute)

The screening rules in the ACL are generally stateless and static. The static nature of ACL rules and their dependence on the IP address and port numbers for packet filtering limit the router's

TABLE 9.1
Summary of learning objectives

Security layers	Technological measures	Sections
Host security	• Host-based firewall	9.3
	• Host intrusion detection system	9.4
Internal network security	• Cyber Threat Intelligence (CTI)	9.7
	• Security Information and Event Management (SIEM)	9.7
	• Honeypot and Honey net	9.7
	• DNS infrastructure protection	9.8
	• Software defined networking (SDN)	9.9
	• Virtualization	9.9
	• Cloud computing network	9.9
Perimeter security	• Access control list (ACL)	9.2
	• Perimeter (or border) firewall	9.3
	• Intrusion Detection System	9.4
	• Demilitarized zone (DMZ)	9.5
	• Proxy server	9.6

effectiveness as a serious counter-threat device. That is, the router's ACL is intended for preliminary screening of disqualified packets, leaving their in-depth examination to the firewall or other specialized defense technologies.

For better customization of filtering rules, an ACL needs to be created for each router's physical port in use. Also, an ACL list needs to be developed for ingress (inbound) and egress (outbound) traffic separately for each physical port (e.g., ethernet0/0). For example, if a border router currently uses two WAN ports (S0/0/0 and S0/0/1), then four customized ACLs should be created – two ACLs for each physical port. This is because subnetworks attached to different router ports may not be identical in their protection requirements.

9.2.1 EXAMPLE: ADDING ACL TO CISCO ROUTER

The following statements in Table 9.2 can be added to the Cisco operating system to create an ACL of *access group 102*. The ACL allows *inbound* TCP traffic on the router's *ethernet0/0* port/interface if the destination port matches 80 (HTTP), 443 (HTTPS), or 25 (SMTP). The message is permitted regardless of 'any' source port. If the ACL 102 includes only the three rules as in Table 9.2, any message arriving at the *ethernet0/0* port will be dropped if it does not match any of three permit clauses (default *deny*).

TABLE 9.2
An illustration of ACL on Cisco router

Interface ethernet0/0	# configure router port ethernet0/0
ip access-group 102 in	# define a filtering group of inbound traffic
Access-list 102 permit tcp any any eq 80	# allow HTTP web traffic
Access-list 102 permit tcp any any eq 443	# allow HTTPS web traffic
Access-list 102 permit tcp any any eq 25	# allow SMTP email traffic

9.3 FIREWALL

The firewall represents software or hardware designed to protect networks (e.g., perimeter, subnet) or computer systems from intruders. It controls inbound (or ingress) and outbound (or egress) traffic and monitors (i.e., keep access logs) the patterns of data flow and of network/system usage by local and remote users. An organization can set up firewalls to form multiple lines of defense:

a. Perimeter security: A border firewall filters out unwanted packets at the entry point to a corporate network. Egress data are monitored and filtered as well.
b. Internal network security: Each segmented internal network can install its own firewall with an access control tailored to the segment functions and requirements.
c. Host security: Each enterprise server and workstation needs to install its own firewall to further fortify host security (thus, host-based firewall). Defining defense rules customized for a particular host provides another protection layer, even when the firewalls deployed to safeguard the entire network and its segments are compromised.

9.3.1 SEPARATING FIREWALL AND BORDER ROUTER

The router intended for individuals and small firms may have firewall functions built in. Very often, however, companies choose to maintain a dedicated firewall device separately from the border router for reasons.

a. If a corporate network is large, it needs a dedicated firewall to take a big load off the router for packet filtering so that the router can focus on its responsibility of routing packets.
b. With its capacity to examine PDUs all the way up to the application layer, the dedicated firewall is better positioned than the border router to detect and stop sophisticated attacks.
c. A firewall may not support the connectivity (e.g., serial port) necessary for the Internet link. When a firewall does not come with built-in support for T-1/T-3 or any other high-speed WAN connections, it has to rely on a router for such connectivity.
d. The router comes with protocols necessary for packet routing over the Internet. The firewall, as a specialized security device, may not have the built-in support for such a packet routing protocol.

When a firewall is detached from the router, popular deployment approaches are shown in Figure 9.1 in which the second method maintains two redundant connections for improved Internet accessibility. Notice that each of the segment between the firewall and the border router and that between the border router and the ISP router is configured as a single subnet.

9.3.2 FIREWALL FUNCTIONS

A firewall's packet filtering generally relies on information relevant to the internet, transport, and application layers. Among the firewall's primary functions are:

a. Inspection of the IP, TCP, UDP, and ICMP protocol data units (PDUs) in their header to apply predefined filtering rules for intrusion prevention.
b. Inspection of the application layer PDU in its header and payload to apply various filtering rules related to email and web contents, URL links, domain names, and malware signatures (i.e., unique fingerprints of malware).
c. Network address translation (NAT) to hide internal IP addresses
d. VPN (virtual private network) gateway to protect remote connections over the Internet

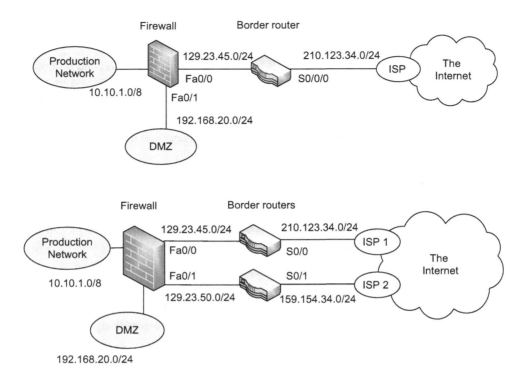

FIGURE 9.1 Two approaches in separating firewall and border router(s)

9.3.3 Managing Firewall

The effective protection of corporate networks demands its adequate configuration and management. For this:

a. The firewall's packet filtering rules should be in sync with a firm's policies on security, risk management, and compliance. The policy details change continuously and the updates should be reflected on the firewall's configuration in a timely manner. As an example, if a firm decides to introduce a telecommuting program for employees, filtering rules (e.g., TCP ports) should be adjusted to allow remote access to corporate systems via VPN connections.

b. A corporate firewall may have hundreds or thousands of filtering rules and, because of the continuous rule updates, outdated or unused filtering rules need to be removed. Also, conflicting rules are to be eliminated. The lack of rule maintenance can pose security risks. For example, if a threat actor finds that a particular TCP port remains open due to a filtering rule no longer used, he/she may be able to exploit it.

c. Fundamental principles used in managing intermediary nodes apply to the firewall as well. For example, any vulnerabilities in the firewall's operating system should be patched immediately and TCP/UDP ports that are either unnecessary or subject to threats should be closed.

d. Just as the router's access control list (ACL), the firewall's filtering rules are developed separately for ingress (inbound) and egress (outbound) traffic. Ingress filtering is important for obvious reasons – intrusion detection and prevention. Egress filtering is also critical because:
   • Internal data must be protected from their theft over the network.
   • Egress packets with an evil code (e.g., a virus) need be stopped from spreading to other networks.
   • Internal systems should be guarded against being exploited (e.g., DDOS attacks, digital currency mining) by threat entities from outside, especially the botnet's command and control server.

9.3.4 STATELESS PACKET FILTERING

Stateless filtering is the packet screening method in which the firewall examines each packet as an isolated case. For this, rules in the filtering list are applied to each arriving packet one by one from top to bottom. If a matching rule is found, it decides the fate of a packet (e.g., either *permit* or *deny*) and the rest of the screening rules are skipped. Generally, if no matching rule is found for a packet, it is dropped (i.e., default *deny*) by the firewall.

For example, complying with the corporate policy, its border firewall may be configured to drop IP packets outright when they meet any of the following conditions:

• If source IP = 172.16.*.* to 172.31.*.* or 192.168.*.*	#Private IP ranges
• If TCP destination port = 21	#FTP connection attempt
• If TCP destination port = 23	#Telnet connection attempt

Also, the border firewall may be set up to allow IP packets when they satisfy any of the following criteria:

• If destination IP = 161.154.23.59 and TCP port = 443	#Webserver connection
• If destination IP = 161.154.23.59 and TCP port = 25	#Email server connection

Stateless packet filtering has limitations. Above all, it is not highly effective in detecting or preventing intrusions as each packet is inspected independently of other inbound or outbound packets. Also, changing an IP packet's sender address (i.e., IP spoofing) is easy and thus the filtering decision of incoming packets based on the source IP address alone should be avoided.

9.3.4.1 Demonstration of Stateless Rules

Table 9.3 demonstrates a partial view of the actual table with stateless filtering rules.

- The 'Rule Name' is the name you choose to call a rule.
- The 'Direction' is either *inbound* or *outbound*.
- The 'Event Name' specifies whether the rule is a(n) *allow* or *deny* rule.
- The 'Protocol' column specifies a protocol to which a rule is applied.
- The 'Source Port' causes a rule to apply to a specific source port of a packet.
- The 'Destination Port' causes a rule to apply to a specific destination port of a packet.

TABLE 9.3

A packet filtering table of stateless rules

Rule name	Direction	Event name	Protocol	Source port	Destination port
Allow HTTP in	inbound	Allow http in	TCP	80	*
Allow HTTPS in	inbound	Allow https in	TCP	443	*
Allow ICMP in	inbound	Allow icmp in	ICMP	*	*
Allow SMTP in	inbound	Allow smtp in	TCP	25	*
Allow POP3 in	inbound	Allow pop3 in	TCP	110	*
…………....	…….	…….	……	…….	…..

For example, the first rule is named 'Allow HTTP in' and 'allows' all inbound HTTP protocol data units (PDUs) when they are encapsulated within a TCP segment containing 80 as the source port. You can guess that the rule covers inbound packets containing webserver responses to browser requests from internal hosts. It is important to remember that the sequence of rules is critical in correctly filtering disqualified packets. Having the same set of rules entered in different orders can result in very different filtering outcomes.

9.3.5 STATEFUL PACKET FILTERING

With stateful filtering, the firewall inspects each packet in the context of previous engagements (e.g., a session, packet exchange history), making the packet screening context-dependent and thus more effective than stateless filtering. For stateful filtering, the firewall maintains and continuously updates the *state* information including source and destination IP addresses, engaging protocols (e.g., TCP, UDP), source and destination ports used, sequence numbers (if TCP) and connection states (see Table 9.4 for an example).

If an arriving packet is consistent with information stored in the state table (e.g., a previously established session), it is allowed to enter the network. Otherwise, it is dropped by the firewall (i.e., default *deny*). The following are general rules of stateful filtering.

- If a packet's source and destination sockets are in the state table, then allow it to *pass*.
- If a packet's source and destination sockets are not in the state table or the packet is not a connection-opening attempt (i.e., no handshaking request), then *deny*.

Although stateful filtering is more powerful than stateless filtering in locating intrusion attempts, the screening process can be more effective if both approaches are used concurrently.

9.3.6 DEEP PACKET INSPECTION

9.3.6.1 Limitations of Stateless and Stateful Filtering

The stateless and stateful filtering methods primarily inspect the header of the internet and transport layer PDUs (e.g., IP, ICMP, TCP, and UDP) to make filtering decisions. They, however, have limitations when the majority of today's cyberattacks target the application layer functions. For example, think of an phishing email or an email attached with malware. The application layer's email protocol, SMTP, is the most heavily targeted attack vector. That is, the stateless and stateful filtering methods are not enough to detect them, and using techniques that filter packets based on the application layer information is fundamental to better prevent cyber threats.

9.3.6.2 Deep vs. Shallow Packet Inspection

The technique that inspects the application layer PDU including its header and contents is called deep packet inspection (or DPI). In contrast, stateless and stateful filtering is called *shallow packet*

TABLE 9.4
An example of the state information table

Source address	Source port	Destination address	Destination port	Connection state
192.168.1.23	1324	183.120.34.75	80	Initiated
192.168.1.30	2357	10.10.1.45	80	Established
192.168.1.213	5437	157.74.231.23	443	Established
192.168.1.43	23578	72.23.167.10	25	Established

inspection, as it does not examine the application layer's rich PDU information. The DPI-enabled firewall is able to scrutinize the following information for filtering decisions:

- An application's digital certificate and signature (also called code sign; more in Chapter 10)
- Application header (e.g., HTTP/HTTPS header for URL filtering, block unapproved applications, SSL session inspections)
- Payload/content for keyword-based content filtering (e.g., pornography, racism, violence), malware signature screening, and spam filtering

9.4   INTRUSION DETECTION SYSTEM (IDS)

9.4.1   IDS vs. FIREWALL

The IDS is a network/host security system often used along with the firewall. As the name indicates, it is a system designed to detect network intrusions. Thus, *there is a fundamental difference in their orientation between the firewall and the IDS* as the former's task is to filter and stop disqualified packets and the latter's task is to detect and alert to suspicious activities.

That is, the firewall generally monitors ingress and egress traffic to keep disqualified packets from entering or leaving the network and do not produce alarms triggered by dropped packets. Whereas, the IDS monitors communications and unusual activities and attempts to detect and alert any suspicious intrusion that has already taken place (e.g., malware already gained a foothold).

9.4.2   INTRUSION DETECTION TECHNOLOGIES

The IDS uses packet detection technologies such as malware signatures, which is similar to the firewall. Additionally, it uses advanced 'anomaly' detection technologies that understand the baseline of normal behaviors or patterns in various aspects and applies the baseline to detect anomalies in network traffic.

Among the different anomaly types the IDS can monitor are as follows.

- Volumetric anomaly (e.g., a database server is sending more data than the average; the data exchange ratio is abnormally skewed; there is an unusually high connection rate).
- Geometric anomaly (e.g., the company's webserver is being probed from certain countries where its products are not sold or have no existing businesses).
- Temporal anomaly (e.g., there are busy database activities on Sunday when the office is closed).
- Protocol anomaly (e.g., FTP to an outbound server has suddenly surged).

9.4.3   NETWORK vs. HOST IDS

There are two different IDS types. The network IDS (or NIDS) monitors network traffic and the host-based IDS (or HIDS) are installed on host devices to watch suspicious activities.

- **Network IDS**: To detect suspicious intrusions, the NIDS relies on such information as: (1) statistical anomaly that is different from the baseline profiling (e.g., connection rate anomaly) and (2) intrusion signatures for pattern matching (e.g., predefined strings). Other types of packet filtering rules used by the firewall such as stateful information and deep packet inspection are also used by NIDS to detect intrusion and to alert.
- **Host-based IDS**: The host-based IDS (or HIDS) uncovers intrusions by tracking such information as *system calls to the operating system* (e.g., print request), *file system access* (e.g., read a file), and *host input/output communications*.

Separately, there is a system called IPS (intrusion prevention system) that differs from the IDS as IPS is able to take more proactive action in its ability to drop suspicious communications (e.g., terminate ongoing sessions). These days, some IDS products can also block suspicious traffic rather than just detecting intrusions and producing alerts to the defense team.

9.5 DEMILITARIZED ZONE (DMZ)

9.5.1 DMZ AND PRODUCTION NETWORK

Some server hosts, especially the webserver and email server, heavily interact with the external systems from the Internet to provide communication and information access services, and thus they are naturally more exposed to cyber threats. To better safeguard an enterprise from possible external threats, these servers are generally separated from the main production network by placing them in the *demilitarized zone* (or DMZ) subnet. The production network is an internal network that needs secure protections and, for this reason, the two network segments need to be separated physically (e.g., separate LAN cabling) or logically (e.g., different subnets). In the case of Figure 9.2, the border router/firewall is dividing the corporate network into two subnets.

9.5.2 IP ADDRESSING OF DMZ

Servers in a DMZ can be configured with private or public IP addresses. When DMZ servers are equipped with private IPs, the *network address translation* (NAT) function is performed by the border router or firewall. As explained, many organizations rely on private IPs for internal nodes because internal resources can be better protected from probing and other threat attempts. Also, NAT offers more flexibility in address management (e.g., more room to handle the growth of a network and subnets).

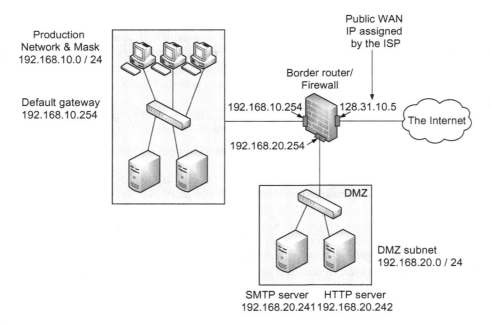

FIGURE 9.2 Border router firewall and DMZ

9.5.3 CASE: FIREWALL ROUTER AND DMZ

This case is derived from the network of a real company with over $30 million in yearly revenue to demonstrate the firewall router and DMZ deployed to protect the main production network. As can be seen, the firewall router joins three subnets; one for the Internet connection, one for the main production network, and one for DMZ. The production network (192.168.10.0/24) and DMZ (192.168.20.0/24) are given private subnet addresses and the firewall's interface (128.31.10.5) connects to the Internet. The firm maintains internal DNS servers for local hosts. For Internet routing, packets are sent to the default gateway that is the firewall's LAN port (192.168.10.254).

The firewall router drops inbound IP packets unless they are a part of ongoing sessions initiated by internal hosts – thus, stateful filtering. However, certain packets such as emails to the SMTP server (192.168.20.241) and HTTP requests to the webserver (192.168.20.242) are allowed into the DMZ. The firewall screens packets based on information pertaining to the internet layer (e.g., IP address-based filtering), transport layer (e.g., port-based filtering), and application layer (e.g., malware removal, web content-based filtering).

The firewall router also performs network address translation (NAT) between the production network and the Internet, and between the DMZ and the Internet. For example, all packets from the production network carry the source address of 128.31.10.5 after NAT. The corresponding responses from the Internet, therefore, contain the destination address of 128.31.10.5 before its translation back into original IP addresses by the firewall router.

When an email arrives from the Internet, the firewall performs initial packet filtering and then forwards it to the SMTP server (192.168.20.241) on DMZ. The SMTP server removes any virus and spam, and forwards cleaner emails to the production network's email server. This two-email server approach (i.e., the primary in the production network and the secondary in DMZ) adds extra security to email communications.

9.6 PROXY SERVER

9.6.1 PRIMARY FUNCTIONS

The proxy server is a computer or an application set up by an organization to improve network performance and also to serve security functions. Its primary functions include:

a. Keep internal computers anonymous by hiding their IP addresses through IP spoofing
b. Block access to restricted or blacklisted Internet sites
c. Scan inbound and outbound traffic to detect any malicious activities
d. Cache external websites frequently visited by employees to accelerate their downloading

As can be seen, it performs some of the security functions of the router's access control list and the firewall. Access to the proxy server deployed on the network perimeter can be configured in the host's web browser or operating system.

9.6.2 PROXY SERVER TYPES

There are three different proxy server types an organization deploys on-site (Figure 9.3):

a. **Forward proxy**: It is the Internet-facing proxy server that intercepts user requests from internal sources and carries them out them on behalf of the user hosts. It is, thus, generally intended to protect internal client hosts that initiate communications.
b. **Reverse proxy**: It receives requests from client hosts coming from external networks and forwards them to the correct internal server. It is, therefore, meant primarily to protect internal server hosts through obscurity.
c. **Transparent proxy**: It is used much for content filtering in such locations as schools or libraries to selectively censor or monitor traffic.

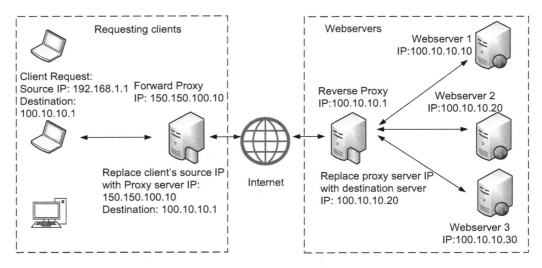

FIGURE 9.3 Forward proxy and reverse proxy servers

9.6.3 THIRD-PARTY PROXY SERVICE

The IP proxy service is also offered by third-party websites so that ordinary web users can surf the Internet while maintaining personal privacy by blocking the visited sites from gathering their personal information (e.g., source IP, user location). The online proxy service has limitations, especially as it can create potential security vulnerabilities at an organization. For instance, an employee of a company can use the public proxy service to bypass firewall rules that keep him/her from visiting rogue or distractive (e.g., social networking) websites while at work. What happens if the rogue site is infested with malware?

9.7 CYBER THREAT INTELLIGENCE (CTI)

9.7.1 RISE OF CTI

Conventional cybersecurity efforts have been only partially successful against sophisticated adversaries. This is because the traditional security paradigm of deploying *general* countermeasures (e.g., firewall, anti-virus, proxy server, VPN) is not enough in safeguarding a firm from sophisticated and highly persistent threats. Amid the growing challenge, more organizations are adding the *cyber threat intelligence* (CTI) component to their existing cybersecurity program these days. CTI is intended to supplement the traditional security solutions, and create their synergy.

For the CTI program, an organization can hire CTI analysts or re-train existing IT security staff. The staffing arrangement for CTI efforts at an organization varies depending on its circumstances such as the firm size, industry type, and available IT budget. The majority of large corporations with a CTI function maintain dedicated CTI positions and even create a dedicated CTI team, separated from the traditional IT security team.

9.7.2 WHAT IS CTI?

In a nutshell, CTI is intended to improve the *situational awareness* of the potential or looming cyber threats *particularly relevant* to an organization/business. To grow the situational awareness, for example, a firm needs to learn who are the cyber adversaries that may attack its business, where

TABLE 9.5

Types of threat intelligence an organization can act on

CTI categories	CTI items	Description
Threat actor/agent	Identity	Attribution of an attacker or attacker group's identity that may be a real name (e.g., BlackOasis) or an alias (e.g., APT12)
	Goal	What motivates attacks (e.g., ransom extortion, stealing intellectual assets, hack government facility, cripple utility infrastructure)?
Traces of attack (or indicators of compromise)	Hash value	Hash values (e.g., MD5, SHA1) of malware strains, signatures
	IP address	IP addresses of threat sources
	Domain name	Domain names such as malignant webservers and rogue DNS servers
	Network/host artifact	Information on suspicious or malicious activities such as the discovery of a back door, an illegal user account, network or host probing, and malware infection.
Attack execution method	Tool	Exploit tools (e.g., executables) used, which may be developed by threat actors or freely available.
	Tactics, techniques, and procedures (TTPs)	Behavioral patterns of a threat agent in orchestrating attacks. For example, it describes technical and non-technical details an attacker uses in executing one or more steps of the cyber kill chain (see Section 2.12).

they are coming from, and what tools, tactics, techniques, and procedures they may use to launch attacks and cause damages.

CTI thus represents *actionable* threat information including threat types, sources, actors, technologies, and attack surface relevant to a particular firm and thus require the firm's immediate attention to reduce risks. The CTI drive aims to add more *proactive* (not reactive), *preventive* (not remedial), and *timely* (not belated) defense orientation to compensate for traditional threat detection and response security measures.

There are many different types of threat intelligence on which an organization can take active countermeasures. Some are easier to obtain, and others are most difficult to derive as they take data analysis such as data correlations and pivoting. There are three different types of cyber threat intelligence: *threat actor/agent-related*, *traces of attack-related* (also called *indicators of compromise* or IOCs), and *attack execution method-related* (Table 9.5).

9.7.3 Examples: CTI in Practice

A few examples illustrate how CTI differs from the traditional cybersecurity paradigm and how CTI can further strengthen the protection of an organization (Table 9.6).

9.7.4 Security Information and Event Management (SIEM)

As shown in the preceding examples, the CTI analyst of a company gathers internal and external threat data, particularly relevant to the company and its industry, and performs analysis. Very often, the analysis tasks mobilize advanced analytical methods using statistical, machine-learning, visual, and heuristics methods to overcome the challenges of sifting through a large, messy volume of data to uncover relevant CTI. Organizations use a software platform generally called SIEM to undertake the analytical task of CTI.

TABLE 9.6

Examples – traditional vs CTI-powered security activities

Examples	Traditional approach	CTI added approach
Construction of firewall/border router filtering rules	Gather a relatively static and general packet filtering rules and implement them. Once the access rules are in place, they may stay relatively stable.	In addition to the general filtering rules, additional filtering rules (e.g., blacklisted IPs, domains, malware hashes) are obtained from CTI service sources dynamically and added to the firewall in an automated fashion. Examples of CTI service sources include IBM's X-Force and AT&T's AlienVault.
Ransomware defense in the finance industry	Rely on the commercial anti-virus program installed on the network node and the client and server hosts	In addition to using the anti-virus program, the CTI analyst can actively learn what particular ransomware strains are wreaking havoc in the finance industry currently and their technical details (e.g., malware signatures, techniques used to compromise victims). Then, work with the security team to deploy countermeasures to protect a bank from particular ransomware strains that have a high chance of attacking it.
A hacker or insider is trying to sell confidential information (e.g., business secrets) stolen from a company in the dark web's marketplace.	There is no effort to actively find and prevent the hacker or insider from selling the confidential information, which could inflict severe damages to the victim company.	The CTI analyst can do the routine search of the dark web's marketplace and discover that the company's valued assets are being sold. Once that is uncovered, the company can take quick remedial actions including contacting law enforcement.

9.7.4.1 SIEM's External and Internal Data Sources

SIEM can use internal and external data sources to derive CTI of various types as summarized in Table 9.5. Among the most significant threat information sources are CTI subscription services, open source intelligence, and internal log data.

a. The external CTI service (e.g., AT&T's AlienVault and IBM's X-Force) provides up-to-date information on threat sources (e.g., IPs, threat domains, malware hashes) and software vulnerabilities reported. Correlating the external information with internal assets (e.g., software inventory) to find 'actionable' information is the responsibility of CTI analysts.

b. Another external data source is *open source intelligence* (or OSINT), which categorically means any legally gathered information without infringing on others' privacy. The data gathering generally uses free and publicly available sources such as public information feeds, comments of potential threat actors/hacking groups, and government-provided information (e.g., InfraGard, European Network and Information Security Agency).

c. SIEM can analyze traffic data obtained from internal network nodes. The nodes (e.g., firewall, proxy server, router, IDS, decoys) as internal CTI sources provide rich security-related 'log' data to SIEM for analysis. The log includes such information as probes to TCP/UDP ports, unsuccessful login attempts, outbound connections, traffic dropped, changes in firewall/IDS/router configurations, and administration access granted (see Figure 9.4).

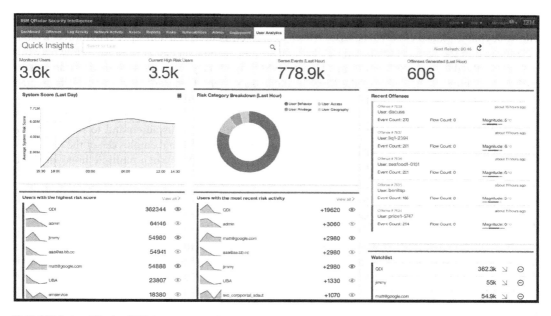

FIGURE 9.4 QRadar SIEM screenshot (Source: IBM.com)

9.7.4.2 SIEM's Analytical Capabilities

SIEM's analytical capabilities include:

a. Aggregation that combines data from multiple internal and external sources to enable their slicing and dicing for data analysis from different angles

b. Correlation of data from different sources in order to search for suspicious activities. Some of the correlation analysis is to finding similar alerts over time, revealing the order of similar events, and searching for events detected by multiple network nodes.

c. Automated alerting of threats or similar network activities to CTI analysts or system administrators for immediate remedial actions.

d. Analysis of log data from network nodes (e.g., IDS, firewall, proxy server) to determine the company's compliance with regulations and laws.

One critical aspect of CTI analysis is assessing the impact (e.g., benign, low, medium, high, critical) and confidence (e.g., unknown, low, medium, high) of uncovered threats highly relevant to an organization. For this, several assessment techniques (e.g., confidence matrix, common vulnerability scoring system) have been introduced. Of course, the CTI of both significant impact and high confidence will have to be taken most seriously by an organization.

9.7.5 HONEYPOT AS CTI SOURCE

The honeypot is a decoy or bait system (computer) that is installed by an organization to attract and monitor an attacker's intrusion behaviors (e.g., techniques, tactics, and procedures). Also, by engaging with the honeypot, the attacker is going to reveal the *indicators of compromise* such as the attacker's IP address and domain name. This way, the honeypot can deflect attacks by distracting the adversary's attention from other real targets. As can be seen, the honeypot can provide valuable CTI and also triggers timely and accurate alerts to the security team if an organization is attacked.

9.7.5.1 Honeypot Deployment

The honeypot is placed close to the asset it tries to protect. That is, if a honeypot is to protect a database located in the data center, it can be positioned in the same data center or on the same network segment as the database. As an example, HoneyMySQL is a honeypot that is designed to trap attackers by mimicking the behavior of the MySQL database system. Generally, the honeypot is created on a virtual machine (VM) so that it can be quickly restored if compromised.

One challenge of installing a honeypot is that it should closely emulate the real system in terms of available services and high interactivity to avoid the attacker's suspicion and to provide more security protection to the 'real' system. Also, it is important that internal employees of the organization are fully aware of the honeypot deployment to avoid accidents. When multiple honeypots are created, they form a *honey net*, another defense line to monitor the corporate network.

9.8 DEFENDING DNS INFRASTRUCTURE

We already know that DNS provides the mapping between a domain name and an IP address. In this section, we go deeper into DNS, one of the most critical infrastructures for the Internet to function. DNS, as a whole, is a complex system and thus has been exposed to cyberattacks on many fronts.

9.8.1 DOMAIN AND NAME RESOLUTION

A *domain* such as *purdue.edu* defines a boundary within which an organization (e.g., university) manages or controls its network resources. Within the boundary, hosts are labeled with human-readable *domain names* such as *www.purdue.edu* (for a webserver) that is paired with an IP address.

For *name resolution*, the DNS server maintains a database of the domain name and IP address pairs, and the list is continuously updated. With the rapid growth of hosts attached to the network, the DNS database entries need to be dynamically updated. Name resolution can be both forward (e.g., www.facebook.com → 12.34.56.78) and backward/reverse (e.g., 12.34.56.78 → www.facebook.com), although DNS queries are mostly for the forward resolution.

9.8.2 DOMAIN HIERARCHY AND MANAGEMENT

The domain name itself is formed in a hierarchical structure composed of *root-level*, *top-level*, *second-level*, and *lower-level* domains. The root domain is the highest level of the domain hierarchy, literally indicating the whole Internet space. The next is the *top-level domain* (TLD), which includes the *generic TLD (or gTLD)* such as *.com*, *.edu*, *.gov*, and *.org*, and the *country code TLD (ccTLD)* such as *.kr* (for Korea) and *.uk* (for United Kingdom).

The second-level domain is the sub-domain of a top-level domain. For example, in *texas.edu, texas* is its second-level domain. The majority of the second-level domains represent organizations, schools, and businesses. Once the second-level domain name is registered, an organization can freely create lower-level or sub-domain names. As an example, *cba.sdsu.edu* consists of the *edu* top-level domain, the *sdsu* (university) second-level domain, and the *cba* (college of business) sub-domain.

Then, there is the *Fully Qualified Domain Name* (or FQDN) at the bottom of the domain hierarchy. Also called *Absolute Domain Name*, it is the name that points to the precise location (e.g., host computer) in the DNS hierarchy. A couple of hypothetical examples are 'www.cba.sdsu.edu' and 'mail.sdsu.edu', which represent the webserver (www) and the email server (mail) respectively. DNS maps an FQDN to an IP address. When a domain name is preceded by a protocol such as *http*, *https*, or *ftp*, it becomes a URL. Thus, URL = protocol + FQDN. For example, *https://www.yale.edu* becomes a URL in which *www.yale.edu* is a fully qualified domain name.

The *Internet Assigned Numbers Authority* (IANA) manages top-level domains as well as the IP address space. Specifically, it manages generic (*gTLD*) and country code (*ccTLD*) top-level domains and delegates their control to *domain name registrars* who process domain name applications from businesses and individuals. There are a number of IANA-accredited registrars in the world (refer to *www.icann.org* for the list). Businesses and individuals who want an Internet presence are required to register the second-level domain name through the registrar. As for country-code TLDs, the domain registry is generally controlled by each country's government.

9.8.3 DNS ARCHITECTURE

For name resolution, several server types including *local DNS* and *root DNS* servers are necessary. An organization maintains its own *local DNS* server(s) that keeps a database of local hostnames and their IP addresses, and also caches information of frequently visited external sites to serve local inquiries. An organization may be one domain that may be comprised of several sub-domains logically divided (e.g., colleges within a university). A domain maintains primary and secondary (for backup) DNS servers, and the DNS database of the primary server is routinely copied into the secondary server, a procedure known as *zone transfer*.

On receiving the DNS inquiry, the local DNS server attempts name resolution by searching its database and cache. If the local server is unable to resolve the inquiry, it is forwarded to a root DNS server that covers the root domain, which is on top of the domain hierarchy as explained. There are currently 13 root servers in the world, and each root server has multiple instances geographically dispersed (Details are on www.root-servers.org).

The root server does not have the answer to the local inquiry either, but it provides the *authoritative* name server(s) of the top-level domain pertaining to the inquiry (see Figure 9.5). The ensuing inquiry to the top-level name server may lead to another referral of the authoritative name server for the second-level domain. The general-to-specific referral process repeats from the root server to the authoritative server of a target sub-domain and until the IP address of a FQDN is found.

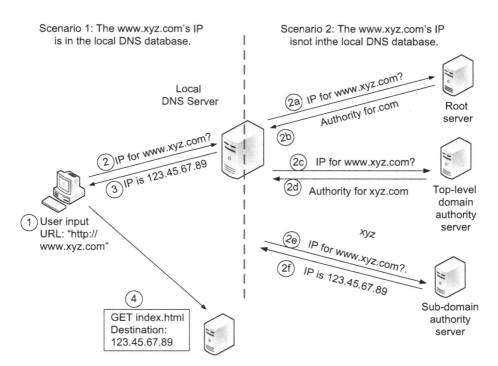

FIGURE 9.5 An iterative process of name resolution

9.8.4 Host DNS File

The operating system of a host has a DNS file that can be edited for the *initial* name resolution. For example, in Windows, the file name is *hosts* and available at *C:\windows\system32\drivers\ etc*. The file is automatically loaded into the memory during system bootup. The file's initial entry only includes IPv4 (127.0.0.1) and IPv6 (::1) loopback addresses that redirect packets to itself (see Figure 9.6).

When a user enters a website on the browser, the Windows computer first searches its own *hosts* file to see if has a corresponding IP address. If the IP is not found, then the computer sends an inquiry to the default local DNS server, as in Figure 9.5. Having DNS entries in the *hosts* file offer benefits:

- Web access speed improves by bypassing the iterative DNS queries, as in Figure 9.5.
- A newly developed system can be pilot-tested without having an entry in the local DNS server.

9.8.5 DNS Poisoning/DNS Spoofing

DNS poisoning is an act of substituting DNS entries in an attempt to redirect traffic to the system owned or arranged by the attacker. The attacker can take advantage of the redirected traffic to mount various attacks including stealing data, spreading malware, performing man-in-the-middle, attracting users to a spoofed website, and staging denial of service. DNS poisoning can target both the local hosts file (Figure 9.6) and external DNS servers.

First, the *hosts* file has been subject to cyberattacks in which malware (e.g., 'FreeVideo Player' Trojan) secretly changed its entries to redirect user inquiries to malignant websites. Second, threat actors can target a registrar system that handles domain registration to alter DNS records. On compromising the registration system, the attacker can change the authoritative server of the target domain to his/her own server. For example, Twitter and the *New York Times* were victims of such attacks in the past.

Third, an attack can be directed at the authoritative or local DNS server of a target domain. On taking over the DNS server, the attacker can alter the DNS records in order to redirect user traffic to a malignant site. When the records of an authoritative DNS server are forged with bogus resolution information, this inevitably results in the poisoning of the local DNS cache. With cache poisoning, the local DNS server supplies the false IP address to clients. For example, Figure 9.7 demonstrates how the rogue server's IP address is provided by the local DNS server whose cache is poisoned when the authority server is compromised by an attacker.

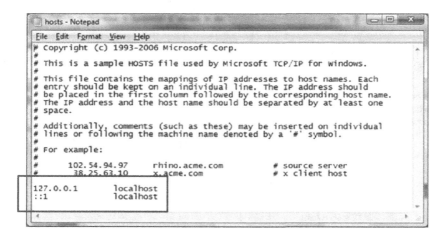

FIGURE 9.6 Demonstration of *hosts* file in Windows

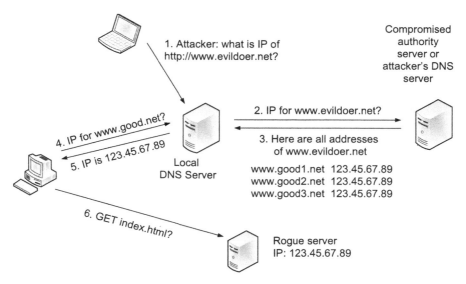

FIGURE 9.7   Demonstration of DNS poisoning

9.8.6   DNS PROTECTION MEASURES

Defense measures need to be taken to prevent such DNS attacks by following the best security management practices. Among them are:

- The DNS server login needs to be protected with a strong password.
- Adequate access control to the DNS server needs to be in place. For example, only qualified local clients can be allowed to query the local DNS server, and any external requests to the local DNS server can be outright rejected.
- Deploy the DNSSEC (*Domain Name* System Security Extensions) standard to authenticate all communications between DNS servers (e.g., *zone transfer*). DNSSEC adds a layer of security to the DNS infrastructure by implementing a suite of security protocols.

9.9   CYBERSECURITY AMID NEW NETWORKING PARADIGMS

New computing and networking paradigms continue to emerge, opening opportunities and at the same time posing challenges in strengthening security management. Among them, software defined networking, virtualization, and cloud computing are discussed.

9.9.1   SOFTWARE DEFINED NETWORKING (SDN)

9.9.1.1   Traditional Networking vs. SDN

As explained, intermediary devices perform networking functions defined in two or more layers. For example, the layer 2 switch and the Wi-Fi access point implement data link and physical layer functions, and the highest layer of the router is layer 3. Here, while the physical layer's mission is to physically move packets over the network, layers 2 and 3 are responsible to manage packet movements including switching/routing path decisions. That is, each intermediary device (except layer 1 hubs and repeaters) implements both the *management* (i.e., layer 2 and 3) and *packet delivery* (i.e., layer 1) functions, frequently called *control plane* and *data plane* activities respectively.

Now, let's imagine the situation in which the control plane functions of each intermediary device are physically separated from those of the data plane and then *consolidated* and *centrally managed*

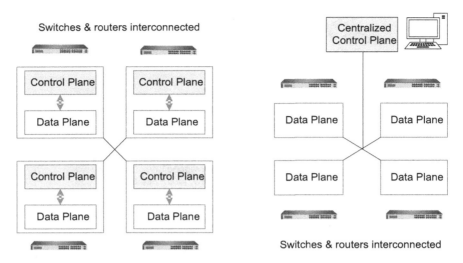

FIGURE 9.8   Traditional network (left) vs. SDN (right)

by an independent system (see Figure 9.8). This consolidated control plane system is able to communicate with the intermediary devices over the network. In this arrangement, the intermediary devices largely maintain only data plane functions (i.e., physically transporting packets) and their packet forwarding instructions come from the control plane system. This is a new emerging paradigm called SDN, which is radically different from the traditional paradigm of computer networking.

9.9.1.2   Control Plane

In SDN, the control plane node is called the *SDN controller* and acts like the computer's operating system that centrally controls all activities of its hardware components including the memory, CPU, storage, and peripheral devices. Hence, SDN becomes the framework to automatically manage a collection of data plane devices through the control plane's programmable SDN controller. With the centralized management of networking, the SDN controller has a complete view of the whole network nodes and their interconnectivity. The SDN paradigm thus can significantly improve network security.

The SDN controller can provide various services to the data plane, which include the:

- Network 'topology' service that provides data plane devices with information on how they are interconnected with each other.
- Inventory service that tracks the details of all SDN-enabled data forwarding devices.
- Host tracking service that furnishes IP and MAC addresses of hosts to data plane devices.
- Traffic engineering and load balancing that optimize network performance by regulating the details of data transmissions.
- Decisions of packet routing and frame switching.
- Security monitoring and regulation/policy compliance.
- Management of virtual LANs (VLANs) and Spanning Tree Protocol (STP).

9.9.1.3   Data Plane

The primary responsibility of data plane devices is to physically transport packets following instructions from the control plane's SDN controller. For this, the data plane devices (1) keep instructions coming from the control plane in their cache and use them to forward packets; and (2) examine arriving packets and apply the instructions.

If the data plane device does not have instructions to apply against an arriving packet, it sends an inquiry to the SDN controller for guidance. On receiving the request, the SDN controller verifies that the packet is permitted to enter, satisfying the firm's security policy. Once approved, the SDN controller computes a route for the packet to take and sends instructions to each of the data plane nodes along the packet delivery path.

9.9.1.4 Management Plane

Then, there is one more SDN layer called the *management plane*, operating on top of the 'core' control and data planes. The *management plane* is where the policy and rules of network management used by the control plane are created by IT professionals through user/business applications. Among the examples are those related to packet filtering and routing, network security, load balancing, and traffic monitoring. That is, through management plane applications, network admins and cybersecurity professionals create the detailed logic and instructions used by the control plane node to manage the behaviors of data plane nodes.

9.9.1.5 Operational Mechanism of Three Planes

The relationship between the three planes is precisely the same as that of software and hardware components of a computer. To better grasp how the three planes work together, let's look at their relationship through the operational mechanism of a computer. A computer is basically composed of an operating system and hardware resources (e.g., CPU, storage). The OS controls hardware resources through hardware-dependent device drivers, which mirrors the relationship between the SDN's control plane and the data plane. For this reason, the SDN controller is also called the network operating system (or NOS).

Then, on the computer, a user installs various user applications as needed (e.g., word processor, browser, database) to undertake user tasks through the interaction with the OS and hardware resources. Similarly, on SDN, the user application accepts human inputs (e.g., security rules) and passes them to the control plane, which issues relevant instructions to the data plane nodes (see Figure 9.9). In sum, different applications of the SDN's management plane mirror what the ordinary computer's user applications do.

9.9.1.6 SDN and Network Security

The SDN can provide stronger network security protections mainly for two reasons:

a. The SDN controller becomes a central node to *enforce consistent and centralized security rules*. In the traditional networking environment in which the control plane is in every network node (e.g., switch and router), every node needs to be configured for the node and

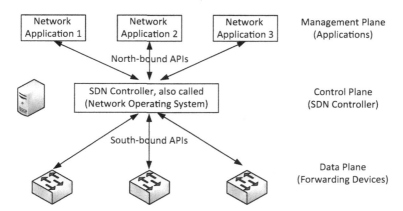

FIGURE 9.9 SDN's management, control, and data planes

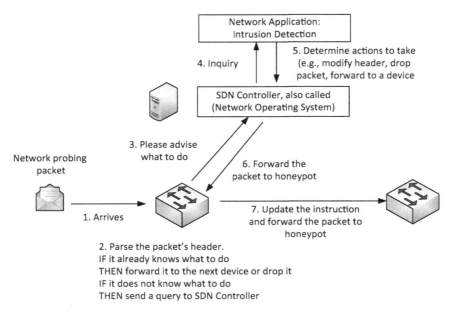

FIGURE 9.10 SDN's cyber threat handling scenario

network security. This way, enforcing consistent security rules becomes difficult. Imagine the task of maintaining the security of hundreds of switches and routers deployed on a number of subnets and VLANs of a corporate network. SDN is expected to handle the challenging task better. For example, despite the network's architectural complexity, SDN can ensure that all network traffic including Wi-Fi packets is routed through a single dedicated firewall for their inspections.

b. The SDN controller simplifies network configurations, making it *less prone to human mistakes*. This differs much from the conventional network management environment in which each node's control plane needs to be configured one by one. As an example, VLANs are one of the mechanisms that enhance network security. Creating and maintaining VLANs, however, can be a complex task when each switch and router is programmed for all VLANs to function adequately. The SDN controller can simplify the task, curtailing the chance of human mistakes in the security configuration of network nodes.

Figure 9.10 illustrates how SDN can handle a hypothetical situation in which a probing packet sent by a malicious hacker arrives at the corporate network.

9.9.2 Virtualization

Virtualization has become a dominant computing paradigm these days because of its significant benefits to adopting organizations. In computing, virtualization hides the physical characteristics of a computer from its users, thus hardware virtualization. This reduces the cost of computing and increases flexibility and effectiveness in allocating system resources. Two different types of hardware virtualization are explained: *server virtualization* and *network function virtualization*.

9.9.2.1 Drawbacks of Traditional Model

The traditional, old-fashioned model of enterprise computing without virtualization is shown first (Figure 9.11). In the model, a physical server is equipped with a host OS and is generally dedicated to a particular business application such as the email server, webserver, and database server. In that

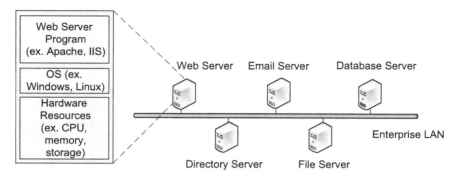

FIGURE 9.11   Traditional approach in deploying server hosts

arrangement, hardware resources including CPU, memory, and storage are utilized by the single OS and dedicated application. The approach, however, incurs excessive business costs when a company has to operate a large group of server machines, each dedicated to a particular application. This results in the problem of underutilizing each server's capacity.

9.9.2.2   Types of Server Virtualization

With virtualization, one powerful physical machine houses multiple virtual machines (VMs), each of which behaves just as a standalone computer. This creates an environment where several *independent* server applications run in parallel on a single physical host. With VMs, the number of physical computers necessary to run server applications is reduced significantly and the utilization of each physical server increases, curtailing the waste of server resources. Three different VM approaches are being used: hosted virtualization, hypervisor-based virtualization, and container-based virtualization.

a.   **Hosted Virtualization**

In this less popular mode, the host machine has its own server OS (e.g., Windows, Linux). Then the virtualization software (e.g., VMware, VirtualBox) is installed on top of the host OS, and subsequently multiple VMs each with its own OS are created on top of the virtualization software. Each VM thus created becomes a totally independent (logical) server machine with its own OS, application(s), and IP and MAC addresses. Figure 9.12, for example, demonstrates a scenario in which five VMs run in parallel on one physical machine sharing its

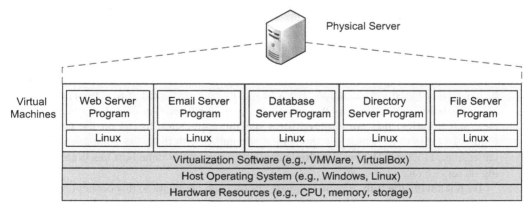

FIGURE 9.12   Hosted server virtualization

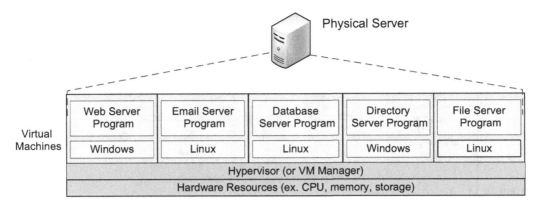

FIGURE 9.13 Hypervisor-based server virtualization

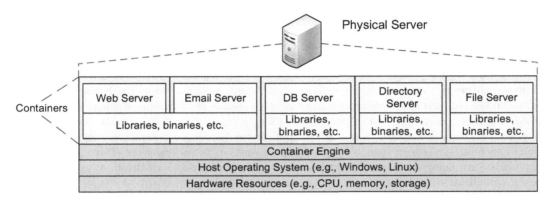

FIGURE 9.14 Container-based virtualization

hardware resources. Clearly, the more powerful the physical machine is, the more VMs can be created without having performance issues.

b. **Hypervisor-Based Virtualization**

In this solution, the physical machine does not need to have its own host OS (see Figure 9.13). Instead, the so-called *hypervisor* program (or VM manager) is used so that multiple VMs can run on top of it sharing hardware resources. Although it is a shared environment, each VM has its own OS and acts as if it has its own dedicated processor, memory, and other resources. The hypervisor ensures that conflicts do not occur in resource sharing between VMs. Its main advantage over hosted virtualization is a better system performance because it skips the host OS layer that bridges hardware elements (e.g., CPU, storage) and VMs.

c. **Container-based virtualization**

The container concept has become popular to enjoy benefits similar to the traditional hosted or hypervisor-based virtualization. The VM has its own dedicated guest OS. The container, however, holds only essential OS components (e.g., configuration files, binaries, dependencies, and libraries) that are required for a specific application to run on the host OS (see Figure 9.14). In other words, an application is bundled with these OS components in a container (e.g., Docker). This way, multiple containers run on the same host machine's OS, sharing its services for operation.

By not having the fully functional guest OS for each application, this concept enjoys obvious benefits. First, there is less need for storage and memory to create the virtualization environment. Second, the business application starts more quickly than the traditional VM because the container image is lightweight, only a few MBs compared to GBs of the whole OS. Third, the host computer's resources (e.g. CPU time) are not wasted to start and run the whole guest OS. Fourth, as the container image is much smaller in size, it is easier to transfer than VM (i.e., higher portability).

d. **Shared Infrastructure**

The virtualization technology has progressed to realize *shared infrastructure* in which hardware resources of server computers are pooled and managed as a whole (e.g., 32 CPUs, 7000 TB storage, and 2000 GB RAM). The resources in the inventory are controlled by the virtualization manager program and dynamically allocated to different server applications over the network. In this shared dynamic environment, thus, physical computers are transparent to VMs/containers and system users.

For instance, a database application can use hardware resources available from other computers. Also, the VM/container can be easily moved from one physical host to another (e.g., a form of drag and drop through the management program) when a situation arises. For example, a physical machine needs to be retired or shut down for regular maintenance and upgrades. With the centralized inventory management of computing resources, the workload of physical machines can be easily redistributed (see Figure 9.15).

9.9.2.3   Network Function Virtualization

Now, let's extend the server virtualization concept to another form of virtualization, called network function virtualization or simply NFV. There are numerous network functions such as the firewall packet filtering, intrusion detection, packet switching and routing, network address translation, deep packet inspection, VPN tunneling, virus scanning, and spam filtering. As can be seen, many of them are cybersecurity-related. Today, each of the functions is generally implemented on a specialized proprietary appliance that you can buy from vendors such as Cisco and Juniper. Naturally, an enterprise network is crowded with many different proprietary physical devices, each providing a particular network service function.

What if each device function is implemented in a software application and multiple applications performing different network functions are mounted on the off-the-shelf server platform? This is the same as mounting several VMs on a physical server, each VM undertaking a particular network function. This is what NFV does and, this way, NFV can realize benefits similar to server virtualization. An organization may install the NFV system in house or use the service offered by a telecom service provider (e.g., Verizon) or cloud service provider (e.g., Amazon AWS) in an arrangement called Infrastructure as a Service (or IaaS) (see Figure 9.16).

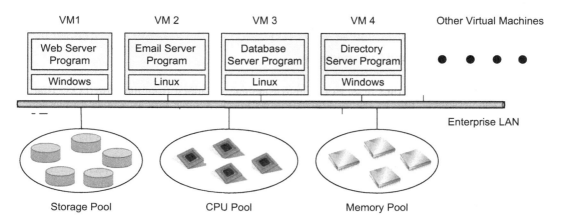

FIGURE 9.15   Virtualization with shared infrastructure

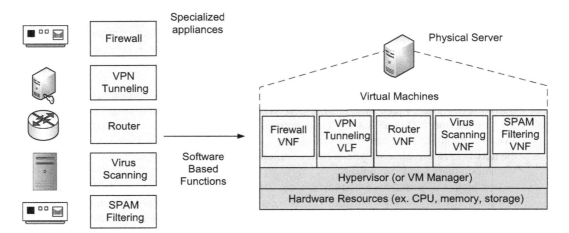

FIGURE 9.16   Network function virtualization

9.9.2.4   Benefits of Virtualization

Virtualization offers a multitude of benefits to adopting enterprises.

a. *Cost savings*: The number of physical servers necessary to deliver equivalent tasks can be reduced significantly, resulting in considerable savings of business costs. They include setup costs (e.g., hardware acquisition, OS licensing, installations), operational costs (e.g., floor space, power consumption), software upgrade and update costs, and infrastructure costs (e.g., deployment of high-speed networks and intermediary devices).

b. *Increased span of control*: With virtualization, the number of servers and the span of network monitoring an IT professional can handle increases significantly. For example, the amount of time necessary for server building and application loading significantly shrinks. The same efficiency applies to server maintenance and updates.

c. *Operational flexibility and efficiency*: VMs/containers can be easily moved from one physical machine to another, and therefore the disruption of computing and network monitoring services due to maintenance and IT outages is reduced.

d. *Reduced maintenance of physical network*: With one physical machine housing multiple VMs/containers, there is less physical cabling and maintenance of the network.

e. *Improved usage of existing resources*: Virtualization results in much better usage of existing computer resources by optimizing their utilization. For example, even relatively outdated hardware resources can become a part of the production infrastructure.

9.9.2.5   Virtualization and Cybersecurity

VM security: The VM runs in an isolated environment, separated from the hosted OS. That is, although VMs share hardware resources of the host computer, they are separate computers with their own IP and MAC addresses. Thus, if the VM is able to access the Internet, it can be infected with malware or be compromised by the adversary just like the regular host machine.

If the VM is infected with malware, however, the host OS is generally not affected as they are two independent nodes. I use the term 'generally' because, although rare, attackers can exploit the VM to attack the host machine, and this can happen if there is a vulnerability in the hypervisor. However, malware on a VM rarely escapes it, reaching the host machine.

Container security: The container has its own share of drawbacks, especially in its security. Most notably, any vulnerability in *the host OS* affects all containers running on the platform. This is because all containers installed on a host computer cannot run in isolation but *depend on the host OS* for their operations. As explained, the container bundles a business application with only the OS files not supported by the host OS but necessary to run the application.

As for the VM, it has its own fully functional OS, and thus it comes with its own security features and functions (e.g., firewall) that can protect the running application. This is not the case for the container, making it more challenging to keep it secure when the host OS is vulnerable. Thus, containers do not provide the same level of security as fully independent VMs.

9.9.3 Cloud Computing Network

The cloud network has become a dominant IT service paradigm. Among the various types of the cloud network, the most visible these days is the commercial cloud service from Amazon, Google, Microsoft, IBM, and others. To understand the cloud concept, think of the conventional business network and various IT services offered to its employees through the infrastructure. Among the services are storage, email, databases, backup, conferencing, and cybersecurity functions (e.g., anti-virus, packet filtering, spam filtering, proxy service). Now, imagine that a commercial company such as IBM creates a cloud service platform and makes most of the conventional in-house IT service functions available to business clients. To many organizations, using such commercial cloud services could be attractive because it could cost less than deploying and maintaining them in-house.

In reality, organizations take the hybrid approach in which they maintain their own internal IT service functions and selectively use the commercial cloud on a need basis, thus frequently called 'pay-as-you-go'. For service provisions, the cloud company maintains one or more giant data centers that are strategically distributed within a country or across the world. Each data center houses thousands of server machines whose hardware and software resources are dynamically utilized by millions of business customers. Managing resources through the virtualization of shared infrastructure (Figure 9.15) is essential for cloud providers to allocate computing resources to satisfy dynamically changing demands.

9.9.3.1 Service Categories

The commercial cloud uses various service models to meet customer needs. They include:

a. *Software/application as a Service (SaaS)*: Customers can selectively use *software applications* available in the cloud but the whole infrastructure is managed by the cloud vendor.
b. *Platform as a Service (PaaS)*: Customers are allowed to manage their *own applications* and *data* on the cloud network.
c. *Infrastructure as a Service (IaaS)*: Customers manage their *own operating systems, software applications,* and *data.*
d. *Security as a Service (SECaaS)*: *Security services* (e.g., anti-virus) are outsourced to the cloud, and thus they are delivered from the cloud to the client.

9.9.3.2 Cloud Security

The cloud service resembles the physical network service deployed at the local premise, except that the former is created in the virtual space using the cloud provider's physical platform. As an example, think of the *network function virtualization* explained (Section 9.9.2.3). Naturally, the cloud is subject to many security risks that the traditional enterprise network platform faces and thus defense measures commonly used to protect the physical network need to be applied to the cloud as well. Among the frequently listed risk factors of the cloud network are system breaches or loss of data stored in the cloud. To counter the risk, strong authentication and access control needs to be in place by using well-known security measures such as intrusion detection system, firewall, strong passwords, data encryption, and regular audits.

CHAPTER SUMMARY

- Ordinary routers come with the capacity to create and maintain an *access control list* (ACL) that includes a collection of inbound or outbound packet filtering rules. With the ACL, a router grants or denies IP packets based on the header information of the transport and internet layer PDUs.
- The firewall represents software or hardware designed to protect networks (e.g., perimeter, internal network) or computer systems from intruders.
- Packet filtering can be either stateful (i.e., the context of previous communications is used) or stateless (i.e., filtering rules are applied to a packet as an isolated case).
- The technique that inspects the application layer PDU including is called deep packet inspection. In contrast, stateless and stateful filtering is called *shallow packet inspection*.
- The IDS monitors traffic flows, attempts to detect and alert any suspicious intrusion that has already taken place.
- Servers that are more exposed to cyber threats are separated from the main production network by placing them in the *demilitarized zone* (or DMZ).
- The proxy server is a computer or an application set up by an organization to improve network performance and also to serve security functions. The forward proxy, reverse proxy, and transparent proxy are popular proxy types.
- More organizations are adding the *cyber threat intelligence* (CTI) function to their existing cybersecurity program these days. It is intended to improve the *situational awareness* of the potential or looming cyber threats *particularly relevant* to an organization/business.
- The CTI types are divided into three categories: threat actor/agent-related, traces of attack-related, and attack execution method-related.
- An organization can use an in-house software platform called SIEM to undertake the analytical task of CTI.
- The honeypot is a decoy system that is installed by an organization to attract and monitor an attacker's intrusion *techniques, tactics*, and *procedures* (or TTPs).
- DNS provides the mapping between a domain name and an IP address, and has been exposed to cyberattacks on many fronts and thus its protection is fundamental.
- DNS poisoning/spoofing is an act of substituting DNS entries in an attempt to redirect traffic to the system owned or arranged by the attacker.
- In the software defined network (SDN), the control plane functions of each and every intermediary device are physically separated from those of the data plane.
- In SDN, the control plane node is called *SDN controller* and acts like the computer's operating system that centrally controls all activities of its hardware components
- In SDN, the primary responsibility of data plane devices is to physically transport packets following instructions from the control plane's SDN controller.
- Virtualization enables one physical machine to house multiple virtual machines or containers, each behaving just like a standalone computer.
- The cloud network has become a dominant IT service paradigm. Among the various types of the cloud network, the most visible these days is the commercial cloud service.

KEY TERMS

access control
access control list (ACL)
authoritative name server
border firewall
cloud computing
container
container-based virtualization
control plane
country code TLD (ccTLD)
cyber threat intelligence (CTI)
data plane
deep packet inspection
demilitarized zone (DMZ)
DNS poisoning
DNS spoofing
DNSSEC
domain name system (DNS)
egress traffic
firewall
forward proxy
Fully Qualified Domain Name (or FQDN)
generic TLD (gTLD)
honey net
honeypot
host DNS file
host-based intrusion detection system
hosted virtualization
hypervisor-based virtualization
indicators of compromise (IOC)

Infrastructure as a Service (IaaS)
ingress traffic
intrusion detection
intrusion prevention
local DNS server
management plane
name resolution
network function virtualization
network intrusion detection system
Platform as a Service (PaaS)
proxy server
reverse proxy
root DNS server
SDN controller
Security as a Service (SECaaS)
security information and event management (SIEM)
shallow packet inspection
shared infrastructure
software defined networking (SDN)
Software/application as a Service (SaaS)
stateful packet filtering
stateless packet filtering
tactics, techniques, and procedures (TTPs)
top-level domain (TLD)
transparent proxy
virtual machine (VM)
virtualization
zone transfer

CHAPTER REVIEW QUESTIONS

1. Which is considered a complete stateful filtering rule?
   A) If source address, destination address, source port, and destination port are in the connection table, and the connection state is *initiated*, then PASS the packet.
   B) If protocol = TCP and destination port number = 25, then PASS the packet.
   C) If IP address = 10.47.122.79, protocol = TCP, and destination port number = 80, then PASS the packet.
   D) If source address, destination address, source port and destination port are in the connection table, and the connection state is *null*, then PASS the packet.
   E) If source address and source port are in the connection table, and the connection state is *initiated*, then PASS the packet.

2. The router's access control list examines PDUs of the following protocols EXCEPT:
   A) IP
   B) TCP
   C) UDP
   D) ARP
   E) ICMP

3. Which describes the DMZ network?
   A) The DMZ and production networks generally belong to a single subnet.
   B) The SMTP email and HTTP webservers are frequently placed in the DMZ network.
   C) The DMZ and production networks should be physically separated.
   D) Servers in the DMZ should use public IP addresses.
   E) The border router is unable to perform network address translation when the DNZ is set up.
4. The firewall may undertake the following functions EXCEPT the _____.
   A) VPN gateway to protect remote connections
   B) network address translation
   C) detection of denial-of-service attacks
   D) deep packet inspection of application layer information
   E) provision of packet routing
5. Which is a top-level domain name?
   A) .com
   B) whitehouse.gov
   C) www.stanford.edu
   D) sdsu.edu/mis
   E) microsoft.com
6. When 'hypervisor-based virtualization' and 'hosted virtualization' are compared:
   A) The host machine needs its own host operating system ONLY when 'hosted virtualization' is used.
   B) The virtual machine (VM) needs to have its own operating system ONLY when 'hosted virtualization' is used.
   C) The VM running on 'hosted virtualization' has better performance than that on 'hypervisor-based virtualization'.
   D) The maintenance cost of 'hosted virtualization' is lower than that of 'hypervisor-based virtualization'.
   E) Moving VMs from one physical computer to another is easier on 'hosted virtualization' than on 'hypervisor-based virtualization'.
7. Choose an INCORRECT statement regarding Domain Name Service (DNS).
   A) The root domain is the highest level of the Internet domain hierarchy, literally indicating the whole Internet space.
   B) The country code is a top-level domain.
   C) Once a top-level domain name is registered by a university, it can freely create second-level and lower-level domain names.
   D) A university may be one domain that includes several sub-domains logically divided.
   E) The uniform resource locater (URL) combines a protocol and a fully qualified domain name.
8. The following describes server virtualization EXCEPT:
   A) The virtual machine installed on a host computer can have its own operating system.
   B) The number of servers an IT professional can manage declines.
   C) The number of physical servers necessary to deliver the equivalent amount of computing is reduced.
   D) The need for physical cabling of server computers to the network decreases.
   E) IT service disruptions due to maintenance and outages are reduced.
9. The following DNS information is kept in a file of the _____.

| '127.0.0.1 | localhost' | (for IPv4) |
| '::1 | localhost' | (for IPv6) |

   A) local DNS server
   B) root DNS server

    C) DNS local authority server

    D) host computer

    E) DHCP server

10. The following describes the proxy server EXCEPT:

    A) The website connection can be expedited as it caches frequently visited sites.

    B) The reverse proxy protects internal servers through obscurity.

    C) For improved network defense, the proxy server heavily relies on the cloud network service.

    D) The proxy may protect hosts from malware.

    E) The proxy can hide IP addresses of host systems inside a secured network.

11. Technical measures to improve the perimeter security of an organization do NOT include the:

    A) access control list

    B) proxy server

    C) border firewall

    D) demilitarized zone (DMZ)

    E) server virtualization

12. Which describes packet filtering by firewalls?

    A) They typically do either ingress or egress filtering, but not both.

    B) In stateful packet filtering, filtering rules are applied to each packet in isolation.

    C) Packet filtering rules use both hostnames and IP addresses for filtering decisions.

    D) Both stateless and stateful filtering can be used concurrently.

    E) 'Default permit' is recommended over 'default deny' if no specific filtering rule matches.

13. Which is considered a 'complete' rule included in the firewall list?

    A) If source IP = 172.16.x.x to 172.31.x.x or 192.168.x.x.

    B) If TCP destination port = 21.

    C) If HTML message contains 'entertainment'.

    D) If destination IP = 161.154.23.59 and TCP port = 25.

    E) If there is a duplicated packet, drop it.

14. Which information may be LEAST used by the firewall's deep packet inspection function?

    A) URL included in the message

    B) Keyword-based web content

    C) Time to live value of a packet

    D) An application's signature

    E) SSL session information

15. What could be the biggest difference between the firewall and the IDS?

    A) While the firewall monitors ingress traffic, the IDS examines both ingress and egress traffic.

    B) While the firewall focuses on perimeter security, the IDS is designed for internal network security.

    C) While the firewall uses both stateful and stateless packet filtering rules, the IDS relies on stateless rules only.

    D) While the firewall uses the information of the transport and internet layers, the IDS uses data link layer information for packet filtering decisions.

    E) While the firewall does not produce alarms when packets are dropped due to the rule mismatch, the IDS focuses on alerting any suspicious intrusion that has already taken place.

16. When a firewall router uses two ports (interfaces) for WAN and Internet connections, how many separate access control lists (ACLs) may be created for adequate packet filtering?

    A) 1

    B) 2

    C) 4

D) 6

E) 8

17. Maintaining dual Internet connections improves what aspect of security requirements?

A) confidentiality

B) data integrity

C) authentication

D) authorization

E) availability

18. Which may be the least relevant anomaly scenario the IDS uses for packet filtering?

A) Volumetric anomaly: A database server is sending more data than the average.

B) Geometric anomaly: The webserver is being probed from certain countries where its products are not sold or that have no existing businesses.

C) Temporal anomaly: There are busy database activities on Sunday when the office is closed.

D) Volumetric anomaly: There is an unusually high connection rate.

E) Protocol anomaly: There is a sudden surge of packets that combine TCP and UDP headers.

19. There are three different types of cyber threat intelligence: *threat actor/agent*, *traces of attack*, and *attack execution method*. Which is paired CORRECTLY?

A) Hash values (e.g., MD5, SHA1) of malware – *attack execution method*

B) Domain names such as malignant webservers – *traces of attack*

C) Exploit tools used by attackers – *threat actor/agent*

D) Behavioral patterns of a threat agent in orchestrating attacks – *threat actor/agent*

E) Attack motivation – *attack execution method*

20. The intrusion detection system (IDS) can use different methods for monitoring cyberattacks. Assume that ICMP packets on a network generally represent less than 1% of normal traffic, but they just increased to 20%, triggering an alert by the IDS. This is an example of:

A) profile monitoring

B) signature monitoring

C) overflow monitoring

D) anomaly monitoring

E) dynamic monitoring

21. On the Software Defined Network (SDN), what specific unit gives the permission to forward a packet to a device to another device on the network?

A) SDN router

B) SDN firewall

C) SDN gateway

D) SDN controller

E) SDN application

22. An attacker can substitute a DNS address record so that a user computer is redirected to a malicious site. This is _____.

A) DNS poisoning

B) zone transfer

C) DNS man-in-the-middle

D) DNS overloading

E) DNS session hijacking

23. Which of the following is performed by the SDN's data plane?

A) Provides information on how network nodes are interconnected (network topology).

B) Physically transports packets between intermediary devices.

C) Furnishes host IP and MAC addresses to intermediary devices.

D) Decides packet delivery routes among intermediary devices.

E) Manages virtual LANs

24. The cyber threat intelligence (CTI) program aims to improve security driven by the following orientations EXCEPT:
    A) proactive (rather than reactive) defense
    B) timely (rather than belated) defense
    C) preventive (rather than remedial) defense
    D) defense based on generalized (rather than specific) rules
    E) actionable information-driven defense
25. Which CORRECTLY describes the cloud network service?
    A) *Infrastructure as a Service (IaaS)*: Customers can selectively use *software applications* available while the cloud infrastructure is managed by the service provider.
    B) *Platform as a Service (PaaS)*: Customers are allowed to manage their *own applications* and *data* on the cloud computing network.
    C) *Software/application as a Service (SaaS)*: Customers can manage their *own operating systems*, *software applications*, and *data*.
    D) *Security as a Service (SECaaS)*: Customers are allowed to manage their *own applications* and *data*
    E) *Software/application as a Service (SaaS)*: *Security services* are outsourced to the cloud.

HANDS-ON EXERCISES

Exercise 9.1

Firewall rule construction: The XYZ Company hired you to improve the security of its corporate network. They purchased a firewall that can perform packet inspections. Your job is to create a stateless packet filtering table similar to Table 9.3. Use best practices to lock down firewall security as much as possible without blocking legitimate traffic. In developing a static ruleset, you are required to develop both outbound (egress) and inbound (ingress) screening rules. XYZ's business requirements are translated into the following:

a. The XYZ company has several remote offices that access the webserver located in the main office network. Remote office 1 accesses the XYZ's webserver on port 443, from the source port of 8724. Remote office 2 accesses the XYZ' webserver on port 443, from the source port of 7323.
b. The company wants to restrict its employees' ability to send ICMP messages to the Internet.
c. XYZ has an SMTP email server operating on its corporate network. The mail server exchanges emails with other email servers using the SMTP's default port.
d. XYZ wants to deny all other traffic coming into its corporate network.

Exercise 9.2

Experience online proxy service. For this:

a. Search a web-based proxy service site on the Internet.
b. Experience how you can use the proxy website to spoof your computer's IP address while visiting different websites.
c. Discuss pros and cons of utilizing such a spoofing service.

Exercise 9.3

In this exercise, you examine DNS information stored in the local cache.

a. At the command prompt of your computer (assuming Windows), enter '*C:\>ipconfig/all*' to learn the IP addresses of local DNS servers.

b. The host maintains in its cache DNS information on previously visited sites. Find out the paired list of domain names and IPs using the command '*C:\>ipconfig/displaydns*'.

c. What is the main benefit of storing DNS information in cache?

d. Clear the name resolution table with '*C:\>ipconfig /flushdns*' and confirm the clearance with '*C:\>ipconfig/displaydns*'. You should see only the entries of *localhost* paired with the loopback IP (e.g., 127.0.0.1) after the flush. If your computer displays '*The requested operation requires elevation*', complete the following procedure: go to *All Programs, Accessories*; right click *Command Prompt*; and click *Run as administrator*.

e. Assuming that the DNS list is empty, visit a website of your university. Then, observe additions of TCP connections with 'C:\>*netstat –n*' at the command prompt. Also, display the name resolution table with '*C:>ipconfig/displaydns*'. Can you explain why several DNS entries are added after visiting just one site?

EXERCISE 9.4

Hosts file exercise on Windows OS.

1. Open the *hosts* file in *Notepad* (run the program as administrator if necessary). Search the IP address of your ISP's website with the nslookup command (e.g., c>nslookup www.cox.com). At the end of the file, add the IP, press Tab, enter www.crcpress.com, and save the file. Open a browser, enter *www.crcpress.com*, and explain what happens. Restore the original by removing the *www.crcpress.com* entry and then save.

2. Entering '*127.0.0.1 ad.doubleclick.net*' into the host file results in blocking of all ad/banner files from *ad.doubleclick.net* (DoubleClick advertising server) and their displays on your browser. It also has the effect of preventing the ad server from tracking your movements (e.g., other visited websites) through cookies. Explain why. Understand that there are many other ad servers on the Internet.

EXERCISE 9.5

Malware detection with VirusTotal: VirusTotal.com is a Google-owned service that runs submitted file against every listed antivirus software, which includes those from McAfee, Microsoft, Kaspersky, and FireEye. It currently uses about 60+ antivirus engines. When you use either a utility program such as Autoruns or the online service option, each file will be automatically inspected by all of the antivirus engines and then the ratio will be returned.

If three or more anti-virus engines alert, then chances are that the submitted file is malicious. If there are one or two alerts, it is usually a false-positive by a relatively unknown antivirus engine. If you follow the rules, VirusTotal is quite accurate. Submit different local files to the online VirusTotal site and observe their screening results.

10 Cybersecurity

Data Protection

10.1 INTRODUCTION

This chapter explains various concepts directly or indirectly related to cryptography, an essential technology used ubiquitously to ensure data security whether data are in storage or in transit over the network. Simply speaking, cryptography represents a procedure that transforms a message into an unreadable code. Cryptography is highly versatile and fundamental to meet the various requirements of data security, including confidentiality, integrity, authentication, nonrepudiation (i.e., proves that a user performed an action), and obfuscation (i.e., making data/message obscure or unclear).

The objectives of this chapter are to learn the fundamentals of cryptography-related technologies in their role to protect data and communications.

- Steganography
- Essential elements of cryptography
- Symmetric and asymmetric cryptography technologies
- Hashing
- Digital signature
- Digital certificate
- Certificate authorities
- Wi-Fi security protocols (WEP, WPA, WPA2, and WPA3)
- Virtual private network protocols (IPsec and SSL)

10.2 STEGANOGRAPHY

Steganography is a technique that *hides* data within an ordinary file or message, and thus it is designed to protect data through *obscurity*. Steganography does not encrypt messages to make them unreadable but just uses a clever technique to make them difficult to detect with the naked eye. There are many different steganography techniques available to obfuscate data within the text, image, audio, or video files. Among them, embedding data inside the unused portion of an image has been one of the well-known methods.

Let's look at a couple of sample steganography techniques for demonstration. Each alphanumeric character of a message to hide can be embedded inside a text using such techniques as every first-letter or every n-th character of each word. For example, to email a confidential password, a person may include 'He was born in London in 2020' somewhere in the message. When both parties know the recovery rule to derive the password by combining the first letter of each word, *HwbiLi2* can be easily obtained.

As another technique, a message can be hidden in the metadata section of an image file. Metadata represents the data (attributes) about other data such as an image. For instance, the metadata of an image file can be the creation date, image resolution and size, image width and height, and image compression method used. Many files such as e-books, photographs, movies, music and documents

FIGURE 10.1　Metadata of an image file (Windows OS)

contain metadata, and the unused portion of the designated metadata space can hide a secret message. For example, in the Windows OS, the metadata information of an image file can be viewed through its *properties* tab (see Figure 10.1) and its metadata can be easily edited to hide a secret message.

10.3　CRYPTOGRAPHY

This section explains the fundamentals of cryptography, a process to convert a regular plain text into an incomprehensible text or vice versa, and the types of the cryptography system.

10.3.1　Essential Elements

A cryptography system is composed of four basic elements: plaintexts, ciphertexts, a cipher, and key values (see Figure 10.3).

10.3.1.1　Plaintext and Ciphertext

The *plaintext* is an original, unencrypted message in various formats including text, voice, data, and video. The *ciphertext* is an encrypted plaintext and thus unintelligible unless decrypted.

10.3.1.2　Cipher

The *cipher* is an encryption algorithm used to convert plaintexts to ciphertexts and vice versa. Simple cipher techniques include the *transposition* that reorders the letters of a message and the *substitution* that replaces a character with another. For example, ROT13 ('rotate by 13 places') is a substitution cipher that replaces an alphabetical letter with the 13th letter after it (see Figure 10.2).

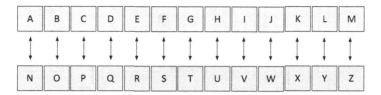

FIGURE 10.2 ROT13 substitution cipher

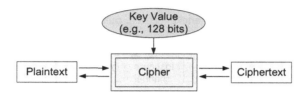

FIGURE 10.3 Components of cryptography

Today's cryptography standards (e.g., DES, RC4, RSA) use much more sophisticated ciphers, and they are largely divided into *stream ciphers* and *block ciphers*. The stream cipher such as RC4 encrypts a message one byte (or character) at a time, and the block cipher performs encryption per block of characters (e.g., 128-bit block). The majority of ciphers today including DES, IDEA, AES, and RC5 are block ciphers. Besides, as a relatively new cipher, the so-called *sponge function* takes a bitstream of any length as input and returns a bitstream of any desired variable length.

10.3.1.3 Key Value

The *key* represents a value the cipher applies to encrypt/decrypt a plaintext. A ciphertext is, therefore, compromised when a third party obtains the secret key one way or another. A cryptography system generally uses a fixed-size key value. These days, a key size of at least 128 bits is recommended to safeguard encrypted messages. With the rapid advancement of computers in their processing speeds, it takes less time to recover the key and a longer key will be necessary soon.

The key can be generated randomly or derived from user passwords/passphrases. As an example of the second type, a password (or passphrase) is entered into the wireless access point and client hosts during the initial setup of a Wi-Fi home network. The password is subsequently used to derive a secret key for data encryption.

10.3.2 SYMMETRIC-KEY CRYPTOGRAPHY

Cryptography standards use either *symmetric* or *asymmetric* keys. With the symmetric-key system, a *secret key* is shared by communicating parties to encrypt and decrypt data (see Figure 10.4a). The key, therefore, should remain confidential to protect encrypted data. A drawback of the secret key-based encryption is that, when multiple parties need to exchange data over the network using one secret key, its distribution and subsequent management becomes problematic.

A distinctive advantage of the symmetric key system is its fast throughput in encrypting and decrypting data, putting less process burden on network nodes. Among the well-known standards are DES (Data Encryption Standard), 3DES, AES (Advanced Encryption Standard), RC4, Blowfish, and IDEA (International Data Encryption Algorithm).

As a type of the secret symmetric key, the *session* key is used for a particular session (e.g., TCP session) only. For example, the browser-enabled online transaction (e.g., online banking,

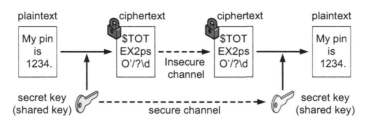

(a) Symmetric Key Cryptography

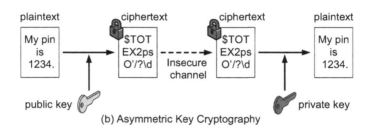

(b) Asymmetric Key Cryptography

FIGURE 10.4   Symmetric-key vs. asymmetric-key cryptography

e-commerce) relies on a symmetric and one-time session key to encrypt exchanged data. For this, a randomized session key is produced by the browser and shared with the online server for secure client-server communications.

10.3.3   ASYMMETRIC-KEY CRYPTOGRAPHY

10.3.3.1   Private and Public Keys

In asymmetric cryptography, each party has a *private* and *public* key pair (see Figure 10.4b) in place of using just one secret key. This means that it takes two *private* and *public* key pairs (i.e., one pair for each communicating party) when asymmetric cryptography is used for secure data exchange. The private key is kept by the owner and not shared with anybody else. Meanwhile, his/her public key is shared with the world just like phone numbers in the telephone directory. To maintain the confidentiality of an exchanged message, the sender encrypts it with the receiver's public key, and then the receiver decrypts it with his/her own private key.

10.3.3.2   General Features

With asymmetric cryptography, a message encrypted with a public key cannot be decrypted with the same public key. Likewise, a plaintext encrypted with a private key cannot be decrypted with the same private key. If a sender uses his/her own private key to encrypt a message, then the receiver can decrypt the ciphertext using the sender's public key. This practice, however, defeats the purpose of keeping message confidentiality as anybody can decrypt the ciphertext (This method can be used to authenticate the sender, though).

10.3.3.3   Popular Standards

RSA is one of the most well-known standards. RSA uses long keys (e.g., 2048, 3072 bits) and thus it takes heavy computations for message encryption and decryption. This much computation, however, makes RSA less ideal for mobile devices (e.g., smartphones, IoT devices) that have less processing capability and also rely on limited battery hours.

Elliptic curve cryptography (ECC) is another popular standard for mobile and wireless devices as it offers data security comparable to RSA using smaller keys. For example, ECC's 256- and 384-bit keys provide data protection roughly equivalent to RSA's 3072- and 7680-bit key sizes. Smaller keys result in faster computations for encryption/decryption and less power consumption.

10.3.4 HYBRID APPROACH

Because of the pros and cons inherent to both symmetric and asymmetric cryptography technologies, they are widely used in combination to complement each other's weaknesses and to make the most of their strengths. In the hybrid solution:

a. Symmetric cryptography is utilized for encrypting/decrypting lengthy messages to ensure their *confidentiality* and fast performance.
b. Asymmetric cryptography is used to securely exchange the symmetric session key, to *authenticate* communicating parties and messages, and to check message *integrity*.

Let us see how that works in two actual technologies.

10.3.4.1 Scenario 1: HTTPS

A wildly popular example of their combined usage is HTTPS, in which the browser receives the public key of a server website and uses it to securely exchange a symmetric session key. Once both parties have the session key, it is used to encrypt and exchange messages for a particular session. The high-level procedure is in Figure 10.5.

Procedure:

1. The web browser contacts a website (server) to use its service.
2. The server sends its digital certificate that contains the server's public key. The browser validates the authenticity of the public key by examining the *certificate revocation list* it maintains or dynamically querying the website that issued the certificate.
3. On validating the server's digital certificate, the browser generates a symmetric session key, encrypts it with the server's public key, and sends it to the server.
4. From thereon, data exchanged between the browser and the webserver are encrypted with the session key until the session is terminated.

10.3.4.2 Scenario 2: PGP

As another way of combining symmetric and asymmetric cryptography, think of this scenario wherein a confidential document is exchanged between two parties (Figure 10.6).

1. The sender can encrypt the document using a symmetric session key, which is fast.
2. If the receiver does not have the symmetric session key already, the sender encrypts it with the receiver's public key. Encrypting a relatively short session key (e.g., 128 bits) with the public key does not take a significant toll on the sender's system.

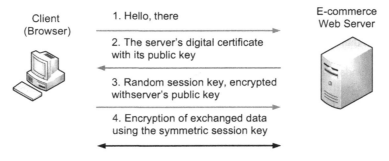

FIGURE 10.5   Scenario 1: Hybrid use of asymmetric and symmetric cryptography

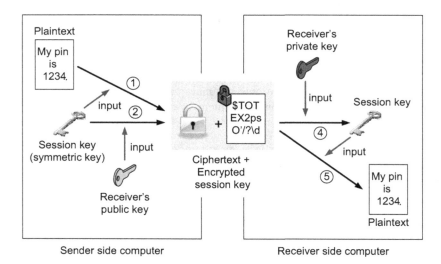

Sender side computer   Receiver side computer

FIGURE 10.6   Scenario 2: Hybrid usage of symmetric and asymmetric cryptography

3. Both the symmetric-key encrypted document (ciphertext) and the asymmetric-key encrypted session key are dispatched to the receiver.
4. On their arrival, the receiver decrypts the encrypted session key using his/her own private key.
5. The decrypted session key is then used to decode the ciphertext back to the original document.

Pretty Good Privacy (PGP) is an encryption system that relies on the hybrid method.

10.3.5 HASHING

Hashing creates a unique digital fingerprint of data/message using a mathematical algorithm and is extensively used as a cryptographic tool. Hashing has unique features that make it distinct from other cryptography technologies.

a. **Fixed size**: It takes an input (e.g., password, plaintext) of any length and produces a fixed-length hash value known as a *message digest*. For example, MD5 and SHA-512 hash functions produce unique 128-bit and 512-bit hash values regardless of the input size.
b. **Unique**: The probability of different datasets to produce the same hash value (called a collision) is extremely low.
c. **Secure**: A hash value cannot be reversed to restore the original input, making hashing a one-way function.
d. **Original**: A dataset cannot be created in order to produce a predefined hash value.

Several hash standards are currently used, including MD (Message Digest) family, SHA (Secure Hash Algorithm) family, RIPEMD (Race Integrity Primitives Evaluation Message Digest) and Whirlpool. The usage of hashing is primarily limited to ensuring *data integrity* because a hash value cannot be reversed to restore the original data. This is much different from other cryptography (especially asymmetric) technologies that can be flexibly used for data *confidentiality*, *integrity*, and *authentication*. Table 10.1 demonstrates sample inputs and their corresponding outputs in hex produced by MD5 for the sake of illustration.

TABLE 10.1

Sample inputs and MD5 produced hash values

Inputs (e.g., passwords)	Outputs (hash values in hexadecimal)
Stealth	899db408cba5858a0f1701a2caef2628
She	1a699ad5e06aa8a6db3bcf9cfb2f00f2
I am a student.	2f1f75e8bb00643cb05aed57f7bdb4a8

10.4 DIGITAL SIGNATURE

The digital signature is a solution used for *message authentication* and *sender authentication*. In computer networks, passwords (or passphrases) are a prevalent solution for user authentication. However, passwords can be accidentally revealed, forgotten, or, even worse, stolen in various manners. For this reason, very often, a more reliable authentication technology is required between communicating parties. This is where the *digital signature* (or *electronic autograph*) comes in as an electronic equivalent of the handwritten signature.

Figure 10.7 demonstrates a scenario of how the *digital signature* works to authenticate engaging parties and exchanged messages. In that scenario, it is assumed that each party has his/her own public-private key pair.

10.4.1 ON THE SENDER SIDE

1. A sender's computer uses a hash function (e.g., MD5) to compute a hash value (e.g., 128 bits for MD5) from the original message to be transported. The hash value is also called a *message digest*, as it is derived from the source message.
2. The *message digest* is encrypted with the sender's private key. The output becomes a sender's *digital signature* because it can be created only by the sender's private key – making it perfect for sender *authentication*. Observe that the digital signature changes with the original message.
3. The original message and digital signature are then encrypted with a symmetric session key generated by the sender's computer.
4. The session key itself is encrypted with the receiver's public key.
5. The encrypted *original message*, *digital signature*, and *session key* are dispatched to the receiver's computer over the Internet.

10.4.2 ON THE RECEIVER SIDE

On accepting the encrypted units from the sender,

6. The encrypted session key is first decrypted by the receiver's own private key (reverse of step 4).
7. Using the restored session key, the original message and digital signature are decrypted (reverse of step 3). Thus, message *confidentiality* has been achieved.
8. The restored digital signature is decrypted by the sender's public key and the original message digest is obtained (reverse of step 2).

Sender's computer

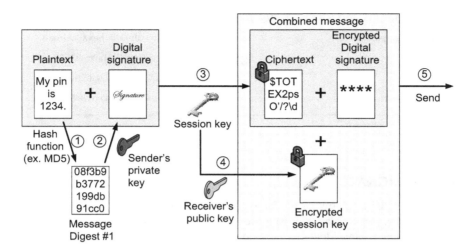

Receiver's computer

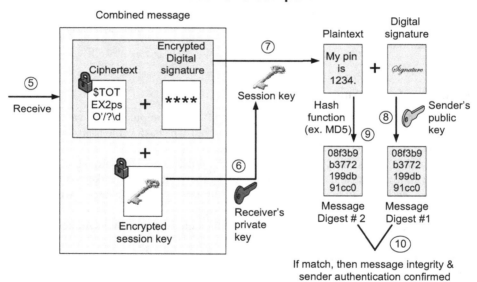

FIGURE 10.7   Usage of a digital signature for data integrity and authentication

9. The receiver hashes – using the same hash function – the original message to generate his/her own message digest.

10. The receiver compares the delivered message digest (i.e., hash value) with the locally produced one. Their matching confirms that the original message has not been changed, confirming *message integrity*. The matching also validates that the sender indeed owns the public-private key pair – which is confirmation of *sender authentication*.

This complex process, summarized in Figure 10.7, is automatically executed by computer systems.

10.5 DIGITAL CERTIFICATE

The *digital certificate* is a digital equivalent ID card and is used in conjunction with the asymmetric encryption system. More specifically, it verifies the holder of a particular *public key* (not the private key) and is an extremely important mechanism to authenticate communicating parties. You might wonder why not just use the digital signature for authentication. The digital signature is a good authentication mechanism in cyberspace, but it comes with a caveat. The digital signature only shows that the sender's private key was used to produce it and does not definitively prove who the sender was. That is, an imposter can post his/her public key under the sender's name (e.g., Tom in Figure 10.8) to impersonate. Then, the imposter can do man-in-the-middle by intercepting the real sender's message and passing a forged message digitally signed with his/her own private key. The question is, how to prevent this?

One way is to formally validate the true owner of a public key by issuing a 'digital certificate' to the communicating party. Remember that a digital certificate is not an indicator of the owner's 'integrity' but simply validates who the real owner of a particular public key is. That is, a malicious hacker or a con artist can certainly have his/her own digital certificate.

10.5.1 X.509 DIGITAL CERTIFICATE STANDARD

The digital certificate contains such information as the owner of a particular public key, certificate's serial number, certificate's expiration, the issuer (i.e., certificate authority), and the certificate authority's digital signature to prevent spoofing. X.509 from the *International Telecommunications Union* (ITU) is a widely accepted standard of the digital certificate. Figure 10.9 lists information items of the X.509 standard. Remember that the digital certificate does not reveal the private key of a person or a system.

10.5.2 DIGITAL CERTIFICATE TYPES

Various digital certificate types are used to prove the authenticity of online systems and infrastructure entities. Among the prevalent types are:

a. **End-user certificate** that is used by clients and server hosts for public key-based authentication. The webserver certificate that proves the authenticity of a website to the browser is a ubiquitous example (see Figure 10.5).
b. **Code-signing certificate** that validates the developer/vendor of particular software. For example, in Figure 10.10, the Adobe program installed on Windows is digitally signed by its

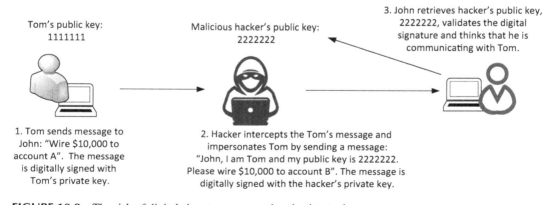

Tom's public key:
1111111

Malicious hacker's public key:
2222222

3. John retrieves hacker's public key, 2222222, validates the digital signature and thinks that he is communicating with Tom.

1. Tom sends message to John: "Wire $10,000 to account A". The message is digitally signed with Tom's private key.

2. Hacker intercepts the Tom's message and impersonates Tom by sending a message: "John, I am Tom and my public key is 2222222. Please wire $10,000 to account B". The message is digitally signed with the hacker's private key.

FIGURE 10.8 The risk of digital signature as an authentication tool

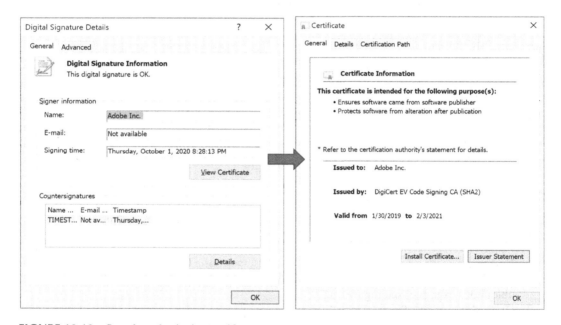

```
Version: 3
Serial number: 123456
Algorithm: RSA
Issuer name: VeriSign
Validity period: start / expiration dates
Subject name: John Doe
Subject public key: XXXXXXXXXX
CA digital signature: XXXXXXX
```

FIGURE 10.9   Key X.509 attributes (left) and sample public key and CA digital signature (right) (Source: SSL.com)

FIGURE 10.10   Sample code-signing certificate

private key (left) and the code-signing certificate was issued to Adobe by DigiCert (right). The certificate contains the public key that matches the private key used for code signing, and thus Windows will be able to validate the software's (more specifically, the '.exe' file's) integrity.

c. **Domain certificate** that shows the real owner of a particular domain name (e.g., www.github. com). This proves the integrity of a domain visited by people.

10.5.3   Certificate Authorities

Digital certificates are issued by *certificate authorities* (CAs) such as VeriSign and Microsoft through their *public key infrastructure* (or simply PKI) servers. The PKI represents a collection of hardware, software, technical and non-technical policies, and procedures that are integral to manage the asymmetric cryptography system. A CA's PKI server creates, distributes, and manages digital certificates. An organization may choose to set up its own PKI server to issue digital certificates to employees instead of purchasing them from a trusted third-party CA. By not using the commercial CA service, the company becomes its own CA and can save service costs.

10.5.3.1 Creating a Chain of Trust

As digital certificates are issued by CAs through their PKI, a digital certificate is only as good as the CA. In other words, if a CA is not a reliable or trusted business (e.g., imagine a CA established by organized crime), certificates issued by it cannot be trusted either. Because a single CA is hard to be trusted, multiple CAs are chained together to form 'a chain of trust'.

In the chain, there are two CA types, *root CAs* and *intermediate CAs*, and they are chained by linking their digital certificates together. The endpoint of a chain is an end-user certificate such as the one issued to a website (e.g., Yahoo.com) and the top (or beginning) of the chain is a root CA. There are one or more intermediate CAs between the root and the user certificates.

Using Figure 10.11 as an example (available on Windows OS), the root CA is *Entrust.net* and it is a self-signing entity as it is not chained to any higher-level CA. The intermediate CA in the chain is the *Entrust Certification Authority*. The end of the chain is end-user digital certificate issued to *www.bankofamerica.com*. The root CA uses its private key to sign the intermediate CA's digital certificate in the chain. The intermediate CA, in turn, uses its own private key to sign the end user digital certificate. Again, remember that more than one intermediate CA can be in the chain of trust between the root CA and the end-user digital certificate.

10.5.4 Obtaining a Digital Certificate

To obtain a digital certificate, you can use your computer's OS that has a built-in function to generate your own private and public key pair, and subsequently submit the form called *Certificate Signing Request* (or CSR) to a CA. On receiving the CSR, the CA first verifies its accuracy, signs it using the CA's own private key, and returns the signed end-user digital certificate to you. As can be seen, the generation of the private and public key pair is done on the user computer, and the CA's role is just to validate and sign it.

FIGURE 10.11 Chaining CAs to form trust in a digital certificate

10.5.5 Certificate Revocation List

CAs can revoke a person's digital certificate for various reasons including its expiration, compromised private key, and policy violation. Revoked certificates are placed in the *certificate revocation list* (CRL). The verifier (e.g., user computer) of a digital certificate must check with the certificate issuer to determine if the certificate is on the CRL list. Without the CRL check, the integrity of a digital certificate is not guaranteed.

In today's web environment, the browser becomes a 'verifier'. If a web browser connects to a webserver (e.g., abcnews.com), the webserver returns its digital certificate to the browser for server authentication. Then, the browser validates it by examining the certificate revocation list (CRL). The browser can obtain the CRL in different ways depending on how the logic is programmatically implemented. It can contact the CA's PKI server that issued the certificate, or the CRL can be pushed to the browser as a software update. The digital certificate assures a server site's authenticity and, thus, its validation is critical to protect consumers when they engage in e-commerce transactions.

10.5.5.1 CAs Trusted by OS and Web Browser

Operating systems and web browsers maintain a list of certificate authorities they trust. Figure 10.12 demonstrates the list of CAs trusted by Google Chrome.

If a CA itself is not recognized by a browser (e.g., see Figure 10.13a) or if there is a problem with a presented certificate such as an expired or revoked certificate or revocation information not available (see Figure 10.13b), the browser alerts the user. Facing such a warning, it is generally safer to bypass the website unless the user positively identifies and trusts it.

10.6 SECURITY PROTOCOLS

The cryptography, digital signature, and digital certificate technologies explained thus far perform their intended functions by being embedded into security protocols. Many different security

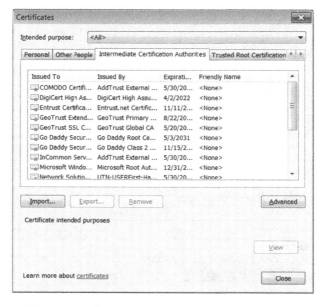

FIGURE 10.12 Trusted CAs: Chrome browser

(a) Warning for a digital certificate (Internet Explorer)

(b) Warning for inaccessibility of certificate revocation list (Google Chrome)

FIGURE 10.13 Warnings associated with digital certificates

protocols have been introduced in different layers, each with its own strengths and weaknesses. The following lists popular ones defined in each layer:

- Application layer: S/MIME, PGP
- Transport layer: SSL/TLS
- Internet layer: IPSec
- Data link layer: WEP, WPA, WPA2, WPA3

In general, each of the protocols supports security requirements of *authentication*, *data integrity*, and *data confidentiality* (or privacy) altogether to facilitate secure data exchange. To support the security requirements, each protocol takes advantage of several standardized technologies such as pre-shared keys, digital certificates, cryptography, and hashing. In this section, the focus is on explaining Wi-Fi security, and then the transport and internet layer security protocols of IPSec and SSL/TLS that power VPN security are explained subsequently.

10.7 WI-FI SECURITY

The security elements of the Wi-Fi network and the enabling security protocols are explained.

10.7.1 AUTHENTICATION: THREE-STAGE PROCESS

The relationship between a user station and an access point (AP) is in one of three states: (1) unauthenticated/unassociated, (2) authenticated/unassociated, and (3) authenticated/associated (see Table 10.2). Prior to the exchange of data between an AP and a host station, the two nodes should complete the *authentication* and *association* process. This is intended for access control that prevents unauthorized hosts or people from entering a Wi-Fi LAN. For the eventual binding, therefore, the two nodes should undergo the three-step sequence for which several frames are exchanged.

TABLE 10.2

Three stages of authentication and association

Stage	State	Description
1	Unauthenticated/ Unassociated	No relationship between a client station and an AP
2	Authenticated/ Unassociated	• The client is authenticated by the AP. • For this, the client submits an authentication frame to the AP. • At an enterprise, there is generally a designated authentication server. This centralized control of Wi-Fi access improves network security.
3	Authenticated/ Associated	• Upon successful authentication, the client sends an association request frame to the AP. • The AP's association response completes the binding. • At this stage, other options including security and data transmission rate are finalized.

10.7.2 Authentication Methods of a Station

There are different options available to authenticate a client station, each with its own pros and cons. Among them, *open authentication*, *pre-shared key authentication*, and *authentication server* solutions are explained here. Open authentication and pre-shared key authentication of client stations are performed by the AP. With the authentication server approach, the authentication is handled by a designated server, and the AP's role is reduced to the relay of authentication frames between the server and host stations.

10.7.2.1 Open Authentication

Open authentication uses SSID for authentication. In this mode, a client station furnishes such basic information as its MAC address and SSID to a target AP to request authentication. The AP responds with either success or failure, making the authentication a two-step process. For this mode of authentication, depending on the context, communicating nodes can be pre-configured with an SSID so that the AP's periodic broadcasting of the SSID is turned off.

Open authentication uses clear texts making it easy to intercept them with a software tool, and thus it is not a serious form of authentication. With open authentication, both parties (i.e., client and AP) may be pre-programmed with a *pre-shared* secret key to encrypt data exchanged after authentication, but the encryption function is not utilized for initial authentication (see Figure 10.14).

10.7.2.2 Pre-Shared Key Authentication

To authenticate user stations, a pre-shared secret key of a certain length (e.g., 128 bits) is used. The pre-shared key may be derived from a user-provided password/passphrase, which is stored in the

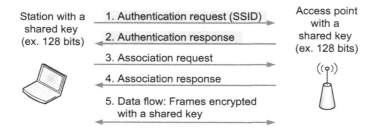

FIGURE 10.14 Two-way open authentication (steps 1 and 2)

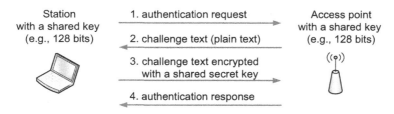

| Station
with a shared key
(e.g., 128 bits) | 1. authentication request | Access point
with a shared key
(e.g., 128 bits) |

1. authentication request

2. challenge text (plain text)

3. challenge text encrypted
   with a shared secret key

4. authentication response

FIGURE 10.15 Four-way shared-key authentication

client nodes and AP to avoid re-entries. With the direct derivation of the pre-shared key, choosing a strong password/passphrase is important to make it difficult to break the pre-shared key.

The pre-shared key-based authentication requires four-way communications (see Figure 10.15). First, when a client station initiates an association request to an AP, the AP sends a random challenge text back to the requesting station. Then, the client station encrypts the challenge text with the pre-shared secret key and returns the encrypted challenge text back to the AP. On receiving it, the AP validates the encrypted text and determines the client's eligibility to grant an association.

This seemingly secure authentication method has a weakness because hackers can recover the shared secret key by monitoring the traffic. To make it much more difficult to recover the pre-shared key, current Wi-Fi standards use technology where, once a client is authenticated, the pre-shared key does not stay the same but is dynamically changed.

10.7.2.3 Authentication Server

Many organizations deploy a central authentication server to manage the authentication process. Such protocols as RADIUS (Remote Authentication Dial-in User Service) and TACACS+ (Terminal Access Controller Access-Control System Plus) are used to manage communications between an authentication server and an AP that forwards authentication requests coming from client stations. Besides the authentication of Wi-Fi clients, the server can handle other security-related functions such as the authorization of remote access through dial-in or through the virtual private network (VPN) link over the Internet (see Figure 10.16).

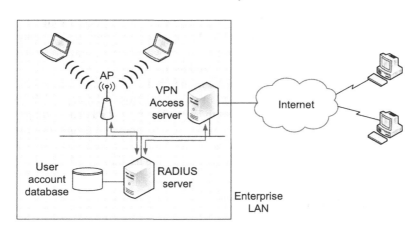

FIGURE 10.16 Authentication of Wi-Fi stations with RADIUS

10.7.2.4 Notes on Additional Security

In addition to authentication, an AP may come with another layer of security that filters client devices or device users based on such information as the destination IP address, protocol in the data field, TCP/UDP port, and MAC address. Also, an AP may be configured to turn off application services deemed unnecessary. For example, if a corporation does not allow such application services as Telnet (for remote access) or FTP (for remote file transfer), they should be disabled by APs. As a no-brainer, using data encryptions on Wi-Fi should be mandatory unless it is for public usage (e.g., store visitors). Lastly, any Wi-Fi open for guest access should be completely disengaged from the production network.

10.7.3 Wi-Fi Security Protocols

Different authentication schemes explained in Section 10.7 are all embedded in the Wi-Fi security protocol. This section summarizes how the security standards have evolved in generations and their distinctive features.

10.7.3.1 Wired Equivalent Privacy (WEP)

WEP, the first generation and legacy standard introduced in 1997, was intended to offer Wi-Fi security comparable to that of wired networks, although it was proved otherwise. Both the AP and qualified client stations share a manually entered secret key for client authentication and the encryption of exchanged data. Client stations are authenticated by the pre-shared key derived from the user-provided password. The pre-shared key is used to encrypt messages, but the key remains the same, making it vulnerable to decipher attacks if the attacker captures enough messages as a sample.

WEP delivers the level of security that can deter casual snooping. However, the shared secret key can be compromised using software tools that perform the brute force or dictionary-based search. WEP is especially vulnerable if it uses short encryption keys such as 40 bits or 64 bits, instead of 128 bits. Due to the inherent risk, setting up Wi-Fi LANs with WEP should be avoided.

10.7.3.2 Wi-Fi Protected Access (WPA and WPA2)

WPA and WPA2 offer stronger security than WEP. With WPA and WPA2, Wi-Fi nodes initially use the same pre-shared key – just as WEP does – entered into both the AP and user stations. As pre-shared keys are oftentimes derived from user-provided passwords/passphrases, they must be long and difficult to guess. Unlike WEP that uses a static pre-shared key, the WPA/WPA2 key is changed by the AP after exchanging a certain number of frames or after a while (e.g., every 10 minutes). This dynamic and periodic alteration of key values makes WPA/WPA2-guarded networks more difficult to penetrate than WEP-based ones.

WPA is not an official IEEE standard, as it was intended to be an interim solution for the transition from WEP to WPA2, which is the IEEE 802.11i standard offering government-grade protections. The network in compliance with IEEE 802.11i is known as a Robust Security Network (RSN), as it generally allows Wi-Fi access only to authorized users.

One key difference between WPA and WPA2 is the choice of encryption technology, making WPA2 more secure than WPA. WPA relies on the same encryption technology as WEP and, thus, a wireless NIC that supports WEP can be updated to WPA. The backward compatibility was a reason for having WPA as an interim solution. WPA2, meanwhile, is not upgradeable from WEP or WPA. Although WPA2 offers a higher security assurance, WPA still remains viable for Wi-Fi users if strong passphrases/passwords (e.g., 13 characters or more) are used to withstand password-cracking attempts.

10.7.3.3 Wi-Fi Protected Access (WPA3)

As a new arrival, WPA3 offers stronger authentication and encryption improved over WPA2. Its usage is mandatory for the Wi-Fi 6 (or IEEE 802.11ax) standard that can connect more devices simultaneously. WPA3 supports *opportunistic wireless encryption* in which data will be auto-encrypted in layer 2 without human interventions, especially in the public Wi-Fi. In the public setting, Wi-Fi users can be subject to such attacks as man-in-the-middle and dictionary password cracking, and WPA3 performs better than WPA2 in protecting users from the attacks.

Also, with WPA3, nodes will be able to use the QR code to access the network rather than using the traditional password. That is, a Wi-Fi network's SSID and password are encoded in a QR code, and your smartphone will be able to join the Wi-Fi network by just scanning the access point's QR code. This password portability is going to be increasingly important with the arrival of the IoT (Internet of Things) paradigm. IoT alone explains the critical importance of improved security for WPA3.

10.7.4 Wi-Fi Security Modes: Enterprise vs. Personal Mode

Wi-Fi security can be implemented in the *enterprise mode* or *personal mode*. The personal mode is designed to offer Wi-Fi security for homes and small offices and supports WPA-Personal, WPA2-Personal, and WPA3-Personal types. The Wi-Fi AP is responsible for the authentication of client stations and key management.

The enterprise modes (i.e., WPA-Enterprise, WPA2-Enterprise, and WPA3-Enterprise) are to offer boosted Wi-Fi security for corporations. The enterprise mode uses a central server for authentication and key management via such protocol as RADIUS (see Section 10.7.2.3). The central server ensures consistency in client authentication and reduces security risks resulting from mismanaged access points.

10.7.5 Example: Wi-Fi Security Options on Windows OS

Here Wi-Fi security options available on Windows OS are reviewed. Figure 10.17a shows a screenshot in which users can choose different authentication options including open authentication, shared key authentication with WEP, WPA (i.e., WPA-Personal and WPA-Enterprise), and WPA2 (i.e., WPA2-Personal and WPA2-Enterprise). The network security key (Figure 10.17b) is the password entered and used to derive a pre-shared key in the WPA2-personal mode. Figure 10.17b also indicates that AES (Advanced Encryption Standard) is an encryption technology option available for the WPA2-Personal mode.

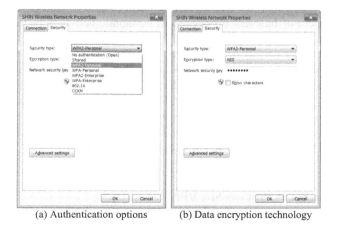

(a) Authentication options   (b) Data encryption technology

FIGURE 10.17   Wi-Fi security standards (Windows 10)

10.8 VPN SECURITY

10.8.1 BACKGROUND

The Internet, with its global coverage, has become an ideal platform for creating WAN connections through which corporate networks can be accessed by authorized people (e.g., traveling salesmen, business partners) from anywhere in the world. Despite the obvious benefits (e.g., low cost of connections) of the Internet as a WAN platform, enterprises have been somewhat slow in embracing it because of security concerns, uncertain network reliability (e.g., packet delays, packet delivery errors), and limited quality of service in packet transportation. VPN (virtual private network) has changed much of that negativity.

VPN uses *tunneling* to securely transport IP packets, the process of encapsulating an encrypted IP packet within another packet for its secure delivery. It is like transmitting packets within a secured pipe over the Internet. The encapsulation includes encrypting the original packet and adding a new IP header. At the receiving end, a router/VPN gateway performs the packet de-encapsulation and forwards the decrypted, original packet to the destination host. With VPN, mobile workers, home-based workers, telecommuters, and branch offices are effectively integrated into the virtual enterprise network.

10.8.2 VPN BENEFITS AND DRAWBACKS

a. **Cost Effectiveness**: The Internet is a very cost-effective communication platform because most businesses already have Internet access and VPN does not incur additional costs. Empirical data indicate that, compared to the private WAN services, VPN considerably curtails costs associated with network equipment, maintenance, administration, and communications. When a public or private organization maintains a large contingent of mobile workers, telecommuters, or branch offices, cost savings are even more significant.

b. **Accessibility and Scalability**: The Internet with its global reach offers accessibility that no other private carrier WAN network can match. Organizations can add VPN-based remote links anywhere, anytime, and any-to-any connectivity because of the Internet's ubiquity. Also, VPN has bandwidth scalability in which the data rate between a client site and an ISP can grow as needed, taking advantage of various services available for Internet access.

c. **Flexibility**: VPN offers ideal flexibility in business operations as a remote link can be formed and terminated as needed using Internet connectivity. For example, remote workers (e.g., traveling salesman), suppliers, or customers of a firm can be easily added to its enterprise network. This will benefit the firm in various ways such as improved customer service and better management of business processes. As economic activities become more distributed and global, firms can take advantage of VPN for cost-effective communications with global partners.

d. **Reliability**: While a VPN can bring about significant benefits to adopting organizations, there are potential drawbacks. Above all, VPNs depend upon the speed, reliability, and performance of the Internet. The Internet can be vulnerable to congestion, and maintaining the reliability of data transmissions for mission-critical applications could be challenging. Also, Internet-based connections can compromise their stability because the majority of IP packets have to cross multiple ISP networks to reach their destinations.

10.8.3 REMOTE-ACCESS VS. SITE-TO-SITE VPN

Different approaches are used in setting up the VPN, and they are largely divided into remote-access VPN and site-to-site VPN (see Figure 10.18).

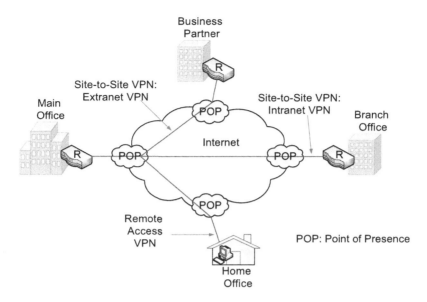

FIGURE 10.18   VPN types

10.8.3.1   Remote-Access VPN

The remote-access VPN allows workers in remote locations to take advantage of the Internet to reach back to their corporate sites and conduct tasks (e.g., transfer field data or download necessary information) in a timely manner. It implements a person-to-LAN connection in which the person may be a telecommuter, mobile worker, or traveling salesman.

10.8.3.2   Site-to-Site VPN

In this type, secure connections are established between two geographically separated LANs to protect IP packets in transit using encryptions. On arriving at the destination, packets are decrypted and forwarded to destination hosts. In this mode, the border router (or VPN gateway/firewall) does the work of encrypting and decrypting packets to protect their privacy. The site-to-site VPN comes in two modes: intranet-based and extranet-based.

The intranet-based VPN interconnects a firm's internal LANs (e.g., headquarter and branch location) over the Internet. Thus, the *LAN-to-LAN* connections are assumed to have minimal security risks. The extranet-based VPN, also known as the *business-to-business* VPN, connects LANs of two different companies to streamline business processes such as supply chain management. While the intranet-based VPN involves trusted endpoints, the extranet-based VPN interconnects a firm with business partners, customers, suppliers, or consultants.

10.8.4   VPN Protocol: IPSec (IP Security)

Several VPN protocols have been introduced, and *SSL/TLS* (shortly SSL) and *IPSec* are among the well received. IPSec was developed by the *Internet Engineering Task Force* (IETF). IPSec operates at the internet layer and therefore can protect all protocol data units (PDUs) coming down from the transport and application layers (see Figure 10.19). This protection is necessary because the IP protocol itself has no such capability. IPSec can encrypt data exchanged between network nodes (e.g., router-router, firewall-router, client-router, client-server) as long as the necessary software is installed on them. A dedicated, independent IPSec server may be set up at the corporate boundary, or it may be installed on the firewall/border router.

| Application layer (e.g. HTTP, SMTP) |
| Transport layer: TCP/UDP |
| Internet layer: IPSec Protocol |
| Internet layer: IP Protocol |

FIGURE 10.19　The IPSec layer

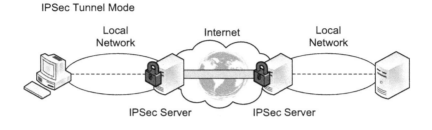

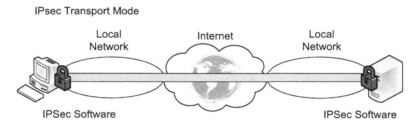

FIGURE 10.20　IPSec tunnel mode vs. transport mode

The IPSec standard is implemented in two different modes: *tunnel mode* and *transport mode* (see Figure 10.20).

10.8.4.1　IPSec Tunnel Mode

IPSec implemented in the tunnel mode has the following features:

a. IPSec servers are placed at the boundary of local sites, securing all inter-site transactions through data encryptions (site-to-site security).
b. Internal hosts are not aware of the IPSec server's existence, making it transparent to them.
c. No security is provided for IP packets outstanding within a local network. In other words, packets inside of a corporate network remain unprotected.
d. The tunnel mode is popular in implementing both remote-access and site-to-site VPNs.

In terms of packet encryption/decryption, the IPSec server encrypts an outgoing IP packet and encapsulates the encrypted packet within another IP packet (see Figure 10.21). In doing so, the IPSec server adds another IPSec header to the encrypted original IP packet for packet routing over the Internet. In this mode, therefore, the original IP packet is entirely encrypted and protected from eavesdropping. The new IP header is used only for the packet routing between two IPSec servers.

10.8.4.2　IPSec's Transport Mode

IPSec in the transport mode provides end-to-end (or host-to-host) security. For this, IPSec software needs to be installed on each *host* station, making its implementation considerably costlier and

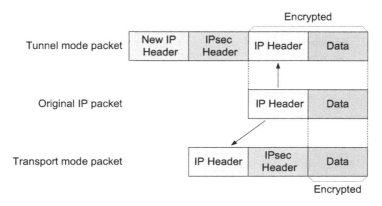

FIGURE 10.21   IP packet encapsulation: tunnel mode vs. transport mode

more labor-intensive than the tunnel mode. With the transport mode, a packet remains encrypted even while it traverses inside a LAN (see Figure 10.21). In this mode, however, only *the data field* of a packet is protected by encryption. The IP header is not encrypted because its information (e.g., destination IP address) is necessary to deliver a packet to its destination host.

IPSec's tunnel mode and transport mode can be combined to offer double protection of IP packets. When the two IPSec modes are used together, hosts communicate in the end-to-end transport mode so that nobody else is able to read encrypted data. In addition, the site-to-site tunneling is established between LAN boundaries for further protection of the encrypted data. This, however, results in a considerable process overhead and is also costly.

10.8.5   VPN Protocol: SSL

10.8.5.1   Broad Acceptance

Secure Socket Layer (SSL) is a popular protocol that also performs authentication, data encryption, and data integrity, offering a secure means to transport data over the Internet. SSL was initially developed by Netscape Co. for secure communications between the web browser and the webserver based on HTTP. When HTTP is combined with SSL to enhance transactional security, it becomes HTTPS (or HTTP over SSL). When a browser visits a sensitive website (e.g., online banking), the webserver enforces the browser to use HTTPS to protect exchanged data. Formally, SSL became TLS (*Transport Layer Security*), a standard from the Internet Engineering Task Force (IETF). All browsers use TLS standards under the hood, although they are still being called SSL.

SSL rose quickly because the protocol is built into the web browser and thus there is no need to install the program separately to use its security features. Besides HTTPS, SSL has been applied to turn other insecure protocols into secure ones. For instance, FTP (File Transfer Protocol) and SMTP (Simple Mail Transfer Protocol) exchange data and files in clear text, making them vulnerable to interceptions. With the addition of SSL, FTPS (FTP over SSL) and SMTPS (SMTP over SSL) protect FTP and SMTP data.

10.8.5.2   VPN Implementation

SSL has become the most popular VPN standard as it is embedded in the browser. As is the case with IPSec, SSL-based VPN can be flexibly implemented in both transport- and tunnel modes (see Figure 10.22). When SSL is used for VPN, ideally both the browser (client) and the SSL server should authenticate each other by exchanging their credentials (e.g., digital certificate). This is to

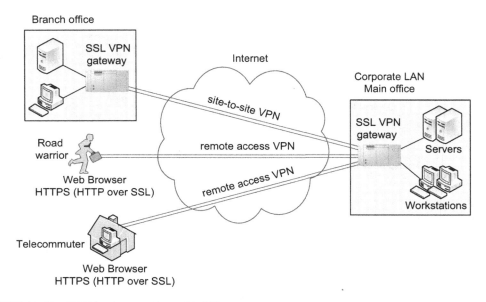

Branch office

SSL VPN gateway

Internet

site-to-site VPN

Corporate LAN
Main office

SSL VPN gateway

Servers

Road warrior

remote access VPN

Web Browser
HTTPS (HTTP over SSL)

remote access VPN

Workstations

Telecommuter

Web Browser
HTTPS (HTTP over SSL)

FIGURE 10.22   VPN implementations with SSL

avoid such risk as *man-in-the-middle*, in which a session is hijacked by an attacker. Especially, the prevalence of Wi-Fi networks makes the mutual authentication in VPN important.

10.8.6 IPSec vs. SSL/TLS

IPSec and SSL as two most popular VPN standards have their own pros and cons, and the key differences are summarized in Table 10.3. In fact, IPSec and SSL can be used in tandem to provide enhanced VPN security.

TABLE 10.3
Comparison: IPSec vs. SSL

	IPSec (IP security)	SSL (secure socket layer)
Operational layer	Internet layer	Transport layer
Software need (if used without VPN server)	Installation of IPsec software on the user station required.	It is already built into the web browser.
Setup and maintenance	High setup cost as software needs to be separately installed. Maintenance and updates become a burden if there is a large installation base.	Low maintenance and update cost as it is pre-loaded in the web browser.
Ease of use	End-user training is necessary for its usage.	It is integrated into the browser and thus its usage is transparent to the user.
Overall security	Generally, it provides a higher level of security than SSL.	Considered less secure than IPSec.
VPN implementation	Its security configuration in each station requires expertise.	On the client side it works more like plug-and-play, as the software is built into the browser.

CHAPTER SUMMARY

- Steganography is a technique that *hides* data within an ordinary file or message and thus it is designed to protect data through *obscurity*.
- Cryptography transforms a plaintext into an unreadable ciphertext. A cryptography system is composed of four basic elements: plaintexts, ciphertexts, a cipher, and key values.
- While symmetric-key encryption uses one secret key (e.g., session key) to encrypt and decrypt data, asymmetric-key cryptography relies on a private and public key pair.
- Because of pros and cons inherent to both symmetric and asymmetric cryptography technologies, they are widely used in combination to complement each other's weaknesses and to make the most of their strengths.
- Hashing based on such standards as MD and SHA are extensively used as cryptographic tools. The usage of hashing is, however, generally limited to the provision of data integrity.
- The digital signature is an electronic equivalent of the handwritten signature and is produced by encrypting the hash value of a message with the sender's private key.
- The digital certificate is the traditional ID card's digital equivalent and is used in conjunction with an asymmetric encryption system to verify the holder of a particular public key (not the private key).
- Digital certificates are issued by *certificate authorities* through their *public key infrastructure* (or simply PKI) servers.
- The public key infrastructure (PKI) represents a collection of hardware, software, policies, and procedures managed by a certificate authority to create, issue, monitor, and revoke digital certificates.
- Because a single *certificate authority* (CA) is hard to be trusted, multiple CAs are chained together to form 'a chain of trust.' In the chain, there are two CA types, *root CAs* and *intermediate CAs*, and they are chained by linking their digital certificates together.
- Each computer has a built-in function to generate a private and public key pair and can submit a form called *Certificate Signing Request* (or CSR) to a CA.
- CAs can revoke a person's digital certificate for various reasons, including its expiration, compromised private key, and policy violation.
- The relationship between a user station and an AP of a Wi-Fi network can be in one of three states: unauthenticated and unassociated, authenticated and unassociated, and authenticated and associated.
- Wi-Fi uses three different approaches to authenticate client stations: open authentication, preshared key authentication, and authentication server.
- The security standards of Wi-Fi include WEP, WPA, WPA2, and WPA3.
- The virtual private network (VPN) represents a technology that uses tunneling to protect IP packets in transit. Tunneling is the process of encapsulating an encrypted IP packet within another packet for its secure delivery over the Internet.
- 'Remote-access' and 'site-to-site' are two different setup modes of VPN.
- Among several VPN standards, SSL/TLS (or SSL) and IPSec are broadly used.
- IPSec is implemented in two different modes: tunnel mode and transport mode.

KEY TERMS

3DES	certificate authority
Advanced Encryption Standard (AES)	certificate revocation list (CRL)
asymmetric-key encryption	certificate signing request (CSR)
block cipher	chain of trust
Blowfish	cipher

ciphertext
code-signing certificate
cryptography
Data Encryption Standard (DES)
digital certificate
digital signature
domain certificate
elliptic curve cryptography (ECC)
encryption key
end-user certificate
hashing
IEEE 802.11i
International Data Encryption Algorithm (IDEA)
IPSec
MD5
message digest
plaintext
pre-shared key (PSK)
Pretty Good Privacy (PGP)
private key
public key
public key infrastructure (PKI)
RC4
remote-access VPN

Robust Security Network (RSN)
RSA
Secure Hash Algorithm (SHA)
Secure Socket Layer (SSL)
session key
site-to-site VPN
steganography
stream cipher
symmetric-key encryption
Transport Layer Security (TLS)
transport mode
tunnel mode
virtual private network (VPN)
VPN tunneling
Wi-Fi Protected Access (WPA)
Wi-Fi Protected Access2 (WPA2)
Wi-Fi Protected Access3 (WPA3)
Wired Equivalent Privacy (WEP)
WPA-Enterprise
WPA-Personal
WPA2-Enterprise
WPA2-Personal
WPA3-Enterprise
WPA3-Personal
X.509

CHAPTER REVIEW QUESTIONS

1. Which can protect data through an *obscurity* solution?
   A) steganography
   B) symmetric cryptography
   C) message authentication function
   D) hashing
   E) sponge function

2. The following are benefits of VPN EXCEPT:
   A) VPN offers flexibility in forming and terminating secure connections over the Internet.
   B) When an organization maintains a large contingent of mobile workers, telecommuters, or branch offices, cost savings could be significant.
   C) VPN supports anytime, anywhere, and any-to-any accessibility.
   D) VPN performance is unaffected by Internet congestions.
   E) VPN uses tunneling to securely transport IP packets.

3. Which is CORRECTLY paired between a VPN standard and its operational layer?
   A) IPSec: internet, SSL: data link
   B) IPSec: internet, SSL: application
   C) IPSec: transport, SSL: data link
   D) IPSec: internet, SSL: transport
   E) IPSec: transport, SSL: application

4. The four components of a cryptography system include the following EXCEPT:
   A) plaintext
   B) ciphertext

    C) digital signature

    D) key value

    E) encryption algorithm

5. The PKI (public key infrastructure) is maintained and operated by _____.

    A) governments

    B) certificate authorities

    C) Internet Engineering Task Force

    D) Internet service providers

    E) WAN service providers

6. When a digital signature is used for authentication, a session key can be utilized concurrently to _____.

    A) generate a message digest by the sender

    B) encrypt the original message and digital signature

    C) generate a digital signature by the sender

    D) generate a digital signature by the receiver

    E) generate a message digest by the receiver

7. Choose an ACCURATE statement on asymmetric vs. symmetric key encryption.

    A) In the asymmetric key encryption, both parties encrypt and decrypt messages using the same single key.

    B) In the symmetric key encryption, each party should have two keys – a public key and a private key.

    C) In the asymmetric key encryption, only one key must be shared between communicating parties.

    D) Symmetric keys are longer than asymmetric keys.

    E) The asymmetric key encryption is slower than the symmetric key encryption.

8. An applicant is sending an encrypted message with her/his digital signature appended. To authenticate the sender, the verifier (message receiver) uses a/the _____.

    A) private key of the verifier

    B) public key of the verifier

    C) private key of the applicant

    D) public key of the applicant

    E) session key

9. The X.509 standard defines information items to be included in the _____.

    A) digital signature

    B) digital certificate

    C) public key encryption

    D) symmetric key encryption

    E) message digest

10. The digital certificate _____.

    A) is an alternative authentication method when encryption is unavailable

    B) validates the owner of a particular public key

    C) delivers a private key to its owner

    D) is a method to securely exchange session keys

    E) is an electronic receipt of an online transaction

11. The digital signature attached to a message can authenticate _____.

    A) both the message sender and the message itself

    B) the message sender only

    C) the message only

    D) both the message sender and receiver

    E) both the message receiver and the message itself

12. What type of cipher can take a character and replace it with another character, working one character at a time?
    A) stream cipher
    B) block cipher
    C) Triple Data Encryption System (3DES)
    D) RSA cipher
    E) elliptic curve cryptography (ECC)

13. Which is NOT a characteristic of hashing?
    A) The results of a hash function should not be reversed as it is a one-way function.
    B) The hash value of a particular standard (ex. MD5) should always be the same fixed size.
    C) Collisions between two hash values of two different hash algorithms are normal.
    D) A message cannot be produced from a predefined hash value.
    E) Hashing creates a unique digital fingerprint of data or message.

14. Which describes the transport mode of IPSec?
    A) IPSec servers are placed at the boundary of local sites.
    B) Hosts internal to a site are not aware of IPSec servers.
    C) When a packet in transition is in a corporate network, it remains unencrypted.
    D) It is a popular choice for implementing intranet-based site-to-site VPNs.
    E) The data field of an IP packet is protected by encryption, but not the IP header.

15. When Bob needs to send Alice a message with a digital signature, which two technologies can be used by Bob's device?
    A) SHA-512 and Alice's private key
    B) SHA-512 and Bob's public key
    C) MD5 and Bob's public key.
    D) SHA-512 and Alice's public key
    E) MD5 and Bob's private key

16. Cryptography can be a tool for _____.
    A) confidentiality and authentication
    B) authentication and integrity
    C) integrity and confidentiality
    D) confidentiality, authentication, and integrity
    E) confidentiality

17. Which of the following uses an asymmetric cryptography?
    A) Data Encryption Standard (DES)
    B) elliptic curve cryptography (ECC)
    C) Advanced Encryption Standard (AES)
    D) Blowfish
    E) Triple Data Encryption Standard (3DES)

18. Which system uses the hybrid approach that utilizes both symmetric and asymmetric cryptography technologies to make the most of their strengths?
    A) RSA cryptography
    B) elliptic curve cryptography (ECC)
    C) Triple Data Encryption Standard (3DES)
    D) Advanced Encryption Standard (AES)
    E) Pretty Good Privacy (PGP)

19. The WPA standard has one major advantage over WPA2/WPA3. What is it?
    A) WPA offers stronger authentication than WPA2/WPA3.
    B) WPA offers better a quality of service than WPA2/WPA3.
    C) Wireless NICs that support WEP can be upgraded to WPA, but not to WPA2/WPA3.
    D) WPA has been standardized by IEEE but WPA2/WPA3 has not.

E) WPA is supported by more Wi-Fi standards, including 802.11g and 802.11n, than WPA2/WPA3.

20. Which information may NOT be included in a digital certificate?
   A) Owner's private key
   B) Issuer company
   C) Expiration date
   D) Name of its owner
   E) Owner's public key

21. Which VPN requires additional purchase and installation of security software in user computers?
   A) SSL in the tunnel mode
   B) IPSec in the transport mode
   C) IPSec in the tunnel mode
   D) IPSec in the site-to-site mode
   E) SSL in the regular mode

22. The framework for all of the entities (e.g., software, hardware, roles, policies, protocols, procedures) involved in the digital certificate and asymmetric cryptography management is called _____.
   A) certificate authority standards
   B) certificate authority policy
   C) public key infrastructure
   D) asymmetric cryptography Infrastructure
   E) digital certificate management

23. _____ is a popular security standard built into web browsers.
   A) SSH (Secure shell)
   B) PPTP (point-to-point tunneling protocol)
   C) SSL (Secure Socket Layer)
   D) SET (Secure electronic transaction)
   E) IPSec (IP security)

24. Choose a CORRECT statement regarding VPN standards.
   A) SSL offers the most secure VPN solution among available standards.
   B) IPSec's tunnel mode is more cost-effective to implement than its transport mode.
   C) Implementing IPSec's tunnel mode requires software installation in each user computer.
   D) IPSec's security software is embedded in web browsers.
   E) When SSL is combined with HTTP, the mutual authentication of both client and server is mandated.

25. When a person has a 20MB message to transmit electronically, how can she/he add a digital signature for sender authentication?
   A) By scanning her handwriting signature
   B) By encrypting the message with her own public key
   C) By encrypting the message with her own private key
   D) By encrypting the message digest with her own public key
   E) By encrypting the message digest with her own private key

HANDS-ON EXERCISES

Exercise 10.1

In this exercise, we simulate how a message can be hidden in the metadata section of a file (a form of steganography). There are free online metadata viewing and editing sites such as 'https://products.groupdocs.app/metadata'.

   a. Drag files of two different types (e.g., image, audio, document) to the site.
   b. Browse what metadata are extracted from each file type, and observe which file properties are allowed to change.
   c. Now, change the editable metadata (to hide a message) and save the modified files to simulate steganography.

EXERCISE 10.2: VIEW SOFTWARE CODE SIGN

In this exercise, you will examine a software program's digital signature that validates its authenticity by the vendor. The signature is produced by encrypting the software's hash value with the vendor's own private key. Then, the digital certificate that contains the vendor's public key is attached to the software program. This way, the program's integrity (more precisely, its .exe executable file) can be automatically examined by the operating system before its installation. As an example, let's check the code sign of *Notepad++* on Windows:

   1. Go to 'Program Files' folder, then 'Notepad++' folder.
   2. Right click on the .exe file of '*Notepad++*' and then open *Properties*
   3. Open the *Digital Signatures* tab
   4. Highlight the signature on the list and answer the following questions.
      a. What hash was used to produce the Notepad's code signature?
      b. When was it signed?
      c. Which certificate authority issued the digital certificate associated with the signature?
      d. When does the certificate expire?
      e. What asymmetric encryption standard was used to produce the code sign?
      f. What are the root and intermediate CAs that form the chain of trust (or certification path)?

EXERCISE 10.3

Answer the following questions on Wi-Fi security standards.

   1. What are differences between WEP and WPA/WPA2/WPA3?
   2. What are differences between the personal mode and the enterprise mode of WPA/WPA2/WPA3?
   3. How does WPA2/WPA3 differ from WPA?
   4. What information is exchanged for the open authentication of a Wi-Fi client?
   5. What is RADIUS?
   6. What is a popular approach used to derive a pre-shared key in the WPA family?
   7. With the pre-shared key (PSK) approach, which Wi-Fi network nodes are configured with a password/passphrase?
   8. What are the two primary functions of Wi-Fi security standards such as WPA2 and WPA3?

EXERCISE 10.4

Deploy a QR code on your Wi-Fi network's AP and use it to connect your smartphone to the Wi-Fi network. There are websites (e.g., qrcode-monkey.com) that you can use to create your QR code based on SSID and password information. Again, YouTube is your best friend if you need help.

11 Fundamentals of Packet Routing

11.1 INTRODUCTION

This chapter explains key infrastructure and architectural aspects of the Internet and then key issues relevant to the routing decision process of IP packets. To forward IP packets, the router develops and periodically updates its routing table as a reference table. The table is placed in the router's main memory to allow a quick look-up whenever an IP packet arrives. The router searches routing table entries when it receives an IP packet and determines the packet's best forwarding path. So, there is a resemblance in the roles of the switch table and the routing table as two different reference sources: the one for *frame switching* decisions for intra-networking (layer 2) and the other for *packet routing* decisions for inter-networking (layer 3). The summary of their procedural equivalence is:

A frame arrives at a switch port		A packet arrives at a router port
→ The switch refers to its *switch table*		→ The router refers to its *routing table*
→ Decide the frame's exit port		→ Decide the packet's exit port

The router constructs and maintains a routing table that enables decision-making regarding the delivery path of IP packets across an internet. To update the routing table, routers periodically advertise and exchange information using the so-called *dynamic routing protocol*. The protocol performs functions necessary to maintain and update the routing table and, thus, fundamentally differs from the IP protocol whose responsibility is packet development and delivery. This chapter explains the structural details of the routing table and demonstrates how the dynamic routing protocol updates its entries.

An enterprise, such as a business firm, or an ISP can have multiple internal routers to couple its subnetworks, and this makes the enterprise network an internet as a whole. Routers are divided into two types: internal and border routers. Internal routers provide the connectivity of network segments within an enterprise (called intra-domain routing) and border routers are responsible for dispatching packets to destinations beyond the enterprise boundary (called inter-domain routing).

Internal and border routers rely on different types of dynamic routing protocols to exchange (or advertise) information necessary to update their routing tables. The focus of this chapter is the internal (or intra-domain) routing decision. The external (or inter-domain) routing is briefly covered at the end of this chapter, but much of its technical details are beyond the scope of this textbook.

11.1.1 LEARNING OBJECTIVES

The key learning objectives of this chapter are to understand:

- The general architecture of the Internet – Internet service provider, Internet exchange point, and autonomous system
- Fundamentals of the routing mechanism
- The internal structure of the routing table
- The process of IP packet forwarding decisions
- Types of routing table entries – directly connected, static, and dynamic routes
- The interior dynamic routing protocol for intra-domain routing and its fundamentals
- The basics of external (or inter-domain) routing
- Traceroute/tracert utility program

11.2 INTERNET ARCHITECTURE

The Internet is a truly global network that is joined by wired and wireless (e.g., satellite) networks of many ISPs (e.g., AT&T, British Telecom, Verizon). With its enormity and complexity, numerous routers on the Internet move IP packets between corporate networks and ISP networks, and between ISP networks. Depending on the geographical location of communicating hosts, IP packets have to pass through several ISP networks to reach their destinations. For the packet delivery across networks, ISPs have to work together, although they also have to compete with each other to attract more individual and corporate clients to their Internet access service. This section covers the Internet's important architectural components in terms of *Internet service providers* (ISPs), *Internet exchange points* (IXPs), and *autonomous systems* (AS).

11.2.1 INTERNET SERVICE PROVIDER (ISP)

11.2.1.1 National ISPs

ISPs use their own networks to offer Internet access to large and small businesses as well as to individual clients. In the US, there are three types of ISPs – *national ISPs* (or Tier 1 ISPs) and *regional/local ISPs* (Tier 2/Tier 3 ISPs) (see Figure 11.1). The network infrastructure operated by each national ISP constitutes the Internet *backbone*. The Internet is, therefore, a gigantic entity as a whole, made up of many backbone networks owned and operated by national ISPs. National ISPs provide regional/local ISPs with access to the Internet in exchange for contracted service fees. AT&T, Level 3 Communications, British Telecomm, UUNet, and Sprint are some of the largest backbone providers. The backbone network of a national ISP is comprised of trunk links of bundled optical fibers, transporting data at high speeds defined by the optical carrier (OC) hierarchy (more in Chapter 13). ISPs are continuously adding network capacity to keep up with the rapid increase in Internet traffic.

11.2.1.2 Regional/Local ISPs

The *local* and *regional ISPs* provide Internet access to individual and business clients in a relatively limited geographical area (e.g., San Diego metropolitan area) by forwarding their IP packets to national ISPs' backbone networks. In the US, many local ISPs connect to national ISPs via regional ISPs. With the local and regional ISPs' role to bridge customer LANs and the Internet backbone, their networks are frequently called *feeder networks*. The connectivity between local, regional, and national ISPs is based on contracted business relationships that include service fees. In other words, service fees local/regional ISPs pay to access the Internet become an important source of revenue for backbone providers. Individual and organizational customers, on the other hand, pay subscription fees (e.g., monthly charge) to local/regional ISPs for Internet access. Many Tier 1 carriers (e.g., AT&T) offer Internet access to local/regional ISPs and also individual/corporate customers.

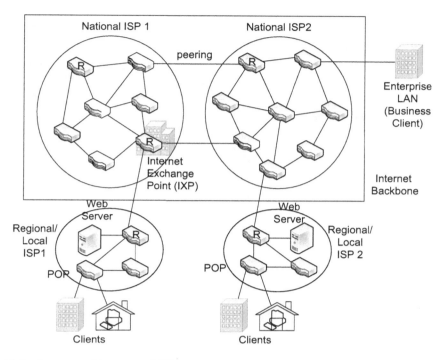

FIGURE 11.1 Internet architecture and ISPs

11.2.1.3 ISP Network Architecture

An ISP network is composed of one or more Point-of-Presence (or POPs) as customer gateways to the Internet. The large ISP owns a number of POPs, each of which is literally a large structure (e.g., building) with its own internal high-speed LAN. Each POP houses different types of routers, including:

a. One or more access routers that connect to customer premises (individuals/organizations).
b. Core routers that connect to other POPs of its own.
c. Border routers that connect to other ISP networks.
d. Hosting routers that link webservers stationed inside a POP. The webservers provide Internet surfers with accelerated web access. You might have noticed that popular portal sites such as Google.com and Yahoo.com respond much faster than most other sites. It is because portal servers are strategically placed at POPs right next to customer premises, making it unnecessary for user requests to cross the Internet backbone, cutting response time considerably.

POPs of an ISP are primarily interconnected by the SONET ring (see Chapter 13) implemented on optical fibers at such high speeds as 100 Gbps. Tier 1 ISPs generally use circuit speeds higher than those of Tier 2 and Tier 3 as Tier 1's backbone should handle a large influx of IP packets from its Tier 2 and Tier 3 feeder networks.

11.2.2 INTERNET EXCHANGE POINT (IXP)

ISP networks are coupled together for IP packets to travel across them to reach destinations. ISPs interconnect each other through designated access locations called *Internet Exchange Points* (IXPs) or through *peering* (see Figure 11.1). The IXP, also known as a *network access point* (NAP) for a historical reason, is itself a high-speed LAN running on such speed standard as 10 Gigabit Ethernet installed in a building and becomes a junction point of participating ISP networks.

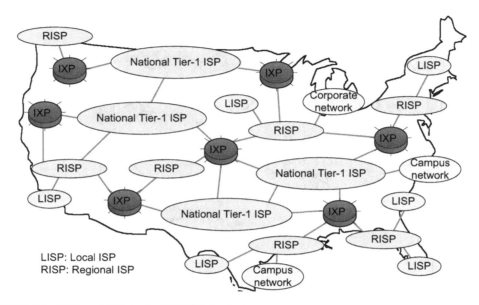

FIGURE 11.2 IXPs and ISPs in the US (high-level views)

There are a number of IXPs throughout the world (see Figure 11.2 for the interconnectivity between IXPs and ISPs). ISP networks joined together through an IXP are bound by bi- or multi-lateral commercial contracts. In the US, there were initially four NAPs in New York, Washington, D.C., Chicago, and San Francisco when the Internet was born. Now, there are many more IXPs across the country, mostly owned and operated by national-level carriers.

With the continuous growth of Internet traffic, IXPs oftentimes become bottlenecks, and relying solely on them as gateways to the Internet can be problematic. As a result, ISPs also use *private peering* in which ISPs directly interconnect their networks bypassing IXPs to improve Internet accessibility and to gain other benefits such as link redundancy and lower cost of Internet access. For the arrangement of private peering, ISPs agree on contract terms.

11.2.3 AUTONOMOUS SYSTEM (AS)

The *autonomous system* (AS) represents a collection of interconnected networks of a region or an organization that is under one 'administrative' control. An AS, therefore, adopts a consistent packet routing policy in which routers use the same routing protocol(s) internally and are programmed with a uniform set of packet routing rules. For this reason, the AS is also called a *routing domain*. A large enterprise or university is assigned an AS because there is a natural boundary within which it can decide its own consistent routing policy. For example, MIT's campus network is an *autonomous system*.

Relatively smaller campus networks, corporate networks, and home networks belong to the *autonomous system* of their ISP. As of December 2020, there are more than 99,000 autonomous systems in the world. Each AS is assigned an *autonomous system number* (ASN) by the *Internet Assigned Numbers Authority* (IANA) to represent the network. In other words, the ASN uniquely identifies an 'administrative' domain on the Internet. Note that the DNS domain, previously explained (revisit Section 9.8), fundamentally differs from the AS domain here. ASNs can be searched from a registry website such as *www.arin.net*.

Each autonomous system consists of a number of subnets held together by internal routers and autonomous systems are interconnected through border routers. Routers within an AS rely on an

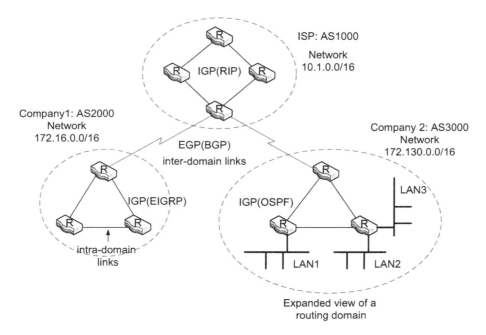

FIGURE 11.3 An illustration of autonomous systems

Interior Gateway Protocol such as OSPF to develop their routing tables for the intra-domain (or local) routing of IP packets (see Figure 11.3).

Meanwhile, border routers of autonomous systems use the *Exterior Gateway Protocol*, most notably BGP (Border Gateway Protocol), to develop their routing table entries necessary for the inter-domain routing of IP packets. Although the details are beyond the scope of this book, the ASN becomes a key information piece that enables inter-domain (or between autonomous systems) routing of packets. So, the delivery of an IP packet over the Internet between two remotely distanced hosts takes a combination of both intra-domain routing and inter-domain routing.

11.3 ROUTING MECHANISM

In Chapter 3, it was explained that routing moves packets across multiple subnetworks based on their destination IP addresses. Then, the differences between switching and routing and how they work together to transport IP packets between any two hosts across subnetworks were explained. In this section, the focus is on explaining how the router uses its routing table entries to make forwarding (or routing) decisions of IP packets.

11.3.1 SCENARIO 1: TWO SUBNETS

Let us begin with a hypothetical corporate network where two subnets are joined by the router R1 (see Figure 11.4). Imagine a situation in which PC1 (172.20.1.1) exchanges IP packets with the Server (172.20.2.1) via the router. The packet delivery between the two hosts needs *routing* across the two subnets and, to make it possible, R1 should maintain a routing table as a reference table. R1's two ports (interfaces) are configured with an IP address pertaining to each attached subnetwork (recall that the IPs are manually set up). They are:

172.20.1.254 (Fa0/0) attached to the 172.20.1.0/24 subnet,
172.20.2.254 (Fa0/1) attached to the 172.20.2.0/24 subnet.

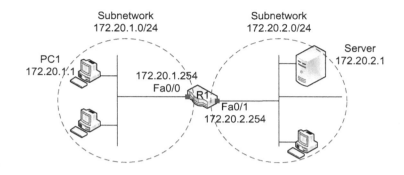

Destination Subnetwork/Mask	Exit Port/ Interface	Next hop IP	Metric
172.20.1.0/24	FastEthernet0/0	N/A	0
172.20.2.0/24	FastEthernet0/1	N/A	0

FIGURE 11.4   A case of two subnets and a router

On sending a packet to the Server, PC1 learns from the Server's IP address (172.20.2.1) that the destination is on a different subnet and therefore dispatches the packet (encapsulated within a frame) directly to Fa0/0 of R1 for routing. Once the packet arrives at Fa0/0, R1 refers to its routing table as in Figure 11.4, finds that the routing table's entry 172.20.2.0/24 matches the Server IP's first three numbers (**172.20.2.**1) and uses the corresponding Fa0/1 as the exit port of the packet. Note that host nodes including laptops and Servers are generally connected to the router through one or more switches and/or access points, but they are not shown in Figure 11.4 for visual brevity.

Observe that, to enable packet routing, subnet addresses (not host IP addresses) and their subnet masks are listed in the routing table. Among the columns of the routing table, you don't have to worry about the *next-hop IP* and *Metric* variables for now. Given that there are only two subnets in Figure 11.4, R1's routing table only needs two entries to enable packet routing.

11.3.2 Scenario 2: Three Subnets

Building on the very simple demonstration in Figure 11.4, let us take a look at a little more expanded internet in Figure 11.5. It illustrates a small enterprise network made up of three subnets (172.20.1.0/24, 172.20.2.0/24, and 172.20.3.0/24) joined by two routers, R1 and R2. The table in Figure 11.5 illustrates R1's routing table. For all host stations to be able to exchange IP packets, the routing tables of both R1 and R2 have to contain entries of all three subnets.

Again, don't forget that each subnetwork in Figure 11.5 includes one or more switches or access points between hosts and a router and between two routers. That is, although not shown, R1 and R2 are *indirectly* connected through intra-networking devices.

11.4 ROUTING TABLE

11.4.1 Background and Dynamic Routing Protocol

One key function performed by the router is to develop its own routing table as in Figure 11.5, a reference table necessary to decide forwarding paths of IP packets. The routing table has subnet entries that are manually added or automatically created. When there are a small number of routers

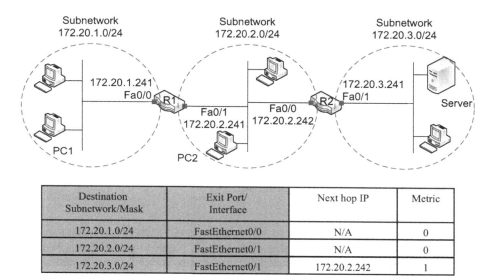

Destination Subnetwork/Mask	Exit Port/ Interface	Next hop IP	Metric
172.20.1.0/24	FastEthernet0/0	N/A	0
172.20.2.0/24	FastEthernet0/1	N/A	0
172.20.3.0/24	FastEthernet0/1	172.20.2.242	1

FIGURE 11.5   A case of three subnets and R1's routing table

within a network and/or when there is little need for updating the routing table, the manual addition of its entries makes sense. However, when a network has a number of routers in it, the manual construction and maintenance of each routing table becomes costly and also prone to mistakes. For this reason, a majority of routing table entries are dynamically created by the router itself based on information obtained from other routers.

To enable the auto-creation of the routing table and dynamic updates of its entries, routers advertise their status information based on a (or sometimes more than one) standard protocol called a *dynamic routing protocol*. Several dynamic routing protocols have been introduced to specify what status information is shared and how to share it. By now, you should be able to see the difference between the routing protocol and the IP protocol (oftentimes called a *routed protocol*) in their functional orientation:

- The routing protocol is intended to advertise information necessary to construct and update the routing table.
- The routed protocol, IP, is responsible for packet movements for which the routing table becomes a reference source.

The internet layer's essential and fundamental responsibility is the forwarding of IP packets according to the routing table information. As for routing protocols, their details are not necessarily defined in the internet layer. In fact, confusing enough to readers, several of them belong to the application layer – yes, application layer. This means that constructing the routing table by a router is not necessarily the work of the internet layer. Even if it conducts non-internet layer functions, the router becomes a layer 3 device because its primary function is moving packets across subnets based on the IP protocol, and other functions are rather supplementary to it.

11.4.2 ROUTING TABLE ELEMENTS

In this section, information elements stored in the routing table are described. As explained, its entries can be manually inserted (i.e., static entries that stay unchanged) or dynamically added/updated based on the status information regularly advertised by other routers. The frequent routing table updates reflect changes in network conditions and topology. In Figure 11.5, the routing table is shown to contain such information fields as *destination network*, *subnet masks*, *exit ports*, *next-hop IPs*, and *metric* values. Among them, the *destination network*, *subnet masks*, and *exit ports* variables are most fundamental to enable packet routing. The role of the remaining columns (i.e., *next-hop IPs* and *metric*) is supplementary or informational. They are explained later in this section.

11.4.2.1 Destination Subnetwork Addresses and Subnet Masks

Remember that this column contains subnet addresses, not host addresses.

11.4.2.2 Exit Ports (Interfaces)

This is the router port used to forward an IP packet to ultimately reach the destination subnetwork or, less frequently, the destination host (e.g., server).

11.4.2.3 Next-Hop IP

This is the port address of the next router to which a packet is forwarded to reach the destination host eventually. The *next-hop* may be cabled directly (e.g., router-to-router over a WAN link) or indirectly via one or more switches. The switches between two routers are not included in the hop count (Remember that switches are layer 2 devices that do not understand IP).

Figure 11.6 demonstrates the exit port and next-hop IP address. According to the figure, two routers, R1 and R2, interconnect two LANs (i.e., 10.10.1.0/24 and 172.16.1.0/24) via the WAN link (192.168.10.0/24). If the PC (10.10.1.1) sends an IP packet to the server (172.16.1.20), R1 will route the packet to R2 after referring to its routing table entries. In this situation, 192.168.10.2 of R2 becomes the next-hop IP address for R1 and R1's S0/0/1 becomes the exit port. You can observe that the exit port and next-hop are two ends of a subnetwork. In the case of Figure 11.4, there are no other routers except R1, and thus the R1's routing table has exit ports but not next-hops.

11.4.2.4 Metric

The metric represents a value obtained from such cost factors as the *hop count*, *bandwidth*, *network load*, and *delay*. Some of the cost items such as *bandwidth* and *delays* can be manually configured on the router (e.g., S0/0/1 is linked to T-1 at 1.54 Mbps). Other cost items (e.g., *network load*) are dynamically computed by the router based on sampled data (e.g., the amount of data arrived at S0/0/1 during a measured time period). *The metric value is used to break a tie when a router finds more than one optimal routing path to a particular destination in its routing table.* The metric value is thus a measure of transmission 'costs' and the routing path of a lower cost is always better. For consistency, some metric values (e.g., bandwidth, reliability) are inversely (e.g., 3 → 1/3) entered into the routing table so that a high original value translates into a low-cost value.

A dynamic routing protocol can use one or more factors to compute the overall 'cost' of a particular route. For example, the RIP standard relies on *hop count*; the OSPF's preferred choice is

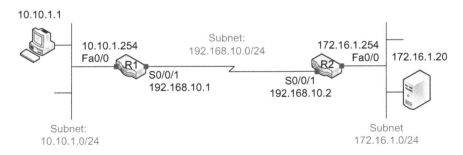

FIGURE 11.6 Exit port (interface) and next-hop IP address

bandwidth; and EIGRP (Cisco's proprietary protocol) uses *bandwidth* and *delay* as the default cost factors. Among the cost variables frequently used to compute the metric value are:

- **Hop count**: The number of routers an IP packet has to pass through before reaching the destination network. The lower the hop count, the better (i.e., lower cost) the route path becomes. For instance, in Figure 11.6, delivering a packet from R1 to the server (172.16.1.20) via R2 takes one hop.
- **Bandwidth**: It represents the connection speed of a route and generally a static value that is pre-assigned. For this, the lowest speed of all links of a delivery path can become the path's bandwidth value. For instance, if a particular end-to-end route takes four LAN and WAN links of 100 Mbps (Fast Ethernet), 1.5 Mbps (T-1), 155 Mbps (OC-3), and 2.0 Mbps (DSL), its bandwidth is 1.5 Mbps, the slowest link. Alternatively, the combined bandwidth of all links of a delivery path can be used to decide the metric value. In both approaches, the higher the bandwidth value, the better (i.e., lower cost) the route path becomes. In the previous example, the combined bandwidth of four links is 258.5 Mbps.
- **Delay**: The estimated delay of a particular path is decided by the type of link to a router port. The estimated delay is therefore primarily static rather than dynamic. For example, the delay of 100 Mbps Fast Ethernet is 100 microseconds and that of 1.5 Mbps T-1 line is 20,000 microseconds. With this metric, the lower the delay value, the better a route path becomes.
- **Reliability**: This metric is an indication of a network link's dependability in which the lower the probability of link failure, the higher the link reliability. It can be computed dynamically by a router based on the average network performance of sampled values during a certain duration (e.g., 5 minutes) and presented as a percentage out of 100 (e.g., 80% reliable out of 100%). The higher the reliability, the better a route path becomes.
- **Load**: This metric reflects the rate of link utilization as a percentage out of 100 (i.e., fully utilized). It can be examined dynamically during a sampled interval (e.g., 5 minutes). For instance, the load value of 80% of a link means 80 percent of the link capacity was used during the measurement period. The lower the load, the better a route path becomes.

11.5 PACKET FORWARDING DECISION

This section explains the general mechanism used by routers to determine the forwarding paths of IP packets. Before doing so, the *default route* concept is briefly introduced. A routing table can include the *default route* indicated by 0.0.0.0/0 (subnet IP address: 0.0.0.0, subnet mask 0.0.0.0). When the router cannot find the destination network of an incoming IP packet among the entries of its routing table, it releases the packet through the port assigned to the default route. The default route is generally tied to the port that eventually leads to the border router for a WAN or an Internet connection.

11.5.1 FINDING MATCHING ROUTES

When a packet arrives at a router port, the router searches its routing table going through all entries from top to bottom to locate all subnetwork addresses that match the packet's destination address. Here, *a match is found when an IP packet's destination address contains a bitstream identical to a particular subnet address in the routing table*. The router performs this matching process for every IP packet it receives. The router table search can result in a single match, multiple matches, or no match. Given the three different scenarios in matching, the following rules are applied for packet forwarding decisions.

11.5.1.1 Single Match

When there is a single match between routing table entries and a packet's destination address, the packet is dispatched through the corresponding exit interface. For example, if the routing table includes *any* one of the following entries, the packet with the destination address of 100.50.30.10 has a match (pay close attention to the subnet mask):

100.50.30.0/24
100.50.0.0/16
100.0.0.0/8.

11.5.1.2 Multiple Matches

When multiple matches are found in the routing table, the router chooses the network path that has the most 'explicit' or the 'longest' match with the destination IP address. If there is more than one best path, the metric value is used to break the tie.

For example, assume that an IP packet with the destination address of 100.50.30.10 arrives at a router port and the router table contains the following subnet address/mask entries:

[1] 100.50.30.0/24
[2] 100.50.0.0/16
[3] 100.0.0.0/8
[4] 0.0.0.0/0 (default route)

Of course, the router understands only binary values of 0s and 1s, and finding the longest match is always based on the string of 0s and 1s. The destination address, 100.50.30.10, is equivalent to: 01100100.00110010.00011110.00001010.

Meanwhile, the four routing table entries in binary are (with subnet ID bits in bold):

[1] **01100100.00110010.00011110.**00000000
[2] **01100100.00110010.**00000000.00000000
[3] **01100100.**00000000.00000000.00000000
[4] 00000000.00000000.00000000.00000000

Among the four entries, the subnet address of [1] has the longest (thus most explicit) match with the destination address, followed by [2] and then [3]. Therefore, the IP packet is dispatched to the 100.50.30.0 network. It is important to remember that the longest match does not have to be a multiple of 8 bits.

11.5.1.3 No Match

If there is no matching entry in the table, the router forwards the packet through the exit port assigned to the *default route* (0.0.0.0/0). When there is neither a matching entry nor a *default route* in the routing table, the router has no choice but to abandon the IP packet. As said, if any of the subnet address bits differ from the arriving packet's destination address bits, there is no match. For instance, there is no match between the destination address of 100.50.30.10 (01100100.00110010.00011110.0000 1010) and the following routing table entries:

01100100.00100000.00000000.00000000/16
01100100.00110010.00010101.00000000/24

Let us extend the example further. If the routing table only includes the entries that follow, the packet with the destination address of 100.50.30.10 has no match because of a discrepancy between their subnet address bits and the packet's destination address. Then, the router releases the packet through the exit port of 0.0.0.0/0:

100.50.20.0/24
100.40.40.0/24

100.40.0.0/16
90.0.0.0/8
0.0.0.0/0

11.6 ENTRY TYPES OF ROUTING TABLE

The routing table entry can be one of three types: *directly connected routes, static routes,* and *dynamic routes.* Understanding their differences helps you to better comprehend what mechanisms are utilized to develop and update the routing table.

11.6.1 DIRECTLY CONNECTED ROUTES

With the *directly connected route*, the destination subnetwork of an IP packet is directly linked to a router port. In other words, all subnets physically connected to router ports are entered into its routing table as directly connected routes. For example, in Figure 11.4, two subnets, 172.20.1.0/24 and 172.20.2.0/24, are routes directly connected to R1 through Fa0/0 and Fa0/1. *A directly connected route is added to the routing table whenever the IP address and subnet mask of a router port is manually configured.* This means that a router has as many directly connected routes in its routing table as the number of ports that are physically cabled and activated.

11.6.1.1 Example: Adding a Directly Connected Route

This example demonstrates how the directly connected route is added to the routing table of Cisco routers by issuing several relatively simple commands. Using Figure 11.4 as an example, three commands assign an IP address and its subnet mask to *Fastethernet0/0* and activate the port. On their completion in succession, the router enters the directly connected subnet (172.20.1.0/24) into its routing table.

1. R1(config)# *interface Fastethernet0/0*
   Comment: This command points to a particular port of R1 to be configured.
2. R1(config-if)# *ip address 172.20.1.254 255.255.255.0*
   Comment: This command assigns an IP address and a subnet mask to *Fastethernet0/0*. With this, R1 automatically learns that the subnet 172.20.1.0 is physically connected to its *Fastethernet0/0* port.
3. R1(config-if)# *no shutdown*
   Comment: This command activates the *Fastethernet0/0* port. The router port is not operational unless it is manually activated.

11.6.2 STATIC ROUTES

11.6.2.1 Static Routes of a Router

With the static route, the routing path to a destination network is manually added to the routing table and it remains there unless manually changed or removed. Although this definition bears a close resemblance to the directly connected routes discussed previously, the key difference is that the destination network of a static route is not directly cabled to the router port. There are situations where such manual addition of static routes makes much sense:

- Adding a default route to the routing table
- When there is little need for changing an entry (or entries)
- Configuring a small network with a limited number of routers

TABLE 11.1
Default route as a static route

Destination network/subnet mask	Exit port/interface	Next-Hop IP	Metric
172.20.1.0/24	FastEthernet0/0	N/A	0
172.20.2.0/24	FastEthernet0/1	N/A	0
0.0.0.0/0	FastEthernet0/0	N/A	1

As an extension of R1's routing table in Figure 11.4, for example, Table 11.1 demonstrates two directly connected routes and one static entry of the default route (IP address = 0.0.0.0 and subnet mask = 0.0.0.0). As explained, if there is no matching between an incoming IP packet's destination address and routing table entries, then the router will forward the packet to the *default route* via the FastEthernet0/0 port.

11.6.2.2 Example: Adding a Default Route on Cisco Router

Adding the static, default route in Table 11.1 to the routing table is done by issuing a simple statement as the one that follows. The statement basically tells the router that the default route path (destination IP: 0.0.0.0 with subnet mask: 0.0.0.0) is through the exit port, *FastEthenet0/0* (or shortly *Fa0/0*).

$$\text{R1}(\text{config})\# \textit{ip route 0.0.0.0 0.0.0.0 Fa0 / 0}$$

11.6.2.3 Static Routes of a Host

So far, the explanation of static entries has focused on the router's routing table. Host devices (e.g., laptops, smartphones) also have their own routing table whose entries generally stay unchanged. As an example, Figure 11.7 demonstrates the routing table of a PC running Windows OS. To display it, issue '*C:\>route print*' or '*C:\>netstat –r*' at the command prompt. A recent OS version including Windows 10 provides two routing tables (one for IPv4 and another for IPv6).

Although there are a number of entries in the table, the first line is the most important one that enables the computer to route IP packets to the Internet. Basically, the first line says that the default routing path (subnet address 0.0.0.0 with subnet mask 0.0.0.0) of IP packets from the host station (192.168.1.135) is through the (*default*) *gateway* of 192.168.1.1.

The default gateway (or just *gateway* as in Figure 11.7) is the IP address of the router port to which a host station sends IP packets when their destination addresses are not in the same subnet (revisit Section 4.10.1). Packets arriving at the default gateway are relayed to the outside of the subnet and a majority of them reach the Internet (see Figure 11.8). The default gateway can be viewed with the command, '*C:>ipconfig*'.

11.6.3 DYNAMIC ROUTES

The router adds dynamic entries to its routing table using information obtained through communications with other routers. Adding and updating dynamic entries into the routing table requires that routers advertise their status information using the dynamic routing protocol. The advertising takes place periodically or is triggered when there is a change in the network such as router crash/rebooting or unexpected corrections in the network topology. On receiving advertisements from other

Command Prompt

IPv4 Route Table

===

Active Routes:

Network Destination	Netmask	Gateway	Interface	Metric
0.0.0.0	0.0.0.0	192.168.1.1	192.168.1.135	45
127.0.0.0	255.0.0.0	On-link	127.0.0.1	331
127.0.0.1	255.255.255.255	On-link	127.0.0.1	331
127.255.255.255	255.255.255.255	On-link	127.0.0.1	331
169.254.0.0	255.255.0.0	On-link	169.254.229.231	281
169.254.0.0	255.255.0.0	On-link	169.254.229.226	281
169.254.229.226	255.255.255.255	On-link	169.254.229.226	281
169.254.229.231	255.255.255.255	On-link	169.254.229.231	281
169.254.255.255	255.255.255.255	On-link	169.254.229.231	281
169.254.255.255	255.255.255.255	On-link	169.254.229.226	281

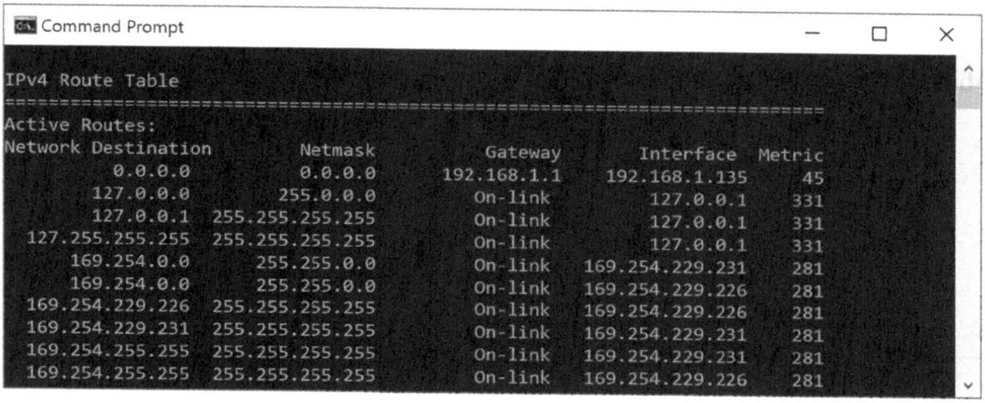

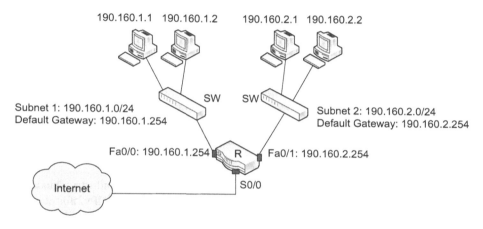

FIGURE 11.7 A sample IPv4 routing table of a host station

FIGURE 11.8 Demonstration of default gateway

routers, a router uses a built-in algorithm to compute the best delivery path and its metric value to each destination subnet and updates them to its routing table.

Depending on the dynamic routing protocol activated, advertised information items vary. Several routing protocols are being used. They are not compatible and, generally, one routing protocol is activated within an enterprise network, although routers can rely on more than one routing protocol to gather information. When there are two or more protocols activated on a router, each routing protocol comes up with its own best path to a subnetwork, resulting in as many best paths as the number of routing protocols in action. The routing table, however, includes only one path chosen according to the preference order.

The entries of a routing table represent the combination of directly connected routes, static routes, and/or dynamic routes depending on how it is constructed. Some routing tables may have only directly connected routes and static routes; some only directly connected routes and dynamic routes; and others with all three types.

In addition, although not shown previously for brevity, the routing table can contain an 'information' column that tells how each entry was created. As an example, the routing table in Table 11.2 has the 'Type' column in which the first two entries (C) are directly connected routes; the next two entries (O) are added by the OSPF dynamic routing protocol; and the last (S) is a static default route manually added.

TABLE 11.2
Routing table with entry *Type* information

Type	Destination subnetwork/mask	Exit port/interface	Next-Hop IP	Metric
C	192.168.10.0/24	FastEthernet0/1	N/A	0
C	172.20.1.0/24	FastEthernet0/0	N/A	0
O	10.10.1.0/24	FastEthernet0/1	192.168.10.254	120
O	192.168.1.0/24	Serial0/1	172.16.10.254	120
S	0.0.0.0/0	Serial0/1	172.16.10.254	1

11.7 DYNAMIC ROUTING PROTOCOLS

Dynamic routing protocols that enable the dynamic and automated additions and updates of routing table entries are divided into two types of the Interior Gateway Protocol (IGP) and Exterior Gateway Protocol (EGP).

11.7.1 INTERIOR GATEWAY PROTOCOLS

The *Interior Gateway Protocol* (IGP) is activated on internal routers placed inside the autonomous system to exchange their status information necessary to develop the routing table and thus to facilitate the intra-domain routing of packets. Among the popular IGPs are RIP (Routing Information Protocol), EIGRP (Enhanced Interior Gateway Routing Protocol), OSPF (Open Shortest Path First), and IS-IS (Intermediate System to Intermediate System).

- RIP was originally developed by Xerox and later adopted as an industry standard. It has evolved with the Internet from RIPv1 for classful IPv4 networks to RIPv2 for classless IPv4 networks. RIPng (or RIP next generation) for IPv6 has been released as well. RIP is a good choice for relatively small networks.
- OSPF, as a popular IGP, was developed for the TCP/IP protocol suite by the *Internet Engineering Tasks Force* (IETF), and two versions are available currently: OSPFv2 for IPv4 and OSPFv3 for IPv6.
- IS-IS was introduced by *International Organization for Standardization* (ISO) for the OSI protocol suite and is used widely by large network service providers including ISPs and telcos.
- EIGRP is a proprietary protocol from Cisco.

11.7.2 EXTERIOR GATEWAY PROTOCOLS

The *Exterior Gateway Protocol* (EGP) is used for routing table updates of border routers to facilitate inter-domain routing between *autonomous systems*. In other words, border routers use EGPs to exchange their status information with other border routers placed at autonomous system boundaries. *Border Gateway Protocol* (BGP) is the dominant EGP.

11.7.3 DELIVERY OF ADVERTISEMENT

The advertisements by dynamic routing protocols are conveyed in IP packets (see Figure 11.9). For example, the RIP's advertising message is encapsulated within the UDP datagram in the transport layer, which then becomes an IP packet in the internet layer and subsequently a frame in the data link layer. Meanwhile, the encapsulation process of OSPF messages slightly differs from that of

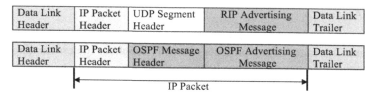

Data Link Header	IP Packet Header	UDP Segment Header	RIP Advertising Message	Data Link Trailer

Data Link Header	IP Packet Header	OSPF Message Header	OSPF Advertising Message	Data Link Trailer

FIGURE 11.9 Encapsulation of dynamic routing protocol advertisement

RIP in that the IP packet encapsulates OSPF advertisement in its data field (therefore no UDP header). Despite the relatively minor differences, all advertisements are delivered to other routers in IP packets.

11.8 DETERMINATION OF DYNAMIC ROUTES

What mechanism is used by the Interior Gateway Protocol to determine the best path from the router to all subnetworks within an autonomous system? Routing protocols use different algorithms. Among them, the so-called *link-state* protocol approach utilized by OSPF is demonstrated in a simplified manner. The process takes the following steps: (1) learn directly connected links; (2) form adjacency; (3) build link-state information; (4) advertise link-state information; (5) construct a map; and (6) update the routing table.

11.8.1 LEARN DIRECTLY CONNECTED LINKS

A router learns about subnets directly connected to its ports (or interfaces). This includes: the IP address and subnet mask of a port; subnet type (e.g., Ethernet, WAN link); and the cost of a link (e.g., bandwidth). The router learns the information when a network administrator manually configures its ports.

For example, from the manual input, R1 in Figure 11.10 learns that its Fa0/0 port has the IP address and subnet mask of 172.17.20.1/24 (therefore, 172.17.20.0 is the subnet address), and connects to Fast Ethernet at 100 Mbps. R2 and R3 also obtain such information through the same process.

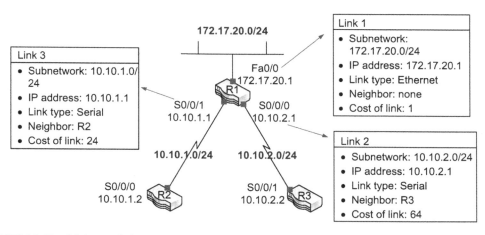

FIGURE 11.10 Link-state information of R1

11.8.2 FORM ADJACENCY

Each router sends out *hello* messages through its connected ports to learn if any directly connected router runs the same dynamic routing protocol of OSPF. Neighbor routers running the same OSPF protocol respond with *hello* messages, thus forming adjacency.

11.8.3 BUILD LINK-STATE INFORMATION

Each router builds an advertisement message with link-state information, which includes:

- IP address and subnet mask of a port
- Link type (e.g., Ethernet, WAN serial)
- Neighboring router (if it exists)
- Cost metric of a link (e.g., bandwidth)

As a demonstration, Figure 11.10 shows link-state information of R1's three links that are directly cabled to its Fa0/0, S0/0/0, and S0/0/1 ports.

11.8.4 ADVERTISE LINK-STATE INFORMATION

The *link-state* information is advertised to all routers running OSPF. For example, in Figure 11.10, R1 floods the link-state information to adjacent R2 and R3. R2 and R3 store the received information in their *database* and then flood R1's link-state information to other adjacent routers (if there are any). This flooding repeats until all routers in the autonomous system receive the R1's link-state information. R2 and R3 also flood their own link-state information to other routers. With the periodic link-state advertisements by all routers, each router possesses link-state data of all the other routers in its database.

11.8.5 CONSTRUCT A MAP

Once a router receives link-state information from all the other routers, it uses the database to develop a complete map (or graph) of router/subnet interconnectivity and also uses the map to determine the best packet routing path to each subnet based on the *shortest path first* principle (thus called OSPF – Open Shortest Path First).

For instance, Figure 11.11 demonstrates a map developed by R1 with the transmission cost of each link (Note that the transmission cost such as link bandwidth is also included in the advertisement). When bandwidth is used as the cost metric, for example, the higher the bandwidth of a link, the lower the transmission cost becomes. Given the principle of *shortest path first*, the optimal routing path between any two routers should have the lowest cumulative cost. For example, the best route from PC1 to the Server becomes 'PC1-R1-R2-R5-R4-Server' with a total cost of 24.

11.8.6 UPDATE ROUTING TABLE

Once the best route from R1 to each subnet is calculated based on the shortest path first principle, it is entered into the R1's routing table to assist the router's packet forwarding decision. For example, if the Server in Figure 11.11 is in the subnet address and subnet mask of 192.168.20.0/24, R1 will add an entry '192.168.20.0 (subnet), /24 (subnet mask), and Fa0/1 (R1's exit port)' to its routing table. The entry means that packets are released through its Fa0/1 port to reach 192.168.20.0/24 through the shortest path.

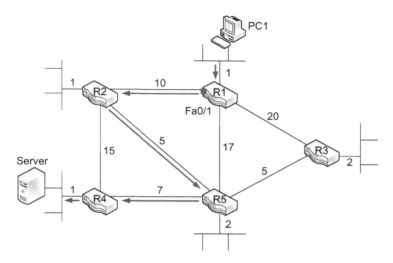

FIGURE 11.11   A sample router map

11.9   SECURITY MANAGEMENT

There are security risks in creating and updating routing table entries relying on information advertised by other routers. For example, what if a malicious attacker can advertise falsified link-state
information? Also, a misconfigured router can be mistakenly added to the network by someone other
than authorized people. It can advertise flawed link-state information and subsequently corrupt other
routers' routing table entries. This will disrupt the integrity of packet routing, negatively affecting
network performance (e.g., more lost packets).

11.9.1   MESSAGE AUTHENTICATION

To reduce potential security risks, routers can be configured to authenticate and encrypt advertisements. For this, all routers can be set up with the same authentication information including
the password. Then, using the password, a router with an advertisement message (e.g., R1 in
Figure 11.12) can produce an *electronic signature* unique to the message. To generate it, the
password and the advertisement message in combination can be fed into a hash function such as
MD5 that produces a one-way, unique value of a certain size (e.g., MD5 produces 128-bit hash
values).

The hash value as an electronic signature and the advertisement message are, then, sent to neighboring routers (e.g., R2 in Figure 11.12). The router (e.g., R2), on receiving them, repeats the same
process of producing an electronic signature using its own password that is identical to the sender's.
If the locally computed signature is identical to that from the sender, then this completes sender
authentication. The authentication process is summarized in Figure 11.12.

11.10   ACTIVATING DYNAMIC ROUTING PROTOCOL

The Cisco router is used to demonstrate how a dynamic routing protocol is activated (see
Figure 11.13). Dynamic routing protocols (e.g., RIP, OSPF) are the same in that their activation on a
router requires the listing of all subnets *directly connected* to it. For example, in Figure 11.13, each

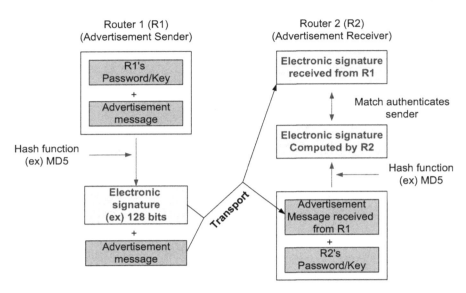

FIGURE 11.12   Authentication of advertisement

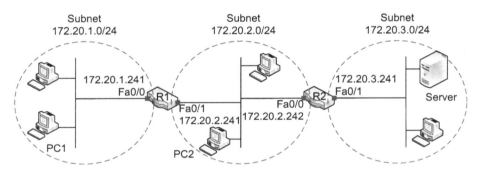

FIGURE 11.13   A hypothetical network

router should be given all *directly connected* subnets. The activation of RIP on R1, thus, takes the following commands:

R1(config) #*router rip*	: Enter the RIP configuration mode
R1(config-router) #*network 172.20.1.0*	: Add 172.20.1.0 as a directly connected network
R1(config-router) #*network 172.20.2.0*	: Add 172.20.2.0 as a directly connected network
R1(config-router) #*end*	: Exit the RIP configuration mode

11.11   COMPARISON – STATIC VS. DYNAMIC ROUTING

As explained, a router's routing table can have a combination of directly connected, static entries, and dynamic entries. Dynamic entries are continuously updated by the dynamic routing protocol to reflect situational changes (e.g., traffic volume, network topology). This dynamic update is important for the effective forwarding of IP packets to their ultimate destinations. Dependence on the

TABLE 11.3

Static vs. dynamic updates of a routing table

	Comparison	
Compared Aspects	**Static Approach**	**Dynamic Approach**
Difficulty in configuration	More difficult	
Chance of configuration errors	Higher chance	
Security of routing table entries	More secure	
Responsiveness to changes in network topology		More responsive
Burden (overhead) on network		Higher burden
Burden on router (e.g., CPU, memory)		Higher burden

advertisement of dynamic routing protocols, however, results in a considerable overhead in the network (e.g., increased network traffic due to periodic advertisements) and routers (e.g., processing of received advertisements to update the routing table).

On the other hand, although the static configuration of the routing table does not burden the network and routers, it results in higher administrative costs and a greater chance of making configuration mistakes, especially as the number of routers grows. The pros and cons of static (manual) versus dynamic (automated) addition and update of routing table entries are summarized in Table 11.3.

11.12 INTER-DOMAIN ROUTING

As inter-domain routing is an advanced concept even in the networking field, it is briefly explained here hiding the complex details in order to provide readers with a general understanding of how it enables global routing of IP packets. As explained, the Border Gateway Protocol (BGP) is the most widely used Exterior Gateway Protocol (EGP) developed for the inter-domain (i.e., between autonomous systems) routing of IP packets.

Each autonomous system (AS) has a network address and an AS number (or ASN). Each border router contains, in its routing table, network addresses of entire autonomous systems in the world. Relying on BGP, the border router of each AS develops a routing table that contains such a long list of entries.

11.12.1 PROCESS VIEW

A simplified example is presented here to demonstrate how border routers learn the existence of other networks and their autonomous systems. For the sake of explanations, let's assume that the entire Internet is composed of only five autonomous systems (see Figure 11.14), although there are more than 99,000 autonomous systems in reality. The following describes the learning process in a nutshell:

1. Each ASN is given a network address. For example, assume that AS10 is 100.0.0.0/8.
2. AS10's border router advertises its 'AS10 and 100.0.0.0/8' to its neighboring AS20 and AS30.
3. AS20 and AS30 relay 'AS10 and 100.0.0.0/8' to their neighbors. Also included in the relay is the information regarding the AS chain to AS10. For example, AS40 gets the chain information of 'AS20-AS10' from AS20, and AS50 gets 'AS40-AS20-AS10' from AS40 and 'AS30-AS10' from AS30.

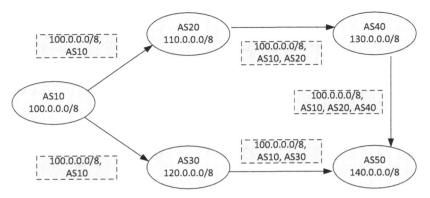

FIGURE 11.14   A demonstration of BGP mechanism

4. Now, AS50 (its border router) knows that there are two paths to AS10: one through AS40 and the other through AS30, and its routing table entries include AS10's 100.0.0.0/8 and the AS chain information.
5. When an IP packet originating from AS50 is destined to AS10, AS50's border router delivers it through the path that involves the smallest number of ASes (i.e., AS50-AS30-AS10) on the way.

11.13   TRACEROUTE AND TRACERT

As a useful utility function that runs on ICMP, *traceroute* shows a packet's end-to-end routing path and propagation delays while traversing the Internet. The function is activated by slightly different commands depending on the operating system (e.g., *tracert* in Windows, *traceroute* in Linux). For example, Figure 11.15 demonstrates the result of *C:\>tracert -d www.yahoo.com* targeting the Yahoo webserver. The command issues an ICMP packet three times to each router – shown as a hop

```
Command Prompt                                    —    □    ×

C:\Users\bshin>tracert -d www.yahoo.com

Tracing route to new-fp-shed.wg1.b.yahoo.com [2001:4998:24:120d::1:0]
over a maximum of 30 hops:

  1     1 ms     1 ms    <1 ms   2604:5500:5036:da00:6238:e0ff:feb2:1f32
  2     3 ms     2 ms     2 ms   2604:5500:5036::1
  3     3 ms     2 ms     3 ms   2604:5500:5034::1
  4    19 ms     2 ms     2 ms   2604:5500:5080::1
  5     6 ms    30 ms     2 ms   2604:5500:507f::1
  6     2 ms     1 ms     2 ms   2604:5500:5030:10::1
  7     6 ms     5 ms     6 ms   2a00:86c0:124:1::2
  8     6 ms     5 ms     6 ms   2001:504:13::195
  9    13 ms    13 ms    13 ms   2001:4998:f02f:f::
 10    30 ms    30 ms    30 ms   2001:4998:f005:202::1
 11    35 ms    35 ms    35 ms   2001:4998:f007::1
 12    33 ms    50 ms    33 ms   2001:4998:f00f:207::1
 13    35 ms    36 ms    35 ms   2001:4998:c:fe20::1
 14    37 ms    35 ms    35 ms   2001:4998:c:fa7d::1
 15    35 ms    34 ms    34 ms   2001:4998:24:ce05::1
 16    35 ms    35 ms    35 ms   2001:4998:24:ce11::1
 17    35 ms    34 ms    34 ms   2001:4998:24:120d::1:0

Trace complete.
```

FIGURE 11.15   A demonstration of *tracert*

number in the first column – on the way to the destination host. Each record in Figure 11.15 indicates three different round-trip delays in milliseconds. The 1st and 17th entries are IPv6 addresses of the source host and the destination 'www.yahoo.com' server. This means, the request to 'www. yahoo.com' went through 15 routers before reaching the destination server.

11.14 PERSPECTIVES ON PACKET ROUTING

Packet forwarding is highly process-intensive because the router needs to look up its routing table to find the best delivery path whenever a packet arrives at one of its ports (interfaces). When the routing table has a large number of entries, searching through them from top to bottom for each arriving IP packet causes latency affecting the router's packet forwarding performance. When the end-to-end transportation of an IP packet needs to go through a number of routers as in Figure 11.15, the aggregate delay can be substantial and may become intolerable to certain applications, especially when they are time-sensitive in nature (e.g., VoIP, online gaming, video conferencing, online movies).

As a measure to alleviate shortcomings of the conventional *routing* technology, especially to enhance the delivery speed of IP packets, the industry has heavily embraced the MPLS (Multi-Protocol Label Switching) technology. As the name implies, MPLS takes advantage of *switching* as a substitute for *routing* to transport IP packets. To refresh the *switching* concept, recall that the Ethernet LAN relies on the layer 2 switching technology to transport frames. For this, the LAN switch table contains layer 2 MAC address and exit port pairs, which enable the rapid relay of an incoming frame to its destination host or next switch. The switch table lookup process is significantly simpler and faster than that of the routing table (see Section 5.7). MPLS is explained in Chapter 12 as a popular WAN standard.

CHAPTER SUMMARY

- The Internet's important architectural components include Internet service providers (ISPs), Internet exchange points (IXPs), and autonomous systems (AS).
- There are national ISPs (or Tier 1 ISPs) and regional/local ISPs (Tier 2/Tier 3 ISPs). The network infrastructure operated by each national ISP constitutes the Internet backbone.
- The Internet exchange point is itself a high-speed LAN running on such speed standard as 10 Gigabit Ethernet installed in a building and becomes a junction point of participating ISP networks.
- The autonomous system represents a collection of interconnected networks of a region or an organization that is under one 'administrative' control.
- The routing table is a reference table necessary for a router to decide the forwarding path of an IP packet. The dynamic routing protocol facilitates the automated creation of routing table entries and their updates.
- The routing table contains destination networks, subnet masks, exit ports, next-hop IPs, and metric values as cost indicators.
- Among the cost variables frequently used to compute the metric value are the hop count, bandwidth, delay, reliability, and load.
- When an IP packet arrives at a router port, the router searches its routing table going through all entries from top to bottom to locate all subnet addresses that match the packet's destination address. The routing table search can result in a single match, multiple matches, or no match.
- The routing table entry can be one of three types: directly connected routes, static routes, and dynamic routes.
- There are two types of dynamic routing protocols: Interior Gateway Protocols (IGP) and Exterior Gateway Protocols (EGP).
- Routers use the IGP (e.g., RIP, OSPF, IS-IS) to share status information necessary in updating the routing table entries pertaining to the intra-domain routing of IP packets.

- Border routers use the EGP (e.g., BGP) to share information necessary to update routing table entries that support inter-domain (i.e., between autonomous systems) routing of IP packets.
- Updating routing table entries takes several steps. For example, OSPF takes the following procedure: learn directly connected links, form an adjacency, build link-state information, advertise link-state information, construct a map, and update the routing table.
- There are security risks in creating and updating routing table entries relying on information advertised by other routers. To reduce the risks, routers need to be configured to authenticate and encrypt advertisements.
- As a useful utility function that runs on ICMP, *traceroute* and *tracert* show a packet's end-to-end routing path and propagation delays while traversing the Internet.

KEY TERMS

advertisement
autonomous system (AS)
AS number (ASN)
bandwidth
Border Gateway Protocol (BGP)
default gateway
delay
directly connected route
dynamic route
dynamic routing protocol
Enhanced Interior Gateway Routing Protocol (EIGRP)
exit port/interface
Exterior Gateway Protocol (EGP)
gateway
hard boundary
hop count
Internet exchange point (IXP)
Internet service provider (ISP)
Interior Gateway Protocol (IGP)
Intermediate System to Intermediate System (IS-IS)

intra-domain routing
inter-domain routing
link-state information
local ISP
metric
national ISP
network access point (NAP)
next-hop IP
Open Shortest Path First (OSPF)
packet routing
point of presence (POP)
regional ISP
route print
router map
routing
Routing Information Protocol (RIP)
routing table
soft boundary
static route
traceroute, tracert

CHAPTER REVIEW QUESTIONS

1. The router's packet forwarding decision is based on the IP packet's _____.
    A) source IP address
    B) destination IP address
    C) source MAC address
    D) destination MAC address
    E) source and destination ports
2. To determine the metric values of the routing table, a protocol gathers information on the *failure rate of router links*. Then, the protocol is using the _____ factor to determine metric values.
    A) load
    B) reliability
    C) delay

    D) bandwidth

    E) throughput

3. If multiple entries in the routing table match a packet's destination IP address, the router ___.

    A) forwards the packet to the default gateway

    B) forwards the packet to the path with the longest match

    C) discards the packet

    D) forwards the packet to the first-matched path

    E) forwards the packet to the last-matched path

4. Entries (routes) of the routing table are divided into _____.

    A) directly connected routes, indirectly connected routes, and remotely connected routes

    B) directly connected routes, static routes, and remotely connected routes

    C) directly connected routes, static routes, and dynamic routes

    D) directly connected routes, dynamic routes, and remotely connected routes

    E) directly connected routes, indirectly connected routes, and dynamic routes

5. The _____ is a router port that relays IP packets of a host beyond the subnet boundary.

    A) default path

    B) direct route

    C) static route

    D) default gateway

    E) dynamic route

6. Border routers use _____ to exchange (or advertise) information needed to develop the routing table.

    A) Exterior Gateway Protocol (EGP)

    B) Routing Information Protocol (RIP)

    C) Open Shortest Path First (OSPF)

    D) Intermediate System to Intermediate System (IS –IS)

    E) Transmission Control Protocol (TCP)

7. Which routing table entry may NOT be a dynamic route?

Destination Subnetwork/Subnet Mask	Exit Port/Interface
A) 192.168.0.0/16	FastEthernet0/1
B) 130.0.0.0/8	FastEthernet0/0
C) 10.10.1.0/24	FastEthernet0/1
D) 192.192.0.0/10	Serial0/1
E) 0.0.0.0/0	Serial0/1

8. Which is a popular exterior gateway protocol?

    A) Intermediate System to Intermediate System (IS –IS)

    B) Open Shortest Path First (OSPF)

    C) Border Gateway Protocol (BGP)

    D) Routing Information Protocol (RIP)

    E) Enhanced Interior Gateway Routing Protocol (EIGRP)

9. How often does the router make the packet forwarding decision?

    A) Once for every packet that it receives.

    B) Once for a group of arriving packets with the same source and destination addresses.

    C) Once for a group of arriving packets with the same source address.

    D) Once for a group of arriving packets with the same destination address.

    E) Once for a group of arriving packets with the same source port number.

10. Which dynamic routing protocol is a good choice for a relatively small network?
    A) RIP
    B) BGP
    C) OSPF
    D) EIGRP
    E) IS-IS

11. Routers use the _____ to share status information necessary to update their routing table.
    A) IP protocol
    B) dynamic routing protocol
    C) address resolution protocol
    D) advertising protocol
    E) domain name protocol

12. Which describes a routing protocol-related technology CORRECTLY?
    A) To interior dynamic routing protocols, the *default gateway* of a subnet is equivalent to the border router address.
    B) The Border Gateway Protocol is an interior dynamic routing protocol.
    C) Routers rely on unicasting to advertise information necessary to update routing table entries.
    D) A university can have a number of internal routers that run the same interior gateway routing protocol.
    E) RIP, OSPF, and EIGRP are designed to help manual updates of the routing table.

13. When a router receives a packet with the following IP addresses, what should be the exit interface?
    [Source IP address: 171.56.73.25] [Destination IP address: 183.69.53.151]

(Routing Table)		
Network Address	Mask	Exit Interface
183.69.48.0	/20	S0/0/0
183.69.32.0	/19	S0/0/1
183.69.0.0	/18	Fa0/0
183.69.52.0	/22	Fa0/1
0.0.0.0	/0	S0/0/2

    A) S0/0/0
    B) S0/0/1
    C) Fa0/0
    D) Fa0/1
    E) S0/0/2

14. When a router receives a packet with the following IP addresses, what should be the exit interface?
    [Source IP address: 141.56.73.25] [Destination IP address: 200.100.150.140]

(Routing Table)		
Network Address	Subnet Mask	Exit Port
200.100.150.0	255.255.0.0.	S0/0/0
200.100.150.0	255.255.224.0	S0/0/1
200.100.150.0	255.255.128.0	Fa0/0

(Routing Table)		
Network Address	**Subnet Mask**	**Exit Port**
200.100.150.0	255.255.240.0	Fa0/1
0.0.0.0	0.0.0.0	S0/0/2

   A) S0/0/0
   B) S0/0/1
   C) Fa0/0
   D) Fa0/1
   E) S0/0/2

15. When using the metric value to break a tie between routing table entries, the router _____.
   A) selects the entry with the highest metric value
   B) selects the entry with the lowest metric value
   C) selects the entry with the latest update value
   D) selects the entry with the oldest update value
   E) selects the entry with the highest or the lowest value depending on the metric

16. What information is LEAST used to compute the metric value of a routing table?
   A) hop count to a destination
   B) bandwidth of a link
   C) network load of a link
   D) estimated delay of a link
   E) physical distance to the next router

17–18. Answer questions based on the hypothetical network in Figure 11.16.

17. Link-state protocols such as OSPF advertise link status information of a router to other routers. When R1 advertises link-state, information of how many links should be included?
   A) 1
   B) 2
   C) 3
   D) 4
   E) 5

18. Which may NOT be link information related to S0/0/0 (Link 1) of R1?
   A) Subnet address of the link
   B) Subnet mask of the link
   C) Type of the link (e.g., Ethernet)

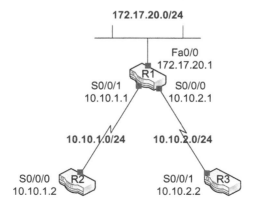

FIGURE 11.16 A hypothetical network

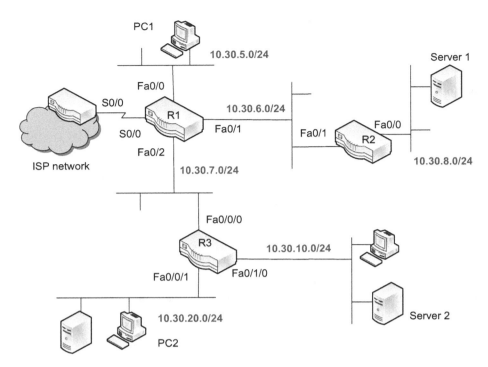

FIGURE 11.17   A hypothetical enterprise network

D) Transmission cost (metric) of the link
E) Operating system of the router
19–25. Answer questions based on the hypothetical enterprise network in Figure 11.17.

19. How many subnets do you see in the enterprise network? (Exclude the connection between R1 and the ISP router.)
   A) 4
   B) 5
   C) 6
   D) 7
   E) 8

20. Assume that there are three subnets in the enterprise network: 10.30.165.0/24, 10.30.145.0/24, and 10.30.185.0/24. The firm's network administrator decided to configure the border router R1 using a supernet that represents all three subnets. Which can be a supernet address and its subnet mask?
   A) 10.30.0.0/16
   B) 10.30.128.0/20
   C) 10.30.128.0/21
   D) 10.30.192.0/24
   E) 10.30.192.0/18

21. Which address can become the default gateway of PC2?
   A) 10.30.20.255
   B) 10.30.7.1
   C) IP address of R1's S0/0
   D) IP address of S0/0 of the ISP router
   E) 10.30.20.254

22. The following is Server 1's IP configuration:
    - IP address: 10.30.8.254
    - Subnet mask: 255.255.255.0
    - Default gateway: 10.30.6.254
      If PC2 pings Server 1, what should happen? Assume that all routing tables and IP addresses of router ports are correctly configured.
    A) The ping request is blocked by R3 and PC2 will not receive the ping response.
    B) The ping request is blocked by R2 and PC2 will not receive the ping response.
    C) The ping request is blocked by R1 and PC2 will not receive the ping response.
    D) The ping request is delivered to Server 1, but PC2 will not receive the ping response.
    E) The ping request is delivered to Server 1 and PC2 will receive the ping response.

23. The following is Server 2's IP configuration:
    - IP address: 10.30.10.254
    - Subnet mask: 255.255.255.0
    - Default gateway is not entered.
      If PC1 pings Server 2, what should happen? Assume that all routing tables and IP addresses of router ports are correctly configured.
    A) The ping request is blocked by R1 and PC1 will not receive the ping response.
    B) The ping request is blocked by R3 and PC1 will not receive the ping response.
    C) The ping request is delivered to Server 2, but PC1 will not receive the ping response.
    D) The ping request is delivered to Server 2 and PC1 will receive the ping response.
    E) PC1 does nothing.

24. If the following command is entered on a router's command prompt, what type of entry this statement creates in the routing table? (Assume that the command is issued to a Cisco router.)
    '#ip route 0.0.0.0 0.0.0.0 Serial0/0'
    A) directly connected route
    B) static route
    C) dynamic route based on RIP
    D) dynamic route based on OSPF
    E) It can create any of directly connected, static, or dynamic route.

25. Which information is NOT included in the OSPF advertisement from R3? (Think logically.)
    A) Fa0/0/0's network address and subnet mask
    B) Fa0/0/0's IP address
    C) Fa0/0/0's neighbor is R1
    D) Fa0/0/0's link is Ethernet
    E) Fa0/0/0's MAC address is 1A.B4.56.8A.36.9C

HANDS-ON EXERCISES

Exercise 11.1

Identify the autonomous system number(s) of the following companies and universities from such websites as *www.arin.net* and *spyse.com*: Apple, Google, Facebook, MIT, and Stanford University.

Exercise 11.2

Imagine a corporate LAN composed of six subnetworks interconnected by three routers.

a. Draw a network topology in which three routers interconnect six subnetworks. (There can be several solutions).

b. Choose a network address of the company.

c. Create six subnet addresses and subnet masks, and assign them to the network. Clearly indicate which router port (e.g., Fa0/0) connects to which subnet.

d. Construct routing tables of the three routers to enable inter-networking among host stations. The routing table should include three columns of *destination subnet*, *subnet mask*, and *exit port* only.

EXERCISE 11.3

1. Construct R2's routing table in Figure 11.5. The routing table should include the *destination subnet address*, *subnet mask*, *exit port*, *next-hop IP*, and *metric* (based on *hop count*) columns.

2. Answer the following questions.
   a. If R1 routes a packet from PC1 to Server, what is R1's next-hop address?
   b. If R2 routes a packet from PC2 to Server, what is R2's next-hop address?
   c. If R1 routes a packet from PC1 to Server, what is R1's exit port?
   d. If R2 routes a packet from Server to PC1, what is R2's exit port?
   e. If R2 routes a packet from Server to PC2, what is R2's next-hop address?
   f. If R2 routes a packet from Server to PC1, what is R2's next-hop address?

EXERCISE 11.4

Figure 11.18 is a hypothetical enterprise network in which three routers are interconnected by a high-speed switch.

1. How many subnetworks do you see in the enterprise network and what are the subnet addresses?
2. If R1 routes a packet from PC1 to Server1, what is R1's next-hop address?
3. If R2 routes a packet from PC2 to Server1, what is R2's next-hop address?
4. If R1 routes a packet from PC1 to PC2, what is R1's exit port?
5. If R3 routes a packet from Server1 to PC2, what is R3's exit port?
6. Construct routing tables of R2 and R3. The routing tables should include columns of the *destination network*, *subnet mask*, *exit port*, *next-hop IP*, and *hop count* as the metric. Hint: Below is the routing table of R1.

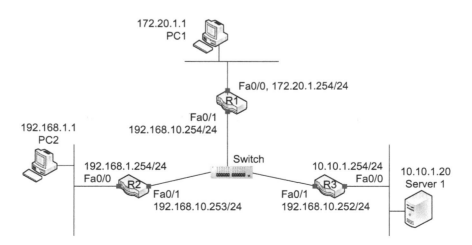

FIGURE 11.18 A hypothetical enterprise network

Destination network/subnet mask	Exit port/interface	Next-Hop IP	Metric
192.168.10.0/24	FastEthernet0/1	....	0
172.20.1.0/24	FastEthernet0/0	......	0
10.10.1.0/24	FastEthernet0/1	192.168.10.252	1
192.168.1.0/24	FastEthernet0/1	192.168.10.253	1

EXERCISE 11.5

1. Decide if the destination address, 100.50.30.10, of a packet matches the following routing table entries.

100.50.30.0/16	100.40.30.0/16	100.50.30.0/8	100.50.30.0/25
100.50.15.0/16	100.50.30.0/24	100.50.10.0/24	100.50.0.0/24
100.0.0.0/16	100.50.0.0/18	100.48.30.0/21	100.27.0.0/15

2. A router receives packets. What should be the exit port (interface) of each packet?
   a. Packet destination: 172.164.32.25

Subnet/mask	Exit port
172.164.30.0/21	S0/0/0
172.154.24.0/20	S0/0/1
173.140.21.0/7	Fa0/0
173.120.21.0/15	Fa0/1
0.0.0.0/0	S0/0/1

   b. Packet destination: 142.66.39.125

Subnet/mask	Exit port
142.64.130.0/16	S0/0/0
142.62.39.0/24	S0/0/1
142.140.21.0/7	Fa0/0
142.66.39.64/25	Fa0/1
0.0.0.0/0	S0/0/1

   c. Packet destination: 11.87.234.111

Subnet/mask	Exit port
11.87.234.60/27	S0/0/0
11.87.200.60/22	S0/0/1
11.85.234.60/15	Fa0/0
11.87.234.160/25	Fa0/1
0.0.0.0/0	S0/0/1

Exercise 11.6

Assume that you are configuring a Cisco router.

1. In Figure 11.4, what three commands are issued to create the directly connected route (172.20.2.0/24) on R1's routing table?
2. In Figure 11.6, how many directly connected routes should be entered into R1's routing table?
3. In Figure 11.6, what three commands are issued to create the directly connected route (192.168.10.0/24) on R1's routing table?

Exercise 11.7

1. Refer to Figure 11.13. What are commands you need to issue on R2, another Cisco router, so that the two routers (R1 and R2) begin to advertise status information based on RIP? Don't worry about the difference of the prompt [e.g., R1(config) vs. R1(config-router)].
2. Refer to Figure 11.16. What commands are issued on R1, R2, and R3 so that the three routers begin to advertise their status information based on RIP?

Exercise 11.8

The static PC routing table entries can be modified using commands including *route print*, *route add* and *route delete* as shown below. Keywords are in upper characters.

C:\>route **PRINT**
C:\>route **DELETE** *network*
C:\>route **ADD** *network* **MASK** *mask gateway-IP address*

For example, you can erase the default gateway in Figure 11.7 by issuing '*C:\>route DELETE 0.0.0.0*' Then, the first entry '*0.0.0.0 0.0.0.0 192.168.1.1 192.168.1.135*' will be removed from the routing table. Also, you can add the default route back with '*C:\>route ADD 0.0.0.0 MASK 0.0.0.0 192.168.1.1.*'

Now, you are repeating the process using your own computer.

1. At the command prompt, issue a ping request to a well-known portal site such as *www.yahoo. com* and see if there are responses. If there is no response, then try other sites until you come up with one that responds.
2. Bring up the routing table of your computer.
3. Delete the default route from the routing table (ensure to write down the original statement before its deletion). Use the *route print* command to confirm the removal of the default route.
4. After removing the default route, ping again the webserver identified in Step 1 and describe what happens. Explain why.
5. Now add the deleted default route back to the routing table. Use the *route print* command to confirm the addition.
6. After the addition, ping the webserver again and describe what happens.
7. Explain what you have learned from this.

Note: If you are using recent Windows versions, you may be alerted that '*The required operation requires elevation.*' This means that you can run the command with an administrator privilege. To do this, go to: ***All Programs > Accessories > right click Command Prompt and click Run as administrator***.

Exercise 11.9 (Challenge)

Mobile phones, as host devices/end nodes, have their own routing table similar to Figure 11.9, although it is not readily accessible. One way to see the table is to use a 'terminal emulator' app. Download an app of either Android or iPhone and display its routing table. Search the Internet for commands necessary to change the directory and display the routing table. Also, chances are that there are two routing tables: one when mobile data is active and the other (e.g., wlan0) when Wi-Fi is active.

Exercise 11.10 (Challenge)

Refer to Figure 11.19 and answer the following questions.

1. The list of permanent IP addresses and subnet masks available is given in the following table. Assign them to all user stations, servers, the printer, and router ports of the enterprise network.

Available IP ranges	Subnet masks
192.168.5.251 ~ 192.168.5.252	255.255.255.0
192.168.10.253 ~ 192.168.10.254	255.255.255.0
192.168.20.1 ~ 192.168.20.6	255.255.255.0
172.18.10.1 ~ 172.18.10.3	255.255.255.0
172.19.110.1 ~ 172.19.110.3	255.255.255.0

2. Once IP addresses and subnet masks are assigned, then identify default gateways of all hosts including workstations, servers, and the printer.
3. Based on the results, develop a routing table of R1, R2, R3, and R4. Each table should contain columns of the *destination subnet*, *subnet mask*, *exit port*, and *next-hop IP*. Also, add a default route to each routing table so that it enables the forwarding of IP packets to the Internet.

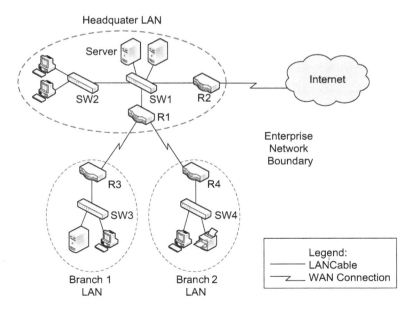

FIGURE 11.19 A hypothetical enterprise network

EXERCISE **11.11** (CHALLENGE)

The Green Tech Co's enterprise network in Figure 11.20 interconnects LANs in four business locations through several leased line WAN links.

1. What topology is used to interconnect the four routers?
2. How many subnets do you see in the enterprise network?
3. Assign adequate names to all router ports in use.
4. Assuming that there are 100 hosts that need an IP address in each business location, assign a subnet address and subnet mask to all subnetworks. Then allocate an IP address to each router port being connected. Use a private IP range for the subnetworks.
5. Once all subnetworks have their own subnet addresses, then each router should have a router table to route IP packets. Develop the routing table of each router that contains columns of the *destination network, subnet mask, exit port, next-hop IP,* and *hop count* as the metric.

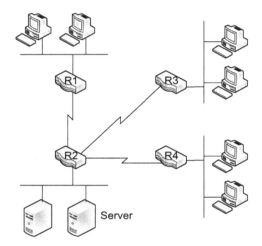

FIGURE 11.20   Enterprise network of Green Tech Co.

12 Wide Area Network

12.1 INTRODUCTION

The WAN link spans a state, a nation, or across nations, covering a large geographical region. Unlike the LAN installed by a business, university, or government organization, the WAN infrastructure is owned and maintained by carriers (or common carriers) in order to provide WAN link services to the general public. Common carriers include traditional telephone companies (or telcos), cable companies, and satellite service providers that offer various voice and data services to individuals and businesses.

WAN services offered by carriers are generally regulated by the government. In the US, for example, the *Federal Communications Commission* (FCC), as an independent agency of the US government, regulates carriers that offer interstate and international WAN services. These carriers have the right-of-way to install networks necessary to offer WAN services to clients. Remotely dispersed branch locations and mobile workers of an organization can reach each other through the carrier's WAN service.

With more carriers offering both voice and data WAN services, the traditional distinction between carriers and ISPs is becoming less meaningful as they are competing with each other to grow businesses. The WAN service is fee-based, in which service costs are decided by various factors including the standard technology utilized, connection speed, quality of service, and link distance. This chapter is to explain popular WAN services offered on the private infrastructure wholly owned by the carrier.

Aside from the 'private' WAN infrastructure of the carrier, the Internet that no single service provider has an exclusive ownership, is also a wildly popular platform for low-cost WAN connections. However, remind that the focus of this chapter is WAN services available from the private infrastructure, not the Internet.

12.1.1 LEARNING OBJECTIVES

The primary learning objectives of this chapter are to understand:

- Different scenarios of WAN link usage
- Principal components of WAN infrastructure
- Key WAN topologies and design considerations
- Layers of WAN technologies: physical and data link layers
- IP addressing for WAN links
- WAN access link services: leased lines and broadband services
- WAN layer 2 standards

12.2   WAN AND ENTERPRISE NETWORK

12.2.1   WAN Connection Scenarios

As structural entities of an organization are becoming more distributed (e.g., from local to national and global) and the business relationship (e.g., inter-firm partnerships, supply chains, and business outsourcing) gets more complicated, the demand for WAN connection services keeps growing to better manage intra- and inter-business communications and operations. Some of the prevalent situations where the WAN service (both private and public) becomes instrumental are portrayed in Figure 12.1.

a. A company has its main office and several branch offices across the nation or world. The company's distributed business locations and their local networks (LANs) are interconnected by WAN links available through a carrier's 'private' WAN infrastructure and the Internet.

b. Firms of a partnership (e.g., part suppliers, manufacturers, and wholesalers) may tie their networks over the WAN link so that they can electronically conduct business transactions. For instance, inter-firm database access and updates, inventory monitoring, product ordering, and invoicing over the WAN link can transform business processes cheaper, faster (e.g., real-time), and more accurate because of reduced manual engagement. They are important activities of supply chain management between partnership firms and, not surprisingly, the WAN link has become an artery of the practice.

c. Telecommuters working at home can access their corporate systems to conduct job-related functions such as file uploading and downloading, updating databases, and business communications. Their computers remotely connect to corporate systems over various broadband WAN technologies including DSL, Cable, and cellular.

d. Mobile workers including traveling salesmen and onsite customer service agents can access corporate systems to perform business tasks over WAN connections. Mobile workers may be in one location today but in another location tomorrow. Unlike those that stay unchanged (e.g., inter-LAN connections), WAN links for mobile workers are dynamically established and terminated as needed.

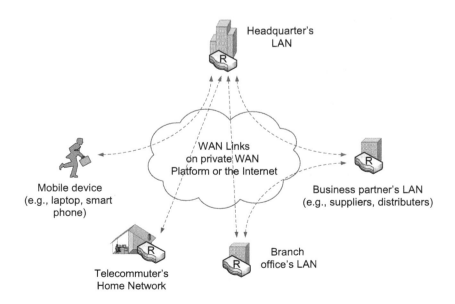

FIGURE 12.1   WAN links over the private platform or the Internet

12.2.2 SERVICE LEVEL AGREEMENT

The WAN connection scenarios in Figure 12.1 include both the private WAN service and the Internet-based WAN links. If a business client subscribes to the WAN service purely running on the carrier's private infrastructure, two parties generally exchange a formal *service level agreement* (SLA) that specifies service terms and conditions. Detailing the SLA is important to both parties because their expectations (e.g., service quality) do not necessarily coincide and disputes can occur regarding the service provision. Among agreed terms and conditions of the WAN service are:

- Data rate (speed)
- Latency (e.g., round-trip transmission delays) and how it is measured (e.g., average latency should be less than 90 milliseconds based on sample measurement)
- Acceptable error rates and how they are measured (e.g., average percentage of packets dropped by the carrier network based on sample measurement)
- Availability of network service and its calculation method (e.g., uptime of network should be at least 99.95%)
- Penalty provisions for service failures (e.g., compensation of service credits to clients)
- Details of scheduled/unscheduled maintenance
- Customer support options and service call procedure
- Service cancellation terms

12.2.3 CPE vs. SPF

The WAN link is formed by the *customer premises equipment* (CPE) that resides at a client site and the *service provider facility* (SPF) that enables WAN connectivity between remote client sites (see Table 12.1). The CPE contains such networking equipment as the modem, CSU/DSU, and router. The SPF includes: (1) Central Offices that are local ending points of a carrier's WAN backbone network; (2) local access lines that link CPEs to Central Offices; and (3) the WAN backbone that transports customers' data between Central Offices. These days, *Central Offices* and *Point of Presence* (POP), an access point to the Internet, are used interchangeably although they have distinct historical roots: the former for voice and the latter for data communications.

12.2.4 DEMARCATION POINT

The *demarcation point* is where CPE meets SPF. It is generally a cabling junction box (or system) located at the customer premises (both business and individual clients) and becomes a dividing point of network maintenance responsibility. At a business-occupied building, the *building entrance facility* (Chapter 13) becomes the demarcation point. At a house, the junction box is also called a *network interface device* (NID) and is generally attached to its outside wall so that a service technician can

---

TABLE 12.1
Building blocks of the WAN connection

Category	Equipment/facility
Customer premises equipment (CPE)	• Modem (e.g., dial-up, DSL, and Cable modem) • CSU/DSU (channel service unit/data service unit) • Router
Service provider facility (SPF)	• Central Office (CO) • Local access link • WAN backbone network

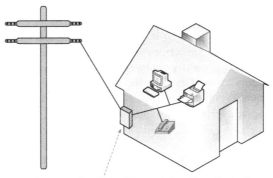

Demarcation Point (Network Interface Device)

FIGURE 12.2 Demarcation point at a house

access it as needed (see Figure 12.2). The WAN provider is responsible for all maintenance and repairs of cabling and equipment up to the demarcation point, and the owner of a house is liable for maintaining the integrity of wiring inside the house leading to the demarcation point.

12.2.5 WAN Design Considerations

A business organization experiences continuous changes (e.g., firm growth or downsizing, business process reengineering, business relocation, forming business partnerships, mergers, and acquisitions). This poses challenges, as the enterprise network, including WAN links, needs to be adapted to changing business requirements. The enterprise network of a company is thus a result of continuous planning, deployments, and adjustments over the time period. Firms may take different approaches in designing their WANs given that each topology has its own strengths and weaknesses. The WAN design of an enterprise, therefore, is contingent on a number of internal and external factors, including:

- Available resources (e.g., budget, internal IT staff)
- Cost assessment (e.g., the total cost of ownership)
- Required data rate of applications (e.g., emails, voice-over IP, and large-scale data backup)
- Required service quality (e.g., best effort service vs. guaranteed QoS for real-time and mission-critical applications)
- Necessary reliability of WAN links
- Scalability (e.g., future growth and expandability) of WAN links
- Importance of protecting data (e.g., data security and privacy)

12.3 LAYERS OF WAN STANDARDS

Similar to LAN standards (e.g., Ethernet and Wi-Fi), a carrier's WAN infrastructure primarily utilizes physical and data link layer technologies.

12.3.1 Physical Layer

The physical layer defines technical details relevant to data transmissions over the WAN link including standard ports, transmission speeds, signal strengths, and bit encoding mechanisms (see Section 1.10). WAN links subscribed by business and individual customers are considerably slower than LAN links. For example, the T-1 (1.54 Mbps) and T-3 that have been popular WAN links are much slower than prevalent LAN standards such as Fast Ethernet (100 Mbps), Gigabit Ethernet (1 Gbps), and 10 Gigabit Ethernet (10 Gbps). However, as WAN links are transporting more time-sensitive and bandwidth-consuming traffic (e.g., multimedia), the demand for Quality of Service (QoS) and higher throughputs is growing.

There are several physical layer standards developed for WAN services including T-carrier and E-carrier, Synchronous Optical Network (SONET), Digital Subscriber Line (DSL), and wireless WANs such as cellular and satellite technologies.

12.3.2 DATA LINK LAYER

The layer is responsible for such functions as addressing, virtual circuit management, and packet encapsulation within the frame. WAN standards in the data link layer support either *circuit switching* or *packet switching*.

12.3.2.1 Circuit Switching

With circuit switching, an end-to-end circuit is created beforehand between the source and destination nodes (or local sites) with certain *bandwidth reserved* for the circuit. For example, imagine the situation in which a car is given a highway lane exclusively reserved for it between Boston and New York. The dedicated lane is the same as the circuit in networking. The end-to-end circuit is established via multiple high-speed WAN switches, and the circuit capacity is exclusively used only by the two communicating parties during the engagement period (e.g., a conference call). The leased line service relies on circuit switching, and *Point-to-Point* (PPP) is a popular data link layer standard for leased lines.

12.3.2.2 Packet Switching

Definition: With packet switching, data are packaged as discrete units and physically transported 'independently' from other units. With this approach, two communicating parties (or sites) do not need reserved capacity as in circuit switching. Signals carrying packets just take advantage of available network space in a more dynamic fashion. For that reason, packets traveling between two sites do not need to take the same delivery path along the way. Packets from the same source are reassembled once they have arrived at the destination. This technology was initially developed for the Internet to physically transport IP packets and was subsequently adopted by WAN carriers.

Advantages: Packet switching has several advantages. Most notably, it utilizes network capacity much more effectively than circuit switching. With the on-demand use of network capacity, the carrier's WAN infrastructure can be dynamically shared by more customers. It resembles the situation in which a highway lane between Boston and New York is shared by many automobiles, using the lane capacity much more effectively. *The packet switched data network* (PSDN) is a carrier's WAN platform that moves clients' voice/data using the packet switching technology. The PSDN is frequently shown to clients as a 'cloud', as they are not responsible for its operation and maintenance.

Virtual circuits: These days, most PSDNs take advantage of *virtual circuits* for data transmissions. The *virtual circuit* represents a *logical* end-to-end path pre-determined between two remote client sites. It, therefore, does not dedicate physical capacity between two distant locations as circuit switching does, but only pre-determines the delivery path formed through high-speed WAN switches. Hence, the virtual circuit is technically analogous to LAN switching for which the delivery path of frames between any two hosts is determined in advance.

Carrier Ethernet and Multi-Protocol Label Switching (MPLS) have been well-received data link layer standards for PSDN. *Frame-Relay* and *Asynchronous Transfer Mode* (ATM) are other PSDN standards although their acceptance has been dwindling. Table 12.2 summarizes primary WAN technologies at layer 1 and layer 2.

TABLE 12.2
Popular WAN standards

Layer	Leased lines	Packet Switched Data Network (PSDN)
Data Link (Layer 2)	• Point-to-Point (PPP)	• Carrier Ethernet • Multi-Protocol Label Switching • Asynchronous Transfer Mode • Frame-Relay
Physical (Layer 1)	• T-carrier and E-carrier (e.g., T-1/E-1, T-3/E-3) • Synchronous Optical Network (SONET) • Digital Subscriber Line (DSL) • Broadband wireless (e.g., WiMax, Cellular)	

12.3.3 COMPARISON: WAN VS. LAN

It is worthwhile to highlight differences between LAN and WAN standards. Each LAN standard defines both data link (e.g., media access methods, frame construction) and physical layer (e.g., speeds, signaling, cabling) details. For instance, Fast Ethernet specifies the transmission speed (e.g., 100 Mbps), available cables (e.g., twisted pairs, optical fibers), each cable's required physical specs (e.g., maximum segment distance, number of twists per foot), and transmission technologies (e.g., encoding methods). Meanwhile, WAN standards generally do not require that a particular data link standard be tied to one or more physical layer standards. For example, T-carrier/E-carrier circuits at the physical layer are used to carry various data link layer frames including those of Frame Relay, ATM, and PPP.

Additionally, to optimize network performance and reduce operational costs, carriers utilize WAN data link standards in a flexible manner (e.g., encapsulation of one data link frame into another data link frame), which can be quite confusing to readers. For example, border routers at customer sites can be configured to transport Frame-Relay frames over T-1, but the carrier's backbone network may be running on ATM as another data link standard. Transporting Frame-Relay frames between two remote client sites through the ATM backbone requires encapsulation of Frame-Relay frames within ATM frames. Putting one frame within another frame in order to make the most of two different WAN standards does not happen in the LAN environment.

Figure 12.3 demonstrates connectivity of Ethernet LANs and Frame Relay WAN, which allows IP packet exchanges between two end stations. In that scenario, the border router should support

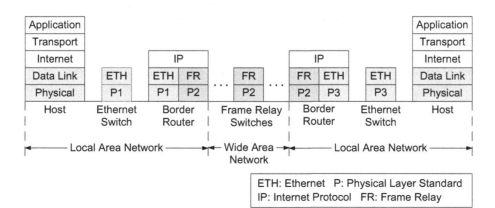

FIGURE 12.3 LAN vs. WAN standard layers

both Ethernet and Frame Relay data link standards for necessary frame translation. In other words, the border router converts Ethernet frames arriving at its LAN port into Frame Relay frames and releases them through a WAN (or serial) port. Of course, both the Ethernet and Frame Relay frames contain the same IP packets produced by the source host computer. On arrival at the destination LAN, the Frame Relay frames are translated back into the Ethernet frames for delivery to the destination host. Remember that physical layer technologies used to transport WAN and LAN frames differ as well.

12.4 IP ADDRESSING FOR WAN LINKS

The WAN links of an enterprise network interconnect geographically dispersed LANs, each with one or more subnetworks. Imagine an enterprise network with offices in three different locations and the border routers from three sites exchange IP packets through a carrier's WAN links that are either leased lines or PSDN (not the Internet). Then, each WAN link between two remote border routers becomes a subnet with its own subnet address and the routers' WAN ports are configured with IP addresses pertaining to the subnet. This means that, in Figure 12.4, there are three subnets created by the three WAN links, and each subnet has two permanent IP addresses assigned to the connecting routers' WAN ports.

As for the IP addressing of leased lines or PSDN-based WAN links, the company can choose either public IPs or private IPs because the links, although subscribed from a carrier, are an integral part of its enterprise network. Many firms opt for private IPs when the WAN link runs on a common carrier's network to enjoy the benefits of private IP assignment such as:

- Improved security (e.g., invisible internal nodes)
- Flexibility in internal IP allocations (e.g., availability of large IP space)
- Consistency in internal IP allocations (e.g., IP addresses of internal hosts are not affected when the firm changes its WAN carrier)

12.4.1 LEASED LINES

If the border router connects to multiple leased lines, a router port (interface) with an IP address is assigned to each leased line. For example, Figure 12.4 shows that R1 of the main office is using two different ports S0/0/0 (10.10.10.1/24) and S0/0/1 (172.16.10.1/24) for two separate leased lines. In this setup, each leased line connection becomes a subnet. Figure 12.4 displays three subnets with

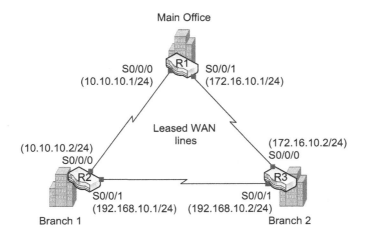

FIGURE 12.4 IP addressing on leased lines

subnet addresses of 10.10.10.0/24, 172.16.10.0/24, and 192.168.10.0/24. Note that all three subnets are on private IP ranges.

12.4.2 PACKET SWITCHED DATA NETWORK (PSDN)

When WAN links are through the PSDN cloud, the border router at a client site needs just one physical link to the carrier network to connect several remote locations through as many virtual circuits. For example, Figure 12.5 shows that R1 just needs one WAN link (e.g., generally a leased line) to the PSDN cloud to exchange packets with R2 and R3 rather than two separate WAN links as in Figure 12.4. Instead, the R1's single physical link attached to the WAN interface S0/0/0 should carry packets to R2 and R3 through the use of virtual circuits. Two different IP addressing approaches are possible to enable this:

1. Each WAN link (e.g., R1–R2) between two locations becomes a single subnet
2. All WAN links (i.e., R1–R2, R1–R3, and R2–R3) are assigned to a single subnet.

The two different addressing approaches are explained next.

12.4.2.1 One Subnet between Two Locations

This approach creates a dedicated subnet address between two locations (or two border routers). R1's S0/0/0, therefore, connects to two separate subnets, one to R2 and one to R3. It was explained that the router port is normally tied to a single subnet. Linking multiple subnets to one physical router port needs the definition of *sub-interfaces*, each with a unique IP address (revisit Section 7.11.2). Remember that, while the ordinary port/interface (e.g., S0/0/0) is a physical entity, the sub-interface does not physically exist but is *logically* defined by a router's operating system. Once defined, the sub-interface acts just like an ordinary router interface/port.

For example, Figure 12.5 shows that R1 at the main office location defines two sub-interfaces (let's say S0/0/0.10 and S0/0/0.20) under the physical interface S0/0/0. Each sub-interface has its corresponding IP address, 10.10.10.1/24 and 172.16.10.1/24, belonging to two different subnets. Then, the two sub-interfaces are assigned to the two virtual circuits (i.e., VC1 and VC3) respectively.

The result is the creation of a mapping table for R1 as Table 12.3. The table can be created either automatically or manually and stored on R1's memory. Remember that the mapping table includes the IP addresses of *destination border routers*. Also, keep in mind that a virtual circuit is

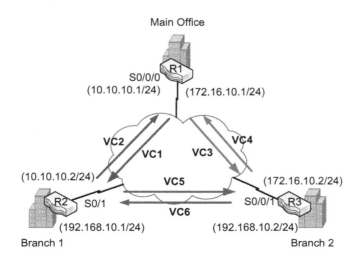

FIGURE 12.5 IP addressing: One subnet between two locations

TABLE 12.3

IP address-to-VC mapping table of R1

IP address of destination routers	Virtual circuit identifier	Exit interface (or sub-interface)
10.10.10.2 (to Branch1)	VC1	S0/0/0.10
172.16.10.2 (to Branch2)	VC3	S0/0/0.20

unidirectional and therefore VC1 and VC3 are used for delivering frames from R1 to R2 and from R1 to R3 respectively, but not reverse directions. This means that the packet delivery from R2 to R1 requires a separate virtual circuit (i.e., V2). R1's table, therefore, keeps only VC1 and VC3 that R1 needs to know to dispatch packets over the WAN links, but does not need to know about VC2, VC4, VC5, and VC6.

To transport an IP packet (e.g., from R1 to R2), R1 refers to the mapping table to find the corresponding virtual circuit (VC1) and encapsulates the IP packet within a data link frame that contains VC1 as the virtual circuit ID (For easier comprehension, imagine that the virtual circuit ID for WANs is equivalent to the MAC address for LANs). The data link frame is released through the exit port of S0/0/0.10, and therefore physically S0/0/0. On receiving the frame, the carrier's PSDN cloud delivers the WAN frame purely based on the virtual circuit information.

So, basically, what the mapping table in Table 12.3 does on WAN connections (i.e., the mapping between VC identifiers and IP addresses) is identical to what the ARP table does on LANs (i.e., the mapping between MAC and IP addresses).

12.4.2.2 One Subnet for All Locations

As another approach, all WAN links of an enterprise can belong to one subnet address. In this setup, each border router's WAN port just needs one IP address belonging to the same subnet. Figure 12.6 demonstrates a scenario in which all three router ports use IP addresses (172.16.10.1/24, 172.16.10.2/24, and 172.16.10.3/24) of one subnet (172.16.10.0/24). The packet delivery process is identical to the previous case.

To transport an IP packet from a site (e.g., R1) to another site (e.g., R2), for example, R1 refers to its mapping table to find the corresponding virtual circuit (VC1) and encapsulates the IP packet within a data link frame that contains VC1 as the virtual circuit ID. The data link frame is released via the exit port of S0/0/0.

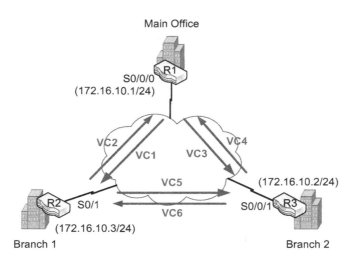

FIGURE 12.6 IP addressing: One subnet for all locations

With two different options available for IP addressing, the question remains, which is a better choice? In a nutshell, the decision should be based on the assessment of the business context and planned WAN link usage. For example, the choice has implications for network security. By having separated subnets as in Figure 12.5, accessibility from one location to other locations can be better controlled. On the other hand, let's assume the situation where frequent broadcasting or multicasting of IP packets between remote locations is necessary. Then, having one subnet for all remote connections makes the job easier.

12.5   PHYSICAL LAYER OPTIONS: LEASED LINES

This section explains physical layer options available to access WAN services. They include *leased lines, Digital Subscriber Lines (DSL), Cable*, and *broadband wireless*. Among the various options, popular leased line technologies are explained here.

12.5.1   LEASE LINE USAGES

The leased line service available from a carrier results in a point-to-point link with dedicated link capacity. There are two main usages of the leased line link.

a. The end-to-end leased line connection between two distant client sites through a carrier network (see Figure 12.4): This end-to-end connection is through the *local loops* that link client sites to the carrier's Central Office (CO) and the carrier's *trunk links* that provide the client with guaranteed channel capacity. (Although not shown in Figure 12.4, the leased lines go through Central Offices.)
b. The local link between a client site and a carrier's Central Office (see Figures 12.5 and 12.6): The local leased line is intended to provide a client with access to the carrier's PSDN platform whose capacity is shared by many customers.

Subscribers of the leased line pay for the link capacity committed by the WAN provider regardless of its usage level. With the dedicated capacity, leased lines pose no such quality problems as packet losses, packet delays, and call dropping (for voice communications). There are many situations where the end-to-end leased line is well justified despite the relatively high cost. This is especially so when packets are highly time-sensitive and mission-critical, demanding guaranteed performance in delivery. For instance, imagine financial networks or online gaming networks that demand real-time or near-real-time relay of traffic. The companies simply cannot risk non-dedicated WAN link capacity. T-carrier/E-carrier and SONET/SDH are two popular leased line technologies.

12.5.2   T-CARRIER/E-CARRIER

The T-carrier service is offered according to the *digital signal* (DS) speed hierarchy (see Chapter 13). Although introduced to support digitized voice communications initially, it is widely used for both voice and data these days. There are two different leased line standards: (1) T-carrier based on the North American digital speed hierarchy, and (2) E-carrier based on the international digital speed hierarchy from ITU-T (*International Telecommunication Union – Telecommunication Standardization Sector*). Their channel speeds are summarized in Table 12.4 only for information.

12.5.2.1   T-1 and T-3 Circuits

As one of the most popular leased line services, T-1 is designed to transport data in the DS1 (1.54 Mbps) speed, which represents 24 digital voice channels of 64 kbps (DS0). Voice and data traffic from 24 channels are combined (or multiplexed) using *Time Division Multiplexing* (TDM) for transmission (see Chapter 13). With full-duplex capacity, one T-1 circuit sends and receives data at 1.54

TABLE 12.4
Leased line speed hierarchies

North American hierarchy	Digital data rate	International (ITU) hierarchy	Digital data rate
T-1	1.5 Mbps	E-1	2.0 Mbps
T-1C	3.1 Mbps	E-2	8.4 Mbps
T-2	6.3 Mbps	E-3	34.3 Mbps
T-3	44.7 Mbps	E-4	139.2 Mbps
T-4	274.1 Mbps	E-5	465.1 Mbps

Mbps in both directions. Channel usage may be voice only, data only, or a combination of voice and data. T-1 is available on both UTP and optical fiber, although UTP tends to be a preferred choice. Service providers also offer *Fractional T-1* in increments of 64 kbps such as 256 kbps and 384 kbps for customers who need lower throughput at a reduced price.

As another popular leased line option, the T-3 circuit delivers the DS3 speed of 44.7 Mbps (28 T-1 channels combined) generally on the fiber-optic cable. Instead of the T-carrier, most international countries adopted the E-carrier for the leased line service. The E-1 channel at the bottom of the E-carrier hierarchy supports 2.0 Mbps for each direction, equating to the multiplexing of 30 DS0 channels.

12.5.3 SONET/SDH

SONET/SDH is intended for high-speed leased line services on optical fiber. The SONET standard is used in North America and its sibling adopted as the international standard is SDH. The SONET speeds are defined by the *optical carrier* (OC) speed hierarchy (see Chapter 13) with the base speed of 51.84 Mbps for OC-1.

SDH's data rate is based on the *Synchronous Transport Module* (or STM) speed hierarchy. The base data rate for STM-1 is 156 Mbps (equivalent to OC-3). Just as with T-carrier/E-carrier, the SONET/SDH technologies are defined in the physical layer. SONET/SDH uses the so-called *Dense Wave Division Multiplexing*, a type of Frequency Division Multiplexing technology, to produce a bigger pipe by multiplexing lower-speed channels.

Although available as a leased line service for business clients, SONET/SDH is widely adopted by carriers to define the bandwidth of their backbone networks to which business customers connect via such lines as T-1 or T-3. The SONET infrastructure generally relies on the dual-ring architecture to improve fault-tolerance so that the network can quickly restore even if the primary ring fails. The *Add-Drop Multiplexer* (ADM) is a device that inserts and removes traffic to/from the SONET ring.

Figure 12.7 demonstrates a SONET architecture that has two SONET rings coupled at the carrier's Central Office: the backbone ring that interconnects access rings and the access ring that provides an entry to the backbone ring from customer sites. The figure displays that, while the access ring's speed runs at 2.5 Gbps (OC-48), the backbone ring has a higher bandwidth such as 10 Gbps (OC-192).

Selected digital circuit speeds of leased lines and their preferred cabling options are summarized in Table 12.5.

12.6 DATA LINK STANDARD: LEASED LINES

Several data link layer protocols have been in use to transport IP packets over the leased line, and *Point-to-Point Protocol* (PPP) has been a popular choice. As explained, the leased line standard in the physical layer (e.g., T-3) is generally not tied to any particular data link protocol. In other words,

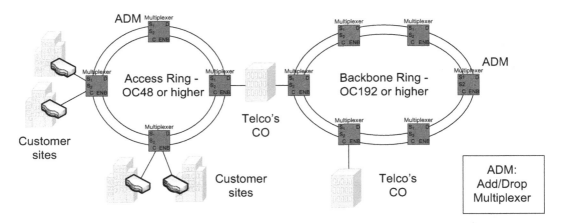

FIGURE 12.7   A demonstration of SONET's ring architecture

TABLE 12.5
Popular leased line options

Standards	Channel speed (bandwidth)	Popular cabling
T-1/E-1	1.54 Mbps/2.04 Mbps	UTP
Bonded T-1	Multiple T-1 lines combined	UTP
T-3/E-3	44.7 Mbps/34 Mbps	Optical fiber
SONET/SDH	Varies (e.g., 51.8 Mbps, 156 Mbps)	Optical fiber

the PPP frame with an IP packet inside can be transported by different physical layer technologies including T-carrier/E-carrier and DSL.

12.6.1 PPP FRAME STRUCTURE

The general structure of the PPP frame is shown in Figure 12.8.
    The function of each information field is summarized as follows:

- *Flag* bits, 01111110, mark the beginning of a PPP frame.
- The *Address* field becomes meaningless for the point-to-point link (as there is only one possible destination) and communicating devices fill it with all 1s.
- The *Control* field plays little role and is filled with the value of 00000011.
- The *Protocol* field identifies the protocol (e.g., IP) included in the *Information* field.
- The *Information* field contains an IP packet from the Internet layer. Its size varies and generally runs up to 1500 bytes.
- The *FCS* (*Frame Check Sequence*) field carries an error detection code.

Flag	Address	Control	Protocol	Information	FCS
8 bits	8 bits	8 bits	16 bits	Variable	16/32 bits

FIGURE 12.8   PPP frame structure

12.6.2   ROUTER AUTHENTICATION

PPP has several features designed to maintain the performance and reliability of a WAN link. These include monitoring of link quality, data compression for effective use of available bandwidth, and peer router authentication. Among them, *router authentication* as a measure to maintain network security is briefly explained here.

Assuming that border routers at two remotely distanced customer sites are already configured with the same username and password, they can authenticate each other prior to exchanging data frames. This is an important function as more networks are exposed to security risks today. For router authentication, the *Challenge Handshake Authentication Protocol* (CHAP) is used.

12.6.2.1   CHAP

As shown in Figure 12.9, CHAP takes three steps for the process. On receiving a challenge text from a remote router, the local router produces a hash value based on the combination of the pre-configured password and the challenge text. The hash value thus produced is sent back to the challenger. On receiving the hash value, the remote router computes its own hash value using the challenge text and its own pre-configured password. If they match, then the local router is authenticated and allowed for WAN connectivity.

12.6.3   EXAMPLE: ENABLING PPP ON CISCO ROUTER

Figure 12.10 displays two routers (R1 and R2) connecting through the T-3 lease line. Assuming that each router is already set up with the same access password, the point-to-point protocol (PPP) is activated on *Serial0/0/1* by issuing the following commands to R1 and R2.

R1(config)#**interface serial 0/0/1**	#	At R1, choose the Serial0/0/1 interface.
R1(config-if)#**encapsulation ppp**	#	Instruct R1 to use the PPP frame to encapsulate IP packets.
R1(config-if)#**ppp authentication CHAP**	#	Enable router authentication using CHAP.

These commands are repeated on R2. Once complete on both R1 and R2, all IP packets exchanged between them are encapsulated in the PPP frame. Also, router authentication based on CHAP is performed prior to data exchange.

12.7   DATA LINK STANDARDS: PSDN

The leased line service is highly reliable because of the dedicated circuit capacity between two locations. However, when the number of remote sites to be interconnected grows and the network topology of an organization becomes more complex, creating WAN links of an enterprise network relying

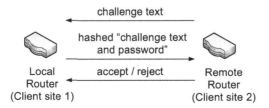

FIGURE 12.9   Router authentication with CHAP

FIGURE 12.10   Using PPP frames on T-3 leased lines

exclusively on the leased line becomes costly. Besides the leased line, carriers also offer WAN services using their own PSDN infrastructure that takes advantage of the packet switching technology. The service paradigm of PSDN is fundamentally different from that of the leased line because, in PSDN, the available capacity of the carrier's WAN platform is dynamically shared (rather than dedicated) among clients, significantly lowering the service cost.

12.7.1   Two Segments of a PSDN-Based WAN Link

The PSDN-based WAN link that connects two distant customer sites is composed of two network segments: local access links and the PSDN backbone cloud. The PSDN backbone is presented as a cloud because the carrier fully controls its operation and maintenance, making it virtually transparent to business customers. PSDN customers generally use leased lines to reach the carrier's Central Office (CO), an entry point to the PSDN cloud. The cloud's network capacity is, therefore, shared by WAN service users. Figure 12.11 offers a general view of the 'inside cloud' in which many high-speed WAN switches (or routers) are interconnected to become the backbone network and a customer site connects to the backbone by linking its border router to a router of a Central Office.

12.7.2   PSDN Attributes

12.7.2.1   Shared Capacity

With capacity sharing, more clients can be served using the same network capacity. As an example, think of the following scenario in which 1.54 Mbps, equivalent to T-1 capacity, can serve 24 dedicated data sources concurrently with each source transmitting at 64 kbps. When the same 24

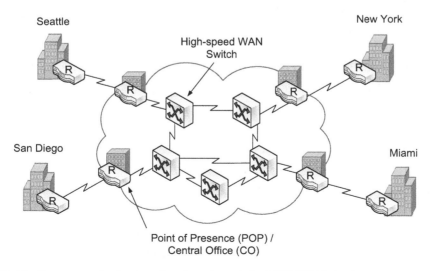

FIGURE 12.11   Interconnecting business locations through the PSDN WAN cloud

channels are dynamically allocated, more than 40 different data sources can be served because chances are that not all connected user systems transmit data simultaneously (Refer to *Statistical Time Division Multiplexing* in Chapter 13 as a related concept). The shared usage of available capacity lowers the cost of WAN services.

12.7.2.2 Customizability of Subscribed Speeds

PSDN is more flexible than leased lines in meeting customer demands. With the leased line service, the bandwidth available to clients is generally in the increment of 64 kbps (one voice call capacity). However, with PSDN, the increment can be much smaller than 64 kbps, offering better customization of client needs. For example, a business client may want a WAN link of 30 kbps between its two branch locations. With a leased line, however, Fractional T-1 at 64 kbps or 128 kbps may be the closest speed available from a carrier. When PSDN is chosen instead, a carrier can offer a much smaller increment such as 4 kbps, which results in significant cost savings for clients.

12.7.2.3 Support for Data and Voice

With non-dedicated capacity for WAN links, PSDN was originally designed for data rather than voice that cannot afford transmission delays. However, with technology maturation, more businesses are using PSDN for voice communications as well. That is, telephone calls and faxed documents are digitized and packaged in frames for delivery.

This offers at least two significant benefits. It is a cost-effective solution compared to the traditional voice service offered on the carrier's *Public Switched Telephone Network* (PSTN) that adopts more expensive circuit switching technology. An organization does not need to maintain two separate voice and data networks and equipment. Their convergence in the corporate network curtails costs associated with operation and maintenance, subscription of WAN connections, and hiring of specialized IT skills.

12.7.2.4 Frame Multiplexing

The PSDN cloud of a carrier consists of high-speed WAN switches that interconnect trunk lines. These switches are arranged in a mesh to have redundant paths between user locations. WAN frames, each containing an IP packet, are *multiplexed* (or bundled together) at Central Offices and transported over the cloud's trunk links.

12.7.2.5 Unreliable Transmissions

PSDN generally depends on the *unreliable* transmission in the data link. That is, there is no error control during packet delivery. The WAN cloud can detect faulty frames using the *Frame Check Sequence* (FCS) error detection code and drop them from the network. The correction of transmission errors, however, is left to host stations (i.e., TCP of the transport layer). Delivering IP packets in an unreliable manner results in cost savings of WAN services. Besides, the PSDN service is generally full-duplex (simultaneous flow of packets in both directions) and symmetric (identical transmission speeds in both directions).

12.7.2.6 Use of Virtual Circuits

PSDN relies on the virtual circuit, a logically defined delivery path, to transport frames between remote locations. The virtual circuit is therefore different from the leased line's physical circuit that is a dedicated channel capacity between two ending points.

There are two virtual circuit types: *permanent virtual circuits* (PVCs) and *switched virtual circuits* (SVCs). With the PVC, once a client's virtual circuit is configured on WAN switches by the carrier, it remains unchanged, lasting months or years. Meanwhile, the SVC is transient as it is dynamically decided in the beginning of a communication session and lasts only until the session ends. For practical reasons (e.g., easy to maintain, less process burden on WAN switches), carriers use PVCs these days. Each PSDN service uses its own unique naming of the permanent virtual circuit. For example, it is called *data link connection identifier* in Frame Relay and *virtual path identifier/virtual channel identifier* in ATM.

12.7.2.7   Use of WAN Switch Table

The virtual circuit (VC) identifier between the two remote sites of a business client is manually configured on the WAN switches of the PSDN cloud. Also, the business client adds the same VC identifier to its own border router that connects to the PSDN cloud. Then, all frames originating from the client's premise carry the pre-configured VC identifier in the frame header. The router at the customer premise produces WAN frames, each encapsulating an IP packet. WAN switches (or routers) in the cloud forward the frames purely based on the VC identifier. In Section 12.8, the virtual circuit mechanism is explained in more detail based on the Frame Relay service, as the mechanism is similar to other PSDN services.

12.7.2.8   Access Link Speeds

As stated, the access links between customer premises and Central Offices are primarily leased lines such as T-1/E-1 and T-3/E-3. The access link should be faster than the contracted WAN throughput in order to fully capitalize on the VC's bandwidth. Also, if a local client site sets up multiple PVCs with remote locations, its access link to the WAN cloud should have enough bandwidth to allow simultaneous flows of WAN frames through the PVCs.

Next, major PSDN technologies including Frame Relay, ATM, Carrier Ethernet, and MPLS are explained. *Currently, Carrier Ethernet, and MPLS are the two most popular WAN services in the US; however, countries differ in their popularity.*

12.8   FRAME RELAY

12.8.1   GENERAL CHARACTERISTICS

Frame Relay used to be a popular PSDN service as it satisfies the speed range most enterprises demand at a competitive price. It, however, has lost its market to MPLS and Carrier Ethernet. Its technical details are explained *to demonstrate how virtual circuits work.* Frame Relay is characterized by the use of *permanent virtual circuits* between client sites; *low overhead* (simple header structure) and efficient frame delivery; and *unreliability*, as there is no acknowledgement from WAN switch nodes when a frame is lost or dropped.

12.8.2   FRAME STRUCTURE

Frame Relay accepts an IP packet from the internet layer, encapsulates it, and passes the frame down to the physical layer for delivery. As in Figure 12.12, the frame has a lean structure because Frame Relay is designed to minimize network overhead in exchange for low service cost to customers. Among the frame fields, Flags (01111110 bits), FCS (detection of transmission errors), and Data fields perform functions identical to other protocols. The address field contains the *data link connection identifier* (DLCI), a virtual circuit identifier.

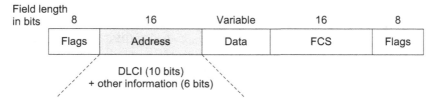

FIGURE 12.12   The frame structure of Frame Relay

12.8.3   DATA LINK CONNECTION IDENTIFIER (DLCI)

A particular DLCI is used to transport Frame Relay frames 'over a single physical link' between two neighboring network nodes. In other words, although the virtual circuit between two remote client locations can pass through any number of WAN switches in the cloud, the DLCI is only *locally significant*, meaning that a unique DLCI is assigned to a direct connection between any two nodes. The DLCI of a frame is, therefore, changed whenever it passes through a carrier's WAN switch. As a result, an end-to-end *permanent virtual circuit* is composed of multiple DLCIs.

12.8.3.1   How DLCI Works

To illustrate how DLCIs are used to form an end-to-end virtual circuit, an example is presented in Figure 12.13 in which a permanent virtual circuit is established between two remote routers of a company: Houston main office (*A*) and Toronto branch location (*E*). Assume that a frame is sent from *A* to *E*, and the pre-established virtual circuit enables frame forwarding through three WAN switches, *B*, *C*, and *D*. The router *A*'s and *E*'s S0/0/1 port is assigned DLCI 101 and 210 respectively, and four different DLCIs (i.e., 101, 203, 301, and 210) form the end-to-end virtual circuit. It can be seen that each physical link uses a unique DLCI (therefore, locally significant). For example, DLCI 101 is for the link between *A* and *B*, DLCI 203 for the link between *B* and *C*, and so on, and the DLCIs are entered into the cloud's WAN switches.

12.8.3.2   FR Switch Table

Each WAN switch in the cloud maintains a switch table just as the LAN switch has its own switch table. To enable frame forwarding based on the virtual circuit, the carrier adds DLCIs on WAN switches. The structure of the WAN switch table is explained based on Switch B in Figure 12.13. The switch table contains four different columns: incoming port#, incoming DLCI#, outgoing port#, and outgoing DLCI#. The switch table's general structure is demonstrated in Table 12.6.

The first entry of Table 12.6 means that if a frame with DLCI 101 arrives at port#0 of Switch B, the switch changes the frame's DLCI value to 203 and then sends it out through port#2. The second

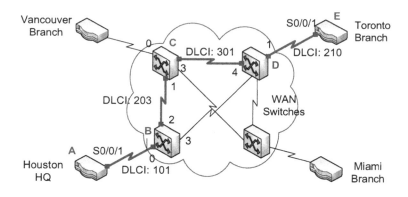

Nodes	Arrival		Departure		
	DLCI	Port (Interface)	DLCI	Port (Interface)	
A			101	S0/0/1	
B	101	0	203	2	
C	203	1	301	3	
D	301	4	210	1	
E	210	S0/1			

Summary of DLCI changes within the virtual circuit from A through E router

Source DLCI: 101
Destination DLCI: 210

FIGURE 12.13   Change of DLCIs from router A to router E

TABLE 12.6
Switch table entries (Switch B of Figure 12.13)

Incoming port #	Incoming DLCI #	Outgoing port #	Outgoing DLCI #
0	101	2	203
2	203	0	101
...	...	...	...

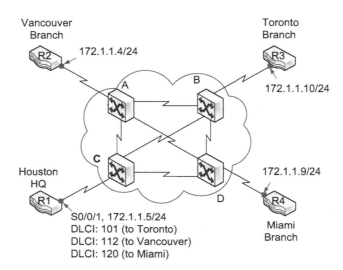

FIGURE 12.14 A physical circuit with three virtual circuits

entry enables frame forwarding in the reverse direction. The two entries in Switch B enable frame delivery following the bidirectional virtual circuit established between the Houston and Toronto offices.

12.8.3.3 Multiple VCs and DLCIs

The access line that connects a customer's local router to the Frame Relay network can carry multiple permanent virtual circuits (PVCs), each with a unique DLCI number. For instance, a company (headquartered in Houston) with three branch offices (Vancouver, Toronto, and Miami) can set up three PVCs from the main office to branch locations. In this case, Figure 12.14 shows three virtual circuit numbers (101, 112, and 120) assigned to the router port S0/0/1 at the Houston location. DLCI 101 is for the virtual circuit to Toronto; DLCI 112 to Vancouver; and DLCI 120 to Miami.

12.9 ASYNCHRONOUS TRANSFER MODE (ATM)

12.9.1 Background

ATM is another well-known data link layer standard for WAN services. ATM supports higher data rates than Frame Relay. The ATM network's bandwidth is specified in terms of the optical carrier (OC) hierarchy that has a base speed of about 52Mbps. With its high-speed connectivity, the ATM technology has been largely adopted by the carrier's backbone network. Figure 12.15, for example,

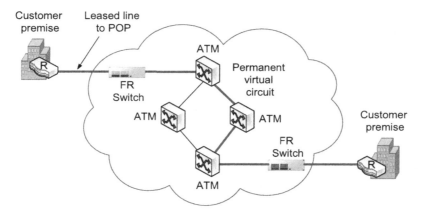

FIGURE 12.15   Transporting Frame Relay frames over ATM cloud

demonstrates that the ATM backbone provides Frame Relay links to business customers. In this case, the border routers or frame relay access devices (FRAD) at the customer premises produce FR frames. Arriving at the carrier's ATM backbone, however, the FR frames are moved through the cloud by the high-speed ATM technology. For the 'Frame Relay over ATM', such methods as *header translation* can be used.

12.9.2   CELL SWITCHING

ATM also uses permanent virtual circuits (PVC). In ATM, the virtual circuit identifier is the combination of the *virtual path identifier* (VPI) and the *virtual channel identifier* (VCI) (see Figure 12.16). The ATM's virtual circuit identifier is, therefore, equivalent to the Frame Relay's DLCI. ATM uses fixed-size frames called *cells* with 48 octets of payload (data) and 5 octets of header (there is no trailer), making each cell 53 octets or bytes. The fixed payload size is what makes ATM different from Frame Relay and other WAN standards that allow the data field of variable size.

ATM's packet switching is called *cell switching*. With the fixed-size cell, ATM switching becomes very effective, especially when switches handle real-time traffic that cannot afford delays. When the ending point of an arriving cell is anticipated in advance, switching becomes faster.

12.9.3   QUALITY OF SERVICE (QoS)

The ATM technology is designed to handle both real-time voice/multimedia traffic and non-real-time data traffic efficiently. For this, ATM defines several service classes and offers *Quality of Service* (QoS) that guarantees certain performance in network service (e.g., maximum latency for

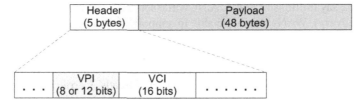

FIGURE 12.16   ATM cell and virtual circuit identifier in the header

time-critical applications). The four representative classes are CBR, VBR, ABR, and UBR, and each class defines a set of parameters regarding network performance. A brief description of each class is:

- *Constant bit rate* (CBR) for video and voice applications that demand fixed channel capacity
- *Variable bit rate* (VBR) for high-priority applications
- *Available bit rate* (ABR) for applications that need a minimum guaranteed data rate
- *Unspecified bit rate* (UBR) for applications that can use remaining (or unused) network capacity

Despite the technical sophistication and early anticipation of its ultimate supremacy as a WAN standard, it has lost its market to other technologies, especially Carrier Ethernet and Multi-Protocol Label Switching (MPLS) in the US. Several factors have contributed to the slow adoption of ATM despite its technological advancement. Among them are ATM's technical complexity; expensive intermediary devices; and high overhead in which 5 bytes out of the 53-byte frame are taken up by the header to support cell switching. Finally, as the WAN carrier's backbone network (cloud) runs on optical fibers with literally unlimited bandwidth, effective management of network capacity through such advanced but complicated technology as ATM has become a less pressing matter.

12.10   CARRIER ETHERNET

12.10.1   BACKGROUND

WAN carriers have been heavily investing to bring the Ethernet technology to the world of WAN, thus called Carrier-Ethernet. Riding on the enormous popularity of Ethernet as a LAN standard, it was initially adopted by carriers to offer MAN service, called Metro Ethernet. Intended to cover a city or a suburban area, Metro Ethernet's main usage has been:

- To interconnect distributed LANs within a particular metropolitan area
- To connect a business client's LAN to the Internet
- To bridge a business client's LAN to the carrier's WAN backbone

When it was first introduced in early 2000, Metro Ethernet had several relative shortcomings compared to other, more established WAN counterparts (e.g., Frame Relay, ATM, SONET) in provisioning:

- Network reliability expected to run MAN services
- Network scalability that can handle growing traffic in a graceful manner
- Quality of Service (QoS) that guarantees network performance

This is not surprising because Ethernet was initially designed as a LAN technology while others were intended for WANs from the beginning.

WANs demand technical and service features much different from LANs. For example, a LAN may connect hundreds or thousands of network nodes, but a carrier's WAN infrastructure should scale it much bigger, say millions of nodes. Also, while service types available for LANs are limited (e.g., best effort delivery), WANs should be able to support several service options tailored to various needs (e.g., QoS provisions) of large enterprise clients, small/medium-size businesses, SOHO/residential customers, and even mobile workers.

With the rapid rise of Metro Ethernet in the past, carriers have been upgrading the technology to offer a truly global WAN platform – Carrier Ethernet. Already, Carrier Ethernet has become an extremely popular WAN service platform in the US, largely driven by its capacity to provide customers with competitively priced, high-performance connectivity.

12.10.2 STRENGTHS

Among the notable strengths of Carrier Ethernet are:

a. Ethernet already has a massive installation base, and its advanced features such as Virtual LAN (see Chapter 7) enables the handling of mission-critical applications better than before (e.g., VLAN's priority bits).
b. Compared with other WAN platforms (e.g., SONET), the service costs of Carrier Ethernet are very competitive. One main reason is that Carrier Ethernet uses intermediary devices (e.g., Ethernet switches) whose manufacturing costs already enjoy a significant economy of scale.
c. Carrier Ethernet offers high bandwidth leading up to 100 Gbps between sites separated by several hundred miles apart. Supports for 400 Gbps and 1 Tbps are on the horizon. Corporate customers can purchase bandwidth incrementally to meet their needs.
d. Carrier Ethernet provides flexible WAN design choices to business clients, which include simple point-to-point as well as multipoint-to-multipoint connections.
e. The service provision is not limited by a single WAN provider's network span. That is, clients can build global scale, end-to-end WAN connections on multiple providers' Carrier Ethernet platforms. After all, carriers are offering their services on the standardized Ethernet platform.
f. Corporate clients are already familiar with Ethernet and, thus, linking their Ethernet LANs to Carrier Ethernet is relatively easy. If the end-to-end WAN connectivity between two client LANs is purely through Carrier Ethernet, there is no need to make protocol translations (e.g., frame conversion) at the connecting points.
g. Carrier Ethernet's technological compatibility with Ethernet LAN makes it highly cost-effective for business clients to set up and operate WAN connections. For instance, the network administrators of a client firm do not need separate training to manage Carrier Ethernet-based WAN links.

12.10.3 SERVICE PROVISION

WAN carriers have been using different approaches in provisioning the Metro- or Carrier Ethernet service.

a. Relying on pure Ethernet in which the WAN platform is composed of layer 2 Ethernet switches. Just as the Ethernet LAN, frames are forwarded referring to the switch table that contains MAC addresses and exit ports. When the switch table is kept relatively small, the WAN should be able to perform well. When the table size gets larger, however, switching performance can suffer considerably, having ripple effects on service quality for corporate customers. As pure Ethernet is not dependable to support the large-scale WAN platform, its usage was limited to early Metro-Ethernet.
b. These days, carriers transport Ethernet frames relying on other WAN standards primarily SDH/SONET and MPLS (see Section 12.11). Unlike Ethernet, SDH/SONET and MPLS were developed as WAN standards and, thus, provide necessary reliability and scalability in transporting WAN data. This hybrid approach is especially attractive when a carrier already has SONET/SDH or MPLS infrastructure in the service area.

12.11 MULTI-PROTOCOL LABEL SWITCHING

Multi-Protocol Label Switching (MPLS) is another WAN technology that has become extremely popular. MPLS has been adopted by carriers as a solution to 'fast forward' IP packets using a mechanism similar to *layer 2 switching* rather than traditional *layer 3 routing*. With MPLS in place, therefore, the traditional IP-based routing is skipped in a network. This is what makes it different from other WAN technologies conceived as layer 2 standards from their inception.

To make that possible, MPLS relies on the *label,* conceptually similar to the *virtual circuit,* as a way to expedite forwarding of IP packets by MPLS-enabled *routers.* The router refers to its MPLS table with *labels* for quick IP packet forwarding decisions, bypassing the traditional routing decision. Standardized by the *Internet Engineering Task Force* (IETF), MPLS has been well received by US carriers as a measure to improve WAN performance.

12.11.1 LABELS AND LABEL INFORMATION BASE (LIB)

As stated, the *label* itself plays the role of the virtual circuit identifier. The label is added between the IP packet header and the layer 2 frame header (see Figure 12.17) so that MPLS-enabled routers can forward IP packets relying on the label rather than the destination IP address. As MPLS-enabled 'routers' are used for packet forwarding, it is different from the layer 2 switching explained in Chapters 3 and 5. For this reason, MPLS is considered a 2.5-layer technology.

12.11.1.1 Label Information Base

For label switching, each MPLS-enabled router called a *label switching router* (LSR) maintains a *label information base* (LIB) (see Figure 12.18). The LIB keeps pairing information of label numbers and exit ports/interfaces. This pairing literally turns connectionless IP routing into connection-oriented *virtual* switching. The label is *locally significant,* meaning that each link between two MPLS routers uses a unique label. For instance, the first entry of the LIB in Figure 12.18 indicates that when a packet containing 10 as its label arrives at S0/0/0, it will be re-labeled as 15 and released through S0/0/1. This re-labeling repeats until the packet completes its journey inside a WAN cloud or an ISP network. Can you observe that the working mechanism of the label-based switching closely resembles that of the *virtual circuit*?

Edge LSRs are routers that insert or remove the label. Figure 12.18 demonstrates that when an MPLS-enabled router (as edge LSR) in the cloud receives an IP packet from a client network, it adds a label to the packet. Each intermediate LSR reads only the label information, instead of the IP header, to re-label and dispatch the packet to the next router. The last LSR (as edge LSR) in the cloud removes the label before passing the packet to the destination network. So, the packet routing decision on each router in the cloud is entirely skipped.

12.11.2 BENEFITS OF MPLS

MPLS offers several benefits. Among the most noticeable are:

a. IP packet forwarding gets significantly faster when routers rely on labels rather than IP addresses, and this is the primary reason for the popularity of MPLS.
b. It allows traffic engineering or traffic load balancing. With traffic engineering, the packet delivery path between two locations can be pre-planned for balanced use of network links and nodes. It addresses weaknesses of traditional IP packet routing in which routing paths are decided by such factors as the *shortest delivery path* (see Chapter 11). Using such criteria to prioritize the packet routing path can result in uneven utilization of routers and develop congestions in heavy traffic areas, adversely affecting the network's overall performance.

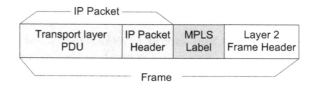

FIGURE 12.17   IP packet with a MPLS label

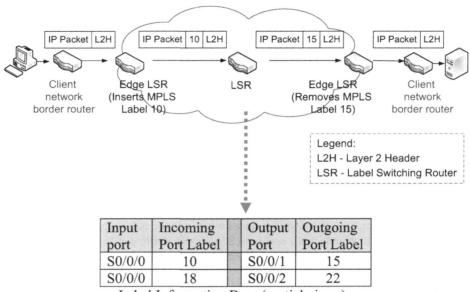

Input port	Incoming Port Label		Output Port	Outgoing Port Label
S0/0/0	10		S0/0/1	15
S0/0/0	18		S0/0/2	22

Label Information Base (partial views)

FIGURE 12.18 MPLS-enabled ISP network

c. MPLS can offer better Quality of Service (QoS) for different data types by utilizing more than one label type between two locations so that the IP packet carrying time sensitive or mission critical information (e.g., voice-over IP, video streaming) gets a higher priority in delivery.

CHAPTER SUMMARY

- This chapter covers, non-Internet based, WAN services offered on the private WAN infrastructure owned by a common carrier.
- In order to use a common carrier's WAN service, a client organization exchanges a formal service level agreement (SLA) with the carrier, which specifies service terms and conditions.
- A WAN link consists of the customer premises equipment (CPE) and service provider facility (SPF). The demarcation point is where the CPE meets the SPF.
- Similar to LAN standards, the common carrier's WAN service primarily utilizes physical and data link layer technologies.
- There are several physical layer standards developed for WAN services including T-carrier and E-carrier, Synchronous Optical Network (SONET), Digital Subscriber Line (DSL), and wireless WANs such as cellular and satellite technologies.
- WAN standards in the data link layer support either circuit switching or packet switching.
- In circuit switching, an end-to-end circuit is created beforehand between remote sites with certain bandwidth reserved for the circuit.
- With packet switching, data are packaged in discrete units, and each is transported independent of other units. PSDN is a carrier's WAN platform that moves clients' voice/data using packet switching.
- If the border router connects to multiple leased lines, a router port (interface) with an IP address is assigned to each leased line.
- When WAN links are through the PSDN cloud, the border router at a client site needs just one physical link to the carrier network to connect several remote locations through as many virtual circuits.

- The leased line service available from a carrier results in a point-to-point link with dedicated link capacity. Subscribers of the leased line pay for the link capacity committed by the WAN provider regardless of its usage level. T-carrier/E-carrier and SONET/SDH are two popular leased line technologies.
- *Point-to-Point Protocol* (PPP) has been a popular data link layer choice to transport IP packets over the leased line. It uses the *Challenge Handshake Authentication Protocol* (CHAP) for router authentication.
- Common attributes of PSDN services include the shared capacity, customizability of subscribed speeds, support for data and voice, frame multiplexing, unreliable transmissions, use of virtual circuits, and use of the WAN switch table.
- Frame-Relay, Carrier Ethernet, Multi-Protocol Label Switching (MPLS) and Asynchronous Transfer Mode (ATM) are well-known PSDN standards.
- Frame Relay is characterized by the use of *permanent virtual circuits* between client sites; *low overhead* (simple header structure) and efficient frame delivery; and *unreliability*, as there is no acknowledgment from WAN switch nodes when a frame is lost or dropped.
- ATM is designed to handle both real-time voice/multimedia traffic and non-real-time data traffic efficiently. For this, ATM defines several service classes in terms of their *Quality of Service* (QoS).
- Carrier Ethernet has become an extremely popular WAN service platform in the US, largely driven by its capacity to provide customers with competitively priced, high-performance WAN connectivity.
- MPLS has been adopted by carriers as a solution to 'fast forward' IP packets using a mechanism similar to *layer 2 switching* rather than traditional *layer 3 routing*.

KEY TERMS

add-drop multiplexer (ADM)	label information base (LIB)
Asynchronous Transfer Mode (ATM)	label switching router (LSR)
available bit rate (ABR)	leased line
Carrier Ethernet	local loop
cell	Metro Ethernet
cell switching	Multi-Protocol Label Switching (MPLS)
Central Office	network interface device (NID)
Challenge Handshake Authentication Protocol (CHAP)	optical carrier (OC)
circuit switching	packet switching
common carrier	packet switched data network (PSDN)
constant bit rate (CBR)	permanent virtual circuit (PVC)
customer premise equipment (CPE)	point of presence (POP)
data link connection identifier (DLCI)	Point-to-Point (PPP)
demarcation point	service level agreement (SLA)
E-carrier	service provider facility (SPE)
fractional T-1	switched virtual circuit (SVC)
Frame Relay	Synchronous Optical Network (SONET)
frame relay access device (FRAD)	Synchronous Transport Module (STM)
label (MPLS)	T-carrier
	traffic engineering

traffic load balancing

unspecified bit rate (UBR)

variable bit rate (VBR)

virtual channel identifier

virtual circuit

virtual path identifier

CHAPTER REVIEW QUESTIONS

1. Which item may be included in the service level agreement?
   A) minimum latency
   B) minimum number of hops in packet forwarding
   C) maximum availability
   D) minimum error rate
   E) maximum delay in service response time

2. Chose a CORRECT statement regarding the WAN service.
   A) Most firms use leased lines to create a full mesh network.
   B) The WAN link is generally faster than the LAN link.
   C) T-carrier/E-carrier and SONET/SDH are PSDN services.
   D) T-carrier/E-carrier is faster in downstream than in upstream.
   E) A carrier may offer Frame Relay service on its ATM backbone cloud.

3 Which is customer premise equipment of the WAN link?
   A) Central Office
   B) backbone network
   C) local access link
   D) Point of Presence
   E) border router

4. The following are general attributes of PSDN EXCEPT:
   A) PSDN generally depends on the reliable transmission in data link for which transmission errors are detected and corrected.
   B) With capacity sharing, more clients can be served using the same network capacity.
   C) PSDN is more flexible than leased lines in meeting customer demands (e.g., bandwidth).
   D) PSDN serves both voice and data communications.
   E) WAN frames, each containing an IP packet, are multiplexed (or combined) at local POPs and transported over the cloud's trunk links.

5. The demarcation point is a junction point where _____.
   A) the access link of a customer meets the carrier's Point-of-Presence (POP)
   B) the local network of an ISP meets the Internet backbone
   C) the customer premise equipment meets the service provider facility
   D) the access link of a customer meets the Internet
   E) ISP networks are joined together

6. The Carrier Ethernet standard is defined in the _____ layer.
   A) application
   B) data Link
   C) transport
   D) internet
   E) session

7. Choose an INCORRECT statement in regards to the WAN connection service.
   A) The access link that connects a customer premise to a carrier's WAN platform is a service provider facility.
   B) PPP (point-to-point) is a popular layer 2 standard for the leased line service.
   C) The access line of a customer is connected to the carrier's WAN cloud through the POP.

D) The demarcation point of the WAN service is located at the POP.

E) The permanent virtual circuit is more popular than the switched virtual circuit in PSDN.

8. Which standard defines several classes of QoS (Quality of Service) to offer more customized WAN services?
   A) ATM
   B) Frame Relay
   C) T-carrier
   D) Carrier Ethernet
   E) Multi-Protocol Label Switching

9. The technical details of leased lines such as SONET and T-carrier are defined in the _____ layer.
   A) application
   B) transport
   C) internet (or network)
   D) data link
   E) physical

10. The permanent virtual circuit is or becomes
    A) available when a corporate customer enrolls for the leased line service.
    B) less used than the switched (or dynamic) virtual circuit due to its inflexibility.
    C) established when a communication session starts between two hosts.
    D) created between two communicating hosts within a campus site.
    E) set up by a carrier in its WAN cloud.

11. SONET/SDH generally adopts the _____ architecture in implementing the WAN service platform.
    A) hierarchical
    B) dual ring
    C) mesh
    D) point-to-point
    E) star (hub-and-spoke)

12. Which statement is CORRECT about the Frame Relay service?
    A) It uses the virtual circuit established at the beginning of each communication session.
    B) To connect to the carrier network, customers configure their WAN router with the virtual circuit identifier (DLCI) provided.
    C) ATM is a popular connection standard between client sites and the Frame Relay cloud.
    D) Its technical details are defined in the Internet (or network) layer.
    E) It is the most popular leased line standards.

13. The SONET leased line determines its bandwidth according to the _____ speed hierarchy.
    A) DS (digital signal)
    B) T-carrier
    C) E-carrier
    D) OC (optical carrier)
    E) T-carrier or E-carrier

14. Refer to Figure 12.19. If a computer in Dallas sends an IP packet to a server in Toronto, how many different virtual circuit identifiers are used to reach the destination over Frame Relay?
    A) 1
    B) 0
    C) 3
    D) 4
    E) Cannot decide

15. The DLCI (Data Link Connection Identifier) is the ___.
    A) virtual circuit number
    B) destination router address

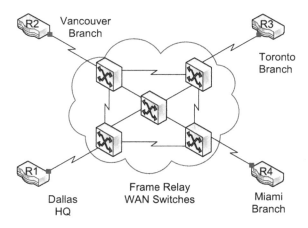

FIGURE 12.19   A Frame Relay WAN network

C) sender's authentication code
D) router's layer 2 address
E) unique identification of an ISP

16. Which statement describes MPLS?
A) MPLS is designed to replace layer 2 switching by LAN switches.
B) The MPLS link is a physical layer link.
C) MPLS is used whenever a TCP session is established between two hosts.
D) MPLS treats all IP packets equally in their transportation priority.
E) MPLS supports load balancing that moves traffic from congested links to less congested ones.

17. Which may NOT be a service provider facility (SPF) of WAN links?
A) Central Office (CO)
B) border router on the customer premise
C) Point of Presence (POP)
D) access link
E) WAN cloud network

18. Which does NOT represent the responsibility of carriers that provide WAN services?
A) day-to-day operations of the WAN cloud
B) QoS guarantees for 'all' WAN services
C) service administration including client billing
D) programming virtual circuits on the intermediary nodes in the cloud
E) maintenance of access links

19. The service classes of Constant Bit Rate and Variable Bit Rate are defined in _____.
A) Carrier Ethernet
B) VPN (virtual private network)
C) ATM (Asynchronous Transfer Mode)
D) Frame Relay
E) MPLS (Multi-Protocol Label Switching)

20. Which statement is CORRECT regarding the T-carrier service (e.g., T-1)?
A) Its technology details belong to the data link layer.
B) It can carry Frame Relay frames.
C) Its channel bandwidth is generally large enough to match that of Gigabit Ethernet.
D) It is an international standard from ITU (International Telecommunications Union).
E) It is designed to support the OC speed hierarchy.

21. Which of the following is NOT designed as a packet switching technology?
    A) Frame Relay
    B) point-to-point (PPP)
    C) Carrier Ethernet
    D) Multi-Protocol Label Switching
    E) Asynchronous Transfer Mode
22. Which is INCORRECT with regard to MPLS?
    A) Traffic engineering blocks certain IP packets from entering the WAN network.
    B) To transport IP packets with MPLS, routers should be MPLS-enabled.
    C) The MPLS label of an IP packet is locally significant.
    D) MPLS results in faster IP packet forwarding than conventional routing.
    E) MPLS is a popular standard adopted by ISP networks.
23. When the leased line and PSDN services are compared:
    A) Transmission capacity can be better tailored to client needs by the PSDN service.
    B) Unlike the leased line that relies on digital transmissions, PSDN uses analog transmissions.
    C) The leased line is more cost-effective than the PSDN service.
    D) The leased line generally offers faster data rates than the PSDN service.
    E) Both offer reliability of data transmissions through the frame acknowledgement.
24. *CHAP* is used for node (e.g., router) authentication by the _____ standard.
    A) Carrier Ethernet
    B) PPP (Point-to-Point)
    C) ATM (Asynchronous Transfer Mode)
    D) Frame Relay
    E) MPLS (Multi-Protocol Label Switching)
25. A firm has three business sites remotely separated. It decided that each site is going to have a permanent virtual circuit to two other sites by using the AT&T PSDN service. What is the total number of PVCs the company will have?
    A) one
    B) two
    C) three
    D) six
    E) Cannot decide

HANDS-ON EXERCISES

EXERCISE 12.1

Refer to Figure 12.5.

1. Develop the IP address-to-VC mapping table of R2 and R3, referring to Table 12.3.
2. How many virtual circuits are needed to fully interconnect (full mesh) the three business locations?

EXERCISE 12.2

Refer to Figure 12.6.

1. Develop the IP address-to-VC mapping table of R1, R2, and R3 referring to Table 12.3.
2. How many virtual circuits are necessary to fully interconnect (full mesh) the three business locations?

Exercise 12.3

Figure 12.20 demonstrates a hypothetical enterprise network where WAN links interconnect distributed LANs through the carrier's PSDN cloud. The client's border router at the Houston location has three PVCs (one PVC to each branch office) on one physical link, with three different speeds. What is the minimum data rate of the physical link necessary to avoid transmission delays?

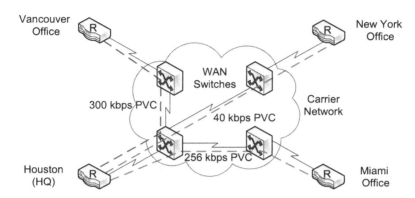

FIGURE 12.20 A physical link with three permanent virtual circuits

13 Physical Layer Data Transmissions

13.1 INTRODUCTION

This chapter explains technology elements and their standards necessary to physically propagate data-carrying signals over wired and wireless networks. Hence, technology concepts introduced in this chapter belong to the physical layer of the TCP/IP and OSI architectures. Despite the fact that the concepts are highly hardware-driven, they still form fundamental knowledge in understanding computer networking. Recall that data transmission technologies explained in Section 1.10 of Chapter 1 are all physical layer concepts. They were covered in advance as their comprehension is fundamental in studying subsequent chapters.

13.1.1 LEARNING OBJECTIVES

The objectives of this chapter are to learn:

- Signal encoding devices of WAN links (modems and CSU/DSU)
- Concepts of baseband and broadband
- Synchronous transmissions vs. asynchronous transmissions
- Frequency division multiplexing and time division multiplexing technologies
- International standards in digital speed hierarchies
- Networking media with focus on twisted pairs and optical fibers
- Structured cabling system and its subsystems

13.2 DATA TRANSMISSION TECHNOLOGIES

13.2.1 LAN SIGNAL ENCODING

The digital and analog signal encoding and decoding, as physical layer technologies, are explained in Section 1.10. Wired LANs, including the dominant Ethernet, primarily take advantage of digital encoding these days. On the wired Ethernet LAN, the network interface card of host stations and intermediary devices is responsible for the production and release of standardized digital signals. On the Wi-Fi LAN, the wireless LAN card uses analog signal encoding based on the spread spectrum technology such as Orthogonal Frequency Division Multiple Access (OFDMA) (revisit Sections 6.2.2 and 6.12.2.4).

13.2.2 WAN SIGNAL ENCODING

Just as with LANs, Wide Area Network (WAN) connections also use both digital (e.g., T-carrier, E-carrier) and analog (e.g., satellite links, cellular networks) signal encodings to transport bitstream data. On the wired WAN link, there are two different device types that enable signal encoding: CSU/

DSUs (*Channel Service Unit/Data Service Units*) for digital encoding and modems (*modulators* and *demodulators*) for analog encoding.

13.2.2.1 Modem and Analog Signal Encoding

Dial-up, Digital Subscriber Line (DSL), and Cable services enable an individual/business client to access the carrier's private WAN platform or the Internet over the local access line (e.g., telephone or cable lines). With relatively higher speeds than the conventional dial-up connection, DSL and Cable links are considered *broadband access services*. In the US, the *Federal Communications Commission (FCC)*, which regulates interstate and international telecommunications, officially recognizes 25 Mbps download and 3 Mbps upload as thresholds for broadband speeds currently.

Here, the responsibility of dial-up, DSL, and Cable modems is to conduct necessary translations between digital and analog signals. The modem uses such technologies as amplitude or frequency modulation (revisit Section 1.10.2.2.1) to convert a computer's digital signals to analog signals necessary for transmissions.

13.2.2.1.1 Dial-Up Modem

The dial-up modem takes advantage of the traditional landline telephone infrastructure (called *public switched telephone network* or PSTN) to transport computer-produced data. The computer's NIC port releases digital signals and they are converted to analog signals by the dial-up modem for transmissions through the phone line's 'voice channel' in the frequency range of 0–4000 Hz (see Figure 13.1). This conversion is necessary because the carrier's (e.g., AT&T) landline telephone equipment processes only analog signals of that frequency range coming from the local telephone line.

As the dial-up modem utilizes the limited single voice channel (0–4000 Hz) to transport both voice and data, the user can use only one service at a time. This may sound too old-fashioned to the vast majority of people who are used to using a smartphone on the cellular network. The landline-based dial-up service is still available even in developed countries.

Once computer data delivered through the voice frequency channel (0–4000 Hz) of the landline arrives at a carrier's switching office, they are directed to the Internet. Using analog signal encoding through the limited voice frequency range (0–4000 Hz) restricts the maximum speed of the dial-up connection to 64kbps (DS-0 speed), unless other measures, typically data compressions, are used to boost the transmission speed.

13.2.2.1.2 DSL and Cable Modems

As a broadband service, DSL takes advantage of separate voice and data channels occupying different frequency ranges of the phone line. This approach eliminates the need for channel sharing by voice and data traffic, and thus affords simultaneous access to the telephone network and the Internet. Furthermore, there are two separate data channels for simultaneous flows of upstream and

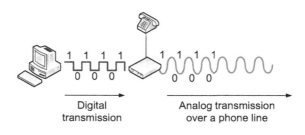

FIGURE 13.1 Data transmissions with a dial-up modem

downstream traffic. *DSL modems* take advantage of 'analog signal encoding' to transport digital source data as well as telephone calls, making the naming somewhat confusing to readers.

There are several variants of DSL, and they are largely divided into two groups: symmetric (SDSL) and asymmetric (ADSL). Unlike SDSL that offers the same speed in both upstream and downstream channels, ADSL has a downstream channel capacity larger than that of upstream, allowing faster downloading of files from the Internet (see Figure 13.7). Similar technical approaches apply to Cable service in which the cable capacity (or bandwidth) is divided into several frequency channels to transport voice, Internet traffic (data), and cable TV concurrently.

13.2.2.2 CSU/DSU and Digital Signal Encoding

Unlike the modem that provides conversion between digital and analog signals in the physical layer, the *CSU/DSU* (Channel Service Unit/Data Service Unit) translates a digital signal generated by the customer premise equipment (e.g., router) into another digital signal format required by the WAN/Internet access link. That is, unlike the dial-up and DSL modems that connect to an analog circuit (i.e., traditional telephone landline), the CSU/DSU is used when the access link runs a digital circuit such as T-1 or T-3.

Figure 13.2 demonstrates a situation in which the CSU/DSU equipment translates the digital signal coming from the border router's WAN port to another digital signal format required by the T-3 access line. The CSU/DSU comes with different standard ports. Many routers' *WAN interface card* (WIC) has a built-in CSU/DSU, and thus these routers do not need a separate external CSU/DSU for WAN connectivity. In fact, CSU/DSU, as an independent external unit, has been largely disappearing as it is increasingly integrated into the router.

13.2.3 DIGITAL SIGNAL ENCODING STANDARDS

Here, a few digital encoding standards are demonstrated as in Figure 13.3 to provide readers with some basic understanding of 'how it works'. As can be seen, the three standards (i.e., *NRZ – None Return to Zero*, *Manchester Encoding*, and *Differential Manchester Encoding*) use different rules in converting the same bitstream. The difference in the encoding rules results in their discrepant effectiveness of data transmissions. Their conversion rules are not important to the readers and thus are not explained (but, you can find the encoding rule yourself).

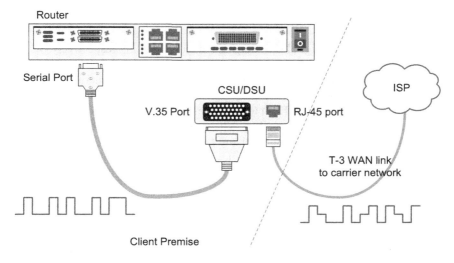

FIGURE 13.2   Demonstration of external CSU/DSU device

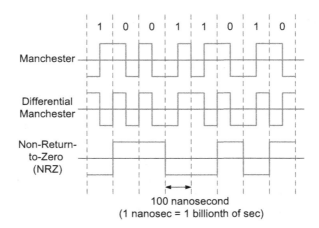

FIGURE 13.3 Select standards of digital signal encoding

TABLE 13.1
Signaling and conversion devices

Input	Output	Select encoding standards for conversion	Conversion devices
Digital signal	Digital signal	• Manchester • Differential Manchester • Non-Return-to-Zero	CSU/DSU
Digital signal	Analog signal	• Amplitude Modulation • Frequency Modulation • Phase Modulation	Dial-up, DSL, and Cable modems

Table 13.1 summarizes the input and output data types, signal encoding methods, and devices that perform the conversion.

13.2.4 BASEBAND VS. BROADBAND

Baseband and broadband mean digital signaling and analog signaling respectively. With baseband (or digital) transmission, only one digital signal flows at a time using the full bandwidth of a cable to transport data (see Figure 13.4). Today's wired computer networks generally take advantage of the baseband technology. For example, the early generation of Ethernet with 10 Mbps speed relied on Manchester Encoding (see Figure 13.3) to translate a digital bitstream into a digital signal that uses the entire bandwidth of the copper cable. When multiple sources of data are to be combined and delivered concurrently based on the baseband technology, so-called *time division multiplexing* (TDM) is utilized (see Figure 13.4a). Multiplexing is a technology to combine distinct signals and transport them just like a single signal through the cable's shared space (to be explained in Section 13.2.6).

When the broadband (or analog) transmission is utilized, several frequency channels can be created within a cable to transport multiple analog signals concurrently through separated frequency ranges (see Figure 13.4b). Frequency channels can carry different data types such as text, voice, and video. Naturally, the wider the bandwidth of a medium, the more channels or sub-channels can be accommodated allowing concurrent flows of multiple data streams.

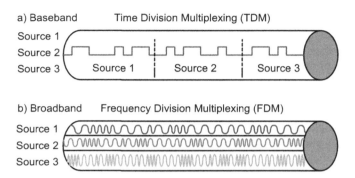

FIGURE 13.4   Baseband vs. broadband transmissions

Using the coaxial cable, for instance, the cable TV broadband service feeds a number of TV channels along with Internet traffic and telephone calls. Also, DSL offered on the landline to transport both voice (telephone calls) and data (Internet traffic) concurrently is another example. When multiple sources of data are pulled together and transported concurrently over the network based on the broadband technology, *Frequency Division Multiplexing* (FDM) is utilized.

To confuse matters more, the term *broadband* is also used to indicate a high-speed connection as opposed to *narrowband*. For instance, DSL, Cable, and T-3 are broadband technologies, and the dial-up connection with its maximum speed of 64 kbps (without using compression) and T-1 (1.54 Mbps) are narrowband technologies.

13.2.5   Synchronous vs. Asynchronous Transmission

13.2.5.1   Asynchronous Transmission

Digital bits can be moved either asynchronously or synchronously. With asynchronous transmission, each character (7 or 8 bits in ASCII) becomes a unit of delivery (see Figure 13.5a). Its focus is on safely conveying one alphanumeric character at a time. For this, each character is added by the *start* (indicating the starting point), *stop* (indicating the ending point), and *parity* (for error detection) bits. If a character uses 7-bit ASCII, the delivery of each character takes 10 bits after adding the 3 overhead bits. With the large 30% overhead, the asynchronous transmission is ineffective and its usage in computer networking has been largely limited to low-speed circuits such as those connecting a computer to the terminal, keyboard, and dial-up modem.

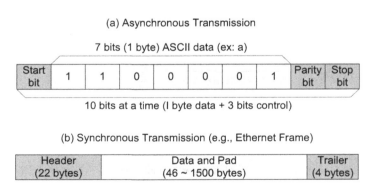

FIGURE 13.5   Asynchronous vs. synchronous transmissions

13.2.5.2 Synchronous Transmission

With synchronous transmission, each message unit is essentially a long string of characters rather than a single character (see Figure 13.5b). In Chapter 3, for example, it was explained that there are three different types of the protocol data unit (PDU). The data link layer PDU (or frame) generally includes the header, data, and trailer sections. The maximum size of the data field (also called payload) and overhead varies depending on the technology standard. The Ethernet frame, for instance, can contain up to 1500 bytes in the data field with the maximum overhead (header and trailer) size of 26 bytes. With synchronous transmission, therefore, a set of data characters are transported in their entirety within a single PDU. Computer networking these days relies mostly on synchronous transmission.

When the PDU with bundled data characters is transported at once, the delivery becomes more effective than asynchronous transmission. For instance, unlike the 30% overhead of asynchronous transmission, the overhead of synchronous transmission becomes much smaller (generally less than 5%), consuming less bandwidth to move the same amount of data. The start, stop, and parity bit functions of asynchronous transmission are also built into each PDU for synchronous transmission. For instance, with the Ethernet frame, these functions are realized through bits included in such fields as *preamble*, *start frame delimiter,* and *frame check sequence* (revisit Section 7.3.1).

13.2.6 MULTIPLEXING

Multiplexing is another fundamental and important physical layer technology that is heavily used in modern networks. Multiplexing represents the process of combining signals (either analog or digital) from multiple sources to channel them over a single shared line or circuit. When multiple signals are merged and transported over a single line or channel, each signal takes up a portion of the available bandwidth. The multiplexer device performs multiplexing and the de-multiplexer separates combined signals.

The main benefits of multiplexing are:

- It dramatically increases effectiveness in capitalizing network capacity.
- It cuts the number of necessary links or circuits between two points.
- It lowers the cost of networking without sacrificing performance.

Several advanced multiplexing technologies have been developed, and many of these are derived from the fundamental technologies of *frequency division multiplexing* (FDM) and *time division multiplexing* (TDM). Although already explained in Figure 13.4 without formally introducing them, FDM and TDM are further elaborated here.

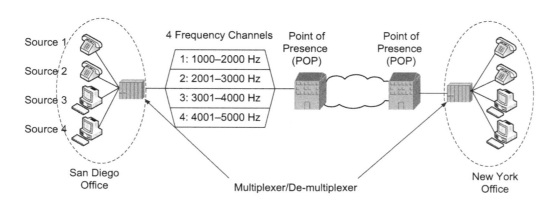

FIGURE 13.6 Frequency division multiplexing

13.2.6.1 Frequency Division Multiplexing (FDM)

For FDM, the line or channel bandwidth available is divided into several, non-overlapping frequency ranges, and a data source (e.g., IP phone, computer) is assigned to one of the available frequency ranges so that multiple data sources share the line or channel capacity for concurrent network access (Figure 13.6). As the data source takes advantage of a pre-assigned frequency range, analog signaling is used. (Remember that frequency is an analog concept.) The multiplexing method takes advantage of the fact that analog signals of different frequency ranges do not interfere with each other even when they travel through the same space.

13.2.6.2 FDM Example: DSL

As an example, ADSL as a popular broadband service creates three non-overlapping channels through a telephone landline: one (0~4 kHz) for the traditional *plain old telephone service* (POTS) and the other two channels (around 20 kHz~1 MHz) for *upstream* and *downstream* data traffic (see Figure 13.7). Then, the multiplexing of three signals allows simultaneous flows of voice and data over a twisted pair cable. The three separate channels, though, consume a small fraction of the twisted pair's entire bandwidth. For example, category 7 twisted pair cable has the bandwidth of 600 MHz (see Table 13.4), and you can observe that the three channels are taking up less than 1% of the available capacity.

With DSL's FDM, both voice traffic and data traffic are transported concurrently between the carrier's *Central Office* and the customer premise. At the Central Office, the signals are decoupled. Then, voice traffic is forwarded to the traditional public switched telephone network while data traffic is channeled to the Internet (see Figure 13.8).

As another example of FDM, Cable TV service providers divide the bandwidth of a coaxial cable into at least three different frequency ranges: one for TV channels, one for voice, and one for Internet access. Clients may subscribe to all three services at a discounted rate or a subset of the three available services.

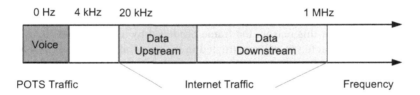

FIGURE 13.7 Frequency usage with the ADSL modem

TABLE 13.4
Twisted pair categories and supported bandwidth

Categories	Bandwidth (approx.)
CAT5	100 MHz
CAT5e	100 MHz
CAT6	250 MHz
CAT6a	500 MHz
CAT7	600 MHz
CAT7a	1000 MHz

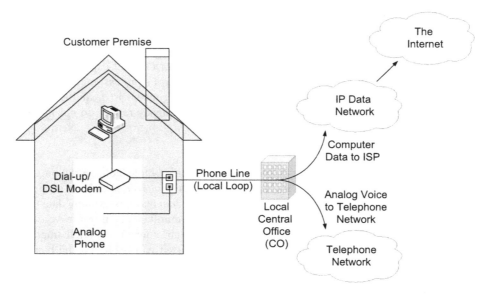

FIGURE 13.8 Internet connection with DSL

13.2.6.3 Time Division Multiplexing (TDM)

TDM uses the entire bandwidth of a line for the transmission of a single digital signal that aggregates data from multiple sources (e.g., phones, computers). For this, inputs from data sources are interwoven one after the other within a frame that is transmitted every certain time interval regulated by the clock speed (see Figures 13.4a and 13.9). The frame, therefore, contains multiple time slots, with each slot containing data from a transmitting source.

Here, the term 'frame' is used to indicate a physical transmission unit produced when digital signals from multiple sources are combined (or multiplexed). This assemblage process is literally a mechanical procedure. For this reason, the frame produced by a multiplexer (a layer 1 device) is fundamentally different from the frame constructed in the data link layer by a LAN/WAN standard such as Ethernet. Once the physical layer frame is assembled, it is directly injected into the network for transmission, making multiplexing a physical layer technology.

13.2.6.4 Synchronous vs. Statistical TDM

Two different approaches are used in utilizing available time slots of a frame: *synchronous TDM* and *statistical TDM*. With synchronous TDM, each data source is assigned a dedicated time slot of the frame. If there is no incoming data assigned to a particular time slot, the frame is released, leaving the slot empty. The number of data sources, therefore, equals the number of time slots in the frame. Figure 13.9 demonstrates synchronous TDM in which each frame carries data from four different sources in every clock cycle of the multiplexer. With the dedication of a time slot (therefore network bandwidth) to a data source, synchronous TDM does not result in transmission delays.

Statistical TDM (see Figure 13.10) is designed for more effective utilization of frame slots. To that end, available slots of the frame are dynamically allocated to incoming traffic on a first-come-first-served basis. Without committing a particular time slot to a particular source, statistical TDM can serve more data sources than the number of available time slots, because chances are that not all sources release data simultaneously. That way, statistical TDM increases the occupancy of available time slots. However, you can also observe that if more sources than available slots send data at the same time, transmission delays are inevitable.

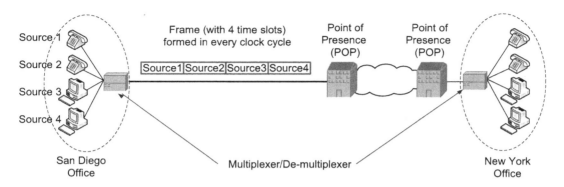

FIGURE 13.9 Synchronous time division multiplexing

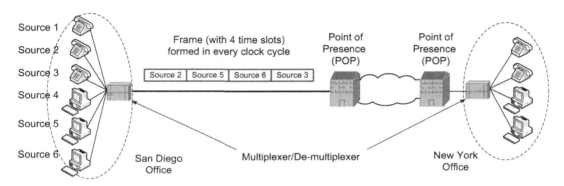

FIGURE 13.10 Statistical time division multiplexing

13.2.6.5 TDM Example: T-1 Line

For a more in-depth look at TDM, T-1's TDM approach is illustrated in Figure 13.11. T-1, as a narrowband service, is used by medium to small businesses for WAN connections. It is offered on the twisted pair or optical fiber to connect a local network to the Internet or to other remote locations (e.g., branch offices) geographically dispersed. Using digital signal encoding, it achieves the data rate of 1.54 Mbps and can convey both voice and data traffic. T-1 uses the physical layer *frame*, a discrete unit of the bitstream produced in every clock cycle by bundling bits from several data sources.

Each T-1 physical layer frame has 24 time slots (for 24 different voice and/or data sources) in which each slot can carry 8 bits (or 1 byte). As there are 24 slots in each frame, the size of a frame becomes 193 bits (24 × 8 bits/slot = 192 bits + 1 bit overhead = 193 bits). The T-1 multiplexer

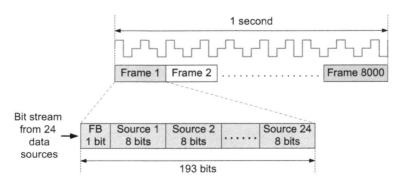

FIGURE 13.11 Time division multiplexing with T-1

quickly scans data sources in every clock cycle to fill up the time slots and the completed frame is dispatched. If a particular data source does not produce bits, its assigned time slot remains empty. With T-1, 8000 frames are produced per second, effectively reaching the speed of $193 \times 8000 = 1.54$ Mbps. Alternatively, the entire T-1 bandwidth of 1.54 Mbps may be used as a single channel without having time slots.

13.2.7 DIGITAL SPEED HIERARCHIES

Multiplexing by multiplexers (e.g., T-1 multiplexer) is conducted according to a standard hierarchy of digital speeds. *Digital signal* (DS) and *optical carrier* (OC)/*synchronous transport module* (STM) are two different digital speed hierarchies. DS was introduced when cabling options for the computer network were mainly copper wires such as twisted pairs and coaxial cables. The OC/STM hierarchy specifies a set of channel speeds on fiber-optic-based cabling.

13.2.7.1 Digital Signal (DS)

DS-0 at 64 Kbps is the base speed of the digital speed hierarchy. The speed of 64 Kbps represents the digital data rate produced when a single voice call (that is analog) is digitized by the standard conversion method called *Pulse Code Modulation* (PCM). Then, the capacity of higher-level digital channels is decided by the multiples of DS-0 (64 kbps). For example, DS-1 combines (or multiplexes) 24 DS-0 channels achieving the data rate of 1.54 Mbps.

Now, you can relate why the T-1 line is designed to provide DS-1 data rate and supports up to 24 channels of 64 kbps. DS speeds, therefore, represent the number of digitized phone calls (equivalent to DS-0) that can be transported simultaneously. Table 13.2 summarizes the hierarchy levels, their corresponding speeds, and the number of voice channels supported.

13.2.7.2 Optical Carrier/STM

The hierarchies of *optical carrier* (OC) (as the North America standard) and *synchronous transport module* (STM) (as the ITU-T international standard) define various channel speeds on the fiber-optic-based network. With the huge bandwidth of an optical fiber, their base speed starts at 51.84 Mbps (OC-1) and 155.5 Mbps (STM-1), and higher OC and STM levels are the multiples of OC-1 and STM-1 respectively. For example, OC-12 is about 622 Mbps (12 channels of 51.8 Mbps). As can be seen, the base speed of STM-1 is equivalent to three OC-1s.

You can observe that, although OC and STM are two different standards, there is a correspondence between their hierarchy levels (see Table 13.3). Also, there is contiguity from the DS hierarchy to the OC/STM hierarchies. For instance, the OC-1 data rate is the result of multiplexing 28 DS-1 channels.

TABLE 13.2
Digital signal (DS) hierarchy

Digital signal (DS) hierarchy	Digital data rate	# of Voice channels
DS-0	64 kbps	1
DS-1	1.54 Mbps	24
DS-1C	3.15 Mbps	48
DS-2	6.31 Mbps	96
DS-3	44.74 Mbps	672
DS-4	274.17 Mbps	4032

TABLE 13.3
OC/STM hierarchy – select speeds

Select OC/STM levels	Digital speed	Note (OC vs. DS)
OC-1	51.84 Mbps	28 DS-1 (1.54 Mbps)
OC-3/STM-1	155.52 Mbps	3 OC-1s/84 DS-1s
OC-12/STM-4	622.08 Mbps	4 OC-3s/336 DS-1s
OC-48/STM-16	2.48 Gbps	16 OC-3s/1344 DS-1s
OC-192/STM-64	9.95 Gbps	64 OC-3s/5376 DS-1s

13.3 NETWORKING MEDIA

Copper wires (twisted pairs and coaxial cables), *optical fibers*, and the earth's *atmosphere* (for wireless networking) are dominant media types these days. This section covers two most important media for wired (or guided) networking: twisted pairs and optical fibers. As explained, all details about networking media such as their physical properties, signal and transmission characteristics, and interfaces/ports and connectors are standardized in the physical layer.

The networking media differ in many ways, including:

- Transmission characteristics including the susceptibility to noise and interference; signal propagation effects including signal attenuation and distortion; and bandwidth supported
- Physical properties such as size, flexibility, number of wires, and ease of installation
- Costs of purchase, setup, maintenance, and operation
- Security of data in transition

With their varying characteristics, each medium has its right place when it comes to the design and deployment of a network.

13.3.1 PROPAGATION EFFECTS

All media have propagation effects especially in the form of signal attenuation and distortion.

13.3.1.1 Attenuation

Attenuation means that the strength or intensity of a signal (e.g., electronic currents, lights, radios) traveling through the media gets weaker as it progresses, and the rate of attenuation differs depending on the medium type. The light signal propagating through the optical fiber has the lowest attenuation rate. It can propagate a few miles without restoring its shape and strength. The electrical signal moving through the copper wire has much faster attenuation than the optical fiber's light signal. As a result, the effective distance of twisted pair cabling between two network nodes, generally up to 100 meters, is considerably shorter than that of the optical fiber. Wireless signals have the steepest attenuation compared to those traveling through the guided or wired media.

13.3.1.2 Distortion

Distortion refers to the fact that a signal's original shape cannot be maintained when it propagates because of several factors including signal attenuation, added noise, and transmission interferences. That is, the longer a signal travels, the greater distortion of its shape that takes place. If there is too much distortion, the receiving node may not recognize the signal pattern, or it may misinterpret the encoded meaning, resulting in data transmission errors.

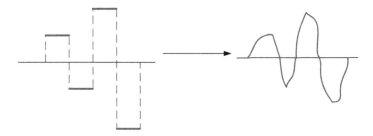

FIGURE 13.12 Attenuation and distortion effects of a digital signal

In digital signaling where there is only a limited number of signal *states* (e.g., Figure 13.12 has four states), the network node can better recognize and reproduce the original signal even if there is a certain degree of distortion and attenuation. In contrast, the reproduction of an analog signal is much more challenging because of difficulties in separating the original signal pattern from any noise added during its propagation. The relative ease of restoring digital signals makes digital transmission a better choice for retaining the integrity and quality of data (e.g., music) being transported.

13.3.2 Twisted Pairs

13.3.2.1 UTP vs. STP

The twisted pair is an ordinary copper wire that uses electrical currents to encode data. With low cost, high durability, and easy installation, it has become a popular choice for network cabling. Twisted pairs are either unshielded or shielded (see Figure 13.13). The *shielded twisted pair* (STP) has an extra metal shield over copper pairs to further protect signals inside from external noise and, thus, can support higher data rates.

The STP, however, has not been successful in the marketplace because the advantages over the *unshielded twisted pair* (UTP) generally do not compensate for its higher cost. The UTP satisfies the performance requirements of most local networks. Naturally, the STP's usage has been limited

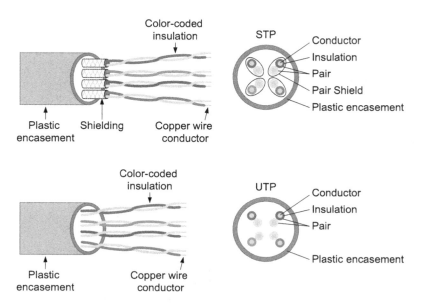

FIGURE 13.13 STP versus UTP

to atypical situations such as very high-speed connectivity (e.g., 10 Gbps) and the presence of significant noise sources in the installation area.

13.3.2.2 Cable Structure and Categories

The twisted pair is composed of eight copper wires with two copper wires twisted to become a pair. Thus, each UTP/STP cable has four twisted pairs inside. The twisting has an effect of canceling out external noise known as *electromagnetic interference* (or EMI). The UTP cable has different twist rates depending on the category (e.g., three times per inch for CAT5). More twisting results in reduced interference and noise, and better protection from EMI, which improves signal quality.

Twisted pairs come in different categories including CAT5, CAT5e (CAT5 enhanced), CAT6, CAT6a, CAT7, and CAT7a. Though all copper wires, they differ in such properties as the number of twists per foot, copper purity, electrical resistance, bandwidth, and type of insulation. Some categories use UTP while others rely on STP to be able to handle very high data rates in a reliable manner. Given that there are four twisted pairs inside, some categories utilize one pair for sending and another pair for receiving, but other categories take advantage of all four pairs (two pairs for each direction) to support faster transmission speeds.

Twisted pairs in higher categories offer better quality and support higher bandwidth, and thus are adequate for faster connections (see Table 13.4). For instance, although the same twisted pairs, CAT7a has bandwidth 10 times higher than CAT5, making the former ideal for high-speed networks. Twisted pair cabling is prevalent in Ethernet LANs and in the traditional telephone system, especially local access lines.

FIGURE 13.14 CAT6 patch cable with RJ-45 connectors (Source: connection.com)

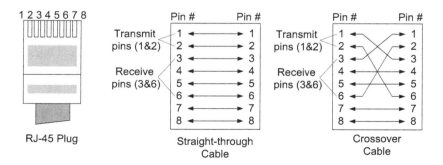

FIGURE 13.15 RJ-45 connector and pin pairing of a patch cable (10/100 Mbps cable)

13.3.2.3 Twisted-Pair Patch Cable

Twisted-pair *patch cables* (or *patch cords*) (see Figure 13.14) are used to link network nodes located within a few meters from each other, and they are in the *straight-through* or *cross-over* mode.

On both ends of the patch cable, eight wires are connected to eight pins of the RJ-45 plug, where pin 1 and pin 2 are for transmitting and pin 3 and pin 6 are for receiving (see Figure 13.15). With the straight-through cable, pin 1 and pin 2 of both ends are directly connected, and so are the receiving pins 3 and 6. With the direct link of the same pins, the straight-through cable is designed to relay signals from one node to another node. On the other hand, the crossover cable directly connects transmitting pins (1 and 2) of one end to the receiving pins (3 and 6) of the other end and vice versa. Oftentimes, the crossover cable has a red sheath to differentiate it from the straight-through cable that comes in several colors including yellow, blue, and gray.

Straight-through cables: They are used to interconnect different node types such as:

- Switch–Router
- Hosts (clients/servers)–Switch
- Wireless access points–Router

Crossover cable: Connecting two similar devices requires the crossover cable. For example, two computers can exchange data (without intermediary nodes) by directly linking their NICs with the crossover cable. Also, crossover cables are necessary to join:

- Switch–Switch
- Router–Router
- Host (server)–Router

It may sound odd that the crossover cable is used for 'host–router' connectivity. As a matter of fact, they are considered similar devices in the networking field. Although linking a host (mostly server) directly to a router is not a frequent practice, it certainly is an option. Why are hosts and routers regarded as similar devices? Unlike the switch port that has only a MAC address, both the host's NIC port and the router's LAN port require the pairing (or binding) of IP and MAC addresses to function.

These days, manufacturers offer intermediary devices whose ports can auto-sense the attached node and the type of cabling, and internally adjust its configuration automatically. This function, called *medium dependent interface crossover* (MDIX), makes the choice of crossover versus straight-through cable irrelevant and thus reduces the risk of disconnection between network nodes due to cabling mismatch.

13.3.3 OPTICAL FIBERS

The fiber-optic cable has emerged as a medium of choice for high-speed networking. Over the last two decades, optical fibers have replaced most of the copper lines for WAN and Internet backbone links, dramatically lowering communication costs. Also, fibers are replacing copper cables for the trunk links of LANs and campus networks.

Unlike twisted pairs and coaxial cables made of copper that transport data in electronic currents, optical fibers take advantage of light pulses to transmit data through the core made of extremely pure glass. The light transmitter device, primarily the *laser*, switches on and off rapidly according to a clocked cycle to send digital bits (see Figure 1.23). The signaling method is analogous to turning a flashlight on and off to exchange Morse codes that convey a message; but, the laser can do the altering of on and off at an amazing speed, several billions of times per second.

13.3.3.1 Advantages

The optical fiber enjoys several advantages over the copper wire as summarized here:

a. **Bandwidth**: It has a huge bandwidth. A single fiber strand can transmit billions of bits per second. If the advanced multiplexing technology called *dense wave division multiplexing* is applied to inject a number of light signals concurrently into one fiber strand, this can boost its data rate to terabits per second.

b. **Security**: Light signals are more difficult to tap without disrupting them than electrical currents and therefore are ideal for the link that needs heightened security.

c. **Lower interference**: Electrical currents in neighboring copper wires can interfere with each other, and wire twisting is used to reduce the interference. But, light signals traveling through multiple fibers do not interfere with each other even when they are bundled, resulting in a better quality of data delivered.

d. **Low attenuation**: The fiber-optic cable can carry signals much longer than the copper wire before their reproduction becomes necessary due to the propagation effect (e.g., attenuation). According to the IEEE's recommendation, the maximum segment length of the twisted pair between two nodes is generally limited to 100 meters to maintain signal integrity. Meanwhile, the effective segment length of fiber stretches several miles. Telecom service providers place signal repeating/reproduction equipment every 40 to 60 miles on long-haul fiber lines.

e. **Cost effectiveness**: Several miles of fiber can be manufactured more economically than the copper wire of equivalent length. Also, unlike copper wires that rely on high-voltage electrical transmitters, optical fibers can use low-power transmitters because signals degrade much more slowly.

13.3.3.2 Physical Structure

Physically, the optical fiber has a cylindrical structure composed of three elements: *core*, *cladding*, and *protective jacket* (see Figure 13.16). Core and cladding are mostly made of glass. The core, especially, uses glass with extreme purity to preserve the integrity of light signals. Cladding is designed to keep light signals from escaping the glass core, creating the effect of a mirrored tube that reflects lights back into the tube. As a result, lights traveling through the core bounce at shallow angles, staying in the core.

13.3.3.3 Single-Mode vs. Multi-Mode Types

The fiber-optic cable is either *single-mode* or *multi-mode* (see Figure 13.17). The single-mode fiber is very thin in its core, with a diameter typically less than 10 microns (1 micron is one-millionth of a meter). With the narrow core, light signals in the single-mode fiber travel in a straight line (therefore only one mode of propagation). The multi-mode fiber has a larger core diameter at around 50/62.5 microns, making it considerably cheaper to produce than the single-mode fiber.

With the relatively large diameter, the multi-mode fiber allows light signals to travel through the core at different angles (thus multi-modes in propagation). But, this does not mean that the

A single fiber: side view   A sheath with 3 fibers: end view

FIGURE 13.16   General structure of a fiber-optic cable (simplified views)

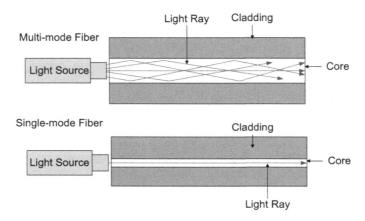

FIGURE 13.17 Optical fibers: single-mode vs. multi-mode

multi-mode fiber has a larger transmission capacity than the single-mode counterpart. The multi-mode and single-mode types have nothing to do with data rates, especially in a short range.

13.3.3.4 Comparing Single-Mode and Multi-Mode Fibers

When light pulses from a source travel in different modes through the multi-mode fiber, their arrivals at a destination may not be in sync. This problem of arrival gaps, called *modal dispersion*, gets worse as the travel distance extends further, increasing the chance of transmission errors or miscommunications between communicating nodes. Modal dispersion, thus, restricts the effective segment length of multi-mode fibers substantially shorter than that of single-mode fibers, making the former adequate for LANs but not for WANs. Modal dispersion is not a significant issue for the single-mode fiber, as there is only one mode in signal propagation. Carriers (e.g., AT&T) deploy WAN and Internet backbone links using the single-mode fiber. Table 13.5 compares the single-mode and multi-mode fibers.

13.3.3.5 Fiber Patch Cable

To link closely placed network nodes, the full-duplex patch cord with two fiber strands can be used. Different optical fiber connectors have been introduced, and Figure 13.18 demonstrates a fiber patch code with a particular connector at each end.

TABLE 13.5
Multi-mode vs. single-mode fibers

Comparative dimensions	Multi-mode fiber	Single-mode fiber
Usage for networking	Popular for LAN	Popular for Carrier WAN (LAN standards available, too)
Max segment length	200~300 meters	Several kilometers or miles
Cable cost	Significantly lower than single-mode fibers	Significantly higher than multi-mode fibers
Core diameter in micron (one millionth of a meter)	50~62.5 micron	8~10 micron
Propagation effect	Higher modal dispersion	Less modal dispersion
Select standards for LAN-cabling	1000BASE-SX 10GBASE-SR	1000BASE-LX 10GBASE-LR

FIGURE 13.18 Optical fiber patch cord and connectors (Source: tecratools.com)

13.3.4 LAN CABLING STANDARDS

As Ethernet is the dominant wired LAN standard, this section explains its standard cabling options defined in the physical layer. Ethernet's three most popular speed standards are Fast Ethernet (100 Mbps), Gigabit Ethernet (1 Gbps), and 10 Gigabit Ethernet (10 Gbps); 100 Gigabit Ethernet has been announced as well. In each of the speed categories, several cabling standards are available for both twisted pairs and optical fibers.

The cabling standards are expressed in the combination of the *rated speed*, *signaling method* (*baseband* for digital signaling and *broadband* for analog signaling), and *cable type* (twisted pair or optical fiber). For example, as one of the most popular Fast Ethernet options, the 100BASE-TX cabling standard has the following specs:

- 100 means the transmission speed of 100 Mbps.
- BASE means baseband (or digital) signal encoding.
- TX means the unshielded twisted pair (UTP) that is category 5 (CAT5) or higher

As explained, the twisted pair cable has four pairs inside but uses only two pairs for Fast Ethernet (100 Mbps): one pair for sending and another for receiving data. This results in two remaining pairs unused. Gigabit Ethernet, however, uses all four pairs, each pair operating in the full-duplex mode transmitting at 250 Mbps in each direction to achieve the aggregate speed of 1 Gbps.

In LANs, UTP cabling still dominates access links between host stations and access (or workgroup) switches. However, the optical fiber is popular for trunk links that interconnect core (backbone) and access switches. Several physical layer standards based on the optical fiber have been introduced to support different data rates (e.g., 100 Mbps, 1 Gbps, 10 Gbps, 100 Gbps). Table 13.6 summarizes select Ethernet standards available. Although both UTP and fiber cabling options are available to support various speeds, the fiber-optic cable has become a preferred medium for high-speed links.

13.4 STRUCTURED CABLING

13.4.1 BACKGROUND

With its importance in practice, the *structured cabling* concept is explained in this section. In a nutshell, network cabling complying with published standards is called structured cabling. The published standards specify recommended practices on all aspects of network cabling, including cabling

TABLE 13.6
Ethernet's physical layer standards

Ethernet speed standards	Select physical layer standards	Speed and cabling	Minimum UTP categories recommended
Fast Ethernet	100BASE-TX	100 Mbps/UTP	CAT5
Fast Ethernet	100BASE-FX	100 Mbps/fiber	
Gigabit Ethernet	1000Base-T	1000 Mbps/UTP	CAT5e/CAT6
Gigabit Ethernet	1000BASE-SX	1000 Mbps/fiber	
10 Gigabit Ethernet	10GBASE-T	10 Gbps/UTP	CAT6a/CAT7
10 Gigabit Ethernet	10GBASE-SR	10 Gbps/fiber	
100 Gigabit Ethernet	100GBASE-SR10	100 Gbps/fiber	

types available, effective segment distance of a cable type, connectors, installation requirements, and testing methods of installed cables. For structured cabling, it is important to use nationally and internationally standardized media, connection interfaces, and the layout.

EIA/TIA568: Widely adopted, EIA/TIA568 defines a set of standards for planning and implementing structured cabling. EIA/TIA568 standards include:

- 568-B.1: Commercial cabling standards – general requirements
- 568-B.2: Components of the twisted pair cable system
- 568-B.3: Components of the optical fiber cable system

EIA/TIA568 has been superseded by the international standard, ISO/IEC 11801.

Benefits of structured cabling: By complying with the structured cabling principle, an organization can enjoy several benefits:

- The practice reduces the initial costs of network implementation.
- IT staff can respond quickly and cost-effectively to changing needs of the network infrastructure as they face fewer problems in hardware compatibility.
- Network reliability and performance are ensured.
- The network can better support broadband applications in the future.

13.4.2 STRUCTURED CABLING SYSTEM

The *structured cabling system* of a building includes cabling, voice and data network components, and other building system components (e.g., safety alarms, lights, security access, energy systems), implemented according to the standard principles of high-performance structured cabling. The structured cabling system divides the cabling infrastructure of a building into six segments called subsystems:

1. Work area
2. Horizontal cabling
3. Wiring closet (or intermediate distribution facility – IDF)
4. Backbone cabling
5. Main equipment room (or main distribution facility – MDF)
6. Building entrance facility

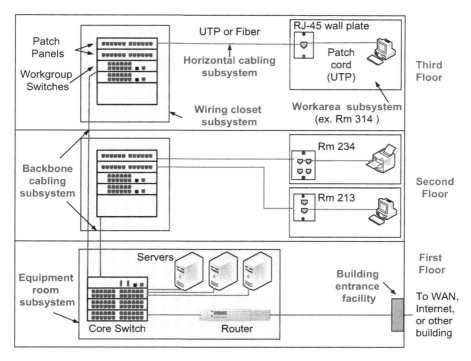

FIGURE 13.19   Structured cabling system and subsystems

Figure 13.19 demonstrates a general layout of the six subsystems within a building of three floors. For the demonstration, the figure focuses on the data networking side. However, remember that the telephone system including telephones and telephone switches (called private branch exchange or PBX) is also an integral part of the structured cabling system.

13.4.2.1   Work Area Subsystem

The work area subsystem covers structured cabling between wall plates of a room and various end nodes attached to them, including computers, wireless access points, telephones, and network printers.

13.4.2.2   Horizontal Cabling Subsystem

The horizontal cabling subsystem connects wall plates of a room to the wiring closet. The subsystem is, therefore, pre-installed in the building structure and enables the physical connectivity of end nodes in the work area to intermediary devices (generally switches) placed in the wiring closet. The popular cabling choice is 100 Mbps or 1 Gbps UTP or optical fiber.

Through horizontal cabling, each room on a floor is cabled to a patch panel installed in the wiring closet. The patch panel (see Figure 13.20) comes with many network ports (primarily RJ-45 ports) and enables easy connectivity between a switch of a wiring closet and end nodes distributed throughout the floor. Each occupied port of a patch panel is labeled for easy identification of its assigned room. For example, Figure 13.21 demonstrates that the host stations in three rooms (i.e., Room1, Room2, and Room 3) are joined by the workgroup switch via the 12-port patch panel. You can observe that patch cords are used to link the patch panel's ports and the switch ports.

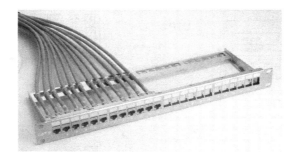

FIGURE 13.20   A Cat6 patch panel (Source: excel-networking.com)

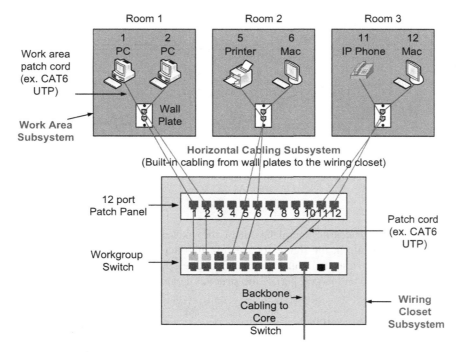

FIGURE 13.21   Work area, horizontal cabling, and wiring closet subsystems on a floor

13.4.2.3   Wiring Closet Subsystem

The wiring closet located on a floor is the cross-connection point of horizontal cabling and backbone cabling that leads to the main equipment room. The wiring closet houses one or more intermediary devices (e.g., workgroup switches) available for host stations in the adjacent work area. There is no limit to the number of wiring closets installed on a building floor, and the decision largely rests on the floor plan. The wiring closet houses a rack(s) that mounts intermediary devices and patch panels (see Figure 13.23). The rack mounting and concentration of intermediary nodes reduces the length of patch cables that interconnect them and simplifies cable management.

As an example of the structured cabling concept, let me use an EIA/TIA recommendation in coupling the horizontal, work area, and wiring closet subsystems with UTP cables. The standard suggests that:

• The maximum horizontal distance between a patch panel and wall plates is 90 meters (297 feet).

- Patch cables used in the wiring closet and work area can be up to 6 meters (20 feet) each, but the combined length of patch cables may not exceed 10 meters (33 feet).
- The overall length between an end node in the work area and a switch in the nearby wiring closet may not exceed 100 meters (330 feet), which represents the combined length of 90 meters and 10 meters above. This structured cabling guidance thus reflects the UTP's maximum segment length of 100 meters.

13.4.2.4 Backbone Cabling Subsystem

Backbone cabling (or vertical cabling) ties wiring closets, the main equipment room, and the building entrance facility together (see Figure 13.19). Backbone cabling runs through floors to cross-connect them. As trunk links (not access links), backbone cables require a larger capacity than horizontal cables because the former transport much data traffic that enters or leaves a building. Also, host stations in a work area depend on backbone cabling to access servers located outside the work area (e.g., another floor, main equipment room). To accommodate the large bandwidth consumption, backbone cabling primarily relies on optical fibers running Gigabit or 10 Gigabit Ethernet these days.

Although unclear in Figure 13.19 as it shows the general layout of subsystems, backbone cabling takes advantage of the hierarchical topology (see Figure 13.22) to interconnect wiring closets and the main equipment room.

13.4.2.5 Main Equipment Room Subsystem

The main equipment room houses routers, telecom devices (e.g., private branch exchanges or PBXs), and core switches that interconnect workgroup switches located in wiring closets (see Figure 13.23). The main equipment room is located on the first floor of a building and becomes the termination point of backbone cabling to which wiring closets are attached. Some firms may choose to place the main equipment room on a higher floor out of such concern as flooding.

The router in the equipment room becomes a gateway to the WAN or Internet connection outside of the building. If the building belongs to a campus network, the router may connect to another campus facility. Many organizations also choose to house enterprise-level servers in the main equipment room to directly link them to core switches.

13.4.2.6 Building Entrance Facility Subsystem

The building entrance facility is a dividing point between the external and internal cabling of a building. It becomes a junction point to the campus backbone or a demarcation point that couples the building's internal network with a WAN carrier's or ISP's local link(s). The building entrance facility connects to the equipment room (see Figure 13.19). As a concept similar to the building entrance subsystem, the demarcation point of a house is shown in Figure 12.2.

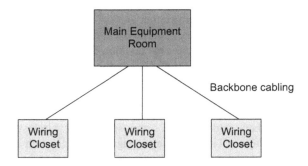

FIGURE 13.22 Connectivity between wiring closets and the main equipment room

FIGURE 13.23   A wiring closet (L) and main equipment room (R) (Sources: tennexcom.com, web.engr. oregonstate.edu)

CHAPTER SUMMARY

- On the wired Ethernet LAN, the network interface card of host stations and intermediary devices is responsible for the production and release of standardized digital signals. On the Wi-Fi LAN, the wireless LAN card uses analog signal encoding based on the spread spectrum technology.
- On the wired WAN link, there are two different device types that enable signal encoding: CSU/DSUs *(Channel Service Unit/Data Service Units)* for digital encoding and modems *(modulators and demodulators)* for analog encoding.
- Dial-up, DSL, and Cable modems use such technologies as amplitude or frequency modulation to convert a computer's digital signals to analog signals necessary for transmissions.
- *CSU/DSU* (Channel Service Unit/Data Service Unit) translates a digital signal generated by the customer premise equipment (e.g., router) into another digital signal format required by the WAN/Internet access link.
- The baseband transmission uses the full bandwidth of a medium to transport data using digital signal encoding. In broadband transmissions, meanwhile, frequency channels are created within a medium to transport multiple analog signals concurrently.
- In asynchronous transmissions, a character (7 or 8 bits in ASCII), added by the start, stop, and parity bits, is transported one by one. In synchronous transmissions, a long string of characters (e.g., frame) containing a data field and a header/trailer is moved at once as a discrete unit.
- Multiplexing is the process of combining either analog or digital signals from multiple sources in order to channel them over a single shared physical line or circuit. Among the technologies are frequency division multiplexing and time division multiplexing.
- Digital signal (DS) and optical carrier (OC)/synchronous transport module (STM) are different digital speed hierarchies. DS was introduced when cabling options for the computer network were mainly copper wires and the OC/STM hierarchy specifies a set of channel speeds on fiber-optic-based cabling.
- Copper wires, optical fibers, and the earth's atmosphere (for wireless networking) are dominant media types these days. All media have propagation effects such as signal attenuation and distortion.

- The twisted pair is an ordinary copper wire that uses electrical currents to encode data. Twisted pairs are either unshielded or shielded.
- The fiber-optic cable has emerged as a medium of choice for high-speed networking. It takes advantage of light pulses to transmit data through the core made of extremely pure glass, and has two types of *single-mode* and *multi-mode*.
- The cabling standards of Ethernet are expressed in the combination of the *rated speed, signaling method* (*baseband* for digital signaling and *broadband* for analog signaling), and *cable type* (twisted pair or optical fiber).
- Network cabling practice executed in accordance with published standards is called structured cabling. The standards define recommended practices on all aspects of cabling including cabling types, effective transmission distances, installation requirements, and testing methods of installed cables.
- The structured cabling system divides the cabling infrastructure of a building into six subsystems: work area, horizontal cabling, wiring closet, backbone cabling, main equipment room, and building entrance facility.

KEY TERMS

10 Gigabit Ethernet
100 Gigabit Ethernet
asymmetric DSL (ADSL)
asynchronous transmission
attenuation
backbone cabling subsystem
baseband
broadband
building entrance subsystem
CAT5
CAT6
CAT7
Central Office (CO)
coaxial cable
copper wire
crossover cable
CSU/DSU
dense wave division multiplexing
digital signal (DS)
distortion
EIA/TIA568
encoding
equipment room subsystem
Fast Ethernet
gigabit Ethernet
horizontal cabling subsystem
intermediate distribution facility (IDF)
main distribution facility (MDF)
main equipment room

medium dependent interface crossover (MDIX)
modal dispersion
modem
multi-mode fiber
optical carrier (OC)
parity bit
patch cable (patch cord)
patch panel
plain old telephone service (POTS)
public switched telephone network (PSTN)
shielded twisted pair (STP)
single-mode fiber
spread spectrum
start bit
statistical time division multiplexing (STDM)
stop bit
straight-through cable
structured cabling
structured cabling system
symmetric DSL (SDSL)
synchronous TDM
synchronous transmission
synchronous transport module (STM)
T-1 line
T-3 line
unshielded twisted pair (UTP)
wiring closet subsystem
work area subsystem

CHAPTER REVIEW QUESTIONS

1. Choose a FALSE statement regarding the wiring (or telecommunications) closet.
   A) It is a connecting point between horizontal cabling and backbone cabling.
   B) It houses intermediary devices to connect end nodes in the adjacent area.
   C) It has one or more patch panels that are normally rack-mounted.
   D) It is generally located on the bottom floor of a building.
   E) It simplifies cable management within a building.
2. Which describes the synchronous (ST) or asynchronous (AT) transmission?
   A) ST utilizes the start, stop, and parity bits.
   B) ST is used for communications between a computer and its keyboard.
   C) The data link layer frame is an example of ST.
   D) ST has a higher overhead than AT.
   E) In ST, each character becomes a unit of delivery.
3. Signals attenuate most quickly when they travel through the _____.
   A) single-mode fiber
   B) multi-mode fiber
   C) air (or atmosphere)
   D) unshielded twist pair
   E) coaxial cable
4. Which signal conversion device is placed between the border router and the T-3 line, if any?
   A) codec
   B) CSU/DSU
   C) switch
   D) digital converter
   E) modem
5. Which link needs cross-over cabling (assume MDIX not available)?
   A) switch–router
   B) user PC–switch
   C) server–switch
   D) wireless access point–router
   E) switch–switch
6. DS-0 represents the unit speed of a voice-grade channel. Then, its speed must be:
   A) 64 kbps
   B) 128 kbps
   C) 32 kbps
   D) 45 kbps
   E) 10 kbps
7. Structured cabling is achieved in a building when _____
   A) voice and data communications depend on digital signaling.
   B) network nodes are interconnected in the 'star' topology.
   C) trunk links utilize optical fibers.
   D) its cabling is designed to integrate voice and data traffic.
   E) its cabling is conducted according to published standard practices.
8. The advantage of optical fibers over twisted pairs is NOT _____.
   A) higher bandwidth
   B) better security
   C) lower interference
   D) higher attenuation
   E) longer signal propagation

9. The number of twists per foot, copper purity, and electrical resistance are properties that determine _____.
   A) the category of a twisted pair
   B) the mode of an optical fiber (single-mode vs. multi-mode)
   C) the type of a patch cable
   D) the category of an optical fiber
   E) the type of a twisted pair (cross-over vs. straight-through)

10. Which is INCORRECT about digital speed hierarchies?
    A) DS (digital signal) is an international standard mainly for copper wires.
    B) STM (Synchronous Transport Module) is an international standard for optical fibers.
    C) The base speed of DS is 1.54 Mbps, and higher speeds are its multiples.
    D) OC (optical carrier) is the North American standard for optical fibers.
    E) The base speed of OC is 51.84 Mbps, and higher speeds are its multiples.

11. Two main propagation effects of a signal include _____.
    A) attenuation and distortion
    B) attenuation and interference
    C) distortion and interference
    D) distortion and proliferation
    E) interference and proliferation

12. Six components (or subsystems) of the structured cabling system do NOT include _____.
    A) main equipment room
    B) backbone (vertical) cabling
    C) telecommunications (or wiring) closet
    D) horizontal cabling
    E) cross-connect cabling

13. The straight-through cable should be used to connect two nodes EXCEPT:
    A) switch–router
    B) PC–switch
    C) wireless access points–router
    D) server–switch
    E) server–router

14. The T-1 line combines multiple signals using ____ for their concurrent deliveries.
    A) frequency division multiplexing
    B) time division multiplexing
    C) wavelength division multiplexing
    D) dense wave division multiplexing
    E) code division multiple access

15. Patch panels are used widely in the ____ subsystem to connect host stations and switches.
    A) building entrance
    B) wiring closet
    C) backbone cabling area
    D) work area
    E) switch room area

16. The access (or workgroup) switch is generally placed in the _____.
    A) wiring closet subsystem
    B) work area subsystem
    C) horizontal cabling subsystem
    D) backbone cabling subsystem
    E) equipment room subsystem

17. When multi-mode and single-mode fibers are compared:
    A) Multi-mode supports full-duplex transmissions, but single-mode does not.
    B) Multi-mode is more reliable than single-mode in maintaining signal integrity.
    C) Single-mode is easier to multiplex than multi-mode.
    D) Multi-mode is adequate for LANs and campus networks, but not for WANs.
    E) Multi-mode has a higher capacity than single-mode.
18. When baseband and broadband transmissions are compared:
    A) Baseband allows the flow of only a single data type (e.g., sound) at a time.
    B) Baseband is slower than broadband.
    C) Wired networks such as Ethernet primarily rely on broadband transmissions.
    D) With baseband, several frequency channels can be created within a cable.
    E) Using broadband, multiple analog signals can travel through a cable concurrently.
19. The _____ is used to make a physical connection between two closely placed network nodes.
    A) parallel cord
    B) patch cord
    C) conversion cord
    D) horizontal cord
    E) vertical cord
20. When light signals travel in different modes (angles) through the fiber-optic cable, they may not reach the destination in exact time intervals, this is _____.
    A) multimode transmission
    B) propagation conversion
    C) modal bandwidth
    D) modal dispersion
    E) optical interference
21. What could be a major reason that multi-mode fibers are used instead of single-mode fibers for LANs?
    A) higher speed
    B) longer propagation distance
    C) lower cost
    D) lower error rate
    E) lower dispersion
22. The main equipment room subsystem _____ .
    A) is a demarcation point between the internal network and an ISP network
    B) is typically located on the top floor of a building
    C) houses workgroup switches that directly connect user stations
    D) is the termination point of backbone cabling
    E) is the ending point of horizontal cabling
23. The transmission power of a signal weakens as it progresses. This is called _____.
    A) attenuation
    B) distortion
    C) interference
    D) withdrawal
    E) dispersion
24. Which is CORRECT regarding the fiber-optic cable?
    A) The cable's properties are defined in the data link layer.
    B) The cable does not require repeaters to boost the signal strength.
    C) Carriers normally use multi-mode fibers to develop their backbone infrastructure.
    D) It uses light signals to move data.
    E) It is the most popular medium for the access link that connects a host computer to a switch.

25. If a digital device should transmit data over the analog signaling line (e.g. telephone line), what physical layer device should be used?
    A) coder
    B) CSU/DSU
    C) multiplexer
    D) decoder
    E) modem

HANDS-ON EXERCISES

EXERCISE 13.1

Refer to Figure 13.5. Compute the Ethernet frame's overhead in percentage and compare it with that of asynchronous transmissions. Assume that the Ethernet's data field contains the maximum number of characters possible.

EXERCISE 13.2

1. What is the data rate of each source (e.g., computer, IP phone) assigned to a particular time slot in Figure 13.11?
2. Given that 8000 frames are produced per second, what is the time interval of each frame produced in Figure 13.11?

EXERCISE 13.3

Imagine a hypothetical LAN with various network nodes and UTP connections, as in Figure 13.24. Decide the patch cord type (either straight-through or crossover) that should be used for each link. Assume that the nodes do not support MDIX capability.

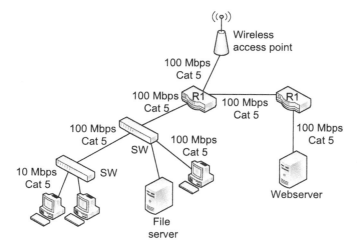

FIGURE 13.24 A hypothetical LAN

Index

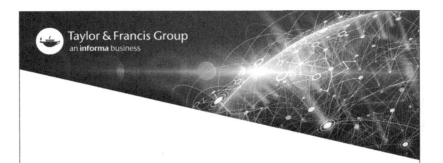

Printed in the United States
by Baker & Taylor Publisher Services